# STATISTICS AND DATA INTERPRETATION FOR SOCIAL WORK

**James Rosenthal** has taught at the Anne and Henry Zarrow School of Social Work at the University of Oklahoma, Norman, since 1985. His primary teaching areas have been in research methods and statistics. He has written two books, *Special Needs Adoption: A Follow-up Study of Intact Families* (1992 with Victor Groza) and *Statistics and Data Interpretation for the Helping Professions* (2001). He has written more than 40 journal articles and book chapters, primarily in the area of child welfare services (adoption, foster care, child maltreatment, children's mental health). He has published in leading social work journals including *Children and Youth Services Review*, *Social Service Review*, *Social Work*, *Child Abuse and Neglect*, and *Child Welfare*. His master's in social service administration is from the University of Chicago (1977) and his doctorate in research and evaluation methods is from the School of Education at the University of Colorado, Boulder (1984).

Jim lives in Norman, Oklahoma, with his wife, Cindy. He enjoys hiking, baseball, golf, and his dogs, Lenny and Sandy. He has two children, Catie and Aaron.

# STATISTICS AND DATA
# INTERPRETATION FOR SOCIAL WORK

James A. Rosenthal, PhD

SPRINGER PUBLISHING COMPANY
NEW YORK

Copyright © 2012 Springer Publishing Company, LLC

Springer Publishing Company, LLC
11 West 42nd Street
New York, NY 10036
www.springerpub.com

*Acquisitions Editor:* Jennifer Perillo
*Composition:* Absolute Service, Inc.

ISBN: 978-0-8261-0720-6
E-book ISBN: 978-0-8261-0721-3

11 12 13/ 5 4 3 2 1

Choose the appropriate disclaimer:
The author and the publisher of this Work have made every effort to use sources believed to be reliable to provide information that is accurate and compatible with the standards generally accepted at the time of publication. The author and publisher shall not be liable for any special, consequential, or exemplary damages resulting, in whole or in part, from the readers' use of, or reliance on, the information contained in this book. The publisher has no responsibility for the persistence or accuracy of URLs for external or third-party Internet Web sites referred to in this publication and does not guarantee that any content on such Web sites is, or will remain, accurate or appropriate.

Library of Congress Cataloging-in-Publication Data

Rosenthal, James A.
  Statistics and data interpretation for social work / James A. Rosenthal.—1st ed.
    p. cm.
  ISBN 978-0-8261-0720-6 -- ISBN 978-0-8261-0721-3 (ebook)  1.  Social sciences—Statistical methods.
2.  Social service—Statistical methods. 3.  Social sciences--Research. 4.  Statistics. I. Title.
  HA29.R796 2011
  519.5--dc23
                                        2011039348

Special discounts on bulk quantities of our books are available to corporations, professional associations, pharmaceutical companies, health care organizations, and other qualifying groups.

If you are interested in a custom book, including chapters from more than one of our titles, we can provide that service as well.

**For details, please contact:**
Special Sales Department, Springer Publishing Company, LLC
11 West 42nd Street, 15th Floor, New York, NY 10036-8002
Phone: 877-687-7476 or 212-431-4370
Fax: 212-941-7842
E-mail:sales@springerpub.com

Printed in the United States of America by Bradford and Bigelow

# CONTENTS

*Preface*     xv

*Acknowledgments*     xvii

## PART I: INTRODUCTION AND DESCRIPTIVE STATISTICS

**1.** Introduction and Overview     *3*
   1.1   Chapter Overview     *3*
   1.2   Statistics and Social Work     *3*
   1.3   Science and Research     *4*
   1.4   Variables and Measurement     *4*
   1.5   Samples and Populations     *5*
   1.6   Descriptive and Inferential Statistics     *6*
   1.7   Univariate, Bivariate, and Multivariate Statistics     *6*
   1.8   Random Assignment     *8*
   1.9   Levels of Measurement     *9*
       1.9.1  Basics     *9*
       1.9.2  Fine Points     *10*
   1.10 Chapter Summary     *11*
   1.11 Problems and Questions     *12*

**2.** Data Presentation     *19*
   2.1 Chapter Overview     *19*
   2.2 Frequency Distributions and Tables     *19*
   2.3 Figures     *21*
   2.4 Chapter Summary     *24*
   2.5 Problems and Questions     *25*

**3.** Central Tendency     *29*
   3.1 Chapter Overview     *29*
   3.2 Key Concepts in Univariate Descriptive Statistics     *29*
   3.3 Three Key Measures of Central Tendency     *29*
   3.4 The Mode     *30*
   3.5 The Median     *30*
   3.6 The Mean     *31*

3.7  Choosing Between Measures    *32*
3.8  Chapter Summary    *33*
3.9  Problems and Questions    *34*

**4.** Measures of Variability    *39*
4.1   Chapter Overview    *39*
4.2   The Concept of Variability    *39*
4.3   Assessing the Variability of Categorical Variables    *40*
4.4   The Range    *41*
4.5   The Interquartile Range    *41*
4.6   The Mean Deviation    *41*
4.7   The Standard Deviation    *42*
4.8   The Variance    *44*
4.9   Chapter Summary    *45*
4.10  Problems and Questions    *45*

**5.** Shape of Distribution    *51*
5.1   Chapter Overview    *51*
5.2   The Normal Distribution    *51*
5.3   Skewed Distributions    *53*
        5.3.1  Characteristics    *53*
        5.3.2  Skewness and Measures of Central Tendency    *55*
5.4   Kurtosis    *57*
5.5   Uniform and Bimodal Distributions    *58*
5.6   Percentages and the Normal Distribution    *58*
5.7   Introduction to $z$ Scores    *61*
        5.7.1  $z$ Score Calculation    *61*
        5.7.2  Basics of $z$ Scores    *61*
        5.7.3  Uses of $z$ Scores    *62*
5.8   $z$ Scores and the Normal Distribution    *63*
        5.8.1  Problems About Percentages of Cases    *63*
        5.8.2  Reminders and Cautions    *65*
5.9   Chapter Summary    *66*
5.10  Problems and Questions    *67*

**6.** The Concept of Relationship and Relationship
Between Categorical Variables    *75*
6.1   Chapter Overview    *75*
6.2   Definition of Relationship    *75*
6.3   Comments on Relationship    *76*
6.4   Contingency Tables and Categorical Variables    *77*
        6.4.1  Reading a Contingency (Crosstabs) Table    *77*
        6.4.2  Assessing Relationship Using a
                 Contingency Table    *78*
6.5   Size of Association    *80*
6.6   Difference in Percentages ($D\%$)    *80*
6.7   Qualitative Descriptors of Size of Association    *81*
6.8   Risk Ratio ($RR$)    *82*
6.9   Difference in Percentages or Risk Ratio?    *84*
6.10  Chapter Summary    *84*
6.11  Problems and Questions    *85*

**7.** The Odds Ratio and Other Measures for Categorical Variables    *93*
    7.1  Chapter Overview    *93*
    7.2  Odds Ratio    *93*
        7.2.1  Basics and Formula    *93*
        7.2.2  Interpretation    *95*
        7.2.3  Advantages    *96*
    7.3  Relationship in Contingency Tables Larger Than $2 \times 2$    *97*
    7.4  Directional Relationship    *98*
    7.5  Measures of Directional Association Between Categorical Variables    *100*
    7.6  Chapter Summary    *100*
    7.7  Problems and Questions    *101*

**8.** Correlation and Regression    *107*
    8.1  Chapter Overview    *107*
    8.2  Positive and Negative Correlation    *107*
    8.3  Scatterplots    *108*
    8.4  Formula for the Correlation Coefficient, $r$    *109*
    8.5  Understanding $r$    *111*
    8.6  Interpretations Using $r$ and $z$ Scores    *115*
        8.6.1  Predictions With $z$ Scores    *115*
        8.6.2  Predicted Change in Standard Deviation Units    *115*
    8.7  Curvilinear Relationship    *116*
    8.8  A Caution in Interpreting $r$    *117*
    8.9  Regression    *118*
        8.9.1  Regression Equation and Regression Line    *118*
        8.9.2  Contrast Between $r$ and $B$    *119*
    8.10  Correlation for Nominal-Level and Ordinal-Level Variables    *120*
    8.11  Chapter Summary    *120*
    8.12  Problems and Questions    *121*

**9.** Standardized Mean Difference    *127*
    9.1  Chapter Overview    *127*
    9.2  Introduction to the Standardized Mean Difference    *127*
    9.3  Graphical Interpretation of the Standardized Mean Difference    *128*
    9.4  A Caution Regarding the Standardized Mean Difference    *130*
    9.5  More Measures of Differences Between Two Means    *130*
    9.6  Differences Between Three or More Means    *131*
    9.7  Chapter Summary    *131*
    9.8  Problems and Questions    *132*

**10.** Research Design and Causality    *135*
    10.1  Chapter Overview    *135*
    10.2  Introduction to Causality    *135*
    10.3  What Does "Cause" Mean in Social Science?    *136*
    10.4  Confounding Variables    *136*
    10.5  Experimental and Survey Designs    *138*
        10.5.1  Experiments Versus Surveys    *138*
        10.5.2  Random Assignment to Groups    *138*
    10.6  Random Assignment and Causality    *139*
    10.7  Chapter Summary    *140*
    10.8  Problems and Questions    *140*

**11.** Controlling for Confounding Variables    *143*
    11.1  Chapter Overview    *143*
    11.2  Controlling for a Variable    *143*
        11.2.1  Basic Concepts    *143*
        11.2.2  Different Patterns Following Control    *145*
        11.2.3  Initial Relationship Persists    *145*
        11.2.4  Initial Relationship Weakens    *146*
        11.2.5  Initial Relationship Disappears    *146*
    11.3  Causal Models and Additional Considerations    *147*
    11.4  Control for Multiple Variables and Causality    *149*
    11.5  Interaction Effects    *150*
    11.6  Chapter Summary    *151*
    11.7  Problems and Questions    *152*

## PART II: INFERENTIAL STATISTICS AND DATA INTERPRETATION

**12.** An Introduction to Inferential Statistics    *161*
    12.1    Chapter Overview    *161*
    12.2    Descriptive Versus Inferential Statistics    *161*
    12.3    Characteristics of Random Samples    *161*
    12.4    The Advantage of Random Samples    *163*
    12.5    Statistics and Parameters    *164*
    12.6    Characteristics of Estimators    *165*
    12.7    Sampling Error and Sampling Distributions    *166*
        12.7.1  Concepts    *166*
        12.7.2  Sampling Distribution of the Mean    *168*
    12.8    Sample Size and the Sampling Distribution of $\overline{X}$    *170*
    12.9    Chapter Summary    *172*
    12.10  Problems and Questions    *173*

**13.** Confidence Intervals for Means and Proportions    *179*
    13.1  Chapter Overview    *179*
    13.2  What Is a Confidence Interval?    *179*
    13.3  Confidence Intervals for Means    *179*
        13.3.1  Theory    *179*
        13.3.2  Formulas and Computation    *181*
    13.4  Confidence Intervals for Proportions and Percentages    *184*
        13.4.1  Theory    *184*
        13.4.2  Formulas and Application    *185*
    13.5  Five More Things to Know    *187*
    13.6  Chapter Summary    *188*
    13.7  Problems and Questions    *189*

**14.** The Logic of Statistical Significance Tests    *195*
    14.1    Chapter Overview    *195*
    14.2    Introduction to Significance Testing    *195*
    14.3    Probability    *195*
        14.3.1  Definition and Formula    *195*
        14.3.2  Probability and the Normal Distribution    *196*
    14.4    Null and Alternative Hypotheses    *196*

14.5    A Common Pattern for Hypothesis Pairs    *197*
14.6    Directional and Nondirectional Hypothesis Pairs    *199*
    14.6.1  Definitions and Examples    *199*
    14.6.2  Guidelines for Usage    *200*
14.7    Sampling Error and the Null Hypothesis    *201*
14.8    Statistical Significance Levels    *202*
14.9    Examples of Statistical Significance Testing    *203*
    14.9.1  An Example in Which We Reject the Null    *203*
    14.9.2  An Example in Which We Fail to Reject (Accept) the Null    *205*
    14.9.3  More Interpretations of *p*    *205*
    14.9.4  What Does It Mean to Reject the Null?    *206*
    14.9.5  What Does It Mean to Fail to Reject (Accept) the Null?    *207*
14.10  Null and Alternative Hypotheses and Scientific Inquiry    *208*
14.11  What Is a Statistically Significant Result?    *209*
14.12  Chapter Summary    *209*
14.13  Problems and Questions    *210*

**15.** The Large Sample Test of the Mean and New Concepts    *219*
15.1    Chapter Overview    *219*
15.2    A Model for Hypothesis Testing    *219*
15.3    Assumptions of Statistical Significance Tests    *220*
    15.3.1  Definition and Assumptions of the Large Sample Test of $\overline{X}$    *220*
    15.3.2  Assumptions Common to All Tests    *220*
15.4    The First Two Steps of the Hypothesis Testing Model    *220*
15.5    Statistical Tests and Sampling Distributions    *221*
15.6    Directional Versus Nondirectional Hypothesis Pairs    *224*
    15.6.1  Overview    *224*
    15.6.2  Nondirectional Hypothesis Pair    *224*
    15.6.3  Directional Hypothesis Pair    *225*
15.7    Carrying Out the Significance Test Using the Sampling Distribution    *226*
15.8    Finishing the Example Using the Formula    *227*
    15.8.1  Step 3: Carry Out the Test    *227*
    15.8.2  Decision Rules    *227*
    15.8.3  Step 4: Make a Decision    *228*
15.9    Effect of Choice of Significance Level on Decision Making    *228*
15.10  Type I and Type II Errors    *230*
15.11  Two-Tailed Versus One-Tailed Tests    *231*
    15.11.1  Carrying Out Our Example    *231*
    15.11.2  Determining the Exact Value of the Study Sample Result (*p*)    *233*
15.12  More Decision Rules for the One-Tailed, Large Sample Test of $\overline{X}$    *234*
15.13  Rejecting the Null and "Real" Things    *236*
15.14  Chapter Summary    *237*
15.15  Problems and Questions    *238*

**16.** Statistical Power and Selected Topics    *247*
16.1    Chapter Overview    *247*
16.2    Definition of Power    *247*
16.3    Sample Size and Power    *247*
16.4    Examples of How Sample Size Affects Power    *248*
    16.4.1  The Parenting Skills Example    *248*
    16.4.2  More Examples of Sample Size and Power    *250*

16.5   Factors Other Than Sample Size That Influence Power   *252*
   16.5.1 Overview   *252*
   16.5.2 Size of Relationship or Difference in the Population   *252*
   16.5.3 Reduced Variability of Independent or Dependent Variable   *254*
   16.5.4 Control for Third Variables   *255*
   16.5.5 Significance Level   *256*
   16.5.6 Directional Hypotheses and One-Tailed Tests   *256*
   16.5.7 Statistical Significance Test   *257*
16.6   How Much Power is Enough?   *257*
16.7   How Large Should Sample Size Be?   *257*
16.8   Nonrandom Samples and Significance Tests   *260*
16.9   Reporting Statistical Significance   *260*
16.10  What Statistical Significance Is (And Is Not)   *261*
16.11  Chapter Summary   *261*
16.12  Problems and Questions   *263*

17. The *t* Distribution and One-Sample Procedures for Means   *269*
17.1   Chapter Overview   *269*
17.2   Small Sample Size and Distributions   *269*
17.3   Degrees of Freedom   *269*
17.4   The Family of *t* Distributions   *270*
17.5   Confidence Intervals for Means for Small Samples (and Large)   *271*
17.6   Introduction to the One-Sample *t* Test   *273*
   17.6.1 Assumptions, Hypothesis Pairs, and Formula   *273*
   17.6.2 Decision Rules   *274*
17.7   Carrying Out the One-Sample *t* Test   *274*
17.8   Chapter Summary   *277*
17.9   Problems and Questions   *278*

18. Independent Samples *t* Test and Dependent Samples *t* Test   *283*
18.1   Chapter Overview   *283*
18.2   Introduction to the Independent Samples *t* Test   *283*
   18.2.1 Purpose and Sampling Distribution   *283*
   18.2.2 Hypothesis Pairs   *283*
   18.2.3 Assumptions and Formulas   *284*
18.3   Carrying Out the Independent Samples *t* Test Using
   the SPSS Software Package   *285*
18.4   The Independence Assumption   *287*
18.5   The Dependent Samples *t* Test   *288*
   18.5.1 Dependent Samples and Statistical Power   *288*
   18.5.2 Requirements   *288*
   18.5.3 Example Demonstrating Increase in Power
       from Positive Correlation   *289*
18.6   Chapter Summary   *289*
18.7   Problems and Questions   *290*

19. One-Sample Tests of Proportions   *295*
19.1   Chapter Overview   *295*
19.2   One-Sample Test of a Proportion   *295*
   19.2.1 Introduction   *295*
   19.2.2 Theory and Basics   *295*
   19.2.3 Carrying Out the Behavior Problems Example   *296*

19.3  The Binomial Test    *297*
    19.3.1  Background    *297*
    19.3.2  Carrying Out the Test    *299*
19.4  The One-Variable Chi-Square Test    *300*
    19.4.1  Background    *300*
    19.4.2  The Chi-Square Distribution    *300*
    19.4.3  Observed and Expected Frequencies    *301*
    19.4.4  Particulars for the Test    *301*
    19.4.5  Completing Our Example    *302*
19.5  Chapter Summary    *303*
19.6  Problems and Questions    *304*

20.  The Chi-Square Test of Independence    *311*
20.1  Chapter Overview    *311*
20.2  Introduction to the Chi-Square Test of Independence    *311*
20.3  Selected Characteristics of $\chi^2$ Test    *311*
    20.3.1  Hypothesis Pair    *311*
    20.3.2  Distribution and Degrees of Freedom    *312*
    20.3.3  Observed and Expected Proportions    *312*
    20.3.4  Formula, Observed and Expected Frequencies,
            Decision Rule, and Requirements    *313*
20.4  Carrying Out the $\chi^2$ Test    *314*
    20.4.1  Hypothesis Testing Model and Calculations    *314*
    20.4.2  Comments on the Example    *316*
20.5  Comments on the $\chi^2$ Test    *316*
20.6  The $\chi^2$ Test is *Not* a Measure of Size of Association    *317*
20.7  Chapter Summary    *318*
20.8  Problems and Questions    *318*

21.  Analysis of Variance    *323*
21.1  Chapter Overview    *323*
21.2  Introduction to Analysis of Variance    *323*
21.3  The Logic of Analysis of Variance    *323*
    21.3.1  Hypothesis and Overview    *323*
    21.3.2  Two Estimates of the Population Variance    *324*
    21.3.3  The *F* Distribution    *325*
21.4  Particulars of Analysis of Variance    *325*
    21.4.1  Assumptions and Level of Measurement    *325*
    21.4.2  Hypothesis Pair    *326*
    21.4.3  Critical Values and Decision Rules    *326*
21.5  Calculation Example Using SPSS    *326*
21.6  Multiple Comparison Procedures    *328*
21.7  Fishing Expeditions    *329*
    21.7.1  The Dangers of Fishing    *329*
    21.7.2  The Dangers of Not Fishing    *330*
21.8  Chapter Summary    *330*
21.9  Problems and Questions    *331*

**22.** More Significance Tests and Reasoning with Test Results    *337*
   22.1   Chapter Overview    *337*
   22.2   Statistical Significance Test of Pearson's $r$    *337*
       22.2.1 Basic Logic    *337*
       22.2.2 Assumptions and Levels of Measurement    *337*
       22.2.3 Hypothesis Pair    *338*
       22.2.4 Decision Rules and Degrees of Freedom    *338*
       22.2.5 Carrying Out the Hypothesis Testing Model    *338*
       22.2.6 A Look at the Sampling Distribution of $r$    *340*
   22.3   A Correlation Matrix    *340*
   22.4   Comments on Hypothesis Testing and Confidence Intervals    *343*
       22.4.1 Hypothesis Testing    *343*
       22.4.2 Confidence Intervals    *343*
   22.5   Parametric and Nonparametric Tests    *343*
   22.6   Selected Parametric Tests    *345*
       22.6.1 Significance Test of Spearman's $r$    *345*
       22.6.2 Tests of Association Between Two Ordinal-Level
             Categorical Variables    *345*
       22.6.3 Tests for Independent Samples    *345*
       22.6.4 Tests for Dependent Samples    *345*
   22.7   Parametric or Nonparametric Test?    *346*
   22.8   Data Transformation    *347*
   22.9   Single-Case Designs    *349*
       22.9.1 Basic Applications    *349*
       22.9.2 Comments on Single-Case Designs    *351*
       22.9.3 Serial Dependency    *351*
   22.10 Qualitative Methods and Statistics    *352*
   22.11 Reasoning with Data: A Brief Review    *354*
   22.12 Chapter Summary    *356*
   22.13 Problems and Questions    *357*

**23.** An Overview of Selected Multivariate Procedures    *365*
   23.1 Chapter Overview    *365*
   23.2 Multiple Regression Analysis    *365*
       23.2.1 Equation and Introduction    *365*
       23.2.2 Assumptions of Multiple Regression    *368*
   23.3 Advantages of Multivariate Analyses    *370*
   23.4 Logistic Regression    *374*
   23.5 Factorial Analysis of Variance    *375*
   23.6 Multivariate Procedures Related to Analysis of Variance    *378*
   23.7 A Glimpse at Selected Procedures    *379*
   23.8 Chapter Summary    *380*
   23.9 Problems and Questions    *381*

**24.** Generalizability, Importance, and a Data Interpretation Model    *387*
   24.1 Chapter Overview    *387*
   24.2 Generalizability    *387*
       24.2.1 Inferential Statistics and Generalizability    *387*
       24.2.2 Generalization Using Nonstatistical Tools    *390*
   24.3 Importance    *392*
   24.4 The Balanced Model for Data Interpretation    *393*
   24.5 Chapter Summary    *395*
   24.6 Problems and Questions    *396*

**Appendix A**  Tables    *401*
   A.1 Percentage of Cases in Selected Areas of the Normal Distribution    *401*
   A.2 Critical Values for the *t* Distribution and Values for Confidence Intervals    *403*
   A.3 Critical Values (Frequencies) for the Binomial Distribution:
       One-Tailed Test, Alpha = .05    *404*
   A.4 Critical Values for the Chi-Square Distribution    *405*
   A.5 Critical Values for the *F* Distribution    *406*
   A.6 Critical Values for Pearson's *r*    *407*

**Appendix B**  Review of Basic Math    *409*
   B.1　Basic Operations, Terms, and Symbols    *409*
   B.2　More Symbols    *409*
   B.3　Order of Operations    *410*
   B.4　Positive and Negative Numbers and Absolute Values    *410*
   B.5　Squares and Square Roots    *411*
   B.6　Fractions    *411*
   B.7　Algebra    *412*
   B.8　Ratios, Proportions, Percentages, and Percentiles    *413*
   B.9　Rounding    *413*
   B.10 Math Review Problems    *413*
   B.11 Math Review Answers    *414*

**Appendix C**  Appropriate Measures for Different Situations    *415*
   C.1 Selected Univariate Measures and Measures of Association    *416*
   C.2 Selected Statistical Significance Tests for Univariate, Bivariate,
       and Multivariate Situations    *417*

**Appendix D**  Symbols in the Text    *419*

**Appendix E**  Formulas in the Text    *421*

**Appendix F**  Answers To End-Of-Chapter Problems and Questions    *425*

*Notes*    *453*
*References*    *467*
*Index*    *469*

# PREFACE

## OVERVIEW

*Statistics and Data Interpretation for Social Work* differs from most statistics texts in several key ways:

- It provides pragmatic examples in real-world settings and situations.
- It emphasizes that data assessment builds on but is not limited to statistics.
- It builds strong links to research methods courses, in particular demonstrating how social workers
  - assess whether study results reflect the effects of programs and interventions rather than extraneous factors (bias);
  - assess the applicability of research findings to the practice and policy situations in which they work; and
  - assess the importance (practical significance) of statistical results for clients and communities.

This text is a thorough rewrite of *Statistics and Data Interpretation for the Helping Professions* (2001). It presents less theory and more examples than did its predecessor. Even so, it is not a "baby statistics" text, one that is watered down and that avoids key (and sometimes difficult) concepts. If not a baby text, it is an introductory one; it provides the fundamentals for carrying out straightforward statistical analyses in basic research designs. It emphasizes concepts and skills much more than math and formulas. Scanning the text, the reader will observe the many problems and questions at the end of each chapter—indeed, 140 pages are devoted to problems and questions. These provide considerable opportunity to put the text's content into practice. The text works well in a stand-alone statistics course or in a research methods course in which statistics is a major content area. It is appropriate at both undergraduate and graduate levels. Although designed for social work students, it will work well in related professions such as human relations, counseling, criminology, sociology, and public administration.

The text is accompanied by a 200-plus page online companion guide for the IBM SPSS statistical software program. This companion introduces SPSS and then gears SPSS exercises to particular chapters in the text. It is (to my knowledge) the most visual SPSS guide available. It is

---

*This book tries to minimize the use of gender-related pronouns. When such usage is necessary, it uses feminine pronouns because most social workers are women.*

filled with screen shots (large and small) that walk the reader through key steps of data analysis with SPSS. Although designed for use with *Statistics and Data Interpretation for Social Work*, the companion stands well on its own as a basic SPSS primer.

## CONTENTS

The text's first chapter emphasizes that the profession of social work seeks to build its interventions on scientific knowledge—this is *evidence-based* practice. The second chapter involves data presentation, both with tables and figures (graphics). The next six chapters focus on *descriptive statistics*, tools for describing the data in one's sample. Some of the key topics covered here include measures of *central tendency* (i.e., the mean), measures of *variability* (i.e., the standard deviation), *distributions* (normal distribution, skewed distributions, *z* scores), and measures of *association* (difference in percentages, odds ratio, correlation, standardized mean difference). Chapters 6–9 direct considerable attention to size of relationship (*effect size*), that is, to how researchers assess whether observed relationships and differences are "large" or "small." Chapters 10 and 11 focus on how researchers determine whether one variable (say, for instance, a behavior modification intervention) actually *causes* another (say, a child's school behavior).

The text's second (and longer) half presents *inferential statistics*, tools for drawing conclusions about populations that are larger than one's sample. Chapters 12 and 13 deal with *confidence intervals* (much like the margins of error presented in newscasts for political polls). Chapters 14–16 present the logic behind *statistical significance tests*—how a researcher decides whether a difference or relationship may just be due to the luck of the draw (to chance). Chapters 17–22 present a wide array of statistical significance tests for use in many different situations. These include *t* tests, chi-square tests, analysis of variance (ANOVA), and tests for small samples and single-case designs. Chapter 23 enters the realm of *multivariate statistics* and presents multiple regression, logistic regression, factorial ANOVA, and other selected tests. The final chapter integrates the book's content and focuses on the qualitative (nonstatistical) aspects of data interpretation.

## SUMMING UP

*Statistics and Data Interpretation for Social Work* provides a solid introduction to statistics and data analysis. It has abundant problems on which students can test their knowledge. The 200-page plus online SPSS guide is filled with screenshots that guide students visually through the steps of data analysis. The text has strong, purposive links to research methods and to social work practice. It emphasizes reasoning. This reasoning begins with statistics, but moves beyond towards more comprehensive assessment that can guide social work practice. The strong foundation in statistics and data interpretation can help you (the student) as you begin to help people and the communities in which they live.

# ACKNOWLEDGMENTS

My great thanks go to my family: **Cindy**, Catie, and Aaron (and also Charlie, Don, and Lee, and Mom and Dad). And I should also mention great canine companionship: Chip, Monza, Hogan, Rainbow, Koal, Mui-Mui, and now, Lenny and Sandy. All deserve medals (or bones) for putting up with me and my bad jokes.

I have had and still have wonderful colleagues at the Anne and Henry Zarrow School of Social Work. Rather than taking a chance on missing someone, I say, simply, many thanks to all.

Thanks to Jennifer Perillo at Springer who encouraged me to begin this project and to Sheri W. Sussman and Michael O'Connor who, with the able assistance of Jessica Jonas at Absolute Service Inc., helped bring it "home."

This text states that there is no such thing as a normal distribution in the real world. I am blessed to have had a truly abnormal distribution of family, friends, and experiences both in growing up and—this presumed to have occurred by now—continuing onward.

*James Rosenthal*
*Norman, OK*
*October 2011*

# Part I

# INTRODUCTION AND DESCRIPTIVE STATISTICS

Part 1 begins by introducing concepts and terms to give you a solid footing in the field of statistics. Next, it discusses how to present data. Its major focus is on *descriptive statistics*, the tools that researchers use to describe and summarize data. Chapters 3, 4, and 5 present tools for describing a single variable. Some examples of *variables* (things that vary) include height, political party affiliation, and whether one is employed (yes or no). Among the most important tools for describing single variables are the *mean*, the *median*, and the *standard deviation*. Chapters 6–9 present tools for assessing the relationship between variables. For instance, amount of time studying for a test and grade earned on that test have a *relationship* because (in most cases) those who study longer earn higher grades. One of the most important tools for assessing relationship is the *correlation coefficient* (*r*). Finally, Chapters 10 and 11 shift the focus away from relationship per se to how researchers determine whether one variable in a relationship actually *causes* (affects) the other.

# INTRODUCTION AND OVERVIEW

## 1.1 ■ CHAPTER OVERVIEW

Social work strives to develop *evidenced-based practice*, practice grounded in scientific knowledge. Chapter 1 begins with examples that demonstrate how *statistics* contributes to this endeavor. Next, it discusses the basics of *science* and *research*. It introduces *variables* and contrasts *categorical* and *numeric variables*. As it moves along, it overviews key topics covered in this book. It distinguishes between *samples* and *populations* and between *random* and *nonrandom samples*. It presents the two major branches of statistics—*descriptive statistics* and *inferential statistics*—and contrasts *univariate*, *bivariate*, and *multivariate* statistical procedures. It discusses *relationships* among variables and sketches how researchers draw conclusions about whether one variable *causes* another. *Random assignment* is important in this endeavor. The chapter provides a glimpse on how *statistical significance* tests examine the role of luck (chance) in study results. It closes with discussion of the four *levels of measurement*: *nominal*, *ordinal*, *interval*, and *ratio*. These provide guidance on which procedures to use in different situations.

## 1.2 ■ STATISTICS AND SOCIAL WORK

"Social work is a profession . . . committed to the pursuit of social change, to quality of life, and to the development of the full potential of each individual, group, and community in a society" (Wikipedia, 2010a). Statistics is "the science of making effective use of numerical data" (Wikipedia, 2010b). Why do social workers need statistics?

Social workers need to learn what "works" and what does not. A couple of examples can make this point. Fisher, Gunnar, Dozier, Bruce, and Pears (2006) developed a therapeutic intervention to help foster parents better meet the emotional and behavioral needs of preschool children in their care. Preliminary study results suggest that this intervention promotes capacity for attachment in foster children and, for some children, actually increases levels of the hormone cortisol. Because cortisol is involved in the regulation of stress, this suggests that the intervention may help children handle stress more effectively. A second example: Social workers have long been concerned about possible long-term negative impacts of foster care. A recent study compared young adult outcomes—high school graduation, public assistance use, criminal behavior, drug use, teenage pregnancy, and homelessness—for about 300 young adults who had spent time in foster care at some time during their childhood and about 9,000 who had never been in such care (Berzin, 2008, p. 181). Preliminary statistical analyses indeed found worse outcomes for those who had been in foster care. Yet, more sophisticated analyses suggested that these worse outcomes were not caused primarily by foster care experiences but rather by a host of factors that those who had experienced foster care had been exposed to prior to entering care. These factors included poverty, having a very young birth mother, and a birth family environment with less opportunity for learning and socialization.

The two just-discussed studies are part of a growing knowledge base for effective social work practice in foster care. This knowledge is grounded in *science*. Expanding our focus from foster care to social work as a whole, the increased grounding of social work practice in *scientific* knowledge is one of the most important trends in the field over the past 30 or so years. Social work practice based on the "best scientific evidence available" is termed **evidence-based practice**[1] (Rubin, 2010, p. 315). The effective use of statistics is essential in this endeavor.

The two studies mentioned earlier were both large ones, involving many participants. Yet, statistics is also important in work with individual clients. For instance, you will need ways to assess whether your clients are making effective progress toward their treatment goals.

I would be lying to tell you that statistics is easy. But, on the other hand, introductory statistics is not so difficult. It is much more about key ideas than complicated math. This text emphasizes *interpretation* more than calculation. I want you to *understand* the conclusions that can—and cannot—be drawn in different situations.

So let us get started building statistical tools for social work practice. You will need to know what works and what does not.

## 1.3 ■ SCIENCE AND RESEARCH

**Science** comprises "systematic knowledge gained through observation and experimentation" (*Random House Webster's Dictionary*, 1987, p. 1716). It has two sides: a theoretical side based on theory, concepts, and ideas; and an applied side built on real-world observations. The theoretical side is termed **theory**. The gathering of real-world observations (i.e., **data**) is termed **research**.

Social science research uses two basic methods, quantitative and qualitative. **Quantitative research methods** are characterized by **objective measurement**, which is the assigning of numbers or classifications to observations. Both of the just-discussed foster care studies used quantitative methods. **Qualitative research methods** "emphasize depth of understanding and the deeper meanings of human experience" (Rubin & Babbie, 2008, p. 643). An example might be *in-depth* interviews of persons who grew up in poverty, experiencing multiple risks and stressors, who, nevertheless, experienced success as adults. These interviews would probe for the *particular perspective* of each person and would not include questions that could be answered by checking a box such as "yes" or "no" or, say, "strongly agree." Checking responses in boxes is a quantitative method.

Social work research is, almost without exception, *applied research*—research focused on real-world problems. This contrasts with *pure research*, research that seeks to build knowledge for its own sake. Much research in social work is **program evaluation**, research carried out to judge the usefulness of a social program or intervention.

## 1.4 ■ VARIABLES AND MEASUREMENT

Each unit on which measurements are recorded is a **case**. In social work research, cases are typically individual people. For instance, if you distribute a questionnaire to the students in your statistics or research class, each student is a different case. But cases are not always individuals. If you study child abuse rates in the 50 different states, then each state is a different case.

**Variables** are the "ingredients" of data, the different things that are measured. So, if you measure the gender, height, and academic major of each student in your class, each of these is a different variable.

The just-provided definition of variable is a general one. There is also a more specific definition: A **variable** is something with more than one value. For instance, gender takes on the values, female and male. Height can assume many different values, say, 5 ft. 4 ½ in., 5 ft. 7 in., 6 ft. 2 ¼ in., and so on. Before going further, let us define value: **Value(s)** (*attributes*) are the different numbers or classifications that a variable assumes.

We may contrast a variable with a **constant**, something that takes on only one value. For instance, the number "2" is a constant. If all cases have the same value on a given "variable," (here, we use the general definition) then that "variable" is not actually a variable but is, instead, (using our more specific definition) a constant. For instance, if all persons in a study are female, then sex is a constant rather than a variable.

Variables may be either categorical or numeric. **Categorical variables** (**qualitative variables**) have nonnumeric values. For instance, sex is a categorical variable because its values (female, male) are nonnumeric. Eye color (brown, blue, hazel, green, gray, etc.) is another example of a categorical variable. A categorical variable with exactly two values—for instance, sex has the values female and male—is a **dichotomous variable** (*binary variable*). **Numeric variables** (**quantitative variables**) have numeric values. Height, as measured in the previous example is numeric. On the other hand, if persons categorized their height as "short," "medium," or "tall," then height measured in this way is categorical. How many cars (0, 1, 2, 3, 4, etc.) that a family owns is a numeric variable, as is, for instance, the percentage correct that you earned on your most recent test (83, 91, 88, etc.). Values of numeric variables are often termed *scores*.

## 1.5 ■ SAMPLES AND POPULATIONS

A **population** consists of *all* of the objects that possess a specified set of characteristics. For instance, if there are 30 students in a class, these 30 students are the population of students in the class.

A **sample** consists of *some* but not all of the objects in a population. For instance, the students enrolled in, say, one or more social work courses this semester are a sample of students at your college; they are some of the students at the college. And, for instance, the students who sit in the front row in a given class are a sample of students in that class.[2]

**Random samples** (**probability samples**) are selected by methods of chance (picking names out of hat, a computer program selects names at random, etc.). When methods of chance are not used, the sample is a **nonrandom sample** (**nonprobability sample**). So, if your professor picks from a hat the names of 10 students who will participate in a special class exercise, the selected students are a random sample of students in the class. On the other hand, if she asks for 10 volunteers, the volunteering students are a nonrandom sample of students in the class.

In addition to referring to "some but not all of the objects in a population," the term *sample* has a second meaning in research. Sample is also used to refer to the participants in a research study. To reduce confusion, I typically refer to those selected to be in a research study as the **study sample**. So, if 100 persons fill out, for instance, a web-based survey, these persons are the study sample. In a general sense, **sampling** refers to the method used, **random sampling** (methods of chance used) or **nonrandom sampling** (methods of chance not used), to select participants for the study sample.

## 1.6 ■ DESCRIPTIVE AND INFERENTIAL STATISTICS

The field of statistics was defined previously as "the science of making effective use of numerical data" (Wikipedia, 2010b). A **statistic** is a numerical summary of data (Toothaker & Miller, 1996). For instance, if the average age of students in a class is 20 years old, then "20 years" is a statistic because it summarizes data pertaining to the class. And, by the same logic, if 80% of students respond that they like rock music, then "80%" is also a statistic.

Statistics has two major branches:

■ **Descriptive statistics** (*descriptive statistical procedures*) describe the study sample.

■ **Inferential statistics** (*inferential statistical procedures*) are used to draw conclusions about a population based on a random sample selected from that population.

So, suppose a professor reports the following: "The average age of students in my class is 20 years old and 80% of these students enjoy rock music." The professor is simply describing the study sample—in particular, she is not drawing any conclusions that go beyond this sample. As such, the professor is engaging in descriptive statistics. Chapters 3–9 focus on descriptive statistics.

Now, suppose a researcher takes a *random* sample of students at a university and finds that 72% of persons in the study sample support a proposed change in immigration policy. Based on this sample (and using skills to be taught in Chapters 12 and 13), the researcher states, "I am 95% confident that the percentage of all students in the university who support the change is between 64% and 80%." This example demonstrates inferential statistics as the researcher is drawing a conclusion about a population based on a sample randomly selected from that population.

Although an important exception will be discussed in Chapter 16, Section 8, formally speaking, inferential statistics may not be used with nonrandom samples. For instance, suppose that a social work professor finds that 90% of students in a social welfare policy class support proposed legislation to offer additional services to the homeless. Based on this sample, the professor may not use statistical procedures to draw a conclusion about the percentage of students at her university who support this legislation. She may not do so because the study sample is not a random sample of students at the university.

At the risk of oversimplifying with a random sample, only the "luck of the draw" causes differences between the characteristics and opinions of those in the sample and the characteristics and opinions of those in the population from which the sample was drawn. As such, inferential statistical procedures may be used. Chapter 12 presents more on how the "luck of the draw" operates and on when inferential statistics are used.

## 1.7 ■ UNIVARIATE, BIVARIATE, AND MULTIVARIATE STATISTICS

In addition to dividing the field of statistics into the two branches of descriptive and inferential statistics, we may classify statistical procedures as univariate, bivariate, or multivariate. These procedures may be used in either descriptive or inferential applications.

**Univariate statistics** pertain to a *single* variable at a time. For instance, it was reported earlier that 72% of students supported a change in immigration policy. As only a single variable (opinion on immigration policy) is involved, this is an example of univariate statistics. Chapters 3–5 present univariate descriptive statistics methods.

**Bivariate statistics** convey the relationship (or lack thereof) between *two* variables. Two variables are **related** (**associated**) when the values of one variable vary, differ, or change according to those of the other. For instance, sex and length of hair are related because (at least in most cultures) women have, on average, longer hair than do men. As another example of bivariate statistics, if a researcher writes "60% of Democrats but only 40% of Republicans voted for Legislation Z," she is engaging in bivariate statistics because she is communicating about a relationship between two variables, political party (Democratic or Republican) and vote on Legislation Z, (for the legislation vs. against it). In this example, because Democrats and Republicans vote differently, party affiliation and the vote on Z are related (associated).

The examples earlier involve variables that are related. If the same percentage of women and men respond that they like rock music—say, 80% of women and 80% of men like rock— then sex and liking rock music are **unrelated** (**unassociated**). Suppose that batting averages of left-handed hitters and right-handed hitters are the same (.283 for each group), then "batting handedness" (left vs. right) and batting average are unassociated. The idea here is that being a left-handed or right-handed batter does not tend to "go with" being a better (high average) or a worse (low average) hitter. Chapters 6–9 present bivariate, descriptive statistical methods.

As is discussed in depth beginning in Chapter 14, relationships in study samples can occur simply by luck (chance). For instance, suppose that in the full population of students at your university, the same percentage of women and men are vegetarians; for the sake of argument, suppose that this percentage is 10.7%. Thus, in this population, sex and being vegetarian are not related. Suppose that you draw a random sample of 25 women and 25 men for your study sample. Because of the luck of the draw, the percentages of vegetarians in your study sample will almost surely differ from the percentages in the population. Let us say that in your study sample, 12.4% of women and 9.8% of men are vegetarians. Hence, in your study sample, sex and being vegetarian are related (because the percentage of vegetarians differs). This is so, even though there is no relationship in the population.

Sometimes, relationships observed in study samples are caused only by the luck of the draw. Other times, researchers find relationships in study samples because the variables are actually related in the population. Trying to determine whether a relationship in a study sample reflects only luck or, instead, reflects an actual relationship in the population is a fundamental issue in inferential statistics. The key tool in this task is the statistical significance test. **Statistical significance tests** are used to determine whether study sample results are likely to be due to the luck of the draw. Most of the second half of the text covers significance tests.

**Multivariate statistics** involve three or more variables at a time. Multivariate statistics often concerns whether one variable actually affects (i.e., **causes**) another.

For instance, suppose that a study demonstrates a relationship between eating vegetables and longevity; those who eat more vegetables, on average, live longer. Perhaps this relationship is not a **causal relationship** (**causal association**), one in which one variable affects the other. Instead, it may be caused by a *third* variable. For instance, perhaps those who eat lots of vegetables exercise more intensely than do those who eat less. This being so, the relationship between vegetables and longevity may not be due to the effects of vegetables but instead to those of exercise. In other words, those who eat more vegetables live longer not because they eat vegetables but because they exercise more. The third variables that bring about relationships between other variables, termed **confounding variables** (*third variables*), are discussed in Chapters 10 and 11.

Because we are discussing *causality* (what causes what), it is a good time to define two common terms, independent variable and dependent variable. An **independent variable** affects another variable. A **dependent variable** is affected by another variable. So, suppose that visiting persons who are in nursing homes reduces depression. In this example, because visiting does the "affecting" (the causing), it is the independent variable. Because depression is affected (caused), it is the dependent. Chapter 23 demonstrates that several independent variables can be entered simultaneously into a single equation to see which of these most affects a dependent variable. This is an example of multivariate statistics.

Returning to our discussion of independent and dependent, sometimes, two variables that are related cannot be classified easily as independent and dependent. For instance, how high persons can jump in the high jump and how far they can jump in the long jump are related. On average, persons who jump "high" tend to jump "long" and those who jump "low" tend to jump "short." But it does not make sense to say that long jumping causes high jumping or that high jumping causes long jumping. So, in this case, there is no independent or dependent variable; the two variables are simply related.

## 1.8 ■ RANDOM ASSIGNMENT

Prior to examining random assignment, some terms need to be introduced. A *group* consists of those who possess some characteristic. A *treatment group* consists of those who receive a particular intervention (treatment). An **intervention** (**treatment**) is, broadly speaking, the "things that are done" to the research participant or client. Examples of social work interventions include a behavior modification program for a child, marital therapy for a couple experiencing difficulty, parenting skills training for a new parent, or a community intervention for a community under stress.

**Assignment** refers to the method used to assign participants to groups. It is distinct from sampling, which pertains to how participants were selected to be in the study sample. **Random assignment** (**randomization**) is the use of methods of chance to assign participants to groups.

The following is an example of a study that uses random assignment: A statistics professor puts students' names in a hat. She picks names randomly from the hat, assigning (at random) half to receive a software-based intervention to enhance statistics skills and half to have extra time with a teaching assistant. At the end of the semester, the professor compares scores on the final exam in the two groups.

An example of the same study but with a nonrandom assignment process is as follows: A statistics professor asks students which of the two interventions they want to sign up for: (a) the software-based intervention or (b) the teaching assistant. Students select an intervention and are assigned to it. At the end of the semester, the professor compares scores on the finals in the two groups.

Studies that use random assignment are termed **randomized studies** (**randomized clinical trials**). The great strength of the randomized study is that (at the risk of oversimplifying) the only thing that distinguishes treatment groups as the intervention begins is the luck of the draw of the assignment process. More precisely, confounding variables are not a concern. So, if a researcher sees a difference in outcomes between two treatment groups, that researcher knows that this difference is caused by either (a) the luck of the draw of the assignment process or (b) the greater effectiveness of the intervention received in one group than of that received in the other. The researcher may conduct a significance test to see whether luck alone is a plausible explanation and, if it is not, may be confident that the results reflect the effects of the intervention.

Contrast this with a nonrandomized study. In a nonrandomized study, confounding variables cannot be ruled out as an explanation for study results. So, if a researcher sees a difference in outcomes between the two groups, that difference may be caused by (a) the luck of the draw of the assignment process, (b) the greater effectiveness of the intervention received in one group than of that received in the other, or (c) a confounding variable(s). Consider, for instance, the second version of the professor's study, the one in which students choose their own group. Suppose that those instructed by the computer do better on the course finals than those instructed by the teaching assistant. Presume also that the difference is substantial enough so that the professor can be confident that it is not caused by luck. The problem is that the researcher will never know with confidence whether the result is caused by the greater effectiveness of the computer program over the teaching assistant or to a confounding variable(s).

What confounding variables might be at work? Well . . . for instance . . . relative to those who chose the teaching assistant, those who chose the computer program may have (a) been more motivated in the course, (b) had better math skills as the course began, and (c) had more time to study. The researcher will not be able to unravel whether one of these variables—or perhaps some other confounding variable not mentioned—or the greater effectiveness of the software package explains the better performance of the computer group on the statistics finals.

Suffice it to say that, in the absence of randomization, drawing conclusions about *causality*—that is, about what causes what—is a hazardous undertaking. On the other hand, with randomization, that researcher can, almost always, be confident that results that are larger than those that might be due to luck are indeed caused by the intervention. Chapters 10 and 11 discuss these issues in depth.

## 1.9 ■ LEVELS OF MEASUREMENT

### 1.9.1 ■ Basics

As discussed earlier, variables may be classified as categorical (qualitative) or numeric (quantitative). In addition, variables may be measured at four different **levels of measurement** (*scales of measurement*). These levels may be ordered from low to high. As one moves from lower to higher levels, greater precision is gained and new conclusions can be drawn. Ordered from low to high, the levels of measurement are nominal, ordinal, interval, and ratio. All categorical variables are at the nominal or ordinal level.

At the **nominal** level of measurement, one may *classify* a variable's values into separate categories, but these categories may not be ordered. For instance, sex is measured at the nominal level. One may classify sex as female or male. However, these values may not be ordered (Female is not higher than male. Male is not higher than female.). Another example is eye color (brown, blue, hazel, or green). The values of eye color may be classified but not ordered. It makes no sense to ask, "Which is higher, brown, blue, hazel, or green?" This question asks for an ordering that is neither possible nor logical.

At the **ordinal level** of measurement, one may classify and *order* values. For instance, consider the responses on a class evaluation question excellent, good, fair, or poor. "Excellent" is higher than "good," which is higher than "fair," which is higher than "poor." As such, the class evaluation question is at the ordinal level of measurement. Most questions probing agreement represent ordinal-level measurement. For instance, the responses strongly agree, agree, disagree, and strongly disagree may be ordered to convey level of agreement or disagreement.

At the ordinal level, the researcher may not measure the difference between values. For instance, one may not measure the difference between excellent and good. One knows that excellent is higher than good but does not know by how much. More formally, to find differences, one must be able to subtract one value from another value, but subtraction is not possible with nonnumeric values.

In **rank ordering**, objects are ordered on some characteristic from highest to lowest. The object's position in that ordering is their **rank**. Rank orderings are at the ordinal level.

For instance, suppose that there are 37 students in your current class. We could order them from tallest to shortest and assign ranks to each—"1" to the tallest, "2" to the next tallest, and so on down to "37" to the shortest. We would then know, for instance, that the student assigned Rank 5 was taller than the student assigned Rank 6. Yet, we would not know the actual difference in height between any two ranks. For instance, we would not know how much taller Rank 5 was than Rank 6.

At the **interval level**, the researcher can order values and, in addition, can *measure differences* between values. Differences can be measured because the values of interval-level variables represent numeric quantities, and thus, subtraction is valid. Temperature in degrees Fahrenheit is an example of an interval-level variable. To find the difference between, say, 50 and 40 degrees, subtract: $50 - 40 = 10$.

Ratios cannot be interpreted meaningfully at the interval level of measurement. For instance, suppose that it is 8 °F one day and 4 °F the next day. Dividing 8 by 4 yields the ratio "2" ($8 / 4 = 2$ or 2 to 1). This ratio (falsely) conveys that there was twice the quantity of heat on the first day as on the second—obviously, this was not so. For a ratio to be valid and meaningful, the zero point on the measurement scale must be a *true zero*, one that conveys the absence of the quantity being measured. The zero point on the Fahrenheit scale is an *arbitrary zero*, and thus, ratios involving degrees Fahrenheit are not meaningful.

When the zero (0) on the measurement scale is a true zero, ratios are meaningful and, hence, measurement is at the **ratio level**. Variables at the ratio-level measurement are, on balance, more common than are those at the interval level. For instance, physical quantities such as height and weight are typically measured at the ratio level. Let us use weight as an example. If Fred weighs 200 lb, and Yi weighs 100 lb, dividing Fred's weight by Yi's ($200 / 100 = 2$ or 2 to 1) yields a valid and meaningful ratio. We may indeed conclude that Fred weighs twice as much as Yi. *Counts* are at the ratio level of measurement. For instance, if Professor $X$ published nine articles and Professor $Y$ published three articles, then Professor $X$ published three times as many articles as Professor $Y$, $9 / 3 = 3$.

Observe that ratio-level measurement does not require that any case actually has the value "0." For instance, no real person weighs 0.00 lb. The key idea is that zero on the measurement scale conveys the absence of the quantity being measured. This is so for weight; if something weighs "0.00" lb, it has no weight.

Different statistical procedures are used with variables at different levels of measurement. For instance, given nominal-level measurement, one procedure is likely appropriate. Given ordinal-level measurement, another may be indicated. An exception is that, at least in introductory statistics, the same statistical procedures are used for interval- and ratio-level variables. This being so, from this point forward, this text groups these levels into a single level—the **interval/ratio level**.

Because greater precision is gained at higher levels of measurement, it is generally advisable to measure at the highest possible level. As an example, do not simply obtain rank orderings of height (ordinal level) when you can measure using, say, a tape measure (interval/ratio level). A helpful tip: To remember the ordering of levels of measurement from low to high, think of the letters of the French word for night, "noir": nominal, ordinal, interval, ratio.

It may be useful to relate the levels of measurement to the two types of variables: categorical and numeric. All variables at the nominal level are categorical. Most ordinal-level variables do indeed have categories and thus are categorical. Examples of categorical ordinal-level variables include those measuring, for instance, level of agreement (strongly disagree, disagree, agree, strongly agree), ratings (poor, fair, good, excellent), social class (lower, middle, upper), how often things happen (never, sometimes, often, always), and education level (less than high school, high school, college, graduate). Although at the ordinal level, rank orderings are numeric. However, remember that mathematical operations (for instance, calculating differences between values) are not valid with rank orderings. Finally, all variables at the interval/ratio level are numeric.

### 1.9.2 ■ Fine Points

Sometimes, researchers assign numbers to the values of categorical variables as, for instance, *strongly agree* = 4, *agree* = 3, *disagree* = 2, and *strongly disagree* = 1. The assigning of numbers does *not* make the level of measurement interval/ratio. In particular, ordinal-level variables remain ordinal-level variables whether numbers have been assigned. You should think of (and we will term) the numbers assigned to categories as *codes* rather than as numeric quantities.

A **multi-item scale** consists of multiple *items*, each of which probes some aspect of a concept. For instance, a multi-item self-esteem scale might consist of, say, 20 items, each probing some aspect of self-esteem. Examples might be "My opinions are valued," "I take pride in what I do," and so on. These items are almost always at the ordinal level of measurement. Researchers create scores on multi-item scales by summing codes for the items. For instance, for our self-esteem scale, the researcher would sum the codes for the 20 items.

The following question arises: What is the level of measurement of multi-item scale scores? Formally, these scores are *not* at the interval/ratio level. This is because summing together codes to derive a numeric score is not valid mathematically. Pragmatically, however, most researchers regard multi-item scores as being "almost" at the interval-ratio level. As such, they take the position that the statistical procedures designed for this level of measurement may be appropriately used to analyze them. I take this position in this text. I treat multi-item scale scores as interval-ratio level variables and use procedures appropriate for such variables with these scores.

## 1.10 ▨ CHAPTER SUMMARY

**Statistics** is "the science of making effective use of numerical data . . . " (Wikipedia, 2010b). A solid understanding of introductory statistics is important for *evidence-based practice*, practice based on "the best scientific evidence available" (Rubin, 2010, p. 315).

*Science* comprises "systematic knowledge gained through observation and experimentation" (*Random House Webster's Dictionary*, 1987, p. 1716). Its theoretical side is termed *theory*. The gathering of real-world observations is termed *research*. The observations gathered are *data*.

*Quantitative research methods* are characterized by objective *measurement*, which is the assigning of numbers or classifications to observations. *Qualitative research methods* "emphasize depth of understanding and the deeper meanings of human experience" (Rubin & Babbie, 2008, p. 643). *Program evaluation* is carried out to judge the usefulness of a social program or intervention.

Individual units are *cases*. Variables are the "ingredients of data." A *variable* is something with more than one value. *Value(s)* are the different numbers or classifications that a variable takes on or assumes. A *constant* takes on only one value. *Categorical variables* (*qualitative variables*) have nonnumeric values. A categorical variable with exactly two values is a *dichotomous variable*. *Numeric variables* (*quantitative variables*) have numeric values.

A *population* consists of *all* of the objects that possess a specified set of characteristics. A *sample* consists of *some* but not all of the objects in a population. *Random samples* (*probability samples*) are selected by methods of chance. When methods of chance are not used, the sample is a *nonrandom sample* (*nonprobability sample*). Participants in a study form the *study sample*. In a general sense, *sampling* refers to the methods used to select the study sample.

A *statistic* is a numerical summary of data (Toothaker & Miller, 1996, p. 7). *Descriptive statistics* describe the study sample. *Inferential statistics* are used to draw conclusions about a population based on a random sample selected from that population. With a random sample, only the luck of the draw causes differences between the sample and the population from which the sample is drawn. Although an important exception is presented later, inferential statistics should not be used with nonrandom samples.

*Univariate statistics* pertain to a *single* variable at a time. *Bivariate statistics* convey the relationship (or lack thereof) between *two* variables. Two variables are *related* (*associated*) when the values of one variable vary, differ, or change according to those of the other. Relationships in study samples can occur simply by the luck of the draw. *Statistical significance tests* determine whether study sample results are likely to be due to the luck of the draw.

*Multivariate statistics* involve three or more variables at a time. In a *causal relationship*, one variable affects the other. *Confounding variables* are third variables that bring about relationships between other variables. An *intervention* (*treatment*) is the "things that are done" to the research participant.

*Sampling* refers to how participants were selected to be in the study sample. *Assignment* refers to how participants are assigned to groups. *Random assignment* (*randomization*) is the use of methods of chance to assign participants to groups. In a randomized study, the only thing that distinguishes groups as the intervention begins is the luck of the draw of the assignment process. Confounding variables are not a concern.

In a nonrandomized study, confounding variables can cause differences between groups. It can be difficult, if not impossible, to determine whether a difference is caused by a confounding variable(s) or by the effects of the intervention. In a randomized study, given that a difference is sufficiently substantial so that "luck" alone is an unlikely explanation, the researcher can be confident that such difference is caused by the intervention.

An *independent variable* affects another variable. A *dependent variable* is affected by another variable.

Ordered from low to high, the *levels of measurement* are nominal, ordinal, interval, and ratio. At the *nominal* level, one may classify a variable's values into separate categories but these categories may not be ordered.

At the *ordinal level*, one may classify and order values but one may not determine differences between values. In a *rank ordering*, objects are ordered on some characteristic from highest to lowest. The object's position in that ordering is their *rank*. Rank orderings are at the ordinal level.

Variables measured at the *interval level* have numeric values, and hence, using subtraction, differences between values can be determined. Because the zero point of the measurement scale is not a true zero, one that conveys the absence of the quantity being measured, ratios are not meaningful for interval-level variables. When the zero (0) on the measurement scale is a true zero, ratios are meaningful, and hence, measurement is at the *ratio level*.

Different statistical procedures are used with variables at different levels of measurement. An exception is that the same statistical procedures are almost always used for interval- and ratio-level variables. This being so, these levels are grouped into a single level, the *interval/ratio level*. Almost always, one should measure at the highest possible level of measurement.

A *multi-item scale* consists of multiple items, each of which probes some aspect of a concept. Adapting a pragmatic stance, this text treats scores on multi-item scales as being at the interval/ratio level of measurement.

## 1.11 ▓ PROBLEMS AND QUESTIONS

### Section 1.2

1. Social work practice based on the "best scientific evidence available" (Rubin, 2010, p. 315) is termed _____-_____ practice.

### Section 1.3

2. The theoretical side of science is termed _____, and the applied/observational side is termed _____.

3. The observations that one gathers are termed _____.

4. The two basic social science research methods are _____ methods and _____ methods.

5. _____ research methods emphasize objective measurement. _____ research methods emphasize depth of understanding and deeper meaning.

6. Indicate whether each of the following demonstrates quantitative or qualitative research methods.

   a. Questions on a questionnaire ask respondents to choose between the responses "yes," "no," or "not sure."

   b. A researcher conducts in depth, deeply probing interviews asking children placed in foster care to share their personal feelings about the foster care experiences.

   c. A scientist records how long it takes rats to run a maze in two different situations.

   d. A researcher interviews in depth seven children who were adopted when older and produces "vignettes" of the unique experience of each one.

   e. A researcher rides motorcycles for a year with members of a motorcycle club. She gains first-hand, personalized experience of the "culture" of the club and develops an article on this.

   f. Youth who have been delinquent take part in a program designed to reduce delinquency. A researcher examines arrest records for these youth and develops a report based on these records.

   g. Some students in a statistics class receive tutoring from a teaching assistant. Others complete a computer-based statistics module. The professor compares grades on the final exam for the two groups and develops a report.

7. Indicate whether each of the following is applied research or pure research.

   a. A researcher examines whether a change in the nutritional content of school lunches leads to better health in an elementary school.

   b. A scientist studies the structure of the atom for the pure joy of learning.

   c. A social worker examines whether a behavior management program leads to better behavior among school children.

**Section 1.4**

8. Each individual unit on which measurements are recorded is a _____.

9. A variable is something that takes on different _____.

10. What are the values of the variable sex?

11. _____ take on only one value.

12. Is 3.1416 (*pi*) a variable or a constant?

13. _____ variables are numeric. _____ variables are nonnumeric.

**14.** Is the variable height (as it is most often measured) a quantitative or a qualitative variable?

**15.** Is the variable sex qualitative or quantitative?

**16.** A term synonymous with qualitative variable is _____ variable.

**17.** Indicate whether each of the following variables (as they are most commonly measured) is a quantitative (numeric) or a qualitative (categorical) variable.
   **a.** Number of movies seen in the last month.
   **b.** Whether (yes or no) you enjoy football games.
   **c.** Your score (percentage correct) on your last test.
   **d.** Favorite kind of music: rock, jazz, classical, hip-hop, and so on.
   **e.** Eye color (blue, brown, green etc.).

**18.** A _____ variable has exactly two categories. Another name for a dichotomous variable is a _____ variable.

## Section 1.5

**19.** _____ samples, also known as _____, are selected by methods of chance.

**20.** This text refers to those selected to be in a research study as the _____ _____.

**21.** Indicate whether each of the following is a random sample or a nonrandom sample.
   **a.** A computer program generates a random list of clients who will participate in a follow-up study.
   **b.** Social workers, working from memory, provide a list of clients who they believe would want to participate in a follow-up study.
   **c.** Clients who keep their appointments participate in a study. (Those who do not participate.)
   **d.** One hundred students are selected by "the luck of the draw" to take part in a campus opinion survey.
   **e.** An interviewer at a shopping mall stops shoppers, asking them if they want to complete a questionnaire.

## Section 1.6

**22.** A statistic is a _____ _____ of data (Toothaker & Miller, 1996).

**23.** Indicate whether the researcher is engaging in descriptive statistics or inferential statistics.
   **a.** A student organization studies responses of a random sample of university students for the purpose of drawing conclusions about the population of students at the university.
   **b.** A professor administers a questionnaire to students in her class and writes an article about these opinions.

    **c.** A researcher obtains data about the residents in a nursing home and writes about their situations.

    **d.** The National Association of Social Workers (NASW) selects a random sample of its members and mails them a survey. It studies the sample's responses to learn about the full NASW membership.

**24.** Indicate whether each of the following demonstrates a correct or incorrect use of inferential statistics. Consider the use as correct only if the researcher uses a *random* sample to draw conclusions about the *particular* population from which the sample was selected.

    **a.** A professor determines the opinions of social work students who are taking her class in social welfare policy and, based on this sample, draws conclusions about all social work students at her university.

    **b.** Community residents who attend a community meeting about violence in their community fill out a questionnaire on violence. The meeting's organizers tabulate responses and, based on them, draw conclusions about all members of the community.

    **c.** A random sample of students from University *X* responds to a poll on political attitudes. A professor uses these responses to write a report about the political attitudes of all students at University *X*.

    **d.** A random sample of students from University *X* responds to a poll on political attitudes. A professor uses these responses to write a report about the political attitudes of all students at University *Y*.

    **e.** A mental health clinic administers a survey on client satisfaction to a random sample of its clients. It uses this survey to draw conclusions about all of its clients.

**25.** Indicate which variable in each pair is the independent variable and which is the dependent variable. Or it may be that the variables cannot be classified as independent or dependent, in which case respond "cannot be classified."

    **a.** A researcher studies the effect of therapy (one variable) on assertiveness (other variable).

    **b.** A researcher monitors the relationship between amount of exercise (one variable) and blood pressure (other variable).

    **c.** A professor examines the association between number of hours studying for an exam (one variable) and grade on the exam (other variable).

    **d.** A researcher finds an association between self-esteem (one variable) and happiness (other variable). (Hint: Difficult one to answer.)

    **e.** A "token economy" (one variable) is developed to help an elementary school student reduce disruptive classroom behavior (other variable).

## Section 1.7

**26.** Indicate whether the application demonstrates univariate, bivariate, or multivariate statistics.

    **a.** A researcher examines the relationship between visiting of nursing home residents and the level of happiness of these residents.

    **b.** A poll reports that 57% of respondents support Legislation *X*.

    **c.** A researcher examines whether handedness (right vs. left) is associated with the choice of major (natural sciences vs. social sciences vs. humanities).

    **d.** A researcher finds a relationship between levels of exercise and blood pressure but wonders whether this relationship may be caused by a confounding variable, and therefore examines this possibility.

    **e.** In a single equation, a researcher examines the effects of several variables—income level growing up, family structure (one parent vs. two parent family), education level—on income earned at age 30.

    **f.** A professor finds that the average number of movies seen by students in her class in the last month is 3.7.

**27.** *Respond true or false.*

    **a.** Whenever one finds that two variables are associated in a random sample, one knows assuredly that these variables are associated in the population from which the sample was selected.

    **b.** At the risk of oversimplifying, with a random sample, only the "luck of the draw" causes differences between the characteristics and opinions of those in the sample and the characteristics and opinions of those in the population from which the sample was drawn.

**28.** _____ _____ _____ examine whether study sample results are likely to be caused by the luck of the draw.

**29.** The third variables that bring about relationships between other variables are often termed _____ variables.

**30.** See if you can think of a confounding variable or variables that might provide an alternative to the conclusion the "researcher" reaches about the cause of each relationship. There is no right or wrong answer to these.

    **a.** Some students volunteer to take part in a health fitness program. Others do not volunteer for this program. After the program has ended, those who took part (the volunteers) have, on average, lower blood pressure than those who did not take part. A researcher concludes that the fitness program caused the low blood pressure.

    **b.** A student researcher finds that students who volunteer in community projects score higher on a "happiness" scale than do students who do not volunteer. The researcher concludes that participation increases happiness.

    **c.** A child welfare researcher finds that children adopted by their foster parents are less likely to require mental health services than are children adopted by "new" adoptive parents. The researcher concludes that adoption with new adoptive parents (rather than with prior foster parents) causes mental health problems.

**Section 1.8**

**31.** _____ refers to the methods used to assign participants to groups.

**32.** _____ _____ is the use of methods of chance to assign participants to _____.

33. Indicate whether each of the following studies uses random assignment.
    a. One group consists of persons who volunteer to participate in a stop smoking program. A second group consists of persons who smoke about the same number of cigarettes but who do not volunteer.
    b. A researcher studies children in foster family homes (one group) and children in group homes (the other group), looking to see which group has better outcomes.
    c. Some elderly persons have pets (one group). Others do not (the other group). A researcher examines happiness in these groups.
    d. Fifty nursing home residents are selected to participate in a study. One half are randomly selected to receive visitation by a therapy pet and one half are randomly selected not to receive such visitation. Depression levels are studied.
    e. A professor selects randomly from a hat some students to receive tutoring on a computer and (again randomly) some students to receive tutoring from a teaching assistant. Scores on the final exam are compared.

34. *Respond true or false.*
    a. In studies that use random assignment, the researcher should be quite concerned that a confounding variable or variables is affecting study results.
    b. In studies that do not use random assignment, it can be extremely difficult if not impossible to determine whether a study result is caused by the intervention or by a confounding variable.
    c. Generally speaking, random assignment to groups increases the researcher's confidence that the study results are caused by the intervention rather than by a confounding variable.

## Section 1.9

35. When variables are at the nominal level, one may _____ responses into categories. At the ordinal level, one may also _____ responses/categories. At the interval level, one may speak meaningfully about the _____ between values. At the ratio level, _____ become meaningful.

36. All rank orderings are at the _____ level of measurement.

37. At the ratio level of measurement, "0" may be regarded as a _____ zero rather than an arbitrary one. Zero on a ratio-level scale conveys the _____ of the quantity being measured.

38. In your own words, why does not it make sense to say that 10 °F is twice as hot as 5 °F?

39. Indicate the level of measurement for each of the following:
    a. Shoe size as measured in the United States
    b. Social class (lower, middle, upper)
    c. Weight measured with a scale

    **d.** Political party (Republican, Democratic, etc.)

    **e.** Students rank order themselves according to the amount of time that they spent studying

    **f.** Religion (Christian, Hindu, Buddhist, Native American Church, other)

**40.** This text recommends treating the numbers that are sometimes assigned to the values of categorical variables as _____ rather than numeric quantities.

**41.** As a general rule of thumb, one should measure at the _____ possible level of measurement.

**42.** *Respond true or false.*

    **a.** Many statistical procedures are appropriate only for variables at particular levels of measurement.

    **b.** Whether a variable is considered to be at the interval level versus the ratio level often has important consequences for the basic introductory statistical procedures that may be used.

    **c.** The *individual items* that are summed together to develop scores on multi-item scales are at the interval/ratio level of measurement.

    **d.** In a formal and mathematical sense, scores on multi-item scales are (without question) regarded as being at the interval/ratio level of measurement.

    **e.** Pragmatically, most researchers view scores on multi-item scales as being at or very nearly at the interval/ratio level of measurement.

    **f.** So far, statistics is fun.

2

# DATA PRESENTATION

## 2.1 ▪ CHAPTER OVERVIEW

Chapter 2 defines some new terms and presents univariate (one variable at a time) *tables* and *figures*. It presents *frequency distribution tables* and *grouped frequency distribution tables*, and then *bar charts*, *histograms*, *frequency polygons*, *box plots*, and *pie charts*. If you need refreshing in the math of percentages, proportions, or ratios, see the Review of Basic Math in Appendix B before you read this chapter.

## 2.2 ▪ FREQUENCY DISTRIBUTIONS AND TABLES

The number of cases in the study sample is the **sample size**, symbolized by $N$. Thus, if there are 42 cases in the study sample, the sample size is 42 (i.e., $N = 42$). The number of cases with a given value is that value's **frequency**, symbolized by $f$. Thus, if 28 of the 42 persons in a sample are women, the frequency of women is 28, that is, $f = 28$. If three persons are 5 ft. 6 in. tall, then $f = 3$ for that height. The symbol $n$ is an alternative to $f$, particularly to refer to the number in a group. For instance, the earlier mentioned frequency of women may be symbolized either as $f = 28$ or as $n = 28$.

A **distribution** is a group of values that have been organized in some way (Toothaker & Miller, 1996, p. 23). A **frequency distribution** groups together cases with the same values. Table 2.1 presents a frequency distribution and thus is termed a **frequency distribution table**. In addition to frequencies, frequency distribution tables almost always present percentages. The formula for the percentage of cases with a given value is

$$\% = (f / N) \times 100 \tag{2.1}$$

In Table 2.1, the frequency of women is 11 and the percentage of women is $11/20 = .55 \times 100 = 55\%$.

When values can be ordered, frequency distribution tables present lower values first. For instance, Table 2.2 presents the age of sexual abuse perpetrators at a child protective services agency in this way. When values can be ordered, cumulative frequencies and cumulative percentages are often presented. A value's **cumulative frequency** is the number of cases with that value or a lower value. For instance, in Table 2.2, the cumulative frequency of perpetrators aged 17 years and younger is five. Two perpetrators were 14, one was 15, and two were 17: $2 + 1 + 2 = 5$.

Table 2.1 ■ Gender of Persons in a Hypothetical Class (*N* = 20)

| Value | Frequency | Percentage |
|---|---|---|
| Female | 11 | 55 |
| Male | 9 | 45 |
| *Note. N* = 20 | | |

A value's **cumulative percentage** is the percentage of cases with that value or a lower value. The formula for cumulative percentage is

$$\text{cumulative percentage} = \frac{\text{cumulative frequency}}{\text{sample size}} \times 100 \tag{2.2}$$

This formula divides the cumulative frequency by the sample size and then multiplies by 100. Thus, the cumulative percentage of perpetrators aged 17 years and younger is 5/20 = .25 × 100 = 25%.

Observe that calculations of cumulative frequency and cumulative percentage require that values be ordered from low to high. These procedures are not valid for nominal-level variables because the values of these variables cannot be ordered. For instance, cumulative frequency and cumulative percentage cannot be calculated in Table 2.1 because the values of sex cannot be ordered.

A **grouped frequency distribution** groups cases with similar values to form categories. This is done to make the data easier to manage and interpret. Table 2.3 presents a **grouped frequency distribution table** for the sexual abuse perpetrator data.

Table 2.2 ■ Ages of Sexual Abuse Perpetrators

| Age | Frequency | Percentage | Cumulative Frequency | Cumulative Percentage |
|---|---|---|---|---|
| 14 | 2 | 10 | 2 | 10 |
| 15 | 1 | 5 | 3 | 15 |
| 17 | 2 | 10 | 5 | 25 |
| 21 | 2 | 10 | 7 | 35 |
| 23 | 1 | 5 | 8 | 40 |
| 26 | 1 | 5 | 9 | 45 |
| 32 | 1 | 5 | 10 | 50 |
| 37 | 1 | 5 | 11 | 55 |
| 38 | 1 | 5 | 12 | 60 |
| 42 | 1 | 5 | 13 | 65 |
| 44 | 1 | 5 | 14 | 70 |
| 55 | 3 | 15 | 17 | 85 |
| 63 | 1 | 5 | 18 | 90 |
| 67 | 1 | 5 | 19 | 95 |
| 77 | 1 | 5 | 20 | 100 |
| *Note. N* = 20. Hypothetical data. | | | | |

Table 2.3 ■ Grouped Frequency Distribution of Perpetrator Age

| Age | Frequency | Percentage | Cumulative Frequency | Cumulative Percentage |
|---|---|---|---|---|
| 19 or younger | 5 | 25 | 5 | 25 |
| 20–29 | 4 | 20 | 9 | 45 |
| 30–39 | 3 | 15 | 12 | 60 |
| 40–49 | 2 | 10 | 14 | 70 |
| 50 and older | 6 | 30 | 20 | 100 |
| *Note. N* = 20. Hypothetical data. | | | | |

## 2.3 ■ FIGURES

**Tables** do not include pictures or graphics. On the other hand, when pictures or graphics are used, one has a **figure**. We examine six types of figures. The examples for figures are taken from a random sample of 1,494 cases from the National Longitudinal Study of Youth (NLSY). The NLSY's study sample comprises persons born in the years 1980–1984. They were aged 12–17 when first interviewed in 1997. The figures were generated by the IBM SPSS Statistics software package.[1]

**Bar charts** display frequencies of categorical variables. A variable's values are typically displayed on the horizontal axis. The height of each *bar* (*column*) conveys frequency. To estimate a value's frequency, trace from the top of its bar over to the vertical axis. Figure 2.1 presents a bar chart for the ethnicity of youth in a random sample from the NLSY. In Figure 2.1, the term *count* is a synonym for frequency. Ethnicity is broken down into four categories.

FIGURE 2.1 ■ Ethnicity of Youth in the National Longitudinal Study of Youth

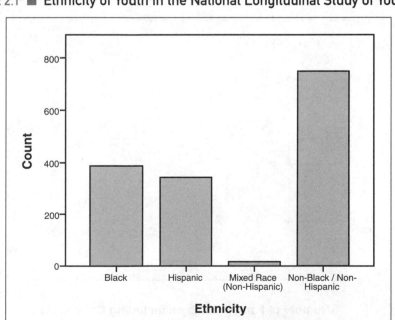

To estimate, for instance, the frequency of Hispanic youth, trace from the top of the bar labeled Hispanic to the vertical axis. This reveals that about 350 youth are Hispanic. Observe that the bars in a bar chart do not touch. This conveys that each bar represents a separate and distinct value. As you know, the values of nominal-level variables cannot be ordered. This being so, the ordering of the values from left to right for nominal-level variables is arbitrary, essentially at the researcher's discretion. On the other hand, the values of ordinal-level variables can be ordered. Thus, for categorical ordinal-level variables, the bar chart presents lowest value first (the leftmost bar), then the next highest value and so on up to the highest (the rightmost bar).

**Histograms** display frequencies of numeric variables. Like bar charts, histograms have bars and, like bar charts, the bars' heights convey frequency. Obviously, numeric variables' values can be ordered. The order of a histogram bars is the same as that of bar chart for ordinal-level data; lowest values are on the left and values ascend as one moves to the right. Unlike the bar chart, a histogram's bars touch or come close to doing so. This touching (or near touching) of the bars signifies that adjacent bars have similar values.

Figure 2.2 presents the number of family members, including cohabitators, residing in the NLYS sample families when the study began in 1997. The most common number of family members was four, about 400 families being of this size.

Just as histograms, frequency polygons are used with numeric variables. **Frequency polygons** represent with lines the same information as do histograms with bars. Frequency is conveyed by the height of the line. Figure 2.3 presents the NLSY family size information using a frequency polygon.

As histograms and frequency polygons convey the same information and as both are used with numeric variables, the researcher chooses which to use. I tend to prefer histograms as these are more common and perhaps easier to understand. However, histograms start to get quite

FIGURE 2.2 ■ **Histogram of Number of Family Members Residing in the Home in National Longitudinal Study of Youth**

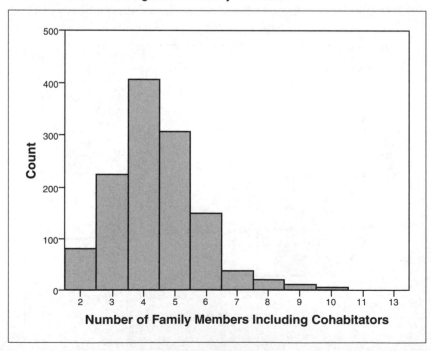

FIGURE 2.3 ■ **Frequency Polygon of Number of Family Members in the National Longitudinal Study of Youth**

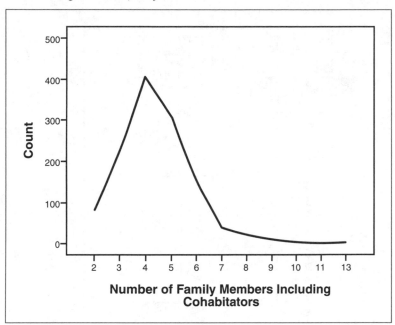

"crowded" when the number of categories exceeds, say, 20. So, perhaps using histograms when there are 20 or fewer categories and frequency polygons when there are more than 20 categories is a sensible guideline.[3]

**Box plots** (*box and whisker plots*) are used with numeric data and consist of a box, whiskers, and fences. The edge at the top of the box conveys the value at the 75th percentile. The edge at the box's bottom conveys the value at the 25th percentile. The line inside the box represents the 50th percentile. A case's *percentile* (*percentile rank*) is the percentage of cases with lower values.[2] For instance, if Fred's height is at the 72nd percentile, this conveys that Fred is taller than 72% of the persons in the sample. A box plot's *whiskers* are the lines that extend out from the edges of the box. The horizontal lines at which the whiskers end are *fences*.

Figure 2.4 is a box plot of the number of days during the past 30 days on which NLSY study participants had drunk alcohol. This question was asked in 2007, at which time the participants ranged in age from about 23 to about 27. This question was not asked of participants who indicated that they had not drunk alcohol since a prior interview.

Looking at the top edge of the box, we can see that the value at the 75th percentile is 10 days. The bottom edge of the box indicates that 2 days is at the 25th percentile. The line through the box's middle indicates that the 50th percentile is four days. The fence at the end of the whisker below the box is located at 0 days while that at the top is located at 20 days. Conceptually, values located beyond the fences are regarded as being extremely different from most other values. Figure 2.4 lists case numbers for values beyond the fences. In Figure 2.4, all such values are above the upper fence. Sometimes, extreme values such as these may reflect a mistake in entering data. Often, researchers examine such values closely as they can have large effects on the results of statistical procedures. I discuss the implications of extreme values in subsequent chapters.

FIGURE 2.4 ■ Box Plot of Number of Drinking Days in the National Longitudinal
Study of Youth

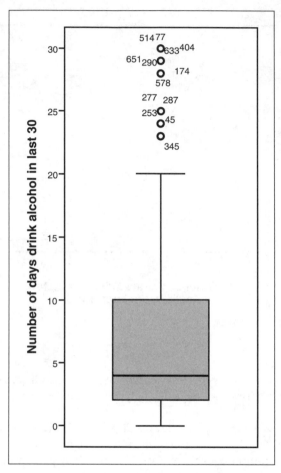

**Pie charts** provide another way to present frequencies and percentages. Figure 2.5 presents the number of days drinking in the past 30 days as a grouped frequency distribution. In a pie chart, the size of a category's "slice" conveys the percentage of cases in that category. For instance, the less than or equal to one (≤1) slice comprises about 25% of the area of the pie. This informs us that about 25% of youth drank on 1 day or less. Pie charts are used with categorical variables.

## 2.4 ■ CHAPTER SUMMARY

*Sample size* is the number of cases and is symbolized by *N*. *Frequency*, symbolized by *f*, is the number of cases with a given value.

A *distribution* is a group of values that has been organized in some way (Toothaker & Miller, 1996, p. 23). A *frequency distribution* groups together cases with the same values and is presented by a *frequency distribution table*. A value's *cumulative frequency* is the number of cases with that value or a lower one. A value's *cumulative percentage* is the percentage of cases with that value or a lower one.

FIGURE 2.5 ■ **Pie Chart of Number of Drinking Days in the National Longitudinal Study of Youth**

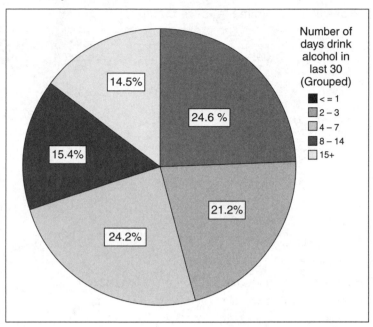

In a *grouped frequency distribution*, cases with similar values are grouped together to form categories. A table that presents a grouped frequency distribution is a *grouped frequency distribution table*.

*Tables* do not include pictures or graphics while *figures* do. *Bar charts* use bars to display frequencies of categorical variables. *Histograms* also use bars but are used with numeric variables. The columns of the bar chart do not touch while those of the histogram do (or nearly do). *Frequency polygons* present the same information as do histograms but do so using lines rather than bars. Another way to present frequencies is with *pie charts*.

The line at the bottom of a *box plot*'s box conveys the 25th percentile. The line in the middle of the box conveys the 50th percentile. The line at the top conveys the 75th percentile. *Pie charts* present frequencies and percentages for categorical variables.

## 2.5 ■ PROBLEMS AND QUESTIONS

**Section 2.2**

1. The symbol for the number of cases in the study sample is _____.

2. The number of cases with a given value is the _____

3. The symbol for frequency is _____.

4. An alternative symbol for frequency, often used to indicate the number in a group is _____.

The next series of questions pertain to the following table.

Table 2.4  ■  **Ages of Students in Statistics Class**

| Age | Frequency | Percentage | Cumulative Frequency | Cumulative Percentage |
|---|---|---|---|---|
| 18 or below | 2 | | 2 | 10 |
| 19 or 20 | 6 | 30 | | |
| 21 or 22 | 5 | | 13 | 65 |
| 23–29 | 3 | 10 | 16 | |
| 30 and older | 4 | | 20 | 100 |
| *Note. N* = 20. | | | | |

5. Regarding Table 2.4 . . .
   a. What is the sample size?
   b. What is the percentage aged 18 or younger?
   c. What is the cumulative frequency aged 19 or 20 or younger?
   d. What is the cumulative percentage aged 19 or 20 or younger?
   e. What is the percentage aged 21 or 22?
   f. What is the cumulative percentage aged 23–29 or younger?
   g. What is the percentage who are 30 or older?

6. As it groups together cases with common values, Table 2.4 is an example of a _____ _____ distribution table.

7. A study sample consists of 30 persons, 14 of whom are women and 16 of whom are men.
   a. What is *N*?
   b. What is the frequency of women?
   c. Assume that a frequency distribution table lists women first and then men. This being so, what is the cumulative frequency of men? (Trick question?)

8. A _____ is a group of values that have been organized in some way (Toothaker & Miller, 1996, p. 23).

**Section 2.3**

9. _____ do not include pictures or graphics while _____ do include these.

10. Among clients at a mental health center, 33 receive individual therapy, 72 receive group therapy, and 22 receive an innovative service entitled computer-assisted therapy. For the variable type of therapy . . .
    a. What is the level of measurement?
    b. Is a histogram or a bar chart the better choice?

    **c.** Should the columns of the chart "touch"? Why or Why not?

    **d.** Draw (by hand) a bar chart.

**11.** Regarding Figure 2.1, what is the approximate frequency of Hispanic youth?

**12.** Regarding Figure 2.1, is the ordering of the bars arbitrary (choice of researcher) or must the groups be displayed in a particular order?

**13.** *Respond true or false.*

    **a.** Histograms are used with numeric data rather than with categorical data.

    **b.** Frequency polygons and histograms present the same information in different ways.

**14.** Thinking about the number of values that a variable has: When is a histogram preferred and when is a frequency polygon preferred?

**15.** Yuan is taller than 83% of persons in a population. What is Yuan's percentile rank in height?

**16.** Regarding the box plot . . .

    **a.** The line at the bottom of the box represents the _____ percentile.

    **b.** The line at the top of the box represents the _____ percentile.

    **c.** The thick line located inside the box represents the _____ percentile.

    **d.** The lines that extend away from the box are termed _____.

    **e.** The lines at which the whiskers end are termed _____.

**17.** In a sample of 90 clients at a family support agency, 25 participate in a "job search skills" focused program, 45 in a "basic skills training" program, and 20 in a "mentor" program. For this data . . .

    **a.** What is the percentage in the job search skills program?

    **b.** In drawing a pie chart, what percentage of the area of the pie should the "slice" representing the job search skills program represent?

    **c.** Draw a pie chart.

**18.** Regarding Figure 2.5 . . .

    **a.** About what percentage of the total pie is represented by the slice for respondents who drank from 8–14 days of the last 30 days?

    **b.** About what percentage of respondents drank from 8–14 days?

# 3

# CENTRAL TENDENCY

## 3.1 ▧ CHAPTER OVERVIEW

Chapter 3 focuses on the three key measures of central tendency: the *mode*, the *median*, and the *mean*. It discusses when each is used and their advantages and disadvantages. It shows how *outliers* influence the mean. In closing, this chapter introduces a fourth measure, the *trimmed mean*.

## 3.2 ▧ KEY CONCEPTS IN UNIVARIATE DESCRIPTIVE STATISTICS

Univariate statistical procedures describe the characteristics of a single variable. Three different characteristics can be described. **Central tendency** refers to the value around which most values tend to cluster or converge. **Variability** refers to the degree to which values are dispersed (spread out) around some central value. And, finally, **shape of distribution** refers to the particular way (pattern) in which values vary. This chapter addresses central tendency.

## 3.3 ▧ THREE KEY MEASURES OF CENTRAL TENDENCY

Measures of central tendency inform us about the typical, the common, the middle, the "everyday"—if you will, the "run of the mill." The three key measures of central tendency are as follows:

- ▧ The **mode** is the most frequently occurring value, that is, the value with the greatest frequency.
- ▧ The **median** is the value with the same number of values greater than and less than its value.
- ▧ The **mean** (or *average)* is the sum of all values divided by the number of cases.

Consider the values: 5, 8, 5, 10, 9, 11, and 43. Perhaps these represent the number of books read by the seven members of the first-grade Chickadees reading group.

The mode is 5, which occurs twice, more than any other value.

To find the median, order the values from low to high: 5, 5, 8, 9, 10, 11, and 43. The median is 9 because there are three lower values and an equal number (three) of higher values.

The mean is 13: (5 + 8 + 5 + 10 + 9 + 11 + 43) / 7 = 13.

## 3.4 ■ THE MODE

The mode may be used with variables at all levels of measurement. For categorical variables, it is ordinarily a nonnumeric value. For instance, if there are 15 women and 5 men in your class, the mode for sex is female because this value occurs more than any other. For numeric variables, the mode is numeric. For instance, in the Chickadees reading example, the mode was 5.

The great advantage of the mode is its simplicity and easily understood meaning. A disadvantage is that it fluctuates a lot just by luck, particularly in small samples. It is perhaps the least used of the three key central tendency measures.

Be careful not to confuse mode and frequency. For instance, in the just-presented example pertaining to your class, the frequency of women is 15 and the mode is female; the mode is a value, not the frequency of that value. Similarly, in the Chickadees example, the mode is 5, and the frequency for this value is 2.

## 3.5 ■ THE MEDIAN

The median can be calculated for ordinal-level and interval/ratio-level variables but not for nominal-level data. Consider, for instance, the question: "What is the median sex of students in your class?" This question is nonsensical. Calculation of the median requires that values be ordered from low to high. Because the values of nominal-level variables cannot be ordered, these variables have no median. The values of sex (female and male) cannot be ordered, and thus, there is no "median" sex.

The Chickadees example demonstrated calculation given an odd number of cases (one orders cases and finds the middle case). When the number of cases is even and the variable is numeric, the median is the mean of the two "middlemost" values. For instance, consider these values, which have already been ordered from low to high: 2, 3, 6, 8, 9, 10. The two middlemost values are 6 and 8. Hence, the median is $(6 + 8) / 2 = 7$.

The most common mistake made in computing the median is forgetting to order the values from low to high. For instance, what is the median of these values: 2, 9, 3, 7, and 4? The temptation is to respond "3" because this value is in the middle of the values as just listed. But, the values must be ordered from low to high prior to determining the median: 2, 3, 4, 7, 9. The middle value in the ordered values is 4; this is the correct median. Indeed, a good definition for the median is the middle value in a set of ordered values.

Still, another definition for the median is the value at the 50th percentile. When a value is at the 50th percentile, one half of values are lower and one half are higher. If Jack's height is at the 50th percentile, he is taller than one half of his peers and shorter than one half—he is right in the middle.

In the examples presented so far, we have not dealt with situations in which several or more cases have the same values. These are commonly encountered with ordinal-level categorical variables. When several or more cases have the same values, the median is the first value for which the cumulative percentage equals or exceeds 50.

Table 3.1 presents responses of adoptive parents to the question: "Overall, has the impact of this child's adoption on your family been . . .?" The children in the study in which the just-presented question was asked were adopted through public child welfare agencies (Rosenthal & Groze, 1992). Many of these children had special needs. Special needs include characteristics such as older age, behavior problems, handicapping condition, and being a member of an

Table 3.1 ■ **Impact of Adoption on Family**

| Value and Numeric Code Assigned to Value | Frequency | Cumulative Frequency | Percentage | Cumulative Percentage |
|---|---|---|---|---|
| Very negative 1 | 10 | 10 | 1 | 1 |
| Mostly negative 2 | 24 | 34 | 3 | 4 |
| Mixed 3 | 163 | 197 | 21 | 25 |
| Mostly positive 4 | 218 | 415 | 28 | 53 |
| Very positive 5 | 365 | 780 | 47 | 100 |

*Note. N = 790.*

adoptive sibling group. In Table 3.1, the first value that has a cumulative percentage equal to or exceeding 50 is "Mostly positive," which has a cumulative percentage of 53. Hence, mostly positive is the median.[1,2]

Cumulative percentage and percentile, both introduced in Chapter 2, are, essentially, equivalent terms. Hence, for data in which many cases share the same value, the median can be thought of as the first value for which percentile rank equals or exceeds 50.

The median is used more often than the mode but less often than the mean. Shortly, a situation in which the median is preferred to the mean will be presented.

## 3.6 ■ THE MEAN

The formula for the mean is as follows:

$$\overline{X} = \frac{\Sigma X}{N} \tag{3.1}$$

where $\overline{X}$ is the mean, $X$ is the value (score) of an individual case, and $N$ is the number of cases (the study sample size). The summation sign, $\Sigma$, instructs one to sum together all of the $X$'s (all of the individual values) in the study sample. Hence, the formula directs one to (a) sum the values and then (b) divide by the sample size.

The mean requires measurement at the interval/ratio level. For instance, it is obvious that there is no such thing as the "mean" sex of students in a class. And, shifting our focus to ordinal-level data, one may not calculate a mean when the response choices are, for instance, excellent, good, fair, or poor. This is because these values are nonnumeric.

Formally speaking, when a variable is at the ordinal level of measurement, the mean cannot be calculated. This is so even when numbers (codes) have been assigned to values. As discussed in Chapter 1, Section 1.9.2, these assigned numbers are codes rather than numeric quantities.

Pragmatically, however, some researchers do use these codes to calculate means. For instance, in Table 3.1, the "mean" numeric code computes to 4.16. The code 4 corresponds to *mostly positive* and the code 5 to *very positive*. So, the mean response in Table 3.1 is a little more positive than mostly positive (4.16 is a little bit higher than 4). Formally, this mean is not valid because it was computed using codes and, as just mentioned, these are not numeric quantities. Pragmatically, however, some researchers contend that, given straightforward and reasonable codes, means calculated from codes provide useful information. Most would agree that the codes used in Table 3.1—1, 2, 3, 4, 5—are straightforward and reasonable. Hence, some would indeed contend that the mean (code) of 4.16 conveys useful information.

My opinion is that, given straightforward codes, the mean of a categorical ordinal-level variable helps one "get a feel" for what that variable conveys. For instance, the just-calculated mean of 4.16 helps me get a feel for the distinctly positive responses regarding the impact of adoption and, by so doing, increases understanding.

Any mean calculated using numeric codes should be viewed as an approximation rather than as a firm numeric quantity. Further, such means are rarely appropriate for formal publication or reporting. In reports, the symbol $M$ is preferred over $\overline{X}$.

## 3.7 ■ CHOOSING BETWEEN MEASURES

Table 3.2 summarizes the required level of measurement for the three key central tendency measures. An "X" indicates that the measure may be appropriately used at a given level of measurement. Note that the mode may be used with variables at all levels, the median may be used only with those at the ordinal and interval/ratio levels, and, formally, the mean may be used only with those at the interval/ratio level.

A different question from when a given measure may be used is "Which measure is the *best* measure?" In part, because its value fluctuates so much in small samples, the mode is perhaps the least preferred measure. The discussion that follows presumes interval/ratio level measurement.

The mean is the most commonly used measure of central tendency and, in most situations, is the preferred measure. The median is preferred over the mean in a specific situation, that being when one's data has an outlier or outliers. An **outlier** (*extreme value*) is a value that is markedly higher or lower than other values. For instance, the Chickadees reading data has an outlier—that being the 43. Outliers "pull" the mean toward their own value. For instance, the 43 (a *positive outlier* because its value is higher than other values) pulls the mean upward, that is, in a positive direction. *Negative outliers*, on the other hand, pull the mean downward, that is, in a negative direction.

One wants a measure of central tendency to convey the typical, common value, if you will, "the middle." An outlier can pull the mean so much that it no longer conveys the middle. For instance, because of the influence of the outlier (43), the mean number of books read by the Chickadees, $(5 + 8 + 5 + 10 + 9 + 11 + 43) / 7 = 13$, does not convey the typical, common number of books that students read. This mean potentially misleads the unwary person into thinking that the typical, average Chickadee reads 13 books. The median value of 9 books clearly does a better job of conveying the common, typical number of books read.

Observe that the mean can be influenced greatly by the values of the lowest and highest cases. On the other hand, the median is not influenced by these values. For instance, changing the value of

Table 3.2 ■ **Levels of Measurement at Which the Measures of Central Tendency May Be Used**

| Level of Measurement | Mode | Median | Mean |
| --- | --- | --- | --- |
| Nominal | X | | |
| Ordinal | X | X | |
| Interval/ratio | X | X | X |

the highest case from 43 to 15 reduces the mean in our Chickadees example from 13 to 9: (5 + 8 + 5 + 10 + 9 + 11 + 15) / 7 = 9. On the other hand, this change does not affect the median. When the highest value was 43, the median was 9. With the highest value changed to 15, it continues to be 9, the middle value in the ordering: 5, 5, 8, 9, 10, 11, and 15.

Viewing things from just a little bit different perspective, the median is affected hardly at all by outliers. An outlier is just one more case in the ordering of cases that determines the median. In this sense, it has no more and no less influence on the median than any other case. This "resistance" of the median to the effects of outliers is why it is preferred over the mean when they are present.

One more example of a situation where the median is preferred over the mean may be useful. Family income in the United States is almost always reported using the median because the astronomically high incomes of a few (for instance, Microsoft co-founder Bill Gates) pull the mean upward so much that it ceases to convey the typical, common income.

In sum, the mode is rarely preferred. The median is preferred when outliers pull the mean to such a degree that it does not convey the middle. The mean is the most commonly used measure and is preferred, except when outliers are present.

A final measure of central tendency is the trimmed mean. A **trimmed mean** is a mean with a percentage of the lowest values and highest values excluded from its computation; the same percentage of lowest and highest values is excluded. For instance, a 10% trimmed mean is a mean with the lowest 5% and highest 5% of values excluded. And, for instance, a 5% trimmed mean excludes the lowest and highest 2.5% of values. The trimmed mean is an excellent alternative to the median for data that contains outliers. By excluding extremely high and extremely low values from computation, the influence of outliers is eliminated or reduced.

## 3.8 ■ CHAPTER SUMMARY

Univariate statistical procedures describe the characteristics of a single variable. *Central tendency* refers to the value around which other values cluster. *Variability* refers to the degree to which values are dispersed around some central value. *Shape of distribution* refers to the particular way in which values vary.

The *mode* is the most commonly occurring value. The *median* is the value with the same number of values above and below it. The *mean* is the sum of all values divided by the number of cases.

The mode may be used with variables at all levels of measurement. Its key advantages are simplicity and straightforward meaning. A disadvantage is that it fluctuates considerably, particularly when sample size is small.

The median is also defined as the value at the 50th percentile. Calculation requires measurement at the ordinal level or above. It is preferred over the mean when outliers are present. Given an even number of cases, the median is the mean of the two middlemost values.

The mean is the most commonly used measure of central tendency. Generally, it is the preferred measure. Formally, it requires measurement at the interval/ratio level. Some researchers use numeric codes to calculate means for categorical, ordinal-level variables. Such means are rarely acceptable in formal reports.

*Outliers* can pull the mean toward their own values and, by so doing, make it a misleading measure. The median is resistant to the effects of outliers and, for this reason, is preferred when they are present. The *trimmed mean* excludes cases with very high and very low values.

## 3.9 ■ PROBLEMS AND QUESTIONS

### Section 3.2

1. Three important characteristics of a variable are: _____ _____, _____, and _____ of distribution.

2. Central tendency refers to the value(s) around which most values tend to _____. Variability refers to the degree to which values are _____ around central value. _____ of _____ refers to the particular way in which values vary.

### Section 3.3

3. The three major measures of central tendency are the _____, the _____, and the _____.

4. The mode is the value with the greatest _____. The median is the value with the same number of values _____ _____ and _____ _____ its value. The median is the _____ value in an ordering of values. The mean is the _____ of the values of all cases divided by the _____ of cases, that is, divided by the _____ _____.

5. Consider these values: 2, 6, 1, 2, 5, 4, and 29. Regarding these values:
   a. The mode is _____.
   b. The median is _____.
   c. The mean is _____.

6. Consider these values: 5, 2, 7, 3, and 3. Regarding these values:
   a. The mode is _____.
   b. The median is _____.
   c. The mean is _____.

### Section 3.4

7. The mode "makes sense" (is appropriate) for variables at what levels of measurement?

### Section 3.5

8. Calculation of the median requires measurement at the _____ level or above.

9. In a state legislature, there are 22 Democrats, 19 Republicans, and 2 Independents. What is the median? (Think carefully.)

**10.** Consider the following observations: 9, 4, 7, 6, 8.
- **a.** Order the observations from low to high.
- **b.** What is the value of the "middle" case in the ordering of cases?
- **c.** What is the median?

**11.** Consider the following observations: 29, 18, 13, 62, 41.
- **a.** Order the observations from low to high.
- **b.** What is the value of the "middle" case in the ordering of cases?
- **c.** What is the median?

**12.** What is the median of these observations: 3, 8, 1, 5, 4?

**13.** Consider the following observations: 14, 12, 8, 16, 9, 15.
- **a.** Order the observations from low to high.
- **b.** What are the two "middlemost" values in the ordering?
- **c.** What is the mean of the two middlemost cases?
- **d.** What is the median?

**14.** What is the median of these observations: 4, 9, 7, 8, 5, 1?

**15.** Twenty persons respond to a questionnaire about height: five respond that they are short, eight respond that they are medium height, and seven respond that they are tall. (Note: order the values from short to medium to tall.)
- **a.** What is the percentage for each value (response)?
- **b.** What is the cumulative percentage of each value?
- **c.** In the just-calculated cumulative percentages, what is the first cumulative percentage greater than or equal to 50?
- **d.** What value (category) does the first cumulative percentage greater than or equal to 50 correspond to?
- **e.** What is the median?
- **f.** What is the mode?
- **g.** What is the mean?

**16.** Ten persons respond to a question evaluating a workshop: one person responds poor, two persons respond fair, three persons respond good, and four persons respond excellent.
- **a.** What is the percentage for each value (response)?
- **b.** What is the cumulative percentage of each value?
- **c.** In the just-calculated cumulative percentages, what is the first cumulative percentage greater than or equal to 50?
- **d.** What value (category) does the first cumulative percentage greater than or equal to 50 correspond to?
- **e.** What is the median?

   **f.** What is the mode?

   **g.** What is the mean?

17. Consult Table 2.2 in Chapter 2. What is the median age of sexual abuse perpetrators?

## Section 3.6

18. The most commonly used measure of central tendency is the _____. In the formula for the mean, _____ symbolizes the score for an individual case and _____ symbolizes the mean. In reports, the symbol _____ is often used for the mean.

19. (*True or False*) In a formal sense, the mean is a valid and appropriate measure for variables at the ordinal level of measurement.

20. In a formal sense, the mean is a valid and appropriate measure of central tendency only for variables at the _____ / _____ level of measurement.

21. *Respond true or false.*

   **a.** No researchers at all use numeric codes to calculate means for ordinal-level categorical variables.

   **b.** Means calculated from numeric codes for ordinal-level data may be used without hesitation or concern in formal publications and reports.

22. What is the mean of the following observations: 18, 22, 38, 17, 12?

23. Consider the following distribution: 8, 10, 11, 12, 14, 83?

   **a.** What term describes the value 83?

   **b.** Is the median or the mean preferred?

   **c.** What is the median?

   **d.** The outlier 83 pulls the mean in a _____ direction.

   **e.** In your own words, why is the mean ($\overline{X} = 23$) a misleading measure of central tendency?

## Section 3.7

24. *The next series of questions are true or false.*

   **a.** The mode is typically preferred over both the mean and the median for analyzing interval/ratio-level data.

   **b.** Outliers typically have very little effect on the value of the mean.

   **c.** When outliers are present, the median is often preferred over the mean.

   **d.** Outliers can pull the value of the median so much that it ceases to be a useful measure of central tendency.

   **e.** The median is "resistant" to outliers; that is, it is not affected much by them.

**25.** Positive outliers pull the mean _____; negative outliers pull it _____.

**26.** Consider this data: 1, 2, 3, 5, 29.
   **a.** What is the mean?
   **b.** What is the median?
   **c.** Is the median or the mean preferred?

**27.** Compare this data to the data in the prior question, noting that the value of the highest case has changed: 1, 2, 3, 5, 9.
   **a.** What is the mean?
   **b.** What is the median?
   **c.** Is the median or the mean preferred? (Actually, a tough question.)
   **d.** (True or False) The mean of this data is the same as that in the prior question.
   **e.** (True or False) The median of this data is the same as that in the prior question.

**28.** A 10% trimmed mean excludes the lowest _____ % of cases and the highest _____ % of cases.

# 4

# MEASURES OF VARIABILITY

## 4.1 ■ CHAPTER OVERVIEW

Chapter 4 begins with a discussion of the concept of *variability*. Next, it demonstrates how to assess variability for categorical variables. It presents five measures of variability, all of which are used predominantly with variables at the interval or ratio level. These are the *range*, the *interquartile range*, the *mean deviation*, the *standard deviation*, and the *variance*. Its primary focus is on the standard deviation.

## 4.2 ■ THE CONCEPT OF VARIABILITY

*Variability* refers to the degree to which a variable's values are dispersed around a measure of central tendency. Consider, for instance, the following two distributions:

Distribution 1: 5, 6, 7, 7, 7, 8, 9

Distribution 2: 1, 4, 6, 7, 8, 10, 13

The mean of both distributions is 7:

$(5 + 6 + 7 + 7 + 7 + 8 + 9) / 7 = 7; (1 + 4 + 6 + 7 + 8 + 10 + 13) / 7 = 7$

Scores in the Distribution 2 are more dispersed (spread out) around the mean than are those in Distribution 1. Therefore, Distribution 2 has greater variability.

Two more distributions follow. The observations in Distribution 2 were created by adding the constant "1" to each observation in Distribution 1. Which distribution, if either, has greater variability?

Distribution 1: 1, 3, 4, 4, 5, 7

Distribution 2: 2, 4, 5, 5, 6, 8

Observe first that the distributions' means differ. The mean of Distribution 1 is 4 $(1 + 3 + 4 + 4 + 5 + 7) / 6 = 4$, whereas that of Distribution 2 is 5 $(2 + 4 + 5 + 5 + 6 + 8) / 6 = 5$. However, with respect to variability, the key point to see is that observations in the two distributions are spread out around their respective means to precisely the same degree. Thus, though their means differ, these distributions have the same amount of variability.

As we head forward into the chapter, let me remind you that, just as with the two prior chapters, this chapter concerns univariate statistical procedures, those that deal with a single variable at a time. We begin by examining variability for categorical variables.

## 4.3 ■ ASSESSING THE VARIABILITY OF CATEGORICAL VARIABLES

Pragmatically speaking, there are no widely known, commonly used measures of variability for categorical variables. As such, this section describes how to assess variability for these variables but does not present any measures. Consider the three distributions for the variable eye color presented in Table 4.1.[1]

In Distribution 1, everyone has blue eyes. When all cases have the same value as in Distribution 1, a categorical "variable" has *no* variability. In fact, in Distribution 1, eye color is not a variable, but instead, because it takes on only one value, is a constant.

In Distribution 2, a very high percentage (92%) of participants have blue eyes. When a very high percentage of cases have the same value, a categorical variable has low variability.

In Distribution 3, cases are quite equally distributed among the three eye colors, with 38% having blue eyes, 32% having brown eyes, and 30% having green eyes. When percentages for the different values of a nominal variable are reasonably equal, as in Distribution 3, then that variable has high variability.

In assessing the variability of categorical variables, I recommend focusing on percentages rather than frequencies. Now, one may also use frequencies. For instance, in Distribution 3, rather than reasoning that percentages are reasonably equal and, thus, variability is high, one could also observe that frequencies are also reasonably equal (19, 16, and 15) and, by so doing, reach the same conclusion. I recommend percentages because of issues raised in the next paragraph.

Consider Distribution 4 in which percentages are identical to Distribution 2 but frequencies are 1,000 times larger: blue eyes, 46,000 (92%); brown eyes, 2,000 (2%); and green eyes, 2,000 (2%). Which distribution has greater variability, Distribution 2 or Distribution 4? The answer is that they have the same amount of variability because the percentages are the same. And one more problem: Consider Distribution 5: blue eyes, 20,000 (40%); brown eyes, 17,000 (34%); and green eyes, 13,000 (26%). Which has greater variability, Distribution 3 or Distribution 5? The answer is Distribution 3, because its percentages are slightly more equal than are those of Distribution 5 (38, 32, and 30 vs. 40, 34, and 26).

In sum, the best way to assess variability of categorical variables is through percentages rather than frequencies. You may use frequencies to assess variability. However, if you do, do not make the mistake of concluding that one variable's variability is greater or lesser than another's simply because its frequencies are larger or smaller than those of the other.

Table 4.1 ■ **Three Distributions With Differing Variability in Eye Color**

| Eye Color | Distribution 1 | | Distribution 2 | | Distribution 3 | |
|---|---|---|---|---|---|---|
| | Frequency | Percentage | Frequency | Percentage | Frequency | Percentage |
| Blue | 50 | 100 | 46 | 92 | 19 | 38 |
| Brown | 0 | 0 | 2 | 4 | 16 | 32 |
| Green | 0 | 0 | 2 | 4 | 15 | 30 |

It would be helpful to have guidelines regarding when the variability of a categorical variable is low or high. Because this text does not present a formal measure of variability for categorical variables, the best guidance that I can provide is as follows:

■ If 90% or more of cases have the same value, variability is low.

■ A guideline for what constitutes high variability is impractical; in general, the more equal the percentages, the greater the variability.

## 4.4 ■ THE RANGE

We now examine measures of variability for variables at the interval or ratio level. We begin with the range.

The **range** equals the highest value minus the lowest value. Consider the values: 3, 5, 6, 7, 7, 8, 9. The highest value is 9 and the lowest value is 3. Hence, the range is $9 - 3 = 6$. The formula for the range is as follows:

$$\text{Range} = X_{highest} - X_{lowest} \tag{4.1}$$

where $X_{highest}$ is the highest value and $X_{lowest}$ is the lowest value.

In reporting the range, researchers typically present the actual highest and lowest values rather than the range per se. For instance, a researcher would likely report "ages of participants ranged from 10 years to 70 years," rather than reporting "the range in age was 60 years." The second statement is correct but conveys less information than the first.

The great advantage of the range is its easily understood meaning. It is a commonly used measure.

## 4.5 ■ THE INTERQUARTILE RANGE

The **interquartile range** (*IQR*, *midrange*) equals the value at the 75th percentile minus the value at the 25th percentile. Its formula is as follows:

$$IQR = X_{75\%} - X_{25\%} \tag{4.2}$$

where $X_{75\%}$ is the score at the 75th percentile and $X_{25\%}$ is that at the 25th percentile.

Therefore, if the value at the 75th percentile is, say, 20 and that at the 25th percentile is, say, 12, then $IQR = 20 - 12 = 8$. The *IQR* is used occasionally, less so than is the range.

## 4.6 ■ THE MEAN DEVIATION

The **mean deviation** conveys the average amount by which values differ from the mean. Its formula is as follows:

$$MD = \frac{\Sigma |X - \overline{X}|}{N} \tag{4.3}$$

where *MD* is the mean deviation, $\overline{X}$ is the mean, $X$ is the score of an individual case, and $N$ is the sample size. The two vertical bars "| |" indicate absolute value. The $\Sigma$ symbol is the summation sign.

Prior to carrying out the formula, let us define "deviation score from the mean." A case's **deviation score from the mean** (or simply its **deviation score**) equals the case's value (score) minus the mean. Expressed as a formula:

$$\text{Deviation score from the mean} = X - \overline{X} \tag{4.4}$$

where $\overline{X}$ is the mean and $X$ is the score of an individual case.

Therefore, suppose that a case's value is 6 and that the mean is 9. This case's deviation score is $6 - 9 = -3$. As another example, if a case's value is 14 and the mean is 8, its deviation score is $14 - 8 = 6$.

To calculate the mean deviation:

1. find the mean;
2. for each case, subtract the mean from the case's value to determine its deviation score;
3. find the absolute value of each deviation score;
4. sum these absolute values; and
5. divide by the sample size ($N$).

Consider the scores "1, 4, 5, 6, and 9." Note that there are five cases and thus $N = 5$. Carrying out the formula's steps:

1. The mean is $(1 + 4 + 5 + 6 + 9) / 5 = 5$.
2. The deviation scores from the mean are $1 - 5 = -4, 4 - 5 = -1, 5 - 5 = 0, 6 - 5 = 1, 9 - 5 = 4$.
3. The absolute values of the deviation scores are $|-4| = 4, |-1| = 1, |0| = 0, |1| = 1, |4| = 4$.
4. The sum of the absolute values is $4 + 1 + 0 + 1 + 4 = 10$.
5. $N$ is 5; dividing the sum from Step 4 by $N$ yields the $MD$: $MD = 10 / 5 = 2$

As mentioned earlier, the mean deviation conveys the average amount by which scores differ from the mean. Study of its formula reveals that it may also be interpreted as conveying the mean (average) absolute value of the deviation scores from the mean.

Variability refers to the degree to which values are dispersed (spread out) around a measure of central tendency. Among all measures, the mean deviation provides the most straightforward and intuitively pleasing measure of variability. In other words, the most straightforward way of measuring how spread out scores are around a measure of central tendency is to determine the average amount by which scores differ from that measure. This is precisely what the $MD$ does with respect to the mean. By conveying the average amount by which scores differ from the mean, the $MD$ does perhaps the best possible job of conveying mathematically what variability means in an intuitive, nonmathematical sense.

The $MD$'s major disadvantage is that it is hardly ever used. In fact, it is used so rarely in real-world research that most statistics books do not cover it. Indeed, its major use seems to be in preparing statistics students for the standard deviation, which we cover now.

## 4.7 ■ THE STANDARD DEVIATION

The **standard deviation** is the most commonly used and most useful measure of variability. One formula is as follows:

$$s = \sqrt{\frac{\Sigma(X - \overline{X})^2}{N-1}} \tag{4.5}$$

where $s$ is the standard deviation, $\overline{X}$ is the mean, $X$ is the score of an individual case, $N$ is the sample size, and $\Sigma$ is the summation sign. This formula directs one to:

1. find the mean;
2. for each case, subtract the mean from the case's score to determine the case's deviation score from the mean;
3. square each deviation score;
4. sum the squared deviation scores;
5. divide the sum of the squared deviation scores by $(N - 1)$; and
6. calculate the square root.

Let us calculate a standard deviation. Suppose that seven residents in a shelter for the homeless spent the following numbers of nights on the street during the prior month: 19, 24, 7, 22, 14, 29, 11. What is the standard deviation of nights spent on the street? The first step is to calculate the mean:

$$19 + 24 + 7 + 22 + 14 + 29 + 11 = 126; 126 / 7 = 18 \text{ nights}$$

At this point, calculations are expedited by a grid as in Table 4.2.

The grid's first column lists individual scores and its second column lists the mean. The second step, computing deviation scores from the mean, is accomplished by subtracting the second column from the first. The resulting deviation scores are presented in the third column. The third step is to square each deviation score. The resulting squared deviation scores are presented in the fourth column. The fourth step is to sum the squared deviation scores. This sum, 360, is presented at the bottom of the fourth column. The fifth step is to divide by $(N - 1)$: $360 / (7 - 1) = 60.0$. The sixth and last step is to calculate the square root: $s = \sqrt{60.0} = 7.7$.

Study the standard deviation's formula to see that the more the scores differ from the mean, the greater is the standard deviation's value. Here is a *very rough* guide for interpreting the standard deviation: The standard deviation is often a little bit larger than the mean deviation, that is, a little bit larger than the average amount by which scores differ from the mean. For instance, in the nights-on-the-street data, the mean deviation is 6.3 (calculations not shown). As just calculated, the standard deviation is 7.7, a little bit larger than 6.3.

Observe that adding or subtracting a constant to all scores does not affect the value of the standard deviation. For instance, suppose that each person in our sample spends, say, two more nights on the street. Adding the constant "2" to reflect this, these data become 21, 26, 9, 24, 16,

Table 4.2 ■ **Grid for Calculating the Sum of Squared Deviation Scores**

| $X$ | $\overline{X}$ | $X - \overline{X}$ | $(X - \overline{X})^2$ |
| --- | --- | --- | --- |
| 19 | 18 | 1 | 1 |
| 24 | 18 | 6 | 36 |
| 7 | 18 | −11 | 121 |
| 22 | 18 | 4 | 16 |
| 14 | 18 | −4 | 16 |
| 29 | 18 | 11 | 121 |
| 11 | 18 | −7 | 49 |
| | | | $\Sigma = 360$ |

29, and 13. Even though the mean number of nights on the street has increased by 2 from 18 to 20 nights, the standard deviation remains the same, 7.7 nights.

Because the standard deviation is used so frequently, one more computation example may be helpful. This time, calculations will be carried out without a grid. What is the standard deviation of the following scores: 1, 4, 6, and 9?

We will make use of the numbered steps as we proceed. Because there are four cases, the sample size is four ($N = 4$).

1. The mean is $(1 + 4 + 6 + 9)/4 = 20/4 = 5$.
2. The deviation scores from the mean are $1 - 5 = -4$,   $4 - 5 = -1$,   $6 - 5 = 1$, $9 - 5 = 4$.
3. The squared deviation scores are $(-4)^2 = 16$,   $(-1)^2 = 1$,   $1^2 = 1$,   $4^2 = 16$.
4. The sum of the squared deviation scores is $16 + 1 + 1 + 16 = 34$.
5. Dividing the sum of the squared scores by $(N - 1)$: $34/(4 - 1) = 10.33$.
6. Calculating the square root: $s = \sqrt{10.33} = 3.21$.

Thus, the standard deviation is 3.21. The mean deviation for the just-presented data is 2.5, demonstrating again that the standard deviation is often "a little bit larger" than the mean deviation. Thus, if you think of the standard deviation as conveying an amount that is a little bit larger than the average amount by which scores differ from the mean, you will typically be on target in your thinking.

The standard deviation is important to the normal distribution (presented in the next chapter) and in inferential statistics (presented in the second half of this text). Although more difficult to interpret than the mean deviation, it is indeed the "workhorse" measure of central tendency and is the primary measure emphasized in this text.

This text uses the symbol $s$ for the standard deviation. In formal reports, $SD$ is often used (American Psychological Association, 2010).

## 4.8 ■ THE VARIANCE

To compute our final measure of variability—the variance—we simply omit the final step (the calculation of the square root) from the formula for the standard deviation. The formula for the **variance** thus is

$$s^2 = \frac{\Sigma(X-\bar{X})^2}{N-1} \tag{4.6}$$

where $s^2$ is the symbol for the variance.

For our nights-on-the-street data, the result for the next to last step (Step 5) was 60.0. Thus, the variance is 60.0, that is, $s^2 = 60.0$. For the more recent example that did not use the calculation grid: $s^2 = 10.33$.

As study of their formulas (4.5 and 4.6) reveals, the variance equals the square of the standard deviation (the standard deviation squared) and, in turn, the standard deviation equals the square root of the variance. For instance, if a variable's standard deviation equals 7, its variance equals $7^2 = 49$. Or, working in the opposite direction, if a variable's variance equals 64, its standard deviation equals $\sqrt{64} = 8$. Expressing the just demonstrated examples using symbols: If $s = 7$, then $s^2 = 49$; and if $s^2 = 64$, then $s = 8$.

The variance is encountered increasingly as one progresses from basic to advanced statistics. Its major disadvantage is that its "meaning" is mathematical; that is, it has no straightforward, intuitive interpretation. In this sense, it is just the opposite of the mean deviation that (though hardly ever used) conveys variability in a straightforward, "commonsense" way.

## 4.9 ■ CHAPTER SUMMARY

*Variability* is the degree to which values are dispersed (spread out) around a measure of central tendency. The greater that dispersion, the greater the variability.

There are no widely used measures of central tendency for categorical variables. For these variables, variability is assessed primarily by percentages. If a high percentage of cases have the same value, variability is low. If cases are distributed more equally across different values, variability is greater.

The five measures summarized as follows are all used with interval- or ratio-level variables.

The *range* equals the highest value minus the lowest value. It is commonly used and easy to interpret.

The *IQR* equals the score at the 75th percentile minus that at the 25th percentile. It sees occasional usage.

A case's *deviation score from the mean* equals the case's score minus the mean. The *mean deviation* conveys the average amount by which scores differ from the mean and, thus, is a straightforward, intuitive measure of variability. Its formula is $MD = (\Sigma|X - \overline{X}|) / N$. It is rarely used in actual research.

The standard deviation is the most commonly used and most useful measure of variability. Its formula is $s = \sqrt{\Sigma(X - \overline{X})^2 / (N - 1)}$. The standard deviation's value is typically a little bit larger than that of the mean deviation, that is, a little bit larger than the average amount by which scores differ from the mean. Adding or subtracting a constant to all scores does not change the standard deviation's value.

The *variance* ($s^2$) equals the square of the standard deviation. In turn, the standard deviation equals the square root of the variance. It is difficult to make intuitive sense of the variance.

## 4.10 ■ PROBLEMS AND QUESTIONS

**Section 4.2**

1. Variability concerns the degree to which observations are _____ around a measure of _____ _____.

2. Which set of observations has greater variability?
   a. 6, 7, 8, 9, 10
   b. 4, 6, 8, 10, 23

3. Which set of observations has greater variability?
   a. 2, 6, 9, 11, 12, 13, 15, 18, 22
   b. 7, 9, 10, 11, 12, 13, 14, 15, 17

4. Which set of observations has greater variability (or does either)?
   a. 1, 2, 3, 4, 5
   b. 3, 4, 5, 6, 7

5. Which set of observations has greater variability (or does either)?
   a. 4, 6, 6, 7
   b. 923, 924, 924, 925

## Section 4.3

6. *Respond true or false.*
   a. Pragmatically speaking, there are no well-known, very commonly used measures of variability for categorical variables.
   b. In assessing the amount of variability for categorical variables, this text recommends examining percentages rather than frequencies.

7. Distribution A: 8 students succeed (80%) and 2 (20%) fail.
   Distribution B: 80 students succeed (80%) and 20 (20%) fail.
   *Choose the best response:*
   a. Distribution A has more variability than does B.
   b. Distribution B has more variability than does A.
   c. A and B have the same amount of variability.

8. Distribution A: 8 students succeed (80%) and 2 (20%) fail.
   Distribution B: 90 students succeed (90%) and 10 (10%) fail.
   *Choose the best response:*
   a. Distribution A has more variability than does B.
   b. Distribution B has more variability than does A.
   c. A and B have the same amount of variability.

9. For each of the following, indicate "high" if the variable has high or reasonably high variability, "low" if it has low or reasonably low variability, or "constant" if the variable has no variability at all (and thus is a constant).
   a. 47% of students choose burgers for lunch and 53% choose salads.
   b. 94% of students choose meals with meat and 6% choose vegetarian meals.
   c. 50% of social work students choose the community practice concentration and 50% choose the direct practice concentration.
   d. 95% of social work students choose the direct practice concentration and 5% choose the community practice concentration.
   e. Ten social work students choose the community practice concentration and 10 choose the direct practice concentration. (Hint: Although frequencies rather than percentages are presented, you can do this problem. You can, if you wish to, calculate the percentages.)
   f. Ninety-five social work students choose the community practice concentration and five choose the direct practice concentration.
   g. Twenty-three social workers (100%) pass a competency exam and zero (0%) fail.

   **h.** Field of practice choice of students in a social work master's program: children and families, 37%; mental health, 34%; health and aging, 29%.

   **i.** Evaluations of a workshop: excellent, 91%; good, 6%; fair, 3%; poor, 0%.

   **j.** 96% pass the course; 2% fail; 2% withdraw.

## Section 4.4

**10.** In your own words, what is the definition of the range?

**11.** (*True or False*) The range is a univariate statistical procedure.

**12.** Calculate the range of each set of observations.

   **a.** 6, 4, 7, 2, 9, 5

   **b.** 23, 8, 41, 13, 17, 22

   **c.** 114, 888, 22, 9, 672, 3, 47

   **d.** 2, 9, 3, 5, 12

## Section 4.5

**13.** Consider the following distribution of scores: 7, 4, 6, 3.

   **a.** What is the mean?

   **b.** What is the deviation score of each of the scores?

**14.** Consider the following distribution of scores: 2, 6, 2, 1, 4.

   **a.** What is the mean?

   **b.** What is the deviation score of each of the values?

**15.** *Indicate whether each statement is true or false.*

   **a.** In the author's opinion, the mean deviation is a straightforward, easily understood measure of variability.

   **b.** The mean deviation measures the average amount by which scores differ from the mean.

   **c.** The mean deviation conveys the mean (average) absolute value of difference scores from the mean.

   **d.** The mean deviation is a frequently used measure.

**16.** Calculate the mean deviation of each set of observations. The formula is $MD = (\Sigma|X - \overline{X}|) / N$.

   **a.** 2, 4, 6, 8

   **b.** 3, 5, 7, 9

   **c.** 2, 3, 7, 6, 12

   **d.** 2, 3, 7, 1, 3, 1, 4

   **e.** 5, 5, 5, 5, 5, 5

**Section 4.6**

17. Calculate the standard deviation of each set of observations in the prior problem. The formula is $s = \sqrt{\Sigma(X - \overline{X})^2 / (N-1)}$ (Label your answers "a" through "e.")

18. For each just completed calculation of the standard deviation, indicate whether the standard deviation is "a great deal larger," "a little bit larger," "the same size as," "a little bit smaller," or "much smaller" than the mean deviation. (Label your answers "a" through "e.")

19. Calculate the standard deviation of these observations: 18, 19, 20, 21, 22.

20. Consider the following observations: 19, 20, 21, 22, 23. Without carrying out any calculations, what is the standard deviation. (Hint: Consider the observations in the prior problem.)

21. *Indicate whether each statement is true or false.*
    a. The standard deviation is a commonly used measure of variability.
    b. For a given set of observations, the value of the standard deviation is typically a little bit smaller than that of the mean deviation.
    c. Adding or subtracting a constant to or from each score does not affect the value of the standard deviation.
    d. The more the scores differ from the mean, the greater the value of the standard deviation.
    e. The standard deviation is a measure of central tendency.
    f. The standard deviation is a univariate rather than a bivariate statistical procedure.

**Section 4.7**

22. *Indicate whether each statement is true or false.*
    a. The variance is easily interpreted in nonmathematical, intuitive fashion.
    b. The variance equals the square of the standard deviation.
    c. The standard deviation equals the square root of the variance.
    d. The variance is a measure of variability.

23. In each of the following, the standard deviation is provided. For each, calculate the variance.
    a. 3
    b. 10
    c. 6
    d. 5
    e. 2

24. In each of the following, the variance is provided. For each, calculate the standard deviation.
    a. 36
    b. 121
    c. 49
    d. 100
    e. 9

25. The symbol for the standard deviation is _____. The symbol for the variance is _____. In formal reports, the standard deviation is often symbolized by _____.

# 5

# SHAPE OF DISTRIBUTION

## 5.1 ■ CHAPTER OVERVIEW

As you study distributions, you will see that different *distributions* have different *shapes*. Chapter 5's key focus is on the bell-shaped, *normal distribution*. It also presents *positively* and *negatively skewed* distributions and those with differing degrees of *kurtosis*. In closing, it introduces *z scores* and shows how to calculate percentages of cases in various regions of the normal distribution.

## 5.2 ■ THE NORMAL DISTRIBUTION

As presented in Chapter 2, a **distribution** is a group of values that have been organized in some way (Toothaker & Miller, 1996, p. 23). A distribution's **shape** refers to the *pattern* of the distribution of its scores, that is, to *how* its scores are distributed. The most important and best-known distribution is the normal distribution.

The **normal distribution** is not an *empirical distribution*, one of actual scores, but instead a *theoretical distribution*, one that is defined mathematically. Because the normal distribution is a theoretical ideal, it has an infinite number of cases. No real-world research variable conforms *precisely* to the normal distribution. On the other hand, many approximate it. For instance, the distributions of physical characteristics such as height and weight often correspond reasonably well with a normal distribution. The normal distribution is shown in Figure 5.1. Because its shape resembles a bell, it is termed the *bell-shaped curve* (*normal curve*).

The vertical axis in Figure 5.1 depicts frequency; the higher the curve, the greater the frequency. The horizontal axis presents values (scores). Lower values are to the left and higher ones to the right. In a normal distribution, frequency is greatest in the "middle" of the distribution and then tapers off in both the negative (left) and positive (right) directions, as shown in Figure 5.1. Three defining features of the normal distribution are as follows:

1. Its mean, median, and mode all have the same value.
2. **Sixty-eight percent** (68.26%; i.e., about two-thirds of the cases) are located within one standard deviation of the mean.
3. It is **symmetric**; that is, its left and right sides are mirror images.

Figure 5.2 illustrates Point 1. We know that the vertical line in Figure 5.2 conveys the mode because it passes through the normal curve's highest point—the value with the greatest frequency. We know that it conveys the median because the median and the mode (by Point 1) have the same value.

FIGURE 5.1 ■ The Normal Distribution

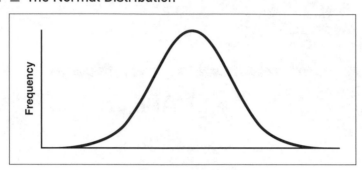

Recall that the median is located at the 50th percentile. Hence, 50% of cases are located below the line (to its left) and 50% are located above it (to its right). Finally, (by Point 1) the line also conveys the mean. Thus, Figure 5.2 demonstrates that 50% of cases in a normal distribution have values below the mean and 50% have values above it. We make frequent use of this fact later in the chapter.

To illustrate Point 2, suppose that the height of women is normally distributed with a mean of 5 ft. 6 in. and a standard deviation of 3 in. Given this information, we know that about 68% of women are between 5 ft. 3 in. (the mean minus one standard deviation: 5 ft. 6 in. − 3 in. = 5 ft. 3 in.) and 5 ft. 9 in. (the mean plus one standard deviation: 5 ft. 6 in. + 3 in. = 5 ft. 9 in.).

In a normal distribution, about **95%** of cases (95.44%) are located within two standard deviations of the mean. Hence (continuing to assume that $\overline{X}$ = 5 ft. 6 in., $s$ = 3 in., and a normal distribution), about 95% of women are between 5 ft. 0 in. and 6 ft. 0 in.: 5 ft. 6 in. − 2(3 in.) = 5 ft. 0 in.; 5 ft. 6 in. + 2(3 in.) = 6 ft. 0 in. *Almost all* cases (99.74%) in a normal distribution have values within three standard deviations of the mean. Hence, almost all women are between 4 ft. 9 in. and 6 ft. 3 in. Figure 5.3 presents the percentages of cases within one, two, and three standard deviations in a normal distribution.

Before considering distributions with shapes other than normal, we need to define the tails of a distribution. The **tails** of a distribution are its extreme left and extreme right areas. The extreme left area is the **lower tail** (*negative tail*, *left tail*). The extreme right area is the **upper tail** (*positive tail*, *right tail*). Some distributions have long, stretched out tails while others may have short, stubby ones. Sometimes, one tail is stretched out and the other is stubby. The arrows in Figure 5.2 point to the tails of the normal distribution. A normal distribution's tails extend infinitely, although this cannot be displayed by a figure.

FIGURE 5.2 ■ Measures of Central Tendency and Tails

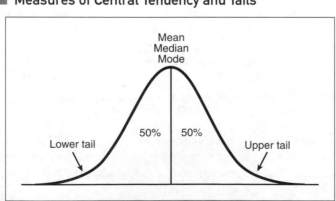

FIGURE 5.3  ■  **Percentage of Cases in Selected Areas of Normal Distribution**

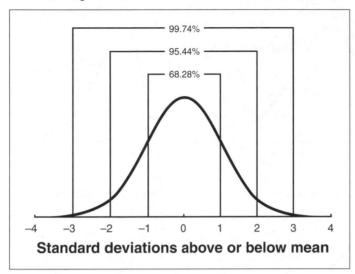

99.74%

95.44%

68.28%

−4    −3    −2    −1    0    1    2    3    4

**Standard deviations above or below mean**

## 5.3  ■  SKEWED DISTRIBUTIONS

### 5.3.1  ■  Characteristics

Many distributions have a *nonnormal* shape, a shape that is different from that of a normal distribution. Some distributions are **skewed**. **Skewness** (*skew*) is the degree to which a distribution's shape departs from symmetry (Toothaker & Miller, 1996, p. 90). The greater the departure, the greater the skew.

Symmetric distributions have no skew. For instance, the normal distribution is symmetric and thus is not a skewed distribution.

Some distributions are **positively skewed**. In a positively skewed distribution, scores cluster at the lower (left, negative) end. The lower tail of a positively skewed distribution is short and stubby, and the upper tail is large and stretched out. Figure 5.4 presents four distributions with differing degrees of positive skew.

It is easy to think of variables whose distributions are positively skewed. A common example is family income in the United States, a variable also used in Chapter 3, Section 3.7, to demonstrate how outliers pull the value of the mean in their direction. Figure 5.5 presents the distribution of family income. Because most families have moderate or low incomes, the frequency distribution is higher on the left side. A smaller number have high incomes and, hence, the distribution is lower on the right side. A few families with extremely high incomes (like Bill Gates' family) cause the upper tail to stretch far to the right.

Another example of a positively skewed variable is the number of chin-ups that people can do. Most can do only a few (or no) chin-ups. This makes the left side of the distribution higher than the right. A few people can do many chin-ups (say, 15 or more). As such, the upper tail is elongated.

In **negatively skewed** distributions, the lower tail is large and stretched out and the upper tail is short and stubby. Cases in a negatively skewed distribution cluster in the right (positive) side while, in contrast, fewer cases are located on the left (negative) side. Figure 5.6 presents four distributions with different degrees of negative skew.

Negatively skewed variables are harder to think of than are positively skewed ones. A good example of a negatively skewed distribution is length of gestation (time from conception to birth) of infants born in the United States. To simplify discussion, let us consider only infants who survive childbirth. The modal gestational time is about 9 months, and, as such, the frequency

FIGURE 5.4 ■ Differing Degrees of Positive Skew

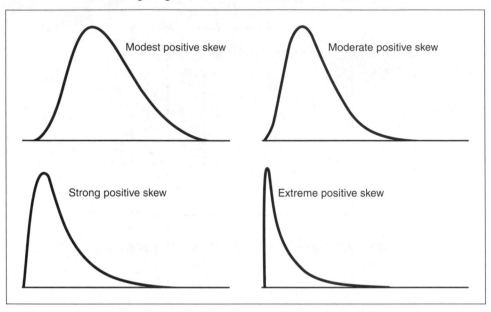

distribution curve is highest at this value. In the United States, it is extremely rare for gestational time to exceed 10 months. (If a mother has carried her baby that long, almost always the baby will be delivered by cesarean section or labor will be induced.) Thus, the frequency of births at 10 months is markedly lower than that at 9 months. Gestational time never reaches 11 months. Hence, the upper tail of the distribution ends by this time.

On the other hand, the frequency distribution curve declines more slowly on the left side of the distribution. For instance, more babies are born at 8 months than at 10 months. Indeed, some babies who are born at 5 months or even earlier survive. As such, the lower tail stretches out more than does the upper tail. Figure 5.7 presents a hypothetical frequency distribution curve for age of gestation.

FIGURE 5.5 ■ Family Income in the United States

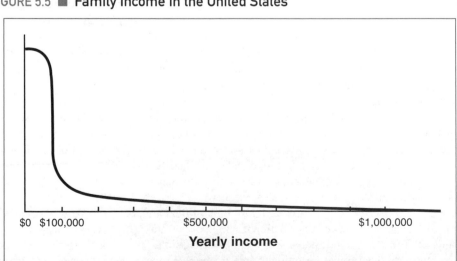

FIGURE 5.6 ■ Differing Degrees of Negative Skew

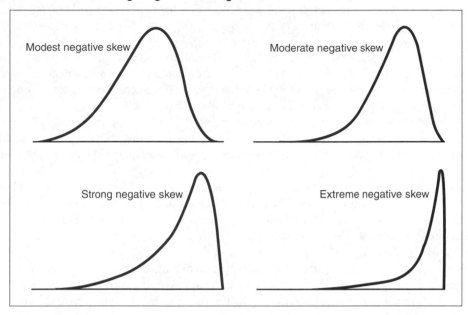

Students sometimes mix up positively and negatively skewed distributions. To avoid this, remember this saying: "The tail tells the tale." In other words, a skewed distribution's correct name corresponds to the location of the elongated tail. In a positively skewed distribution, the upper (positive) tail is elongated. In a negatively skewed distribution, the lower (negative) tail is elongated.

### 5.3.2 ■ Skewness and Measures of Central Tendency

As presented in Chapter 3, Section 3.7, an outlier is an *extremely* high or an *extremely* low value. Saying that a distribution has outliers located in the positive (right) side of the distribution says

FIGURE 5.7 ■ Length of Gestation

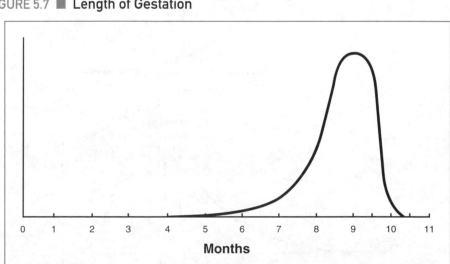

much the same thing as saying that the distribution is positively skewed. Thus, when a distribution is positively skewed, most of its outliers are located in the upper (positive) tail. By the same line of reasoning, when a distribution is negatively skewed, most of its outliers are located in the lower (negative) tail.

Skewness exerts predictable effects on the measures of central tendency. Skewness has minimal impact on the mode and median. For instance, the degree of stretch in a distribution's tail does not affect the median. Each case in the tail, whatever its value, simply counts as one more case in locating the middle case, that is, the case at the 50th percentile.

However, skewness can *greatly* affect the mean. The value of the mean is pulled in the direction of the elongated tail. The greater the skew—that is, the more stretched out and elongated the tail—the greater the impact. When the degree of skew is sufficiently large, the mean can be pulled so much that it becomes a misleading measure of central tendency, that is, one that no longer conveys a common value. In such situations, the median is preferred to the mean. Although there is no hard-and-fast point at which the mean is pulled so much that the median becomes preferred, the degree of skew in the strongly and extremely skewed distributions in Figures 5.4 and 5.6 is sufficient for this to be so. Hence, for strongly and extremely skewed distributions, the median is preferred over the mean.

When we study inferential statistics, you will learn that the degree of skew can have important implications regarding the appropriateness or lack thereof of various statistical procedures. In general, it is important to learn whether or not the variables in one's study have skewed distributions and, if so, to what degree.

In a normal distribution, the three measures of central tendency all have the same value. In a skewed distribution, these values (almost without exception) differ. Figure 5.8 presents positively and negatively skewed distributions. Each distribution has three vertical lines, corresponding

FIGURE 5.8 ■ **Measures of Central Tendency in Skewed Distributions**

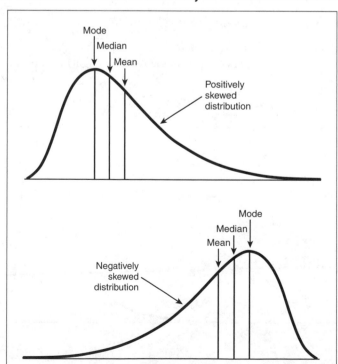

to the mode, the mean, and the median. Suppose that these lines were not labeled. One could logically reason out which line represents which measure. Consider the positively skewed distribution. The tallest (highest) line represents the mode because the mode is the value with the greatest frequency. The rightmost line represents the mean because the value of the mean is pulled toward the elongated tail. By the process of elimination, the remaining line (the middle line) represents the median. In the negatively skewed distribution in Figure 5.8, the right line represents the mode, the left line represents the mean, and the middle line represents the median.

## 5.4 ■ KURTOSIS

One of the two major characteristics of shape of distribution is skewness. The second is **kurtosis**, the degree of "peakedness" of a distribution relative to that of the normal distribution (Toothaker & Miller, 1996, p. 90). A distribution with high kurtosis has, relative to a normal distribution, a higher proportion of cases in the very center. This gives it its peaked shape. A distribution with high kurtosis also has, relative to the normal distribution, a higher proportion of cases in its tails. Thus, its tails (both tails) are thick and elongated. A distribution with low kurtosis has, relative to the normal distribution, a flatter shape. Its center is broad and rounded (sometimes almost flat), and its tails are short and stubby. Figure 5.9 presents a distribution with high kurtosis, the normal distribution, and one with low kurtosis.[1,2]

As mentioned earlier, skewness can have important implications regarding the appropriateness of various statistical procedures. In general, kurtosis, at least for the introductory procedures discussed in this text, does not have important implications regarding which procedures are or are not appropriate.

FIGURE 5.9 ■ **Distributions with Differing Kurtosis**

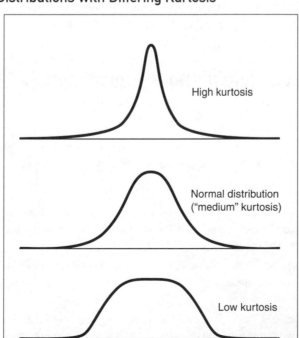

FIGURE 5.10 ■ A Distribution with a Shape Close to Uniform

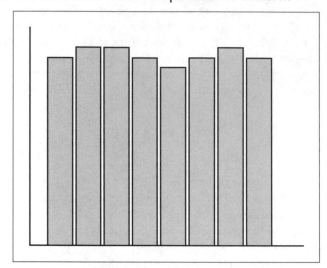

## 5.5 ■ UNIFORM AND BIMODAL DISTRIBUTIONS

When each value of a distribution has the same frequency, the resulting distribution is a **uniform distribution** (*flat distribution*, *rectangular distribution*). In a precisely uniform distribution, each column of the distribution's histogram would be exactly the same height (as each value would have the same frequency) and thus the histogram would have a rectangular shape. Figure 5.10 presents a distribution that is nearly uniform.

In a **bimodal distribution**, cases cluster around two distinct values. Figure 5.11 presents a bimodal distribution.

## 5.6 ■ PERCENTAGES AND THE NORMAL DISTRIBUTION

Recall that in a normal distribution, 68.26% of cases are within one standard deviation of the mean, 95.44% are within two standard deviations of the mean, and 99.74% are within three standard deviations of the mean. Recall also that the mean is located at the 50th percentile and that the normal distribution is symmetrical. Putting these points together in a normal distribution,

■ 34.13% of cases (68.26% / 2 = 34.13%) are located between the mean and one standard deviation above the mean, and 34.13% are located between the mean and one standard deviation below the mean;

■ 47.72% of cases (95.44% / 2 = 47.72%) are located between the mean and two standard deviations above the mean, and 47.72% are located between the mean and one standard deviation below the mean;

■ 49.87% of cases (99.74% / 2 = 49.87%) are located between the mean and three standard deviations above the mean, and 49.87% are located between the mean and three standard deviations below the mean.

FIGURE 5.11 ■ Bimodal Distribution

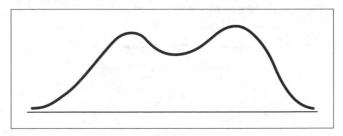

Figure 5.12 presents these percentages and also shows visually that 50% of cases in a normal distribution are located above the mean and 50% are located below it.
Given these percentages, you should be able to answer the following questions. Solutions are provided as you move through each question.

1. Given a normal curve, what percentage of cases are located more than one, two, and three standard deviations *above* the mean?

Let us calculate the percentage of cases more than one standard deviation above the mean. Given that the mean is at the 50th percentile, 50% of cases are above the mean. Of these, 34.13% are between the mean and one standard deviation above the mean. The percentage of cases more than one standard deviation above the mean is calculated by subtraction: 50.00% − 34.13% = 15.87%. The percentage more than two standard deviations above the mean is 50.00% − 47.72% = 2.28%. And more than three standard deviations above is 50.00% − 49.87% = 0.13%. Figure 5.13 presents visually the calculation of the percentage of cases located more than one standard deviation above the mean.

FIGURE 5.12 ■ Areas Above and Below Mean in a Normal Distribution

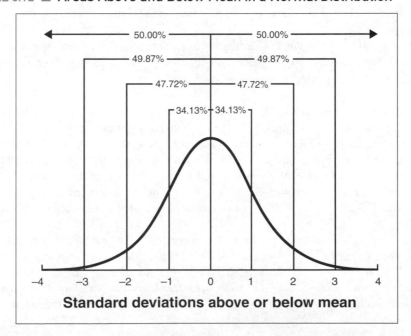

FIGURE 5.13 ■ **Calculation of Percentage of Cases More Than One Standard Deviation Above the Mean**

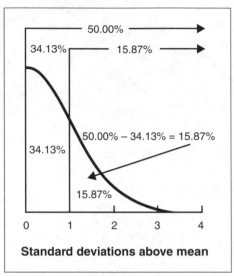

2. Given a normal curve, what percentage of cases are located more than one, two, and three standard deviations *below* the mean?

Because the normal curve is symmetric, it *must* be the case that percentages for cases in given areas below the mean will be the same as those for the corresponding areas above the mean. As such, we know already that 15.87%, 2.28%, and 0.13% of cases are located more than one, two, and three standard deviations below the mean, respectively. Although we already know the answers, let us carry out one problem. For instance, given that 50% of cases are below the mean and 34.13% of cases are between the mean and one standard deviation below the mean, 50% − 34.13% = 15.87% of cases are located more than one standard deviation below the mean.

3. Given a normal curve, what percentage of cases are located more than one, two, and three standard deviations from the mean, *both* directions considered? (In other words, consider both cases above the mean and cases below it.)

Given that we have just finished calculating percentages of cases located above and below the mean, one way to carry out this new set of problems is simply to sum these percentages. For instance, because 15.87% of cases are located more than one standard deviation above the mean and 15.87% of cases are located more than one standard deviation below the mean: 15.87% + 15.87% = 31.74% of cases are located more than two standard deviations from the mean, both directions considered. The percentage of cases located more than two standard deviations from the mean is 2.28% + 2.28% = 4.56%; for three standard deviations, it is 0.13% + 0.13% = 0.26%.

Another way to reason through the earlier presented set of problems is to refer back to Figure 5.3. The total percentage of all cases is 100%. If 68.26% of cases are within one standard deviation of the mean, then 100% − 68.26% = 31.74% of cases are more than one standard deviation away from the mean, both directions considered. For two standard deviations, the necessary subtraction is 100% − 95.44% = 4.56%; and for three standard deviations, it is 100% − 99.74% = 0.26%.

Problems similar to those just presented are important in inferential statistics. Solutions to such problems require a normal distribution. For instance, here is a trick question: Scores on a spelling test are negatively skewed. Shawna's score is one standard deviation above the mean. What percentage of students scored higher than did Shawna? The correct answer should be something similar to "cannot be determined given the information provided." Because the distribution has a nonnormal shape, we do not have the necessary information to solve the problem.

Now, let us reword the problem: Scores on a spelling test are very nearly normally distributed. Shawna's score is one standard deviation above the mean. About what percentage of students scored higher than did Shawna? Now, the problem can be solved. Working through the logic, (a) 50% of scores are above the mean, (b) 34.13% of scores are between the mean and Shawna's score, and (c) 50.00% − 34.13% = 15.87%. In sum, about 16% of students scored higher than did Shawna.

## 5.7 ■ INTRODUCTION TO *z* SCORES

### 5.7.1 ■ *z* Score Calculation

A case's *z* **score** (*standard score*) conveys the number of standard deviations that that case's score (value) is above or below the mean. For instance, if Alice's score on a self-esteem scale is two standard deviations below the mean, her *z* score is −2.00. If Kim's score on the scale is one half of a standard deviation above the mean, her *z* score is 0.50. To compute a case's *z* score, subtract the mean from its score and divide by the standard deviation:

$$z = \frac{X - \overline{X}}{s} \tag{5.1}$$

where *z* is the *z* score for a case, *X* is the score for the case, $\overline{X}$ is the mean score, and *s* is the standard deviation.

Suppose that the mean score on a self-esteem scale is 25 points with a standard deviation of 10 points and that Ann's score is 17 points. Her *z* score is

$$z = \frac{17 - 25}{10} = \frac{-8}{10} = -0.80$$

Thus, Ann's score is 0.80 standard deviations below the mean. Suppose that Rosa scored 37 on this test. Her *z* score is (37 − 25) / 10 = 12 / 10 = 1.2. Hence, Rosa scored 1.2 standard deviations above the mean.

A synonym for a case's score is its raw score. For instance, Ann's raw score on the self-esteem scale was 17; Rosa's raw score was 37. A case's **raw score** is its score as the variable was originally measured, in other words, in the original units of measurement. In contrast, a case's *z* score is its score following "transformation" using the *z* score formula. As already calculated, Ann's *z* score is −0.80 and Rosa's is 1.20. When one carries the *z* score formula for a score, we say that that score has been *transformed* (*converted*) into a *z* score. Thus, the previous calculations transformed Ann and Rosa's scores to *z* scores. Figure 5.14 displays Ann and Rosa's raw scores and *z* scores on the self-esteem measure.

### 5.7.2 ■ Basics of *z* Scores

For *all* variables: (a) scores below the mean have negative *z* scores, (b) scores above the mean have positive *z* scores, and (c) scores exactly at the mean have *z* scores of 0.00.

FIGURE 5.14 ■ **Raw Scores Compared to *z* Scores**

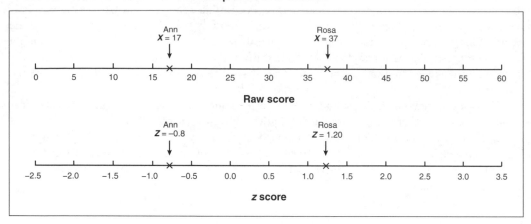

Further, if one transforms *all* cases in a sample or population into *z* scores, the mean of these *z* scores will be 0.00 and the standard deviation will be 1.00. This is so for *all* variables. For instance, suppose that an elementary school teacher gives five tests: a spelling test, a math test, a history test, a reading test, and a science test. Presumably, each test has a different mean and a different standard deviation. Suppose that the teacher uses the *z* score Formula 5.1 to transform all scores on each test into *z* scores. Following transformation, the mean score on each test (i.e., the mean *z* score on each test) will be 0.00 and the standard deviation on each test (that is, the standard deviation of the *z* scores on each test) will be 1.00. In sum, for any distribution of *z* scores: (a) the mean is (always) 0.00 and (b) the standard deviation is (always) 1.00.

Although transforming all scores in a distribution to *z* scores affects the mean and standard deviation (changes these to 0.00 and 1.00, respectively), it does not affect the shape of distribution. In other words, for any variable, the shape of the distribution of its *z* scores will be exactly the same as that of its original (raw) scores.

Adding or subtracting a constant to all raw scores does not affect *z* scores. For instance, suppose that a professor decides that a particular test was too hard and thus adds five points to *each* student's grade. Doing so would not affect any student's *z* score. For instance, if Joe's *z* score was 1.35 prior to the addition of the five points, his *z* score would be 1.35 after this. (Do you see that each student's score remains the same number of standard deviations above or below the mean following the addition of the points as was the case prior to this? Hence, *z* scores are unaffected.) Just as is the case for addition and subtraction, multiplying or dividing all (raw) scores by a constant does not affect *z* scores.

Before we proceed further, let me be sure that you understand what a *z* score conveys by asking two questions with straightforward answers. First, Sally's *z* score on variable *X* is −0.75. How many standard deviations did Sally score above or below the mean? The answer is that Sally scored 0.75 standard deviations below the mean. Second, Fred scored 1.29 standard deviations above the mean on variable *Y*. What is Fred's *z* score? The answer is that Fred's *z* score is 1.29. In sum, a case's *z* score tells you how many standard deviations that score is above or below the mean. A case's *z* score and how many standard deviations that score is above or below the mean are one and the same.

### 5.7.3 ■ Uses of *z* Scores

Researchers use *z* scores to assess a case's relative standing on different variables. For instance, suppose that Sally scored 75% on a math test and 85% on a history test. Which test did she do better on? On the one hand, the answer is the history test, because her percentage of correct answers was higher. Yet, relative to the math test, perhaps the history test was quite easy. Let's say, for instance, that the mean score on the history test was 90% while that on the math test was 70%. If so, then Sally's score was above the mean in math but below the mean in history. Thus, using her peers for comparison, Sally actually did better in math than in history.

Our example, so far, lacks information on standard deviations. Let us say that the standard deviation on the math test was 10% and that that on the history test was 5%. Given that both means and standard deviations have been provided, $z$ scores may be calculated. Sally's $z$ score in math is $(75 - 70) / 10 = 0.50$. Her $z$ score in history is $(85 - 90) / 5 = -1.00$. Hence, Sally scored one half of a standard deviation above the mean in math and one standard deviation below the mean in history. Given that her $z$ score is higher in math ($z = 0.50$) than in history ($z = -1.00$), relative to her peers, Sally did better in math.

Note that the "higher" can be misinterpreted. For $z$ scores, higher conveys a higher relative standing, not a higher absolute value. For instance, a $z$ score of $-0.50$ is higher than (greater than) is one of $-1.00$. And, for instance, a $z$ score of 0.25 is higher than (greater than) is one of $-0.50$.

Using $z$ scores puts all variables on a common metric—all have a mean of 0.00 and a standard deviation of 1.00—and, by so doing, allows comparisons between variables. In essence, $z$ scores allow comparisons between "apples and oranges."

## 5.8 ■ $z$ SCORES AND THE NORMAL DISTRIBUTION

### 5.8.1 ■ Problems About Percentages of Cases

### Problems Involving Only One Side of the Distribution

When a variable is normally distributed, we may draw conclusions about various percentages associated with $z$ scores. We do so using the same logic as we used for cases located exactly one, two, and three standard deviations from the mean and, in addition, a table of percentages for the normal distribution, Table A.1 in Appendix A.

For instance, what percentage of cases in a normal distribution are between the mean and a $z$ score of 1.26? To use Table A.1: (a) trace down the "$z$ or $-z$" column to find 1.26 and (b) move one column to the right to the "Cases Between Mean and $z$ or $-z$" column to locate the percentage 39.6%. This is the percentage of cases between the mean and a $z$ score of 1.26. Suppose that we want to find the percentage of cases between the mean and a $z$ score of $-1.26$. We have already done so. Because the normal curve is symmetric, the columns in Table A.1 list percentages both for cases above the mean and for those below it. Hence, the percentage of cases between the mean and a $z$ score of $-1.26$ is 39.6%.

We have just determined that, in a normal distribution, 39.6% of cases are located between the mean and a $z$ score of $-1.26$. To reinforce the meaning of a $z$ score let me pose the question: What percentage of cases in a normal distribution are between the mean and 1.26 standard deviations below the mean? By definition, a $z$ score conveys how many standard deviations a case is above or below the mean. Hence, the just-posed question is asking for the percentage of cases between the mean and a $z$ score of $-1.26$. We have already answered this question, 39.6%. Similarly, the question "What percentage of cases in a normal distribution are located between the mean and 1.26 standard deviations above the mean?" asks for precisely the same information as does the question "What percentage of cases in a normal distribution are between the mean and a $z$ score of 1.26?" The answer to both questions is 39.6%.

The problems presented so far have asked about percentages between the mean and a given $z$ score. We may also use the table of normal distribution percentages to find percentages of cases that differ from the mean by more than given $z$ scores. For instance, what percentage of cases in a normal distribution have $z$ scores greater than 1.26? (In other words, what percentage of cases are more than 1.26 standard deviations above the mean?) Using Table 1.26, we (a) trace down the "$z$ or $-z$ column" to find 1.26 and (b) move two columns to the right to the "Cases $>$ $z$ or $< -z$" column to locate the percentage 10.4%. Thus, 10.4% of cases have $z$ scores greater than 1.26.

We have just found the percentage of cases with $z$ scores greater than 1.26. What is the percentage of cases with $z$ scores less than $-1.26$? (In other words, what percentage are more than 1.26 standard deviations below the mean?) As you may have guessed, given that the normal curve is symmetric, we already know this percentage; it is 10.4%.

Figure 5.15 presents the percentages of cases in the four areas that we have been discussing: (a) between the mean and a $z$ score of 1.26 (39.6%), (b) between the mean and a $z$ score of $-1.26$ (39.6%), (c) with a $z$ score greater than 1.26 (10.4%), and (d) with a $z$ score less than $-1.26$. (10.4%)

This might be a good time to note that for all $z$ scores in Table A.1, the percentages in the "Cases between Mean and $z$ or $-z$" column and those in the "Cases $>z$ or $< -z$" column always sum to 50%. For instance for "$z$ or $-z$" = 1.26 these percentages are, respectively, 39.6% and 10.4%: 39.6% + 10.4% = 50.0%.

## Problems Involving Both Sides of the Distribution

The questions posed, so far, pertain to only a single side of the normal distribution, so let us do one that pertains to both sides: What percentage of cases in a normal distribution have $z$ scores between $-1.26$ and 1.26? This question can also be stated as: What percentage of cases are located within 1.26 standard deviations of the mean? We have already determined the percentages of cases with $z$ scores between the mean and 1.26 (39.6%) and between the mean and $-1.26$ (39.6%). To answer the question, we sum or, alternatively, multiply by 2: 39.6% + 39.6% = 79.2% or 39.6% $\times$ 2 = 79.2%.

Perhaps we want to find the percentage of cases in a normal distribution with $z$ scores either less than $-1.26$ or greater than 1.26, that is, the percentage that differ from the mean by more than 1.26 standard deviations, both directions considered. We have already found these percentages for each side of the distribution (10.4%) and, thus, may either sum or multiply by 2 to solve the problem: 10.4% + 10.4% = 20.8% or 10.4% $\times$ 2 = 20.8%. Hence, 20.8% of cases in a normal distribution differ from the mean by more than 1.26 standard deviations.

FIGURE 5.15 ■ Normal Distribution and $z$ Scores of ±1.26

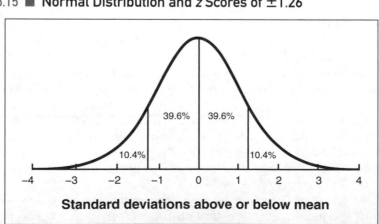

Standard deviations above or below mean

As mentioned in Section 5.6, finding the percentage of cases that differ from the mean by a given amount or more is important in inferential statistics, so let us do one more problem. What percentage of cases differ from the mean by more than 1.74 standard deviations, both directions considered? Locating 1.74 in the "$z$ or $-z$" column of Table A.1 and tracing over to the "Cases $> z$ or $< -z$" column finds the percentage, 4.1% for a single side of the normal distribution. Because the question asks us to consider both directions, we multiply by 2: 4.1% $\times$ 2 = 8.2%.

To this point, we have not carried out any problems concerning either the percentage of cases above a negative $z$ score or the percentage of cases below a positive one; so, let us do so.

What percentage of cases in a normal distribution have $z$ scores of $-0.84$ or higher? One way to do this problem is to: (a) find the percentage of cases between the mean and a $z$ score of $-0.84$ and (b) add 50% (because 50% of cases are above the mean). Table A.1 conveys that 30.0% of cases are between the mean and a $z$ score of $-0.84$: 30% + 50% = 80%. Thus, 80% of cases have $z$ scores of $-0.84$ or higher. Figure 5.16 displays this result.

Now, a problem regarding the percentage of cases located below a positive $z$ score: What percentage of cases have $z$ scores less than 1.42? Following much the same logic as just applied: (a) 42.2% of cases are between the mean and a $z$ score of 1.42 and (b) 50% of cases are below the mean. Hence, the percentage of cases with $z$ scores less than 1.42 is 42.2% + 50% = 92.2%. Figure 5.17 presents this result.

Observe that questions about the percentage of cases located below a $z$ score are one and the same as questions about percentile rank. For instance, we have just established that 92.2% of cases have $z$ scores of 1.42 or lower. This tells us that the percentile rank of this $z$ score is 92.2; stated differently, this score is at about the 92nd percentile. For problems involving negative $z$ scores, questions about percentile rank and about percentages of cases with lower $z$ scores are one and the same. For instance, we determined earlier that 10.4% of cases in a normal distribution have $z$ scores less than $-1.26$. Hence, it follows that (assuming a normal distribution) the percentile rank for a $z$ score of $-1.26$ is 10.4, about the 10th percentile.

### 5.8.2 ■ Reminders and Cautions

$z$ Scores may be used to calculate percentages *only* when the distribution is normally distributed. For instance, consider this problem: "Scores on a family closeness measure are positively

FIGURE 5.16 ■ **Percentage of Cases With a $z$ Score of $-0.84$ or Higher**

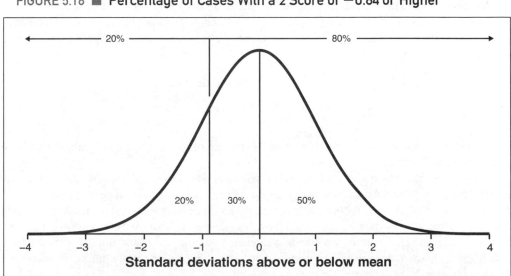

FIGURE 5.17 ■ Percentage of Cases With a *z* score of 1.42 or Lower

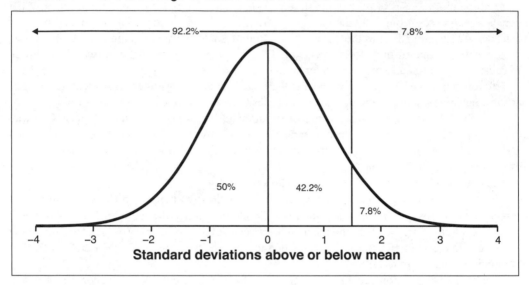

skewed. The *z* score for the Smith family on the measure is 0.70. What percentage of families scored higher than the Smiths?" On the basis of the information available, this question cannot be answered. This is because the percentages in the normal distribution table (Table A.1) apply only to the normal distribution.

Suppose, however, that the family closeness measure has a very nearly normal distribution. Now, assuming that the distribution is sufficiently close to normal, we may use Table A.1. Thus, we conclude that about 24.2% of families scored higher than the Smiths.

Although percentages for *z* scores may be calculated only for variables that are normally distributed, *z* scores convey useful information for nonnormally distributed variables as well. In particular, when a *z* score is positive, one knows that this score is above the mean. When it is negative, one knows that it is below the mean. And when a *z* score equals 0.00, one knows that it is precisely at the mean.

Returning to the family closeness measure and assuming again that family closeness scores are positively skewed, the Smith's *z* score was 0.70. Because 0.70 is greater than 0.00, we may conclude that the Smith's *z* score is above the mean. We may do so even though the distribution has a nonnormal shape.

## 5.9 ■ CHAPTER SUMMARY

The *shape* of a frequency distribution refers to the pattern of the distribution of values, that is, to how values are distributed.

The *normal distribution* is a theoretical distribution. No real-world variable has a *precisely* normal shape. In a normal distribution, (a) the mean, median, and mode all have the same value; (b) 68% of cases are located within one standard deviation of the mean; and (c) the left and right sides are mirror images (that is, the distribution is *symmetric*). About 95% of cases in a normal distribution are located within two standard deviations of the mean and almost all values are within three standard deviations. In a normal distribution, 50% of cases are below the mean and 50% are above it.

The *tails* of a distribution are its extreme left (lower, negative) and extreme right (upper, positive) areas.

*Skewness* refers to the degree to which a distribution departs from symmetry. In a *positively skewed distribution*, cases cluster in the left (negative) side of the distribution and the upper (positive) tail is elongated. In a *negatively skewed distribution*, cases cluster in the right (positive) side and the lower (negative) tail is elongated. When skewness is strong or extreme, the median is preferred over the mean. Skewness can have important implications regarding which statistical procedures are appropriate.

Kurtosis refers to the degree of peakedness relative to a normal distribution. Distributions with high kurtosis have "peaked" centers and large, elongated tails. Distributions with low kurtosis have broad (almost flat) shapes and short, stubby tails. Kurtosis rarely has important implications for introductory statistical procedures.

A *z score* conveys how many standard deviations a score is above or below the mean. For all variables, z scores have a mean of 0.00 and a standard deviation of 1.00. The z score formula is $z = (X - \overline{X}) / s$. z Scores allow comparisons of relative standing. For all variables, negative z scores are below the mean, positive z scores are above the mean, and a z score of 0.00 is exactly at the mean. Scores that have not been transformed to z scores and thus are in their original measurement metric are termed *raw scores*.

Neither adding or subtracting nor multiplying or dividing all scores by a constant affects z scores. Transforming scores to z scores does not affect a distribution's shape.

When variables are normally distributed, z scores may, in conjunction with the normal distribution table (Table A.1), be used to carry out various kinds of problems dealing with percentages of cases. When they are not, such problems may not be carried out.

## 5.10 ■ PROBLEMS AND QUESTIONS

**Section 5.2**

1. A distribution's _____ refers to the _____ of the distribution of its scores, that is, to how its values are distributed. The most important and best-known distribution is the _____ distribution, sometimes called the _____ -shaped curve.

2. Indicate whether each statement is true or false.
    a. The normal distribution is a theoretical distribution, one that is defined mathematically.
    b. Many real-world variables have *precisely* normal shapes.
    c. The normal distribution has an infinite number of cases.
    d. In a normal distribution, the mean, median, and mode have different values.

3. In a normal distribution, _____% of cases are located above the mean and _____% are located below it.

4. Regarding the normal distribution, the _____, _____, and _____ have the same value. _____-_____ percent of cases have values within one _____ _____ of the mean. It is _____, that is, its left and right sides are _____ images.

5. In a normal distribution about _____% of cases are located within two standard deviations of the mean and almost all cases are located within _____ standard deviations of the mean.

6. Suppose that the mean height of seventh-grade girls is 60 in. with a standard deviation of 3 in. and that the shape of the distribution of this variable is normal. About what percentage of these girls are between 54 in. tall and 66 in. tall?

7. The areas located in the extreme right and left sides of a distribution are termed the distribution's _____. The area in the extreme left is termed the _____ tail and that in the extreme right is the _____ tail.

## Section 5.3

8. Skewness is the degree to which a distribution departs from _____.

9. When a distribution is negatively skewed, scores tend to cluster in the _____ side/ area of the distribution. (Choose the best response.)
   a. lower (negative)
   b. upper (positive)
   c. middle

10. When a distribution is positively skewed, the tail that is elongated is on the _____ side of the distribution. When it is negatively skewed, this tail is on the _____ side.

11. Indicate the most likely skew, positive or negative of the distributions of each of the following variables.
   a. The age of students at your college
   b. Number of months of gestation for babies born in the United States
   c. Scores on a very easy test (most scores clustered at the top, but a few are very low)

12. An _____ is a case with an extremely high or extremely low value. If all or most of its outliers are located in the positive tail, a distribution is _____ skewed.

13. When a distribution is negatively skewed, the mean is pulled in a/an _____ direction.

14. (*True or False*) When a distribution is positively skewed, it is typically the case that the mean, median, and mode all have the same value.

15. The measure of central tendency on which skewness exerts the largest effect is the _____.

16. A distribution is negatively skewed. Which is most likely to have a higher value, the mean or the median?

**17.** (*True or False*) A distribution's degree of skewness rarely, if ever, has important implications regarding the appropriateness of statistical procedures.

## Section 5.4

**18.** Kurtosis refers to the degree of _____ of a distribution.

**19.** Indicate whether each statement is true or false.
  **a.** A distribution with high kurtosis has a broadly rounded (possibly even flat) kind of shape.
  **b.** A distribution with high kurtosis has very small, stubby tails.
  **c.** A distribution with low kurtosis has a broadly rounded (possibly even flat) shape.
  **d.** A distribution with low kurtosis typically has small, stubby tails.
  **e.** A distribution's kurtosis, typically, has critically important implications regarding which introductory statistical procedures are appropriate.

## Section 5.5

**20.** A distribution in which each value has the same frequency is termed a _____ distribution. A distribution which has two distinct clustering of values is termed a _____ distribution.

**21.** For each variable, indicate whether you think the shape of its distribution is "close to normal," "positively skewed," "negatively skewed," "close to uniform," or "bimodal." Some of these could have more than one good answer. When this is so, I provide the answer that I think is best. Hints are provided in some situations.
  **a.** The height of women at your university.
  **b.** The height of all students at your university. Hint: Consider the possibility of separate modes for women and men.
  **c.** The number of youth in each of the four grades at your high school.
  **d.** The number of players on your university football (or basketball) team that persons in your class can name.
  **e.** Scores on the ACT or SAT.
  **f.** Weight. Hint: "Close to normal" would be a good response but I am looking for another response.
  **g.** Considering families who have one or more children at a given elementary school, the total number of children in the families.
  **h.** Family income in the United States.

## Section 5.6

**22.** Indicate the percentage of cases in a normal distribution in each area of the normal distribution.
  **a.** Above the mean
  **b.** Below the mean

    **c.** Between the mean and one standard deviation above the mean

    **d.** Between the mean and one standard deviation below the mean

    **e.** Between the mean and two standard deviations above the mean

    **f.** Between the mean and two standard deviations below the mean

    **g.** Between the mean and three standard deviations below the mean

    **h.** More than one standard deviation above the mean

    **i.** More than one standard deviation below the mean

    **j.** More than two standard deviations above the mean

    **k.** More than two standard deviations below the mean

    **l.** More than three standard deviations below the mean

    **m.** More than one standard deviation from the mean, both directions considered

    **n.** More than two standard deviations from the mean, both directions considered

    **o.** More than three standard deviations from the mean, both directions considered.

23. Answer each of the questions in the prior question for both positively and negatively skewed distributions. Hint: This is a tricky question. Can this question be answered? Think before answering.

24. The distribution of scores on a large exam is approximately normal. Sally's score is two standard deviations above the mean. About what percentage of students scored between the mean and Sally's score?

25. On the next large exam, Sally's score is one standard deviation above the mean. Scores on this exam were negatively skewed. What percentage of students scored between the mean and Sally's score?

## Section 5.7

26. A case's $z$ score conveys how many standard deviations that case's score is _____ or _____ the mean. A synonym for $z$ score is _____ score.

27. Yuan's score on $X$ is 2.18 standard deviations above the mean. What is his $z$ score on $X$?

28. Maria's score on $X$ is 0.38 standard deviations below the mean. What is her $z$ score on $X$?

29. James' $z$ score on $X$ is $-1.47$. How many standard deviations above or below the mean is his score?

30. Taylor's $z$ score on $X$ is 0.74. How many standard deviations above or below the mean is her score?

31. A distribution has a nonnormal shape. Jack's $z$ score is $-0.37$. Choose the best response.
    **a.** Jack's score is above the mean.
    **b.** Jack's score is below the mean.

    **c.** Jack's score is precisely at the mean.

    **d.** It cannot be determined whether Jack's score is above or below the mean.

**32.** Regarding the prior question, how many standard deviations is Jack's score above or below the mean?

**33.** The mean score on a self-esteem scale is 44. Andrea scored 57. What is Andrea's $z$ score? Hint: Do you have sufficient information to answer this question?

**34.** The mean score on a self-esteem scale is 44. The standard deviation of scores is 10. Andrea scored 57. What is her $z$ score?

**35.** Daniel scored 38 on the same self-esteem scale. What is his $z$ score?

**36.** The mean score on a test is 78 and the standard deviation is 12. Indicate each student's $z$ score.

    **a.** Heather's test score is 90.

    **b.** Kate's test score is 72.

    **c.** William's test score is 78.

    **d.** Trudy's test score is 87.

    **e.** Dick's test score is 54.

    **f.** Rafe's test score is 96.

**37.** Regarding the prior question, how many standard deviations did each student score above or below the mean?

**38.** Choose the $z$ score from each pair of $z$ scores that has the higher value.

    **a.** $-1.00$ or $0.00$

    **b.** $-2.00$ or $1.00$

    **c.** $-1.00$ or $-0.50$

    **d.** $-1.00$ or $1.00$

**39.** A professor gives an exam and each student gets a score on it. Using Formula 5.1, the professor calculates each student's $z$ score.

    **a.** What is the mean $z$ score on the exam?

    **b.** What is the standard deviation of the $z$ scores on the exam?

    **c.** The professor decides the exam was too tough and adds three points to each student's (raw) score. What is the mean and standard deviation of the student's $z$ scores given the addition of the three extra points?

**40.** When all scores in a sample or population are converted to $z$ scores, these $z$ scores have a mean of _____ and a standard deviation of _____. (*True or False*) This is so for all variables.

**41.** (*True or False*) When scores are transformed to $z$ scores, this changes the shape of the distribution.

**42.** A variable is negatively skewed. Scores are converted to $z$ scores. The shape of the distribution of the $z$ scores is
  **a.** normal
  **b.** negatively skewed
  **c.** positively skewed

**43.** A score expressed in its original unit of measurement is termed a _____ score.

**44.** The mean high jump of fourth graders is 50 in. with a standard deviation of 10 in. Their mean long jump is 120 in. with a standard deviation of 30 in. Sandy high jumps 70 in. and long jumps 130 in.
  **a.** What is Sandy's $z$ score in the high jump?
  **b.** What is Sandy's $z$ score in the long jump?
  **c.** Relative to her peers, is Sandy a better high jumper or long jumper?

**45.** Test 1: $\overline{X} = 88$, $s = 8$; Test 2: $\overline{X} = 75$, $s = 10$. Sondra scored 84 on Test 1 and 77 on Test 2.
  **a.** What is Sondra's $z$ score on Test 1?
  **b.** What is Sondra's $z$ score on Test 2?
  **c.** Relative to her classmates, on which test did she do better?

**46.** In a sample of children who have been in foster care, the mean number of months in foster care is 30 with a standard deviation of 12 months. Determine the $z$ score for each of the following children.
  **a.** Ann, 54 months
  **b.** Ali, 30 months
  **c.** Jim, 34 months
  **d.** Yi, 21 months

## Section 5.8

**47.** Assume a normal distribution. Indicate the percentage of cases in each area of the distribution. You will need to use Table A.1 in Appendix A.
  **a.** Between the mean and 0.78 standard deviations above the mean
  **b.** Between the mean and a $z$ score of 0.78
  **c.** Between the mean and 0.78 standard deviations below the mean
  **d.** Between the mean and a $z$ score of $-0.78$
  **e.** Within 0.78 standard deviations of the mean
  **f.** Between a $z$ score of $-0.78$ and a $z$ score of 0.78

**48.** Assume a normal distribution. Indicate the percentage of cases in each area.
  **a.** More than 0.78 standard deviations above the mean
  **b.** $z$ Score is 0.78 or higher
  **c.** More than 0.78 standard deviations below the mean

**d.** $z$ Score is $-0.78$ or lower

**e.** More than 0.78 standard deviations from the mean

**f.** $z$ Score $< -0.78$ or $> 0.78$ (total percentage in both areas)

49. Assume a normal distribution. Indicate the percentage of cases in each area.
    **a.** Between the mean and 1.56 standard deviations above the mean
    **b.** Between the mean and a $z$ score of 1.56
    **c.** Between the mean and 1.56 standard deviations below the mean
    **d.** Between the mean and a $z$ score of $-1.56$
    **e.** Within 1.56 standard deviations of the mean
    **f.** Between a $z$ score of $-1.56$ and a $z$ score of 1.56

50. Assume a normal distribution. Indicate the percentage of cases in each area.
    **a.** More than 1.56 standard deviations above the mean
    **b.** $z$ Score is 1.56 or higher
    **c.** More than 1.56 standard deviations below the mean
    **d.** $z$ Score is $-1.56$ or lower
    **e.** More than 1.56 standard deviations from the mean
    **f.** $z$ Score $< -1.56$ or $> 1.56$ (total percentage in both areas)

51. Assume a normal distribution. Indicate the percentage of cases in each area.
    **a.** Between the mean and 0.24 standard deviations above the mean
    **b.** Between the mean and a $z$ score of 0.24
    **c.** Between the mean and 0.24 standard deviations below the mean
    **d.** Between the mean and a $z$ score of $-0.24$
    **e.** Within 0.24 standard deviations of the mean
    **f.** Between a $z$ score of $-0.24$ and a $z$ score of 0.24

52. Assume a normal distribution. Indicate the percentage of cases in each area.
    **a.** More than 0.24 standard deviations above the mean
    **b.** $z$ Score is 0.24 or higher
    **c.** More than 0.24 standard deviations below the mean
    **d.** $z$ Score is $-0.24$ or lower
    **e.** More than 0.24 standard deviations from the mean
    **f.** $z$ Score $< -0.24$ or $> 0.24$ (total percentage in both areas)

53. Assume a normal distribution. Indicate the percentage of cases in each area.
    **a.** Between the mean and a $z$ score of $-1.72$
    **b.** Above the mean
    **c.** $z$ Score of $-1.72$ or higher
    **d.** Between the mean and a $z$ score of 1.72
    **e.** Below the mean
    **f.** $z$ Score of 1.72 or lower

**54.** Assume a normal distribution.
   **a.** What is the percentile rank of a $z$ score of 1.72?
   **b.** What is the percentile rank of a $z$ score of $-1.72$?
   **c.** What is the percentile rank of a $z$ score of 0.00?

**55.** Assume a normal distribution. Indicate the percentage of cases in each area.
   **a.** Between the mean and a $z$ score of $-0.64$
   **b.** Above the mean
   **c.** $z$ Score of $-0.64$ or higher
   **d.** Between the mean and a $z$ score of 0.64
   **e.** Below the mean
   **f.** $z$ Score of 0.64 or lower

**56.** Assume a normal distribution.
   **a.** What is the percentile rank of a $z$ score of 0.64?
   **b.** What is the percentile rank of a $z$ score of $-0.64$?

**57.** Indicate the percentage of cases with lower values and the percentile rank of each of the following $z$ scores. Assume a normal distribution.
   **a.** $z = 0.00$
   **b.** $z = -1.92$
   **c.** $z = 1.92$
   **d.** $z = 0.88$
   **e.** $z = -0.88$

**58.** Scores on a test are negatively skewed. The mean on the test is 84 with a standard deviation of eight points. Matt's $z$ score is $-0.62$, Jas' $z$ score is 1.52, and Yzzy's is 0.00. *Respond True or False or "insufficient information" to each statement.*
   **a.** Matt's score is above the mean.
   **b.** Jas' score is above the mean.
   **c.** Yzzy's score is precisely at the mean.
   **d.** Matt's score is 0.62 standard deviations below the mean.
   **e.** Jas' score is 1.52 standard deviations above the mean.
   **f.** Among the three, Matt scored lowest, Yzzy in the middle, and Jas at highest.
   **g.** We may use the normal distribution table to determine the percentile rank of each of the three scores.

**59.** (*True or False*) Even when a distribution is not normally distributed, a $z$ score conveys how many standard deviations a score is above or below the mean.

**60.** Scores on variable *XYZ* are negatively skewed. Antoine's scored 1.68 standard deviations below the mean on Z. (True or False) Antoine's $z$ score on *XYZ* is $-1.68$.

# 6

# THE CONCEPT OF RELATIONSHIP AND RELATIONSHIP BETWEEN CATEGORICAL VARIABLES

## 6.1 ■ CHAPTER OVERVIEW

Chapter 6 focuses on *relationship (association)*, particularly on relationship between categorical variables. It demonstrates how researchers examine *contingency tables* and presents two measures of *size of association (strength of association)*, the *difference in percentages*, and the *risk ratio*.

## 6.2 ■ DEFINITION OF RELATIONSHIP

Two variables are **related** (**associated**) when the values of one vary, differ, or change according to those of the other. For instance, suppose that 30% of Republicans and 80% of Democrats support Legislation Z. As support for the legislation differs by party, party affiliation (Republican or Democrat) and support (yes or no) are related. Stated differently, these variables have a **relationship** (**association**).

A formal definition of relationship is "some values of one variable tend to occur more often with some values of the second variable than with other values of that variable" (Moore, 1997, p. 285). Applying this definition to the just-presented example, support for the legislation occurs more often for Democrats (80% of the time) than for Republicans (30%). This being so, party affiliation and support variables are related.

In a general sense, when two variables are related, given values of one variable tend to "go with" given values of another; that is, the values tend to "vary together." Take shoe size and height. Those who are tall tend to have big feet. Those who are short tend to have small feet. Thus, being tall and having big feet tend to "go together." And, likewise, being short and having small feet also "go together." As their values vary together, height and shoe size are related.

Take another two variables, score on a statistics test and eye color. My best guess is that those with blue, brown, and green eyes are equally likely to receive high, medium, or low scores on the test. Presumably, we will not find a pattern in which those with blue eyes tend to receive certain scores, those with green tend to receive other scores, and those with brown tend to receive still different scores. In this example, particular values of one variable do not tend to go with particular values of another. Viewed differently, the likelihood of receiving a high, medium, or low score does not vary by eye color. In this example, eye color and score on the test are not related (*unrelated, unassociated,* or *independent*).

Similarly, suppose that the same voting patterns on Legislation Y are observed for Democrats and Republicans. Among Democrats, 60% voted yes and 40% voted no, and among Republicans, 60% voted yes and 40% voted no. In this example, votes on Legislation Y do not vary according to party affiliation. Hence, vote and party affiliation are unrelated (*unassociated*, *independent*).

## 6.3 ■ COMMENTS ON RELATIONSHIP

It takes two to tango. Similarly, it takes *two* variables to form a relationship. A "trick" exam question might ask "On Legislation Q, 44% of Republicans voted yes and 56% voted no. Are political party affiliation and votes on Legislation Q associated?" This question presents only one variable, votes on Legislation Q. Political party affiliation takes on only one value, Republican, and, as such, is a constant (something that does not vary) rather than a variable. The exam question is nonsensical. One cannot assess the presence or absence of association unless *two* variables are present. When looked at differently, it is impossible for a constant to have a relationship with a variable.

On the other hand, suppose that the question had asked, "Sixty-six percent of Democrats and 44% of Republicans voted yes on Legislation Q. Are political party and support for the project related?" Now two variables are involved and the question makes sense. Given that Democrats and Republicans demonstrate different voting patterns, votes on Legislation Q and party affiliation are associated.

The fact of relationship between variables demonstrates only a pattern. In a class discussion, I remarked that there is a relationship between smoking and cancer. A student stated that this was not true because both of her parents had smoked heavily since their teens and neither had developed cancer. But pointing out a relationship only identifies the general pattern. Exceptions almost always occur. So to say that smoking and cancer are associated does not say that all smokers develop cancer or that all nonsmokers do not. It says only that smokers and nonsmokers are not equally likely to develop cancer.

A common mistake is to assume that because two variables are related, one variable causes the other, that is, that the relationship is causal. Some relationships are causal but others are not. Recall, for instance, our discussion in Chapter 1 (Section 1.7) regarding a (hypothetical) relationship between eating vegetables and longevity. Perhaps eating vegetables actually increases longevity, in which case the relationship is causal. Yet, our discussion also suggested the possible involvement of a confounding variable, amount of exercise. It was proposed that eating vegetables did not increase longevity, but instead that the relationship between eating vegetables and longevity was caused by the fact that vegetable eaters exercised more. In this case, the relationship between eating vegetables and longevity is not a causal one.

The presence of a relationship between two variables informs us that their values vary together but does not speak to what causes this to be so. Stated differently, the presence of a relationship and the reasons for that relationship are separate issues. The next several chapters (Chapters 6–9) focus on how to assess the presence of relationship. Chapters 10 and 11 discuss how to assess whether relationships are causal and the role of confounding variables in this assessment.

Recall from discussion in Chapter 1 (Section 1.7) that relationships in random samples can occur simply due to luck of the draw. In other words, two variables that are unassociated in a population may—due to the luck of the draw—be associated in a sample randomly selected from that population. For now, hold the notion that relationships can occur due to luck in the back of your mind. It is not germane to our discussion in the next several chapters. Statistical significance tests address the role of luck (chance) in relationships, and the second half of this text covers this in depth.

## 6.4 ■ CONTINGENCY TABLES AND CATEGORICAL VARIABLES

### 6.4.1 ■ Reading a Contingency (Crosstabs) Table

A key tool for assessing relationship between categorical variables is **contingency table analysis** (*cross tabulation, crosstabs*). Table 6.1 is a **contingency table** (*cross tabulation table, crosstabs table*) with hypothetical data pertaining to special-needs adoption. The **column variable**, the variable defining the columns, is type of adoption and takes on two values: (a) adoption by parents who were not previously foster parents to the child, labeled as *new home adoption* and (b) adoption by a child's prior foster parents, labeled as *foster family adoption*. The **row variable**, the variable defining the rows, is adoption outcome which also takes on two values: (a) disrupted, the adoption ends and the child returns to the care of the child welfare agency, and (b) stable, the child continues to reside with the adoptive family, that is, the adoption remains intact. Type of adoption is the independent variable. Adoption outcome is the dependent variable.

In Table 6.1, the independent variable is the column variable and the dependent variable is the row variable. There is no firm convention on this. Thus, as you read the social work research literature, you will encounter some tables in which the independent variable is the row variable and the dependent variable is the column variable. For consistency, *all* tables in this text present the independent and dependent variables as in Table 6.1, that is, with the independent variable as the column variable and the dependent variable as the row variable.

Because it has two rows and two columns, Table 6.1 is a 2 × 2 table. The number of rows and columns corresponds to the number of categories (values) of the variables. The first number indicates rows and the second indicates columns. For instance, a 3 × 4 table has three rows and four columns.

Some guidance in deciphering Table 6.1 is in order. The number 150 in the lower right hand corner conveys the total number of cases, that is, the sample size (*N*). The areas just to the right of and just below the table's boxed in area are the table's **margins**. The number 100 in the bottom margin conveys the number (frequency) of new home adoptions. The 50 in the bottom margin conveys the number (frequency) of adoptions by foster families. These are the **column totals**.

Table 6.1 ■ A Contingency Table Demonstrating the Absence of Relationship Between Variables (Hypothetical Data)

| Adoption Outcome | New Home Adoption | Foster Family Adoption | |
|---|---|---|---|
| **Disrupted** | 10 | 5 | 15 |
| | 10% | 10% | 10% |
| | 67% | 33% | |
| **Stable** | 90 | 45 | 135 |
| | 90% | 90% | 90% |
| | 67% | 33% | |
| | 100 | 50 | 150 |
| | 67% | 33% | 100% |

The 15 in the upper right margin conveys the number (frequency) of disrupted placements. The 135 in the right margin conveys the number (frequency) of stable placements. These are the **row totals**. Both the column totals (100 + 50 = 150) and the row totals (15 + 135 = 150) sum to the total number of cases ($N$ = 150).

The 10 in the upper left box or **cell** conveys the number (frequency) of new home adoptions that ended in disruption. The 5 in the upper right cell conveys the same for foster family adoptions. These are examples of **cell frequencies**. So also are the 90 and 45, respectively, in the lower left and lower right cells. The 90 conveys the number of stable new home adoptions. The 45 conveys the number of stable foster family adoptions. Cell frequencies sum down the columns to the column totals (10 + 90 = 100; 5 + 45 = 50) and across the rows to the row totals (10 + 5 = 15; 90 + 45 = 135).

The 10% in the right margin beside the top row conveys the percentage of all adoptions that ended in disruption. Hence, 10% (15 of 150 = 10%) did so. The 90% in the right margin conveys the percentage of all adoptions that were stable (135 of 150 = 90%). The percentages in the bottom margin convey that 67% (100 of 150) of adoptions were new home adoptions and that 33% (50 of 150) were foster family adoptions.

The percentages in the cells are termed **cell percentages**. The upper (top) of the two percentages in each cell is that cell's **column percentage**, the percentage of cases in the column in which the cell is located that are in the cell. For instance, the 10% in the upper left cell conveys that 10% (10 of 100 = 10%) of new home adoptions ended in disruption. Similarly, the 90% in the lower left cell conveys that 90% (90 of 100 = 90%) of new home adoptions were stable. Column percentages sum to 100 *down* the column. For instance, in the left column, 10% and 90% sum to 100%. The lower (bottom) percentage in each cell is that cell's **row percentage**, the percentage of cases in the row in which the cell is located that are in the cell. For instance, the 33% in the upper-right cell conveys that 33% (5 of 15 = 33%) of disruptions were in foster family adoptions. Row percentages sum to 100 *across* the row. For instance, in the first row: 67% + 33% = 100%.

Some crosstab tables present only cell frequencies. Others present frequencies and either row or column percentages. Others, such as in Table 6.1, present frequencies and both sets of percentages. To determine whether presented percentages are row or column percentages, find the direction in which they sum to 100. If they do so across the rows, they are row percentages. If they do so down the columns, they are column percentages.

Cell *percentages* rather than cell frequencies are the key to assessing the presence or absence of relationship in a contingency table. In most tables, the assessment of relationship is more straightforward using one set of percentages than using the other. The following guideline is recommended:

■ When the independent variable is the row variable, compare row percentages.

■ When the independent variable is the column variable, compare column percentages (Norušis, 1991, p. 203)

As stated earlier, the independent variable in this text's contingency tables is the column variable. Hence, for our purposes, the recommended percentages are always column percentages. Beginning with Table 6.2, this text's contingency tables present column percentages only. These are the recommended ones for assessing association.

### 6.4.2 ■ Assessing Relationship Using a Contingency Table

In Table 6.1, column percentages are identical for the two columns. Focusing first on new home adoptions: 10% disrupt and 90% are stable. Focusing next on foster family adoptions: 10% disrupt and 90% are stable. Adoption outcomes do not differ according to type of adoption. Instead, the

Table 6.2 ■ A Contingency Table Demonstrating Relationship Between Variables (Hypothetical Data)

|  | New Home Adoption | Foster Family Adoption |  |
|---|---|---|---|
| **Disrupted** | 20 | 5 | 25 |
|  | 20% | 10% | 17% |
| **Stable** | 80 | 45 | 125 |
|  | 80% | 90% | 83% |
|  | 100 | 50 | 150 |
|  | 67% | 33% | 100% |

same pattern of outcomes is observed for new home and foster family adoptions: In each type of adoption, 10% disrupt and 90% are stable. In Table 6.1, type of adoption and adoption outcome are unrelated (unassociated).

Table 6.2 presents a different hypothetical situation using the same two variables. In Table 6.2, column percentages differ for new home and foster family adoptions. Focusing first on new home adoptions: 20% disrupt and 80% are stable. Focusing next on foster family adoptions: 10% disrupt and 90% are stable. Adoption outcomes do indeed differ by type of adoption. In Table 6.2, type of adoption and adoption outcome are related (associated).

In summary, variables in a contingency table are unrelated (unassociated) when column percentages are the same (as in Table 6.1). Variables are related (associated) when column percentages differ (as in Table 6.2). As (beginning with Table 6.2) this text's tables present column percentages only, we may simplify and state that

■ categorical variables are unrelated when cell percentages are the same (as in Table 6.1), and

■ categorical variables are related when cell percentages differ (as in Table 6.2).

Although the assessment of relationship was demonstrated only for a $2 \times 2$ table, the same principles apply to larger tables such as, for instance, $2 \times 3$ tables, $3 \times 3$ tables, $3 \times 4$ tables, and so on. When cell percentages are the same, variables are unrelated (unassociated). When percentages differ, variables are related (associated).

Recognize that we do not need contingency tables to assess whether two categorical variables are related. Percentages alone are sufficient. For instance, suppose that 18% of women and 34% of men who earn master's degrees in social work choose careers in administration. This information by itself is sufficient for us to conclude that gender (female vs. male) and career choice (administration vs. other) are associated. On the other hand, if, say, 23% of women and 23% of men choose careers in administration, then we have sufficient information to conclude that gender and career choices are unassociated.

Whenever percentages differ, even by small amounts, variables are, formally speaking, related. Intuitively, one knows that differences of one or two percentage points are very small. If a researcher found that 17% of adoptions in new homes but only 16% of adoptions in prior foster homes ended in disruption, that researcher would not trumpet the finding, "Foster family adoptions are more successful." Instead, the researcher would correctly recognize that the pattern of outcomes was highly similar for the two types of adoption. By formal definition, there is a relationship. Yet, obviously, the relationship is a weak one. How does one assess *size* or *strength* of a relationship? Do the values of the variables go together in a strong, compelling pattern or is the pattern one that can barely be discerned?[1]

## 6.5 ■ SIZE OF ASSOCIATION

Four synonymous terms—**size of association**, **strength of association**, **size of relationship**, and **strength of relationship**—refer to the degree to which the values of one variable vary, differ, or change according to those of the other. When the values of two variables vary together in a compelling pattern, the relationship between these variables is strong or large. When the degree to which the values vary together is modest, the relationship is weak or small.

A term whose meaning is, in essence, identical to that of the just-presented terms is called **effect size**. The usage of effect size has increased markedly in the past 15 or so years; indeed, it is now used more often than are any of the other just-presented terms. Effect size is used most often in studies that examine the relative effects of different interventions. I do not like effect size as a term, at least when it is used in studies that do not assess interventions. The problem, in my view, is that its name (*effect* size) implies that one variable in a relationship affects (causes) another. As discussed in Chapter 1 (Section 1.7) and as emphasized in Chapters 10 and 11, two variables can be related when neither causes the other. I like to keep the presence (or absence) of a relationship distinct from the cause of that relationship. As such, this text uses effect size sparingly.

## 6.6 ■ DIFFERENCE IN PERCENTAGES (*D*%)

The most straightforward measure of size of association between categorical variables is the **difference in percentages** (or *percentage difference*). The difference in percentages is not a formal statistical measure but rather a tool for approximating size of association. It is indeed a workhorse tool. Social scientists examine differences in percentages almost by habit. Interpretation is straightforward: The larger the difference in percentages, the larger (stronger) the relationship. The difference in percentages is used primarily with $2 \times 2$ tables, that is, to assess the size of association between two dichotomous variables. Its formula is

$$D\% = \%_1 - \%_2 \tag{6.1}$$

where $D\%$ is the difference in percentages, $\%_1$ is the percentage in the first category of the independent variable and $\%_2$ is that in the second.

As a calculation example, Table 6.2 conveys that 20% of adoptions in new homes versus 10% of adoptions in prior foster homes end in disruption. The $D\%$ with new adoptive homes designated as the first category and foster adoptive homes as the second is $D\% = 20\% - 10\% = 10\%$.

The $D\%$ may calculate to a negative number. This occurs when the percentage in the first designated category is smaller than that in the second. For instance, had foster family homes been designated as the first category and new adoptive homes as the second, the $D\%$ would have been $D\% = 10\% - 20\% = -10\%$. Negative differences can be counterintuitive. For the most part, this text designates the category with the larger percentage as the first category and that with the smaller as the second. This is probably a good practice for you to follow as well.

The just-presented calculations focused on disruptions. We may equally well focus on stable outcomes. Referencing Table 6.2, 90% of prior foster family adoptions versus 80% of new home adoptions resulted in stability. The $D\%$ with foster homes designated as the first category and new homes as the second is $D\% = 90\% - 80\% = 10\%$. This value of the $D\%$ is the same as was obtained earlier when we focused on disruptions ($D\% = 10\%$). This demonstrates that, assuming that the category with the larger percentage is designated as the first category, for a $2 \times 2$

table, the category of the dependent variable that is used in computing the $D\%$ does not affect its value.

However, in calculating the $D\%$, be sure to use the type of percentages (column or row) recommended in the guideline. For instance, using row percentages when column percentages are recommended can result in a different (and wrong) value. With the exception of Table 6.1, this text's contingency tables present column percentages only. These are the correct percentages for all $D\%$ problems.

## 6.7 ■ QUALITATIVE DESCRIPTORS OF SIZE OF ASSOCIATION

A larger difference of percentages represents a larger relationship than does a smaller difference. But, to this point, no guidelines have been provided for categorizing various differences as conveying small, medium, or large associations. Should such guidelines be provided? Researchers disagree. Some take the position that qualitative descriptors (such as small, medium, or large) should not be used to describe relationships. Some do so because they believe that the numbers "speak for themselves" and that interpretation with words confuses matters. Others contend that a small, medium, or large relationship varies greatly by substantive area. For instance, a 10% difference of percentages may represent a strong relationship in, say, the area of pregnancy prevention but a weak one in, say, the treatment of math anxiety.

Others, including this author, believe that qualitative descriptors are helpful. In this vein, Table 6.3 provides descriptors for assessing size of association for the difference in percentages. Two cautions regarding this table and subsequent tables with qualitative descriptors should be mentioned. First, these tables assess the size of association within the context of social science research rather than in a strict mathematical sense. For instance, a difference of 50% is interpreted as conveying a very large relationship because a difference of this size is larger than most of the differences encountered in social science research. Second, what is large or small does indeed vary by content area. Therefore, use Table 6.3 only as a starting point for assessment. Do not just slap labels on relationships. This will not help you to understand data. Instead, use the table to guide your thinking. The qualitative descriptors presented in this text derive heavily from Cohen's work (1988).

It should be mentioned that relationships that are compellingly strong in a mathematical sense are encountered only occasionally in social science and social work research. There are several reasons for this. First, compared with the physical and biological sciences, social science research is a new endeavor. In many areas, our theories and knowledge base are not yet up to the task of identifying powerful mathematical relationships. Second, the social world is a complex one, one in which multiple variables affect (cause) multiple other ones. This complexity makes

**Table 6.3 ■ Qualitative Descriptors of Size and Strength of Association for the Difference in Percentages**

| Difference in Percentages | Size of Association | Strength of Association |
|---|---|---|
| About 7% (or −7%) | Small | Weak |
| About 18% (or −18%) | Medium | Moderate |
| About 30% (or −30%) | Large | Strong |
| About 45% (or −45%) | Very large | Very strong |

*Note.* When any compared percentage is less than 10% or greater than 90%, the descriptors in this table should not be used.

the identification of powerful relationships between particular variables a difficult task. Indeed, many variables likely have relationships of medium (or small) strength with many other variables rather than a powerful mathematical relationship with only one other variable. Finally, we do not investigate research questions to which we already know the answer. These are the precise questions that most often yield strong mathematical relationships. For instance, we will almost assuredly find a powerful mathematical relationship between having taken a prior statistics class (yes or no) and grade earned on a statistics knowledge exam. (Obviously, those who have taken a course will perform far better on the exam than those who have not.) But we will not investigate this topic because the result is a foregone conclusion.

In summary, the social world is complex and social work research is less than perfect. Recognize that qualitative descriptors of size of association provide broad guidelines only and that they do so in the context of social science research rather than in a strict mathematical way.

Rather than memorizing this and subsequent tables of qualitative descriptors, I recommend directing your closest attention to the descriptors associated with small and very large size of association. For instance, regarding the difference in percentages, if you realize that differences of about 7%, generally speaking, convey quite small (weak) associations and those of about 45% or larger, generally speaking, convey very large ones, you are well on your way to using the table as a straightforward, sensible aid for approximating the size of association between two dichotomous variables.

A caution should be mentioned regarding Table 6.3. The qualitative descriptors in Table 6.3 are recommended for use only when both compared percentages are within the range of about 10%–90%. When one or both compared percentages are not in this range, the descriptors tend to underestimate size of association.

An example can help one make intuitive sense of this. Suppose that 8% of persons who take Vaccine A develop a serious illness compared with 1% of those who take Vaccine B. Observe that both of these percentages fall outside the suggested range. In this example, $D\% = 8\% - 1\% = 7\%$. A difference of 7%, according to Table 6.3 guidelines, conveys a weak association. Yet, common sense suggests something amiss in this characterization. Those who take Vaccine A are *eight times more likely* to develop the illness than are those who take Vaccine B. Common sense correctly informs us that, in this situation, a difference of 7% conveys a strong relationship between type of vaccine and risk for the illness.

## 6.8 ■ RISK RATIO (*RR*)

An alternative to the difference in percentage for assessing size of association between two dichotomous (binary) variables is the risk ratio. The **risk ratio** (*relative risk*, *rate ratio*) is a ratio of percentages. To calculate it, divide the percentage that experiences an *event* in one group by the percentage that experiences it in another:

$$RR = \frac{\%_1}{\%_2} \qquad (6.2)$$

where *RR* is the risk ratio, $\%_1$ is the percentage in Group 1 that experiences the event and $\%_2$ is the percentage in Group 2 that does so.

A mathematically equivalent formula uses proportions:

$$RR = \frac{p_1}{p_2} \qquad (6.3)$$

where $p_1$ is the proportion in Group 1 that experiences the event and $p_2$ is the proportion in Group 2 that does so. The researcher designates one group as the first and the other as the second.

The event used in the formula is a category (value) of a dichotomous dependent variable. For instance, if the dependent variable is a "test result," pass versus fail, the researcher designates one of these categories as the event used in the risk ratio formula. When the designated event represents an undesirable outcome—failing a test, contracting an illness, an unsuccessful treatment outcome, an undesired pregnancy, and so on—the risk ratio conveys the relative risk of that event in the two groups.

Let us use the vaccine and illness example introduced earlier to demonstrate the risk ratio. Recall that 8% who received Vaccine A and 1% who received Vaccine B developed a serious illness. Let us designate those receiving Vaccine A as Group 1 and those receiving Vaccine B as Group 2. The designated event is developing the illness. The risk ratio is $RR = 8\% / 1\% = 8.00$ or, using the proportion-based formula, $RR = .08 / .01 = 8.00$. This risk ratio conveys that the risk of illness among those who received Vaccine A (Group 1) is eight times that of those who received Vaccine B. Or, alternatively, and as stated earlier, we may say that those who received Vaccine A in Group 1 are eight times more likely to develop the illness than those who received Vaccine B.

Suppose that we had designated those who received Vaccine B as Group 1 and those who received Vaccine A as Group 2. (Presume that developing the illness continues to be the designated event.) In this case, $RR = 1\% / 8\% = 0.125$. We conclude that the risk of developing the illness for those who received Vaccine B is 0.125 times (1/8th) that of those who received Vaccine A.

Most people find that risk ratios that are greater than 1.00 are easier to interpret than are those that are less than 1.00. This being so, I recommend designating the group with the larger percentage as Group 1. Doing so results in a risk ratio that is greater than 1.00.

Observe that the risk ratio that resulted with Vaccine B designated as Group 1 (0.125 = 1/8th) is the reciprocal of that with Vaccine A so designated (8.00). Two numbers are reciprocals when their product equals 1.00. In our example, $8.00 \times 0.125 = 1.00$. To find a number's reciprocal, divide 1.00 by that number; for instance, $1 / 8.00 = 0.125$. Designating the "other" group as Group 1 always yields a reciprocal risk ratio. For instance, suppose that a risk ratio calculates to 0.20 with one group designated as Group 1. It will calculate to 5.00 with the other so designated ($1 / 0.20 = 5.00$).

The risk ratio may vary from a lowest possible value of 0.00 to a highest possible value of positive infinity. A risk ratio of 1.00 results when the same percentage in both groups experiences the event. For instance, if 8% in each group experience the event, $RR = 8\% / 8\% = 1.00$. A risk ratio of 1.00 conveys the absence of association between group membership and experience of the event. As the risk ratio moves away from 1.00—either from 1.00 toward 0.00 or from 1.00 toward positive infinity—size of association increases. This is intuitive in a positive direction. For instance, it is intuitive that a risk ratio of 10.0 conveys a larger association than does one of 5.00. But it may not be intuitive in the negative one. For instance, a risk ratio of 0.10 conveys a larger association than does one of 0.20, as it differs more from 1.00.

Risk ratios that are reciprocals convey the same size of association. For instance, a risk ratio of 2.00 conveys the same size of association as does one of 0.50 because these are reciprocals ($2.00 \times 0.50 = 1.00$). As just discussed, changing the group designated as Group 1 results in a reciprocal risk ratio. As reciprocal risk ratios convey the same size of association, changing the group that is designated as Group 1 does not affect size of association. This is advantageous. We would not want something as arbitrary as the designation of groups to affect our assessment of size of association. Here are some other examples of reciprocal risk ratios, ones that convey the same size of association: 1.33 and 0.75, 1.50 and 0.67, 4.00 and 0.25, 2.50 and 0.40, 5.00 and 0.20, 10.0 and 0.10, and 20.0 and .05.

In calculating the $RR$, I recommend *strongly* that you designate the category of the dependent variable with percentages closer to 0% rather than that with percentages closer to 100% as the event. The reason for this recommendation can be demonstrated by not following it.

Suppose that rather than designating developing the illness as the event, we instead designate not developing it. The percentages of persons who did not develop the illness for each vaccine are found with subtraction: $100\% - 8\% = 92\%$ for those who received Vaccine A, and $100\% - 1\% = 99\%$ for those who received Vaccine B. Treating those who received Vaccine B as Group 1 and those who received Vaccine A as Group 2, $RR = 99\% / 92\% = 1.08$. This tells us that the "risk" for *not* developing the illness for those who received Vaccine B is 1.08 times higher than for those who received Vaccine A. This risk ratio is not incorrect. On the other hand, it has no straightforward, intuitive interpretation. Put simply, it is not useful. In summary, always use the category with percentages that are closer to 0% when you calculate a risk ratio.[2]

Table 7.2 in the next chapter presents qualitative descriptors of size of association for the risk ratio. Table 7.2 was developed primarily for use with the odds ratio, to be presented in Chapter 7. Observe that the size of association conveyed by the risk ratio increases as it diverges from 1.00. For each descriptor, Table 7.2 presents two values of the risk ratio. These are reciprocals. For instance, for very large association, $10.0 \times 0.10 = 1.0$. As the pairs of risk ratios are reciprocals, each risk ratio within a given pair conveys the same size of association. Table 7.2 conveys that risk ratios of about 1.5 (or 0.67) convey weak association, whereas those of about 10.0 (or 0.10) convey very strong association.

The qualitative descriptors presented in Table 7.2 are recommended for assessing size of association for the risk ratio only when the percentage experiencing the event in both groups is about 30% or less. For instance, if the percentages experiencing the event in Groups 1 and 2 are 60% and 20%, respectively, then Table 7.2's descriptors should not be used. These descriptors should only be used when the recommendation to use percentages close to 0% rather than to 100% is followed.[3]

## 6.9 ■ DIFFERENCE IN PERCENTAGES OR RISK RATIO?

Table 6.3 for the $D\%$ and Table 7.2 for the $RR$ indicate situations when their descriptors of strength of association should not be applied. When one measure's descriptors may be applied but the other's may not, the measure whose descriptors may be applied is generally preferred for that situation. When descriptors for both the $D\%$ and the $RR$ may be applied, my preference is for the $D\%$. Indeed, researchers employ the $D\%$ almost by habit to get a "feel" for the size of association. As mentioned earlier, the major disadvantage of the $D\%$ is that it is an informal measure. In general,

- ■ the $D\%$ tends to be preferred over the $RR$ when no percentages in the contingency table are close to 0% or 100%, and

- ■ the $RR$ tends to be preferred over the $D\%$ when one or more percentages is close to 0% or 100%.

Taken as a pair, the difference in percentages and the risk ratio cover most situations involving association between two dichotomous variables. Yet, it would be handy to have a single measure of size of association between dichotomous variables that could be applied in almost all situations. That measure is the odds ratio and it is presented in the next chapter.

## 6.10 ■ CHAPTER SUMMARY

Two variables are *related* (*associated*) when the values observed for one variable vary, differ, or change according to those of the other. Relationship demonstrates only a pattern. Some relationships are causal but others are not. Relationships in random samples can occur due to the luck of the draw.

Relationship (or the lack thereof) between categorical variables is presented using a *contingency table*. In a contingency table, the *column variable* defines the columns and the *row variable* defines the rows. *Column percentages* sum to 100% down the columns, and *row percentages* sum to 100% across the rows. Tables in this text make the independent variable the column variable and present column percentages.

*Cell percentages* rather than *cell frequencies* are used to assess relationship. When the column variable is the independent variable, as is always the case in this text, relationship should be assessed using column percentages. When these percentages are the same in all columns, the table's variables are unrelated. When they differ, these variables are related.

*Size of association* refers to the degree to which the values for one variable vary, differ, or change according to those of the other. Size of association, *strength of association*, *size of relationship*, *strength of relationship*, and *effect size* are synonymous terms.

The most straightforward and commonly used measure of size of association between two dichotomous variables is the *difference in percentages* ($D\%$). To compute the $D\%$, subtract the percentage in one group from that in the other: $D\% = \%_1 - \%_2$. The $D\%$ should be calculated using the recommendation for comparing percentages. Column percentages should be used for all problems in this text. The $D\%$ is an informal measure.

Qualitative descriptors provide a starting point for assessing size of association. Researchers disagree about whether such descriptors should be used. A difference in percentages of about 7% indicates a small association, whereas one of about 45% indicates a very large one (see Table 6.3). The qualitative descriptors should not be used to assess the $D\%$ when both compared percentages are not within the range of 10%–90%.

To calculate the *risk ratio*, divide the percentage (proportion) experiencing an event in one group by the percentage experiencing it in the other: $RR\% = \%_1 \, / \, \%_2$. Categories of the event with percentages closer to 0% (rather than to 100%) should be used in calculations. A risk ratio of 1.00 conveys the absence of association. The more that the risk ratio differs from 1.00, the stronger the association that it conveys. The qualitative descriptors for the risk ratio in Table 7.2 should not be used when the percentage experiencing the event in either group exceeds 30%.

Generally speaking, the $D\%$ is preferred over the $RR$ when no percentages are close to 0% or to 100%; when one or more percentages is close to 0% or 100%, the $RR$ is, generally, preferred over the $D\%$.

## 6.11 ■ PROBLEMS AND QUESTIONS

### Section 6.2

1. Two variables are _____ when the _____ observed for one variable vary, differ, or change according to those of the other.

2. For each of the following examples, mark *R* if the variables are related/associated, *U* if they are not related/unassociated, or *I* if necessary information is insufficient for making a decision (i.e., a "trick question")
   a. Seventy percent of women and 40% of men drink diet soft drinks.
   b. Eighty percent of women and 60% of men choose the direct (clinical) practice track for the second year of their social work master's.

    **c.** The batting average in the American (baseball) League is .287 whereas that in the National League is .272 (hypothetical data).

    **d.** The mean grade point average (GPA) of men is 3.22. The mean GPA of women is 3.22.

    **e.** The greater the number of compliments given, the greater the number of chores completed. (As compliments go up, so also do chores completed.)

    **f.** Eighty percent of social work students choose direct practice and 20% choose community practice.

    **g.** In a sample of left-handed college students from the southern United States, all of whom like country music, 38% prefer burgers and 62% prefer salads.

    **h.** The greater the number of visits by family members, the lower the depression level of nursing home clients.

    **i.** Fifteen percent of women in Program 1 for pregnancy prevention become pregnant within 1 year. Fifteen percent in Program 2 become pregnant within 1 year.

    **j.** Thirty-three percent in Program A require rehospitalization. Twenty percent in Program B require rehospitalization.

**Section 6.3**

  **3.** *Indicate whether each statement is true or false.*

    **a.** A constant may be involved in a relationship with a variable.

    **b.** Overall, students who study more for an exam receive better grades than do those who study less. However, because a couple of students who studied hardly at all did well, the professor concludes that studying and grades are unassociated. (*True or False*) The professor's conclusion is correct.

    **c.** The presence of a relationship and the cause of that relationship are synonymous (the same) issues.

    **d.** When two variables are related, one may safely conclude that at least one of these variables causes (affects) the other.

    **e.** Relationships in random samples can occur simply due to luck of the draw.

    **f.** The terms "relationship" and "association" mean the same thing (are synonyms).

**Section 6.4**

Table 6.4 ■ **Readmission to Psychiatric Hospital by Program**

| | Mental Health Program 1 | Mental Health Program 2 | |
|---|---|---|---|
| **Readmitted to hospital** | 40 | 20 | 60 |
| | 40% | 33% | 37.5% |
| **Not readmitted to hospital** | 60 | 40 | 100 |
| | 60% | 67% | 62.5% |
| | 100 | 60 | 160 |
| | 67% | 33% | 100% |

**4.** Answer regarding Table 6.4

    **a.** This table is an example of a/an _____ table.

    **b.** The column variable is _____.

    **c.** The row variable is _____.

    **d.** The independent variable is _____.

    **e.** The dependent variable is _____.

    **f.** (*True or False*) The independent variable is the column variable.

    **g.** What are the values (categories) of type of mental health program?

    **h.** What are the values (categories) of readmission to hospital?

    **i.** As this table has _____ rows and _____ columns, it is an example of a _____ × _____ table (all of these answers are numbers).

    **j.** The total number of cases (*N*, sample size) is _____.

    **k.** The areas just to the right of and just subsequent to the boxed in areas are the table's _____.

    **l.** The boxes within the table are termed _____.

    **m.** The row total for the top row is _____.

    **n.** In all, how many persons were readmitted?

    **o.** Among all persons, what percentage was readmitted?

    **p.** The column total for the second column is _____.

    **q.** In all, how many persons were in Program 2?

    **r.** What is the cell frequency for the upper left cell?

    **s.** How many persons in Program 1 were readmitted?

    **t.** What is the cell frequency for the upper right cell?

    **u.** How many persons in Program 2 were readmitted?

    **v.** (*True or False*) The cell percentages sum to 100 down the columns.

    **w.** (*True or False*) Column percentages are presented.

    **x.** What is the (column) cell percentage for the upper left cell?

    **y.** Among those in Program 1, what percentage was readmitted?

    **z.** Show the calculation for the cell percentage for the upper left cell.

  **aa.** What is the cell percentage for the upper right cell?

  **bb.** Among those in Program 2, what percentage was readmitted?

  **cc.** Show the calculation for the cell percentage for the upper right cell.

  **dd.** (*True or False*) The percentages in the two columns are the same (those in the left column are identical to those in the right).

  **ee.** (*True or False*) Those in Program 1 and those in Program 2 are equally likely to be readmitted.

   **ff.** (*True or False*) Those in Program 1 are more likely to be readmitted than those in Program 2.

  **gg.** (*True or False*) Types of program and readmission status (readmitted vs. not readmitted) are associated.

  **hh.** (*Yes or No*) Can one be confident just from the information provided in Table 6.4 that Program 2 actually *causes*, as compared with Program 1, reduced likelihood of hospital readmission?

5. *Respond true or false to each statement.*
   a. In assessing relationship, cell percentages rather than cell frequencies should be compared.
   b. The independent variable is the column variable in all (or almost all) contingency tables presented in this text.
   c. All (or almost all) of the contingency tables in this text present column percentages rather than row percentages.
   d. When the independent variable is the column variable, column percentages rather than row percentages should be compared to assess relationship.
   e. In assessing relationship in the contingency tables presented in this text, one should compare column percentages rather than row percentages.
   f. When column percentages are the same in all columns, the variables in a contingency table are associated.
   g. When column percentages differ in the different columns, the variables in a contingency table are associated.

## Section 6.5

6. (*True or False*) Size of relationship and strength of relationship have very similar rather than very different meanings.

7. A frequently used term with the same meaning as size/strength of relationship/association is _____ _____.

8. Define size/strength of relationship in your own words.

## Section 6.6

9. Calculate the difference in percentages ($D\%$) in Table 6.4 according to each set of instructions.
   a. With Program 1 designated as the first group and using percentages readmitted
   b. With Program 2 designated as the first group and using percentages readmitted
   c. With Program 1 designated as the first group and using percentages not readmitted
   d. With Program 2 designated as the first group and using percentages not readmitted

10. Twenty-seven percent of Republicans and 52% of Democrats voted for Legislation Z. What is the difference in percentages? Calculate so that the $D\%$ computes to a positive percentage.

11. Eighty-three percent of children in Program A successfully reunite with their families of origin. Seventy-four percent of those in Program B do so. What is the difference in percentages? Calculate so that the $D\%$ computes to a positive percentage.

12. On Bill Z, 71% of Democrats voted yes and 29% voted no. What is the $D\%$? (Hint: Be careful here.)

13. *Respond true or false to each statement.*
   a. In general, the larger the difference in percentages, the larger the size of relationship.
   b. In calculating the $D\%$, it does not matter whether one uses the percentages (column or row) suggested in the guideline because its value is always the same regardless of which is used.

**Section 6.7**

14. *Respond true or false to each statement.*
   a. All researchers concur that qualitative (nonmathematical) interpretation of size of association is an appropriate and useful undertaking.
   b. The qualitative descriptors of size/strength of association in Table 6.3 interpret the size of association within the context of social science research rather than in a strict mathematical sense.
   c. According to this text, the qualitative descriptors in Table 6.3 do not need to be adjusted to take into account the particular content/substantive area.
   d. The qualitative descriptors presented in the book's tables provide strict, exact definitions of size of association.
   e. A difference in percentages of 50% represents a weak relationship between two variables.
   f. A difference in percentages of 7% represents a weak relationship between two variables.

15. The qualitative descriptors of the difference in percentages are not recommended when both compared percentages do not fall in the range of about _____% to _____%.

16. Using the qualitative descriptors in Table 6.3, indicate the approximate size of association conveyed by each of the following differences in percentages.
   a. 31%
   b. 19%
   c. 6%
   d. 67%
   e. 0%
   f. 8%
   g. 47%

**Section 6.8**

17. The _____ _____ also known as the _____ _____ is a ratio of percentages.

18. Calculate the risk ratio in each of the following situations.
   a. Twelve percent in Program A versus 3% in Program B experience an unsuccessful treatment outcome. Treat Program A as the first group.

    **b.** Twenty-four percent of boys versus 12% of girls engage in aggressive behavior during recess according to a behavioral observation tool. Treat boys as the first group.

    **c.** Twenty percent of men and 5% of women pass the firefighters physical exam on the first try. Treat men as the first group.

    **d.** Five percent of women and 20% of men pass the firefighters physical exam on the first try. Treat women as the first group.

    **e.** Two percent of youth who are mentored in school versus 20% of those who are not earn a failing grade in at least one course. Treat mentored youth as the first group.

    **f.** Same example as prior question but with nonmentored youth designated as the first group.

**19.** Using your own words, interpret the first three risk ratios in the prior question.

**20.** Using the descriptors in Table 7.2 in Chapter 7 (Section 7.2), indicate the approximate size of association conveyed by each risk ratio presented in Question 18.

**21.** (*True or False*) A risk ratio of $-10.0$ conveys a very large association. (Think carefully.)

**22.** The risk ratio in a given situation calculates to 4.00. Had the "other" group been designated as Group 1, what would the risk ratio have been? (Hint: To calculate a number's reciprocal, divide 1.00 by that number.)

**23.** Which risk ratio, 4.00 or 0.25, conveys the stronger association?

**24.** For each pair of risk ratios, choose the risk ratio that conveys the stronger association.
    **a.** 3.0 or 4.0
    **b.** 0.20 or 0.30
    **c.** 10.0 or 5.00
    **d.** 10.0 or 0.10
    **e.** 0.8 or 0.9

**25.** In Group 1, 90% experience the event. In Group 2, 80% do so. A researcher calculates the risk ratio: $RR = 90\% / 80\% = 1.125$. Respond to the following questions about this situation.
    **a.** In terms of math only (arithmetic), is this risk ratio correct (yes or no)?
    **b.** Was this risk ratio calculated in accord with the recommendation to use percentages closer to 0% rather than those closer to 100%?
    **c.** Is interpretation of this risk ratio straightforward?
    **d.** As calculated, may the qualitative descriptors be used to interpret the size of association conveyed by this risk ratio?
    **e.** If 90% in Group 1 experienced the event, what percentage did not? If 80% in Group 2 experienced the event, what percentage did not? (Hint: Use subtraction.)
    **f.** With the other category of the dependent variable considered to be the event, calculate the risk ratio. (In other words, use the percentages that you just calculated to calculate the risk ratio.)

    **g.** Continuing to use the just-calculated percentages, calculate the risk ratio with Group 1 designated as Group 2 and Group 2 designated as the Group 1.

    **h.** Which risk ratio, 2.0 or 0.5, conveys the larger size of association.

    **i.** Using the descriptors in Table 7.2, what is the size of association?

**26.** This text recommends against using the descriptors of size of association for the risk ratio when either or both compared percentages exceeds _____%.

**27.** Indicate whether the qualitative descriptors for the *RR* are appropriate in each of the following situations.

    **a.** Four percent in Program A and 24% in Program B experience a given outcome.

    **b.** Twenty percent in Program A and 40% in Program B experience a given outcome.

    **c.** Thirty-six percent in Program A and 12% in Program B experience a given outcome.

**28.** Treating Program 1 as Group 1 and treating readmission as the event, what is the risk ratio in Table 6.4? May the qualitative descriptors be appropriately applied in this situation?

### Section 6.9

**29.** (*True or False*) The difference in percentages is a highly formal rather than informal measure of size of association.

**30.** If the qualitative descriptors for the *D%* may be appropriately used in a situation, mark "*D%*." If those for the *RR* may be appropriately used, mark "*RR*." Hint: Descriptors for both may be used in some situations; descriptors for neither may be used in one.

    **a.** Sixteen percent in Group 1 and 48% in Group 2 experience an outcome.

    **b.** Four percent in Group 1 and 16% in Group 2 experience an outcome.

    **c.** Twenty-two percent of women and 6% of men experience an outcome.

    **d.** Sixty-three percent of Democrats and 28% of Republicans voted for a given legislation.

    **e.** Twenty percent of adoptions in new homes versus 10% in foster family homes end in disruption.

    **f.** Four percent without mental health problems versus 62% with such problems experience at least 1 day without adequate food in a given month.

Portions of this chapter originally appeared in James Rosenthal's "Qualitative Descriptors of Strength of Association and Effect Size." *Journal of Social Service Research 21*(4), 1996, pp 37–49. Reproduced with permission.

# THE ODDS RATIO AND OTHER MEASURES FOR CATEGORICAL VARIABLES

## 7.1 ■ CHAPTER OVERVIEW

Chapter 7 begins with the discussion of *odds ratio* (*OR*), the most versatile measure of association between dichotomous variables. This discussion introduces *odds*, presents a formula, and interprets size of association. We move on to variables with more than two categories and overview measures for these situations. Finally, this chapter introduces *directional association* and overviews measures for assessing this.

## 7.2 ■ ODDS RATIO

### 7.2.1 ■ Basics and Formula

The odds ratio (*OR*) is certainly the most versatile and, in my opinion, the preferred measure for assessing size of association between two dichotomous variables. As its name suggests, an **odds ratio** is a ratio of odds. To calculate the **odds** of an event, divide the number that experiences an event (outcome) by the number that does not.

$$\text{odds} = \frac{\text{number that experience event}}{\text{number that does not experience event}} = \frac{n_e}{n_{ne}} \tag{7.1}$$

Another formula for the odds is

$$\text{odds} = \frac{\text{percentage that experience event}}{\text{percentage that does not experience event}} = \frac{\%_e}{\%_{ne}} \tag{7.2}$$

Formula 7.2 can also be expressed using proportions:

$$\text{odds} = \frac{\text{proportion that experience event}}{\text{proportion that does not experience event}} = \frac{p_e}{p_{ne}} \tag{7.3}$$

where *p* symbolizes proportion. Just as with the risk ratio (*RR*), the researcher designates one of the two categories of the dependent variable as the event.

The contingency table in Table 7.1 presents support for a proposed child welfare services bill by political party affiliation for a sample of state legislators. We will choose supporting the legislation (rather than not supporting it) as the event. The odds of a Democrat supporting the legislation are 30 / 20 = 1.5. The just-completed calculation used cell frequencies (numbers; Formula 7.1). We get the same result using percentages: 60% / 40% = 1.5 (Formula 7.2) or proportions, .60 / .40 = 1.5 (Formula 7.3).

Table 7.1 ■ **Support for Child Welfare Legislation by Political Party Affiliation (Hypothetical)**

|  | Democratic | Republican |  |
|---|---|---|---|
| **Supports** | 30 | 15 | 45 |
|  | 60% | 43% | 53% |
| **Does not support** | 20 | 20 | 40 |
|  | 40% | 57% | 47% |
|  | 50 | 35 | 85 |
|  | 59% | 41% | 100% |

Odds may vary from 0.00 to positive infinity. Negative odds (i.e., odds less than 0.00) do not exist. Odds greater than 1.00 convey that the event occurs more than 50% of the time; those of 1.00 convey that it occurs exactly 50% of the time; and those less than 1.00 convey that it occurs less than 50% of the time.

Our primary interest is not in the odds for each group but rather in the *OR*. To calculate the *OR*, we also need to find the odds for Republicans. The odds that a Republican will support the legislation are $15/20 = 3/4 = 3$ to $4 = 0.75$.

As mentioned earlier, the *OR* is a ratio of odds. Its formula is

$$OR = \frac{\text{odds for Group 1}}{\text{odds for Group 2}} = \frac{\text{odds}_1}{\text{odds}_2} \qquad (7.4)$$

The researcher decides which group to designate as Group 1 and which to designate as Group 2.

We will designate Democrats as Group 1 and Republicans as Group 2. We have already calculated odds for both groups and thus we use these to calculate the *OR*: $OR = 1.5 / 0.75 = 2.0$. This *OR* conveys that the odds that a Democrat will support the child welfare bill are two times the odds that a Republican will do so.

The just-carried out calculation of the *OR* used odds that have already been calculated. One may simply "plug" numbers (cell frequencies) directly into the formula

$$OR = \frac{30}{20} \div \frac{15}{20} = \frac{30}{20} \times \frac{20}{15} = \frac{600}{300} = 2.0$$

Or, one may simply plug in percentages (cell percentages). Using percentages:

$$OR = \frac{60}{40} \div \frac{43}{57} = \frac{60}{40} \times \frac{57}{43} = \frac{3420}{1720} = 1.99$$

The prior *OR* differs to 2.0 because of a rounding error. Finally, one may plug in proportions:

$$(0.60 / 0.40) / (0.43 / 0.57) = 1.99.$$

So far, we have treated Democrats as Group 1. This decision was arbitrary. Instead, let us make Republicans Group 1. The resulting odds ratio is $OR = .75 / 1.5 = 0.50$. Hence, the odds that a Republican will support the legislation are one half (0.5) those that a Democrat will do so.

Observe that the *OR* differed depending on whether Democrat or Republican was designated as Group 1. The two odds obtained *OR*s, 2.0 and 0.5, are reciprocals. Just as for the *RR* (see Chapter 6, Section 6.8), the *OR* obtained with one group designated as Group 1 is always the reciprocal of that obtained with the other designated group.

One does not need a contingency table to calculate the *OR*: The percentages of each group that experience the event is all that is needed. The percentages that do not experience it can be determined by subtraction. For instance, 90% in Job Program A (Group 1) obtain a job (the event) and 80% in Job Program B (Group 2) do so. What is the *OR*? The percentage not obtaining a job in A is 100% − 90% = 10%, and in B is 100% − 80% = 20%. Thus, the *OR* is

$$OR = \frac{90}{10} \div \frac{80}{20} = \frac{90}{10} \times \frac{20}{80} = \frac{1800}{800} = 2.25$$

Hence, the odds that a participant in A will obtain a job are 2.25 times the odds that a participant in B will do so.

## 7.2.2 ■ Interpretation

Just as odds (and the *RR*) may vary from 0.00 to positive infinity, so also may the *OR*. An *OR* of 1.00 conveys that the odds in each group are equal; in other words, that those in each group are equally likely to experience the event. Such an *OR* conveys the absence of association between group membership (Group 1 vs. Group 2) and experiencing the event (experience it vs. do not experience it).

*OR*s that differ from 1.00 convey the presence of association between group membership and experiencing the event. An *OR* greater than 1.00 conveys that the odds of experiencing the event are greater in Group 1 than in Group 2. An *OR* less than 1.00 conveys that the odds are greater in Group 2.

It is, generally speaking, easier to interpret *OR*s that are greater than 1.00 than those that are less than 1.00. Hence, when convenient to do so, I recommend designating groups so that the *OR* computes to a value greater than 1.00. This is accomplished by designating the group with the larger odds as the first group (the numerator) and that with the smaller as the second group (the denominator).

Just as for the *RR*, reciprocal *OR*s convey the same size (strength) of association. For instance, an *OR* of 6.00 conveys the same size of association as does one of 0.167 as these are reciprocals: 6.0 × 0.167 = 1.00.

As the *OR* differs increasingly from 1.00, the relationship that it conveys becomes stronger. For instance, an *OR* of 5.00 conveys a stronger association than does an *OR* of 2.00. And, for instance, an *OR* of 0.10 conveys a stronger association than does an *OR* of 0.20.

Table 7.2 presents qualitative descriptors for the *OR*. Two *OR*s are listed for each descriptor, one greater than 1.00 and one less than 1.00. The two *OR*s for each descriptor are reciprocals and thus convey the same size of association. Table 7.2 indicates that an *OR* of about 1.5 (or 0.67) conveys weak association whereas an *OR* of about 10 (or 0.10) conveys strong association.

Table 7.2 ■ **Qualitative Descriptors of Size and Strength of Association for the Odds Ratio and Risk Ratio**

| Odds Ratio or Risk Ratio | Size of Association | Strength of Association |
|---|---|---|
| About 1.5 or 0.67 | Small | Weak |
| About 2.5 or 0.40 | Medium | Moderate |
| About 4.0 or 0.25 | Large | Strong |
| About 10.0 or 0.10 | Very large | Very strong |

*Note.* For the *RR*, do not use these descriptors if the percentage experiencing the event in either group is greater than 30%. For the *OR*, do not use these descriptors if any percentage in the contingency table is less than 1% or greater than 99%.

In our political party and voting example with Democrats treated as Group 1, the *OR* was 2.0. Referencing Table 7.2, this *OR* is between 1.5, which conveys small association, and 2.5, which conveys medium association. Thus, the association between party affiliation and support for the legislation is roughly between small and medium in size.

Recall from our discussion in Chapter 6, Section 6.7, that the tables of qualitative descriptors interpret size of association in the context of social science research. So, adding a bit more context to our interpretation, let us conclude that, relative to the size of associations often found in social science research, our *OR* of 2.0 reflects a relationship of small to medium size.

### 7.2.3 ■ Advantages

This chapter introduced the *OR* by stating that it is the most versatile measure for assessing association between dichotomous variables. Let us see some of its advantages.

One advantage is that the qualitative descriptors for the *OR* may be applied in just about any 2 × 2 table. In contrast, the descriptors for the difference in percentages (*D%*) and *RR* are not recommended in some situations (for the *D%*, when one or more compared percentages are less than 10% or greater than 90%; for the *RR*, when one or more percentages exceed 30%).

Recall that for the *RR*, it is important to designate as the event the category of the dependent variable whose percentages are closer to 0%. Failure to do so changes the value of the *RR* and makes interpretation difficult at best. For the *OR*, designating the "other" category of the dependent variable as the event has the same effect as designating the "other" group as Group 1—that is, the *OR* calculates to its reciprocal. For instance, with *not* supporting the legislation designated as the event and Democratic as Group 1, the odds ratio is *OR* = (20 / 30) / (20 / 15) = 0.50. This is the reciprocal of 2.00, the *OR* that results when supporting the legislation is the event. As discussed previously, reciprocal *OR*s convey the same size of association. Thus, reversing the categories does not change the size of association—a nice feature.

Let us give one more example to demonstrate that changing the category that conveys the event yields a reciprocal *OR*. Twenty youth participate in a mentoring program. Sixteen graduate from college and four do not. Among the 20 youth who are not mentored, 12 graduate and 8 do not. With mentoring treated as the first group and graduating as the event, the *OR* is (16 / 4) / (12 / 8) = 2.67. Treating not graduating as the event yields: *OR* = (4 / 16) / (8 / 12) = 0.375.). The result 0.375 is indeed the reciprocal of 2.67, as 2.67 × 0.375 = 1.00.

Recall that the *D%* can calculate to an incorrect value when the wrong set of percentages is used (row percentages when column percentages are recommended, or vice versa). In contrast, either set of percentages may be used to compute the *OR*. To demonstrate this, let us designate Democratic as the event and supporting the legislation as Group 1. The *OR* is (30 / 15) / (20 / 20) = 2.00. Interpreting the odds of being a Democrat among those who support the legislation are 2.00 times the odds of those who do not. Now, I do not recommend carrying out the *OR* formula in such a counterintuitive fashion, with a category of the *independent* variable treated as the event and a category of the *dependent* variable treated as Group 1.

On the other hand, in some situations, neither variable is clearly the independent or the dependent. In such situations, the fact that either set of percentages may be used is a convenient feature.

In sum, although more difficult to calculate than the *D%* and the *RR*, the *OR* has numerous advantages. The multivariate statistical procedure *logistic regression* is becoming increasingly popular. Both odds and *OR*s are important in logistic regression (see Chapter 23, Section 4). (For more advantages of the *OR*, see Fleiss [1994, pp. 251–258].)

## 7.3 ■ RELATIONSHIP IN CONTINGENCY TABLES LARGER THAN 2 × 2

Researchers often peruse their way, almost by habit, through contingency tables. The special needs adoption study (Rosenthal & Groze, 1992) found that

■ 29% of minority children adopted by minority families had serious behavior problems (minority inracial group);

■ 47% of White children adopted by White families had such problems (White inracial group); and

■ 37% of children adopted transracially by White families (transracial group) had such problems.

Given that percentages differ, family ethnicity and the presence of versus the absence of serious behavior problems are associated. Table 7.3 presents the just-described relationship. Because it has two rows and three columns, it is a 2 × 3 contingency table. (See Chapter 3, Section 3.5, for information on the special-needs adoption study.)

In perusing Table 7.3, a researcher might compute (or perhaps informally estimate) the differences in percentages between the different family groups. For instance, comparing the minority inracial and white inracial groups, $D\% = 47\% - 29\% = 18\%$, an association of medium size (see Table 6.3). The other two family group comparisons result in smaller differences ($D\% = 47\% - 37\% = 10\%$; $D\% = 37\% - 29\% = 8\%$) and thus indicate smaller relationships. Thus, Table 7.3 contains a medium-size difference and two smaller ones. So, on balance, the overall size of association between family ethnicity and child behavior can perhaps be characterized as small to medium, that is, as a rough average of the different comparisons in the table.

It is hoped that this discussion gives you a glimpse of how researchers examine larger contingency tables. They peruse the various differences in percentages, often thinking about whether these are larger or smaller than expected. Although no formal measure works per se as just described, such a perusal is exactly what I recommend carrying out to get a beginning understanding of the data in contingency tables. In examining differences in percentages, be sure to use the correct percentages—always column percentages for tables in this text.

Although the examination of differences in percentages helps one to "get a feel for" the data in contingency tables that are larger than 2 × 2, there is an excellent measure of size of association between nominal-level variables in tables larger than 2 × 2, that being **Cramer's V**. Cramer's *V* may vary from a minimum possible value of 0.00, indicating the absence of association between variables to a maximum possible value of 1.00, indicating the strongest possible association. For the family ethnicity and behavior problems data presented in Table 7.3, Cramer's *V* calculates to 0.16.

Table 8.2, used primarily for the correlation coefficient, also provides qualitative descriptors for Cramer's *V*. In Table 8.2, the "0.10" conveys a small association and "0.30" conveys a medium

Table 7.3 ■ **Family Ethnicity by Severity of Child Behavioral Problems**

| | Minority Inracial | White Inracial | Transracial |
|---|---|---|---|
| **Child has serious behavior problems** | 59 | 194 | 20 |
| | 29.4% | 46.6% | 37.0% |
| **Child does not have serious behavior problems** | 142 | 222 | 34 |
| | 70.6% | 53.4% | 63.0% |

one. Hence, size of the association between family ethnicity and behavior problems is interme-diate between small and medium. This assessment agrees well with the earlier assessment that we formed from perusing Table 7.1's percentages. The descriptors for Cramer's *V* in Table 8.2 should be viewed as approximating size of association. (See Cohen [1988, pp. 215–272] for more on measures of size of association for contingency tables.)

Although its primary use is with tables larger than 2 × 2, Cramer's *V* may also be used with 2 × 2 tables (for more on Cramer's *V*, see Blalock [1979, pp. 305–315]). A final measure of size of association[1] between categorical variables, *phi*, is discussed in Chapter 8.

## 7.4 ■ DIRECTIONAL RELATIONSHIP

A relationship between two variables has **direction** if as one variable increases (or decreases) and so also does the other. Such a relationship can be termed a **directional relationship** (**directional association**, *ordinal relationship*, *ordinal association*).[2] In a **positive relationship** (**positive association**), both variables change in the *same* direction—as one increases, so does the other (which is the same as saying that as one decreases, so does the other). In a **negative relationship** (**negative association**), the variables change in *opposite* directions—as one increases, the other decreases (or, to be redundant, as one decreases, the other increases).

For a variable to be involved in a directional relationship, one must be able to order its values from high to low. Consider the variable eye color with the values of brown, blue, green, gray, and other. Because these values cannot be ordered, this variable cannot form a directional relationship with any other variable.

As presented in Chapter 1, Section 1.9.1, by definition, the values of a nominal-level variable cannot be ordered. It follows then that nominal-level variables may not be involved in directional relationships. However, there is an exception. When a nominal-level variable is dichotomous (has exactly two values), we may view (albeit arbitrarily) one value as high and the other as low. For instance, we may view "yes" as high and "no" as low. Or (again arbitrarily) we may view "female" as high and "male" as low. As their values may be ordered (even if arbitrarily), dichoto-mous variables may be involved in directional relationships.

Dichotomous variables are the only nominal-level variables that may be involved in direc-tional relationships. When a nominal-level variable has three or more values, it may not have a directional relationship with any other variable. All variables at the ordinal- and interval-ratio levels of measurement can be involved in a directional relationship. This chapter examines rela-tionship for categorical ordinal-level variables.

Table 7.4 presents two hypothetical examples of relationship between the categorical ordi-nal-level variables: age of graduate student and level of motivation. In both examples, percent-ages differ and thus the variables are related.

Example 1 illustrates a directional relationship because as age of students increases, so also does level of motivation. To discern this pattern, examine the percentages. For instance, the per-centage of highly motivated students increases as age group increases from 25 years and younger (30% are highly motivated), to 26–34 years old (40%), to 35 years and older (50%). Similarly, as age group increases, the percentage of unmotivated students decreases from 25% to 20% to 10%.

As mentioned earlier, direction may be positive or negative. Because both variables in Example 1 change in the same direction—as age goes up, motivation goes up—it demonstrates positive directional relationship.

Example 2 demonstrates a *nondirectional relationship* (*nondirectional association*). Percentages differ in the different columns, and thus age and motivation are related. However, this relationship does not have a directional pattern. For instance, the middle group in age

Table 7.4 ■ **Examples of Association Between Variables at the Ordinal Level (Percentages)**

|  | Age of Graduate Student | | |
|---|---|---|---|
|  | **25 Years and Younger** | **26–34 Years Old** | **35 Years and Older** |
| Example 1 | | | |
| Level of motivation | | | |
| Unmotivated | 25 | 20 | 10 |
| Not very | 25 | 20 | 15 |
| Somewhat | 20 | 20 | 25 |
| Highly | 30 | 40 | 50 |
| Example 2 | | | |
| Level of motivation | | | |
| Unmotivated | 5 | 25 | 10 |
| Not very | 25 | 25 | 15 |
| Somewhat | 20 | 20 | 25 |
| Highly | 50 | 30 | 50 |

(26–34 years old) is less motivated than both the youngest and oldest groups. Although it is possible for two ordinal-level variables to have a directional relationship, Example 2 demonstrates that their actual relationship (if any) need not take this form.

On the other hand, as mentioned previously, a nominal-level variable with three or more categories may not be involved in a directional relationship. Hence, any relationship involving such a variable is, by definition, nondirectional.

An example of directional association in which one variable is dichotomous may be helpful. Our two variables are pass a test (yes vs. no, a dichotomous variable) and number of hours studied (an ordinal-level categorical variable with five categories). Suppose that the percentages passing for the five categories of study hours are study 0–1 hour, 40%; study 2–4 hours, 55%; study 5–9 hours, 75%; study 10–19 hours, 90%; and study 20 or more hours, 100%. The pattern is clear; as hours studied increases, so does the percentage passing the exam. Thus, we may say that there is a positive association between hours studied and passing the exam. Now consider the following results (not really expected results but presented for the purposes of illustration): study 0–1 hour, 80%; study 2–4 hours, 55%; study 5–9 hours, 75%; study 10–19 hours, 95%; and study 20 or more hours, 65%. The percentages passing the test differ for the differing categories of hours studied. Hence, hours studied and passing the exam are related. However, there is no directional trend to the data. In other words, as hours studied increases, there is no trend for the percentage passing the exam to either increase (positive relationship) or decrease (negative relationship).

As discussed in the prior section, Cramer's *V* is an excellent measure of size of association between nominal-level variables in contingency tables that are larger than $2 \times 2$. Let us now build on that statement: Cramer's *V* is an excellent measure of size of relationship in contingency tables larger than $2 \times 2$ whenever relationship is nondirectional. That nondirectional relationship may be observed either when directional relationship is not possible (as in Table 7.3 as family ethnicity is a nominal level variable with three categories) or when directional relationship is possible but not observed (as in Example 2 in Table 7.4).

Cramer's *V*, however, is not the preferred measure of size of directional association between categorical variables as in, for instance, Example 1 in Table 7.4. Preferred measures of directional association between categorical variables are presented in the next section.

## 7.5 ■ MEASURES OF DIRECTIONAL ASSOCIATION BETWEEN CATEGORICAL VARIABLES

Four preferred measures of directional relationship between categorical variables are Kendall's tau-*b* ($\tau_b$), Kendall's tau-*c* ($\tau_c$), gamma ($\gamma$), and Somers' *D*. All of these may vary in value from −1.00 (strongest possible negative relationship) to 1.00 (strongest possible positive relationship). The closer the value to 0.00, the weaker the relationship. The value 0.00 conveys the absence of directional relationship. For a rough gauge of size of association, see Table 8.2.[3] Selected advantages and disadvantages of these measures are now overviewed.

**tau-*b*** is an excellent choice in square tables, that is, when both variables have the same number of categories (for instance, in a 3 × 3 table). When the number of categories differ, **tau-*c*** is preferred over tau-*b* as the latter cannot achieve values of either −1.00 or 1.00 in tables that are not square. **Somers' *D*** is often the best choice when variables can be classified as independent and dependent. It yields different values depending on how the variables are classified. In general, I do not recommend **gamma** because it can attain values that are artificially high. For more information, see Rosenthal (2000, pp. 165–168) or Blalock (1979).

For Example 1 in Table 7.4, the values of the just-presented measures are tau-*b* = .18, tau-*c* = 0.19, gamma = 0.26, and Somers' *D* = 0.19. Because Table 7.4 is not a square one, tau-*c* is preferred to tau-*b*. The value of Somers' *D* is the value with age group treated as the independent variable.

The fact that all of these measures compute to positive values confirms for us that the association between student age and motivation level is indeed a positive association. Consulting the qualitative descriptors in Table 8.2, 0.10 conveys a small association and 0.30 conveys one of medium size. Hence, we conclude that the association between age and motivation is positive and small to medium in size.

## 7.6 ■ CHAPTER SUMMARY

When both variables are dichotomous, the *OR* is an excellent measure of size of association. As its name suggests, an *OR* is a ratio of odds. *Odds* may be defined as the number that experience an *event* divided by the number that do not. To calculate the *OR*, divide the odds for the first group by those for the second: $OR = \text{odds}_1/\text{odds}_2$.

Just as is the case for odds, the *OR* may vary from 0.00 to positive infinity. *OR*s greater than 1.00 indicate that the odds for the event are greater for the first group than for the second. *OR*s less than 1.00 convey that these odds are less for the first group than for the second. An *OR* of exactly 1.00 conveys that the event is equally likely in both groups and that group membership and experience of the event are unassociated.

Changing the group designated as Group 1 changes the *OR* to its reciprocal. Reciprocal *OR*s convey the same size of association.

Table 7.2 presents qualitative descriptors for the *OR*. An *OR* of about 1.5 (or 0.67) indicates a small (weak) association whereas one of about 10.0 (or 0.10) indicates a very large (very strong) association.

Assuming that both variables are dichotomous, the *OR* is an effective measure of size of association for almost all situations. Changing the category of the dependent variable that is designated as the event changes the *OR* to its reciprocal. The *OR*'s value is unaffected by whether column or row percentages are used. Whether or not one uses percentages that are closest to 0.00 does not affect the *OR*.

Researchers peruse contingency tables, almost by habit, assessing differences between percentages.

A relationship between two variables has *direction* if as one variable increases (or decreases) and so also does the other. Direction of relationship may be either *positive* (both variables change in the same direction) or *negative* (they change in opposite directions).

Only those variables whose values can be ordered can be involved in directional relationships. Specifically, any nominal-level variable with three or more categories may not be involved in a directional relationship.

Cramer's *V* is used predominantly with contingency tables that are larger than 2 × 2. It is an excellent measure of *nondirectional relationship* (relationships that do not have a directional pattern) but is not a preferred measure of *directional relationship*.

Four measures designed specifically to assess the size of directional relationship in contingency tables are Kendall's tau-*b* ($\tau_b$), Kendall's tau-*c* ($\tau_c$), gamma ($\gamma$), and Somers' *D*. These may vary in value from −1.00 (strongest possible negative relationship) to 1.00 (strongest possible positive relationship). The closer the value to 0.00, the weaker the relationship. Kendall's tau-*b* ($\tau_b$) is an excellent measure for square tables whereas Kendall's tau-*c* is preferred for tables that are not square. *Gamma* sometimes yields values that are artificially high. *Somers' D* is an excellent measure when the variables can be classified as independent and dependent.

## 7.7 ■ PROBLEMS AND QUESTIONS

### Section 7.2

1. Odds may vary from _____ (minimum possible value) to positive _____ (maximum possible value). When odds are greater than _____, the event occurs more than 50% of the time.

2. Nine (75%) children served by a child welfare program are reunited with their families and three (25%) are not. Respond accordingly.
   a. What are the odds of being reunited? Calculate using percentages.
   b. What are the odds of being reunited? Calculate using numbers.
   c. What is the odds ratio? (This is a trick question. Can the odds ratio be calculated in this situation? Why or why not?)

3. Six (50%) professors at a human services education program indicate a preference for behavioral theory and six (50%) indicate a preference for psychosocial theory. What are the odds that a professor favors behavioral theory?

4. Twenty (25%) of 80 clients classified as having "low skills" versus 50 (62.5%) of 80 classified as having "high skills" obtain employment within 6 months of beginning to receive welfare assistance.
   a. Given that 20 of 80 (25%) clients with low skills obtain employment, how many of these did not obtain employment? What percentage did not?
   b. Given that 50 of 80 (62.5%) clients with high skills obtain employment, how many of these did not obtain employment? What percentage did not?

    **c.** Using percentages, calculate the odds of obtaining employment for those with low skills.

    **d.** Using numbers (frequencies), calculate the odds of obtaining employment for those with low skills.

    **e.** Using percentages, calculate the odds of obtaining employment for those with high skills.

    **f.** Using numbers (frequencies), calculate the odds of obtaining employment for those with high skills.

    **g.** With "high skills" treated as Group 1 and obtaining employment as the event, what is the odds ratio?

    **h.** The odds of finding employment for persons with high skills are _____ times those of persons with low skills.

    **i.** With "low skills" treated as Group 1 and obtaining employment as the event, what is the odds ratio?

    **j.** Multiply the two just-computed odds ratios by each other. What is the result? What is the mathematical relationship of the two just-calculated odds ratios?

**5.** Fifteen of 25 students in a social work class versus 10 of 30 students in a business class support legislation to provide increased medical services to those who are poor.

    **a.** What are the odds that a social work student supports the legislation?

    **b.** What are the odds that a business student supports the legislation?

    **c.** What is the odds ratio? Consider social work as Group 1 and support as the event.

    **d.** The odds of a social work student supporting the legislation are _____ times those of a business student.

    **e.** What is the reciprocal of the just-computed odds ratio?

    **f.** What is the odds ratio? Consider business as Group 1 and support as the event. (Hint: You already know the answer.)

    **g.** As a check on your prior answer, compute this odds ratio using the formula for the odds ratio (Formula 7.4).

**6.** Eighty percent of students who study 20 or more hours versus 40% of those who study 19 or fewer hours obtain a grade of A on an examination. What is the odds ratio? Consider studying 20 or more hours as Group 1 and getting an A as the event. Interpret the odds ratio in your own words.

**7.** In Intervention A, 10% do not achieve a criterion; in Intervention B, 20% do not. With not achieving defined as the criterion and Intervention B as the first group, what is the odds ratio? Interpret the odds ratio in your own words.

**8.** (*True or False*) To compute an odds ratio, one must know frequencies (numbers). Stated differently, percentages alone are not sufficient.

**9.** The odds ratio may vary from _____ (minimum possible value) to _____ (maximum possible value). An odds ratio of _____ (number) conveys the

absence of association. When an odds ratio is greater than 1.00, the odds of the event are
_____ for the first group than for the second.

10. Odds ratios that are _____ (mathematical relationship) convey the same size of
association.

11. For each odds ratio, find the odds ratio less than 1.00 that conveys the same size of association.
    **a.** 4.00     **b.** 8.00     **c.** 2.00     **d.** 6.00     **e.** 1.50

12. For each odds ratio, find the odds ratio that is greater than 1.00 that conveys the same size
    of association.
    **a.** 0.25     **b.** 0.10     **c.** 0.333     **d.** 0.80     **e.** 0.667

13. For each odds ratio, find the odds ratio that would have resulted if the other group had been
    designated as the first group.
    **a.** 8.00     **b.** 0.125     **c.** 20.00     **d.** 0.40

14. Choose the odds ratio from each pair that conveys the stronger association.
    **a.** 0.20 or 0.50     **b.** 0.90 or 0.80     **c.** 5.0 or 4.0     **d.** 0.25 or 4.00

15. Characterize the size of association conveyed by each odds ratio.
    **a.** 8.00     **b.** 0.125     **c.** 20.00     **d.** 0.40     **e.** 1.40

16. A research study reports an odds ratio of $-1.75$. What should you conclude?

17. The percentages compared in each group are listed. Consider the odds ratio ($OR$), the
    difference in percentages ($D\%$), and the risk ratio ($RR$). For each set of percentages, indicate
    the measures whose qualitative descriptors may be used to assess size of association.
    **a.** 40% and 80%
    **b.** 3% and 23%
    **c.** 6% and 60%
    **d.** 10% and 25%
    **e.** 5% and 10%
    **f.** 25% and 50%

18. Twenty-five percent in Group 1 and 40% in Group 2 experience Event $X$. Consider
    Group 1 to be the first group.
    **a.** What is the odds ratio? (Event $X$ is the event.)
    **b.** What is the reciprocal of the just-computed odds ratio?
    **c.** What is the odds ratio for *not* experiencing Event $X$?

19. *Respond true or false.*
    **a.** Just as for the risk ratio, using those percentages that are not closest to zero (0%) yields
    an odds ratio that yields nearly meaningless information.

   **b.** Whenever percentages are less than 10%, the descriptors for the odds ratio are not useful.

   **c.** The odds ratio is a good measure of size of association for just about any $2 \times 2$ contingency table.

   **d.** When column percentages rather than row percentages are used (or vice versa), the value of the odds ratio becomes misleading and meaningless.

## Section 7.3

Table 7.5 ■ **Family Ethnicity by Child Has Learning Disability (Hypothetical Data)**

|  | Minority Inracial | White Inracial | Transracial |
|---|---|---|---|
| **Child has learning disability** | 39 | 94 | 16 |
|  | 19% | 23% | 30% |
| **Child does not have learning disability** | 162 | 312 | 38 |
|  | 81% | 77% | 70.0% |

**20.** Referencing the aforementioned hypothetical data: For all questions, calculate the $D\%$ so that it is a positive number.

   **a.** Calculate the $D\%$ comparing minority inracial and White inracial families.

   **b.** Calculate the $D\%$ comparing minority inracial and transracial families.

   **c.** Calculate the $D\%$ comparing White inracial and transracial families.

   **d.** Using the descriptors of size of association, what size of association is conveyed by each just-computed $D\%$?

   **e.** "Synthesizing" together your assessments of size association for the three $D\%$, characterize the overall size of association in the table.

   **f.** (*True or False*) The just-completed procedure is an informal one, designed to give a rough feel for size of association rather than to provide a precise assessment.

**21.** The best measure of size of association between nominal-level variables in a contingency table that are larger than $2 \times 2$ is _____.

**22.** Cramer's *V* may vary from a minimum possible value of _____ (no association) to one of _____ (strongest possible association).

**23.** Indicate the size of association conveyed by each of the following values of Cramer's *V*. (Hint: One value is "bogus.")

   **a.** 0.75

   **b.** 0.28

   **c.** 0.53

   **d.** $-0.53$

   **e.** 0.09

   **f.** 0.32

## Section 7.4

**24.** For each of the following, indicate "positive" if the described relationship is a positive relationship, "negative" if it is a negative relationship, "nondirectional" if it is nondirectional, or "no relationship" if there is no relationship of any kind.

    **a.** As $X$ increases, $Y$ increases.

    **b.** As $X$ decreases, $Y$ decreases.

    **c.** As $X$ decreases, $Y$ increases.

    **d.** As $X$ increases, $Y$ decreases.

    **e.** As $X$ increases, $Y$ changes but not in a directional way.

    **f.** As $X$ goes up, responses on $Y$ change not at all.

    **g.** As eye color changes from brown to blue to green, the percentage who like rock music increases.

    **h.** As hours exercised goes up, weight tends to go down.

    **i.** The percentage graduating from college varies by ethnicity (African American, White, Hispanic, Native American, Asian American).

    **j.** In a health study: Among those who take a low dose of $X$, 40% report symptoms; among those who take a medium dose of $X$, 30% report symptoms; among those who take a high dose of $X$, 20% report symptoms.

    **k.** Categorize the type of relationship in Table 7.5.

**25.** *Respond true or false to each statement.*

    **a.** It is impossible for a nominal-level variable that has three or more categories to be involved in a directional relationship.

    **b.** It is possible for a nominal-level variable with two categories to be involved in a directional relationship.

    **c.** All relationships between categorical ordinal-level variables are directional relationships.

    **d.** Cramer's $V$ is an excellent measure of nondirectional relationship in tables larger than $2 \times 2$ even when both variables in the table are at the ordinal level.

    **e.** Even when relationship in a contingency table is directional, Cramer's $V$ is the preferred measure of association.

    **f.** Cramer's $V$ may not be used to assess association in $2 \times 2$ tables.

## Section 7.5

**26.** Match each measure with the description *tau-b*, *tau-c*, *gamma*, and *Somers' D*.

    **a.** an excellent measure when one variable is clearly independent and the other is clearly dependent

    **b.** an excellent measure for a square table (same number of rows and columns)

    **c.** an excellent measure when the number of rows and columns differ

    **d.** sometimes calculates to a value that is artificially high

**27.** Presume that the value provided is a value for *s tau-b*, *s tau-c*, *gamma*, and *Somers' D*. For each value, indicate whether the relationship that it conveys is positive or negative, as well as the strength (size) of association.

    **a.** 0.53

    **b.** −0.53

    **c.** −0.12

    **d.** 0.31

    **e.** 0.00

    **f.** −0.72

    **g.** −0.28

    **h.** 0.13

Portions of this chapter originally appeared in James Rosenthal's "Qualitative Descriptors of Strength of Association and Effect Size." *Journal of Social Service Research 21*(4), 1996, pp 37–49. Reproduced with permission.

# 8

# CORRELATION AND REGRESSION

## 8.1 ■ CHAPTER OVERVIEW

Chapter 8 addresses *correlation* between interval/ratio-level variables using *Pearson's r (r)*. It shows how researchers use *scatterplots* to interpret *r* and contrasts *curvilinear* and *linear* association. It overviews the *coefficient of determination*. The chapter also examines *regression* and its distinction from correlation. It briefly discusses correlation between nominal- and ordinal-level variables.

## 8.2 ■ POSITIVE AND NEGATIVE CORRELATION

Symbolized by *r*, the **Pearson correlation coefficient** (*Pearson's r*) measures the degree of linear association between two interval/ratio-level variables. A **linear association** is one that can be described by a straight line. Correlational procedures are used primarily with interval/ratio-level variables. Unless otherwise noted, our discussion assumes this to be so; the chapter closes with discussion of correlation with other types of variables. To simplify discussion, this chapter refers to interval/ratio-level variables as numeric variables.[1]

The basic concepts of correlation were introduced in the prior chapter's discussion of positive and negative relationship. If the values of two numeric variables change in the *same* direction, the variables are **positively correlated**. If these values change in *opposite* directions, the variables are **negatively correlated** (*inversely correlated*).

I will present some examples from athletics to demonstrate correlation. Presume that height jumped in the high jump and distance jumped in the long jump are positively correlated. If this is so, then those who jump "high" in the high jump will tend to jump "far" in the long jump, and those who jump "low" in the high jump will tend to jump "short" in the long jump. Not all high high jumpers will be long long jumpers, and not all low high jumpers will be short long jumpers, but this will be the prevailing pattern. When two variables are positively correlated, high scores on one tend to go with high scores on the other, and, similarly, lows on one tend to go with lows on the other. Stated differently, similar scores tend to go together—highs with highs, middles with middles, and lows with lows.

Suppose that height jumped in the high jump and time in the 50-meter run are negatively correlated. If so, then those who jump high in the high jump will tend to have low times (i.e., fast times) in the 50-meter run, and those who jump low will tend to have high times (i.e, slow times). When two variables are negatively correlated, high scores on the first tend to go with low scores on the second, and, similarly, lows on the first tend to go with highs on the second. Stated differently, dissimilar scores tend to go together—highs with lows and lows with highs (although middles will tend to go with middles).

## 8.3 ■ SCATTERPLOTS

**Scatterplots** display correlations visually. Figure 8.1 presents the (hypothetical) correlation between distance jumped in the long jump and height jumped in the high jump. Each marker in Figure 8.1 represents a case. Height in the high jump is conveyed by a marker's position relative to the vertical axis (Y axis) and distance in the long jump is conveyed by its position relative to the horizontal axis (X axis). To learn the height in the high jump that a given marker represents, trace horizontally from that marker to the vertical axis. The point of intersection conveys the height. To learn the distance in the long jump that a marker represents, trace straight down to the horizontal axis. The point of intersection indicates the distance. For instance, the highest marker in Figure 8.1 (located in the upper right corner) represents an individual who high jumped about 6.3 ft and long jumped slightly more than 20 ft. In Figure 8.1, the pattern created by the markers slants upward from the lower left corner toward the upper right corner. This upward slope conveys the basic message of positive correlation: As scores on one variable increase, so do those on the other. When a scatterplot's markers slant upward from lower left to upper right, the displayed variables are positively correlated.

Figure 8.1 also demonstrates that when variables are positively correlated, high scores on one variable tend to go with high scores on the other and, similarly, low scores tend to go with low scores. For instance, the markers near the upper right hand corner convey individuals who had high scores on both variables. Similarly, markers near the lower left convey those who were low on both.

Figure 8.2 displays the (hypothetical) correlation of height jumped in the high jump with time in the 50-meter run. The pattern of the markers slants downward from the upper left corner toward the lower right corner. As time in the 50-meter run increases, height jumped tends to decrease. Such a downward sloping pattern from upper left to lower right conveys negative correlation. Figure 8.2 also conveys that when a correlation is negative, dissimilar values tend to go together. For instance, markers near the upper left corner convey individuals who had high scores

FIGURE 8.1 ■ Scatterplot with Positive Correlation

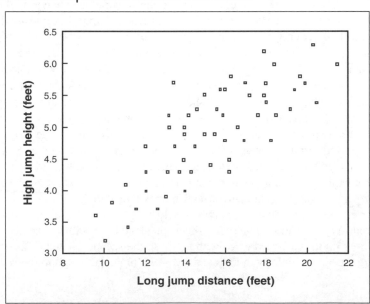

FIGURE 8.2 ■ Scatterplot with Negative Correlation

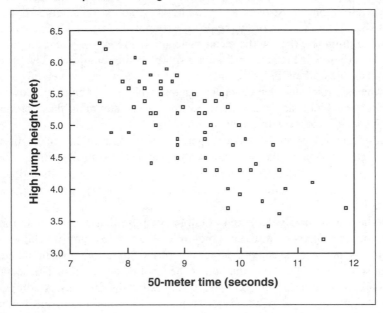

in the high jump but low scores in the 50-meter run. Those in the lower right convey low scores in the high jump and high scores in the 50-meter run.

In the just-presented athletics examples, the variables cannot be easily classified as independent and dependent. When variables can be classified, the independent variable is plotted on the scatterplot's X (horizontal) axis, and the dependent variable is plotted on its Y (vertical) axis.

## 8.4 ■ FORMULA FOR THE CORRELATION COEFFICIENT, *r*

One formula for Pearson's *r* is

$$r = \frac{\Sigma(z_x \times z_y)}{N - 1} \qquad (8.1)$$

where *r* is the correlation coefficient, $z_x$ is the *z* score on variable *X*, $z_y$ is the *z* score on variable *Y*, and *N* is the sample size. The steps in Formula 8.1 are

1. using the *z* score Formula (5.1), transform scores on both variables to *z* scores;
2. for each case, multiply the *z* score on *X* by the *z* score on *Y*;
3. sum the products from the prior step; and
4. divide by $(N - 1)$.

Study of the formula can help you understand correlation. Recall that *z* scores above the mean have positive values, and those below it have negative values.

Let us focus first on positive correlation, continuing to use the high-jump/long-jump example. In positive correlation, similar scores go together. As such, those who jump high (above the mean) in the high jump will, most often, jump long (above the mean) in the long jump. Given that their scores are (most often) above the mean on both variables, these persons will, most often, have positive $z$ scores on both variables. This being so, the product of their $z$ scores (Step 2) will, most often, be positive (a positive times a positive equals a positive). Those who jump low (below the mean = negative $z$ score) on the high jump will, most often, jump short (below the mean = negative $z$ score) in the long jump. The product of their $z$ scores will also, most often, be positive (a negative times a negative equals a positive).

In sum, when similar values tend to occur together—highs with highs and lows with lows—the products of the $z$ scores are, most often, positive. Thus, summing these products (Step 3) yields a positive value, and a positive value of $r$ results.

When dissimilar values tend to occur together—lows with highs and highs with lows—then $z$ scores with opposite signs (positives with negatives; negatives with positives) tend to be paired. The product of these $z$ scores is, most often, negative (a positive times a negative equals a negative). Thus, the summing of the products yields a negative value, and a negative value of $r$ results.

It may be helpful to see a calculation example. Suppose that we have data for eight families on (a) the number of visits in the past month to an extended family member in a nursing home and (b) the score on a measure of depression of the family member in the nursing home; the higher the score on the measure, the higher the level of depression. The second and third columns of Table 8.1 present scores on these variables for the families. A computer software program calculated means and standard deviations. For visiting, the mean is 6.50 visits and the standard deviation is 2.88 visits; for the depression measure, the mean is 48.37 points and the standard deviation is 6.00 points. The fourth and fifth columns list $z$ scores. Although a software program calculated these, we can duplicate its calculations. As you know, to calculate a case's $z$ score, we subtract the mean from the case's raw score and divide by the standard deviation. Thus, the $z$ score in visiting for Family 1 is $(7.00 - 6.50 / 2.88 = 0.17$. Family 1's depression measure $z$ score is $(51.00 - 48.37) / 6.00 = 0.44$. (Check Table 8.1 to see that 0.17 and 0.44 are indeed Family 1's $z$ scores.)

Calculating $z$ scores is the first step in Formula 8.1. The second is multiplication of the $z$ scores. The products from this multiplication are presented in Table 8.1's rightmost column. For instance, for Family 1, $0.17 \times 0.44 = 0.08$. These products sum (Step 4) down the far right column to $-4.15$. Because this sum is negative, we know that Pearson's $r$ will calculate to a negative value. The final step (Step 4) divides by $(N - 1)$: $r = -4.15 / (N - 1) = -0.592$.

Table 8.1 ■ A Grid to Help with Calculation of Pearson's $r$

| Family | Number of Visits | Depression Score | z Score on Visits | z Score on Depression | Product of z Scores |
|---|---|---|---|---|---|
| Family 1 | 7 | 51 | 0.17 | 0.44 | 0.08 |
| Family 2 | 4 | 50 | −0.87 | 0.27 | −0.24 |
| Family 3 | 11 | 39 | 1.56 | −1.56 | −2.44 |
| Family 4 | 2 | 57 | −1.56 | 1.44 | −2.25 |
| Family 5 | 8 | 43 | 0.52 | −0.9 | −0.47 |
| Family 6 | 5 | 44 | −0.52 | −0.73 | 0.38 |
| Family 7 | 6 | 49 | −0.17 | 0.1 | −0.02 |
| Family 8 | 9 | 54 | 0.87 | 0.94 | 0.81 |
| | | | | | $\Sigma = -4.15$ |

FIGURE 8.3 ■ Scatterplot of Negative Correlation Between Family Visits and Depression

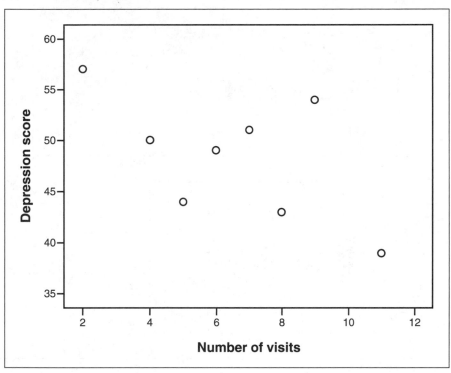

As just mentioned, the correlation between visiting and depression is negative; as visiting goes up, depression goes down. Figure 8.3 is a scatterplot of the data. The upper left to lower right slant of the markers in the scatterplot confirms that the correlation is negative.

## 8.5 ■ UNDERSTANDING *r*

Recall that, when transformed to *z* scores, all variables have a mean of 0.00 and a standard deviation of 1.00. Because *z* scores are used in the formula for *r*, neither multiplication (or division) nor addition (or subtraction) of the original scores (raw scores) by a constant affects the value of *r*. Suppose, for instance, that we wanted to present high jump height in centimeters rather than inches. To convert (transform) our measurements from inches to centimeters, we could multiply all high jump heights by (the constant) 2.54 (2.54 cm equals 1.00 in.). Doing so would not change the correlation between high jump height and any other variable.[2]

Similarly, suppose that we determined that the high jump bar had been one-half inch lower at all heights than we had thought to have been the case. To correct the measurements of height, we could subtract (the constant) 0.5 inches from all scores. Doing so would not change the correlation between high jump height and any other variable.

The value of *r* may vary from −1.00 to +1.00. An *r* greater than 0.00 conveys a positive correlation. One less than 0.00 conveys a negative one. The closer the absolute value of *r* to 1.00, the larger (stronger) the correlation. Correlations of −1.00 and 1.00 are **perfect correlations**. When a correlation is perfect, scores on either variable can be predicted *exactly* from scores on the

FIGURE 8.4 ■ Perfect Correlations and Correlation Close to 0.00

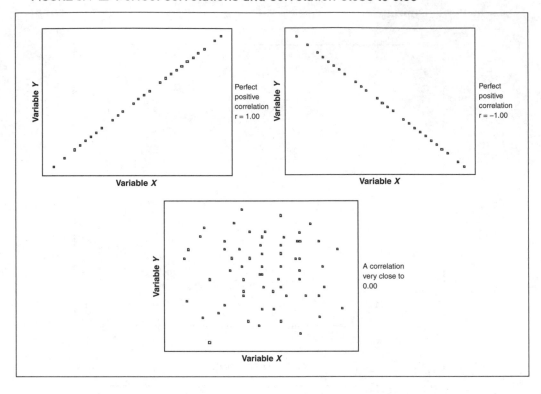

other. Figure 8.4 presents perfect positive and negative correlations. When there is perfect correlation, the scatterplot's markers form a straight line. In a perfect positive correlation, markers slant upward from lower left to upper right. In a perfect negative correlation, they slant downward from upper left to lower right.

Perfect correlations are almost never encountered in real data. In perfect positive correlation, the $z$ scores for each case are precisely equal on both variables.

The "opposite" of a perfect correlation is a correlation of 0.00. When the correlation between two variables is 0.00, there is no linear (straight line) relationship between these variables. The statements in the next paragraph apply except for *curvilinear relationships*, which are discussed in Section 8.7.

With the just-mentioned exception, an $r$ of 0.00 conveys that two variables are unassociated. When $r$ equals 0.00, (a) an increase or decrease in one variable is not accompanied by either an increase or decrease in the other (changes in one variable show no relationship to those in the other); (b) particular values of one variable do not tend "go with" particular values of the other (knowing the value of one variable helps you not at all in predicting that of the other); and (c) the pattern of the scatterplot's markers has neither an upward nor a downward slant but instead takes on a random pattern similar to the scatter of buckshot from a shotgun.

I suspect that the correlation between grades on a statistics test and distance jumped in the long jump would be close to 0.00. Those with low, medium, and high scores on the test will, I suspect, be equally likely to be short, medium, or long long jumpers. Similarly, the correlation between how much one likes spaghetti (measured on a scale from 1 to 100) and political orientation (measured on a scale from 1, extremely conservative, to 100, extremely liberal) is likely to be quite close to 0.00.

Table 8.2 ■ **Qualitative Descriptors of Size and Strength of Association for *r***

| Correlation | Size of Association | Strength of Association |
|---|---|---|
| About 0.10 (or −0.10) | Small | Weak |
| About 0.30 (or −0.30) | Medium | Moderate |
| About 0.50 (or −0.50) | Large | Strong |
| About 0.70 (or −0.70) | Very large | Very strong |

A key advantage of the correlation coefficient is ease of interpretation; −1.00 and +1.00 convey the strongest possible linear (straight line) relationship, and 0.00 conveys the absence of such a relationship. Note that the *absolute value* of *r* conveys size of association. For instance, a correlation of −0.70 indicates a larger (stronger) relationship than does one of 0.50. Table 8.2 presents qualitative descriptors for size of relationship for *r*. As you know, these descriptors can also be used for the measures of directional relationship presented in the prior chapter (see Section 7.5).

Figure 8.5 presents scatterplots for the positive values of *r* that correspond to the qualitative descriptors. As *r* departs from 0.00 and gets closer to 1.00, the shape formed by the scatterplots' markers comes to resemble less a fat wide oval and more a skinny narrow one. The narrower the oval, or stated differently, the more the markers line up in a straight-line pattern, the stronger

FIGURE 8.5 ■ **Four Scatterplots of Positive Correlation**

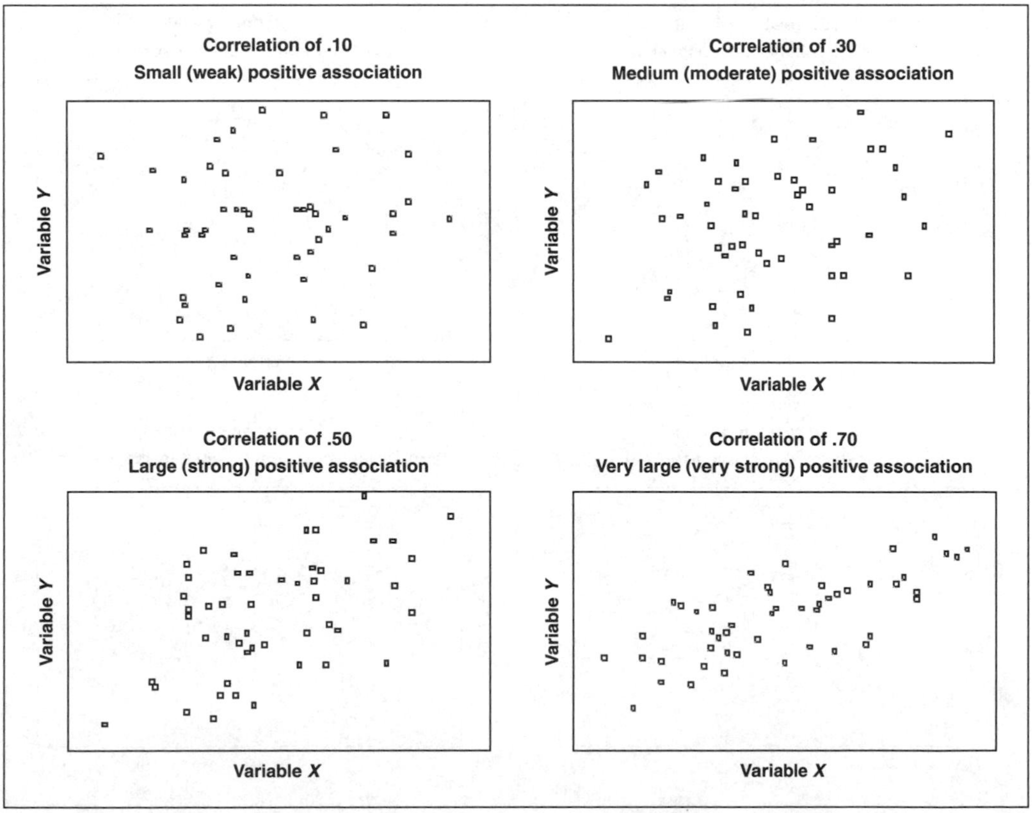

the association and the higher the value of $r$. With some practice, you will be able to examine a scatterplot and estimate the value of $r$. Or conversely, you will be able to note the value of $r$ and picture the shape of the scatterplot.

Figure 8.6 presents scatterplots for the negative values of $r$ that correspond to the descriptors in Table 8.2. Here, the oval formed by the markers gets narrower as $r$ gets closer to $-1.00$.

For your information, the scatterplot in Figure 8.1 (long jump and high jump) conveys a correlation of 0.80 whereas that in Figure 8.2 (50-m run and high jump) conveys one of $-0.78$. Thus, both scatterplots display very strong associations, associations that are stronger than most encountered in social science research. Of course, the variables involved are not typical social science variables. And, further, the data are hypothetical.

Although Table 8.2 interprets strength of association directly using $r$, many researchers prefer to do so using $r^2$. $r^2$, obtained by squaring $r$, is termed the **coefficient of determination**. It conveys the proportion of variance in each variable that is shared with another. For instance, when $r = -0.5$: $r^2 = -0.5 \times -0.5 = 0.25$. In this example, 25% (the proportion 0.25) of the variance in each variable is shared with the other. The minimum possible value of $r^2$ is 0.00, and the maximum possible value is 1.00. When one variable is an independent variable and the other is a dependent, then $r^2$ conveys the proportion or variance in the dependent that is explained by the independent. So, suppose that the correlation ($r$) between independent variable $X$ and dependent variable $Y$ equals 0.60. Then, $r^2 = 0.6 \times 0.6 = 0.36$. This tells us that (independent variable) $X$ explains 36% of the variance in (dependent variable) $Y$.

FIGURE 8.6 ■ **Four Scatterplots of Negative Correlation**

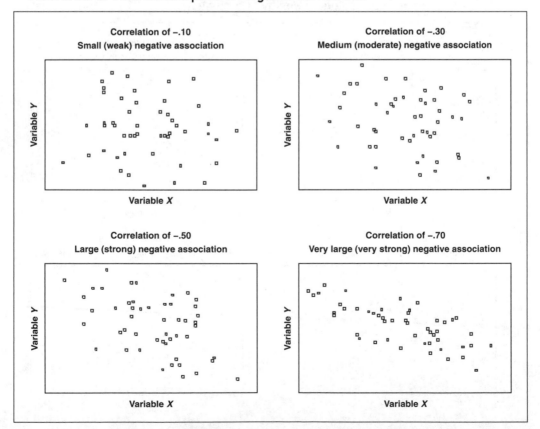

Suppose that one journal article reports that the correlation ($r$) between $X$ and $Y$ equals 0.40 and that a second reports that the coefficient of determination ($r^2$) for the correlation of $X$ and $Y$ equals 0.16. These statistics, $r = 0.40$ and $r^2 = 0.16$, convey the same strength of association. To see this, we can either square $r$, $0.40 \times 0.40 = 0.16$, or take the square root of $r^2$, $\sqrt{r^2} = \sqrt{0.16} = 0.40$. Prior to using Table 8.2 to assess the strength of association conveyed by $r^2$, you should calculate a square root. Should you not do so, your assessment of strength of association will, almost assuredly, be too low.

Now is a good time to comment on correlation and causality. A "famous" saying in research is that "correlation does not imply causality," in other words, the presence of correlation between two variables does not allow one to conclude that either variable *causes* (affects) the other. Perhaps one variable does, indeed, cause the other; the key point is that the presence of correlation does not, per se, let one reach this conclusion. Correlation, as measured by $r$, conveys the presence of linear relationship between (almost always) numeric variables. As Chapter 6, Section 6.3 pointed out, the presence of relationship and the reason(s) for relationship are distinct issues. Chapters 10 and 11 discuss causality, the various reasons why variables may be related.

## 8.6 ■ INTERPRETATIONS USING *r* AND *z* SCORES

### 8.6.1 ■ Predictions With *z* Scores

**Regression** refers to a group of statistical procedures to predict scores on one variable from those on one or more others (Toothaker & Miller, 1996, p. 199). The **standardized regression equation** (*bivariate standardized regression equation*) predicts a case's $z$ score on one variable from its $z$ score on another.

$$\hat{z}_y = r_{xy} z_x \qquad (8.2)$$

In Formula 8.2, $\hat{z}_y$ is a case's predicted $z$ score on $Y$ (the dependent variable); $z_x$ is the case's $z$ score on $X$ (the independent variable); and $r_{xy}$ is the correlation between $X$ and $Y$. The carat symbol, ^, sometimes called a "hat," designates a predicted score.

Formula 8.2 is a *standardized equation* because scores are expressed as standard scores, that is as $z$ scores rather than in their original units of measurement (raw scores). Recall from Chapter 5, Section 5.7.1 that standard score is a synonym for $z$ score.

Equation 8.2 conveys that the best prediction of a case's $z$ score on $Y$ is obtained by multiplying its $z$ score on $X$ by the correlation between $X$ and $Y$. Suppose that Ann's $z$ score on a measure of self-esteem is 0.90 and that the correlation of this measure with a measure of stress is $-0.60$. What is our best prediction of Ann's $z$ score on the stress measure?

$$\hat{z}\,\text{stress} = (-0.60)(0.90) = -0.54$$

Hence, we predict that Ann's score on the stress measure will be slightly more than one half of a standard deviation below the mean. Suppose that Yi's $z$ score in self esteem is $-1.80$. If so, her predicted $z$ score in stress is $(-0.60)(-1.80) = 1.08$, about one standard deviation above the mean.

### 8.6.2 ■ Predicted Change in Standard Deviation Units

Because its formula (Formula 8.1) uses $z$ scores, $r$ conveys the predicted change in standard deviation units for one variable as the other increases by one (1.00) standard deviation. For instance, an $r$ of 0.80 between height jumped in the high jump and distance jumped in the long jump conveys that as height jumped in the high jump increases by one standard deviation, distance jumped in the long jump is predicted to increase by 0.80 standard deviations. As just mentioned, the correlation between high jump height and time in the 50-meter run (see Figure 8.2) is $-0.78$. Thus, as high jump height increases by one standard deviation, time in the 50-meter run is predicted to decrease by 0.78 standard deviations.[3]

The just-expressed predictions work regardless of which variable is treated as the independent and which as the dependent. Thus, for our high-jump/long-jump example, we may view long jump as the independent variable and high jump as the dependent. Viewed this way, as long jump length increases by one standard deviation, high jump height is predicted to increase by 0.80 standard deviations. And for our high-jump/50-meter run example, as 50-m run time increases by one standard deviation, height in the high jump is predicted to decrease by 0.78 standard deviations. Although these predictions work in both directions, when one variable is independent and the other dependent, only one prediction makes conceptual sense. To be specific, if $X$ is the independent variable, then predicting $Y$ as a function of $X$ makes sense, but predicting $X$ as a function of $Y$ does not.

## 8.7 ■ CURVILINEAR RELATIONSHIP

As stated earlier, there is an exception to the statement that a correlation of 0.00 indicates the absence of relationship between variables. Pearson's $r$ measures the degree of *linear* relationship, the degree to which relationship assumes a *straight-line* pattern. For instance, in both Figures 8.1 and 8.2, the scatterplots' markers arrange themselves in straight-line patterns and, thus, the depicted relationships are linear. Indeed, one could picture a straight line that would slice each pattern of markers in half. In Figure 8.1 (positive correlation), such a line would slant from the lower left to the upper right. In Figure 8.2 (negative correlation), it would slant from upper left to lower right.

In social work research, most relationships between numeric variables are linear or approximately so. More than occasionally, however, relationships are curvilinear. In a **curvilinear relationship**, observations take on a pattern that is best described by a curve (very occasionally, that curve has more than one bend).

Let me develop a hypothetical example to demonstrate curvilinear relationship. Suppose that we measure the amount of "flexibility" in rules that parents set for children. Picture at one end of a continuum, an *extremely* high amount of flexibility. Indeed, picture so much flexibility, that, in effect, there are *no rules at all*. Clearly, at this end of the continuum, chaos rules. Now, picture a middle level of flexibility in rules, one at which parents are adaptive and flexible, while still maintaining consistency. And finally, picture an *extremely* low level of flexibility. Indeed, picture such a low level of flexibility that, in effect, there is no flexibility at all. Clearly, at this end of the continuum, rigidity rules. Let us also obtain parental reports on a scale that measures their children's social functioning, that is the quality of their relationships with other children, their behavior, how they are doing in school, and related matters. Presume that high scores on this scale convey high (rather than low) social functioning.

Let us examine the relationship between level of flexibility and children's social functioning. I suspect that we might find a pattern of relationship much like this: At *extremely* low levels of flexibility (chaotic environment), I suspect that, on average, children will have very low social functioning. At middle levels of flexibility (adaptable but still consistent in rules), I suspect that, on average, children's social functioning will be quite high. And finally, I suspect that at *extremely* high levels of flexibility (rigid environment), children, on average, will have very low social functioning. Were we to construct a scatterplot of the relationship between flexibility and social functioning, I suspect that it would look much like Figure 8.7.

FIGURE 8.7 ■ Curvilinear Association—Family Flexibility and Social Functioning

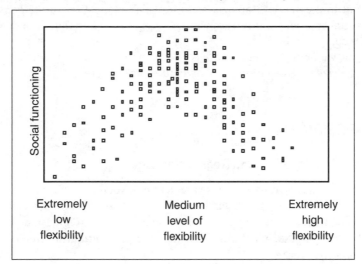

| Extremely low flexibility | Medium level of flexibility | Extremely high flexibility |

Figure 8.7 conveys relationship between level of flexibility and social functioning, that is, particular values of social functioning tend to occur with particular values of flexibility. Specifically, very low levels of flexibility and low levels of functioning tend to occur together; middle levels of flexibility and high levels of functioning tend to occur together; and finally, very high levels of flexibility and low levels of functioning tend to occur together. As the relationship in Figure 8.7 is not described by a straight line, but instead by a curve, it is a curvilinear relationship.

*Pearson's r* is not an effective measure of curvilinear relationship and should not be used with such relationships. Doing so underestimates size of association. For instance, the Pearson's *r* between level of flexibility and children's social functioning as presented in Figure 8.7 computes to −0.02, that is, essentially to 0.00. Clearly, this value of *r* has the potential to mislead. A researcher without access to a scatterplot and who neglected to consider the possibility of curvilinear relationship, might mistakenly conclude that flexibility and social functioning were unassociated. When Pearson's *r* is close to or equal to 0.00, the correct conclusion is that there is no *linear* association, not that there is no relationship whatsoever.

When curvilinear relationship is suspected, one should construct a scatterplot and investigate this possibility. The measure eta squared ($\eta^2$) is often used to assess nonlinear associations. Section 9.6 in the next chapter discusses eta squared.[4]

## 8.8 ■ A CAUTION IN INTERPRETING *r*

The presence of very low variability in one or both variables can markedly reduce the absolute value of *r*. For instance, presume that you are teaching a group of new parents, all of whom are highly motivated to learn about child development. You are also studying the correlation between motivation level and amount learned as measured by a test of child knowledge. Given that *all* parents are highly motivated, motivation varies hardly at all. When a variable varies hardly at all, it is extremely difficult to study its relationship to other variables. In effect, the "variable" is almost a constant, and it is impossible for a constant to be related to any variable.

In our example, the correlation between motivation level and test score will likely be very close to 0.00. But in a child development class in which motivation varied considerably, it is likely that a researcher would find a reasonably strong positive correlation between motivation and amount learned.

In sum, when variability is very low, *r* is not an effective measure. In such a situation, it underestimates the size of association that would otherwise be found.

## 8.9 ■ REGRESSION

### 8.9.1 ■ Regression Equation and Regression Line

As demonstrated earlier, using *r*, we can make predictions involving *z* scores. Sometimes, our goal is not to make a prediction in terms of standardized scores (*z* scores), but instead, in the original units in which the variables were measured, that is, in raw scores. Regression is the appropriate statistical tool for this purpose. The formula for the **regression equation** (the *bivariate unstandardized regression equation*) is

$$\hat{Y} = A + BX \tag{8.3}$$

where $\hat{Y}$ is the predicted value of *Y* (the dependent variable), *X* is the value of *X* (the independent variable), *A* is the constant, and *B* is the regression coefficient. Formula 8.3 is an *unstandardized equation* because *Y* and *X* are expressed as raw scores (unstandardized scores) rather than as *z* scores (standardized scores).

The **constant** (or *intercept*) *A*, conveys the predicted value of *Y* when *X* equals 0.00. The **regression coefficient**, *B*, conveys the change in the predicted value of *Y* as *X* increases by 1.00.

The regression equation (Formula 8.3) is the equation for the **regression line**. It was just mentioned that the constant conveys the predicted value of *Y* when *X* equals 0. It also conveys the regression line's Y intercept, the value at which it intersects the Y (vertical) axis. This interpretation holds only when a graph's Y axis is located at *X* = 0. (Sometimes this is not the case.) The change in one variable as the other increases by 1.00 is a definition for the slope of a line. Thus, in addition to conveying the change in the predicted value of *Y* as *X* increases by 1.00, the regression coefficient conveys the slope of the regression line.

Figure 8.8 presents a scatterplot depicting the (hypothetical) relationship between number of prenatal visits and infant birth weight measured in ounces. It also presents the regression line for this data. This line is described by the regression equation.

Predicted birth weight = 76.86 + 1.73 (number of visits)

In the just-presented equation, 76.86 is the constant (*A*), and 1.73 is the regression coefficient (*B*). These are interpreted as follows:

*A:* The predicted birth weight for a mother who has made no (0) visits is 76.86 oz.
*B:* As number of visits increases by one (1.00)—in other words, for each additional visit— predicted birth weight increases by 1.73 oz.

*A* and *B* may also be interpreted in relationship to the regression line. Observe that the Y axis in Figure 8.7 is indeed located at *X* = 0. Hence, the value of *A*, 76.86 conveys the value at which the line intersects the Y axis (the Y intercept). *B* conveys the slope of the line. The regression line

FIGURE 8.8  ■  Scatterplot and Regression Line for Birth Weight Example

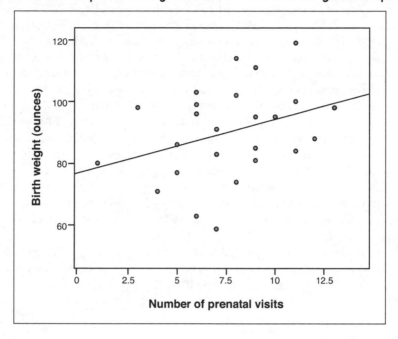

is sometimes called the *best fit line*. Thus, among all possible straight lines, judged by a particular criterion, it does the best job of predicting Y based on X.[5]

The researcher can use the regression equation to make predictions for individual cases. For instance: Mrs. Antonelli made six prenatal visits. What is our best prediction of the birth weight of her child? To determine this, we plug her number of visits—for Mrs. Antonelli, $X = 6$—into the regression equation:

$$\text{Predicted birth weight} = 76.86 + 1.73(6)$$
$$= 76.86 + 10.38$$
$$= 87.24$$

Observe that our prediction of 87.24 oz agrees well with the approximation that we could derive from the scatterplot. Thus, if we (a) trace up from 6 on the X axis to intersect the regression line and (b) then trace left from this point to the Y axis, that axis is intersected at about 87.24.

## 8.9.2  ■  Contrast Between *r* and *B*

The regression coefficient, *B*, and the correlation coefficient, *r*, can be contrasted. The correlation coefficient, *r*, is a **standardized coefficient** and, thus, conveys predicted change with X and Y expressed as z scores (standard scores). As stated earlier, when Y is the dependent variable, *r* conveys the predicted change in Y in standard deviation units as X increases by one standard deviation. The regression coefficient, *B*, is an **unstandardized coefficient**. It conveys predicted change with X and Y expressed in their original, unstandardized units of measurement (as raw scores). As stated earlier, *B* indicates the predicted change in Y as X increases by 1.00.

Observe that the regression coefficient, because it expresses change in unstandardized units, does not convey size of association. On the other hand, the correlation coefficient, because it expresses change in standardized units ($z$ scores), does do so. For the birth weight example, $r = 0.33$ which may be interpreted as a relationship of moderate strength (see Table 8.2).

Interpretation of $B$ is, generally speaking, straightforward and intuitive when variables have tangible, familiar units of measurement. For instance, in our birth weight example, interpretation was intuitive—for each additional visit, predicted weight increases by 1.73 oz.

On the other hand, when variables are intangible or unfamiliar, $B$ typically does not have intuitive meaning. For instance, suppose that you predict scores on a 20-item measure that assesses closeness of parent-child relationship from scores on a 40-item measure that assesses children's behavior problems. Suppose further that $B$ computes to $-0.15$. This tells you that as behavior problems score increases by 1.00 point, predicted parent-child relationship score decreases by 0.15 points. This information has some utility; for instance, it tells you that the two sets of scores have a negative relationship. Yet, unless you happen to be highly familiar with both of these measures, this $B$ does not have easy, intuitive interpretation in the same way as it did in our birth weight example.

When units of measurement are intangible or unfamiliar, $r$ is often preferred to $B$. This is, in large part, because it conveys size of association. For instance, suppose that in the behavior problems/closeness of relationship example $r$ equals $-0.63$. This tells you that there is a large negative relationship between these variables. As stated earlier, $B$ does not convey size of association.

## 8.10 ■ CORRELATION FOR NOMINAL-LEVEL AND ORDINAL-LEVEL VARIABLES

As stated at the beginning of the chapter, correlational procedures are sometimes used with variables that are not at the interval/ratio level of measurement. Two such measures are phi and Spearman's $r$.

Chapter 7 presented various measures of association between two dichotomous variables. Chapter 7 (Section 7.4) pointed out that the researcher may (arbitrarily) designate one category of a dichotomous variable as high and the other as low. With values ordered in this fashion, the correlation between two dichotomous variables can be calculated. The measure **phi** ($r_{phi}$; pronounced as in "five") is the correlation between two such variables. (For more on phi, see Glass & Hopkins, 1996, p. 130).[6]

**Spearman's $r$** ($r_{ranks}$) measures the correlation between two rank orderings. When there are no tied ranks, Spearman's $r$ and Pearson's $r$ have identical values. The formula for Spearman's $r$ is, basically, a shortcut formula for Pearson's $r$ that may be used when both variables are rank orderings.

Both phi and Spearman's $r$ may vary from $-1.00$ to $1.00$. Table 8.2 provides guidelines for interpretation of strength of association for these measures.

## 8.11 ■ CHAPTER SUMMARY

*Pearson's r* conveys the degree of *linear* (straight line) association between numeric variables. If the values of two variables change in the same direction, these variables are *positively correlated*. If their values change in opposite directions, they are *negatively correlated*. In positive correlation, similar values (highs with highs; lows with lows) go together. In negative correlation, dissimilar ones (highs with lows; lows with highs) do so.

Correlation is presented visually using the *scatterplot*. In positive correlation, the slant of the scatterplot's markers is from lower left to upper right. In negative correlation, it is from upper left to lower right. The independent variable is plotted on the scatterplot's X axis and the dependent on its Y axis.

The value of *r* may vary from −1.00 to 1.00. The greater its absolute value, the stronger the linear association. Correlations of −1.00 and of 1.00 are *perfect correlations*. An *r* of 0.00 indicates the absence of linear association. Using Table 8.2, a correlation of about 0.10 (or −0.10) represents a small (weak) linear association, whereas one of about 0.50 (or −.50) represents a large (strong) one. Neither addition (subtraction) nor multiplication (division) by a constant affects the value of *r*.

An *r* conveys the predicted change in standard deviations for one variable as the other increases by one standard deviation. The *standardized regression equation* is $\hat{z}_y = r_{xy}\, z_x$

The *coefficient of determination*, $r^2$, conveys the proportion of variance in one variable that is shared with another.

*Curvilinear relationship* is described by a curve. *r* should not be used to measure curvilinear relationships.

Very low variability in one or both variables reduces the absolute value of *r* that would otherwise be found.

The *unstandardized regression equation* is $\hat{Y} = A + BX$. The *constant*, A, conveys the predicted value of Y when X equals 0.00. The *regression coefficient*, B, conveys the regression line's slope, that is, the predicted change in Y as X increases by 1.00.

The correlation coefficient, *r*, is a *standardized coefficient*. The regression coefficient, B, is an *unstandardized coefficient*. *r* conveys size of association but B does not. Interpretation of B is more intuitive with familiar, tangible variables than with unfamiliar, subjective ones.

*Phi* ($r_{phi}$) measures correlation between dichotomous variables. *Spearman's r* does so for rank orderings.

## 8.12 ■ PROBLEMS AND QUESTIONS

### Section 8.2

1. _____ *r* measures the size of _____ relationship, that is of relationship that can be described by a straight line. In _____ correlation, values change in the same direction. In _____ correlation, values change in _____ directions. Correlation is used predominantly with _____ (type of variable) variables, that is, those at the _____ / _____ level of measurement.

2. In positive correlation, _____ values tend to go together, that is, highs with _____ and lows with _____. In negative correlation, _____ values tend not to go together, that is, highs with _____ and lows with _____.

3. For each of the following, indicate whether the example demonstrates positive correlation or negative correlation.
   a. As number of hours worked goes up, enjoyment of life goes down.
   b. As number of hours worked goes up, so does income.

c. The greater the hours studied, the higher the grade on the test.

d. As confidence goes down, so does self-esteem.

e. As confidence goes up, so does self-esteem.

f. As number of homeless days increases, self-esteem goes down.

## Section 8.3

4. When a correlation is positive, the scatterplot's markers slant from the _____ left to the _____ right. When a correlation is negative, the scatterplot's markers slant from the _____ left to the _____ right.

5. In a scatterplot, the independent variable is plotted on the ___ axis and the dependent is plotted on the ___ axis.

## Section 8.4

6. In your own words, describe how to calculate $r$ using $z$ scores.

7. At Athletic U, students take two free throw shooting tests. On the first test, the mean number of shots made for a group of five students is 5.2 with a standard deviation of 1.789. On the second test, these students make an average of 5.8 baskets ($s = 1.304$). The first two columns of the following grid present the number of baskets made by each student on the two tests. Fill in the grid below or create one yourself and calculate:

   a. Alex's $z$ score on both tests

   b. The product of the $z$ scores for each student

   c. The sum of the product of the $z$ scores (round off to two digits)

   d. The correlation ($r$) of baskets made on Test 1 and baskets made on Test 2

| Student | Number on Free Throw Test 1 | Number on Free Throw Test 2 | z Score on Test 1 | z Score on Test 2 | Product of z Scores |
|---|---|---|---|---|---|
| Alex | 5 | 5 | | | |
| Julio | 7 | 6 | 1.006 | 0.153 | |
| LaKeesha | 4 | 7 | −0.671 | 0.920 | |
| Sandra | 7 | 7 | 1.006 | 0.920 | |
| Rainbow | 3 | 4 | −1.230 | −1.381 | |
| | | | | | $\Sigma =$ |

**Section 8.5**

8. *For each statement, indicate true or false.*
   a. Adding (or subtracting) a constant does not affect the value of *r*.
   b. Multiplying (or dividing) by a constant does not affect the value of *r*.
   c. *r* may range from a lowest possible value of 0.00 to a highest possible value of 1.00.
   d. When a correlation between two variables is 1.00, the markers in the scatterplot form a perfect circle.
   e. Perfect correlations between variables are frequently encountered in real-world research.
   f. The larger the value of *r*, the stronger the relationship conveyed by *r*.
   g. The larger the absolute value of *r*, the stronger the relationship conveyed by *r*.

9. The correlation between $X$ and $Y$ is $-0.30$. The constant 2 is subtracted from all scores on $X$. Following this subtraction, the correlation between $X$ and $Y$ is ___.

10. The correlation between $X$ and $Y$ is $-0.30$. All scores on X are multiplied by 8.34672. Following this multiplication, the correlation between $X$ and $Y$ is ___.

11. For each value of *r*, indicate (a) whether the correlation is positive or negative and (b) the approximate size/strength of association conveyed by *r*
    a. $-0.30$
    b. $0.30$
    c. $-0.68$
    d. $0.11$
    e. $-0.47$
    f. $0.73$
    g. $0.52$

12. You read that the correlation between $X$ and $Y$ equals 1.67. Is this correlation positive or negative? Indicate the strength of association that it conveys. (Hint: What is wrong here?)

13. Indicate which value of *r* from each pair conveys the stronger relationship.
    a. 0.33 or 0.66
    b. $-0.33$ or $-0.66$
    c. $-0.66$ or 0.33
    d. $-0.92$ or 0.29
    e. 0.5 or 0.8

14. As the absolute value of *r* increases, the oval formed by the scatterplot becomes _____ (choose wider or narrower). In a perfect correlation ($r = 1.00$ or $r = -1.00$) the markers in the scatterplot form a _____ _____ (indicate shape).

**15.** When one squares $r$ to obtain $r^2$, the resulting coefficient is termed the coefficient of _____ . $r^2$ conveys the proportion of _____ in each variable that is _____ with the other.

**16.** For each value of $r$, indicate the value of $r^2$.
  **a.** $r = 0.40$
  **b.** $r = -0.40$
  **c.** $r = 0.90$
  **d.** $r = 0.60$
  **e.** $r = -0.60$

**17.** Indicate the proportion of shared variation conveyed by each value of $r^2$.
  **a.** $r^2 = 0.32$
  **b.** $r^2 = 0.27$
  **c.** $r^2 = 0.16$

**Section 8.6**

**18.** The equation for predicting a cases's $z$ score on one variable from its $z$ score on another is termed the (bivariate) _____ regression equation.

**19.** The correlation between variable $X$ and variable $Y$ is provided as is the $z$ score on $X$ for a selected case. Using the standardized regression equation, predict the case's $z$ score on $Y$. (Assume a linear association.)
  **a.** $r_{xy} = 0.5$; $z_x = 0.24$
  **b.** $r_{xy} = -0.5$; $z_x = 0.24$
  **c.** $r_{xy} = 0.8$; $z_x = 2.50$
  **d.** $r_{xy} = -0.8$; $z_x = 2.50$
  **e.** $r_{xy} = 0.6$; $z_x = 1.00$
  **f.** $r_{xy} = 0.00$; $z_x = 2.50$

**20.** The correlation between two variables is $-0.70$ and their relationship is linear. As one variable increases by one standard deviation, the other is predicted to _____ by ___ standard deviations.

**21.** For each listed correlation between $X$ and $Y$, indicate the predicted change in $Y$ in standard deviation units as $X$ increases by one standard deviation.
  **a.** $r = 0.22$
  **b.** $r = -0.22$
  **c.** $r = 0.75$
  **d.** $r = -0.38$
  **e.** $r = 1.00$

## Section 8.7

22. When a relationship between two numeric variables is best described by a curve, that relationship is termed a _____ relationship.

23. *Indicate whether each statement is true or false.*
    a. The Pearson correlation coefficient is *not* an appropriate tool for measuring the degree of curvilinear association between variables.
    b. An $r$ of 0.00 between two variables *always* conveys the absence of relationship between these variables.
    c. An $r$ of 0.00 between two variables conveys the absence of linear relationship between these variables.
    d. When a relationship between two variables is curvilinear, the scatterplot assumes a "buckshot"-like pattern.

24. Think of two variables that you think might have a curvilinear relationship. Explain briefly.

## Section 8.8

25. Extremely low variability in one or more variables typically _____ the absolute value of $r$.

26. Only clients with the highest level of motivation are selected to participate in a treatment program. In this group, the correlation between level of motivation and client rating of the program's effectiveness is 0.20. What is your best estimate of the correlation that would have been observed if clients with more varied levels of motivation had participated?
    a. $r = 0.20$
    b. $r > 0.20$
    c. $r < 0.20$

## Section 8.9

27. In the (unstandardized) regression equation (Formula 8.3), "$A$" is termed the _____. It conveys the predicted value of $Y$ when $X$ equals _____. In this equation, "$B$" is termed the _____ _____. It conveys the change in the predicted value of $Y$ as $X$ increases by ___.

28. In the (unstandardized) regression equation, "$B$" is an _____ coefficient rather than a standardized one. On the other hand, $r$ is a _____ coefficient.

29. *Respond true or false to each statement.*
    a. The regression equation is the equation for the regression line.
    b. Assuming that the Y axis is located at $X = 0$, the constant indicates the value at which the regression line intersects the Y axis.

    **c.** *B* conveys the slope of the regression line.

    **d.** *B* conveys change in terms of *z* scores (standardized scores).

30. Consider the regression equation $\hat{Y} = 3 + (2.5)X$ and respond and indicate the value of each of the following:

    **a.** The constant, *A*

    **b.** Assuming that the Y axis is located at $X = 0$, the Y intercept (the point at which the regression line intersects the Y axis)

    **c.** The regression coefficient

    **d.** The amount by which the predicted value of $Y (\hat{Y})$ changes as *X* increases by 1.00

    **e.** The slope of the regression line

    **f.** $\hat{Y}$ when $X = 4$

    **g.** $\hat{Y}$ when $X = 0$

    **h.** $\hat{Y}$ when $X = -4$

    **i.** Sally's score on *X* is $-4$. What is her predicted score on *Y*?

    **j.** Doug's score on *X* is 6. What is $\hat{Y}$ for Doug?

31. Respond to the same questions as in the prior question but instead for the regression equation: $\hat{Y} = 6 - 3(X)$.

32. Consider the regression equation $\hat{Y} = 3.33 + 77777(X)$. Characterize the relationship between *X* and *Y* as weak, moderate, or strong.

33. *Respond true or false to each statement.*

    **a.** *B* conveys size of association.

    **b.** *B* is a standardized coefficient.

    **c.** *r* conveys size of association.

    **d.** *r* is a standardized coefficient.

    **e.** A *B* of $-0.82$ (necessarily) conveys a strong (large) association.

    **f.** An *r* of $-0.82$ conveys a strong (large) association.

    **g.** Generally, speaking interpretation of *B* is straightforward and highly intuitive with intangible and unfamiliar variables.

### Section 8.10

34. The correlation between two dichotomous variables is measured by _____.

35. The correlation between two rank orderings is termed _____ *r.*

# 9

# STANDARDIZED MEAN DIFFERENCE

## 9.1 ■ CHAPTER OVERVIEW

Chapter 9 presents the *standardized mean difference* (*SMD*), the preferred measure of size of association when one variable is dichotomous (two categories) and the other is numeric. It also gives an overview of measures used when one variable is a nominal-level variable with three or more categories and the other is numeric.

## 9.2 ■ INTRODUCTION TO THE STANDARDIZED MEAN DIFFERENCE

The assessment of relationship when one variable is numeric[1] and the other is categorical most often involves comparison of means. When means are equal, variables are unassociated. When means differ, they are associated. Suppose that the mean score on the *XYZ* self-esteem scale is 45 points in Group A and 45 points in Group B. Because means are equal, group membership (the categorical variable) and self-esteem (the numeric one) are unassociated. Now, suppose instead that the mean self-esteem score is 45 points in Group A and 40 points in Group B. In this example, means differ and, therefore, the variables are associated.

Sticking with this second example, the next question that might be asked is "How large is the association?" or perhaps "How much of a difference in self-esteem is represented by this difference of five points?" Note that self-esteem is abstract and intangible. When the dependent variable is familiar and tangible, one can often answer questions pertaining to size of association based on experience and common sense. For instance, if those in one weight loss group lose, on average, 50 lb more than do those in another, our reaction would likely be, "That is a lot of weight."

But, how does one make sense of a difference of five points in self-esteem? The best way to assess size of association between a categorical variable with two categories and a numeric one is to use the standardized mean difference. A **standardized mean difference** (*SMD*) expresses differences between means in standard deviation units. We will use the following formula for the *SMD*:

$$SMD = \frac{\overline{X}_1 - \overline{X}_2}{s_{wg}}$$

(9.1)

where *SMD* is the standardized mean difference, $\overline{X}_1$ is the mean of Group 1, $\overline{X}_2$ is the mean of Group 2, and $s_{wg}$ is the *within groups standard deviation*. Formula 9.1 assumes that the standard deviations in Groups 1 and 2 are equal, that is, $s_1 = s_2$, and, further, that each of these standard deviations equals the within groups standard deviation, that is, $s_1 = s_2 = s_{wg}$. All examples and problems in this text assume equal standard deviations in the two groups. The researcher designates one group as Group 1 and the other as Group 2.

Table 9.1 ■ Qualitative Descriptors of Size and Strength of Association for the Standardized Mean Difference

| Difference | Size of Association | Strength of Association |
|---|---|---|
| About 0.20 (or −0.20) | Small | Weak |
| About 0.50 (or −0.50) | Medium | Moderate |
| About 0.80 (or −0.80) | Large | Strong |
| About 1.30 (or −1.30) | Very large | Very strong |

Staying with our example, presume that the standard deviation of self-esteem scores in each group equals 10 ($s_1 = s_2 = 10$). As $s_1 = s_2 = 10$, the within groups standard deviation equals 10 ($s_{wg} = 10$) and the *SMD* (with Group A treated as Group 1) is

$$SMD = \frac{45 - 40}{10} = \frac{5}{10} = 0.50$$

On average, the self-esteem of those in Group A is one half of a standard deviation higher than that of those in Group B. Table 9.1 presents qualitative descriptors for the *SMD*. According to Table 9.1, the *SMD* in our example, 0.50, conveys an association of medium size.

As another example of the *SMD*, suppose that a maternal child health clinic implements two programs designed to help teen mothers give birth to healthy babies. Perhaps a program goal is to increase birth weights. Presume that the following results are observed: (a) the mean birth weight of babies of mothers who received Program 1 is 85 oz, (b) that of babies of mothers who received Program 2 is 90 oz, and (c) the standard deviation in each group is 20 oz. In this example, the *SMD* is

$$SMD = \frac{85 - 90}{20} = \frac{-5}{20} = -0.25$$

Thus, the babies of mothers who received Program 1 were, on average, about one quarter of a standard deviation lighter at birth than were those who received Program 2. Referencing Table 9.1, this difference is a small one.

Note that depending on which group is designated as Group 1, the *SMD* may calculate to either a positive or a negative value. The absolute value of the *SMD* conveys size of association; for instance, an *SMD* of −0.65 conveys the same size of association as does one of 0.65.

## 9.3 ■ GRAPHICAL INTERPRETATION OF THE STANDARDIZED MEAN DIFFERENCE

Graphical display of the *SMD* can further understanding. Figure 9.1 presents *SMD*s of 0.2, 0.5, 0.8, and 1.3 standard deviations. (Or, you may equally well think of these as *SMD*s of −0.2, −0.5, −0.8, and −1.3.) These *SMD*s correspond respectively to the qualitative descriptors *small*, *medium*, *large*, and *very large* in Table 9.1. Each of the four parts of Figure 9.1 presents two distributions, one for each of the two groups being compared. Each figure assumes that the distributions (groups) have normal shapes and equal standard deviations.

The figure in the upper left of Figure 9.1 presents an *SMD* of 0.2 (or −0.2) that Table 9.1 classifies as a small difference (small association). Note the extensive overlap between the two

FIGURE 9.1. ■ Graphical Depiction of Standardized Mean Difference

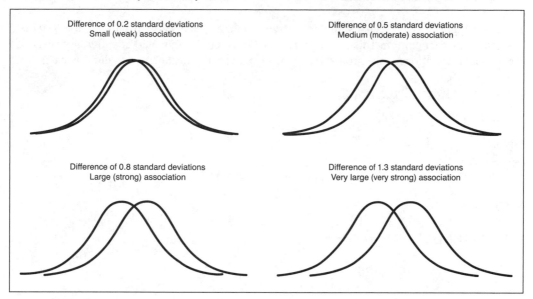

distributions in this figure. In contrast, the figure in the lower right of Figure 9.1 presents an *SMD* of 1.3 (or −1.3), classified as a very large difference (very large association). Note that the two distributions that compose this figure are much more distinct than are those in the upper left figure. Viewed differently, there is much less overlap between the distributions.

The upper right figure in Figure 9.1 presents an *SMD* of 0.5 (or −0.5), classified as a medium difference. As mentioned earlier, in this chapter's first example, those in Group A scored 0.5 standard deviations higher on the *XYZ* self-esteem scale than did those in Group B. This figure represents that size of association. Think of the left distribution in this figure as representing the group with the lower mean score in self-esteem (Group B) and the right distribution as representing the group with the higher mean (Group A). One can see considerable overlap between these distributions. In other words, a reasonably large percentage of persons in Group B (lower mean) have higher self-esteem than do a reasonably large percentage of persons in Group A (higher mean). The degree of overlap is intermediate between that in the two previously described figures. The final figure (lower left) in Figure 9.1 conveys a difference of 0.8 standard deviations (an *SMD* of 0.8 or −0.8), classified as a large difference.

In summary, Figure 9.1 demonstrates that as the absolute value of the *SMD* increases,

■ the degree of overlap between the groups decreases, and

■ scores in the two groups become more distinct.

Observe, however, that even when the association is classified as very large (*SMD* = 1.30), the groups still overlap to a considerable degree. This reinforces that this text's qualitative descriptors characterize size of association in the context of associations typically observed in social science research (see Chapter 6, Section 6.7). Indeed, associations that are compellingly strong—that is, close to "perfect"—in a strict mathematical sense are rarely encountered in social science research. In the case of the *SMD*, a relationship that was close to perfect would be one in which there was almost no overlap between the groups; that is, nearly all scores in the group with the higher mean exceeded nearly all scores in the group with the lower one.

## 9.4 ■ A CAUTION REGARDING THE STANDARDIZED MEAN DIFFERENCE

Although Figure 9.1 presents examples involving normally shaped distributions, the *SMD* is a good measure for nonnormal distributions as well. On the other hand, marked differences between the standard deviations in the groups recommend caution. For instance, consider this data:

| Group | Mean Score on *XYZ* Scale | Standard Deviation |
|---|---|---|
| Group 1 | 45 | 10 |
| Group 2 | 40 | 20 |

Using the standard deviation of Group 1 to compute the *SMD*,

$$SMD = \frac{45 - 40}{10} = \frac{5}{10} = 0.5$$

Using the standard deviation of Group 2,

$$SMD = \frac{45 - 40}{20} = \frac{5}{20} = 0.25$$

These two sets of results differ substantially. This example demonstrates that the *SMD* should not be used when standard deviations within the groups differ greatly. As a pragmatic guideline, do not to use the *SMD* when the standard deviation in the group with the larger standard deviation is more than about one third (33%) larger than that in the group with the smaller standard deviation. As mentioned earlier, the problems and examples in this book assume equal standard deviations.

Although the *SMD* is particularly useful when the units of measure are unfamiliar, it is also an effective measure when units are familiar, as was demonstrated in the birth weight example.

## 9.5 ■ MORE MEASURES OF DIFFERENCES BETWEEN TWO MEANS

As presented in this text, the *SMD* is an informal measure that approximates size of association. When precision is required, two excellent measures of the standardized mean difference are Cohen's *d* and Hedges' *g* (see Rosenthal, 1994, pp. 231–244 for these measures). Another measure of the standardized mean difference, developed by Glass, is often used to assess the size of difference between two groups in experiments. This measure is sometimes simply called "effect size" (and also Glass's delta) but, as this term is so general, we will call it **effect size for means** (**$ES_{means}$**):

$$ES_{means} = \frac{\overline{X}_E - \overline{X}_C}{s_C} \tag{9.2}$$

where $\overline{X}_E$ is the mean in the experimental group, $\overline{X}_C$ is the mean in the control group, and $s_C$ is the standard deviation in the control group. This formula, in effect, standardizes the difference in means using the standard deviation in the control group. Those in the *experimental group* receive some intervention or treatment whereas those in the *control group* do not.

For instance, suppose that we conduct a study in which one group (the experimental group) receives an intervention designed to reduce depression whereas the second group (the control group) receives no such services. Presume that depression is measured by a scale that yields a numeric score. Results are as follows: experimental group, $\overline{X}$ = 20.0, $s$ = 6.0, and control group, $\overline{X}$ = 25.0, $s$ = 5.0. Carrying out Formula 9.2: $ES_{\text{means}}$ = (20.0 − 25.0) / 5.0 = −1.00. Thus, using the standard deviation in the control group for standardization, the mean depression score in the experimental group is one (1.00) standard deviation lower than that in the experimental group. Referencing the descriptors in Table 9.1, this effect size (size of association) is a large one. (For more discussion on $ES_{\text{means}}$, see Glass & Hopkins, 1996, pp. 289–290 or Rosenthal, 1994, pp. 231–244.)

As a reminder, "effect size" is, in essence, a synonym for size of relationship and is used often in studies that seek to determine the effect of an intervention (see Chapter 6, Section 6.5).[2]

## 9.6 ■ DIFFERENCES BETWEEN THREE OR MORE MEANS

The *SMD* assesses size of association when there are two groups and has no easy extension to situations involving three or more groups. When there are three or more groups, **eta squared**, also known as the **correlation ratio** and symbolized by $\eta^2$, is an excellent measure of the size of association. The correlation ratio conveys the proportion of variance in a numeric variable that is explained by a categorical variable. For instance, when $\eta^2$ = .10, 10% of the variance in the numeric variable is explained by the categorical one. The following guidelines, taken from Cohen (1988), can be used for interpreting size of association (effect size) for $\eta^2$: small, about .01; medium, about .06; and large, about .14. See Rosenthal (2001, pp. 164–165), Glass and Hopkins (1996, pp. 180–182), or Cohen (1988, pp. 273–288) for more discussion on $\eta^2$.

We have discussed measures of size of association for relationships involving several combinations of variables, including categorical with categorical, numeric with numeric, and categorical with numeric. Table C.1 in Appendix C summarizes measures of association for different situations.

## 9.7 ■ CHAPTER SUMMARY

When one variable is categorical and the other is numeric, relationship is most often assessed by comparing means. If means are equal, there is no relationship. If means differ, the variables are related.

When one variable is dichotomous and the other is numeric, the *standardized mean difference (SMD)* is the preferred measure of size of association. Its formula is $(\overline{X}_1 - \overline{X}_2) / s_{wg}$. An *SMD* of 0.20 represents a small association, whereas 0.80 represents a large association (see Table 9.1). The less the overlap between the distributions in the two groups, the larger the *SMD*.

The *SMD* is an informal measure. As presented in this chapter, it assumes equal standard deviations in the two groups. In practice, it should not be used when the standard deviations in the groups differ substantially.

In studies involving interventions, researchers sometimes divide the difference between means by the standard deviation in the control group to yield the *effect size for means* ($ES_{\text{means}}$). Given three or more groups *eta squared* (the *correlation ratio*) is a good measure of size of association (effect size).

## 9.8 ■ PROBLEMS AND QUESTIONS

### Section 9.2

1. In your own words, how is the standardized difference between means calculated?

2. In Program 1, the mean level of discomfort experienced by chemotherapy patients on a well-validated instrument is 27. In Program 2, this score is 41. A higher score conveys greater discomfort. Comment on the strength of relationship between program (1 or 2) and level of discomfort. (Tricky question)

3. Regarding the prior question, the standard deviation in both Programs 1 and 2 is 7.0 points. Calculate the standardized mean difference treating Program 1 as Group 1. Assess/interpret the size of association.

4. On an exam of knowledge of the first year of the MSW (masters in social work), a school finds the following results:
   Completed first year in full-time program: mean score on exam = 88.0
   Completed first year in part-time program: mean score on exam = 86.0
   The standard deviation in each program was 12.0 points.

   Consider the full-time program as Group 1. Calculate the *SMD* and interpret the size of association.

5. Compute the *SMD* for each of the following results. ($\overline{X}_1$ is the mean of Group 1 and $\overline{X}_2$ is the mean of Group 2.)
   a. $\overline{X}_1 = 20, \overline{X}_2 = 40, s_{wg} = 10$
   b. $\overline{X}_1 = 40, \overline{X}_2 = 20, s_{wg} = 10$
   c. $\overline{X}_1 = 20, \overline{X}_2 = 40, s_{wg} = 20$
   d. $\overline{X}_1 = 20, \overline{X}_2 = 50, s_{wg} = 10$
   e. $\overline{X}_1 = 20, \overline{X}_2 = 20, s_{wg} = 10$
   f. $\overline{X}_1 = 90, \overline{X}_2 = 80, s_{wg} = 10$
   g. $\overline{X}_1 = 90, \overline{X}_2 = 80, s_{wg} = 20$

6. Using the qualitative descriptors in Table 9.1, characterize the size/strength of association conveyed by each of the following.
   a. $SMD = -0.80$
   b. $SMD = 0.80$
   c. $SMD = 2.00$
   d. $SMD = 0.30$
   e. $SMD = -0.53$
   f. $SMD = -1.23$
   g. $SMD = -0.22$

**Section 9.3**

7. *Respond true or false to each of the following:*
   a. The larger the absolute value of *SMD*, the larger/stronger the relationship.
   b. In graphical depiction of the *SMD* such as in Figure 9.1, the greater the overlap between the two distributions, the larger the *SMD*.
   c. In graphical depiction of the *SMD* such as in Figure 9.1, the more distinct the two distributions, the larger the *SMD*.
   d. Even when the size of association conveyed by the *SMD* is large, there is still considerable overlap between the groups/distributions.
   e. Perfect relationships, those that are compellingly strong in a strict mathematical sense, are encountered frequently in social science research.
   f. In a given situation, *SMD* = 1.00. From a mathematical perspective, this conveys a compellingly strong (almost perfect) relationship.

**Section 9.4**

8. (*True or False*) The *SMD* is an effective and appropriate tool even when the standard deviations of the two groups differ quite markedly.

9. This text advises that *SMD* is not an appropriate tool when the standard deviation in the group with the larger standard deviation is about _____ _____ larger than that in the group with the smaller standard deviation.

10. Using this text's guideline as responded to in the prior question, indicate (yes or no) whether the *SMD* is an appropriate measure in each situation:
    a. Group 1, $\overline{X} = 10$, $s = 8$; Group 2, $\overline{X} = 15$, $s = 18$
    b. Group 1, $\overline{X} = 10$, $s = 8$; Group 2, $\overline{X} = 15$, $s = 10$
    c. Group 1, $\overline{X} = 100$, $s = 20$; Group 2, $\overline{X} = 90$, $s = 10$

**Section 9.5**

11. In the experimental group, the mean number of absences from school is 20.0 ($s = 11$). In the control group, the mean number of absences is 24 ($s = 10$). What is the effect size for means? Interpret/assess the size of the association between intervention (experimental group vs. control group) and number of absences.

12. For each example, calculate the effect size for means and interpret the size of association.
    a. $\overline{X}_E = 20$ ($s = 9$), $\overline{X}_C = 40$ ($s = 10$)
    b. $\overline{X}_E = 20$ ($s = 6$), $\overline{X}_C = 32$ ($s = 6$)
    c. $\overline{X}_E = 50$ ($s = 22$), $\overline{X}_C = 35$ ($s = 20$)

**Section 9.6**

13. The correlation ratio, symbolized by ___ conveys the proportion of _____ in an interval/ratio-level variable that is explained by a categorical variable.

14. Eta squared equals .17. What is the proportion of explained variance?

15. For each value of eta squared, interpret size of association using the descriptors presented in Section 9.6.
    a. $\eta^2 = .06$
    b. $\eta^2 = .15$
    c. $\eta^2 = .013$
    d. $\eta^2 = .04$
    e. $\eta^2 = .27$

Portions of this chapter originally appeared in James Rosenthal's "Qualitative Descriptors of Strength of Association and Effect Size." *Journal of Social Service Research* 21(4), 1996, pp 37–49. Reproduced with permission.

# 10

# RESEARCH DESIGN AND CAUSALITY

## 10.1 ■ CHAPTER OVERVIEW

Chapter 10 discusses how *confounding variables* make the assessment of *causality* difficult. It introduces two major research designs, *experiments* and *surveys*, and discusses how *random assignment* facilitates the drawing of causal conclusions.

## 10.2 ■ INTRODUCTION TO CAUSALITY

Social research often investigates relationships between variables. For instance, several studies have demonstrated a relationship between children's watching of violence on television and their own aggressive behavior (Comstock & Strasburger, 1990; Lazar, 1994; Robinson, Wilde, Navracruz, Haydel, & Varady, 2001). Sometimes, finding relationship is the primary study objective. Other studies seek not only to find relationship but also to determine whether one variable in a relationship *causes* the other—that is, whether the identified relationship is a **causal relationship**. Regarding the relationship between television and behavior, the key research question is perhaps "Does watching violence on television *cause* children to behave aggressively?" In essence, the issue of **causality** (*causation, causal attribution*) boils down to whether the researcher can determine "what causes what."

This chapter presents a framework for establishing when researchers can be confident that observed relationships are causal, when they can be confident that this is not the case, and when—because of study limitations—they cannot be sure about causality. Research design, particularly the distinction between experimental and survey designs, is integral to the assessment of causality. Surveys and experiments are discussed in Section 10.5. Sections 1.7 and 1.8 in Chapter 1 introduced many of the concepts discussed in this chapter, so you may want to review these sections.

As we proceed, let us make two assumptions. Chapter 6, Section 6.4, clarified that even extremely weak (trivial) relationships are technically considered to be relationships. It makes little sense to probe whether a relationship of trivial size is a causal one. As such, we presume that all associations presented in this chapter are at least small in size as defined by the qualitative descriptors presented in the prior several chapters (see Tables 6.3, 7.2, 8.2, and 9.1). Chapter 1, Section 1.7, pointed out that relationships in study samples are sometimes observed simply due to chance (the luck of the draw of random samples). We presume that all relationships presented in this chapter are sufficiently solid for chance alone to be an unlikely explanation. Chapters 14–23 focus on statistical significance tests, including the role of chance in relationships.

## 10.3 ■ WHAT DOES "CAUSE" MEAN IN SOCIAL SCIENCE?

In social science, **cause** is a synonym for "to affect" (to have an effect) or "to influence." Other phrases with nearly identical meanings include "results in," "leads to," "explains," and "increases/decreases the likelihood of." If one variable causes another, it exerts an influence on it. This influence need not be large, although it may be. So, if studying for a test helps even a small amount, we may say that studying *causes* improved test performance. Further, the variable doing the causing (the independent variable) need not be the only one exerting influence. Indeed, in many situations, multiple independent variables affect a dependent variable. For instance, if three variables—studying, having taken a prior course in a similar area, and taking a practice test—all contribute to better test performance, then we may say that each causes improved test performance.

Sometimes, it is intuitively obvious that a relationship is not causal. In New York City, researchers have documented a positive association between ice cream consumption and burglary. On days when New Yorkers eat lots of ice cream, the burglary rate tends to be high. On the other hand, on days when people refrain from ice cream consumption, these rates are much lower. Does eating ice cream cause burglary? Or is it the reverse? Does burglary lead to ice cream eating? The answer to both questions is no. A third variable is responsible for the association between crime and ice cream consumption. That variable is temperature. On hot days, people eat a lot of ice cream. Also on hot days, people are often out of their homes (perhaps on vacation or at the beach). This increases opportunities for burglary. Hence, the association between ice cream consumption and burglary is not causal but is instead was due to temperature.

Another example: I passed out a questionnaire in a class of graduate social work students and found an association between preferring classical music as contrasted to rock music and the reporting of aches and pains upon waking in the morning. Specifically, those who preferred classical music tended to report more aches and pains than did those who preferred rock. Given this association, I concluded that listening to classical music causes aches and pains and recommended that classical fans switch to rock.

Students in this class were of diverse ages. A student informed me that I had failed to consider the possible effects of age. She suggested that older students (30 years and older) were more likely to prefer classical music than were younger students (teens and 20s), and also that older students were more likely to experience aches and pains than were younger students. The association between listening to classical music and aching bones was not causal but instead was due to a third variable—age.

## 10.4 ■ CONFOUNDING VARIABLES

On balance, social scientists are hesitant to conclude that associations are causal. This hesitation stems in part from science's general preference toward the conservative and cautious. Yet, the possible presence of confounding variables is the primary cause. **Confounding variables** were defined in Chapter 1 (Section 1.7) as the third variables that bring about association between other variables. Confounding variables may affect the size of association, the direction (positive or negative) of association, or the presence versus the absence of association. In some situations, a confounding variable may be the sole explanation for the association. In the burglary–ice cream example, temperature is a confounding variable. If one could somehow hold the temperature constant, the association between ice cream consumption and burglary would, presumably, disappear. In the music and aching bones example, age was a confounding variable. Among persons of the *same* age, it is doubtful that there is an association between preferred music and aches and pains.

Returning to the example of the association between children's watching of violent television programs and aggressive behavior, the following question arises: Could this association reflect the effects of confounding variables? Perhaps, for instance, children at homes with high levels of violence (partner abuse, severe and frequent corporal punishment, etc.) tend to watch more violent television programs than those without such violence at their homes. Perhaps such a climate of violence at home, not violent shows on television, is the primary cause of the children's aggressive behavior.

A dictionary defines "confound" as "to fail to discern differences between . . . mix up . . . to increase the confusion of" (Webster's New Collegiate Dictionary, 1979, p. 235). Confounding variables make it difficult to "unscramble" (determine) the causes of relationships. Several other terms have nearly identical meanings. The term **third variable** conveys that an initially observed relationship between two variables (i.e., amount of aches and pains and type of music) may be caused by or influenced by a third variable (i.e., age). Other similar terms include *lurking variable* (here, the idea is that an initially observed relationship is caused by an unsuspected variable that lurks in the background) *extraneous variable, control variable,* and *nuisance variable.* Social science researchers are on constant alert to the possibility that a confounding variable(s) may be the explanation for an association between two others.

It may be helpful to provide an example from the human services field that demonstrates an initially observed relationship that is caused by a confounding variable. Suppose that you are a social worker in a public child welfare agency and read an agency report informing you that 24% (24 of 100) of children in family foster homes versus 36% (36 of 100) of children in group homes have behavior problems as reported by a caregiver at the placement setting. Does this association between types of placement (foster care versus group home) allow you to conclude that foster family care (relative to group home care) *causes* a reduction in behavior problems?

Suppose that you read deeper into the report and come across a table similar to Table 10.1, which introduces child's age at placement into the analysis. Table 10.1 reveals several things. First, it reveals that children aged 10 years and younger were placed more often in family foster care (80 of 100, 80%), whereas children aged 11 years and older were placed more often in group homes (80 of 100, 80%). Second, it reveals that, overall, 20% of younger children versus 40% of children aged 11 years and older had behavior problems (see the percentages in the table's rightmost column). Most important, Table 10.1 reveals that among children in the *same* age group, the same percentage of children in foster family homes and group homes experienced behavior problems. Among children aged 10 years and younger, 20% of children in both foster family and group homes experienced behavior problems. Among children aged 11 years and older, 40% of children in both foster family and group homes experienced behavior problems. Hence, among children in the same age group, type of placement and behavior problems are unassociated.[1]

Table 10.1  ■  **The Confounding Variable Age Creates an Association Between Type of Placement and Behavior Problems**

| | Foster Family Placement | | Group Home Placement | | Totals | |
|---|---|---|---|---|---|---|
| | *n* | % | *n* | % | *n* | % |
| **Aged 10 years or younger** | 80 | 20% | 20 | 20% | 100 | 20% |
| **Aged 11 years or older** | 20 | 40% | 80 | 40% | 100 | 40% |
| **Totals** | 100 | 24% | 100 | 36% | 200 | 30% |

*Note*: Percentage shown is the percentage with behavior problems.

In our example, the initially observed relationship between type of placement and behavior problems is caused by the confounding variable age. In such a situation, we would not want to conclude that group home placement causes increased behavior problems; indeed, had age group not introduced age into the analysis, we might have mistakenly done so. Table 10.1 demonstrates *control* for a confounding variable, that variable being age group. Chapter 11 discusses this topic in greater depth. In this chapter, we examine different types of research designs and conclusions that can and cannot be drawn in these designs.

## 10.5 ■ EXPERIMENTAL AND SURVEY DESIGNS

### 10.5.1 ■ Experiments Versus Surveys

The two basic quantitative research designs are the survey and the experiment. In **experiments** (*experimental designs*), the researcher *manipulates* the environment. In particular, she administers an intervention. As presented in Chapter 1 (Section 1.8), the **intervention** (*treatment*) is, in essence, what is "done to" the participant. For instance, a researcher could administer a desensitization regimen to reduce an irrational fear. In addition to administering an intervention, the experimental researcher determines who receives what intervention, when, where, for how long, how intensely, in what order, and so on. In **surveys** (*survey designs*, *observational studies*), the researcher does not manipulate the environment but instead simply takes measurements or, we could say, makes observations.

Experiments are preferred greatly over surveys for drawing conclusions about causality. In experiments, the key causal conclusion boils down to whether obtained results are caused by the intervention or by a confounding variable(s). As a general rule, the greater the manipulation of the experimental environment, the greater the degree to which confounding variables can be ruled out as possible causes. Given sufficient manipulation and control of the environment, the experimental researcher can sometimes be confident that results are indeed caused by the intervention. On the other hand, in survey designs, the task of determining "what causes what" is far more daunting—indeed often an impossibility. The social world is a complicated place. Potential confounding variables are a constant concern. The survey researcher can hardly, if ever, be confident about causality.

### 10.5.2 ■ Random Assignment to Groups

The three major categories of experimental designs are true experiments, quasi-experiments, and preexperiments. Among these, true experiments are best for drawing causal conclusions. All true experiments have two or more groups, each of which receives a different intervention. **True experiments** (*randomized research designs*, *randomized studies*, *randomized trials*, *randomized clinical trials*, *randomized experiments*) are distinguished by a single characteristic, random assignment. **Random assignment** (**randomization**; first defined in Section 1.8) is the use of methods of chance to assign study participants to groups. Methods of random assignment include flipping coins, drawing names from a hat, using a table of random numbers from a book, and using random numbers generated by a computer software program.

Although many *quasi-experiments* have two or more groups, none randomly assign participants to groups. Quasi-experiments are better than survey designs for drawing conclusions about causality but worse than true experiments. Whereas all true experiments and many quasi-experiments have two or more groups, only a single group participates in the *preexperiment*. With respect to drawing causal conclusions, these designs are hardly an improvement over surveys.

## 10.6 ▉ RANDOM ASSIGNMENT AND CAUSALITY

The pivotal role of random assignment in making it possible to infer causality can be demonstrated by a study that does not use it. The discussion that follows expands on an example introduced in Chapter 1, Section 1.8.

Suppose that a statistics instructor receives a new software program that teaches statistics via computer. To test its effectiveness, the instructor designs an experiment in which half of the class uses the software during their weekly help sessions (the *experimental group*) and the other half completes their help sessions as usual with the graduate teaching assistant (the *control group*). The study's method of assigning students to groups can be termed "student choice," because each student participates in the group of her choice. At the end of the semester, students take their final exam—scores on which are the dependent variable. Data analysis reveals that the mean score on the final is considerably higher in the software group than in the teaching assistant group. Can the instructor be confident that this relationship is causal, that is, that the software program (relative to the teaching assistant) *caused* the better performance on the final exam? The instructor can be confident only if confounding variables can be ruled out.

I can think of at least one such variable that is not ruled out. My hunch is that those with strong math skills more often chose the software group while those with comparatively weaker skills more often opted for the teaching assistant group. I propose that differing math skill as the study began—*not* differential effectiveness of the two interventions—provides the explanation for the final exam results.

What caused the better performance of those in the software program group? Given the absence of random assignment, we cannot unravel whether the intervention (the superiority of the software package to the teaching assistant) or differing math skills (a confounding variable) is the cause.

Perhaps some other confounding variable is at work. Perhaps, for instance, those in the software group were—on average—more motivated in the class than were those in the teaching assistant group. Or possibly, those in the teaching assistant group tended to have higher levels of test anxiety.

It is hoped that this example gives you a feel for the quagmire encountered in drawing conclusions about causality in designs that lack random assignment. The literal definition of *quagmire* is a "soft miry land that shakes or yields under the foot" (Webster's New Collegiate Dictionary, 1979, p. 936). This serves as a good metaphor for drawing causal conclusions in survey and other nonrandomized designs. There is no firm foundation for such conclusions. Each time one thinks that she has put together a solid line of reasoning explaining the cause of a relationship, the land yields underfoot as some new possible confounding variable arises.

As you have likely reasoned, random assignment would greatly improve the instructor's ability to draw a causal conclusion. Let us presume that the instructor lets us design the study. Suppose that we put all students' names in a hat, shake it vigorously, and then (with eyes closed) pick out names and assign students randomly to the two groups. Suppose that the study is carried out again and that the same result is observed (i.e., better performance in the software group).

When students chose their own groups, several possible confounding variables were identified (differing levels of math skills, differing levels of motivation, differing levels of test anxiety). Can we identify any confounding variables now given the random assignment?

Let us consider the just-mentioned variables. Is there reason to think that students in the software group had stronger math skills as the study began? No. All that differentiates the software and teaching assistant groups is the luck of the draw of the random assignment process; there is no reason to think that one set of students picked randomly from a hat will have better math skills than another. Thus, initial level of math skills is not a plausible confounding variable. How about motivation? Clearly, the same logic applies. The luck of the draw will not create groups that differ systematically with respect to motivation. The same logic rules out differing levels of anxiety as a potential explanation for the study result.

*Pragmatically*, random assignment *eliminates all* confounding variables. Stated differently, with random assignment, there are no confounding variables. At the risk of oversimplifying, given random assignment, the researcher may indeed draw causal conclusions. When she sees a difference in outcomes between groups, she need not worry that this difference is caused by confounding variables but may instead be confident that it reflects the effects of the intervention. She is no longer in a quagmire but on a solid ground.

A technical note on random assignment is now in order: *Technically speaking*, random assignment does not eliminate confounding variables but instead *randomly* distributes—"scatters by luck"—them between groups. Just by chance, students randomly assigned to the software group could have had, on average, better math skills than those assigned to the teaching assistant. Random assignment eliminates *systematic bias*, but it does not eliminate differences due to randomness (chance/luck).

As Section 10.2 mentioned, statistical significance tests (Chapters 14–23) examine the role of chance (luck) in study findings. In this chapter and the next, we presume that results are solid enough not to be due to chance.

Having stated that, pragmatically, random assignment eliminates confounding variables but, technically, randomly distributes them, a summary is in order. The pragmatic message is the key one. Pragmatically speaking, random assignment builds equivalent groups and, by so doing, lets researchers draw causal conclusions. In the absence of random assignment, the ground is much softer, and researchers are extremely hesitant to draw causal conclusions.

## 10.7 ■ CHAPTER SUMMARY

The fact of association between two variables is not sufficient for concluding that an association is *causal* (i.e., that one variable causes the other). In social science, to *cause* means to influence or to affect. Often multiple independent variables affect a dependent variable.

*Confounding variables* affect the pattern of association between two other variables. Most often, their effect is on size of association, though they may also affect direction of association, or the presence or absence of association. The relationship between two variables can be due entirely to the effects of a confounding variable.

In *experiments*, researchers manipulate and control the environment. In general, the greater the control, the greater the degree to which causal conclusions can be drawn. In *surveys*, the researcher simply takes measurements. Primarily because of confounding variables, it is extremely difficult to infer causality in surveys.

The *true experiment* is characterized by *random assignment*, the use of methods of chance to assign cases to groups. Pragmatically, random assignment eliminates confounding variables. When random assignment is used, the researcher may be confident that differences in outcome between groups are caused by the *intervention* rather than by a confounding variable(s).

## 10.8 ■ PROBLEMS AND QUESTIONS

**Section 10.2**

1. When one variable causes another, there is a _____ relationship between them.

## Section 10.3

2. What are some terms with meanings highly similar to or synonymous with "cause"?

3. *Respond true or false to each statement:*
    a. All relationships are causal relationships.
    b. For the relationship between *X* and *Y* to be considered causal, *X* must be the *only* cause of *Y* or *Y* must be the *only* cause of *X*.

## Section 10.4

4. *True or false:* Confounding variables may potentially affect . . .
    a. Size of association
    b. Direction of association
    c. Presence or absence of association

5. What are some other terms with meanings highly similar to or synonymous with confounding variable?

## Sections 10.5 and 10.6

6. In experiments, the researcher _____ the environment. In surveys, the researcher simply takes _____.

7. *Respond true or false to each statement:*
    a. Experiments are preferred over surveys for drawing conclusions about causation.
    b. The survey researcher can, quite often, be confident about issues of causation.

8. _____ _____ (randomized studies) are distinguished by a single characteristic, that being _____ _____.

9. *Indicate (yes or no) whether each of the following research designs uses random assignment to groups.*
    a. A staffing committee assigns youth, based on their needs, to Program *A* or Program *B*.
    b. A professor picks names out of a hat to decide which of two curricula students will be assigned to.
    c. Participants choose which of the three smoking prevention programs they will participate in.
    d. An elder care program uses a computer program that randomly picks which worker will be assigned to incoming clients.
    e. Social workers assign children based on their needs to either family foster care or group home care.
    f. Some nursing home residents indicate an interest in pet therapy (visits by certified dogs and their owners), whereas others indicate no such interest. (Those who

indicated interest are visited by dogs; those who do not indicate interest are not visited.)

g. Social workers use a table of random numbers to determine which nursing home residents participate in pet therapy and which do not.

h. A researcher's survey compares psychosocial outcomes for three levels/groups of exercise: low, medium, high (persons reported their exercise levels on the researcher's survey).

10. Indicate (yes or no) whether each research design listed in the prior question is a true experiment (a randomized design).

11. For each example in Question 9, indicate whether the researcher should have, basically, high confidence or low confidence regarding whether observed relationships are causal ones.

12. *Respond true or false to each of the following:*
    a. Random assignment to groups results in groups with *precisely* identical characteristics.
    b. Even when there is random assignment, the luck of the draw (chance) can create differences between groups.
    c. Pragmatically speaking, random assignment eliminates systematic biases that can cause differences between groups.
    d. Most survey designs use random assignment to groups.
    e. In designs with random assignment, the researcher can often (as opposed to hardly ever) draw at least reasonably solid conclusions pertaining to causation.
    f. In general, designs with random assignment are the preferred designs for drawing conclusions about causality.

13. Referring back to Table 10.1, let us change the findings: Suppose that we find that, subsequent to controlling for age group, children in family foster care demonstrate much better behavior than do those in group home care. This being so, would you be willing to conclude that the relationship between type of placement (foster family vs. group home) and behavior problems *is* a causal one? In other words, are you willing to conclude that family foster care *causes* (relative to group home care) reduced behavior problems? Why or why not? Assuming that you are not willing to conclude that the relationship is causal, indicate some confounding variables that might be affecting it.

# CONTROLLING FOR CONFOUNDING VARIABLES

## 11.1 ■ CHAPTER OVERVIEW

Chapter 11 focuses on how researchers *control* for (*hold constant*) confounding variables. Different patterns of results may emerge when this is done, and this chapter discusses how to interpret these patterns. It presents two *causal models*: the *antecedent variable model* and the *intervening variable model*.

## 11.2 ■ CONTROLLING FOR A VARIABLE

### 11.2.1 ■ Basic Concepts

Chapter 10 demonstrated the central importance of random assignment in drawing causal conclusions. Although the absence of random assignment makes drawing causal conclusions a difficult task, some strategies may be followed. This chapter demonstrates how researchers *control for* a variable (*control for a confounding variable*). A term synonymous with control is *hold constant* (*hold a confounding variable constant*). The type of placement/behavior problems example in the prior chapter (see Section 10.4) introduced control for a confounding variable, and we expand on this topic now.

An example from an earlier mentioned study of special-needs adoption can illustrate in greater depth the process of controlling for a confounding variable (see Chapter 3, Section 3.5; Rosenthal & Groze, 1992). The "family ethnicity" variable in this study took on three values: (a) minority, inracial: minority (non-White) parents who adopt a child of the same race as at least one parent; (b) White, inracial: White parents who adopt a White child; and (c) transracial: White parents who adopt a minority child (transracial adoption). Because the transracial group is small (*n* = 61) and for simplicity, we will drop it from our analysis. Also, for simplicity, we will designate the first two groups as "minority families" and "White families," respectively.

In this study, distinctly positive outcomes were observed for minority families. For instance, 58% of respondents in minority families (126 of 219) reported that the adoption's impact on the family was "very positive." In contrast, only 41% of respondents in White families reported this (190 of 465).

I asked myself whether the association was causal. Did some characteristic of minority families or communities—greater experience in raising children outside of the nuclear family, greater tolerance for problems that children experience, reduced stigmatization of adoption, more realistic expectations, stronger social support systems, and so on—*cause* the better outcomes? Or, on the other hand, was a confounding variable responsible? In other words, was the difference in outcomes for minority and White families caused by differential experiences of minority and White children prior to adoption?

How does a researcher hunt for a confounding variable? Basically, the researcher searches for a variable that is associated with *both* variables involved in the initial association. Such a variable has the potential to affect the size of, the direction of, or the presence/absence of that association. Because it is somewhat unusual for a confounding variable to actually reverse the direction of an initial association, our primary foci are on size of association and the presence/ absence of association.

A perusal of variables in the adoption study revealed that the child's age at entry into the adoptive home was associated with both family ethnicity and impact of adoption. As such, it was, at least to some degree, affecting the association between these variables.

Age at entry was associated with perceived impact of adoption on the family: The younger the child's age, the more positive the reported impact. Thus, among children who entered their homes prior to their sixth birthday, 54% (237 of 435) of responses were very positive. Among those who entered their homes after their sixth birthday, this percentage was only 37% (127 of 342). Age at entry into the home was also associated with family ethnicity. Thus, 48% (225 of 467) of children in White families entered the family home subsequent to their sixth birthday; this was the case for only 34% (78 of 227) of children in minority families.

Having identified a potential confounding variable, the next step is to *control* for its influence. When a researcher **controls for** (**holds constant**) a variable, the variable's influence on study results is, in effect, eliminated. Control for a confounding variable changes that variable into a constant (or near constant). For instance, in our example, we can control for age at entry into the home by breaking it down into five age subgroups. Having done so, we then examine the association between family ethnicity and adoption impact *within* each group. Table 11.1 presents these data. Within each age group in Table 11.1, age at entry is nearly a constant. This is so because, within each age group, children's ages vary hardly at all.

The logic behind control for a variable works as follows: For a variable to influence the strength of relationship between two other variables, it must be related to both variables involved in the relationship. But, a constant—because it does not vary—cannot be related to any other variable. Hence, if we make a variable a constant by breaking it into subgroups, within these groups, it will not influence the relationship between the other two variables. Extending the same logic, if we make it a near constant, its influence will necessarily be minimal. In such a case, we can examine the relationship with minimal (negligible) influence from the controlled for variable.

TABLE 11.1  ■  **Impact on Adoptive Family and Family Ethnicity Controlling for Child's Age at Entry**

| Child's Age at Entry into Adoptive Home | Families Reporting "Very Positive" Impact | | | |
| --- | --- | --- | --- | --- |
| | Minority Families | | White Families | |
| | % | *f* | % | *f* |
| **Birth to 2 years** | 63 | 83 | 60 | 113 |
| **3–5 years** | 55 | 60 | 39 | 128 |
| **6–8 years** | 62 | 50 | 36 | 119 |
| **9–11 years** | 35 | 20 | 26 | 73 |
| **12 years and older** | 50 | 4 | 34 | 24 |

As already discussed, within each age subgroup, children's age is nearly a constant. This being so, we know that, within each subgroup, it affects the relationship between family ethnicity and the adoption's impact hardly at all. Viewed pragmatically, within the age groups, we can examine the association between family ethnicity and adoption impact in the absence of any influence from age at entry.

## 11.2.2 ▓ Different Patterns Following Control

Given an initial association between two variables, control for a potential confounding variable can result in several different "patterns" of results. The most common are as follows:

1. *Association persists*: Within each subgroup, the association persists and, further, size of association within each subgroup is nearly the same as (or only modestly smaller than) that prior to control.
2. *Association weakens*: Within each subgroup, the association persists but within each subgroup, size of association is much smaller than that prior to control.
3. *Association disappears*: Within each subgroup, the association disappears; in other words, within each subgroup the variables are unassociated (or their association is extremely weak).
4. *Association varies by subgroup*: Size of association differs markedly in the different subgroups.

The results presented in Table 11.1 perhaps conform best to the first pattern. On balance, the size of the relationships within age groups tends to be only slightly smaller than in the initial relationship. The difference in percentages for the initial relationship was $D\% = 58\% - 41\% = 17\%$. In Table 11.1, the average $D\%$ within the age groups computes to 14%. To compute this (a) subtract the White family percentage from the minority family percentage for each of the five age groups, (b) sum these differences, and (c) divide by five.[1]

Given that the size of association within the groups (an average $D\% = 14\%$) is indeed smaller than that in the initial association ($D\% = 17\%$), the results in Table 11.1 also illustrate the second pattern, a weakening of the association following control.

Note also that the $D\%$ varies from group to group. With real-world data, this is the norm. In particular, notice that the $D\%$ between minority and White families is quite large among those who entered the home between the ages of 6 and 8 years ($D\% = 62\% - 36\% = 26\%$) and quite small among those in the youngest group ($D\% = 63\% - 60\% = 3\%$). Such variability in the $D\%$ between the different groups illustrates the fourth pattern of results. Yet, as just mentioned, real-world data do indeed vary. Many researchers would not regard the degree of variability in Table 11.1 as sufficient for concluding that the results best represent the fourth pattern.

As you proceed through this chapter, recognize that real-world data most often do not perfectly assume one particular pattern. Indeed, the adoption data reflect three of the four patterns. Sections 11.2.3–11.2.5 present the basics of interpreting the first three patterns. Section 11.3 presents considerations, complexities, and cautions. Section 11.5 discusses the fourth pattern.

## 11.2.3 ▓ Initial Relationship Persists

When an initial relationship persists at the same size or weakens only modestly when a potential confounding variable is controlled for, one concludes that the controlled for variable is *not* an important cause of that relationship. In such a situation, one holds open the *possibility* that the initial relationship *may* be a causal one. In the current example, we hold open the possibility that some characteristic of minority families and communities does indeed cause more positive family impact. When an initial relationship persists in a survey or other nonrandomized research design, one may *not* conclude that the initial relationship is causal because *other* confounding variables, not controlled for, may be involved. For instance, in our example, possible differences in child maltreatment histories have not been controlled for.

In our example, the potential confounding variable, age at entry, exerted only a small influence on the association between family ethnicity and family impact. (The association within the subgroups weakened only modestly from that observed initially.) As such, it was almost not a confounding variable at all.

## 11.2.4 ▓ Initial Relationship Weakens

The second pattern, initial association weakens but persists, is encountered frequently. Table 11.2 presents hypothetical adoption data illustrating this pattern. In interpreting Table 11.2, presume that the *D%* in the initial relationship continues to be 17%. In Table 11.2, the average *D%* in the five age groups computes to 8.0%. Hence, control for age at entry markedly reduces size of association—from a *D%* of 17% to an average *D%* of 8% within the groups. Even so, within each age group, family ethnicity and the impact of adoption continue to be associated. When an initial relationship weakens markedly but, nevertheless, persists within the groups when a confounding variable is controlled for, the researcher concludes that (a) the confounding variable is not the *sole* explanation of that relationship (because the relationship persists in the absence of influence from it), and (b) the confounding variable is *partially* responsible for the initial relationship (because the relationship is smaller when it is controlled for than when it is not).

Consider again the part of the initial relationship that persists after control—in our example, the average difference of 8%. This part of the relationship is *not* caused by the controlled for variable. Thus, we hold open the *possibility* that this part of the relationship may be causal. We may not conclude that it is causal because other potential confounding variables have not been controlled for.

## 11.2.5 ▓ Initial Relationship Disappears

The third pattern is for the initial relationship to disappear or to nearly do so. Table 10.1 in Chapter 10 demonstrated this pattern; the association between behavioral problems and type of placement disappeared when age was controlled for.

TABLE 11.2 ▓ **Association Between Family Ethnicity and Impact on Family Decreases in Size when Age at Entry is Controlled For**

| Child's Age at Entry into Adoptive Home | Families Reporting "Very Positive" Impact | | | |
|---|---|---|---|---|
| | Minority Families | | White Families | |
| | % | *f* | % | *f* |
| **Birth to 2 years** | 64 | 83 | 60 | 113 |
| **3–5 years** | 51 | 60 | 42 | 128 |
| **6–8 years** | 57 | 50 | 44 | 119 |
| **9–11 years** | 35 | 20 | 30 | 73 |
| **12 years and older** | 46 | 4 | 35 | 24 |

*Note.* Hypothetical data.

TABLE 11.3 ■ Association Between Marijuana Use and GPA Disappears when Level of Motivation is Controlled For

| | Mean Grade Point Average | |
| --- | --- | --- |
| Level of Motivation | Uses Marijuana | Does Not Use Marijuana |
| Low | 2.07 | 2.09 |
| Moderate | 2.45 | 2.43 |
| High | 2.78 | 2.81 |
| Very high | 3.32 | 3.30 |

*Note.* Hypothetical data. GPA = grade point average.

Another example: Table 11.3 presents hypothetical data on marijuana use and college students' grade point average (GPA), controlling for student motivation level. Presume that prior to controlling for motivation, the mean GPA of those who used marijuana was 2.50 and that that of those who did not was 3.00. Following control for motivation, this association has very nearly disappeared. Stated differently, within each level of motivation, GPAs of users and nonusers are very nearly equal.

When a relationship disappears when a confounding variable is controlled for, the researcher concludes that the initial relationship is not a causal one but, instead, is caused by the controlled for variable. In our example, we conclude that the initial association between low grades and marijuana use occurs because (a) those with low motivation earn lower grades and (b) those with low motivation are more likely to smoke marijuana.

Hopefully, the previous discussion has given you a feel for the "nuts and bolts" (the basics) of reasoning about causality in research studies that do not use random assignment. The next section introduces additional considerations and cautions into our discussion.

## 11.3 ■ CAUSAL MODELS AND ADDITIONAL CONSIDERATIONS

The discussion in Sections 11.2.3–11.2.5 summarizes the basic logic involved in controlling for third variables: The greater the decrease in strength of an initial relationship when a confounding variable is controlled for, the greater the degree to which that relationship is caused by that variable. Yet, the situation is more complex. This complexity can be conveyed using causal models.

A **causal model** (*path diagram*) presents the effects of some variables on others. An arrow from a first variable directly to a second indicates that the first variable (the independent variable) exerts a **direct effect** (directly causes) on the other (the dependent variable). In an **antecedent variable model** (*common cause model*), an **antecedent variable** (*antecedent confounding variable*) directly affects each of two other variables and, by so doing, generates a relationship between these variables. The term *antecedent* conveys that the confounding variable precedes each of the other two in time.

Figure 11.1 presents an antecedent variable model of the association between marijuana use and grades. In this model, low motivation level—the antecedent variable—directly affects both marijuana use and grades. By doing so, it creates an association between them. It creates this association even though marijuana use exerts no direct effect on grades. The absence of such a direct effect is conveyed by the absence of an arrow from marijuana use to grades.

Figure 11.2 presents an **intervening variable model** (*mediation model*) involving marijuana use, motivation, and grades. In this model, marijuana use directly affects motivation level and motivation level, in turn, directly affects grades. In this model, motivation level is an **intervening variable**

FIGURE 11.1 ■ An Antecedent Variable Model of Marijuana Use and Grades

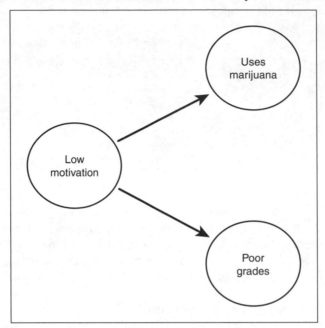

(*mediating variable*), one that passes along the effect of a first variable (in Figure 11.2, uses marijuana) to a second (low grades). According to this model, does marijuana use cause low grades? One is tempted to respond "No" because no arrow points *directly* from marijuana use to poor grades. Yet, there is an *indirect* causal link between these two variables. In Figure 11.2, smoking marijuana does indeed affect grades; it does so by decreasing motivation level, which, in turn, leads to lower grades. In this example, marijuana use has an **indirect effect** on grades, one that is "passed along" (*mediated*) by the intervening variable motivation level.

To identify a pair of variables connected by indirect effects, trace along the arrows going only in the direction that they point. For instance, in Figure 11.1, there is no indirect effect from marijuana use passing through low motivation and on to poor grades because the arrow between marijuana use and low motivation points from motivation to marijuana use rather than in the opposite direction. In Figure 11.1, there is no causal effect whatsoever—direct or indirect—of marijuana use on grades.

Whether an antecedent variable model or an intervening variable model is the correct model can have important implications. For instance, if the causal model in Figure 11.1 is correct, low motivation is an antecedent variable, and, thus, marijuana use does not cause poor grades (either

FIGURE 11.2 ■ An Intervening Variable Model of Marijuana Use and Grades

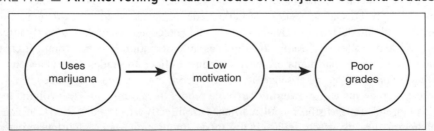

directly or indirectly). If, on the other hand, the model in Figure 11.2 is correct, low motivation is an intervening variable, and, thus, marijuana use does affect grades, even if indirectly.

How does one determine whether an antecedent variable model or an intervening variable model is the better model in a given situation? Suffice it to say that this can be difficult. Often, one's data provides only limited help. In our example, the same pattern of association between marijuana use, motivation level, and grades could equally well suggest either model. Sometimes, common sense or theories recommend one model over the other. Yet, even with careful, thoughtful interpretation, determining the "correct" causal model can be problematic. Often, one simply does not know.

Section 11.2.5 stated that when an initial relationship disappears when a variable is controlled for, the researcher concludes that the initial relationship is not a causal one. This conclusion is correct when the controlled for variable is an antecedent variable. When the controlled for variable is an intervening variable, the disappearance of an initial relationship indicates both (a) the absence of a **direct causal relationship** (one variable in the initial relationship has a direct effect on the other) and (b) the presence of an **indirect causal relationship** (the effects of one variable are passed along to the other through the intervening variable).

One final point should be mentioned. Most researchers consider antecedent variables but not intervening variables to be confounding variables. This is because the "nuts and bolts" interpretations of the effects of confounding variables offered in Section 11.2 apply to the antecedent variable model but not to the intervening variable model; basically, the intervening variable model introduces the complexities discussed in this section.

Our discussion here has only hinted at the complexities involved in assessing causality. On the brighter side, problems from confounding variables simply do not come up in studies with random assignment; in these studies, there are no confounding variables (see Chapter 10, Section 10.6). Further, the discussion of the "nuts and bolts" of confounding variables in Section 11.2 provides solid guidance for most situations. See Cohen (1983) or Rosenthal (2001, pp. 173–212) for more discussion on causal models.[2]

## 11.4 ■ CONTROL FOR MULTIPLE VARIABLES AND CAUSALITY

The examples so far have controlled for only a single variable. One may use contingency tables to control for two or more variables simultaneously. For instance, sticking with the adoption example, suppose that the study had been able to classify the severity of maltreatment sustained by children prior to adoption as (a) none or mild, (b) moderate, or (c) severe. We could then create a table controlling for both age at entry to the home and severity of maltreatment. Having done so, we could compare family impact in minority and White families in 15 different subgroups (3 categories of maltreatment × 5 age groups = 15 subgroups). For instance, one comparison would involve children aged 6–8 years at entry into the home who had sustained severe maltreatment. Suppose that the relationship between minority ethnicity and more positive family impact persisted in each subgroup. If it did, we could conclude that the more positive impact in minority families was not caused by either age at entry or severity of maltreatment.

The researcher encounters at least two problems as she controls for multiple variables in a contingency table. First, the number of subgroups increases rapidly. Second, the number of cases within the subgroups can become so small that the comparisons are of limited value. Pragmatically, it is difficult to control for more than two variables in a single table.

This text began with univariate statistics (means, standard deviations, etc.) and then moved to bivariate statistics (association between two variables). This chapter presents situations involving three or more variables and, thus, involves **multivariate analysis**. Yet, using tables to control for confounding variables provides only the briefest introduction to the capabilities of multivariate analysis. A wide array of multivariate statistical procedures are available for different situations; for instance, for variables at different levels of measurement. These can control simultaneously for six or seven (or more) variables. Chapter 23 introduces the multivariate procedure of *multiple regression analysis* (Section 23.2) as well as other multivariate procedures.

The real limitation in controlling for confounding variables does not lie with choice of methodology, the tabular techniques presented here versus more complex multivariate statistical techniques. The fundamental limitation is that, in a nonrandomized study, one can never control for *all* possible confounding variables. In the absence of random assignment, one can almost *never* have a high degree of confidence that an association is causal.

## 11.5 ■ INTERACTION EFFECTS

To this point, this chapter has demonstrated that control for a potential confounding variable may (a) not affect the size of an initial relationship, (b) weaken that relationship considerably, or (c) cause that relationship to disappear. A fourth pattern is for the size of association to differ markedly between groups. Such a result is an example of an interaction effect. When there is an **interaction effect** (**interaction**, *moderation*), the pattern of relationship between two variables differs according to the value of a third variable. This differing pattern of relationship may be reflected by (a) markedly different size of relationship in the different groups, (b) differing direction of association in the different groups, or (c) the presence of association in some group(s) and the near lack thereof in others. When there is an interaction, the third variable *moderates* the association between the initial two variables.

My statistics professor presented an example that helped me understand interaction. My professor presented results from a study that examined the association of sex of lead characters in children's stories to children's interest in those stories. An initial finding was that, on average, children indicated higher interest when lead characters were male than when they were female. When the researcher controlled for sex of reader, an interesting interaction emerged. For female readers, sex of character did not predict interest; girls were equally interested in stories with female and male lead characters. For boys, the situation was different. They evidenced much greater interest in stories with male lead characters than in those with female lead characters. Thus, the pattern of association between sex of lead character and level of interest differed for girls and boys. When the pattern of association differs according to the value of a third variable, one has an interaction effect. In this example, we may say that sex of reader moderated the relationship between sex of lead character and level of interest.

Table 11.4 presents an example of interaction from the special-needs adoption study (Rosenthal & Groze, 1992). In Table 11.4, the dependent variable is closeness of relationship between parent and child. The higher the closeness score, the closer the relationship.

TABLE 11.4 ■ Closeness of Parent–Child Relationship: An Example of Interaction

| Child's Age at Time of Survey | Minority, Inracial Families | | White, Inracial Families | | Transracial Families | |
|---|---|---|---|---|---|---|
| | Mean | *f* | Mean | *f* | Mean | *f* |
| **Birth to 5 years** | 3.52 | 13 | 3.66 | 60 | 3.80 | 9 |
| **6–11 years** | 3.61 | 112 | 3.35 | 207 | 3.39 | 23 |
| **12–18 years** | 3.46 | 101 | 3.02 | 184 | 2.96 | 26 |

TABLE 11.5 ■ Closeness of Parent–Child Relationship: Association but Not Interaction

| Child's Age at Time of Survey | Minority, Inracial Families | | White, Inracial Families | | Transracial Families | |
|---|---|---|---|---|---|---|
| | Mean | *f* | Mean | *f* | Mean | *f* |
| Birth to 5 years | 3.81 | 13 | 3.51 | 60 | 3.45 | 9 |
| 6–11 years | 3.68 | 112 | 3.38 | 207 | 3.34 | 23 |
| 12–18 years | 3.57 | 101 | 3.30 | 184 | 3.23 | 26 |
| *Note.* Data are hypothetical. | | | | | | |

Observe that for White, inracial families and, even more so for transracial families, as age of child increases, closeness of relationship decreases. Such a pattern would be predicted by the "prevailing wisdom." One expects greater closeness between parents and children when children are younger than when they are in adolescence. The pattern in minority, inracial homes, is distinctly different from that in the other two groups. In minority, inracial families, child's age is essentially unassociated with closeness of association, as indicated by the fact that the mean scores on closeness are virtually identical for the three age groups.

In sum, the pattern of association between age of child and level of closeness differs by family ethnicity. This being the case, there is an interaction. More precisely, there is an interaction between family ethnicity and age in predicting closeness of relationship.

Interaction and association (relationship) are sometimes confused. Table 11.5 presents hypothetical results for the special-needs adoption example. For each of the three family ethnicity groups, closeness of relationship is highest for children aged birth to 5 years, intermediate for children aged 6–11 years, and lowest for children aged 12–18 years. Because closeness differs in the different age groups, family closeness and age are associated. In Table 11.5, the size of association between closeness and age is very nearly the same in each family ethnicity group. This is so because, in each of the three categories of family ethnicity, mean closeness scores decrease by about the same amount as one moves from the youngest, to the middle, and finally, to the oldest age group. Because the pattern of association between closeness and age is the same in each family ethnicity group, there is no interaction between family ethnicity and age. In sum, Table 11.5 conveys association between closeness and age but does not convey interaction.

This chapter has emphasized control for variables as a tool for assessing whether relationships are causal. Yet the methods presented in this chapter are equally important as tools for learning about one's data. By exploring data carefully and by examining associations under varied conditions, the researcher may identify unexpected relationships or interactions. Researchers are often excited to discover interactions, and readers are often intrigued by them (interactions not researchers).

## 11.6 ■ CHAPTER SUMMARY

To determine the influence of a potential confounding variable, one *controls for* that variable, that is, *holds it constant*. Potential confounding variables are associated with both variables in the initial relationship.

A straightforward way to control for a confounding variable is to create subgroups composed of cases with the same (or highly similar) values on that variable. Within each subgroup, the controlled for variable is, effectively, a constant. This being so, one may examine association in the (very near) absence of influence from the variable.

Several patterns may emerge when a potential confounding variable is controlled for. When the size of association *persists* at very nearly the same size, one concludes that the controlled for variable is not a cause of the initial relationship. When the association *weakens* within the groups but, nevertheless, persists, one concludes that the confounding variable is partially but not fully responsible for the initial relationship. When the initial relationship *disappears* within the groups, one concludes, basically, that the controlled for variable is the cause of (explanation for) the initial relationship.

The conclusions in the prior paragraph provide solid guidance in most situations. The next two paragraphs present additional considerations.

A *causal model* depicts causation. A straight arrow connecting two variables conveys that one variable exerts a *direct effect* (cause) on the other. In an *antecedent variable model*, an *antecedent confounding variable* directly affects two other variables and, by so doing, generates a relationship between them. In an *intervening variable model*, an *intervening variable* passes along the effect of a first variable to a second.

In an antecedent variable model, neither variable in the initial relationship has any effect, *direct* or *indirect*, on the other. Thus, there is no causal effect (no *causal relationship*) whatsoever. In an intervening variable model, neither variable in the initial relationship directly affects the other but there is an *indirect effect*. Thus, there is a causal relationship but it is an indirect one (*indirect causal relationship*). It is often difficult to know whether the antecedent variable model or the intervening variable model is correct.

A researcher may control for two or more variables. In designs without random assignment, the researcher does not know whether all possible confounding variables have been controlled for and, thus, can never (hardly ever) be confident about causality.

An *interaction* occurs when the pattern of relationship between two variables differs according to the value of a third variable. Key patterns of interaction are (a) markedly different size of relationship in different groups, (b) differing direction of association in different groups, and (c) the presence of association in some groups and the absence thereof in others.

## 11.7 ■ PROBLEMS AND QUESTIONS

**Section 11.2**

1. A phrase synonymous with controlling for a (confounding) variable is holding a variable _____.

2. (*True or False*) Most confounding variables that exert substantial influence on the size of an initial association are associated with *only one* of the variables in that initial association.

3. When a researcher controls for (holds constant) a variable, the variable's influence on study results is, in effect, _____.

4. When a confounding variable is controlled for (as, for instance, age is in Table 11.1), that confounding variable ceases to be a variable but instead becomes (very nearly) a _____.

5. (*True or False*) Consider the association of $X$ and $Y$ *within* categories (subgroups) of the controlled for confounding variable $Z$. Within categories of $Z$, $Z$ has little (if any) effect on the size of the association between $X$ and $Y$.

6. In various situations, controlling for a (potential) confounding variable may result in which of the following patterns? (*Choose the best response.*)
   a. Only a very small change in size of association (association persists)
   b. A marked reduction in size of association (association weakens)
   c. The disappearance of the association
   d. Any of the above (or a combination of the above or other patterns not described here)

7. $X$ and $Y$ are strongly associated. $Z$ is controlled for. Within categories of $Z$, $X$ and $Y$ are unassociated (or the association is extremely weak). In this example, the association between $X$ and $Y$ _____ when $Z$ was controlled for.

8. In Table 10.1, when age is controlled for the relationship between type of placement (foster family or group home) and number of behavioral problems (*Choose the best response.*)
   a. is just as strong within the age subgroups as in the initial relationship
   b. is somewhat weaker within the age subgroups than in the initial relationship
   c. disappears

9. *Respond true or false to each of the following statements:* (Assume that random assignment is *not* used.)
   a. When an initial relationship persists at about the same size when a potential confounding variable is controlled for, one may conclude that variable is not an important cause of (explanation for) that relationship.
   b. When an initial relationship persists at about the same size when a potential confounding variable is controlled for, one may conclude that the relationship is a causal one.
   c. When a relationship weakens but does not disappear when a confounding variable is controlled for, one concludes that the confounding variable is partially responsible for the relationship.
   d. When a relationship disappears when a confounding variable is controlled for, one concludes that the confounding variable had no effect on the initial relationship.
   e. When a relationship disappears when a confounding variable is controlled for, one concludes that the relationship is caused by (due to) the confounding variable.

10. There are 2,000 children in foster care in a given state, of whom 1,000 are of minority ethnicity and 1,000 are of nonminority ethnicity. Seventy percent of the minority children (700 of 1,000) versus 44% of the nonminority children (440 of 1,000) are placed in kinship foster care. Thirty percent of minority children (300 of 1,000) and 56% (560 of 1,000) of nonminority children were placed in "regular" nonkinship foster care.
   a. Are ethnicity (minority or nonminority) and type of foster care (kinship or nonkinship) associated (yes or no)?

**b.** Calculate the difference in percentages. Treat minority as Group 1 and calculate using the percentages placed in kinship care.

**c.** Characterize the size of association between ethnicity and type of foster care.

**d.** Minority children are more likely to be placed in kinship care than are nonminority children. Identify two confounding variables that you think might be affecting the size of this association. (Think of variables that are associated with both ethnicity and type of foster care.)

Still working with the just-presented example pertaining to ethnicity and foster care, a researcher controls for children's (birth home) environment, that is, whether the child resided in a city environment or another environment. Here are the results:

TABLE 11.6 ■ Percentages of Minority and Nonminority Children Placed in Kinship Foster Care

| Environment | Minority Children | | Nonminority Children | | Totals | |
|---|---|---|---|---|---|---|
| | n | % | n | % | n | % |
| City | 800 | 75 | 400 | 60 | 1,200 | 70 |
| Other than city | 200 | 50 | 600 | 33 | 800 | 38 |
| Totals | 1,000 | 70 | 1,000 | 44 | 2,000 | 57 |

Note: n represents the number in each cell. Percentage (%) is the percentage placed in kinship care.

**11.** Respond to each of the following questions regarding the just-presented table.

**a.** In the city environment, what percentage of (all) children were placed in kinship care? In the other than city environment, what percentage of all children was placed in kinship care? These percentages are provided in the rightmost column.

**b.** Using percentages in the rightmost column, calculate the difference in percentages for the prior question (consider city environment to be Group 1). Is environment (city vs. other) associated with type of foster care (kinship vs. nonkinship)?

**c.** In the city environment, what percentage of children are minority children? In the other than city environment, what percentage of children are minority children? (These percentages are not provided in the table. To determine them, divide the number of minority children by the total number in the row and multiply by 100.)

**d.** Calculate the difference in percentages for the prior question (consider city environment to be Group 1). Is environment (city vs. other) associated with children's ethnicity (minority vs. nonminority)?

**e.** Is environment (city vs. other) associated with both variables in the initial relationship (type of foster care and children's ethnicity)?

**f.** Given that it is associated with both variables in the initial relationship, is environment influencing that relationship, at least to some degree?

**g.** For both subgroups (city and other than city) calculate the difference in percentages for kinship placement between minority and nonminority children. (In calculating the D%, treat minority children as Group 1.)

   **h.** Within the subgroups, is the difference in percentages about the same size as or smaller than the difference in percentages prior to control, or alternatively, within the subgroups has the relationship disappeared? (Hint: The $D\%$ prior to control was $D\% = 70\% - 44\% = 26\%$).

   **i.** Which pattern—association persists, association weakens, association disappears, or association differs markedly within the subgroups—does this data demonstrate?

   **j.** Given the pattern of results, is the association between ethnicity and type of foster care placement
       **a.** entirely due to environment (city vs. other)
       **b.** partially due to environment
       **c.** not affected at all by environment

   **k.** City environment is controlled for in Table 11.6. Can you identify another possible confounding variable that is not controlled for?

   **l.** Is this study an example of a survey design (observational study) or is it a randomized experiment (true experiment)?

   **m.** Based on the information in Table 11.6, can you conclude with confidence that the association between ethnicity and type of foster care placement is causal, that is, it is not caused by a confounding variable.

## Section 11.3

**12.** A _____ _____ is a diagram that presents visually the effects of variables on other variables.

**13.** In your own words, what does an arrow in a causal model convey?

The next two questions pertain to the following causal model:

**14.** This model is termed as _____ variable model, and variable *A* is an example of an _____ variable.

**15.** *Respond true or false to each of the following:*
   **a.** *A* has a direct effect on *B*.
   **b.** *B* has a direct effect on *A*.
   **c.** *B* has no direct effect on *C*.
   **d.** *B* has no indirect effect on *C*.
   **e.** *B* has no effect whatsoever (direct or indirect) on *C*.

    **f.** The relationship between $B$ and $C$ is caused by $A$.

    **g.** The relationship between $B$ and $C$ is a causal relationship.

    **h.** If this model is correct, when $A$ is controlled for, the relationship between $B$ and $C$ will disappear.

The next two questions pertain to the following causal model.

$$A \longrightarrow B \longrightarrow C$$

**16.** The just-presented model is an _____ variable model and variable $B$ is termed as _____ variable.

**17.** *Respond true or false to each of the following:*

    **a.** $A$ has a direct effect on $B$.

    **b.** $B$ has a direct effect on $A$.

    **c.** $B$ has a direct effect on $C$.

    **d.** $A$ has no effect whatsoever on $C$.

    **e.** $A$ has a direct effect on $C$.

    **f.** $A$ has an indirect effect on $C$.

    **g.** Variables $A$ and $C$ have an indirect causal relationship.

    **h.** $B$ "passes along" the effect of $A$ to $C$.

    **i.** If this model is correct, when $B$ is controlled for, the relationship between $A$ and $C$ will disappear.

**18.** Examine Table 10.1. Conceptualize age as an antecedent variable that affects both types of placement and behavior problems. Draw this causal model.

**19.** (*True or False*) Typically, it is extremely easy for the researcher to determine which model, the intervening variable model or the antecedent model, is correct.

**20.** In each of the following situations, a researcher jumps to a conclusion that is not justified given the provided information. For each, (a) briefly describe an antecedent variable model that provides an alternative explanation to that of the researcher for the results and (b) draw this model. Your model will involve identification of a possible confounding variable. As you consider the situations, note that none involves random assignment to groups. Obviously, there are many possible responses to each situation.

    **a.** At a given high school, a researcher finds that youth who are assigned a mentor have lower graduation rates than do youth who are not assigned a mentor. The researcher concludes that the mentor program leads to lower graduation rates.

    **b.** A researcher discovers that children who play chess score higher on achievement tests. She concludes that playing chess causes improved performance on such tests.

    **c.** Lower admission rates are observed for mental health clients served in an intensive community support program than for those served in a transition house program.

Researchers conclude that the community support program is the more effective of the two programs.

**d.** Children from the child welfare system who are placed in adoptive homes by Program A experience lower disruption rates than do those placed by Program B. Researchers conclude that Program A offers more effective services.

**e.** A researcher discovers that those who receive psychotherapy tend to have lower self-esteem than do those who do not. She concludes that psychotherapy reduces self-esteem.

## Section 11.4

**21.** *Respond true or false to each statement:*
  **a.** In nonrandomized designs, control for two or three (rather than just one) confounding variables is sufficient for drawing strong conclusions regarding causation.
  **b.** In the absence of random assignment, it is exceedingly difficult (if not impossible) to control for all potential confounding variables.

## Section 11.5

**22.** *Respond true or false to each statement:*
  **a.** When there is an interaction effect, the association between two variables differs according to value of a third variable.
  **b.** Whenever two variables are related, one knows that there is an interaction effect.
  **c.** For both women and men, Therapy X reduces scores on a depression scale more than does Therapy Y. This example demonstrates interaction.
  **d.** For those with psychosis, Therapy X produces better outcomes than does Therapy Y. For those with neurosis, Therapy Y produces better outcomes than Therapy X. This example demonstrates interaction.

**23.** For each study in Table 11.7, indicate whether there is an interaction effect (Yes or No) and, if there is an interaction effect, describe it in your own words.

TABLE 11.7 ■ Gender and Community Versus Traditional Treatment as Predictors of Hospital Readmission: A Table for Studying Interaction Effects (Percentage Readmitted)

| | Men | | Women | |
| --- | --- | --- | --- | --- |
| Study Number | Community Treatment (%) | Traditional Treatment (%) | Community Treatment (%) | Traditional Treatment (%) |
| 1 | 15 | 25 | 14 | 24 |
| 2 | 15 | 30 | 30 | 15 |
| 3 | 33 | 44 | 33 | 44 |
| 4 | 20 | 20 | 20 | 60 |
| 5 | 5 | 75 | 30 | 35 |

# INFERENTIAL STATISTICS AND DATA INTERPRETATION

Part 2's focus is on *inferential statistics*, that is, on how researchers draw conclusions about whole populations based on data from samples. Chapters 12 and 13 discuss *confidence intervals*, similar to the margins of error often mentioned on newscasts. Chapters 14, 15, and 16 introduce statistical significance tests. *Statistical significance tests* are conducted to see whether differences or relationships may be caused by chance—the luck of the draw of random samples. Chapters 17–22 present different significance tests for examining relationships between different types of variables: categorical with categorical, categorical with numeric, and numeric with numeric. Chapter 23 presents tools for multivariate analyses—analyses that involve three or more variables. Chapter 24 focuses on data interpretation, particularly on how the researcher evaluates the settings to which study results may *generalize* and whether a study result is *important*.

# AN INTRODUCTION TO INFERENTIAL STATISTICS

## 12.1 ■ CHAPTER OVERVIEW

Chapter 12 focuses on key concepts and beginning applications in inferential statistics. It presents characteristics of *random samples* and demonstrates how nonrandom sampling can lead to *sampling bias*. *Sampling error* is introduced and defined. *Sampling distributions* are introduced. This chapter presents the *central limit theorem* and its use in developing the *sampling distribution of the mean*.

## 12.2 ■ DESCRIPTIVE VERSUS INFERENTIAL STATISTICS

Descriptive statistical procedures describe the study sample. Chapters 3–9 presented various univariate and bivariate procedures for doing so.

How a procedure is used rather than the procedure per se determines whether a researcher is engaged in descriptive or inferential statistics. If a researcher uses the mean of a randomly selected study sample to estimate the mean of the population from which that sample was selected, the researcher is not describing her study sample. Instead, she is drawing conclusions about the population and thus has entered the domain of inferential statistics. **Inferential statistical procedures** are tools for drawing conclusions about populations based on observations from samples randomly selected from those populations.

## 12.3 ■ CHARACTERISTICS OF RANDOM SAMPLES

A **random sample (probability sample)** is a sample that is selected by a method of chance. Consider the population of students at a school of social work. Methods of chance for selecting students for a sample include (a) putting the names of *all* students in a hat (shaking well) and drawing names, (b) assigning each student a number and using a table of random numbers to select students, and (c) using a software package to randomly pick the sample from a list of all students. As each of these three examples selects students by chance (luck), the resulting samples are random samples.

Samples that are not selected by methods of chance are **nonrandom samples (nonprobability samples)**. For instance, because chance is not used to select them, the following samples are nonrandom samples: (a) all of the students in your current statistics class, (b) the students in the front three rows of your statistics class, and (c) persons who respond to a newspaper add asking for volunteers in a stop-smoking program.

There are many types of random samples, and presentation of these is beyond our scope. The best known type of random sample is the **simple random sample** (*SRS*). When you think about a random sample, you are likely thinking about an *SRS*. For instance, picking names at random from a hat produces an *SRS*. Three key characteristics of an *SRS* are as follows: (a) selection is by a method of chance, (b) each case has an equal chance of being selected, and (c) the **independence of selection** assumption is met, that is, that the selection of each case is independent of the selection of each other case. The inferential statistical procedures presented in this text are valid only when the study sample is an *SRS*, though Chapter 16, Section 16.8, presents an exception.

The following is an example of a sample that does not possess the independence of selection characteristic: A professor asks all 50 students in her class to write their names on a slip of paper and put them in a hat. She then draws at random 10 slips to determine who will participate in a class activity at a social agency. One of the pieces that she draws has two names written on it, say, Kathleen and Teresa. Kathleen and Teresa explain that they commute together and so they put both their names on a single slip so that they could save on gas money if picked for the activity. Kathleen's and Teresa's selections were not independent of one another. This being the case, the professor's sample is not an *SRS*, and thus, the inferential procedures presented in this text should not be applied to it.

Formally, the inferential procedures in this text should be only used when the independence of observations assumption is met. In essence, the **independence of observations** assumption asserts that pairs or groups of cases do not share some unmeasured factor that makes scores more similar (or, on rare occasions, more dissimilar). Perhaps the most serious violation of the independence of observations assumption occurs when the actions of one case affect those of another. Suppose that grade earned on a test is the dependent variable in a study and that one student copies the answers of another. The test scores for these two students do not meet the independence of observations assumption. Almost assuredly, they are more similar than would have been so in the absence of cheating.

Most situations involving the independence of observations assumption are less clear cut that just presented. For instance, assume that members of a therapy group related to depression participate in a research study in which the dependent variable measures some aspect of mental health. If some members of a therapy group become less depressed and their improvements "rub off" (influence or help) on some other members, this potentially violates the independence of observations assumption.

Often, there is no easy way to know whether the independence of observations assumption has been met. Except for a clear violation such as in the cheating example, the pragmatic approach, the one that I recommend, is to assume that it has been met (see Rosenthal, 2000, pp. 219–220, for more information).

It is important that you do not confuse random sampling and random assignment. *Random assignment* is the use of methods of chance to assign participants to treatment groups and allows researchers to draw causal conclusions in experimental studies (see Chapter 10, Section 10.6). *Random sampling* is the use of methods of chance to select the study sample and is a requirement for the valid use of inferential statistical procedures. As an example, the following study does not use random sampling but does use random assignment: Persons who are HIV positive and attend Clinic X are assigned using methods of chance to one of the three drug treatment regimens: *A*, *B*, or *C*. If this study found substantial differences in outcomes in the three regimens, the researcher could reason as follows: (a) Random assignment rules out confounding variables (with random assignment, there are no confounding variables), and thus (b) the differences in outcomes are likely caused by the differing effectiveness of the three regimens. At the risk of oversimplifying,

- Random assignment bears largely on whether the researcher can conclude that the relationship between the treatment intervention and the dependent variable is a causal one. When random assignment is used, the researcher can often reach such a conclusion; when it is not, almost without exception, she cannot do so.

- Random sampling bears largely on whether the researcher can use inferential statistical procedures to draw conclusions about the population from which the study sample was selected. When random sampling is used, the researcher can do so; when it is not, she cannot do so.

From this point forward, I take a liberty and use "random sample" as a synonym for "simple random sample." Continued use of *SRS* would focus our attention on sampling methods, which are not our central concern.


## 12.4 ■ THE ADVANTAGE OF RANDOM SAMPLES

Because of the luck of the draw, conditions in a random sample almost always vary some from those in the population from which the sample was selected. For instance, if the mean age of all students at your university is 20.0 years, the mean age found in a random sample of 100 students might be 19.2 years. Alternatively, in another such sample, it might be, say, 20.5 years. The means of these two samples differ because of the luck of the draw.

The great advantage of a random sample over a nonrandom one is that the luck of the draw is the *only* factor that causes differences between the sample and the population from which it is selected. Stated differently, in a random sample, only *random* sampling factors affect sample results. One need not be concerned about *systematic* sampling bias.

A sample possesses **sampling bias** if its characteristics differ systematically from those of the population to which the researcher seeks to make inferences. Random samples have no sampling bias. In contrast, when samples are nonrandom, there is typically good reason to suspect sampling bias.

For instance, suppose that a researcher administers a questionnaire regarding support for social welfare programs to a sample of social work students at a given university. Almost assuredly, social work students, taken as a group, support such programs to a greater degree than do most university students. Thus, relative to the full population of students at the university, the social work sample is likely biased in the direction of greater support.

The likely sampling bias in the just-described sample is reasonably straightforward. Yet, when a sample is nonrandom, *one never knows assuredly* that sampling bias is present. Perhaps, for instance, social work and other university students do not differ in their degree of support for social welfare programs. Whereas one never knows for sure that a nonrandom sample is biased, the more important point is that *one never knows for sure that it is not*. On the other hand, as stated previously, random samples do not possess sampling bias and thus only random factors—the luck of the draw—create differences between sample and population conditions.

One caution to the previous discussion should be stated. This discussion has presumed that all cases (100%) selected to be in a random sample do indeed participate in the research study. When some do not participate, *nonresponse bias* can be introduced. This is discussed in Chapter 13, Section 13.5.

Prior to concluding our discussion of random sampling, a final point should be clarified. It is indeed the case that researchers may use inferential statistical procedures to draw conclusions *only* about the population from which the study sample was randomly selected. For instance, a researcher may not study students at one university and, based on their responses, use inferential statistics to draw conclusions about students at another university.

Saying that researchers may not use inferential statistics to draw conclusions about other populations does not say that researchers may not draw conclusions about other populations but only that *inferential statistics* may not be used to do so. Chapter 24, Section 24.2, presents the tools and logic that researchers use to apply study results to varied populations, times, settings, and places.

Unless stated otherwise, from this point forward, "population" conveys the population from which the study sample has been randomly sampled.

## 12.5 ■ STATISTICS AND PARAMETERS

Chapter 1, Section 1.6, provided a general definition of *statistic*: a numerical summary of data (Toothaker & Miller, 1996, p. 7). *Statistic* also has a more specific meaning, one that differentiates it from *parameter*. **Statistics** are numerical characteristics of samples. **Parameters** are numerical characteristics of populations (Toothaker & Miller, 1996, p. 16). For instance, the mean of a sample is a statistic whereas that of a population is a parameter. Much of inferential statistics involves using sample statistics to estimate population parameters. For instance, the mean of a random sample estimates the mean in the population from which it was selected. Similarly, the standard deviation and variance in a random sample estimate their corresponding population parameters. When a sample statistic is used to estimate a population parameter, that statistic is termed an **estimator** (**inferential statistic**).

Often, sample statistics are symbolized by letters from the Roman alphabet (the same letters as are used in English) and population parameters by (usually lowercase) Greek letters. Occasionally, lowercase Roman letters are used for sample statistics and uppercase for population parameters. Some key statistics and their corresponding parameters are presented in Table 12.1.

The formula for the $z$ score of a sample was presented in Chapter 5, Section 5.7.1. As symbols for the mean and standard deviation in a population have been introduced, the formula for the $z$ score in a population may now be presented:

$$z = \frac{\bar{X} - \mu}{\sigma} \tag{12.1}$$

where $X$ is the score of an individual case.

TABLE 12.1 ■ Selected Inferential Statistics and Population Parameters

| Statistic/Parameter | Symbol for Sample Statistic | Symbol for Population Parameter | Spelling of Greek Letter | Pronunciation of Greek Letter |
|---|---|---|---|---|
| Mean | $\bar{X}$ | $\mu$ | mu | mew |
| Standard deviation | $s$ | $\sigma$ | sigma | sigma |
| Variance | $s^2$ | $\sigma^2$ | sigma | sigma |
| Proportion | $p$ | $P$ | | |

## 12.6 ■ CHARACTERISTICS OF ESTIMATORS

Good estimators are both efficient and unbiased (Glass & Hopkins, 1996, pp. 242–247). An **efficient** estimator requires a minimum of cases to generate a good estimate. Efficiency is a matter of relative efficiency. For instance, the mean is a more efficient estimator of central tendency than is the median because, given equal sample size, the sample mean provides more precise estimates of the population mean than does the sample median of the population median. The other estimators in Table 12.1 are also efficient estimators.

An **unbiased** estimator neither *overestimates* nor *underestimates* a parameter. The mean, proportion, and variance of a sample are unbiased estimators of their corresponding population parameters. Given that the sample variance is an unbiased estimator, common sense suggests that the same would be true for the standard deviation. In this situation, common sense leads us astray. The standard deviation in a sample, $s$ (see Formula 4.5), is a biased estimator of the standard deviation in the population, $\sigma$. $s$ tends to underestimate $\sigma$. Fortunately, the degree of underestimation is negligible and thus we may disregard it. In sum, the mean $(\overline{X})$, the proportion $(p)$, the standard deviation $(s)$, and the variance $(s^2)$ of a random sample are all excellent estimators of their respective parameters.[1]

At this point, an example of how to use the just-introduced estimators is in order. Suppose that you work in child welfare services and have access to a large, statewide computerized data file of child abuse and neglect reports. You draw a random sample of 100 reports from this large population of reports and determine that the mean age of children in your sample is 8.5 years with a variance of 24.01 years and a standard deviation of 4.9 years. The mean, the variance, and the standard deviation are all the preferred estimators of their respective population parameters. As such, you would estimate that (a) the population mean $(\mu)$ equals 8.5, (b) the population variance $(\sigma^2)$ equals 24.01 years, and (c) the population standard deviation $(\sigma)$ equals 4.9 years.

Suppose that 40% of reports in your sample involve abuse (physical or sexual) and 60% involve neglect. As you know, proportions and percentages present the same information in different ways. Hence, the points made previously about proportions apply also to percentages. The percentage in a random sample is an unbiased estimate of that in the population from which it has been selected. Thus, 40% (for abuse reports) and 60% (for neglect reports) are the best estimates of the population percentages. Expressed using proportions, the best estimates are that the population proportion $(P)$ equals 0.40 for abuse reports and 0.60 for neglect reports.

In the previous examples, each statistic estimates a single value. When a statistic estimates a specific value, that estimate is a **point estimate**. For instance, 40% is a point estimate of the percentage of abuse cases in the population. A disadvantage of a point estimate is that the researcher does not know how close that estimate is likely to be to the population parameter. Your sample data tells you that 40% is the best estimate of the population percentage. But how good of an estimate is this? Is it likely to be accurate to within 5%, 10%, or 20% of the population percentage? Point estimates do not help with questions such as this.

In addition to point estimates, researchers make interval estimates. Rather than stating a specific value, an **interval estimate** specifies a range within which the population parameter is likely to be located. Thus, rather than stating, for instance, "40%" as would a point estimate, an interval estimate states a likely range, for instance, "between 35% and 45%." The advantage of the interval estimate over the point estimate is that by specifying a range of likely values, it does convey a sense of how "good" an estimate is. In general, as sample size increases, the researcher is able to specify an increasingly smaller (narrower) range of likely values. In other words, as sample size goes up, estimates become more accurate.

## 12.7 ■ SAMPLING ERROR AND SAMPLING DISTRIBUTIONS

### 12.7.1 ■ Concepts

Sample statistics only *estimate* population parameters. For instance, due to the luck of the draw, the mean in your random sample of child abuse and neglect cases almost assuredly differs from that in the population. Indeed, only by pure luck would the mean in your sample *exactly* equal that in the population. The difference between a sample statistic and a population parameter is **sampling error**.

sampling error = sample statistic − population parameter                    (12.2)

The mean in your sample was 8.5 years. Suppose that the mean in the full population of reports in the database was 9.0 years. Then sampling error is 8.5 − 9.0 = −0.5 year.

Observe that the just-described situation is unrealistic because the population parameter is known. In real-world research, only a sample of cases is selected from the population and the population parameter is unknown. As such, the just-provided formula for sampling error cannot be carried out and the exact amount of sampling error cannot be determined. Even if the exact amount of sampling error remains unknown, the researcher can estimate the likely amount of sampling error.

The key tool for so doing is the sampling distribution. A **sampling distribution** is the distribution of a statistic that results from selecting an infinite number of random samples of the same size from a population. The cases in a sampling distribution are statistics from the samples that are drawn to build it. The steps in building a sampling distribution are as follows: (1) select a random sample of a given size from a population, (2) calculate the chosen statistic for this sample, and (3) plot this statistic. The fourth step is to repeat the first three steps an infinite number of times. In a nutshell, a sampling distribution is a frequency distribution composed of statistics from an infinite number of random samples. Some examples involving coin flips can help you get a feel for sampling distributions.

Let us build three sampling distributions of the number of heads obtained from flipping an unbiased coin, one that comes up heads 50% of the time. Specifically, let us build sampling distributions of the number of heads obtained in samples of 1, 2, and 10 flips ($N = 1$, $N = 2$, and $N = 10$). Figure 12.1 presents these distributions.

When sample size is 1 ($N = 1$), the sampling distribution is identical to the frequency distribution for the population. (In practice, researchers do not build sampling distributions when $N = 1$; this distribution is presented for teaching purposes.) As you know, an unbiased coin comes up heads 50% of the time and tails 50% of the time. Thus, the top left distribution in Figure 12.1 shows that, when $N = 1$, we obtain 0 heads in 50% of samples and 1 head in the other 50%.

When $N = 2$, we obtain 0 heads in 25% of samples, 1 head in 50%, and 2 heads in 25% (see the top right distribution in Figure 12.1). Finally, when $N = 10$, we obtain the bottom-pictured sampling distribution in Figure 12.1. In this distribution, the most commonly obtained number of heads is 5 (obtained in 24.6% of samples) and the least commonly obtained numbers are 0 and 10 (.100%) of samples.

It may be helpful to go over the steps in building one of the distributions in Figure 12.1. For instance, to build the sampling distribution of the number of heads obtained when $N = 10$, (1) flip the coin 10 times; (2) count the number of heads; (3) plot this number; and (4) repeat Steps 1, 2, and 3 an infinite number of times.

As you examine the distributions in Figure 12.1, think of the number of heads obtained as a sample statistic, that is, as a numeric characteristic that summarizes each sample. The sampling

FIGURE 12.1 ■ Sampling Distribution of Number of Heads for Three Samples Sizes

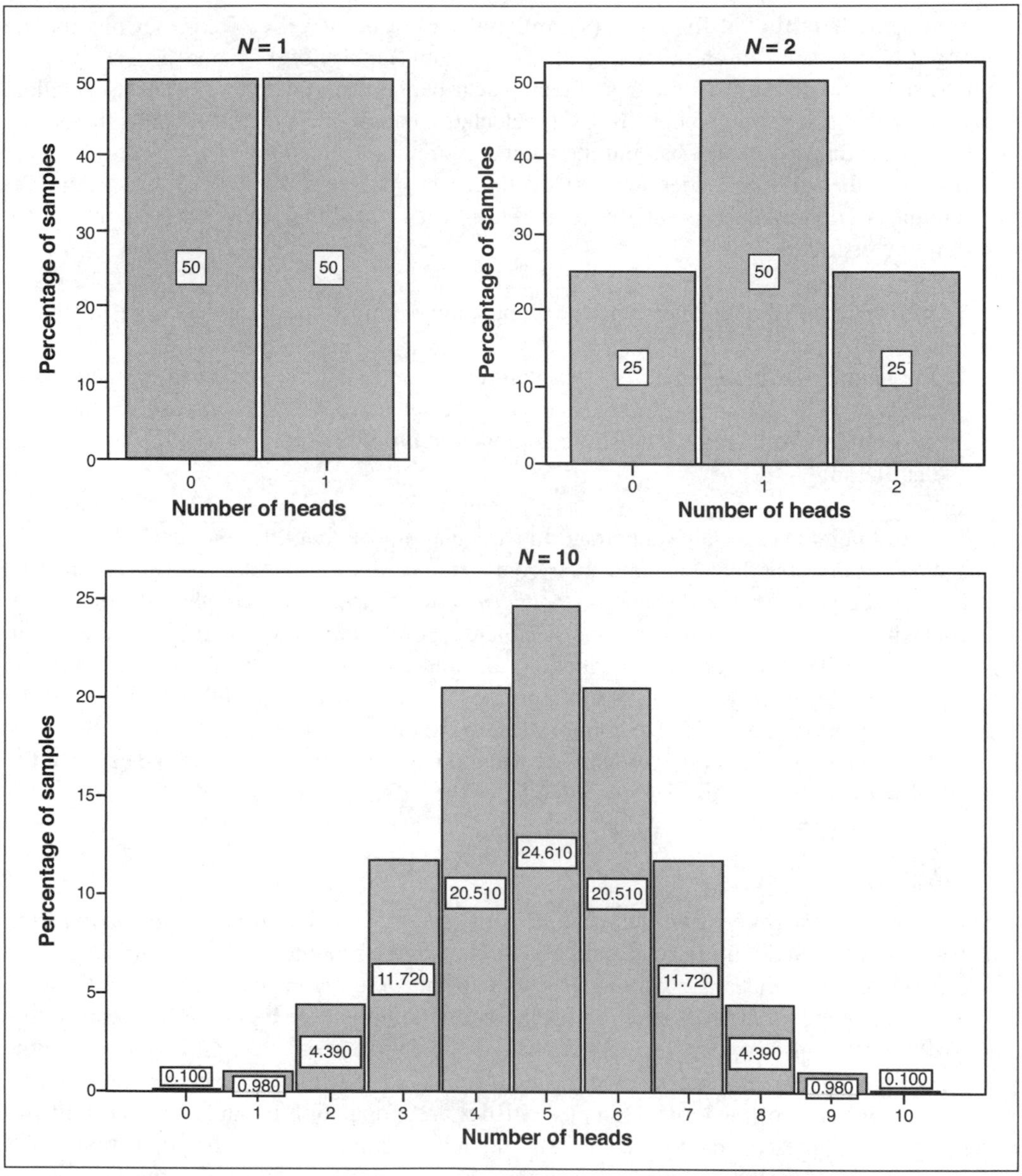

distributions in Figure 12.1 are indeed built from sample statistics; stated differently, their cases are sample statistics.

Observe that each sampling distribution in Figure 12.1 demonstrates the luck of the draw. The same result is not obtained in each sample but instead results vary from sample to sample.

Perhaps these sampling distributions appear "artificial" to you because, after all, selecting an infinite number of samples is an impossibility. Some of the beauty of inferential statistics is that you do not select an infinite number of samples, but instead may rely on statistical theory to build sampling distributions. *Binomial distribution* theory was used to build the sampling distributions in Figure 12.1. We return briefly to this distribution in Chapter 19, Section 19.3. Our key interest now is in the role that the normal distribution plays in building the sampling distribution of the mean.[2]

### 12.7.2 ■ Sampling Distribution of the Mean

A **sampling distribution of the mean** (**sampling distribution of $\overline{X}$**) is a frequency distribution composed of the means of an infinite number of random samples of the same size, all selected from the same population. To build this sampling distribution, the researcher (1) selects a random sample of a given size from a population, (2) calculates that sample's mean, (3) plots that mean, and (4) repeats Steps 1, 2, and 3 an infinite number of times.

In reality, the researcher does not carry out these steps but lets the statistical theory build the distribution. An important theorem, the **central limit theorem** (CLT), makes these points about the sampling distribution of $\overline{X}$:

1. Its mean equals the mean in the population from which samples were randomly selected;
2. Its standard deviation equals the standard deviation in the population from which these samples were randomly selected divided by the square root of the sample size; and
3. As sample size increases, its shape approaches *normality* (approaches that of a normal distribution).

The third point is especially important. In particular, notice that this point does not mention the shape of the distribution in the population from which samples were selected. Thus, even when the shape of the population distribution is *nonnormal*, the shape of the sampling distribution of $\overline{X}$ becomes increasingly normal as sample size increases. We may carry the third point one step further and state that, for almost all distributions that one encounters in social science research—normal, skewed (even very strongly so), flat, bimodal, other shapes as well—the shape of the sampling distribution of $\overline{X}$ is close to normal whenever sample size is 100 or greater.

The standard deviation of the sampling distribution of $\overline{X}$ is termed the **standard error of the mean** and is symbolized by $\sigma_{\overline{x}}$. Based on Point 2 of the CLT, its formula is

$$\sigma_{\overline{x}} = \frac{\sigma}{\sqrt{N}} \tag{12.3}$$

where $\sigma_{\overline{x}}$ is the standard error of the mean, $\sigma$ is the standard deviation in the population from which samples are randomly selected, and $N$ is the size of the randomly selected samples.

Our example on child abuse reports can be used to build a sampling distribution of $\overline{X}$. Presume that the mean age of children in the full population of all child abuse reports is 9.0 years with a standard deviation of 5.0 years. Observe that these population parameters differ some from the statistics of the random sample presented earlier ($\overline{X} = 8.5$, $s = 4.9$). This is expected. Due to sampling error—the luck of the draw—sample statistics and population parameters almost always differ. Figure 12.2 presents the frequency distribution of children's ages in the population.

Be sure to understand that the distribution in Figure 12.2 is *not* the sampling distribution of $\overline{X}$, but rather it is the distribution (the population) from which the infinite number of random samples will be selected. Indeed, three different distributions are involved in our example of building the sampling distribution.

1. The population distribution from which the random samples are selected (see Figure 12.2)
2. The infinite number of random samples that are selected. (These samples are not displayed in any figure presented here.)
3. The sampling distribution that is being created (see Figure 12.3)

In our example, the population distribution (see Figure 12.2) has a distinctly nonnormal shape. Its shape can best be characterized as close to uniform or as flat (see Chapter 5, Section 5.5).

FIGURE 12.2 ■ The Population Distribution

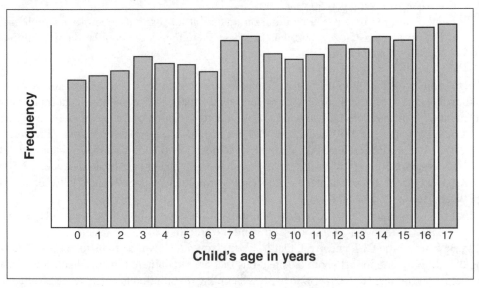

Suppose that we select an infinite number of random samples of size 100 from this population and plot the mean of each. By doing so, we build a sampling distribution of the mean. What will this sampling distribution of $\overline{X}$ look like? More specifically, what will be its mean, its standard deviation, and its shape? The CLT addresses these questions:

1. Point 1 tells us that its mean equals the mean in the population from which the samples were selected. Its mean, therefore, equals 9.0 years ($\mu = 9.0$).
2. Point 2 tells us that its standard deviation (the standard error of the mean, $\sigma_{\overline{x}}$) equals the standard deviation in the population from which samples were selected divided by the

FIGURE 12.3 ■ Sampling Distribution of the Mean for Children's Ages

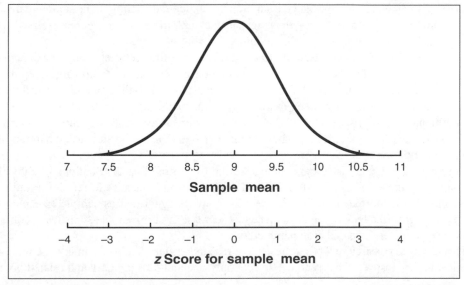

square root of the sample size: $\sigma_{\bar{X}} = 5.0 / \sqrt{100} = 5.0 / 10 = 0.50$ year. Its standard deviation, therefore, equals 0.50 year.

3. Point 3 and the discussion building on this point tell us that, given that sample size is $\geq 100$, its shape is close to normal. This is so even though the population distribution has a nonnormal shape.

As the shape of the sampling distribution of $\bar{X}$ in our example is close to normal, we may use our knowledge of the normal curve to draw additional conclusions about it. In a normal distribution, about 68% of cases are located within one standard deviation of the mean (between a $z$ score of $-1.00$ and a $z$ score of 1.00) and about 95% are within two standard deviations (between a $z$ score of $-2.00$ and a $z$ score of 2.00). Given that its mean is 9.0 years and that its standard deviation is 0.50 year, about 68% of its cases (68% of its sample means) are located between 8.50 and 9.50 years ($9.0 \pm 0.50$) and about 95% of its cases (sample means) are located between 8.00 and 10.00 years [$9.0 \pm (2 \times 0.500)$].

Figure 12.3 presents the sampling distribution of $\bar{X}$ for our example. The X axis in Figure 12.3 has two scales. The top scale uses raw scores and the bottom scale uses $z$ scores.

In sum, using the CLT and given that $N \geq 100$, you now have the tools to describe the sampling distribution of $\bar{X}$ in just about all situations that are encountered in social science research. Of course, you still need to learn how to use this sampling distribution in actual research situations. Chapter 13, on confidence intervals, demonstrates this.

In essence, sampling distributions convey how the luck of the draw (sampling error) affects samples. The more spread out (the wider) the sampling distribution, the greater the effects of luck on sample results. The more compact (narrower) the sampling distribution, the less these effects.

## 12.8 ■ SAMPLE SIZE AND THE SAMPLING DISTRIBUTION OF $\bar{X}$

A fundamental concept in inferential statistics is that as sample size ($N$) increases, sampling error tends to decrease. Stated differently, as sample size increases, sample statistics become better (closer) estimators of population parameters.

We can apply this concept to the sampling distribution of $\bar{X}$. As already discussed, the standard error of the mean ($\sigma_{\bar{X}}$) is one and the same as the standard deviation of the sampling distribution of $\bar{X}$. Study of its formula ($\sigma_{\bar{X}} = \sigma/\sqrt{N}$) reveals that as $N$ increases, $\sigma_{\bar{X}}$ decreases. In words, as sample size increases, the spread of the sampling distribution decreases.

Let us use the child abuse example to demonstrate the link between sample size and sampling error. Recall that the mean age of children in the full population of child abuse reports was 9.0 years with a standard deviation of 5.0 years. We have already built a sampling distribution of $\bar{X}$ based on a sample size of 100 (see Figure 12.3). Let us build two more, first based on a sample size of 400 and next on 1600. Table 12.2 presents the characteristics of these three sampling distributions. Table 12.2 demonstrates that, as sample size increases, the standard deviation of the sampling distribution of $\bar{X}$ ($\sigma_{\bar{X}}$) decreases.

Figure 12.4 presents visual comparisons of the three sampling distributions in Table 12.2. As sample size increases from 100 to 400 to 1,600, the sample means cluster closer and closer around the population mean of 9.0. Figure 12.4 conveys again that as sample size increases, (a) sampling error (the luck of the draw) tends to decrease, and (b) sample statistics become better (closer) estimators of population parameters.

In real-world research involving means, the researcher does not select an infinite number of random samples. Instead, the researcher selects only one and uses the CLT and related points to

TABLE 12.2 ■ Characteristics of the Sampling Distribution of $\overline{X}$ for Children's Ages for Selected Sample Sizes

| Sample size ($N$) | Mean ($\mu$) | Standard deviation, the standard error of the mean ($\sigma_{\overline{x}}$) | Shape |
|---|---|---|---|
| 100 | 9.0 | $5.0 / \sqrt{100} = 5 / 10 = 0.50$ | Very close to normal |
| 400 | 9.0 | $5.0 / \sqrt{400} = 5 / 20 = 0.25$ | Very close to normal |
| 1,600 | 9.0 | $5.0 / \sqrt{1,600} = 5 / 40 = 0.125$ | Very close to normal |

FIGURE 12.4 ■ Sampling Distributions for Different Sample Sizes

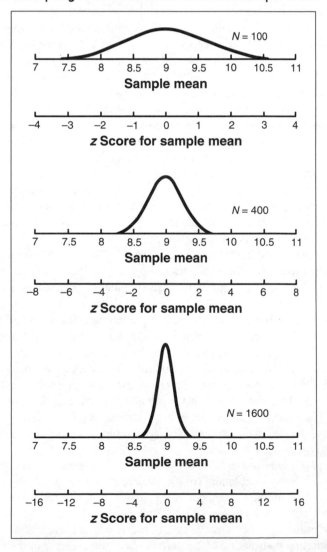

build the sampling distribution. The researcher never knows *exactly* how close her study sample mean is to the population mean. Viewed differently, the researcher never knows which mean in the sampling distribution is her particular sample mean. Yet, using the degree of spread of the sampling distribution as a guide, the researcher can estimate how close to the population mean the study sample mean is likely to be.

When sample size is large, because sample means are often tightly clustered, the researcher can often make a very good (close) estimate of the population mean. When sample size is small, estimates are less precise. The next chapter demonstrates how researchers use sampling distributions to estimate the likely range within which population parameters are located.

## 12.9 ■ CHAPTER SUMMARY

Descriptive statistical procedures describe the study sample. *Inferential statistical procedures* are tools for drawing conclusions about populations based on observations from samples randomly selected from those populations.

The inferential procedures presented in this text should be used only when the study sample is a *simple random sample* (*SRS*; an exception is presented in Chapter 16, Section 16.8). For a sample to be an *SRS*, (a) cases must be selected using a method of chance, (b) each case must have an equal chance of being selected, and (c) the selection of each case must be independent of the selection of each other case (*independence of selection*).

Cases meet the *independence of observations* assumption when they do not share some common unmeasured factor that makes their scores similar (or, very occasionally, dissimilar). Formally, the inferential statistical procedures presented in this text should be used only when the independence of observations assumption is met. Pragmatically, one should assume independence of observations unless there is convincing evidence to the contrary.

A sample is *biased* (possesses *sampling bias*) if its characteristics differ *systematically* from population characteristics. When samples are nonrandom, one typically suspects *sampling bias*. In a random sample, *only* random factors (the luck of the draw) cause differences between sample and population conditions. This is the key advantage of random samples.

*Statistics* are numerical characteristics of samples. *Parameters* are numerical characteristics of populations. When used to estimate a parameter, a statistic is termed an *estimator*. Sample statistics are often symbolized by Roman letters, and population parameters are often symbolized by Greek letters.

Good estimators are efficient and unbiased. An efficient estimator requires a minimum of cases to generate a good estimate. An unbiased estimator neither overestimates nor underestimates a parameter. The sample mean ($\overline{X}$), sample variance ($s^2$), and sample proportion ($p$) are efficient and unbiased. The sample standard deviation ($s$) is efficient and has negligible bias.

*Point estimates* state a specific value. *Interval estimates* state a range of likely values. *Sampling error* is the difference between the sample statistic and the population parameter (sampling error = sample statistic − population parameter). A *sampling distribution* is the distribution of a statistic that results from selecting an infinite number of random samples of the same size from a given population.

The *central limit theorem* states three key points about *the sampling distribution of $\overline{X}$*: (a) its mean equals the mean in the population; (b) its standard deviation equals the standard deviation in the population divided by the square root of the sample size; and (c) as sample size increases, its shape approaches normality. For almost all situations encountered in social science research, the sampling distribution of $\overline{X}$ has a shape that is nearly normal when $N \geq 100$. The standard deviation of the sampling distribution of $\overline{X}$ is termed the standard error of the mean: $\sigma_{\overline{X}} = \sigma/\sqrt{N}$.

As sample size increases, sampling error tends to decrease and sample statistics become better (closer) estimators of population parameters.

## 12.10 ■ PROBLEMS AND QUESTIONS

### Section 12.2

1. Inferential statistical procedures are tools for drawing conclusions about _____ based on _____ that are _____ selected from these _____.

2. For each example, indicate whether the researcher is engaging in inferential or descriptive statistics.
   a. A student summarizes data for residents in a local shelter for those who are homeless.
   b. A student takes a random sample of students at her school of social work and uses responses from this sample to draw conclusions about the population of social work students at this school.
   c. Diana runs 12 rats through mazes and reports their times to fellow students.

### Section 12.3

3. For a sample to be a random sample, it must be selected by a method of _____.

4. For each of the following, indicate whether a method of chance is used in selecting the sample. (Respond yes or no.)
   a. Persons who enter a mall at a given time are asked to respond to a questionnaire.
   b. Students volunteer to participate in a professor's research study.
   c. Names are randomly picked from a hat for participation in a professor's research study.
   d. A computer program randomly selects numbers that determine who will receive a questionnaire.
   e. A therapist works from memory to remember 15 clients that she has served in the prior year and sends a questionnaire to them.
   f. All students in a social work class on gerontology participate in a study.
   g. One hundred students are selected at random from all students at a university.

5. Another name for a random sample is a _____ sample. Another term for a nonrandom sample is a _____ sample.

6. A basic characteristic of a simple random sample is that each case has an _____ chance of being selected.

7. (*True or False*) The inferential statistical procedures presented in this text are valid for both nonrandom and random samples.

8. Provide an example of a sample in which the selection of cases is not independent.

9. Respond "yes," "not sure," or "no" regarding whether the described situation meets the independence of observations assumption. (For some of these, there is probably no single best answer.)

   a. Members of a class ($N = 24$) work in groups of three studying statistics. Later on, they take a statistics test on this material. (Score on the test is the dependent variable.)

   b. One thousand members of a national organization fill out an online survey about their opinions on the organization's work.

   c. Several groups of students copy each others' answers on a test. (Score on the test is the dependent variable.)

   d. One hundred students in a large lecture class fill out an instrument that measures attitudes about volunteerism.

10. What does the author of this text recommend with respect to the independence of observations assumption?

11. Random _____ is the use of methods of chance to assign participants to treatment groups. Random _____ is the use of methods of chance to select the study sample. Random _____ is more important than random _____ in allowing researchers to draw conclusions about causality.

12. Fifty persons volunteer to take part in a smoking cessation study. Methods of chance are used to assign 25 persons to Method A and 25 to Method B. *Respond true or false to each of the following:*

    a. This study uses random sampling.

    b. This study uses random assignment.

    c. This study will allow the researcher to draw causal conclusions about the relative effectiveness of the two methods.

    d. In this research design, many different confounding variables likely bias the results.

    e. The researcher can use inferential statistical procedures to draw conclusions about many different populations across the country.

13. A researcher uses methods of chance to draw a large nationwide sample. She then studies several outcomes, comparing those who grew up in one-parent families (Group 1) to those who grew up in two-parent families (Group 2). *Respond true or false to each of the following:*

    a. This study uses random sampling.

    b. This study uses random assignment to assign to groups.

    c. This study will allow the researcher to draw strong causal conclusions about the impacts of one-parent versus two-parent families.

    d. In this research design, many different confounding variables can affect the results.

    e. The researcher can use inferential statistical procedures to draw conclusions about the large nationwide population from which the sample was drawn.

**Section 12.4**

**14.** *Respond true or false to each of the following:*

    **a.** The characteristics (opinions, responses, etc.) in random samples are precisely the same as those in the populations from which they are selected.

    **b.** Because of the luck of the draw, characteristics of random samples can differ from those of the population from which they are selected.

    **c.** Random samples possess systematic sampling bias.

    **d.** *All* nonrandom samples possess sampling bias.

    **e.** There is often good reason to suspect sampling bias in a nonrandom sample.

    **f.** Inferential statistical procedures may only be used to draw conclusions about the population from which the sample was randomly selected.

    **g.** Researchers may never draw any conclusions at all (by any means whatsoever) about populations other than that from which their sample was selected.

**15.** Indicate (yes or no) regarding whether each of the following demonstrates correct or incorrect reasoning.

    **a.** A random sample of students at a university responds to a questionnaire regarding their attitudes about stem cell research. The researcher uses inferential statistics procedures to draw conclusions about all students at the university.

    **b.** A random sample of students at University A responds to a questionnaire regarding their attitudes about stem cell research. The researcher uses inferential statistics procedures to draw conclusions about students at University B.

    **c.** A researcher at a (highly) prestigious clinic specializing in childhood autism administers a questionnaire to parents. Reasoning (quite appropriately) that almost all of the parents surveyed are highly motivated to improve their children's lives, she uses inferential statistics procedures to draw conclusions about all parents of children with autism.

    **d.** A large national (United States) random sample of children aged 10 years and older who experienced maltreatment in a given time period respond to a questionnaire. A researcher uses inferential statistics procedures to draw conclusions about all children aged 10 years and older in the United States who experienced maltreatment during this time period.

**16.** A student surveys student members of the "Young Republicans Club" regarding their degree of support for public welfare programs. With reference to the population of students at the university, do you think that the degree of support in the sample is similar to that in the population? Do you think sampling bias is present? If you think that bias is present, state its likely nature/direction. Respond in your own words.

**Section 12.5**

**17.** _____ are numerical characteristics of samples. _____ are numerical characteristics of populations.

18. When a sample statistic is used to estimate a population parameter, that statistic is termed an _____ or an _____ _____.

19. Statistics are often symbolized by letters from the _____ alphabet and parameters by (lowercase) letters from the _____ alphabet.

20. Indicate the symbols for both the sample statistic and the population parameter for the following:
    **a.** Mean
    **b.** Standard deviation
    **c.** Variance
    **d.** Proportion

### Section 12.6

21. Good estimators are both _____ and _____.

22. An efficient estimator requires a _____ of cases to generate a good estimate.

23. The quality of unbiasedness conveys that an estimator tends neither to _____ nor _____ the parameter.

24. Assuming random sampling, indicate whether each of the following sample statistics is a biased or unbiased estimate of its counterpart in the population.
    **a.** $\overline{X}$
    **b.** $s$
    **c.** $s^2$
    **d.** $p$

25. The mean of a randomly selected sample is 10 and its standard deviation is 6. Estimate the mean and standard deviation of the population from which the sample was selected.

26. In a random sample, $\overline{X} = 10$ and $s = 6$. What are the best estimates of $\mu$ and $\sigma$?

27. In a randomly selected sample, 28% of adults indicate that they agree with a given statement. What is your best estimate of the percentage of adults who agree with that statement in the population from which the sample was selected?

28. In a given randomly selected sample, $p = .25$. What is your best estimate of $P$?

29. When a statistic estimates a specific value, that estimate is termed a _____ _____. An _____ _____ specifies a range within which a population parameter is likely to be located.

**Section 12.7**

30. The difference between a sample statistic and a population parameter is termed _____ _____.

31. What is the sampling error in each situation?
    a. The mean of a random sample is 18. The mean of the population from which the sample was selected is 20.
    b. The mean of a random sample is 20. The mean of the population from which the sample was selected is 18.
    c. The proportion in a random sample is .62. The proportion in the population from which the sample was selected is .53.
    d. The proportion in a random sample is .53. The proportion in the population from which the sample was selected is .62.

32. Define sampling distribution in your own words.

33. The cases in a sampling distribution are the _____ from the random samples used to build it.

34. In your own words, how would you build a sampling distribution of the number of heads obtained from flipping a coin 5 times? (Assume that you have time to generate an infinite number of samples of coin flips.)

35. In your own words, how would you build a sampling distribution of the mean? (Assume that you have time to pick an infinite number of random samples.)

36. The _____ _____ theorem states three key things about the sampling distribution of the mean.

37. What three things does the CLT state about the sampling distribution of $\overline{X}$?

38. The standard deviation of the sampling distribution of $\overline{X}$ is termed the _____ _____ of the _____ and is symbolized by ____ ____.

39. Whenever $N$ is $\geq 100$, the shape of the sampling distribution of $\overline{X}$ is close to _____.

40. (*True or False*) In "real-world" research, researchers select an infinite number of samples (or at least an exceedingly large number) so that they can construct the sampling distribution of $\overline{X}$.

TABLE 12.3  ■  Examples Involving the Sampling Distribution of $\overline{X}$

| Example | Mean of Population ($\mu$) | Standard Deviation of Population ($s$) | Shape of Population From Which Samples are Randomly Selected | Sample Size (Size of Randomly Selected Samples) ($N$) |
|---|---|---|---|---|
| 1 | 25 | 10 | negative skew | 100 |
| 2 | 25 | 10 | positive skew | 400 |
| 3 | 25 | 10 | negative skew | 16 |
| 4 | 25 | 25 | uniform | 100 |
| 5 | 40 | 16 | bimodal | 256 |

**41.** For each example in Table 12.3, indicate the mean, standard deviation ($\sigma_{\overline{x}}$, the standard error of the mean), and shape of the sampling distribution of the mean. (Hint: For Example 3, observe the sample size.)

**42.** For Example 1 in the prior question, indicate the approximate percentage of means (cases) in the sampling distribution of $\overline{X}$ that are located in the following ranges. Hint: The standard error of $\overline{X}$ is simply the standard deviation of the sampling distribution; call on your knowledge of the normal curve to answer these (see Chapter 5, Section 5.6).
  **a.**  $\mu \pm 1$ standard error of $\overline{X}$
  **b.**  $\mu \pm 2$ standard errors of $\overline{X}$
  **c.**  $\mu \pm 3$ standard errors of $\overline{X}$

## Section 12.8

**43.** In Example 1 in Table 12.3 ($N = 100$), approximately what percentage of means are located between 24 and 26? What is this percentage for Example 2 ($N = 400$)?

**44.** The standard deviation in a population is 20. Indicate the standard error of the mean for the sampling distribution of the mean for this population for the following sample sizes: $N = 25$, $N = 100$, $N = 400$, $N = 1,600$.

**45.** As sample size increases (other things being equal), the spread of the sampling distribution of the mean _____. As sample size increases, $\sigma_{\overline{x}}$ (the standard error of the mean) _____.

# 13

# CONFIDENCE INTERVALS FOR MEANS AND PROPORTIONS

## 13.1 ■ CHAPTER OVERVIEW

Chapter 13 focuses on *confidence intervals*, a key application of inferential statistics. It presents theory, formulas, and calculations for the 95% and 99% *confidence interval of the mean* and the 95% and 99% *confidence interval of the proportion*. In closing, it discusses five issues pertaining to confidence intervals.

## 13.2 ■ WHAT IS A CONFIDENCE INTERVAL?

When researchers use inferential statistics to determine the likely range within which a parameter is located, that estimate is an *interval estimate*. A more common term for interval estimate is *confidence interval*. A **confidence interval** is the likely range within which a population parameter is located. The most common confidence interval is the **95% confidence interval**, the range within which the researcher is 95% confident that the population parameter is located. The **99% confidence interval** is the range within which the researcher is 99% confident that the population parameter is located. Learning how to construct these intervals for means and proportions are the key goals of this chapter. The theory behind confidence intervals for means is presented subsequently.

## 13.3 ■ CONFIDENCE INTERVALS FOR MEANS

### 13.3.1 ■ Theory

The central limit theorem (CLT) and related information from Chapter 12 tell us that the sampling distribution of $\overline{X}$ has (a) a mean equal to the population from which the infinite number of samples have been randomly selected, (b) a standard deviation equal to the population standard deviation divided by the square root of the sample size $\sigma_{\overline{x}} = \sigma/\sqrt{N}$ (where $\sigma_{\overline{x}}$ is the standard error of the mean), and (c) given that $N \geq 100$, a nearly normal shape. As you recall, the cases of the sampling distribution of $\overline{X}$ are the means of the random samples used in building it.

Let us add some new information, when $N \geq 100$, a researcher can, almost without exception, obtain a close (good) estimate of the standard deviation of the sampling distribution (of $\sigma_{\overline{x}}$, the standard error of the mean) by dividing the standard deviation of a random sample ($s$) by the square root of the sample size ($N$). Expressed as a formula

$$s_{\overline{x}} = \frac{s}{\sqrt{N}}$$

(13.1)

where $s_{\bar{X}}$ is the estimate of the standard error of the mean, $s$ is the standard deviation in the researcher's sample, and $N$ is the size of the researcher's sample. This estimate is sufficiently accurate for use in forming confidence intervals for means whenever $N \geq 100$.[1]

Suppose that a researcher selects a single random sample of size 100 or greater from a population. From the CLT and the additional information provided, the researcher knows the following about the sampling distribution of $\bar{X}$ for that population: (a) its mean equals the mean in the population, (b) its standard deviation is closely estimated by $\frac{s}{\sqrt{N}}$, and (c) its shape is close to normal.

Drawing on the just-presented points and using her knowledge of the normal distribution, the researcher knows that about 95% of means (cases) in the sampling distribution are located within two estimated standard errors (two estimated standard deviations of the sampling distribution, $2 \times s/\sqrt{N} = 2 \times s_{\bar{X}}$) of the population mean. From this point forward, I typically do not state "estimated" standard error (or "estimated" standard deviation). As sample size is 100 or greater, the estimate is a good one and, thus, "estimated" is not needed.

Given that 95% of sample means are located within two standard errors (two standard deviations of the sampling distribution) of the population mean, the researcher can be 95% *confident* that this is so for *any particular sample mean*. The mean of the researcher's sample can be (and indeed is) viewed as one of the means (one of the cases) in the sampling distribution. This being so, the researcher can be 95% confident that the mean of her sample is located within two standard errors of the population mean. Because she is 95% confident that the mean of her sample is located within two standard errors of the population mean, she can be 95% confident that the population mean is located within a range that is defined by a line that extends two standard errors in both directions from her sample's mean.

The just-presented discussion comprises the nuts-and-bolts of the formation of 95% confidence intervals for means. By extending a line two standard errors (two standard deviations of the sampling distribution, $2 \times s_{\bar{X}}$) in both directions from the study sample mean, the researcher establishes a range—an interval—within which she is 95% confident that the population mean is located.

Let us now reintroduce the child maltreatment data from Chapter 12 into our discussion of confidence intervals. Recall from Section 12.7.2 that, in the full population of child maltreatment reports: the mean ($\mu$) for children's age equals 9.0 years and the standard deviation ($\sigma$) equals 5.0 years. In Chapter 12, we built a sampling distribution of $\bar{X}$ by drawing an infinite number of random samples of size 100 (see Figure 12.3). (Our example here is less than fully realistic because in real-world research, we do not have information about the population.)

As we know the population standard deviation, we can use it to create a confidence interval. As presented in Chapter 12, the standard deviation of the sampling distribution (the standard error) is given by $\sigma_{\bar{X}} = \sigma/\sqrt{N}$ and, thus, $\sigma_{\bar{X}} = 5.0/\sqrt{100} = 0.50$ years. Following the logic of our discussion, we create a confidence interval by extending a line two standard errors, that is $2 \times 0.50$ years $= 1.00$ year, in both directions from a (randomly selected) sample mean.[2]

Suppose now that we select five random samples ($N = 100$) from the child maltreatment report population and calculate the mean for each. Think of each as the mean from a different study sample. Suppose further that we extend a line 1 year (two standard errors) in both directions from each mean. Figure 13.1 presents the sampling distribution, the means, and the lines.

The lines extended from means A, B, and C include the mean of the sampling distribution and, thus, the population mean. For instance, the line for A extends from about 7.7–9.7 years ($8.7 \pm 1.0$), a range that includes the population mean of 9.0 years. Similarly, the line for B extends from about 8.5–10.5 years ($9.5 \pm 1.0$) and, thus, includes the population mean. On the other hand, the lines for means D and E do not include the mean of the sampling distribution and, therefore, do not include the population mean. For instance, the line around D extends from about 6.8–8.8 ($7.8 \pm 1.0$).

FIGURE 13.1 ■ Five Confidence Intervals

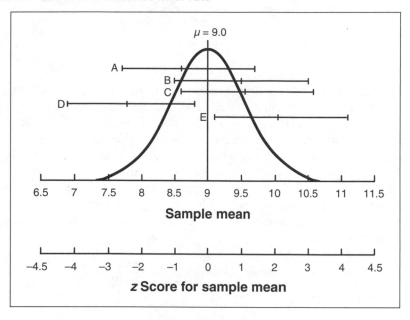

The lines in Figure 13.1 convey 95% confidence intervals. For 95% of sample means in the sampling distribution of $\overline{X}$, the population mean is located within the range that is defined by a line extended two standard errors (two standard deviations) in both directions. Stated differently, 95% of 95% confidence intervals of the mean include the population mean.

The lines extending from means A, B, and C are examples of such 95% confidence intervals, that is, of the 95% that include the mean. For 5% of sample means, the population mean is not located within the range defined by a line extended two standard errors in both directions. Stated differently, 5% of 95% confidence intervals of the mean do not include the population mean. The lines extending from means D and E are examples of such 95% confidence intervals, that is, of the 5% that do not include the mean.

In real-world research, the researcher does not know whether the 95% confidence interval constructed around her particular study sample mean includes the population mean. She can, however, be 95% confident that it does so—or, viewed differently, 5% "confident" that it does not.

### 13.3.2 ■ Formulas and Computation

This chapter has often stated that about 95% of cases in a normal distribution are located within two standard deviations of the mean. To be more precise, 95% of cases in a normal distribution are located within 1.96 standard deviations of the mean (see Table A.1). Hence, 1.96 rather than 2.00 is used in confidence interval formulas. The formulas that follow for confidence intervals of the mean may be used whenever sample size is 100 or greater. Thus, I termed them "large sample" formulas. Chapter 17 (Section 17.5) presents confidence interval formulas for smaller sample sizes. All of the formulas may only be used when the study sample is a random sample.

The **95% confidence interval of the mean** (*95% CI of* $\mu$) is the range within which one is 95% confident that the population mean is located. The first large sample formula is

$$95\% \ CI \ of \ \mu = \overline{X} \pm 1.96\left(\frac{s}{\sqrt{N}}\right) \tag{13.2}$$

where $\overline{X}$ is the mean of the randomly selected study sample, $s$ is the standard deviation of the sample, and $N$ is the sample size. An alternative formula is

*95% CI of* $\mu = \overline{X} \pm 1.96\ (s_{\overline{x}})$                                                                (13.3)

where $s_{\overline{x}}$ is the estimate of the standard error of mean.

Continuing on with the child maltreatment example, let us now compute the 95% confidence interval for the mean age of children. As we proceed, please "forget" that data was provided earlier for the full population of maltreatment reports ($\mu = 9.0$ years; $\sigma = 5.0$ years). In the "real world," you do not have information about the population—if you did, you would not construct a confidence interval. For instance, if you already know the population mean, it makes no sense to build a range within which you are confident that it is located.

In Chapter 12, Section 12.6, you selected a random sample of 100 cases from a large, statewide database of maltreatment reports. The mean age of children in your sample was 8.5 years with a standard deviation of 4.9 years. To calculate the 95% confidence interval for the population mean:

**1.** divide $s$ by $\sqrt{N}$ to estimate the standard error of the mean:

$s_{\overline{x}} = 4.9/\sqrt{100} = 0.49,$

**2.** multiply by 1.96: $0.49 \times 1.96 = 0.96$, and
**3.** add and subtract from $\overline{X}$: *95% CI of* $\mu = 8.5 \pm .96 = 7.54$ to 9.46.

Hence, the *95% CI of* $\mu$ extends from 7.54–9.46 years.

Although one never knows for sure whether a particular 95% confidence interval includes the mean, one knows that *95%* do so, and thus, one can have 95% confidence for any given one. As such, we can be 95% confident that the mean age of children in the population of maltreatment reports is located in the interval that extends from 7.54–9.46 years.

As sample size increases, the width of the 95% confidence interval decreases. For instance, let us compute a 95% confidence interval keeping all things the same, except that let us now assume a sample size of 400. In other words: $\overline{X} = 8.5$, $s = 4.9$, $N = 400$. To compute the confidence interval:

**1.** divide $s$ by $\sqrt{N}$ to estimate the standard error of the mean:

$s_{\overline{x}} = 4.9/\sqrt{100} = 4.9/20 = 0.245,$

**2.** multiply by 1.96: $.245 \times 1.96 = 0.48$, and
**3.** add and subtract from $\overline{X}$: *95% CI of* $\mu = 8.50 \pm .48 = 8.02$–8.98.

The increased sample size results in a narrower 95% confidence interval, that is in a more precise range within which the researcher has 95% confidence that the population mean is located.

As presented earlier, the mean age in the full population of maltreatment reports is 9.0 years. If we continue to presume this to be the case, then this particular confidence interval does not include the population mean. It just misses. Hence, this particular *95% CI* is one of the 5% of such intervals that do not include the mean. Of course, in real-world research, the researcher does not know assuredly that a particular 95% confidence interval includes the mean, although she is 95% confident that this is so.

Sometimes, 95% confidence is not enough. For instance, suppose that a state legislator comes across your study on child maltreatment and phones you about it. Let us presume that your report states that the 95% confidence interval extends from 7.54–9.46 years, the interval when $N = 100$. You explain to the legislator that this indicates that one can be 95% confident that the mean age for the full population of children is within a range that extends from 7.54–9.46 years. She conveys to you that 95% confidence is not sufficient and that, given the importance of the legislative changes in child welfare that she is proposing, 100% confidence is required. You explain to her that, short of studying the full population, there is no way of being *100%* confident about the mean age. It was stated earlier that your sample was drawn from a large, computerized database. You suggest to her that she contact the chief data analyst at the child welfare agency so that she may gain access to data for the full population and, thus, have exact knowledge rather than only some level of confidence. She responds: "There is no time. The hearing is in 2 hours." Perhaps, she suggests, if we could be 99% confident rather than just 95% confident, that would satisfy the legislators who will be voting. You explain that you can calculate such an interval and that you will call her back in 5 minutes.

A **99% confidence interval** is the interval within which the researcher is 99% confident that the population parameter is located. In the long run, 99% of 99% confidence intervals include the population parameter and 1% do not.

The **99% confidence interval of the mean** (*99% CI of* μ) is the interval within which the researcher is 99% confident that the population mean is located. It is constructed using the same logic as is a 95% interval. In a normal distribution, 99% of cases are located within 2.58 standard deviations of the population mean (see Table A.1). Given that $N \geq 100$, if we extend a line 2.58 standard errors ($2.58 \times s_{\bar{X}}$) in both directions from the mean of a randomly selected study sample, we can be 99% confident that this line includes the population mean.

The large sample formula for the 99% confidence interval of the mean requires a sample size of at least 100:

$$99\% \ CI \ of \ \mu = \overline{X} \pm 2.58 \left( \frac{s}{\sqrt{N}} \right) \tag{13.4}$$

An alternative and equivalent formula is

$$99\% \ CI \ of \ \mu = \overline{X} \pm 2.58 \ (s_{\bar{X}}) \tag{13.5}$$

Assume that the child maltreatment data remains the same: $\overline{X} = 8.5$, $s = 4.9$, $N = 100$. The 99% confidence interval is

$$8.5 \pm 2.58(4.9/\sqrt{100}) = 8.5 \pm 2.58(4.9/10) = 8.5 \pm 1.26 = 7.24\text{–}9.76.$$

Having finished your calculation, you phone the legislator back and inform her that you are 99% confident that the mean age of children in the full population is within the interval that ranges from 7.24–9.76 years. Unfortunately, the legislator is again frustrated and responds: "I wanted to be more confident about the children's average age, but you have given me a wider range than before. How can this be?"

Given the same sample size and other things being equal, 99% confidence intervals are always *wider* than are 95% confidence intervals. This should make intuitive sense: To be more confident that the interval contains the population parameter, the researcher must specify a wider range.

Although our state legislator had hoped otherwise, 99% confidence intervals are not "better" than 95% confidence intervals. And, by the same token, 95% intervals are not "better" than 99% intervals. In deciding which interval to use, the researcher has a trade-off. She can either specify a more precise (narrower) interval (the *95% CI*) but have less confidence that it includes the mean (95% vs. 99%) or she can specify a less precise (wider) interval (the *99% CI*) but have greater confidence (99% vs. 95%) that it does so.

The degree of confidence that the researcher has that a confidence interval contains the population parameter is called the **confidence level**. For 95% intervals, the confidence level is 95% and for 99% intervals, it is 99%.

To truly improve an estimate, a researcher cannot simply use a different confidence interval. Instead, she must select a larger sample, which reduces the likely sampling error. Sticking with the current example ($\overline{X} = 8.5$, $s = 4.9$), increasing the sample size to 400 results in a 99% confidence interval of:

$$8.5 \pm 2.58(4.9/\sqrt{400}) = 8.5 \pm (4.9/20) = 8.5 \pm 0.63 = 7.87\text{--}9.13$$

Notice that the increase in sample size reduces the width of the confidence interval. When sample size was 100, the *99% CI* extended from 7.24–9.76 years. Both of the just-mentioned intervals do include the population mean. (Although, as stated several times, in real-world research, you would not know this.)

In summary, calculation of confidence intervals for population means is straightforward and useful. We now move on to confidence intervals for proportions.

## 13.4 ■ CONFIDENCE INTERVALS FOR PROPORTIONS AND PERCENTAGES

### 13.4.1 ■ Theory

Confidence intervals for proportions (percentages) draw on the same statistical theory as do those for means. A researcher builds a **sampling distribution of the proportion (sampling distribution of $p$)** by (a) selecting a random sample of given size ($N$) from a population, (b) calculating the proportion of cases in the sample with some characteristic, (c) plotting this proportion, and (d) repeating the first three steps an infinite number of times. Of course, in real-world research, the researcher does not draw an infinite number of samples but instead, makes use of statistical theory. As we move forward, recall from Chapter 12, Table 12.1 that $P$ symbolizes the proportion in a population and $p$ symbolizes that in a sample.

Earlier, we used the CLT to describe the characteristics of the sampling distribution of $\overline{X}$. The CLT may also be used to describe the sampling distribution of $p$. It states the following about this distribution:

1. Its mean equals the proportion in the population ($P$);
2. Its standard deviation, **the standard error of the proportion (the standard error of $p$)**, symbolized by $\sigma_p$, is:

$$\sigma_p = \sqrt{\frac{P(1 - P)}{N}} \tag{13.6}$$

3. As sample size ($N$) increases, its shape approaches that of a normal distribution.

As discussed earlier, the shape of the sampling distribution of $\overline{X}$ is close to normal whenever $N \geq 100$. The shape of the sampling distribution of $p$ is close to normal whenever both $NP$ and $N(1-P)$ are $\geq 10$.

Let us build a sampling distribution of $p$ using the child maltreatment reports example. Recall that in the population of reports in the state database, the proportion of abuse reports was .43, that is, $P = .43$. Suppose that we pick an infinite number of random samples of size 100 ($N = 100$) and, for each sample, calculate the proportion of abuse reports and plot this proportion. By doing so, we build a sampling distribution of $p$.

FIGURE 13.2 ■ Sampling Distribution of the Proportion of Abuse Reports

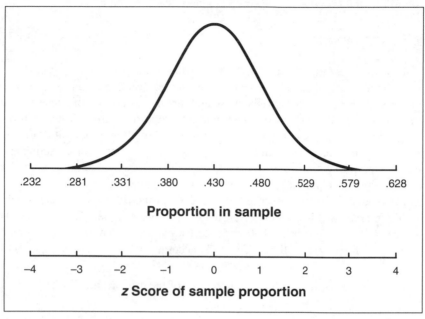

What will be the characteristics of this distribution? Its mean will be 0.43 (from Point 1). Its standard deviation (the standard error of $p$) will be

$$\sigma_p = \sqrt{\frac{.43(1 - .43)}{100}} = \sqrt{\frac{.43(.57)}{100}} = \sqrt{\frac{.245}{100}} = \sqrt{.00245} = .0495 \text{ (from Point 2)}.$$

In our example:

$$NP = 100(.43) = 43, \text{ and } N(1 - P) = 100(1 - .43) = 100(.57) = 57.$$

From Point 3, and because both $NP$ and $N(1 - P)$ are $\geq 10$, its shape will be close to normal. Figure 13.2 presents this distribution.

## 13.4.2 ■ Formulas and Application

Just as is so for the standard error of the mean ($\sigma_{\bar{X}}$, the standard deviation of the sampling distribution of $\bar{X}$) in actual research, the standard error of the proportion ($\sigma_p$) is not known and, thus, is estimated:

$$s_p = \sqrt{\frac{p(1 - p)}{N}} \tag{13.7}$$

where $s_p$ is the estimate of the standard error of the proportion (the estimate of the standard deviation of the sampling distribution), $p$ is the proportion in the sample, and $N$ is the sample size. Whenever both $Np$ and $N(1 - p)$ are greater than 10, the estimate of $s_p$ is sufficiently accurate to use in confidence interval formulas for proportions.[3]

The **95% confidence interval of the proportion** (of $P$) is the interval within which the researcher is 95% confident that the population proportion is located. One formula is

$$95\% \ CI \ of \ P = p \pm 1.96\sqrt{\frac{p(1 - p)}{N}} \tag{13.8}$$

where *95% CI* of *P* is the 95% confidence interval of the proportion, *p* is the proportion in the sample proportion, and *N* is the sample size. An alternative formula is

$$95\% \ CI \ of \ P = p \pm 1.96(s_p) \tag{13.9}$$

where $s_p$ is the estimate of the standard error of the proportion.

Let us continue to use the child maltreatment example. Recall that you selected a single random sample of size 100 from the large database and that the proportion of abuse reports in your sample was .40. It is hoped that it is intuitive that this proportion differs from the proportion in the population of reports ($P = .43$). This is the essence of sampling error, that is, due to the luck of the draw, sample characteristics (almost always) differ from population parameters. Indeed, in a real-world example, you have no information on the population and, thus, do not know the difference between the sample statistic and the population parameter.

Let us calculate a 95% confidence interval for the proportion of abuse cases. First, let us verify that this interval will be sufficiently accurate. In your sample: $Np = 100 \times 0.40 = 40$ abuse cases and $N(1 - p) = 100 \times 0.60 = 60$ cases that are not abuse cases. As both $Np$ and $N(1 - p)$ are $\geq 10$, the interval will be sufficiently accurate. To calculate it, do the following:

**1.** Calculate $s_p$, the estimate of the standard error of the proportion:

$$s_p = \sqrt{\frac{.40(1 - .40)}{100}} = \sqrt{\frac{(.60)(.40)}{100}} = \sqrt{\frac{.24}{100}} = 0.049$$

**2.** Multiply by 1.96:

$$1.96 \times 0.049 = 0.096$$

**3.** Add and subtract from *p* (the sample proportion):

*95% CI* of *P* = .40 ± .096 = .304–.496

The *95% CI* of *P* (the population proportion) spans the interval from .304–.496. We can be 95% confident that the proportion of abuse reports in the large statewide maltreatment database is located within this range. To express this interval in percentages, we multiply by 100. Expressed in percentages, the confidence interval spans from 30.4% to 49.6%.

The **99% confidence interval of the proportion** (of *P*) is the interval within which the researcher is 99% confident that the population proportion is located. One formula is

$$99\% \ CI \ of \ P = p \pm 2.58 \sqrt{\frac{p(1 - p)}{N}} \tag{13.10}$$

An alternative formula is

$$99\% \ CI \ of \ P = p \pm 2.58(s_p) \tag{13.11}$$

We may now calculate the 99% confidence interval for the proportion of abuse reports. We know already that both $Np$ and $N(1 - p)$ are $\geq 10$. Further, the estimate of the standard error of *p* (.049) has been calculated. Hence, we simply insert it into our calculations:

*99% CI* of *P* = .40 ± 2.58(.049) = .40 ± .126 = .274–.526

We can be 99% confident that the proportion of abuse reports in the population is located within the interval that extends from .274–.526. Expressed in percentages, we are 99% confident that the percentage of abuse reports in the population is between 27.4% and 52.6%. As always, given identical data, the 99% interval (.274–.526) is wider than the 95% interval (.304–.496).

## 13.5 ■ FIVE MORE THINGS TO KNOW

First: You have probably heard the term *margin of error* on newscasts. For instance, "The percentage that supports the president on this issue is 44%, with a margin of error of 6%." *Margin of error* and *confidence intervals* are different ways of expressing the same thing. If you listen carefully to a newscast, you might hear something like, "The percentage that supports the president is 44% with a margin of error of 6% with 95% confidence." This is just another way of expressing a confidence interval. In this example, one can be 95% confident that the percentage in the full population is between 44% ± 6%, in other words, between 38% and 50%.

Second: This chapter's formulas assume that samples have been randomly selected from populations that are infinite in size. In the real world, no such populations exist. Pragmatically, the formulas work well when the sample comprises about 10% or less of the population. When the sample comprises more than this, the formulas result in intervals that are too wide and, thus, are not recommended. (See Rosenthal, 2001 for a way to adjust the intervals in this situation.)

As mentioned at the beginning of this chapter, the formulas in the chapter are designed for use with simple random samples. When the sample is not a simple random sample, they should not be used.

Third: Although counterintuitive, the width of the confidence interval for both means and proportions is affected hardly at all by the size of the population from which the sample is randomly selected. For instance, a random sample of 100 persons drawn from a small town of 2,000 will result in a confidence interval (for a mean or for a proportion) of approximately the same width as will a random sample of 100 persons drawn from the *entire* U.S. population. The size of the *sample—not* that of the population from which the sample is selected—is the primary determinant of the width of the confidence interval. The one exception to this occurs when the sample comprises a significant percentage of the population, say 10% or greater, in which case, the confidence interval can be affected. (As just discussed, when a sample comprises 10% or more of a population, the formulas presented in this chapter result in confidence intervals that are too wide; see Rosenthal, 2001).

Fourth: The fourth point concerns nonresponse. So far, this chapter has assumed that all randomly selected cases indeed become part of the study sample. In survey research, however, some percent does not respond. For instance, a response rate of 70% is excellent for a mailed questionnaire (Rubin & Babbie, 1997). One problem with nonresponse is that sample size decreases and, thus, confidence intervals get wider. The much greater problem concerns possible bias. Typically, persons choose not to respond for particular reasons. For instance, those who were dissatisfied with agency services may be less likely to respond to a services satisfaction questionnaire than those who were satisfied. The major issue raised by nonresponse is that the researcher has no way to know whether the opinions of nonresponders are similar to or different from those of responders.

Suppose that one selects a large random sample but there is substantial nonresponse. In such a situation, because of the random selection process, one can be confident that the opinions of the *responding* sample are representative of those in the population who *would also have returned the questionnaire* had it been sent to them. Obviously, this is not the population of interest. When there is substantial nonresponse, opinions in the responding sample may well be biased relative to those in the full population. Bias caused by nonresponse is called **nonresponse bias**.

There is no easy way to deal with nonresponse bias. In general, one should be alert to such bias whenever there is substantial nonresponse, say about 10% or higher.

Fifth: The fifth and final point is that although this text presents confidence intervals only for means and proportions, they are used in many other situations. For instance, suppose that the correlation between the number of visits of family members and the happiness of residents in nursing homes (as measured on some scale) is 0.28 in a random sample of 100 cases. A researcher could calculate a 95% (or 99%) confidence interval for this correlation. In this example, the confidence interval works out to .09 to .45. Hence, the researcher could be 95% confident that the correlation in the population from which the sample was randomly selected is located within this range.

Or, as another example, suppose that in an experimental study, the mean score in the Intervention 1 group is 12 points higher than that in the Intervention 2 group on some outcome measure. The researcher could compute a 95% confidence interval for this difference between the group means. If, for instance, that interval worked out to 7 to 17 points, then the researcher could be 95% confident that, in the population from which persons were randomly sampled, the actual difference in means is somewhere in the range of 7 to 17 points.

## 13.6 ■ CHAPTER SUMMARY

A *confidence interval* is the likely range within which a population parameter is located. The *95% confidence interval* is the interval within which the researcher is 95% confident that the population parameter is located.

When $N \geq 100$, the standard error of the mean ($\sigma_{\bar{X}}$; the standard deviation of the sampling distribution of the mean) can be estimated using information from a single random sample: $s_{\bar{X}} = s/\sqrt{N}$. Extending a line two standard errors ($2 \times s_{\bar{X}}$) from the study sample mean creates a range within which the researcher is 95% confident that the population mean is located. This is a *95% confidence interval of the mean (95% CI of* $\mu$*)*. A formula is

$$95\% \; CI \; of \; \mu = \bar{X} \pm 1.96(s_{\bar{X}})$$

Ninety-five percent of 95% confidence intervals include the population parameter. The researcher never knows for sure whether a particular 95% confidence interval includes the population parameter. However, because 95% do so, the researcher can have 95% confidence for any given one.

A *99% confidence interval* is the interval within which the researcher is 99% confident that the population parameter is located. Ninety-nine percent of 99% confidence intervals include the population parameter. A formula for the 99% confidence interval of the mean is

$$99\% \; CI \; of \; \mu = \bar{X} \pm 2.58(s_{\bar{X}})$$

Other things being equal, as sample size increases, the width of confidence interval decreases. At any given sample size, the 99% confidence interval is wider than the 95% interval. *95% CIs* are not "better" than *99% CIs* and *99% CIs* are not "better" than *95% CIs*.

The CLT describes the characteristics of the *sampling distribution of the proportion (of p)*: its mean equals the proportion in the population ($P$), its standard deviation, the *standard error of the proportion (of p;* $\sigma_p$*)*, is given by

$$\sigma_p = \sqrt{\frac{P(1 - P)}{N}},$$

and, as sample size increases, its shape approaches normality.

The standard error of $p$ is estimated by

$$s_p = \sqrt{\frac{p(1-p)}{N}}$$

The *95% confidence interval of the proportion* (*of P*) is the interval within which the researcher is 95% confident that the population proportion is located. A formula is

$$95\% \ CI \ of \ P = p \pm 1.96 \ (s_p)$$

The *99% confidence interval of the proportion* (*of P*) is the interval within which the researcher is 99% confident that the population proportion (percentage) is located. A formula is

$$99\% \ CI \ of \ P = p \pm 2.58 \sqrt{\frac{p(1-p)}{N}}$$

The confidence interval of the proportion formulas may be used when both $Np$ and $N(1-p) \geq 10$.

The chapter makes five closing points. First, *margins of error* and confidence intervals convey the same information. Second, its formulas work well only when the sample represents about 10% or less of the population. Third, the width of the confidence interval is affected hardly at all by the size of the population from which the sample is selected. Fourth, *nonresponse bias* can bias results. Fifth, confidence intervals can be formed for many applications other than means and proportions.

## 13.7 ■ PROBLEMS AND QUESTIONS

### Section 13.2

1.  A synonym and more common term for interval estimate is _____ \_\_\_\_ \_\_\_\_.

2.  Define confidence interval in your own words.

3.  The _____ _____ _____ is the interval within which the researcher is 95% _____ that the population parameter is located.

4.  The _____ _____ _____ is the interval within which the researcher is 99% _____ that the population parameter is located.

### Section 13.3

5.  The standard deviation of the sampling distribution of the mean is termed the standard _____ of the mean. It is equal to the _____ _____ in the population from which samples are randomly selected and divided by the _____ _____ of the sample _____.

6.  When $N \geq 100$, a researcher may obtain a close (good) estimate of the standard deviation of the sampling distribution by dividing the _____ _____ of the study sample by the _____ _____ of the sample size.

7.  What is the formula for $s_{\bar{x}}$, the estimate of the standard error of the mean?

8.  *The next group of questions are true/false*. Assume that all are random samples and also that sample size is 100 or greater.

    **a.** *All* cases/means in the sampling distribution of the mean are located within 2 standard deviations ($s_{\bar{x}} \times 2$) of the (unknown) population mean, $\mu$.

    **b.** About 95% of cases/means in the sampling distribution of the mean are located within two standard deviations ($s_{\bar{x}} \times 2$) of the (unknown) population mean, $\mu$.

    **c.** A line extended two standard deviations for both directions ($s_{\bar{x}} \times 2$) from the study sample mean *always* includes the population mean, $\mu$.

    **d.** For about 95% of study sample means, a line extended two standard deviations ($s_{\bar{x}} \times 2$) in both directions includes the population mean, $\mu$.

    **e.** The researcher can be 100% confident that a line extended two standard deviations ($s_{\bar{x}} \times 2$) in both directions from the study sample mean includes the population mean, $\mu$.

    **f.** The researcher can be 95% confident that a line extended two standard deviations ($s_{\bar{x}} \times 2$) in both directions from the study sample mean includes the population mean, $\mu$.

9.  The line described in question 8f establishes a _____% _____ _____ of the _____.

10. In your own words, describe the steps in formulating a 95% confidence interval of the mean.

11. What percentage of 95% confidence intervals include the population mean? (Stated differently, what percentage of 95% confidence intervals establish a range within which the population mean is located?) What percentage of 95% confidence intervals do not include the mean?

12. (*True or False*) The researcher can be 100% sure that his or her confidence interval does indeed include the population mean.

13. A researcher selects a random sample size of 144 from a population. The mean of this sample is 24 with a standard deviation of 18. What is the 95% confidence interval for the population mean?

14. Using Formula 13.2 or 13.3, calculate 95% confidence intervals of $\mu$ (the mean) for the following examples in Table 13.1.

TABLE 13.1 ■ Examples for Computing Confidence Intervals of $\mu$

| Example | $\bar{X}$ | N | s |
|---|---|---|---|
| #1 | 50 | 100 | 10 |
| #2 | 50 | 100 | 20 |
| #3 | 50 | 400 | 20 |
| #4 | 50 | 1600 | 20 |
| #5 | 100 | 1600 | 20 |
| #6 | 100 | 400 | 10 |
| #7 | 50 | 9[a] | 6 |

[a]Are the formulas presented in this chapter appropriate when $N = 9$?

15. As sample size increases (other things being equal), the width of the 95% confidence interval of $\mu$ _____.

16. In the long run, what percentage of 95% confidence intervals include the unknown population parameter?

17. What percentage of 99% confidence intervals include the unknown population parameter.

18. The researcher can be _____% confident that a 95% confidence interval includes the population parameter. The researcher can be _____% confident that a 99% confidence interval does so. The degree of confidence that the researcher has that the confidence interval includes the population parameter is termed the _____ _____.

19. Calculate 99% confidence intervals for Examples 2, 3, and 4 in Table 13.1.

20. Given that all other factors are equal, a 95% confidence interval is _____ than a 99% confidence interval.

21. Given that all other factors are equal, a 99% confidence interval is _____ than a 95% confidence interval.

### Section 13.4

22. The symbol for the proportion in a sample is _____; the symbol for that in a population is _____.

23. Describe the steps in creating a sampling distribution of the proportion. (Assume that you have an infinite amount of time to carry out this task.)

24. The central limit theorem states the following about the sampling distribution of the proportion: Its mean equals the _____ in the population; Its standard _____, symbolized by _____ and termed the _____ _____ of the _____ equals $\sqrt{\dfrac{P(1-P)}{N}}$ ; and, as sample size increases, its shape approaches that of a _____ distribution.

25. Using Formula 13.6, $\sigma_p = \sqrt{\dfrac{P(1-P)}{N}}$ , calculate the standard error of the proportion in each situation. Each example provides information on the proportion in the population ($P$) and on the sample size ($N$) used in building the sampling distribution.
    a. $P = .1, N = 50$
    b. $P = .9, N = 50$
    c. $P = .9, N = 100$
    d. $P = .8, N = 100$
    e. $P = .7, N = 100$
    f. $P = .5, N = 100$

26. The estimate of the standard deviation of the sampling distribution of the proportion is symbolized by _____ and equals _____ (provide formula). This estimate is a good one whenever both $Np$ and $N(1 - p)$ are $\geq$ _____.

27. For each of the following situations: (a) calculate $Np$ and $N(1 - p)$ and (b) indicate (yes or no) whether the estimate of $s_p$ is sufficiently accurate for carrying out the confidence interval formulas. Each example provides information on the proportion in the researcher's random sample ($p$) and on the size of the researcher's random sample ($N$).
    a. $p = .2, N = 200$
    b. $p = .2, N = 100$
    c. $p = .8, N = 100$
    d. $p = .8, N = 50$
    e. $p = .1, N = 50$
    f. $p = .1 \ N = 100$
    g. $p = .01, N = 800$

28. For a, b, c, and d in the prior question, calculate the estimate of the standard error of the proportion.

29. For a, b, c, and d in question 27, calculate the 95% confidence interval for the population from which the researcher's sample was selected.

30. For a, b, c, and d in question 27, express the 95% confidence interval in terms of percentages.

31. For a, b, c, and d in question 27, calculate the 99% confidence interval for the population from which the researcher's sample was selected.

32. A researcher selects a random sample of adults in a given state, $N = 600$. In her sample, (exactly) 8% of respondents respond that they have experienced serious depression at some time during the prior year.
    a. What is the estimate of the standard deviation of the sampling distribution ($s_p$)?
    b. What is the 95% confidence interval of the proportion of adults in the state who have experienced serious depression in the prior year?
    c. How confident can the researcher be that the actual population proportion is located within the just-calculated 95% confidence interval of $P$? In other words, what is the researcher's confidence level?
    d. What is the 99% confidence interval of $P$?
    e. How confident can the researcher be that the actual population proportion is located within the just-calculated 99% confidence interval of $P$? In other words, what is the researcher's confidence level?
    f. Which confidence interval in this example establishes a more precise range within which the population proportion is located; in other words, which confidence interval is narrower?

   **g.** In which confidence interval—the 95% or the 99%—do we have a higher confidence level? In other words, which one is more likely to actually include the population proportion?

   **h.** Which confidence interval—the 95% or the 99% (or neither)—is "better"?

## Section 13.5

**33.** Express the 95% confidence interval calculated in the prior question in terms of margin of error. Use percentages rather than proportions in your response.

**34.** You hear on a newscast: "The percentage that supports the Legislation X is 64% with a margin of error of 6% with 95% confidence." What is the 95% confidence interval for the percentage that support X?

**35.** *The next group of questions are true/false.*

   **a.** The formulae presented in this chapter work very well even when the sample comprises up to about 50% of the population.

   **b.** In most situations, the width of the confidence interval (for both means and proportions) is affected hardly at all by the size of the population from which the sample is randomly selected.

   **c.** The greatest problem caused by nonresponse ordinarily does not relate to issues of bias but rather to the increased width of the confidence interval.

   **d.** In actual research, confidence intervals can be calculated in many situations that do not involve means or proportions.

**36.** The bias that can be introduced when persons do not respond to a survey is termed _ _____ bias.

# THE LOGIC OF STATISTICAL SIGNIFICANCE TESTS

## 14.1 ■ CHAPTER OVERVIEW

Chapter 14 discusses the logic and theory of *statistical significance tests* and demonstrates how *chance* (luck) affects study results. It begins with the basics of *probability*. It introduces the *null hypothesis* and the *alternative hypothesis* and also *directional* and *nondirectional hypothesis pairs*. We focus on when to *accept* (*fail to reject*) the null and on what it means for a result to be *statistically significant*.

## 14.2 ■ INTRODUCTION TO SIGNIFICANCE TESTING

Chapters 12 and 13 presented one function of inferential statistics, *estimation*, the key tool for which is the confidence interval. The second function is *decision making*, the primary tool for which is the statistical significance test (Toothaker, 1986, p. 18). As presented in Chapter 1, Section 1.7, a **statistical significance test** (**significance test**, **hypothesis test**) is an inferential statistical procedure conducted to determine how likely it is that a study sample result is due to chance or luck. This chapter and the next help you understand just what this definition means.

## 14.3 ■ PROBABILITY

### 14.3.1 ■ Definition and Formula

Prior to discussing significance tests, an introduction to probability is in order. The **probability** that an event with a given characteristic will occur equals the number of events with that characteristic divided by the total number of events.

$$\text{probability of event with given characteristic} = \frac{\text{number of events with that characteristic}}{\text{total number of events}} \quad (14.1)$$

For instance, suppose that 10 therapists attend a staffing regarding a given case. Suppose further that four of these therapists favor intervention using group therapy and that six favor intervention using individual therapy. You are the supervisor. You put the names of the 10 therapists in a hat, shake the hat, and randomly pick one name.

What is the probability that the therapist whose name is picked favors a group therapy intervention? The number of events with the characteristic of interest (favor group intervention) is four. The total number of events is 10. The probability of randomly selecting a therapist who favors the group intervention is 4 / 10 = .4.

Another example: What is the probability of flipping an unbiased coin and having it turn up heads? The number of events with the characteristic is one (one side of the coin is heads). The number of possible events is two (the coin has two sides). Hence, the probability that the coin will turn up heads is 1 / 2 = .5.

Note that probabilities are expressed as proportions. For instance, in our examples, the probabilities were .4 and .5, respectively. Probabilities are, in essence, proportions. Hence, a second formula for probability is

$$\text{probability of event with given characteristic} = \text{proportion of events with that characteristic} \tag{14.2}$$

For instance, in the first example, the proportion of therapists who favored group intervention was .4: 4 / 10 = .4. This is one and the same as the probability of randomly selecting such a therapist.

Probability may range from 0.00 to 1.00. It is 0.00 when there is no chance of the event and 1.00 when there is certainty. For instance, if no therapists favor group intervention, the probability of randomly selecting such a therapist is 0 / 10 = 0.00. If all 10 favor group intervention, this probability is 10 / 10 = 1.00. Probability is symbolized by $p$. Thus, if the probability of an event is .30, then $p = .30$. Observe that the symbol for probability is the same as that for the proportion in a sample (see Chapter 12, Section 12.5).

### 14.3.2 ▓ Probability and the Normal Distribution

As the next several chapters demonstrate, many statistical significance tests are based on the normal distribution, so let us work through a few probability problems based on this distribution.

What is the probability of randomly selecting from a normal distribution a case that is located within one standard deviation of the mean? As you know, 68% of cases in a normal distribution are located within one standard deviation of the mean. Therefore, the proportion of such cases is .68. Hence, the probability of randomly selecting a case located within one standard deviation of the mean from a normal distribution is .68, that is, $p = .68$.

A second problem: What is the probability of randomly selecting from a normal distribution, a case located 1.50 or more standard deviations below the mean, that is, with a $z$ score of $-1.50$ or lower? As Table A.1 indicates, the percentage of cases in this area of the normal curve is 6.7%. We divide by 100 to determine the proportion: 6.7 / 100 = .067. Hence, $p = .067$.

## 14.4 ▓ NULL AND ALTERNATIVE HYPOTHESES

In **hypothesis testing** (*statistical significance testing*), the researcher decides which of two hypotheses, the null hypothesis or the alternative hypothesis, better conveys a population condition. To keep things simple, this chapter expresses these hypotheses with words rather than mathematical symbols. Just as for confidence intervals, we assume that the study sample has been randomly selected from a wider population. When such is not the case, statistical significance tests are not valid procedures, although an exception is presented in Chapter 16, Section 16.8. As you read, keep in mind that due to chance (sampling error), study sample results almost always differ from population conditions. As you know, chance, sampling error, and the luck of the draw are different terms for the same concept.

The **null hypothesis** states that some condition is true in the population. For instance, a null could state "In the population from which the study sample was randomly selected, the mean score on the XYZ assertiveness scale equals 100 points." The **alternative hypothesis** (*research hypothesis*) states the condition that is "logically opposite" to that stated in the null. In our example, for instance, the alternative hypothesis would state "In the population from which the study sample was randomly selected, the mean score on the XYZ assertiveness scale does not equal 100 points." Null and alternative hypotheses go together as a **hypothesis pair**. For instance, the just-stated hypotheses may be presented together as a hypothesis pair.

Null:       In the population from which the study sample was randomly selected, the mean score on the XYZ assertiveness scale equals 100 points.

Alternative:  In the population from which the study sample was randomly selected, the mean score on the XYZ assertiveness scale does not equal 100 points.

The alternative hypothesis *always* negates the null. If one hypothesis is true in the population, the other, necessarily, is false. If the null is true, the alternative is false. If the alternative is true, the null is false.

The hypothesis pair pertains to the *population* from which the study sample was randomly selected. One carries out statistical procedures using *sample* data. As such, one never knows assuredly which hypothesis is true and which is false. The only way to know this assuredly would be to "sample" the entire population. Yet, if one did so, there would be no need for a significance test (for one would have complete knowledge of the population and thus certainty regarding which hypothesis was correct). Given that the hypothesis pair always pertains to the population, one may state the pair without specific mention of this. For instance, the previous hypothesis pair may be shortened as follows:

Null:       The mean score on the XYZ assertiveness scale equals 100 points.

Alternative:  The mean score on the XYZ assertiveness scale does not equal 100 points.

When the hypothesis pair does not mention the population, we assume that it pertains to it.

## 14.5 ■ A COMMON PATTERN FOR HYPOTHESIS PAIRS

A null hypothesis can state just about whatever the researcher wants it to. However, in social science research, most null hypotheses state that two variables are unassociated. The null's form varies for different combinations of variables.

When both variables are categorical, most null hypotheses state that percentages (proportions) are equal.

When one variable is categorical and the other is numeric, most null hypotheses state that means are equal.

When both variables are numeric, most null hypotheses state that the correlation between these variables (as measured by Pearson's *r*) equals 0.00.

Think back to the discussion of relationships between variables in Chapters 6–9. Recall that two categorical variables are unassociated when percentages are equal (see, for instance, Table 6.1 in Section 6.4.1). Recall from Chapter 9 that when one variable is categorical and the other is numeric, variables are unassociated when means are equal. Finally, recall from Chapter 8 that two numeric variables are unassociated when $r = 0.00$.[1]

Each of three just-presented statements thus conveys the same underlying idea—that two variables are unassociated. Summarizing: In actual social science research, most null hypotheses state that, in the population from which the researcher has randomly sampled, two variables are *unassociated*.

The alternative hypothesis states that the null is false. As most null hypotheses state that variables are unassociated, most alternative hypotheses state that they are associated.

> When both variables are categorical, most alternative hypotheses state that percentages (proportions) are not equal.

> When one variable is categorical and the other is numeric, most alternative hypotheses state that means are not equal.

> When both variables are numeric, most alternative hypotheses state that the correlation between these variables (Pearson's $r$) does not equal 0.00.

Think back again to Chapters 6 through 9 on relationship. Recall that categorical variables are associated when percentages differ. Recall also that when one variable is categorical and the other is numeric, variables are associated when means differ. Finally, recall that two numeric variables are associated when $r$ does not equal 0.00. Thus, each of the three just-presented statements conveys the same idea—that two variables are associated. Summarizing: In actual social science research, most alternative hypotheses state that, in the population from which the researcher has randomly sampled, two variables are associated.

Let us look at some examples of hypothesis pairs for different combinations of types of variables. Observe that the alternative hypothesis always negates the null, that is, states the precisely opposite condition. Observe also that in each pair, the null states that variables are not associated and the alternative states that they are. Although not mentioned explicitly, all pairs pertain to the population from which the study sample was randomly selected.

A "typical" null and alternative hypothesis pair when one variable (gender) is categorical and the other (self-esteem as measured on a scale) is numeric is

Null:        Mean self-esteem scores of women and men are equal.

Alternative:  Mean self-esteem scores of women and men are not equal.

The following null and alternative hypothesis pair involves two categorical variables.

Null:        The percentage of clients who become pregnant in prevention Program A is equal to the percentage of clients who become pregnant in Program B.

Alternative:  The percentage of clients who become pregnant in prevention Program A is not equal to the percentage of clients who become pregnant in Program B.

Both variables in the following pair are numeric:

Null:        The correlation between number of visits of family members and level of depression of nursing home patients equals 0.00.

Alternative:  The correlation between number of visits and level of depression of nursing home patients does not equal 0.00.

Recall from Chapter 1, Section 1.9.1, that categorical variables can be at either the nominal or the ordinal level of measurement. Our discussion so far has not addressed directional association between two ordinal-level variables. This text directs comparatively less attention to statistical tests involving ordinal-level variables than to those for other variables. When two ordinal-level variables are involved, hypothesis statements often take the following form:

Null:          There is no directional relationship between the variables.

Alternative:  There is a directional relationship between the variables.

Observe again that the null states the absence of association and the alternative states its presence. See Chapter 7, Section 7.4, for discussion of directional association.

Null and alternative hypothesis pairs do not always focus on the presence or absence of association. Sometimes, for instance, the null states that a population parameter equals some value and the alternative hypothesis states that it does not. Our example regarding the XYZ self-esteem scale illustrated this pattern. Further, our key examples in this chapter and the next do not involve relationship between variables.[2]

## 14.6 ■ DIRECTIONAL AND NONDIRECTIONAL HYPOTHESIS PAIRS

### 14.6.1 ■ Definitions and Examples

There are two types of hypothesis pairs: nondirectional pairs and directional pairs. As its name suggests, a **nondirectional hypothesis** does not state a direction. In a nondirectional hypothesis pair, the null states "equal" and the alternative states "not equal." All of the pairs presented so far have been nondirectional.

**Directional hypotheses** do state a direction. They make use of the logical operators "less than" and "greater than." To be specific, the null hypothesis in a directional pair states either "less than or equal to" ($\leq$) or "greater than or equal to" ($\geq$). The alternative hypothesis states either "less than" ($<$) or "greater than" ($>$). As is so for all hypothesis pairs, the alternative hypothesis negates the null. Hence, the direction stated in the alternative is always opposite to that stated in the null. The just-presented examples can be restated as directional hypothesis pairs. For instance, for the self-esteem example:

Null:          The mean self-esteem score of men is less than or equal to that of women.

Alternative:  The mean self-esteem score of men is greater than that of women.

This pair may also be stated reversing the direction of the logical operators. Guidance regarding which direction to use in a given situation is presented shortly.

Null:          The mean self-esteem score of men is greater than or equal to that of women.

Alternative:  The mean self-esteem score of men is less than that of women.

Stating the teen pregnancy example as a directional pair:

Null:          The percentage of teens who become pregnant in Program A is greater than or
               equal to the percentage of those who become pregnant in Program B.

Alternative:  The percentage of teens who become pregnant in Program A is less than the per-
               centage of those who become pregnant in Program B.

Stating this example, reversing the direction of the operators:

Null:          The percentage of teens who become pregnant in Program A is less than or equal
               to the percentage of those who become pregnant in Program B.

Alternative: The percentage of teens who become pregnant in Program A is greater than the percentage of those who become pregnant in Program B.

Finally, for our example on family visiting and depression:

Null: The correlation (Pearson's $r$) between family visiting and level of depression of nursing home clients is greater than or equal to 0.00.

Alternative: The correlation (Pearson's $r$) between family visiting and level of depression of nursing home clients is less than 0.00.

Reversing direction:

Null: The correlation (Pearson's $r$) between family visiting and level of depression of nursing home clients is less than or equal to 0.00.

Alternative: The correlation (Pearson's $r$) between family visiting and level of depression of nursing home clients is greater than 0.00.

Observe that, in all of these directional pairs, the alternative hypothesis negates the null. Observe also that the "or equal to" condition is always stated in the null rather than in the alternative.

## 14.6.2 ■ Guidelines for Usage

Although the decision regarding whether to use a directional or a nondirectional hypothesis pair rests with the researcher, guidelines for making this decision are clear. Directional hypotheses are used when prior research, theory, logic, and/or common sense provide a strong (perhaps even compelling) reason for expecting that the study result will be in a particular direction. For instance, a considerable body of research (Comstock & Strasburger, 1990; Lazar 1994; Robinson, Wilde, Navracruz, Haydel, & Varady, 2001) indicates that viewing violent television programs leads to increased violent behavior. A researcher conducting a study in this area would *strongly* expect to find that the greater the amount of violent television viewed, the greater the amount of violent behavior. Given the strong expectation for results to be in a particular direction, a directional hypothesis pair would be preferred.

In a directional hypothesis pair, the *alternative* hypothesis states the direction consistent with expectations and the null states the direction that is counter to expectations. For instance, in the just-presented example,

Null: The correlation ($r$) between the amount of violent television watched and the amount of violent behavior is less than or equal to 0.00.

Alternative: The correlation ($r$) between the amount of violent television watched and the amount of violent behavior is greater than 0.00.

Researchers use nondirectional hypothesis pairs when theory, research, logic, and/or common sense do not provide a strong or compelling reason for expecting that a result will be in a given direction. For instance, regarding the example on self-esteem of women and men, let us presume that there is not a compelling reason for thinking that self-esteem is higher for one gender than for the other. This being so, a nondirectional pair would be preferred. Similarly, presuming that Program A and Program B are both relatively new and untested programs of pregnancy prevention, a researcher would, almost assuredly, use a nondirectional hypothesis pair in a study comparing the effectiveness of these programs. On the other hand, given sufficiently strong reasons for favoring one program over the other, she might use a directional pair.

As stated earlier, the choice of a directional or nondirectional hypothesis pair rests with the researcher. Given doubt regarding which type of pair to use in a given situation, I recommend a nondirectional one. These are much more common in actual research. I recommend that you use a directional pair only when you are extremely confident regarding the direction of results.

## 14.7 ▧ SAMPLING ERROR AND THE NULL HYPOTHESIS

As we move forward, remember once again that due to chance (sampling error, the luck of the draw) sample statistics and population parameters almost always differ. Suppose that a researcher studying self-esteem selects a random sample of students from the population of students at a university and formulates a nondirectional hypothesis pair. So that you do not forget that hypothesis statements apply to populations, the hypothesis pair specifically mentions this:

Null:        In the population of students at the researcher's university, mean self-esteem scores of women and men are equal.

Alternative: In the population of students at the researcher's university, mean self-esteem scores of women and men are not equal.

Presume that, in the study sample, the mean self-esteem score for men is higher than that for women. What is the cause of this difference? Stated differently, what is the cause of the association between gender and self-esteem in the study sample. The two possible causes (explanations) are as follows:

1. The *null hypothesis is true* (mean self-esteem scores of women and men are equal in the population). The association observed in the study sample is due solely to chance (sampling error).
2. The *alternative hypothesis is true* (mean self-esteem scores of women and men differ in the population). The association in the study sample is not due solely to chance (sampling error). Although chance is, almost assuredly, exerting some effect, the fundamental reason for the association between self-esteem and gender in the sample is the fact that these variables are associated in the population.

Short of sampling the entire population, the researcher can never determine with certainty which hypothesis is true. However, a statistical significance test can tell her whether the null or the alternative provides a better explanation for the study result. As stated earlier, a statistical significance test is an inferential statistical procedure conducted to determine how likely it is that a study sample result is due to chance or luck.

Researchers use different significance tests in different situations. For instance, one test examines differences between percentages, another examines differences between means, and another examines correlations. Indeed, there is a test for just about any situation that comes up.

Statistical significance tests yield a probability symbolized by $p$. $p$ (**$p$ value**) conveys the probability of obtaining the study sample result or an even more extreme result given that the null is true in the population from which the study sample was randomly selected. As used in this text, a "more extreme" result is one that differs from the condition stated in the null by more than does the study sample result.

Significance tests test the *null* hypothesis. In essence, every significance test (a) presumes that the null is true and—this presumed to be so—(b) calculates the probability ($p$) of obtaining the study sample result or an even more extreme result.

## 14.8 ■ STATISTICAL SIGNIFICANCE LEVELS

As just mentioned, $p$ conveys, given a true null, the probability of obtaining the study sample result or an even more extreme result. For instance, a $p$ of .17 conveys that, given a true null, the probability of obtaining the study sample result or an even more extreme result equals .17. In other words, if a researcher replicated a study an unlimited number of times (i.e., drew an unlimited number of random samples), she would, given a true null, obtain results as extreme as or even more extreme than the study result 17% of the time.

The researcher's decision regarding the hypothesis pair depends on the value of $p$. When $p$ is sufficiently low, the researcher **rejects the null**; when it is not, the researcher **accepts the null**. A better term than accepts the null is **fails to reject the null**, and this is discussed subsequently.

In essence, a low value of $p$ conveys that, given a true null, the study sample result is an unlikely one. For instance, if $p = .003$, this conveys that, given a true null, results as extreme as or even more extreme than the study result are obtained only three times in every 1,000 random samples (3/1,000 = .003). In essence, a high value of $p$ conveys that, given a true null, the result is not an unlikely one. For instance, a $p$ of .47 ($p = .47$) conveys that, given a true null, results as extreme as or even more extreme than the study sample result are obtained in 47% of random samples.

In addition to making a decision on the null hypothesis, the researcher makes a decision on the alternative hypothesis. This "decision" is almost not a decision at all because it flows automatically from that made on the null. Whenever the researcher rejects the null, she (always) **accepts the alternative hypothesis**. Whenever the researcher accepts (fails to reject) the null, she (always) **rejects the alternative hypothesis**.

We know that the null is rejected when $p$ is sufficiently low. But just how low does $p$ need to be? We need a "cutoff point" for decision making. This cutoff point is termed the **statistical significance level**. Most often, social science researchers use one of two statistical significance levels:

■ At the **.05 statistical significance level**, the researcher accepts (fails to reject) the null hypothesis and rejects the alternative when $p$ (the probability given by the significance test) is greater than .05 ($p > .05$). She rejects the null hypothesis and accepts the alternative when $p$ is less than or equal to .05 ($p \leq .05$).

■ At the **.01 statistical significance level**, the researcher accepts (fails to reject) the null hypothesis and rejects the alternative when $p$ is greater than .01 ($p > .01$). She rejects the null hypothesis and accepts the alternative when $p$ is less than or equal to .01 ($p \leq .01$).

For ease of communication, statistical significance level may be shortened to **significance level** or simply **level**. The probability connected with the selected significance level equals $\alpha$ (**alpha**; a letter from the Greek alphabet.). When the .05 level is selected, $\alpha = 05$; when the .01 level is selected, $\alpha = .01$.

The researcher selects the significance level *prior* to conducting the significance test. The .05 level is used most frequently. Occasionally, researchers use levels different from .05 and .01. Using the *.10 significance level*, the researcher accepts (fails to reject) the null when $p > .10$; when $p \leq .10$, she rejects it. At the *.001 level*, the researcher accepts (fails to reject) the null when $p > .001$; when $p \leq .001$, she rejects it.

Criteria for decision making have been presented for four significance levels. Stated more generally,

The researcher accepts (fails to reject) the null and rejects the alternative when $p$ is greater than the probability associated with the significance level ($> \alpha$). She rejects the null and accepts the alternative when $p$ is less than or equal to the probability connected with the significance level ($\leq \alpha$).

In the just-presented statement, the "probability associated with the significance level ($\alpha$)" is .05 for the .05 level, .01 for the .01 level, .10 for the .10 level, .001 for the .001 level, and so on.

Here are some examples of decision making on hypothesis pairs. Suppose that a researcher selects the .05 level and that $p$ (the probability given by the significance test) equals .17 ($p = .17$). Because .17 is greater than .05, the researcher accepts (fails to reject) the null hypothesis and rejects the alternative hypothesis. As a second example, suppose that the researcher selects the .05 level and that $p = .02$. Because .02 is less than .05, the null is rejected and the alternative is accepted. Finally, suppose the researcher selects the .01 level and that, again, $p = .02$. Because .02 is greater than .01, the researcher accepts (fails to reject) the null and rejects the alternative. The next chapter provides guidance on choosing between the .05 and .01 levels.

## 14.9 ■ EXAMPLES OF STATISTICAL SIGNIFICANCE TESTING

### 14.9.1 ■ An Example in Which We Reject the Null

An example from the world of coin flips can demonstrate the logic of hypothesis testing. Suppose that a particular coin is slightly bent. Curious about whether this affects how it lands (heads vs. tails), you develop a (nondirectional) hypothesis pair:

Null:           The coin comes up heads 50% of the time.

Alternative:  The coin does not come up heads 50% of the time.

Your hypothesis pair pertains to the full *population* of coin flips, that is, to the results that would be obtained if you flipped the coin an infinite number of times. You do not have time to flip the coin indefinitely. Suppose that you flip it 10 times and that it comes up heads nine times.

Just as are confidence intervals, significance tests are based on sampling distributions. We have already encountered the sampling distribution that we need for our example, that being the sampling distribution of the number of heads obtained from tossing an unbiased coin (one that comes up heads 50% of the time) 10 times. We encountered this distribution in Chapter 12, Section 12.7.1, in the discussion that introduced sampling distributions; see Figure 12.1.

A portion of Figure 12.1 is repeated here (see Figure 14.1), but with a small difference; the sample results obtained are presented as proportions rather than as percentages. For instance, the proportion of random samples in which exactly five heads are obtained is .2461. In other words, if you (1) flip an unbiased coin 10 times and (2) count and record the number of heads, and (3) repeat steps 1 and 2 an infinite number of times, the proportion of times that you will obtain (exactly) five heads is .2461.

Our examples here with coin flips actually carry out the *binomial statistical significance test (binomial test)*. I use this test here only to demonstrate the logic of significance testing; we encounter it again in Chapter 19, Section 19.3. As stated previously, you obtained nine heads in your random sample of 10 tosses.

Figure 14.1 shows that the proportion of random samples (cases) in which (exactly) nine heads are obtained is .0098. As probabilities and proportions are one and the same (see Section 14.3.1), the probability of obtaining nine heads is .0098. As discussed earlier, significance tests do not determine the probability of obtaining the study sample result per se but, more precisely, the probability of obtaining that result or an even more extreme one. Obtaining 10 heads is, obviously, more extreme than is obtaining nine heads. The probability of obtaining 10 heads is .0010. We add the probability for nine heads and that for 10 heads to determine that of obtaining nine *or more* heads: $.0098 + .0010 = .0107$. (This probability is .0107 rather than .0108 because of rounding error.)

Our hypothesis pair is nondirectional. When the pair is nondirectional, results that differ in *both* directions from the value stated in the null are considered in determining $p$. The number of

FIGURE 14.1 ■ **Sampling Distribution of Number of Heads for Ten Flips of an Unbiased Coin**

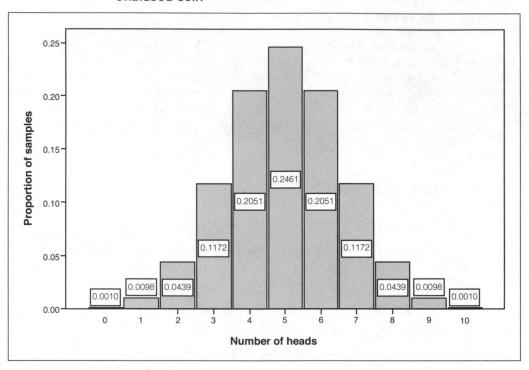

heads that agrees exactly with the null is five heads, as 5 equals (exactly) 50% of the 10 coin flips. Consider that one head differs from five heads by the same amount as does nine heads; in other words, one head and nine heads are equally extreme. Further, zero heads and 10 heads are equally extreme. Thus, we obtain $p$ by summing the probability of obtaining nine or more heads and that of obtaining one or fewer. Because our sampling distribution is symmetric (the left and right sides in Figure 14.1 are mirror images), the probability of obtaining one or fewer heads equals that of obtaining nine or more. This probability is .0107. Thus, $p = .0107 + .0107 = .0215$. (This probability is .0215 rather than .0214 because of rounding error.)

Let us summarize. Given a true null and from the perspective of a nondirectional hypothesis pair—that is, with differences in both directions considered—we have determined that the probability of obtaining our study sample result or an even more extreme result equals .0215 (i.e., $p = .0215$). Given a true null, our study result is an unlikely one. Given a true null, results that differ from the null by as much as does our result or by even more than this are obtained in only about 2% of random samples. What decision should we make regarding the hypothesis pair?

This decision hinges on which statistical significance level we selected. Formally, the researcher selects a significance level prior to conducting the test. Presume that we selected the .05 level—the most commonly selected one. This being the case, our obtained probability ($p = .0215$) is less than the probability connected with the significance level ($.05 = \alpha$). Hence, we reject the null that the coin comes up heads 50% of the time and accept the alternative, that is, we conclude that it does not come up heads 50% of the time.

I note that had we selected the .01 level ($\alpha = .01$), our decision would have been to fail to reject (accept) the null because .0215 is greater than .01. The next chapter discusses the .01 level in depth. Further, I note that we used a nondirectional pair. Directional pairs are discussed in depth in the next chapter.

### 14.9.2 ▨ An Example in Which We Fail to Reject (Accept) the Null

Let us carry out our coin toss experiment again using the same nondirectional hypothesis pair and, again, using the .05 level, but let us presume that we get a different result, say, seven heads in 10 flips. We need to determine, given a true null (an unbiased coin), the probability ($p$) of obtaining our study sample result or an even more extreme result. The probability of obtaining seven or more heads in 10 tosses of an unbiased coin is $.1172 + .0439 + .0098 + .0010 = .1719$ (see Figure 14.1). Three heads differs from the null (50% of $10 = 5$) by the same amount as does seven heads (it is equally extreme). Given that the sampling distribution is symmetric (see Figure 14.1), the probability of obtaining three or fewer heads also equals .1719. We sum to obtain the probability of obtaining seven or more or three or fewer heads: $p = .1719 + 1719 = .3438$. Hence, given a true null (and operating from the perspective of a nondirectional pair, that is, considering both directions), the probability of obtaining our study sample result or an even more extreme result equals .3438 ($p = .3438$). As the obtained $p$ (.3438) is greater than the probability connected with the significance level (.05 = $\alpha$), we accept (fail to reject) the null and accept the alternative.

### 14.9.3 ▨ More Interpretations of $p$

As stated in the prior section, the probability given by a statistical test ($p$) conveys, given a true null, the probability of obtaining the study sample result or an even more extreme result. When the null is true in the population, why do sample results differ from the null? In other words, if our coin is unbiased and thus comes up heads 50% of the time in the population (i.e., if flipped an infinite number of times), why does it come up heads, say, 40% of the time in one random sample of 10 flips and, say, 80% of the time in another? Given a true null, why do sample results differ from the null? You already know the answer: Sample results differ from population conditions due to the luck of the draw—that is, due to chance (sampling error).

As you know, $p$ conveys the probability of obtaining the sample result or an even more extreme result given a true null. This interpretation is clear and precise; it accurately reflects the logic of hypothesis testing. There is, however, another important interpretation of $p$: $p$ conveys the probability of obtaining the study sample result or an even more extreme result due to chance alone (sampling error alone).

In our first coin-flip study (when we obtained nine heads), $p$ equaled .0215. This conveys both (a) that, given a true null, the probability of obtaining our result or an even more extreme result is .0215 and (b) that the probability of obtaining our result or an even more extreme result due to chance alone (sampling error alone) is .0215. Summing up, the probability given by a statistical test, $p$ conveys both,

- ▨ given a true null, the probability of obtaining the study sample result or an even more extreme result and

- ▨ the probability of obtaining the study sample result or an even more extreme result due to chance alone.

Researchers take it as a given that significance tests convey the probability of obtaining the study result *or an even more extreme one*. Hence, we may shorten the just-presented interpretations and state that $p$ conveys,

- ▨ given a true null, the probability of obtaining the sample result and

- ▨ the probability that the study sample result is due to chance alone.

The last interpretation—the probability that the study result is due to chance alone—reflects the "nuts and bolts" meaning that researchers attach to $p$. It is how researchers intuitively think about and interpret $p$. It is likely the interpretation—the kernel of understanding—that you will carry with you beyond this class.

The two just-presented interpretations of $p$ convey the same thing; they are opposite sides of the same coin. Thus, if the null is true, it follows logically that the difference between the value stated in the null and the result obtained in the sample is due *only* to chance (sampling error). And, viewed from the opposite perspective, if chance (sampling error) is the *only* cause of this difference, it follows logically that the null is true.

Let me mention another way in which researchers sometimes interpret $p$. Rather than focusing attention on the study result per se as we have done to this point, researchers sometimes focus their attention on the *difference* between the condition stated in the null and the study result. Viewed from this perspective, $p$ conveys the probability that the difference between the condition stated in the null and the result obtained in the sample is due to chance alone. For instance, our study sample result of nine heads differed from the value expected given a true null, five heads, by four heads. Applying this interpretation, we conclude that the probability that this difference is due to chance alone is .0215.[3]

And finally, a final interpretation of $p$ is simply this: $p$ conveys the probability of the study sample result. In our example, then, we may say that the probability of the study sample result equals .0215. This final interpretation is quick and informal. It is, in essence, "shorthand" and is not recommended for use in formal writing. In particular, it is shorthand for "the probability that the study result is due to chance alone," the nuts-and-bolts meaning of $p$.

### 14.9.4 ■ What Does It Mean to Reject the Null?

The researcher rejects the null when $p$ is less than or equal to the probability connected with the significance level ($\leq \alpha$, alpha). Think of the study sample result as evidence. The most basic meaning of a decision to reject is that the sample result provides strong evidence that the null is false. Stated differently, the sample result is strongly inconsistent with a true null. The researcher reasons something as follows: (1) Given a true null, my study sample result is an unlikely one. (2) Thus, the null is likely false. (3) Thus, I will reject it and accept the alternative.

Consider our first study sample result of nine heads. Given a true null, the probability of getting this result or an even more extreme one is quite low, $p = .0215$. In other words, given a true null, we rarely get results this extreme. (We only get them in about two random samples in every 100.) Chance alone is an *unlikely* explanation for this result. Stated differently, chance alone rarely produces results this extreme.

As our result is unlikely given a true null, we can indeed be confident that the null is false. How confident can we be? To calculate how confident one can be that the null is false, one can (a) multiply $p$ by 100 and (b) subtract from 100%: For our example: $.0215 \times 100 = 2.15\%$; $100\% - 2.15\% = 97.85\%$. Hence, we can be 97.85% confident that the null is false.

When one rejects the null at the .05 level, one can be at least 95% confident that the null is false ($.05 \times 100 = 5\%$; $100\% - 5\% = 95\%$). When one rejects at the 99% level, one can be at least 99% confident that this is so ($.01 \times 100 = 1\%$; $100\% - 1\% = 99\%$).

Significance tests never provide *proof*, that is, *100% certainty*. Researchers never *prove* that the null is true or false. Instead their conclusions are *probabilistic*. For instance, in our example, given a true null, there is a 2.15% chance of getting our result or an even more extreme one due to the "luck of the coin flip," that is, due to chance. The following are some key meanings of a decision to reject the null:

■ The sample results provide strong evidence that the null is false.

■ The study sample result is highly inconsistent with a true null.

■ The null is likely false.

■ The study sample result is unlikely given a true null.

■ The study sample result is unlikely due to chance alone (sampling error alone).

■ The difference between the value stated in the null and the study sample result is unlikely due to chance alone.

■ One can be confident (though not certain) that the null is false.

■ Results do not prove that the null is false.

## 14.9.5 ■ What Does It Mean to Fail to Reject (Accept) the Null?

The researcher fails to reject (accepts) the null when the probability given by the significance test exceeds that connected with the chosen significance level. Interpretation of a decision to fail to reject (accept) the null is tricky. First, let me state some conclusions that do *not* follow from a decision to fail to reject.

■ The null is true.

■ The null is likely true.

■ One can be confident that the null is true.

At its essence, a decision to fail to reject (accept) the null conveys that the study sample result does not provide strong evidence that the null is false. Consider our second random sample in which we obtained seven heads. The probability given by the significance test for this result was .3438 ($p = .3438$). Thus, given a true null, results this extreme or even more extreme occur in 34.38% of random samples. Given a true null, this result is *not a highly unlikely* one. And, correspondingly, chance alone is *not a highly unlikely* explanation for this result.

Observe also that chance alone is *not* a likely explanation for this result. Chance alone produces results as extreme as or even more extreme than this result only 34.38% of the time. The key idea connected with a decision to fail to reject the null is not that chance alone is a likely explanation for the study result but rather that it is *not a sufficiently unlikely one*. As you know, in our example, $p = .3438$. As we are using the .05 level, a probability less than .05 is required for rejection. Our result is not sufficiently unlikely and thus we fail to reject (accept) the null.

When the null is accepted, may the researcher conclude that the study result is consistent with the null? Not necessarily. This interpretation is too strong. The better interpretation is not that the result is consistent with the null but rather that it is not highly inconsistent. More specifically, it is not sufficiently inconsistent for the null to be rejected.

The meaning of a decision to accept (fail to reject) the null is perhaps best conveyed by jury verdicts in criminal trials. A jury does not find the defendant guilty or innocent but rather guilty or not guilty. A finding of not guilty does not convey that a defendant *is* innocent or that it is *likely* that she is innocent. And, similarly, it does not convey that jurors are *confident* in the defendant's innocence. Instead, a finding of not guilty conveys that the evidence does not establish guilt beyond a reasonable doubt. In the same vein, when the researcher accepts (fails to reject) the null, this does not convey that the null *is* true, that it is *likely* that it is true, or that the researcher can be *confident* that it is true. Instead, it conveys only that the study sample result (the evidence) does not provide sufficiently strong grounds for concluding otherwise. Just as the defendant is presumed innocent until proven guilty beyond a reasonable doubt, the null is presumed true—and thus is "accepted" (retained)—unless strong evidence demonstrates otherwise.

Clearly "fail to reject" better expresses the meaning of a decision to accept the null than does "accept." Although I use both terms in this book, I emphasize "fail to reject."

In failing to reject the null, the researcher follows this logic: (a) Given a true null, my study result is not a highly unlikely one; it does not provide strong evidence that the null is false. (b) As such, I will retain (fail to reject, accept) it. The following are some interpretations of what it means to fail to reject (accept) the null:

- The study sample result does not provide strong evidence that the null is false.

- Given a true null, the study sample result is not a highly unlikely (sufficiently unlikely) one.

- Chance alone is not a highly unlikely (sufficiently unlikely) explanation for the study sample result.

- Chance alone is not a highly unlikely (sufficiently unlikely) explanation for the difference between the value stated in the null and the study sample result.

- The study sample result is not highly inconsistent (sufficiently inconsistent) with the null.

In sum, in accepting the null, the researcher does not conclude that the null *is* true but rather acknowledges that the study result does not provide strong evidence otherwise. As such, she retains it; she fails to reject it.

## 14.10 ■ NULL AND ALTERNATIVE HYPOTHESES AND SCIENTIFIC INQUIRY

Peruse through the various null hypotheses presented earlier in this chapter: Null hypotheses, quite simply, are boring. Almost without exception, the null "states" "nothing"—all is the same, things are equal, there is no association, and so on. Indeed, the dictionary definition of null is "amounting to nothing." What is the purpose of the null?"

Science has a deeply rooted preference for the simplest, most straightforward explanation. Consider the study of relationships between variables, perhaps the key focus of scientific inquiry. Researchers often face the task of explaining why two variables are associated in their study sample. The null provides the simplest explanation. It asserts that (a) the variables are unassociated in the population from which the study sample was randomly selected and that (b) the only reason for the association in the study sample is chance (sampling error, the luck of the draw of random samples). Science prefers such a "simplest possible" explanation. So long as chance alone is a sufficient explanation, the null suffices and the researcher accepts (fails to reject) it.

The alternative hypothesis offers a more complex explanation. It asserts that an association is observed in the study sample not only due to chance but also, and more fundamentally, because an association exists in the population. Science will accept this more complex explanation only when the simpler one (e.g., the null—that is, chance alone) does not suffice.

An example of the "logic" of science: If chance alone is a sufficient explanation for the higher self-esteem of male than of female students in a random sample of university students, science does not "permit" consideration of other explanations for this difference. On the other hand, if chance alone is an insufficient (an unlikely) explanation, science gives the researcher "permission" to think about *real* explanations.

*Real* explanations are explanations other than chance. Perhaps men are more assertive in advocating for their rights, and this enhances self-esteem. Perhaps contradictory messages about academic success undermine self-esteem in women. Science permits consideration of real explanations only when the researcher can be confident that an association or other study result is not due simply to chance. When a researcher accepts the alternative hypothesis, she concludes that some *real* difference in the population—something more than chance—explains her result.

## 14.11 ▪ WHAT IS A STATISTICALLY SIGNIFICANT RESULT?

Statistical significance goes hand in hand with rejecting the null. A study sample result is **statistically significant** when $p$ (the probability given by the significance test) is less than or equal to the probability connected to the significance level ($\leq \alpha$). Whenever the researcher rejects the null, the study sample result is statistically significant, and (being redundant) whenever a result is statistically significant, the researcher rejects the null. Statistical significance and rejection of the null are one and the same. When a result is statistically significant, it has achieved **statistical significance**.

Whenever the probability given by the test, $p$, is greater than the probability connected with the significance level ($> \alpha$), the study sample result is *not statistically significant*. The absence of statistical significance goes hand in hand with failing to reject (accepting) the null. Whenever the researcher fails to reject the null, the result is not statistically significant, and (being redundant) whenever a result is not statistically significant, the researcher fails to reject the null. In sum, obtaining a result that is not statistically significant and failing to reject the null are one and the same.

In reporting statistical significance or the lack thereof, researchers often refer to the particular significance level that is used. For instance, suppose that a researcher uses the .05 level and that $p$ equals .14. As the probability given by the test exceeds that connected to the significance level, this result is not statistically significant. In this situation, the researcher could state, "This result is *not statistically significant at the .05 level*." Or, if a researcher uses the .01 significance level and $p$ equals .008, she could state, "The result was statistically significant at the .01 level."

In a general sense, a statistically significant result is one that is unlikely due to chance alone. Suppose that a researcher states, "We found a statistically significant relationship between the amount of time exercising and the amount of weight loss." In essence, this statement conveys that the relationship between these variables in the study sample is unlikely due to chance alone. When a relationship is not statistically significant, it may well be due to chance alone.

## 14.12 ▪ CHAPTER SUMMARY

A formula for *probability* is

$$\text{probability of event with given characteristic} = \frac{\text{number of events with characteristic}}{\text{total number of events}}$$

Probability ($p$) may range from 0.00 to 1.00. It is 0.00 when there is no chance of an event and 1.00 when there is certainty.

Hypothesis statements pertain to the population from which the researcher has randomly selected the study sample. The *null hypothesis* states that a given condition is true in that population. The *alternative hypothesis* states that a logically opposite condition is true. Whenever the null is accepted, the alternative is rejected. Whenever the null is rejected, the alternative is accepted. Most null hypotheses state that variables are not associated and most alternative hypotheses state that they are associated.

Null and alternative hypotheses go together as a *hypothesis pair*. Whereas a *nondirectional hypothesis pair* does not state a direction, a *directional hypothesis pair* does.

Researchers use directional pairs when there is a strong expectation that results will be in a given direction. Nondirectional pairs are much more common. Researchers use these when there is not a strong expectation regarding direction. In a directional pair, the alternative hypothesis states the direction of expectations.

Two explanations for an association between variables in the study sample are (a) the null is true in the population and thus the association is due solely to chance (sampling error); or (b) the alternative hypothesis is true in the population and thus the association is not due solely to chance (sampling error).

The probability given by a *statistical significance test*, *p*, conveys, (a) given a true null, the probability of obtaining the study sample result or an even more extreme result and (b) the probability of obtaining the study sample result or an even more extreme result due to chance alone (sampling error alone). These two probabilities are one and the same. Expressed more succinctly, *p* conveys, (a) given a true null, the probability of obtaining the study sample result and (b) the probability of obtaining the study sample result due to chance alone. The second interpretation conveys the "nuts and bolts" meaning of *p*. Finally, *p* conveys the probability that the difference between the condition stated in the null and the result obtained in the sample is due to chance alone.

The two major *statistical significance levels* are the *.05 statistical significance level* and the *.01 statistical significance level*. The .05 level is used most often. Occasionally, researchers use the *.001 level* and the *.10 level*.

At the .05 level, the researcher accepts (fails to reject) the null and rejects the alternative when *p* (the probability given by the significance test) is greater than .05. She rejects the null and accepts the alternative when *p* is less than or equal to .05. At the .01 level, the researcher accepts (fails to reject) the null and rejects the alternative when *p* is greater than .01. She rejects the null and accepts the alternative when *p* is less than or equal to .01. The probability associated with the significance level is termed $\alpha$ (alpha).

Rejection of the null conveys that (a) the study sample result provides strong evidence that the null is false; (b) given a true null, the study sample result is an unlikely result; (c) the study sample result is unlikely due to chance alone; and (d) the null is likely false.

When a researcher rejects the null at the .01 level, she can be at least 99% confident that the null is false. When she rejects the null at the .05 level, she can be at least 95% confident that this is so.

Failure to reject the null conveys that (a) the study sample result does not provide strong evidence that the null is false; (b) given a true null, the study sample result is not a highly (sufficiently) unlikely one; and (c) chance alone is not a highly (sufficiently) unlikely explanation for the study sample result. Accepting the null does not convey that the null is likely true or that the researcher can be confident that the null is true. Fail to reject is a better term than is accept.

The null offers the simplest explanation—chance alone—for the study sample result. Science permits a more complex one (the alternative) only when the null does not suffice. Acceptance of the alternative conveys that something more than chance—something *real*—is the likely explanation for the study result.

When the researcher rejects the null, the study result is *statistically significant*. *Statistical significance* and rejection of the null are one and the same. When the researcher fails to reject the null, the study result is not statistically significant; these are also one and the same.

## 14.13 ■ PROBLEMS AND QUESTIONS

**Section 14.2**

1. Another term for statistical significance test is _____ _____.

2. A statistical _____ test is an _____ statistical procedure conducted to determine how likely it is that a study sample result is due to _____ or luck.

**Section 14.3**

3. From memory, state the formula for probability.

4. Probability may range from a minimum of _____ to a maximum of _____.

5. A wilderness experience program can serve 16 youth. Forty youth want to participate. Names will be drawn randomly from a hat. For any given youth, what is the probability that she will be selected to participate?

6. What symbol does this text use for probability? For the proportion in a sample?

7. In a normal distribution:
    a. What percentage of cases is located between the mean and one standard deviation below the mean?
    b. What is the proportion of cases that are located between the mean and one standard deviation below the mean?
    c. What is the probability of selecting at random a case that is located between the mean and one standard deviation below the mean?
    d. What percentage of cases is located between the mean and two standard deviations above the mean?
    e. What is the proportion of cases that are located between the mean and two standard deviations above the mean?
    f. What is the probability of selecting at random a case that is located between the mean and two standard deviations above the mean?

8. Given a normal distribution, what is the probability of selecting a case . . .
    a. located at the mean or higher?
    b. located within one standard deviation of the mean?
    c. located one or more standard deviations above the mean?
    d. with a $z$ score of 1.00 or higher?
    e. located two or more standard deviations below the mean?
    f. with a $z$ score of $-2.00$ or lower?
    g. located two or more standard deviations above or below the mean (in other words, consider both directions)?
    h. with a $z$ score $\leq -2.00$ or $\geq 2.00$?

9. Answer each question in the prior question but for a positively skewed distribution rather than for the normal distribution. (Hint: Think carefully before responding.)

**Section 14.4**

10. The _____ hypothesis states that some condition is true in the population.
    The _____ hypothesis, also called the _____ hypothesis, states the condition

that is logically _____ to that stated in the null. Taken together, the null and its corresponding alternative hypothesis form a _____ _____.

11. (*True or False*) Hypothesis statements pertain to the study sample rather than to the population from which that sample was selected.

## Section 14.5

12. (*True or False*) In actual research, most null hypotheses state that variables are associated.

13. When both variables are categorical, most null hypotheses state that _____ are equal.

14. When one variable is categorical and the other is numeric, most null hypotheses state that _____ are equal.

15. When both variables are numeric, most null hypotheses states the _____ between these variables equals _____.

16. The alternative hypothesis, in essence, states that the null is _____.

17. (*True or False*) *All* hypothesis pairs concern the presence or absence of association.

## Section 14.6

18. In a nondirectional hypothesis pair, the null states (the logical condition) _____ to and the alternative states (the condition) _____ _____ to.

19. _____ hypotheses state a direction and make use of the logical operators _____ _____ and _____ _____.

20. Indicate whether the following alternative hypotheses are part of a directional or a nondirectional hypothesis pair.
    a. A higher percentage of women than men choose careers in the human services.
    b. Women and men are not equally likely to choose careers in the human services.
    c. The mean levels of self-esteem of men and women are not equal.
    d. The mean level of self-esteem is higher for women than for men.

21. State a nondirectional hypothesis pair involving two categorical variables.

22. State a nondirectional hypothesis pair involving a categorical variable and a numeric one.

23. State a nondirectional hypothesis pair involving two numeric variables.

24. State a directional hypothesis pair.

25. State the just-stated directional hypothesis pair with the direction reversed.

26. In a directional hypothesis pair, the _____ hypothesis states the direction that is consistent with expectations, and the _____ hypothesis states the opposite direction.

27. The next series of questions are true/false:
    a. Directional (rather than nondirectional) hypothesis pairs are used when theory, research, logic, and/or common sense provide strong reason for expecting that a study result will be in a particular direction.
    b. Ultimately, the choice to use a directional or a nondirectional hypothesis pair rests with the researcher.
    c. In actual research, directional hypothesis pairs are used more commonly than are nondirectional pairs.

## Section 14.7

28. When the null is true, the association observed in the study sample is due solely to _____, also known as _____ _____. When the alternative hypothesis is true, the fundamental reason that an association is observed in the sample is that there is indeed an _____ in the population.

29. (*True or False*) Statistical significance tests allow researchers to determine with certainty which hypothesis is true.

30. Significance tests convey the _____ of obtaining the study sample result or an even more _____ result given that the null is _____ in the _____ from which the study sample was _____ selected. This probability is symbolized by ___ (symbol).

31. Statistical significance tests test the _____ hypothesis.

## Section 14.8

32. When *p* is sufficiently low, the researcher _____ the null and when it is not, the researcher _____ the null. A better term than accepts the null is _____ _____ _____ the null. A low value of *p* conveys that, given a true null, the study sample result is an _____ one.

33. Whenever the researcher rejects the null, she _____ the alternative. Whenever the researcher accepts (_____ to _____) the null, she _____ the alternative.

34. The cutoff point for decision making is termed the _____ _____ _____.

35. At the .05 _____ _____ level, the researcher accepts (fails to reject) the null hypothesis and rejects the alternative when ___ (symbol for the probability given by the significance test) is _____ _____ .05. She _____ the null hypothesis and _____ the alternative when *p* is _____ _____ or equal to .05.

**36.** At the .01 level, the researcher accepts (fails to reject) the null and rejects the alternative when $p$ is _____ _____ ___. She rejects the null and accepts the alternative when $p$ is _____ _____ or _____ _____ ___.

**37.** The probability connected with the selected statistical significance level is termed _____ and is symbolized by ___.

**38.** What does alpha ($\alpha$) equal when the .05 significance level is used? When the .01 level is used?

**39.** (*True or False*) The significance level is customarily selected subsequent to the carrying out of the statistical test.

**40.** For each situation, indicate whether the researcher should fail to reject (accept) or reject the null ($p$ symbolizes the probability given by the significance test):
   **a.** $p = .12$; .05 significance level used ($\alpha = .05$)
   **b.** $p = .02$; .05 significance level used
   **c.** $p = .02$; $\alpha = .05$
   **d.** $p = .02$; .01 significance level used ($\alpha = .01$)
   **e.** $p = .02$; $\alpha = .01$
   **f.** $p = .22$; .05 significance level used
   **g.** $p = .003$, .01 significance level used
   **h.** $p = .0001$; $\alpha = .01$
   **i.** $p = .052$; .05 significance level used ($\alpha = .05$)
   **j.** $p = .04$; .01 significance level used

**41.** The researcher accepts (fails to reject) the null and rejects the alternative when $p$ is _____ _____ the probability associated with the significance level ($> \alpha$). She _____ the null and accepts the alternative when $p$ is _____ _____ or _____ _____ to the probability connected with the significance level ($\leq \alpha$).

## Section 14.9

**42.** The following questions refer to Figure 14.1:
   **a.** What proportion of samples have eight heads?
   **b.** What proportion of samples have eight or more heads?
   **c.** What proportion of samples have two or fewer heads?
   **d.** What proportion of samples have eight or more heads or two or fewer heads?
   **e.** What is the probability of obtaining two or fewer or eight or more heads in 10 tosses of an unbiased coin?

**43.** Answer this in your own words: Given a true null, why do sample results differ from the null?

**44.** *p*, the probability given by a significance test conveys the probability of obtaining the study sample _____ or an even more _____ result due to _____ alone (_____ _____ alone). Stated more simply, *p* conveys the probability that the study result is due to _____ _____.

**45.** *p* also conveys the probability that the _____ between the condition stated in the _____ and the result obtained in the sample is due to _____ _____.

**46.** Assume that *p*, the probability given by the significance test, is less than the probability connected with the significance level and thus the researcher rejects the null. *Respond true or false to each interpretation of this result.*
   **a.** The researcher accepts the alternative.
   **b.** The study sample result provides strong evidence that the null is false.
   **c.** The study sample result is inconsistent with a true null.
   **d.** Given a true null, results as extreme as or even more extreme than the study sample result are obtained quite often.
   **e.** The study sample result is likely due to chance alone.
   **f.** The study sample result is likely due to sampling error alone.
   **g.** Chance alone is an unlikely explanation for the study result.
   **h.** Chance alone is an unlikely explanation for the difference between the condition stated in the null and the study sample result.
   **i.** The researcher can be certain that the null is false.
   **j.** The researcher can be confident that the null is false.
   **k.** The study sample result proves that the null is false.

**47.** Assume that *p*, the probability given by the significance test, is greater than the probability connected with the significance level and, thus, the researcher fails to reject (accepts) the null. *Respond true or false to each interpretation of this result.*
   **a.** The researcher rejects the alternative in this situation.
   **b.** The study sample result provides strong evidence that the null is false.
   **c.** The study sample result (necessarily) provides very strong evidence that the null is true.
   **d.** It is likely that the null is true.
   **e.** The researcher may be confident that the null is true.
   **f.** Given a true null, results as extreme as or even more extreme than the study sample result are hardly ever (essentially never) obtained.
   **g.** Chance alone is a highly unlikely (insufficient) explanation for this result.
   **h.** Chance alone is a highly unlikely (insufficient) explanation for the difference between the value stated in the null and the study sample result.
   **i.** Based on the information provided, the researcher knows that the study result is highly consistent with a true null.
   **j.** The study result is not highly inconsistent with the null.
   **k.** The results prove that the null is true.
   **l.** The results provide insufficient evidence for concluding that the null is false.

**48.** A researcher uses the .05 significance level. The probability given by the statistical significance test is .38, that is $p = .38$. *Respond true or false to each of the following:*
   **a.** The researcher should reject the null.
   **b.** The researcher should fail to reject the null.
   **c.** The researcher should accept the null.
   **d.** The researcher should accept the alternative.
   **e.** The researcher should reject the alternative.
   **f.** The study sample result does not provide strong evidence that the null is false.
   **g.** Given a true null, results as extreme as or even more extreme than the study sample result, are highly uncommon.
   **h.** Chance alone hardly ever produces results as extreme as or even more extreme than the study sample result.
   **i.** Chance alone is a highly unlikely (insufficient) explanation for this result.
   **j.** As the null is accepted, the researcher may be confident that it is true.
   **k.** It is likely that the null is true.

**49.** A researcher uses the .05 significance level. The probability given by the statistical significance test is .02, that is, $p = .02$. *Respond true or false to each of the following:*
   **a.** The researcher should reject the null.
   **b.** The researcher should fail to reject the null.
   **c.** The researcher should accept the null.
   **d.** The researcher should accept the alternative.
   **e.** The researcher should reject the alternative.
   **f.** The study sample result provides strong evidence that the null is false.
   **g.** The null is likely false.
   **h.** Given a true null, results as extreme as or even more extreme than the study sample result are obtained quite often (say in about 20% or more of random samples).
   **i.** The study sample result is likely due to chance alone.
   **j.** The study sample result is unlikely due to chance alone.
   **k.** The difference between the condition stated in the null and the study sample result is unlikely due to chance alone.

**50.** For each value of $p$, the probability given by the significance test, indicate how confident the researcher can be that the null is false.
   **a.** $p = .08$
   **b.** $p = .02$
   **c.** $p = .13$
   **d.** $p = .005$

**51.** A researcher carries out a statistical significance test and rejects the null at the .05 level. *Choose the best response:*
   **a.** $p \leq .05$
   **b.** Given a true null, the probability of obtaining the study sample result is less than or equal to .05.

c. The probability that the study sample result is due to chance alone is less than .05.

d. The probability that the difference between the condition stated in the null and the study sample result is due to chance alone is less than or equal to .05.

e. All of the above are true.

52. When a researcher rejects the null at the .05 statistical significance level, she can be (at least) ___% confident that the null is false. When a researcher rejects at the .01 level, she can be (at least) ___% confident that the null is false.

## Section 14.10

53. The _____ hypothesis offers the simplest, most straightforward explanation of the study sample result. When it deals with association, it asserts that variables are _____ in the population and that the only reason for association in the sample is _____, that is, _____ _____.

54. *Respond true or false to each of the following:*
    a. The alternative hypothesis offers a more complex explanation than does the null.
    b. The alternative asserts that variables are associated in the sample only due to sampling error.
    c. Science prefers complex explanations to simple ones.

55. Real explanations are explanations other than _____.

## Section 14.11

56. When the probability of obtaining the study result is less than or equal to the probability associated with the statistical significance level (less than or equal to $\alpha$), the result is said to be _____ _____.

57. Statistical significance goes hand in hand with _____ the null. When a result is not statistically significant, the researcher _____ to _____ the null.

58. A researcher carries out a significance test using the .05 level. The probability given by the test is less than or equal to .05. *Respond true or false to each.*
    a. The researcher rejects the null.
    b. The study result is statistically significant.
    c. Given a true null, the probability of obtaining the study result or an even more extreme result is less than or equal to .05.
    d. The probability that the result is due to chance alone is less than or equal to .05.
    e. The result is likely due to chance alone.
    f. The probability that the difference between the study result and the condition stated in the null is due to chance alone is less than or equal to .05.
    g. The result is statistically significant at the .05 level.
    h. The result provides strong evidence that the null is false.

**59.** A researcher carries out a significance test using the .05 level. The probability given by the test is greater than .05. *Respond true or false to each.*

    **a.** The researcher fails to rejects the null.

    **b.** The study result is statistically significant.

    **c.** Given a true null, the probability of obtaining the study result or an even more extreme result is greater than .05.

    **d.** The probability that the result is due to chance alone is greater than .05.

    **e.** Chance alone is not a sufficiently unlikely explanation for the study result for the null to be rejected.

    **f.** The probability that the difference between the study result and the value stated in the null is due to chance alone is greater than .05.

    **g.** The result is not statistically significant at the .05 level.

    **h.** The result provides strong evidence that the null is false.

# 15

# THE LARGE SAMPLE TEST OF THE MEAN AND NEW CONCEPTS

## 15.1 ■ CHAPTER OVERVIEW

Chapter 15 presents statistical concepts and uses the *large sample test of* $\overline{X}$ to provide some beginning practice in statistical significance testing. Chapter 15 introduces the *hypothesis testing model, assumptions of significance* tests, *two-tailed* and *one-tailed* tests, *rejection regions*, and *decision rules*. It demonstrates how the .05 and .01 levels are applied. The uncertainty that accompanies decisions on hypotheses is emphasized in a discussion of *Type I* and *Type II errors*.

## 15.2 ■ A MODEL FOR HYPOTHESIS TESTING

Four steps make up the **hypothesis testing model**, the model for carrying out statistical significance tests and making decisions regarding the hypothesis pair (Glass & Hopkins, 1996, p. 258). Chapter 14 introduced some of these steps.

1. State the hypothesis pair (the null and the alternative hypotheses; the pair may be directional or nondirectional).
2. Select a statistical significance level; usually the .05 level ($\alpha = .05$) or the .01 level ($\alpha = .01$) is selected.
3. Select and carry out the appropriate statistical significance test (the appropriate test is determined by the types of variables involved and by other factors that will be presented).
4. Using the results of the significance test, make a decision regarding hypothesis pair:

   ■ If $p$ (the probability resulting from the test) is greater than the probability associated with the selected significance level (> alpha), fail to reject (accept) the null hypothesis and reject the alternative hypothesis.

   ■ If $p$ is less than or equal to the probability associated with the selected significance level (≤ alpha), reject the null hypothesis and accept the alternative hypothesis.

The steps in the model are introduced gradually over the course of this chapter.

The first significance test that we study, the **large sample test of the mean (large sample test of** $\overline{X}$), examines whether the mean of a sample differs from a hypothesized value. It may be used when sample size ($N$) is 100 or greater.

Sometimes, discussion diverges from the large sample test of $\overline{X}$ to illustrate concepts that underlie significance tests. For instance, let us consider now the assumptions of a significance test.

## 15.3 ■ ASSUMPTIONS OF STATISTICAL SIGNIFICANCE TESTS

### 15.3.1 ■ Definition and Assumptions of the Large Sample Test of $\overline{X}$

Statistical significance tests are based on **assumptions**, conditions that must be met for the test to yield an accurate probability (an accurate $p$). Whenever a test assumption is not met (is violated), the probability given by the test differs, at least to some degree, from the actual probability that the study sample result is caused by chance. In other words, when an assumption is violated, the test contains some degree of inaccuracy. A key assumption of the large sample test of $\overline{X}$ is the **normality assumption**, that is that the study sample is selected from a population that is normally distributed.

A statistical test can be either robust or not robust to an assumption. When a test is **robust** to an assumption, carrying out the test when the assumption is violated has only a minor impact on accuracy. For instance, the large sample test of $\overline{X}$ is robust to the normality assumption. When this test is carried out in the absence of normality, the probability given by the test does indeed differ from the actual probability that the result is due to chance. However, presuming that $N \geq 100$, the degree of inaccuracy that is introduced is so small that, pragmatically, we may regard the test's probability as accurate. In sum, given that $N \geq 100$, the large sample test is robust to the normality assumption and we may carry it out even when the normality assumption is violated.

When a test is not robust to an assumption, violation of the assumption can greatly affect accuracy. When a test is not robust to an assumption, the test should be carried out only if the assumption is met.

### 15.3.2 ■ Assumptions Common to All Tests

Random sampling is an implicit assumption of all inferential statistical procedures presented in this text. Specifically, Chapter 12 (Section 12.3) presented three characteristics that random samples possess: (a) selection of cases is by a method of chance, (b) all cases have an equal chance of selection, and (c) the selection of each case is independent from that of each other case. Chapter 12 also presented the independence of observations assumption, in essence, that pairs or groups of cases do not share some unmeasured factor that makes scores more similar (or, on occasion, more dissimilar) than would otherwise be so. Random sampling and independence of observations are assumptions for *all* inferential procedures presented in this text. When these are not present, the procedures should not be carried out, although Chapter 16, Section 16.8 presents an exception.

## 15.4 ■ THE FIRST TWO STEPS OF THE HYPOTHESIS TESTING MODEL

Now for a working example of the large sample test of $\overline{X}$, presume that you are interested in improving the parenting skills of parents of elementary school-age children and that you develop an intervention with this purpose in mind.

From the population of all parents of elementary school children in your city, you randomly select 100 parents, each from a different family, to take part in your program. All agree to do so. Following your implementation of the intervention, you administer a scale that measures parenting skills. Let us say that the scale is scored so that higher scores indicate better parenting skills and lower ones indicate worse skills. Presume also that, in a previous large-scale research project, this scale was administered to a very large, representative sample of parents from across the United States. Finally, presume that the mean scale score in this large representative sample was 100 points.

Let us say that the mean scale score of the 100 parents in your study sample is 105 points, with a standard deviation of 20 points. Your interest is in comparing parenting skills of those in your sample to those in the representative sample. The mean score in your sample is five points higher. Is this difference plausibly caused by chance alone (sampling error alone) or, on the other hand, is chance alone an unlikely explanation for this difference?

The prior chapter did not use statistical symbols in hypothesis statements. I begin to do so now. Let us carry out the first two steps of the hypothesis testing model for our example.

**1.** State the Hypothesis Pair

Let us specify a nondirectional hypothesis pair. In a nondirectional pair for the large sample test of $\overline{X}$, the null states that the mean of the population from which the study sample was randomly selected equals some given value. The alternative states that it does not equal this value. For our example:

Null:          $H_0: \mu = 100$ points

Alternative:  $H_1: \mu \neq 100$ points

Recall that $\mu$ is the symbol for the population mean. $\boldsymbol{H_0}$ symbolizes the null hypothesis; $\boldsymbol{H_1}$ symbolizes the alternative. Expressing the hypothesis pair in words:

Null:          The mean parenting skills score in the population of all parents of elementary school children in your city equals 100 points.

Alternative:  The mean parenting skills score in the population of all parents of elementary school children in your city does not equal 100 points.

The decision to use a nondirectional pair rather than a directional one reflects a conservative approach on our part. It acknowledges that the mean in the population of all parents of elementary school children in your city could potentially be either greater than or less than 100. In essence, the null asserts that if you could administer your parenting intervention to the full population of elementary school parents in your city, the mean score of this population on the parenting skills measure would equal 100 points.

**2.** Select a Statistical Significance Level

We will use the .05 statistical significance level ($\alpha = .05$; alpha = .05).

Having presented the first two steps of the hypothesis testing model for our example, we now discuss the role of sampling distributions in significance testing. This discussion builds on the discussion of sampling distributions in Chapter 14.

## 15.5 ■ STATISTICAL TESTS AND SAMPLING DISTRIBUTIONS

The basic job of a significance test is to determine the probability of obtaining the study sample result under the assumption that the null hypothesis is true. Significance tests use sampling distributions to do so. Different tests use different distributions. The large sample test of $\overline{X}$ is based on the sampling distribution of $\overline{X}$ that was introduced in Chapter 12, Section 12.7.2. Recall that a sampling distribution of $\overline{X}$ is the distribution that would result if one picked an infinite number of random samples of given size from a population and, for each sample, recorded its mean.

What would the sampling distribution of $\overline{X}$ look like for our example if the null was indeed true? In other words, what would the sampling distribution of $\overline{X}$ look like if an infinite number of random samples of size 100 ($N = 100$) were selected from a population with a mean of 100 ($\mu = 100$)? According to the central limit theorem and subsequent discussion in Chapters 12 and 13:

1. Its mean will equal that in the population ($\mu$). Hence, its mean will equal 100 points.
2. Because $N \geq 100$, an accurate estimate of its standard deviation ($\sigma_{\overline{X}}$, the standard error of the mean) can be obtained by dividing the standard deviation in the sample by the square root of the sample size:

$$s_{\overline{X}} = \frac{20}{\sqrt{100}} = \frac{20}{10} = 2.0$$

3. Given that sample size is 100, its shape will be close to normal.

Figure 15.1 presents the sampling distribution of $\overline{X}$ for our example. It has a mean of 100, a standard deviation extremely close to 2.0, and a nearly normal shape. Observe that the X axis in Figure 15.1 has two scales. The top scale uses original measurement units (raw scores) and the bottom scale uses $z$ scores. With all cases (sample means) expressed as $z$ scores, the sampling distribution of $\overline{X}$ has a mean of 0.00 and a standard deviation of 1.00.

We may use our knowledge of the normal distribution to draw conclusions about the sampling distribution of $\overline{X}$ in Figure 15.1. These conclusions help illustrate concepts important in significance testing.

In a normal distribution, 95% of cases are located within 1.96 standard deviations of the mean. Multiplying the estimate of the standard deviation of the sampling distribution ($s_{\overline{X}} = 2.0$) by 1.96 informs us that approximately 95% of sample means are located within 3.92 points

FIGURE 15.1 ■ Sampling Distribution of $\overline{X}$ for Parenting Skills Score

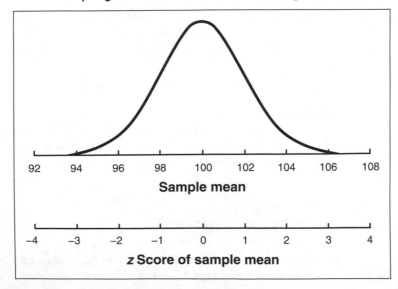

FIGURE 15.2 ■ Sampling Distribution of $\overline{X}$ and 2.5% Tails

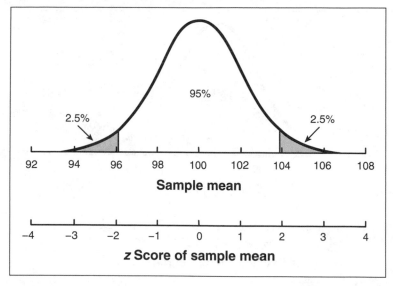

(2.0 × 1.96 = 3.92) of the value stated in the null ($\mu = 100$). Thus, about 95% of means are located between 96.08 and 103.92 ($100 - 3.92 = 96.08; 100 + 3.92 = 103.92$).

If about 95% of sample are within 3.92 points of the value stated in the null, then about 5% of means differ from this value by 3.92 points or more, that is, about 5% of means are either $\leq 96.08$ or $\geq 103.92$. Given that the normal curve is symmetric, about 2.5% (5% / 2 = 2.5%) of means are $\leq 96.08$ and about 2.5% are $\geq 103.92$. Figure 15.2 presents the sampling distribution with its upper and lower 2.5% tails.

In discussing the percentages of cases in given areas, I have used "about" and "approximately." Percentages are approximate because the sampling distribution's standard deviation is estimated rather than exact ($s_{\overline{X}} = \frac{s}{\sqrt{N}}$) and, further, because its shape is close to but not precisely normal. As we move forward, more often than not, I discontinue the use of "about" and "approximately." Because $N \geq 100$, our calculations are sufficiently accurate to justify doing so. We continue to presume that the null is true ($\mu = 100$).

The just-presented conclusions involved percentages. We may also draw conclusions about probabilities. What is the probability of randomly selecting a mean that is either $\leq 96.08$ or $\geq 103.92$? Because 5% of cases have such means, this probability is .05: 5% / 100% = .05, that is, $p = .05$.

To ask another question, "What is the probability of randomly selecting a sample mean that is greater than or equal to the study sample mean, that is, of selecting a mean $\geq 105$?" To determine this probability, we need to compute a $z$ score for the study sample mean and then refer to the normal distribution table, Table A.1 in Appendix A. This $z$ score is $z = (105 - 100) / 2 = 2.50$. Table A.1 indicates that the proportion of cases in a normal distribution with $z$ scores greater than or equal to 2.50 is .0062. Thus, the probability of randomly selecting a mean that is greater than or equal to the study sample mean is .0062, that is, $p = .0062$.

A related question is "What is the probability of randomly selecting a mean that differs from the value stated in the null ($\mu = 100$) by as much as or by more than does the study sample mean, that is, of selecting a mean that differs by five or more points in *either* direction?" Stated differently, what is the probability of randomly selecting a mean that is either $\leq 95$ or $\geq 105$? As the normal curve is symmetric, the proportion of means $\leq 95$ is the same as that for means $\geq 105$. Hence, the probability of randomly selecting a mean $\leq 95$ is .0062.

FIGURE 15.3 ■ **Proportion of Means More Extreme Than the Study Sample Mean**

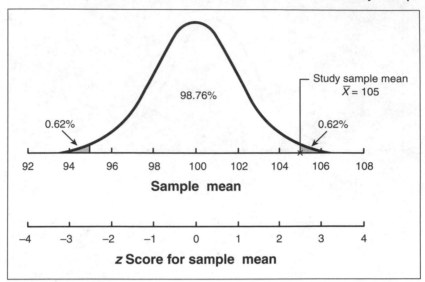

The probability of randomly selecting a mean either $\leq 95$ or $\geq 105$ is $.0062 + .0062 = .0124$, that is, $p = .0124$.

Using terminology introduced in Chapter 14, Section 14.7, the probability of selecting our study sample mean ($\overline{X} = 105$) or an even more extreme one, both directions considered is .0124. Figure 15.3 presents the percentage of means that are more extreme than the study sample mean.

## 15.6 ■ DIRECTIONAL VERSUS NONDIRECTIONAL HYPOTHESIS PAIRS

### 15.6.1 ■ Overview

Interpretation of the study sample result differs for directional and nondirectional hypothesis pairs. The discussion that follows pertains to the large sample test of the mean and (with some exceptions) to significance tests in general.

### 15.6.2 ■ Nondirectional Hypothesis Pair

When the hypothesis pair is nondirectional, study sample results near to the center of the sampling distribution—that is close to the value stated in the null hypothesis—are viewed as consistent with the null. As results move farther away from the center toward the tails, they become increasingly inconsistent with the null, that is, increasingly less likely given a true null and increasingly less likely to be due to chance alone. At some point, the study sample result becomes so extreme that the researcher rejects the null.

When the hypothesis pair is nondirectional, study sample results in both tails (the upper tail and the lower tail) may result in rejection of the null. When results in both tails may result in rejection, the significance test is a **two-tailed test**. When the hypothesis pair is nondirectional, the significance test is typically two-tailed. (Chapter 19, Section 19.4.4 presents an exception.)

The area(s) of the sampling distribution that result in rejection of the null are termed **rejection regions** (Toothaker, 1986, p. 316) or **critical regions**. The proportion of cases located in the rejection regions equals the probability associated with the selected significance level, that is, equals alpha ($\alpha$). When the .05 level is used ($\alpha = .05$), this proportion is .05. When the .01 level is used ($\alpha = .01$), it is .01.

As stated earlier, two-tailed statistical tests have two rejection regions, one in each tail. The proportion of cases in each region is equal. Thus, when the .05 level is used, the rejection regions are the upper 2.5% tail and the lower 2.5% tail (2.5% + 2.5% = 5%); when the .01 level is used, the rejection regions are the upper 0.5% tail and the lower 0.5% tail (0.5% + 0.5% = 1.0%).

A two-tailed test has two rejection regions because, given a nondirectional hypothesis pair, extreme results in both directions are inconsistent with the null. Rejection regions are presented visually as we progress through this chapter.

### 15.6.3 ■ Directional Hypothesis Pair

When the hypothesis pair is directional, study sample results near the center of the distribution *and* those that differ in the direction stated in the null are viewed as consistent with the null. As a result moves away from the center of the distribution *only* in the direction stated in the alternative hypothesis—in a positive direction when the alternative hypothesis states greater than; in a negative one when it states less than—the result becomes increasingly inconsistent with the null. At some point, it becomes sufficiently extreme for the null to be rejected.

When the hypothesis pair is directional, study results in only one tail result in rejection of the null. Only one tail results in rejection because results in only one tail are inconsistent with the null. The tail resulting in rejection is located in the direction stated in the *alternative hypothesis*, the upper tail when the alternative hypothesis states greater than and the lower tail when it states less than. When results in only one tail of the sampling distribution lead to rejection of the null, the significance test is termed a **one-tailed test**. Whenever the hypothesis pair is directional, the significance test is one-tailed.

Just as for the two-tailed test, the proportion of cases in the rejection region for a one-tailed test equals the probability associated with the chosen significance level ($\alpha$). Thus, this proportion is .05 when the .05 level is used ($\alpha = .05$) and .01 when the .01 level is used ($\alpha = .01$).

Table 15.1 presents the rejection region(s) in relationship to the type of hypothesis pair (directional or nondirectional); the expected direction (if any) of the study result, whether the test

### TABLE 15.1 ■ Hypothesis Pair, One- or Two-Tailed Test, Significance Level, and Location of Rejection Region(s)

| Hypothesis Pair | Direction of Expectations for Study Result | Logical Operator | | One- or Two-Tailed Test | Significance Level (alpha, $\alpha$) | Location of Rejection Region(s) |
|---|---|---|---|---|---|---|
| | | Null | Alternative | | | |
| Nondirectional | None | = | ≠ | Two | .05 | Upper and lower 2.5% tails |
| Nondirectional | None | = | ≠ | Two | .01 | Upper and lower 0.5% tails |
| Directional | Greater | ≤ | > | One | .05 | Upper 5% tail |
| Directional | Greater | ≤ | > | One | .01 | Upper 1% tail |
| Directional | Less | ≥ | < | One | .05 | Lower 5% tail |
| Directional | Less | ≥ | < | One | .01 | Lower 1% tail |

is one- or two-tailed; and the selected significance level (.05 or .01). Table 15.1 summarizes the concepts discussed in this section. Observe that

■ two-tailed tests are used with nondirectional pairs, whereas one-tailed tests are used with directional ones;

■ two-tailed tests have two rejection regions, whereas one-tailed tests have only one;

■ for one-tailed tests, the rejection region is in the direction of expectations (the direction stated in the alternative hypothesis); and

■ the proportion of cases in the rejection region(s) equals the probability connected with the significance level (5% =.05 for the .05 level; 1% = .01 for the .01 level).

## 15.7 ■ CARRYING OUT THE SIGNIFICANCE TEST USING THE SAMPLING DISTRIBUTION

We return now to the hypothesis testing model and our parenting skills example. In effect, we carried out the large sample test of $\overline{X}$ test informally in Section 15.5. We now use the sampling distribution to do so more formally.

We have determined that, given a true null, 2.5% of means in the sampling distribution are $\geq$ 103.92 and 2.5% are $\leq$ 96.08. These values define, respectively, the upper and lower 2.5% tails. Recall that our hypothesis pair is nondirectional (Step 1) and, thus, our significance test is two-tailed. We selected the .05 level (Step 2). For a two-tailed test using the .05 level, the upper and lower 2.5% tails form the rejection regions. Figure 15.4 presents these and the study sample mean. Because the sample mean ($\overline{X}$ = 105) is located in a rejection region, we reject the null and, thus, accept the alternative hypothesis. We conclude that the mean score on the parenting skills instrument of elementary school parents in your city—in other words, the mean score if all such parents received your intervention—does not equal 100 ($\mu \neq 100$).

FIGURE 15.4 ■ **Study Sample Mean and Rejection Areas For a Two-Tailed Test, $\alpha$ = .05**

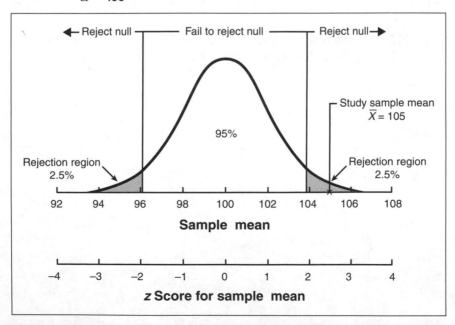

## 15.8 ■ FINISHING THE EXAMPLE USING THE FORMULA

### 15.8.1 ■ Step 3: Carry Out the Test

The prior section carried out the significance test visually using the sampling distribution of $\overline{X}$. All significance tests are based on sampling distributions. When one understands sampling distribution theory, she understands how the test does its job. Yet, just as you need not understand how its engine works to drive a car, you need not understand sampling distribution theory to carry out a statistical significance test. Formulas are provided for doing so. The two formulas for the large sample test of $\overline{X}$ are

$$z \approx \frac{\overline{X} - \mu}{\left(\frac{s}{\sqrt{N}}\right)} \qquad (15.1)$$

where $\approx$ is the approximately equal to sign, $\overline{X}$ is the sample mean, $\mu$ is the value of the population mean stated in the null, $s$ is the standard deviation in the sample, and $N$ is the sample size. A second formula is

$$z \approx \frac{\overline{X} - \mu}{s_{\overline{X}}} \qquad (15.2)$$

where $s_{\overline{X}}$ is the estimate of the standard error of the mean. These two formulas are equivalent (yield identical results).

In essence, Formulas 15.1 and 15.2 transform the study sample mean into a $z$ score with respect to the sampling distribution of $\overline{X}$. The formulas use the approximately equal to sign ($\approx$) because they use estimates of the standard error of the mean ($s_{\overline{X}} \approx \sigma_{\overline{X}}$). Whenever $N \geq 100$, this introduces hardly any inaccuracy.

The value obtained from carrying out a significance test formula is the **obtained statistic** (*test statistic*). As the large sample test formulas calculate a $z$, our value is an obtained $z$.

We move now to Step 3 of the hypothesis testing model.

**3.** Carry Out the Test
First, let us calculate the estimate of the standard error of the mean (the estimate of the standard deviation of the sampling distribution):

$$s_{\overline{X}} = \frac{20}{\sqrt{100}} = \frac{20}{10} = 2.00$$

Next, we use Formula 15.2 to calculate $z$

$$z \approx \frac{105 - 100}{2.00} = 2.50$$

### 15.8.2 ■ Decision Rules

Before moving on to the final step in the model, making a decision on the hypothesis pair, I need to introduce decision rules. Significance tests have **decision rules**, criteria by which the decision to fail to reject (accept) or reject the null is made. Decision rules for the large sample test of $\overline{X}$ vary according to whether a one- or two-tailed test is used and according to the selected significance level. For a two-tailed, large sample test of $\overline{X}$ that uses the .05 significance level (the situation in our example), the decision rule is to:

Fail to reject (accept) the null if the absolute value of the obtained $z$ is less than 1.96.

Reject the null if the absolute value of the obtained $z$ is greater than or equal to 1.96.

The values that determine the researcher's decision to fail to reject or reject the null are the **critical value(s)**. For a two-tailed, large sample test of $\overline{X}$ using the .05 level, the critical values are $-1.96$ and $1.96$.

A test's critical values derive from the sampling distribution that the test uses. As the sampling distribution for the large sample test of $\overline{X}$ has a nearly normal shape, its critical values come from the normal distribution. In a normal distribution, 2.5% of cases have $z$ scores less than $-1.96$ and 2.5% have $z$ scores greater than 1.96% (see Table A.1 in Appendix A). Thus, $-1.96$ ($-1.96$ standard deviations below the mean) defines boundary of the lower rejection region and 1.96 (1.96 standard deviations above the mean) does so for the upper rejection region (see Figure 15.4).

### 15.8.3 ■ Step 4: Make a Decision

As the decision rule has been provided, we may now use it to make a decision on the hypothesis pair. Our obtained $z$ equals 2.50. The absolute value of our obtained $z$, 2.50, exceeds 1.96. Following the decision rule, we reject the null and, thus, accept the alternative. We conclude that, in the population of parents of elementary school students in your city, the mean score on the parenting skills scale does not equal 100 points. In essence, we conclude that if all elementary school parents in the city took your parenting skills intervention, their mean score would not equal 100.

We have rejected the null using the .05 significance level (two-tailed test). Hence, we know that

- given a true null, the probability of obtaining the study sample result ($\overline{X} = 105$) or an even more extreme result given a true null ($\mu = 100$) $\leq .05$; and

- the probability of obtaining the sample result ($\overline{X} = 105$) or an even more extreme result due to chance alone is $\leq .05$.

The various interpretations connected with rejecting the null presented in the prior chapter apply (see Section 14.9.3). Your study result provides strong evidence that the null is false. It is an unlikely result given a true null and is unlikely to be due to chance alone. Your result is inconsistent with a true null. We may be confident, although not certain, that the null is false.

As discussed in Chapter 14 (Section 14.11), rejection of the null and statistical significance go hand in hand. Your result is a statistically significant one. More specifically, it is statistically significant at the .05 level (two-tailed test). Finally, we can be confident that the difference between the value stated in the null ($\mu = 100$) and your result ($\overline{X} = 105$) is not due to chance alone.

### 15.9 ■ EFFECT OF CHOICE OF SIGNIFICANCE LEVEL ON DECISION MAKING

Suppose that rather than selecting the .05 significance level, we had selected the .01 level ($\alpha = .01$) for our parenting skills example. We continue to use a nondirectional hypothesis pair and, thus, a two-tailed test. The decision rule for a two-tailed, large sample test of $\overline{X}$ using the .01 level is to:

Fail to reject (accept) the null if the absolute value of the obtained $z$ is less than 2.58.

Reject the null if the absolute value of the obtained $z$ is greater than or equal to 2.58.

The critical values (stated in the decision rule) are $-2.58$ and 2.58.

We have already calculated the obtained $z$, which is 2.50. The absolute value of the obtained $z$, 2.50, is less than 2.58. Hence, we fail to reject (accept) the null and reject the alternative.

FIGURE 15.5 ■ **Study Sample Mean and Rejection Regions For a Two-Tailed Test,**
$\alpha = .01$

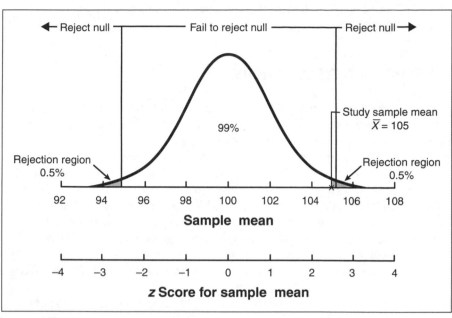

As discussed earlier, the critical values for the large sample test of $\overline{X}$ come from the normal distribution. In a normal distribution, 1% of cases are located 2.58 or more standard deviations from the mean, 0.5% in each tail (see Table A.1 in Appendix A).[1] Thus, the rejection regions for a two-tailed, large sample test at the .01 level begin 2.58 standard deviations away from the value stated in the null.

Because the estimated standard deviation ($s_{\overline{x}}$) is 2.0, the null is rejected for study sample means $\leq 94.84$ or $\geq 105.16$ ($2.00 \times 2.58 = 5.16$; $100 - 5.16 = 94.84$; $100 + 5.16 = 105.16$). Figure 15.5 presents the rejection regions and the study sample mean. The study sample mean is not located in a rejection region—it just misses being in the rejection region in the upper tail.

Given a true null, the probability of obtaining your result or an even more extreme one is $\geq .01$. And, similarly, the probability of obtaining your result or an even more extreme one due to chance alone is $\geq .01$. In summary, given our use of the .01 level (two-tailed test), your results do not provide sufficiently strong evidence for rejecting the null.

We want to be careful not to draw the "mistaken" conclusions that sometimes accompany a decision to "accept" the null. In particular, we do not conclude that the null is likely true and we are not confident that it is true. We presume it to be true only in the sense that our results do not convincingly demonstrate otherwise (just as a jury finds not guilty in the absence of evidence beyond a reasonable doubt).

Given our use of a different significance level, your result now is not a statistically significant one. More specifically, it is not statistically significant at the .01 level using a two-tailed test.

When we used the .05 level, we rejected the null. Now, we accept it. The different decisions reached using the two significance levels demonstrate that, other things being equal, it is more difficult to reject the null when the .01 level is used than when the .05 level is used. This is because rejection at the .01 level requires a larger difference from the value stated in the null than does that at the .05 level. To see this, compare Figures 15.4 and 15.5. At the .05 level, a difference of 3.92 points from this value ($\mu = 100$) results in rejection. At the .01 level, this difference increases to 5.16 points. Choice of the .01 level reduces the likelihood of accepting the alternative hypothesis.

In essence, the alternative asserts that something real—something more than chance alone—is causing the study result. Although one strives to be objective, almost instinctively, one's "human side" "roots for" the alternative. Why would a researcher choose a significance level that lessens the chance of accepting it?

## 15.10 ■ TYPE I AND TYPE II ERRORS

The researcher never knows with certainty whether her decision regarding the null is correct. The selection of significance level, .01 or .05, bears directly on the likelihood of Type I error. When a **Type I error** is made, the researcher rejects a null that is in reality true.

Suppose that a researcher conducts 100 statistical significance tests, in each case using the .05 significance level. Suppose also that in each case (unknown to the researcher), the null hypothesis is true. How often will she mistakenly reject this true null, that is, how often will she make a Type I error? When the .05 level is chosen, 5% of sample results are located in the rejection region(s) of the sampling distribution. Hence (given a true null), the probability of obtaining a result that leads to rejection is .05. Thus, in the long run (given a true null), 5% of study sample results lead to rejection of the null at the .05 level. As such, our best guess is that, given 100 tests, the researcher will mistakenly reject the null five times (5% of 100 = 5). Stated differently, we expect that she will make about five Type I errors.

The probability of a Type I error equals the probability associated with the significance level, that is, alpha ($\alpha$). When alpha equals .05, this probability is .05; when alpha equals .01, it is .01. Choosing the .01 level rather than the .05 level reduces the risk of Type I error by a factor of five (.05 / .01 = 5 times). If the just-described experiment (100 tests, null is true in each case) was repeated using the .01 level, our best guess would be that the researcher would mistakenly reject the null only once (100 $\times$ .01 = 1).

The cause of Type I error is simply sampling error (chance). The researcher has had the "bad luck" of drawing an atypical result in a tail of the sampling distribution. Of course, having drawn only a single sample result and not having access to the population, she has no way to know that she has done so. All that she can know is that, given a true null, the probability of a Type I error is .05 (1 in 20) if she has chosen the .05 level and .01 (1 in 100) if she has chosen the .01 level.

Rejections of the null at the .01 level are more convincing than are those at the .05 level because the probability that the study sample result is due to sampling error alone, that is to Type I error, is lower. Researchers often choose the .01 level when the negative consequences of mistakenly rejecting the null are high.

Consider a new drug with the potential to increase survival rates of those with HIV infection but also with potentially severe side effects. One would not want to market such a drug on a large scale without being thoroughly convinced of its effectiveness. A 1 in 20 (5%) chance of an error may be too great of a risk to accept. The researcher could reduce this risk—the risk of a Type I error—to 1 in 100 (1%) by choosing the .01 level. (Of course, if the drug's side effects were sufficiently severe, even a 1 in 100 chance might not justify a decision to market.)

While choosing the .01 level rather than the .05 level reduces the risk of Type I error, it increases the risk of Type II error. A **Type II error** occurs when the researcher fails to reject (accepts) a null that is in actuality false. Choice of the .01 level increases the probability of a Type II error because the areas of the sampling distribution that result in acceptance of the alternative hypothesis (i.e., the rejection regions) are smaller and further from the value stated in the null. To see this, compare Figures 15.4 and 15.5. The probability of a Type II error is termed beta (pronounced as in [bait-ah]), symbolized by the Greek letter $\beta$. This text does not present a method for calculating $\beta$.

The probabilities of Type I versus Type II error are in tension. Choice of the .01 level (rather than the .05 level) reduces the risk of Type I error but increases that of Type II error. Choice of the .05 level (rather than the .01 level) reduces the risk of Type II error but increases that of Type I

TABLE 15.2 ■ Decision Making and the Null and Alternative Hypotheses

| | | True State of Affairs in the Population | |
|---|---|---|---|
| | | **Null is True** | **Null is False** |
| **Decision** | **Fail to reject (accept) the null** | Correct decision | Incorrect decision (Type II error) |
| | **Reject the null** | Incorrect decision (Type I error) | Correct decision |

error. The trick is to find the right balance between one type of error versus the other. Chapter 16 introduces *statistical power*, which is closely connected with this issue.

As mentioned previously, the .05 level is used most frequently, basically, because of tradition. By tradition, social science seems willing to accept a 5% risk of rejecting a true null.

Decision making in hypothesis testing is probabilistic. Table 15.2 summarizes the possible relationships between the true state of affairs in the population (unknown to the researcher) and the decisions made in hypothesis testing.

Table 15.2 presents four possible scenarios: (a) the null is true and the researcher makes the correct decision (fail to reject), (b) the null is true and the researcher makes an incorrect decision (reject; Type I error), (c) the null is false and the researcher makes a correct decision (reject), and (d) the null is false and the researcher makes an incorrect decision (fail to reject; Type II error).

The researcher knows the decision that she makes but never knows assuredly whether this decision is correct. In a sense, the researcher never makes a decision at all. Her "decision" flows directly from the hypothesis testing model: if $p$ exceeds the significance level, she "decides" to fail to reject the null; if $p$ is less than or equal to the significance level, she "decides" to reject it.

Chapter 14, Section 14.9.4, discusses the degree of confidence that a researcher who rejects the null can have that the null is false. At the .05 level, she may have (at least) 95% confidence that this is so. In other words, she can have 95% confidence that her decision is a correct one. However (at the .05 level and given a true null), there is a 5% chance of obtaining a result in a rejection region and, thus, rejecting the null. Thus, there is a 5% chance that the researcher's decision is incorrect, a 5% chance that she has made a Type I error. At the .01 level, the researcher can have (at least) 99% confidence that her decision to reject the null is correct. On the other hand (given a true null), there is a 1% chance of an incorrect decision, a 1% chance of Type I error.

## 15.11 ■ TWO-TAILED VERSUS ONE-TAILED TESTS

### 15.11.1 ■ Carrying Out Our Example

When the hypothesis pair is directional, the significance test is one-tailed. As you know, a one-tailed test has a single rejection region, its location being in the direction stated in the alternative hypothesis. Let us carry out our parenting skills example using a directional hypothesis pair and, therefore, a one-tailed test:

**1.** State the hypothesis pair.

$H_0: \mu \leq 100$   $H_1: \mu > 100$ or, in words:

Null:        The mean parenting skills score in the population of all parents of elementary school children in your city is less than or equal to 100 points.

Alternative: The mean parenting skills score in the population of all parents of elementary school children in your city is greater than 100 points.

The decision to state a directional hypothesis pair conveys that prior research, theory, common sense, and/or logic indicate convincingly that the result will be in a particular direction. A solid rationale for a directional hypothesis can be generated in our example. Your intervention is designed to improve parenting skills. As such, the common sense expectation is for better parenting skills in your study sample (which has received the intervention) than in the large, representative sample (which has not). Observe that, as always, the alternative hypothesis rather than the null states the expected direction of results.

**2.** Choose the significance level: We will use the .05 significance level ($\alpha = .05$).
**3.** Carry out the test.

The value of the obtained $z$ is not affected by whether the test is one- or two-tailed. Our obtained $z$, calculated earlier, equals 2.50.

**4.** Make a decision.

For a one-tailed, large sample test of $\overline{X}$ when the alternative hypothesis states greater than and the .05 level is used, the decision rule is to:

Fail to reject (accept) the null if the obtained $z$ is less than 1.645.

Reject the null if $z$ is 1.645 or greater.

Because our obtained $z$, 2.50, exceeds 1.645, we reject the null and accept the alternative. Hence, given a one-tailed test using the .05 level, our result is statistically significant.

In making our decision, we simply followed the steps of the hypothesis testing model. It will, however, be helpful to see how the sampling distribution of $\overline{X}$ guided this decision. Because the alternative hypothesis states greater than and because the .05 level is used, the rejection region is the upper 5% tail of the sampling distribution. Five percent of cases in a normal distribution are located 1.645 or more standard deviations above the mean (see Table A.1). Hence, any sample mean located 1.645 or more standard deviations above the mean of the sampling distribution results in rejection of the null. In our example, the sampling distribution's mean is 100 and its standard deviation ($s_{\overline{X}}$) is 2.00. A mean of 103.29 is 1.645 standard deviations above the mean: $100 + (1.645 \times 2.00) = 103.29$. Thus, all means greater than or equal to 103.29 result in rejection. Because our mean is 105, we reject the null. Figure 15.6 presents the sampling distribution and its rejection region.

In Figure 15.6, only means in the upper tail of the distribution result in rejection. Compare Figure 15.6 with Figure 15.4 that presents the rejection regions for a two-tailed test using the .05 level. For both figures, direct your attention to the rejection region in the *upper* tail. Observe that this region is larger for the one-tailed test (it represents 5% of cases) than for the two-tailed test (2.5% of cases). Observe also that for the one-tailed test, results closer to the value stated in the null result in rejection. For the one-tailed test (Figure 15.6), means greater than or equal to 103.29 lead to rejection. For the two-tailed test (Figure 15.4), this value is 103.92.

Comparison of Figures 15.4 and 15.6 demonstrates an important point: Assuming that the (unknown) population parameter (in our example, the population mean, $\mu$) does indeed differ from the null in the expected direction—the direction stated in the alternative hypothesis—use of a one-tailed test rather than a two-tailed one increases the likelihood of rejecting the null. Simply put, given solid expectation of the direction of the study sample result, it is easier to reject the null with a one-tailed test. When the researcher's expectation of direction is solid, a one-tailed test is often the best choice.

FIGURE 15.6  ■  **Study Sample Mean and Rejection Region For a One-Tailed Test,**
**$\alpha = .05$**

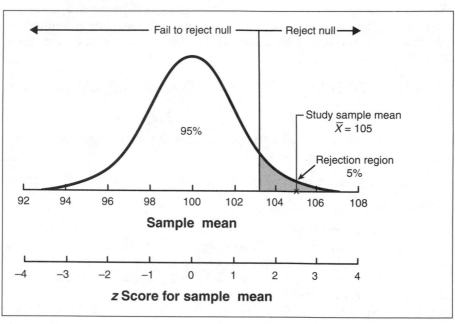

## 15.11.2  ■  Determining the Exact Value of the Study Sample Result (*p*)

When a decision rule calls for rejecting the null, this conveys that *p*, the probability of the study sample result, is less than or equal to the probability connected with the selected significance level (.05 or .01); when one calls for failing to reject, this conveys that *p* is greater than this probability. Yet, as presented here, the hypothesis testing model does not convey the exact value of *p*. This value differs for one- and two-tailed tests.

When a statistical test is two-tailed, cases that are extreme in both directions are considered in determining *p*. Our study sample result ($\overline{X} = 105$) was located 2.50 standard deviations above the value stated in the null. The proportion of cases 2.50 or more standard deviations above the mean in a normal distribution is .0062. Given a two-tailed probability (and because the normal distribution is symmetric), we double this proportion to determine *p*: $p = .0062 + .0062 = 0124$. When a test is one-tailed, only cases that differ in the direction stated in the alternative hypothesis are considered in determining *p*. As has already been determined, for our current example, the proportion of cases that are more extreme in the direction stated in the alternative (the positive direction) is .0062. (This is the proportion of sample means that are greater than or equal to 105.) Hence, from the perspective of a one-tailed test, $p = .0062$.

Assuming that the study result is indeed in the expected direction, the probability of the study sample result for a two-tailed test is double that for a one-tailed one. In our example, for instance, .0062 × 2 = .0124. Or, viewed differently, assuming that results are in the expected direction, the probability for a one-tailed test is one half that for a two-tailed test: .124 / 2 = .0062. The fact that use of a one-tailed test cuts *p* in half demonstrates again that, given solid expectation regarding the direction of difference, use of a directional hypothesis pair and, thus, a one-tailed test makes it easier to reject the null.[1]

Suppose that a researcher uses a one-tailed test and obtains a result in the tail that is opposite to expectations, the tail corresponding to the direction stated in the null. Because a one-tailed test considers only cases in the direction of expectations—the direction stated in the alternative—in determining *p*, this result will not result in rejection of the null.

Such a result conveys that a directional hypothesis pair and, thus, a one-tailed test were used when it should not have been. In such a circumstance, my recommendation is to formulate a non-directional pair and to carry out a two-tailed test. (See the next section for an example.)

Interpretation of one-tailed test results is problematic when results are in the direction opposite to expectations. This is one of the reasons why, in general, two-tailed tests are preferred.

## 15.12 ■ MORE DECISION RULES FOR THE ONE-TAILED, LARGE SAMPLE TEST OF $\overline{X}$

For a one-tailed, large sample test of $\overline{X}$ when the alternative hypothesis states greater than and the .01 level is used, the decision rule is to:

Fail to reject (accept) the null if the obtained $z$ is less than 2.33.

Reject the null if the obtained $z$ is 2.33 or greater.

Sticking with our parenting skills example, our obtained $z$ of 2.50 exceeds 2.33 and, thus, we reject the null and accept the alternative. Observe that when we used the .01 level and, thus, our test was two-tailed, we failed to reject the null (see Figure 15.5). This demonstrates still again that, given solid expectation regarding direction, use of a directional pair (and, thus, a one-tailed test) makes it easier to reject the null.

Figure 15.7 shows the rejection region for a one-tailed, large sample test of $\overline{X}$ using the .01 level when the alternative states greater than; it is the upper 1% tail of the sampling distribution. Given that the estimated standard deviation of the sampling distribution of $\overline{X}$ ($s_{\overline{X}}$) is 2.00 points, the null is rejected for all sample means greater than or equal to 104.66: $100 + 2.33 (2.00) = 104.66$. Consult the normal distribution table (Table A.1 in Appendix A) to see that 1% of cases in this distribution have $z$ scores of 2.33 or greater.[1]

### FIGURE 15.7 ■ Study Sample Mean and Rejection Region For a One-Tailed Test, $\alpha = .01$

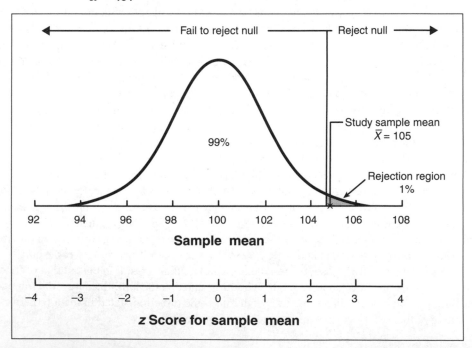

In this chapter's prior examples with directional hypothesis pairs, the alternative hypothesis has stated "greater than." For learning purposes, let us reverse the direction for our ongoing parenting skills example:

$H_0: \mu \geq 100$   $H_1: \mu < 100$ or, in words:

Null:         The mean parenting skills score in the population of all parents of elementary school children in your city is greater than or equal to 100 points.

Alternative: The mean parenting skills score in the population of all parents of elementary school children in your city is less than 100 points.

As the alternative states "less than," we can infer that the researcher (you) is expecting worse parenting skills in the study sample than in the large, representative sample of persons who took the parenting skills measure at an earlier time. This expectation seems nonsensical because, after all, the "common sense" expectation is for a parenting skills intervention to help (or at least not hurt) parenting skills. Of course, our hypothesis pair was developed for learning purposes rather than from solid expectations.

First, let us present the decision rule when the .05 level is used: When the alternative hypothesis states less than and the .05 level is used, the decision rule for a one-tailed, large sample test of $\overline{X}$ is:

Fail to reject (accept) the null if the obtained $z$ is greater than $-1.645$.

Reject the null if the obtained $z$ is less than or equal to $-1.645$.

Do not misinterpret the meaning of "less than" in the decision rule. For instance, $-1.50$ is *greater than* $-1.645$ and $-3.00$ is *less than* $-1.645$.

Because our obtained $z$, 2.50, is greater than $-1.645$, we fail to reject the null. In this example, all means less than or equal to 96.71 result in rejection of the null: $100 - 1.645 (2.00) = 96.71$. Figure 15.8 presents the rejection region and the study sample result. The rejection region is the lower 5% tail.

FIGURE 15.8 ■ **Study Sample Mean and Rejection Region When Result is in Direction Opposite to Expectations**

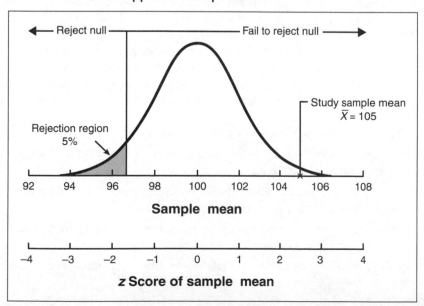

Our study sample result ($\overline{X} = 105$) is located far away from the rejection region. Indeed, our result is in the positive tail and the rejection region is in the negative tail. Our result is in the direction stated in the null. When a result is in the direction stated in the null—the direction *opposite* to expectations—a one-tailed significance test will never reject the null. This is because such tests consider only results in the direction stated in the alternative, the direction of expectations in determining $p$.

The current example illustrates a situation in which the direction of expectations in a directional hypothesis pair was incorrect. Such results are difficult to interpret. To repeat a point made earlier, this is a key reason why nondirectional pairs and, thus, two-tailed tests tend to be preferred. When a result is located in the tail that is opposite to expectations, as is the case here, my recommendation is to repeat the significance test using a nondirectional pair and, thus, a two-tailed test.[2]

When the alternative hypothesis states less than and the .01 level is used, the decision rule for a one-tailed, large sample test of $\overline{X}$ is to:

Fail to reject (accept) the null if the obtained $z$ is greater than $-2.33$.

Reject the null if the obtained $z$ is less than or equal to $-2.33$.

Because our obtained $z$, 2.50, is greater than $-2.33$, we fail to reject the null. The rejection region here is the 1% lower tail. All means less than or equal to 95.34 result in rejection: $100 - 2.33 (2.00) = 95.34$.

The only difference between this situation and the prior one is that we used the .01 level rather than the .05 one. Again, the researcher's direction of expectations is mistaken and, thus, my recommendation is to repeat the significance test using a nondirectional pair.

Observe that, in all of this chapter's examples that involve one-tailed tests, the rejection region is located in the tail that is in the direction stated in the alternative hypothesis. In this regard, it may be helpful to again consult Table 15.1 that summarizes the location of the rejection region in the different situations that come up in significance testing.

## 15.13 ■ REJECTING THE NULL AND "REAL" THINGS

When the null is rejected, chance alone is an unlikely explanation for the difference between the condition stated in the null and the study sample result. Viewed differently, something *real* is causing this difference. Presume that we have rejected the null in our parenting skills example. What real factors are causing the difference between your study sample result ($\overline{X} = 105$ points) and the value stated in the null ($\mu = 100$)? (Recall that the mean score on the parenting skills instrument was 100 in a very large, representative sample; this was the basis for the value in the null.) Some possible real explanations for the difference are

- your intervention did indeed increase parenting skills;
- the parenting skills in your city were very high even prior to your intervention (this, not your intervention, explains the higher score);
- because they "liked" you and sensed how much you wanted to help them, the parents in your sample "fudged" their responses in a positive direction;
- the simple fact of getting some extra attention rather than the scientific components of your intervention led to increased parenting skills; and/or
- any or all of the aforementioned explanations or perhaps something else (or several other things).

Rejection of the null—that is, statistical significance—tells you that *something* real— something more than chance—is the likely cause of the difference between your result and the condition stated in the null. Stated more simply, it tells you that your study sample result is likely caused by something real.

Rejection of the null rules out chance as a likely explanation. This being so, critical thinking about causality—what causes what—as raised in Chapters 10 and 11 is in order. When a researcher's research design does not use random assignment to groups, the "something real" that is causing the study result may well be a confounding variable (see Chapter 10, Section 10.6). On the other hand, pragmatically speaking, confounding variables do not affect results in research designs that use random assignment. (In such designs, there are no confounding variables.) Hence, when a researcher rejects the null in a randomized design, she concludes (with considerable confidence, although not certainty) that the "something real" causing the study result is the treatment invention.

On the other hand, when chance cannot be ruled out with sufficient confidence—in other words, when one fails to reject the null—"real causes" should not be considered. Why think seriously about real cause(s) of a study result when that result may well be due to the luck of the draw (chance)?

## 15.14 ■ CHAPTER SUMMARY

The steps in the *hypothesis testing model* are (1) state the hypothesis pair, (2) select a statistical significance level, (3) carry out the test, and (4) make a decision. The *large sample test of* $\overline{X}$ examines whether the mean of a sample differs from a hypothesized value.

Statistical significance tests are based on *assumptions*, conditions that must be met for the test to yield an accurate probability. When a test is *robust* to an assumption, that assumption may be violated with only a minor impact on accuracy. The large sample test of $\overline{X}$ assumes normality but is robust to this assumption.

The null is designated as $H_0$ and the alternative as $H_1$. When the hypothesis pair is nondirectional, the significance test is *two-tailed* (an exception is presented later in this text). When it is directional, it is *one-tailed*. The areas of the sampling distribution that result in rejection of the null are the *rejection regions*. Two-tailed tests have two such regions, one in each tail. One-tailed tests have a single rejection region located in the tail corresponding to the direction stated in the alternative hypothesis. The proportion of cases in the rejection region(s) equals the probability associated with the significance level, that is, equals *alpha* ($\alpha$). This proportion is .05 when the .05 level is used ($\alpha = .05$) and .01 when the .01 level is used ($\alpha = .01$).

One formula for the large sample test of $\overline{X}$ is $z \approx \dfrac{\overline{X} - \mu}{s_{\overline{X}}}$. The value obtained from carrying out a significance test formula is the *obtained statistic*.

Statistical tests have *decision rules*, criteria by which the researcher decides whether to reject the null. *Critical values* define when to reject the null. It is more difficult to reject the null at the .01 level than at the .05 level.

The researcher never knows for certain whether she has made the correct decision regarding the hypothesis pair. A *Type I error* rejects a true null hypothesis. The probability of Type I error equals the probability associated with the chosen significance level, that is, equals alpha ($\alpha$). This probability is .05 when the .05 level is used and .01 when the .01 level is used.

A *Type II error* fails to reject (accepts) a false null. Its probability equals beta ($\beta$). Choice of the .01 level (rather than the .05) reduces the risk of Type I error but increases that of Type II error. Choice of the .05 level (rather than the .01) reduces the risk of Type II error but increases that of Type I error.

Assuming that the population parameter differs in the expected direction, it is easier to reject the null with a one-tailed test (directional hypothesis pair) than with a two-tailed one (nondirectional pair). Put more simply, it is easier to reject the null with a one-tailed test. When study results are in the direction opposite to expectations, interpretation of results for a one-tailed test is difficult.

Rejection of the null (i.e., statistical significance) conveys that *something* real—something more than chance—is the likely cause of the difference between the study result and the condition stated in the null. It does not convey *what* that particular something is.

## 15.15 ■ PROBLEMS AND QUESTIONS

### Section 15.2

1. State the four steps of the hypothesis testing model.

### Section 15.3

2. In your words, what is an assumption of a statistical significance test?

3. A key assumption of the large sample test of $\overline{X}$ is the _____ assumption, that is, the study sample is selected from a population that is _____ distributed.

4. When a test is _____ to an assumption, carrying out the test when the assumption is violated has only a minor impact on accuracy.

5. The large sample test of $\overline{X}$ is _____ to the normality assumption.

6. (*True or False*) When a test is robust to an assumption, carrying out that test when the assumption is violated *greatly* affects the accuracy of the probability given by the test.

7. _____ sampling and _____ of observations are assumed for all inferential procedures presented in this text.

### Section 15.4

8. ___ symbolizes the null hypothesis. ___ symbolizes the alternative.

9. A researcher's null hypothesis states that the mean of a population is 10 points. In a random sample of 100 cases, $s = 5$. Assume that the null is indeed true. Provide the following for the sampling distribution of $\overline{X}$: mean, standard deviation, and shape of distribution.

## Section 15.5

10. For the presented sampling distribution of $\overline{X}$ in the prior question, what is the probability of randomly selecting a sample with a mean of:
    a. Greater than or equal to 10
    b. Greater than 10.5
    c. Less than 9.5
    d. Either greater than 10.5 or less than 9.5

## Section 15.6

11. With a nondirectional pair, the researcher uses a ___-tailed test. A two-tailed test has two _____ regions. Thus, extreme results in _____ directions may result in rejection of the null.

12. Using the .05 significance level ($\alpha = .05$), the proportion of cases located in the rejection regions equals ___. Given a two-tailed test ($\alpha = .05$), the rejection regions are the upper ___% tail and the lower ___% tail.

13. Using the .01 significance level ($\alpha = .01$), the proportion of cases located in the rejection regions equals ___. Given a two-tailed test ($\alpha = .01$), the rejection regions are the upper ___% tail and the lower ___% tail.

14. When the hypothesis pair is directional, the significance test is a _____-tailed test, that is, there is only _____ _____ rejection region; that region is located in the direction stated in the _____ hypothesis.

15. Indicate the location of the rejection region for each situation. In each situation, assume a directional pair and, thus, a one-tailed test. The information provided for each situation is (a) the direction of expectations (the direction in the alternative hypothesis) and (b) the selected significance level (alpha).
    a. Greater than, .05 level
    b. Greater than, .01 level
    c. Less than, .05 level
    d. Less than, .01 level

16. I am going to develop some *arbitrary* guidelines to help convey the relationship between whether a study result is consistent or inconsistent with the null and the decision to fail to reject or to reject the null. Let us use these (arbitrary) guidelines: $p > .25$, result consistent with the null; $.25 > p > .05$, result neither consistent nor inconsistent with the null; and $p \leq .05$, result inconsistent with the null. Assume that we use the .05 level. For each situation, (a) respond consistent, neither consistent nor

inconsistent, or inconsistent; and (b) indicate your decision on whether to fail to reject (accept) or reject the null:

    **a.** $p = .43$
    **b.** $p = .12$
    **c.** $p = .03$
    **d.** $p = .64$
    **e.** $p = .18$
    **f.** $p = .02$

## Section 15.7

17. The researcher _____ the null and _____ the alternative hypothesis when the study sample result is located in a rejection region. The researcher _____ to _____ the null and _____ the alternative when this result is not located in a rejection region.

## Section 15.8

18. For each situation, calculate $z$ using Formula 15.1 or 15.2. Also, indicate the percentage of cases in the sampling distribution that are more extreme than the study sample result. Consider cases that are more extreme in both directions in calculating this percentage.

    **a.** $\mu = 25.00; \overline{X} = 23.5, s = 10, N = 100$
    **b.** $\mu = 25.00; \overline{X} = 26.5, s = 10, N = 100$
    **c.** $\mu = 25.00; \overline{X} = 27.0, s = 10, N = 100$
    **d.** $\mu = 25.00; \overline{X} = 27.0, s = 10, N = 400$

19. $H_0: \mu = 25.00, H_1: \mu \neq 25; \overline{X} = 23.4, s = 12, N = 144$. The .05 significance level is selected. Based on the just-provided information:

    **a.** Is the hypothesis pair directional or nondirectional?

    Note: The next set of questions guide you to a decision on the hypothesis pair using the sampling distribution and the rejection regions.

    **b.** Given a true null, what are the mean, standard deviation, and shape of the sampling distribution of $\overline{X}$?

    **c.** What is the $z$ score of the study sample mean in the sampling distribution of $\overline{X}$? (Hint: Carry out Formula 15.1 or 15.2.)

    **d.** What percentage of cases in the sampling distribution have scores as low as or even lower than the study sample mean? (Hint: Consult the normal distribution table.)

    **e.** Is the appropriate statistical test one-tailed or two-tailed?

    **f.** In a two-tailed test using the .05 level ($\alpha = .05$), there are _____ rejection regions, one of which is the upper ___% tail and the other of which is the lower ___% tail.

    **g.** Is the study sample mean located in a rejection region? If so, is it located in the region in the upper tail or that in the lower tail?

**h.** Based on the location of the study sample mean, what is your decision on the null? On the alternative?

Note: The next set of questions use the normal distribution table to calculate the probability of the study sample result and, by so doing, guide you to a decision on the hypothesis pair.

**i.** Given a true null, what is the probability of obtaining a mean as low as or even lower than the study sample mean? (Hint: Consult the normal distribution table.)

**j.** Given a true null, what is the probability of obtaining a sample that differs in *either* direction from the value stated in the null by as much as does the study sample mean or by even more than this?

**k.** Given a true null, what is the probability of obtaining the study sample result or an even more extreme result? (Hint: This is the same question as the prior one, expressed with slightly different language; consider both directions.)

**l.** From the perspective of a two-tailed test, given a true null, what is the probability of obtaining the study sample result or an even more extreme result? (Hint: Because a two-tailed test considers both directions, this question restates the prior one.)

**m.** Is the probability of obtaining the study sample result given a true null greater than or less than the probability associated with the significance level ($\alpha$)?

**n.** Comparing the probability of the result ($p$) to the probability connected to the significance level, what is your decision on the null? On the alternative?

Note: The next set of questions guide you to a decision using the decision rule.

**o.** The appropriate decision rule is _____ to _____ (accept) the null if the _____ _____ of the obtained $z$ is _____ _____ 1.96. Reject the null if the absolute value of the obtained $z$ is _____ _____ or _____ _____ _____.

**p.** What is the obtained $z$? (Hint: You have already computed this.) What is the absolute value of the obtained $z$?

**q.** Using the decision rule, what is your decision regarding the null? Regarding the alternative?

Note: The next set of questions has to do with interpreting the result:

**r.** Is this result a statistically significant result?

**s.** Given a true null, what is the probability of obtaining the study result?

**t.** Given a true null, is the study result a highly unlikely one (one sufficiently unlikely for the null to be rejected)?

**u.** What is the probability that the study sample result is due to chance alone?

**v.** What is the probability that the difference between the values stated in the null and the study sample result is due to chance alone?

**w.** Is chance alone a *highly* unlikely explanation for the study sample result (sufficiently unlikely for the null to be rejected)?

**x.** Is the result consistent with the null? (Hint: Not easy to answer.)

**y.** How confident can we be that the null is false?

**z.** Does the study sample result provide strong evidence that the null is false? (Hint: Not easy to answer.)

**Section 15.9**

20. Consider this information: $H_0$: $\mu = 50.00$, $H_1$: $\mu \neq 50$; $\overline{X} = 61.0$, $s = 50$, $N = 100$.
    Respond to the following:
    **a.** Is the hypothesis pair directional or nondirectional?
    **b.** The statistical test is ___-tailed.
    **c.** The obtained $z$ equals ___.
    **d.** Given a true null, what is the probability of obtaining a study sample result that is
    as extreme as or more extreme than the study sample result? (Because the test is
    two-tailed, consider both directions.)
    **e.** (*True or False*) Given a true null, the probability of obtaining the study sample result is
    greater than .01 and less than .05.
    **f.** Suppose that the .05 level is used. This being so, the decision rule calls for rejection if
    the absolute value of the obtained $z$ exceeds ___. Given that the .05 level is used, the
    researcher should _____ the null and _____ the alternative.
    **g.** Suppose that the .01 level is used. This being so, the decision rule calls for rejection
    if the absolute value of the obtained $z$ exceeds ___. Given that the .01 level is used,
    the researcher should _____ to _____ the null and _____
    the alternative.

21. It is more _____ to reject the null when the .01 level is used than when the .05 level
    is used. This is because rejection at the .01 level requires a _____ difference from
    the condition stated in the null than does rejection at the .05 level.

**Section 15.10**

22. When a Type I error is made, the researcher _____ a null that is in reality _____.

23. Suppose that the null is true and that a researcher conducts 1,000 statistical tests (in other
    words, draws 1,000 random samples and carries out a statistical test) using the .05 level.
    **a.** What is your best guess of the number of times that the sample results will lead to
    rejection of the null?
    **b.** What is your best guess regarding the number of Type I errors that will be made?

24. Suppose that the null is true and that a researcher conducts 1,000 statistical tests (in other
    words, draws 1,000 random samples and carries out a statistical test) using the .01 level.
    **a.** What is your best guess of the number of times that the sample results will lead to
    rejection of the null?
    **b.** What is your best guess regarding the number of Type I errors that will be made?

25. Rejections of the null at the .___ level are more convincing than are those at the .___ level,
    because the probability that the study sample result is caused by sampling error (Type I
    error) is _____ (choose lower or higher).

26. While choosing the .01 level rather than the .05 level _____ the risk of Type I error, it _____ the risk of _____ _____. A Type II error occurs when the researcher _____ to _____ a null that is in actuality _____.

27. The probability of a Type II error is termed _____ and is symbolized by _____.

28. *Respond true or false to each question:*
    a. Setting alpha to .01 (rather than to .05) reduces the risk of Type I error.
    b. In any given situation, the higher the risk of Type I error, the lower the risk of Type II error.
    c. The researcher knows assuredly whether her decision is correct or incorrect.

29. When the .05 level is used and the null is rejected, the researcher may have (at least) ___% confidence that the null is false. When the .01 level is used and the null is rejected, the researcher may have (at least) ___% confidence that the null is false.

## Section 15.11

30. What proportion of cases in a normal distribution has $z$ scores greater than 1.645?

31. What is the decision-making rule for a one-tailed, large sample test of $\overline{X}$ when the alternative hypothesis states greater than and the .05 level is used?

32. Consider this information: $H_0$: $\mu \leq 50.0$, $H_1$: $\mu > 50.0$; $\overline{X} = 58.5$, $s = 50.0$, $N = 100$. Respond to the following:
    a. Is the hypothesis pair directional or nondirectional?
    b. Is the appropriate test one-tailed or two-tailed?
    c. Which hypothesis statement, $H_0$ or $H_1$, states the direction of expectations?
    d. Is the study result in the expected direction?
    e. Calculate $z$.
    f. What proportion of cases in the sampling distribution of $\overline{X}$ have means greater than or equal to the study sample mean?
    g. From the perspective of a one-tailed test (i.e., considering only results that are in the direction of expectations), given a true null, what is the probability of obtaining the study sample result or an even more extreme result?
    h. From the perspective of a one-tailed test, what is the probability of obtaining the study result or an even more extreme result due to chance alone?
    i. From the perspective of a one-tailed test, what is the probability that the difference between the conditions stated in the null and the result obtained in the sample is due to chance alone?
    j. Presume that the .05 level is used ($\alpha = .05$). Does the obtained $z$ exceed the value stated in the decision rule? What decision should be made regarding the null? Regarding the alternative hypothesis?

**33.** *Answer true or false for each of the following regarding the just-completed question. (Continue to assume that the null has been rejected.)*

    **a.** The study sample result provides sufficiently strong evidence that the null is false.

    **b.** The null is likely false.

    **c.** Given a true null, results as extreme as or more extreme than the study sample result are obtained quite often (say in about 20% or more of random samples).

    **d.** The study sample result is likely to be due to chance alone.

    **e.** The study sample result is unlikely to be due to chance alone.

    **f.** The difference between the condition stated in the null and the study sample result is unlikely to be due to chance alone.

    **g.** The study sample result is statistically significant at the .05 level.

**34.** Assuming that the (unknown) population parameter does indeed differ from the null in the expected direction, use of a _____-_____ test rather than a two-tailed one _____ the likelihood of rejecting the null. Given solid expectation of the direction of the study sample result, it is _____ to reject the null with a one-tailed test.

**35.** (With some exceptions), assuming that the study result is in the expected direction, the probability of the study sample result for a two-tailed test is _____ that for a one-tailed one. Or, viewed differently, assuming that results are in the expected direction, the probability for a one-tailed test is _____ _____ that for a two-tailed test.

**36.** Assume that the study sample result is in the expected direction. Each situation provides the probability ($p$) given a two-tailed significance test. For each situation, calculate $p$ given a one-tailed test.

    **a.** $p = .06$

    **b.** $p = .22$

    **c.** $p = .40$

    **d.** $p = .08$

**37.** Each situation provides the probability given by a one-tailed test. For each situation, calculate $p$ given a two-tailed test.

    **a.** $p = .02$

    **b.** $p = .04$

    **c.** $p = .16$

    **d.** $p = .03$

**38.** Consider again information presented in Question 32 but presume that the hypothesis pair is nondirectional ($H_0$: $\mu = 50.00$, $H_1$: $\mu \neq 50$). Presume that the .05 level is ($\alpha = .05$) used. Respond to the following:

    **a.** Is the statistical test one-tailed or two-tailed?

    **b.** From the perspective of a two-tailed test, what is the probability of obtaining the study result or an even more extreme result because of chance alone? (Be sure to consider cases that are extreme in both directions.)

   **c.** (*True or False*) Given that a two-tailed rather than a one-tailed test is used, the probability of obtaining the study sample result because of chance alone has doubled.

   **d.** Does the obtained $z$ exceed the absolute value of the value stated in the decision rule (1.96)?

   **e.** What is the decision on the null? On the alternative?

   **f.** Are these the same decisions as were made when the test was one-tailed?

## Section 15.12

**39.** What proportion of cases in a normal distribution have $z$ scores greater than 2.326?

**40.** What is the decision-making rule for a one-tailed, large sample test of $\overline{X}$ when the alternative hypothesis states greater than and the .01 level is used?

**41.** Consider the aforementioned Question 32. $H_0$: $\mu \leq 50.0$, $H_1$: $\mu > 50.0$; $\overline{X} = 58.5$, $s = 50.0$, $N = 100$. Note that the hypothesis pair is directional (the same as presented originally). Presume, however, that the .01 rather than the .05 level is used.

   **a.** What is the obtained $z$? (Hint: This remains unchanged.)

   **b.** The decision rule calls for rejection of the null if the obtained $z$ exceeds ___.

   **c.** What is the decision on the null? On the alternative?

   **d.** Are these the same decisions as were made originally (in Question 32)?

**42.** (*True or False*) When a result is in the direction stated in the null—the direction *opposite* to expectations—a one-tailed significance test will never reject the null.

**43.** Consider the following information: $H_0$: $\mu \leq 50.0$, $H_1$: $\mu > 50.0$; $\overline{X} = 35.0$, $s = 50.0$, $N = 100$. The .05 level is used. Respond to the following:

   **a.** Is the hypothesis pair directional or nondirectional?

   **b.** Is the significance test one-tailed or two-tailed?

   **c.** In what tail (upper or lower) is the rejection region located?

   **d.** What is the direction of expectations (greater than the value stated in the null or less than this value)?

   **e.** Is the study result ($\overline{X} = 35.0$) greater than or less than the value stated in the null ($\mu > 50.0$)?

   **f.** Is the study result in the expected direction or in the direction opposite to expectations?

   **g.** Calculate the obtained $z$ using the formula.

   **h.** What percentage of means in the sampling distribution have values less than that of the study sample mean?

   **i.** The appropriate decision rule calls for rejection of the null if the obtained $z$ is "_____ _____ or _____ _____ _____."

   **j.** According to the decision rule, what decision should be made on the null? On the alternative?

   **k.** (*True or False*) In a situation such as this one, the author of this text recommends repeating the significance test using a nondirectional pair and, thus, a two-tailed test.

**Section 15.13**

**44.** When the null is rejected, _____ _____ is an _____ explanation for the difference between the condition stated in the _____ and the study sample result. Viewed differently, something _____ is causing this difference.

**45.** *The final four questions are true or false.*
   **a.** When a researcher rejects the null in a design that does *not* use random assignment to groups, she can be confident that the study result is not caused by a confounding variable.
   **b.** When a researcher rejects the null in a design that uses random assignment to groups, she can be confident that the study result is not caused by a confounding variable.
   **c.** When a researcher rejects the null in a design that uses random assignment to groups, she can be confident that the study result is caused by the treatment intervention.
   **d.** Even when chance alone is a sufficient (not unlikely) explanation for the study sample result, this text advises the researcher to consider seriously what "real" factors are the likely cause of that result.

# 16

# STATISTICAL POWER AND SELECTED TOPICS

## 16.1 ■ CHAPTER OVERVIEW

Chapter 16 discusses *statistical power* and the factors that affect it. In particular, it focuses on how sample size affects power. Other factors examined include size of relationship in the population, variability, control for third variables, the selected significance level, one-tailed versus two-tailed test, and the particular test used. In closing, this chapter examines misinterpretations of statistical significance.

## 16.2 ■ DEFINITION OF POWER

As presented in Chapter 15 (Section 15.10), the error of failing to reject a false null is termed Type II error and its probability equals beta ($\beta$). Closely related to $\beta$ is the concept of power. The **statistical power** (**power**) of a significance test is the probability that it will reject a false null. Stated differently, a test's power is the probability that it will accept a true alternative hypothesis. Power differs in different situations and much of this chapter discusses the factors that influence it.

Power and $\beta$ are "opposites." Given a false null, power is the probability of making a correct decision (rejecting the null) and $\beta$ is the probability of making an incorrect one (failing to reject it). Power and $\beta$ sum to 1.00. Because power and $\beta$ sum to 1, it is also the case that

$$\text{Power} = 1 - \beta \qquad (16.1)$$

For instance, if $\beta = .40$, then Power $= 1.00 - .40 = .60$.

In the just-presented example, power equals .60. This conveys that given a false null, the researcher has a 60% chance of making the correct decision, that is, a 60% chance of rejecting that null. On the other hand, she has a 40% chance of making an incorrect one, failing to reject it.

As power increases, the risk of Type II error ($\beta$) decreases. In statistics, power is a good thing. The greater the power, the greater the probability of rejecting a false null.

## 16.3 ■ SAMPLE SIZE AND POWER

Although many factors influence power, sample size and size of relationship in the population from which the study sample is selected are the most important. We will focus first on sample size.

When sample size is small, power is often low. Conversely, when it is large, power is often high. How does sample size affect power?

When the null is true (unknown to the researcher), sampling error alone (chance alone) causes the study sample result to differ from the condition stated in the null. When the null is false (again, unknown), both sampling error and a *real difference* are involved. The significance test seeks to detect this real difference (if any) in the presence of sampling error.

As you know, as sample size increases, sampling error tends to decrease. When sample size is small, a great deal of sampling error is likely present. The amount of sampling error can be so large that the test cannot determine whether a real difference is also present. In effect, with very small sample size, the amount of sampling error can be so large that it overwhelms the ability of the significance test to find the real difference.

The analogy of finding a needle in a haystack comes to mind. The haystack represents sampling error, the "noise" that gets in the way of finding the real difference, that is, the needle. When sample size is small, the haystack (sampling error) is large and finding the needle (the real difference) is difficult. In this situation, power is, for the most part, low. When sample size is large, the haystack is smaller and finding the needle becomes easier. Here, power is higher.

## 16.4 ■ EXAMPLES OF HOW SAMPLE SIZE AFFECTS POWER

### 16.4.1 ■ The Parenting Skills Example

Let us examine the effects of sample size using the parenting skills example from the prior chapter, although for variety, let us change the example. Let us say that there is no intervention, you are simply conducting a survey. We will presume that you continue to use the same parenting skills instrument. Your null hypothesis is nondirectional:

Null:         The population mean equals 100 points.

Alternative:  The population mean does not equal 100 points.

Power is the probability of rejecting a false null. So for discussion purposes, presume that the null is false. (In actual research, we would not know this.)

Because the pair is nondirectional, we will use a two-tailed, large sample test of $\overline{X}$. Let us use the .05 level. Let us carry out the study three times, each time with a different sample size: 100, 400, and 1,600. Presume that in each study, the standard deviation of the sample is 20 points ($s = 20$). For all three studies, presume that the study sample mean equals 97 points ($\overline{X} = 97$).

For each study, we estimate the standard deviation of the sampling distribution of $\overline{X}$, the standard error of the mean ($\sigma_{\downarrow}^{-}X$), by dividing the standard deviation in the sample by the square root of the sample size: $s_{\overline{x}} = \frac{s}{\sqrt{N}}$.

Figure 16.1 presents, given a true null, the sampling distribution of $\overline{X}$ for the three studies. As sample size increases, the standard deviation of the sampling distribution decreases and, thus, the sample means cluster closer to 100. For each sample size, Figure 16.1 presents the rejection regions. As sample size increases, sample means closer to the value stated in the null ($\mu = 100$) lead to its rejection. For instance, when sample size equals 100, we reject the null for means that differ by about four points or more. When sample size is 400, we reject for differences of about two points or more. When $N = 1,600$, we reject for differences of about one point or more.

Figure 16.1 presents the location of the study sample mean ($\overline{X} = 97$) with respect to each sampling distribution. When sample size is 100, the study sample mean is not located in a rejection region and, thus, we fail to reject the null. For both of the larger samples, the sample mean is in a rejection region and, thus, we reject the null.

FIGURE 16.1 ■ Sample Size and Power

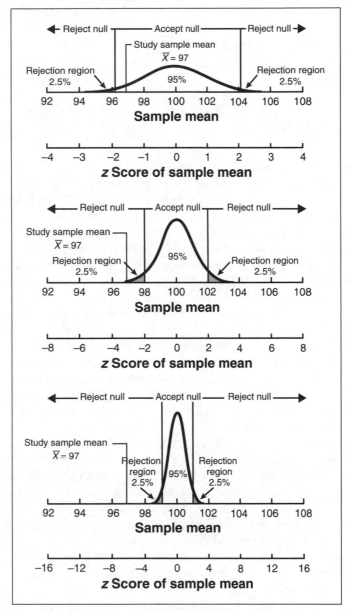

Figure 16.1 illustrates a basic characteristic of sample size: Other things being equal, as sample size increases, increasingly smaller differences are sufficient to reject the null. Given that a null hypothesis is indeed false, as sample size increases, it becomes increasingly easier to reject it.

Having carried out the large sample test of $\overline{X}$ using the sampling distribution of $\overline{X}$, let us now do so using its formula (Formula 15.1). When sample size equals 100:

$$z \approx \frac{97 - 100}{\left(\frac{20}{\sqrt{100}}\right)} = \frac{97 - 100}{\left(\frac{20}{10}\right)} = \frac{-3}{2} = -1.50$$

When sample size equals 400:

$$z \approx \frac{97 - 100}{\left(\frac{20}{\sqrt{400}}\right)} = \frac{97 - 100}{\left(\frac{20}{20}\right)} = \frac{-3}{1} = -3.00$$

When sample size equals 1,600:

$$z \approx \frac{97 - 100}{\left(\frac{20}{\sqrt{1600}}\right)} = \frac{97 - 100}{\left(\frac{20}{40}\right)} = \frac{-3}{.5} = -6.00$$

The decision rule for a two-tailed, large sample test using the .05 level calls for rejecting the null when the absolute value of the obtained $z$ is greater than or equal to 1.96 (see Chapter 15, Section 15.8.2). Hence, we reject the null when sample size equals 400 and 1,600 but fail to reject when it equals 100. As must be the case, our decisions using the formula confirm those made earlier using the sampling distribution.

As sample size increases, other things being equal and assuming that the null is false, so also does power. In our example, power—the opportunity to reject a false null—increased as sample size increased from 100 to 400 to 1,600. Yet, for each of these sample sizes, power was, at the least, adequate. Even when sample size equaled 100, a difference of only four points was sufficient for rejection. In each situation, then we had at least a reasonably good opportunity to reject the null.

When sample size is very small, very large differences are typically required to reject the null. The size of this difference can be so large that the researcher does not have a realistic opportunity to do so. To make this point, let us break from the requirement that the large sample test of $\overline{X}$ should be carried out only when sample size is 100 or greater (see Section 15.3.1). Let us conduct a large sample test with a sample size of nine. All other things stay the same (same hypothesis pair, $s = 20$, .05 level, $\overline{X} = 97$).

Figure 16.2 presents, given a true null, the sampling distribution of $\overline{X}$. Its mean equals 100 and its standard deviation equals $s_{\overline{X}} = 20/\sqrt{9} = 20/3 = 6.67$. (Block from your mind that we have violated a requirement and presume that Figure 16.2 accurately portrays the sampling distribution.)

Observe that a very large difference from the value stated in the null ($\mu = 100$) is now needed to reject it. The study sample mean, $\overline{X} = 97$, is nowhere near either rejection region. Indeed, a difference of about 13 points necessary for rejection. This difference is much larger than in our other examples (see Figure 16.2).

As the wide span of the sampling distribution in Figure 16.2 conveys, when sample size is very small, sampling error alone can be the cause of extremely large differences. In such situations, the significance test almost always cannot effectively distinguish a real difference—a false null—from sampling error. In such situations, statistical power is almost always low and the risk of Type II error is, thus, almost always high.

Low power, primarily caused by small sample size, is a common problem in human services research. When sample size is small, the researcher often fails to reject the null not because it is true, but rather because power is low.

### 16.4.2 ■ More Examples of Sample Size and Power

Let us again demonstrate the effects of small sample size on power. Suppose that the human services agency where you work designs an experiment to test the effectiveness of a program to prevent out-of-home placement of children. Ten families are randomly assigned to the new family preservation unit and 10 to traditional ongoing services. One year later, you discover that

FIGURE 16.2 ■ **Effect of Small Sample Size on Power**

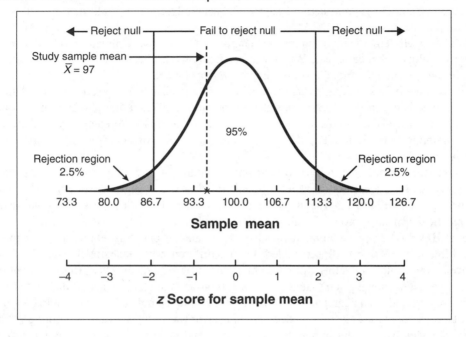

only 3 of 10 children (30%) in the new program but 7 of 10 (70%) in the traditional program required out-of-home placement. Enthusiastic about the new program's apparent success, you conduct the appropriate significance test for determining whether the difference in percentages ($D\% = 70\% - 30\% = 40\%$) is statistically significant. (This test is the chi-square test of independence presented in Chapter 20.) The test indicates that the probability that this difference is due to chance is .13 ($p = .13$; calculations not presented). Because this probability is greater than that associated with your chosen significance level (presume that you had chosen the .05 level), you fail to reject the null.

The likely problem here is low statistical power caused by the very small sample size ($N = 20$). As sample size is very small, a very large difference is required to reject the null—a $D\%$ of 40% is not sufficient to do so.

Your agency continues the experiment for a second year. By the end of the second year, only 6 of 20 children (30%) in the new program in contrast to 14 of 20 (70%) children in the traditional program require placement. In this example, the size of the difference ($D\% = 70\% - 30\% = 40\%$) continues to be the same but sample size has increased. This time, the chi-square test results indicate that $p = .009$. Because .009 is less than .05, the null is rejected. This example demonstrates that (other things staying the same), as sample size increases, so does the likelihood of rejecting the null—that is, so does the statistical power.

Recall that rejection of the null and statistical significance are one and the same, as are failure to reject and the absence of statistical significance (see Chapter 14, Section 14.11). As the just-presented example demonstrates, when sample size is small, even large associations in the study sample (large differences) may not achieve statistical significance.

Conversely, when sample size is large, even small associations often do achieve significance. For instance, my research on the adoption of children with special needs found a negative correlation of −0.10 between family income and the parents' report of their child's enjoyment of school. (Thus, the higher the family income, the lower the child's enjoyment of school; Rosenthal & Groze, 1992). Although this correlation was a small one, it was statistically significant at the

.01 level using a two-tailed significance test of Pearson's *r*. (This tests the null that the population correlation is 0.00 and is presented in Chapter 22, Section 22.2.) How could such a small correlation be statistically significant?

A statistically significant difference or relationship is one that is unlikely to be due to sampling error alone (chance alone). When sample size is large, there is typically little sampling error. In the current example, the study sample size was indeed large ($N = 599$). As such, there was presumably little sampling error. This made the significance test's job an easy one. Although the difference between the correlation stated in the null (0.00) and that obtained in the sample ($-0.10$) was small, the significance test could discern that this difference was unlikely to be due to sampling error alone. (It could do so because the effects of sampling error were minimal because of the large sample size.)

One more example can reinforce your understanding of how large sample size enhances power. My statistics professor informed my statistics class that in a given academic achievement test for high school students, female students outscored males by an *extremely* small margin. As I recall, the mean score of female students was about one fortieth of a standard deviation higher ($SMD = 0.025$), an amount about seven times smaller than this text's categorization of a small difference ($SMD = 0.18$; see Table 9.1). This difference was statistically significant at the .01 level. How could such a tiny difference be statistically significant? My professor went on to say that the test had been given to tens and tens of thousands of students across the United States and that results had been aggregated to form one huge study sample of several hundred thousand students. Because of the huge sample size, sampling error was reduced to almost nothing. As such, the tiniest difference in achievement between female and male students could be discriminated from sampling error and, thus, was sufficient for rejecting the null

The statistical power in the just-described study was extremely high, close to 1.00. In practical terms, a difference of one fortieth of a standard deviation has no real-world importance.

In studies with very large samples, the null is often rejected even for very small relationships. Hence, when you read about results in such studies, focus not just on statistical significance but also on size of the relationship. In particular, verify that statistically significant relationships are not of trivial size. You can use the guidelines of size of association to do so; see Tables 6.3, 8.2, and 9.1.

## 16.5 ■ FACTORS OTHER THAN SAMPLE SIZE THAT INFLUENCE POWER

### 16.5.1 ■ Overview

Power is the probability that a significance test will reject a false null. Sample size and the size of relationship or difference in the population are the most important factors that affect power. Other factors include reduced variability of the independent or dependent variable, whether important third variables are controlled for; the selected significance level, whether the hypothesis pair is directional (one-tailed test) or nondirectional (two-tailed test); and the particular significance test that is used.

### 16.5.2 ■ Size of Relationship or Difference in the Population

Other things (in particular, sample size) being equal, the larger the difference between the actual condition in the population from which the study sample is randomly selected and the condition stated in the null, the greater the power. Very often, researchers examine relationships. When this is the case, and assuming that the null states "no relationship," the larger the relationship in the population from which the study sample is randomly sampled, the greater the power.

To illustrate the effect of size of relationship on power, let us imagine two studies, Study 1 and Study 2, each of which investigates the effects of Treatment A and Treatment B on depression as measured by the *XYZ* Depression Scale. Table 16.1 lists mean scores in the populations from which the Treatment A and Treatment B samples were drawn. Each population mean in Table 16.1 is the mean that would be found if the treatment (A or B) could be administered to all persons in the population.

Table 16.1 calculates the standardized mean difference (*SMD*) for both studies. (These *SMDs* differ from others covered to this point because they measure differences between populations rather than between groups.) Means differ by 1.00 standard deviation in Study 1 but by only 0.50 standard deviations in Study 2. Thus, the difference in means—or stated differently, the relationship between treatment approach (A or B) and *XYZ* Depression Scale score—is larger in Study 1 than in Study 2.

Let us now state the hypothesis pair. The pair is the same for both studies and is nondirectional:

Null:          Mean scores on the *XYZ* depression scale for those who receive Treatment A and those who receive Treatment B are equal.

Alternative:  Mean scores on the *XYZ* depression scale for those who receive Treatment A and those who receive Treatment B are not equal.

Observe that this hypothesis pair is typical of those used when one variable is dichotomous (treatment approach) and the other is numeric (*XYZ* score). Chapter 18 (Sections 18.2 and 18.3) presents the appropriate significance test for this situation, the independent samples *t* test. As the pair is nondirectional, this test is two-tailed.

Presume that we implement both studies and carry out the just-mentioned *t* test. Presume that sample sizes are equal—for instance, if 30 receive A and 40 receive B in Study 1, then 30 receive A and 40 receive B in Study 2. Presume also that we use the same significance level (say, the .05 level) in both studies.

All of the just-mentioned conditions—same hypothesis pair, same significance test, same sample sizes, same significance level, same type of test (one- or two-tailed)—presumed to be met, in other words, all other things being equal, the probability of rejecting the null is greater in Study 1 than in Study 2. Stated differently, statistical power is greater in Study 1 than in Study 2. This is because the size of relationship in the population is larger in Study 1 than in Study 2.

Although the just-presented example dealt with a difference between population means, the underlying idea—other things being equal, the larger the difference or relationship in the

TABLE 16.1 ■ Population Characteristics and Standardized Mean Difference in Two Hypothetical Studies

| Study | Mean ($\mu$) | Standard Deviation ($\sigma$) | SMD |
|---|---|---|---|
| | | Characteristics in Population | |
| Study 1 | | | |
| Treatment A | 50 | 10 | $SMD = \dfrac{50 - 40}{10} = 1.00$ |
| Treatment B | 40 | 10 | |
| Study 2 | | | |
| Treatment A | 50 | 10 | $SMD = \dfrac{50 - 45}{10} = 0.50$ |
| Treatment B | 45 | 10 | |

population, the greater the power—holds across all situations (differences in percentages, correlations, multivariate analyses, etc.).

Hopefully you find it intuitive that a larger relationship in the population brings greater power. The larger the population relationship that the significance test searches for, the easier it is to find. When the population relationship is large, the job of the significance test is akin to searching for a *big* needle in the haystack. Even when sample size is small and, thus, sampling error (the haystack) is large, given a large enough population relationship (a big enough needle), the significance test will likely find it. In other words, the test will likely reject the null.

Let me propose a preposterous research study to demonstrate that power can be high even when sample size is small. Suppose that we study reading proficiency among two groups of students, first graders and college seniors. Obviously, the population difference in reading proficiency between these two groups is absolutely **huge**. Presuming this to be so, then even "tiny" sample sizes (let us just "guess" five in each group) will almost assuredly be sufficient to reject the null. Stated differently, power will be high even when sample size is small. Obviously, we would not implement the just-proposed research study because we would know the study result (huge difference) prior to doing so.

On the other hand, in some real research situations, the researcher has solid grounds for thinking that the population difference or relationship is very large. Suppose that a given behavioral intervention has produced very large decreases in classroom misbehavior in several well-conducted studies. This being so, a modest sample size may be sufficient for good power. On the other hand, in some situations, the size of the population relationship is likely quite small. In such situations, large sample sizes are needed for adequate power.

Size of relationship in the population is instrumental for calculating power. Yet, the researcher never knows the exact size of this relationship. (If she did, there would be no reason to conduct the significance test.) Instead, she estimates it using a combination of theory, prior research knowledge, logic, and common sense. As size of relationship in the population is estimated, so is power. In other words, the power that a researcher calculates is, in essence, a best estimate of the actual power, which ultimately is unknown.

Summing up, (a) when the population relationship or difference is very large, a small sample size is often sufficient for adequate power; and (b) when this relationship or difference is very small, the required sample size is often quite large.

### 16.5.3 ■ Reduced Variability of Independent or Dependent Variable

When variability of either the independent or dependent variable is very low, power is reduced. For instance, suppose that you are interested in the association between the independent variable minority/majority status (minority ethnicity vs. White) and employment status (obtained a human services job vs. did not) among recent graduates of your educational program. Presume that the graduating class consists of 94 (94%) White students but only 6 (6%) minority students. Because of the limited variability of minority/majority status (and assuming that sample size is not very large), a statistical test of its association to employment status will almost assuredly have very low power. Only an extremely large difference between the percentages of White and minority students who obtain employment will lead to rejection of the null.

More equal percentages of minority and majority students in the sample—that is, greater variability in minority/majority status—would increase the likelihood of rejection, that is, would increase power. When a variable is dichotomous (binary) such as is minority/majority status, variability and thus power is maximized when 50% are in each group.

In the just-presented example, an independent variable's variability was very low. A decrease in power also occurs when this is the case for the dependent variable. Suppose that you study factors associated with graduating college with a 4.0 ("perfect") grade point average (GPA). Suppose further that of the 1,000 students in your college graduating class, only 10 (1%) obtain a 4.0. Because 1% have "perfect" GPAs, 99% do not. Thus, the variability of your dependent variable, perfect GPA (yes, 1% vs. no, 99%), is extremely low. This low variability will reduce the power of significance tests that examine whether given independent variables—say student age, gender, motivation level, and so forth—are associated with GPA.

In a situation like this, rather than using perfect GPA as your dependent variable, you could perhaps use students' actual GPAs as your dependent variable and examine what factors predict GPA measured in this way. Unlike perfect GPA, actual (numerically measured) GPAs vary considerably from student to student. This being so, you would have greater statistical power with GPA measured in this way.

When a variable's variability becomes extremely low, that variable (almost) ceases to be a variable and, instead, becomes a near constant. It is impossible for a constant to be related to a variable, and it is almost always exceedingly difficult to study the relationship of a near constant to other variables (see Chapter 11, Section 11.2.1). In such a situation—in other words, when a variable has almost no variability—the researcher almost always has extremely low power.

## 16.5.4 ■ Control for Third Variables

In almost all research situations, many independent variables affect the dependent variable of interest. On the other hand, the researcher's central interest is often in only one of these.

Suppose again that a researcher studies which of two treatment approaches is more effective at reducing depression among clients with this problem. Although treatment approach is the independent variable of central interest, many other variables affect depression. These might include whether the participant in the study has a partner, living situation, stressors, work situation, economic well-being, support systems, family connections, social skills, exercise, diet, sleep habits, health, spiritual life, exposure to discrimination, events of the particular day, and so forth.

Saying that an independent variable causes a dependent variable says much the same thing as saying that it causes variability in that variable. The variability caused by variables that are not of central interest (i.e., by *extraneous variables*) is, in essence, sampling error. The greater is that variability, the larger is the sampling error.

Control for key extraneous third variables reduces sampling error and, thus, increases power. Again, looking for a needle in a haystack provides a good analogy. The effect of the variable of central interest (in our example, treatment approach) is the needle and the variability caused by extraneous variables is the haystack. Control for extraneous variables—in other words, including these variables in the analysis—makes the haystack smaller (reduces sampling error) and, thus, makes the needle easier to find. Hence, if our researcher can control for key extraneous variables that affect depression, her significance test of the relationship of treatment approach to depression will have greater power than would otherwise be so.

A particularly effective way to increase power is to include a *pretest*, that is, a measurement prior to intervention. Consider again our example on treatment approaches A and B for clients with depression. Clients' depression levels will differ (vary) as they enter treatment. Hopefully you find it intuitive that depression level at entry into treatment will affect that at treatment conclusion. Basically, those most depressed at entry will tend to be among those more depressed at conclusion, and similarly, those least depressed at entry will tend to be among those less depressed at conclusion. By measuring depression at entry—that is, by administering a *pretest* of depression—and then including this measurement in her analysis, the researcher controls for depression level at entry and, thus, increases the power of a significance test that examines the relationship of treatment approach to depression at conclusion. If the null of equal mean depression scores for the two treatments is indeed false, the researcher will be more likely to reach the correct decision; she will be more likely to reject the null and accept the alternative.[1]

Some cautions should be mentioned regarding the increased power that comes from controlling for a third variable. In general, such control increases power substantially only when the controlled for variable (a) has a low correlation with the independent variable of central interest and (b) a high correlation with the dependent variable. As you know, researchers can control for more than one variable at a time. At the risk of oversimplifying, the increase in power that comes from controlling for a subsequent third variable—say for a second, third, or fourth—"third" variable is typically less than that which comes from controlling the prior one. In summary, adding one or two judiciously chosen variables to an analysis can often increase power. Beyond this, gains in power are often minimal.[2]

Chapters 10 and 11 demonstrated how control for third variables enhances the researcher's ability to draw causal conclusions in nonrandomized designs. (As you know, in such designs, the researcher can never control for all such variables, and, hence, the strength of causal conclusions is limited.) The current section demonstrates that in addition to contributing to the drawing of causal conclusions, control for key third variables can increase statistical power. Chapters 10 and 11 and the discussion in this chapter provide only a glimpse at how researchers control for third variables. Chapter 22 presents multiple regression analysis and other multivariate procedures that use multiple independent variables. You will have to wait until then to get a better feel for the most common ways of controlling for third variables.

### 16.5.5 ▥ Significance Level

As you know, other things being equal, rejecting the null is easier at the .05 level than at the .01 level. This is because rejection at the .05 level requires a smaller difference from the condition stated in the null than does that at the .01 level. To see this point, compare Figures 15.4 and 15.5 in Chapter 15. When the .05 level is used (Figure 15.4), a difference of 3.92 points from the condition stated in the null ($\mu = 100$) is sufficient for rejection. When the .01 level is used (Figure 15.5), this difference is 5.16 points.

As rejection of the null is easier at the .05 level, using this level rather than the .01 level increases power. Using the .10 level increases power still more. And, at the risk of being redundant, using the .01 level rather than the .05 level reduces power. Using the .001 level reduces power still more.

Social work researchers often deal with small sample sizes. This is particularly the case for practitioners conducting studies in agency settings. As discussed earlier, very small sample size often leads to low power. When sample size is very small—providing an exact size is difficult, but let us say less than about 40—use of the .05 (or even the .10 level) is recommended. Use of these levels increases the opportunity to reject a false null, that is, increases power.

On the other hand, when sample size is large, power is often high. In such situations, even very small relationships are often sufficient to reject the null. Indeed, the null can be rejected for relationships that are trivial in size (see, for instance, the academic achievement example in Section 16.4.2). Use of the .01 level (rather than the .05 level) reduces the risk that this will occur. In general, with very large sample sizes—let us say larger than about 1,000—use of the .01 level rather than the .05 level is recommended.

### 16.5.6 ▥ Directional Hypotheses and One-Tailed Tests

Sometimes theory, prior research, common sense, and/or logic indicate strongly that the population parameter differs in a particular direction from the condition stated in the null. Assuming that the population parameter does indeed differ in the expected direction, power is increased by using a directional hypothesis pair and, therefore, a one-tailed test. This is the case because when a one-tailed test rather than a two-tailed one is used, smaller differences from the condition stated in the null are sufficient for rejecting the null. To see this point, compare Figures 15.4 and 15.6, focusing on the upper halves of the sampling distributions. When the one-tailed test is used (Figure 15.4), a difference of 3.29 points (a score of 103.29 or greater) results in rejection. When the test is two-tailed (Figure 15.6), this difference is 3.92 points (103.92 or greater).

As you know, when sample size is very small, power is often low. When this is the case, and assuming solid grounds for expecting that the population parameter differs in a particular direction, you may want to formulate a directional hypothesis pair and, thus, use a one-tailed test. Doing so increases the opportunity to reject a false null, that is, increases power.

On the other hand, when sample size is very large, the researcher usually does better to use a nondirectional pair (two-tailed test) rather than a directional one. Doing so reduces the risk that a trivial-sized relationship will lead to rejection of the null.

### 16.5.7 ▒ Statistical Significance Test

Some statistical tests have greater power than others. In general, the higher the level of measurement required by the test, the greater its power. In particular, tests designed for numeric variables tend to have higher power than do those designed for categorical data. The practical implication is that the researcher should strive for interval/ratio-level measurement whenever possible. By so doing, she can often use a more powerful test and, thus, increase the likelihood of rejecting a false null.

## 16.6 ▒ HOW MUCH POWER IS ENOUGH?

By tradition, social science has reached a consensus that power of about .80 or higher is good (high) and that power considerably lower than about .80 is poor (low). When power is .80, the researcher has an 80% chance of rejecting a false null. In this situation, the risk of Type II error ($\beta$), failing to reject a false null, is .20.

Just as .80 sets the "traditional" standard for power, the .05 significance level does so for statistical significance. At the .05 level, the risk of a Type I error, rejecting a true null, is .05. The traditions of science thus accept a risk of Type II error that is four times higher than that for Type I error (.20/.05 = 4 times). This reflects the conservative bias of science in favor of the null. The error of rejecting a true null is regarded as a more costly mistake than that of failing to accept (rejecting) a true alternative.

Social work researchers often deal with small samples and, thus, power is often low. Sometimes, the pragmatic thing to do is to go ahead and conduct the research study even though power may be less than adequate. In such situations, the researcher should recognize that failure to reject the null may well be due to low power. Stated differently, in such situations, the risk of Type II error, failing to reject a false null, is high.

## 16.7 ▒ HOW LARGE SHOULD SAMPLE SIZE BE?

Researchers use either power tables or software power calculators to determine power. The authoritative reference for statistical power and the best source of power tables is Jacob Cohen's (1988) classic *Statistical Power Analysis for the Behavioral Sciences*. As this text is written, several free online powers can be accessed by googling "statistical power calculator."

Let us walk through the steps in determining power with a power calculator. We will use our treatment for depression example to do so. The first step is to estimate the size of relationship in the population from which the study sample will be randomly selected. Our depression/therapy example involves two groups (two treatments) and a numeric dependent variable. This being so, we estimate the *SMD*. Let us presume that we estimate the *SMD* to be 0.5, that is, we estimate that the mean depression score on the *XYZ* depression scale is 0.50 standard deviations higher in the Treatment A population than in the Treatment B population. To estimate power, the researcher specifies a significance level and whether the significance test is one-tailed (e.g., directional pair) or two-tailed (nondirectional pair). We will use a two-tailed test and the .05 level. Finally, the sample size is specified. Let us presume that 25 persons receive each treatment. We now "plug" this information into a power calculator.

A particularly good calculator, developed by Russ Lenth (2006) may be found at http://www.stat.uiowa.edu/~rlenth/Power/. Given our situation—an estimated *SMD* of 0.50, a two-tailed test at the .05 level, and 25 participants in each group—our power calculates .41. In other words (presuming that our estimate of the *SMD* is correct), we have a 41% chance of rejecting the null. Our probability of making a Type II error, failing to reject a false null, is $1.00 - .41 = .59$. Thus, we have a 59% chance of making such an error.

Clearly, our power is low. We want to increase it. Let us calculate power keeping all things the same except for sample size, which we will increase to 50 for each treatment group. Doing so increases our power to 0.70 and decreases our risk of Type II error to 0.30. So, things improve considerably with the larger sample size. Perhaps we do not have the resources to increase sample size still more. This being so, how might we increase our power? One way would be to form a directional pair. With a directional pair specified, power increases to 0.80.

Still, another way to increase power is to include a pretest. A different online calculator indicated that given a correlation within each treatment group of 0.70 ($r = 0.70$) between pretest and posttest depression scores, power of 0.80 could be achieved with only 33 persons per group (McDonald, 2009; available at http://udel.edu/~mcdonald/statancova.html). This assumes a two-tailed test using the .05 level. Hence, a pretest would help power considerably.

As presented earlier, restricted variability decreases power. Variability of treatment approach is maximized in our example as 50% of participants receive each treatment. What if, for instance, 60% (that is, 60 participants) received Treatment A and 40% (40 participants) received Treatment B? This modest reduction in variability reduces power to .68 (two-tailed test, .05 level used), hardly a reduction at all from .70, the power when 50% received each treatment. On the other hand, how would a much more substantial reduction in variability affect power? Suppose that 90% (90 participants) received Treatment A and 10% (10 participants) received Treatment B. Now, power calculates to .32 (two-tailed test, .05 level), much less than when percentages were equal.

To help you get a feel for power, I created a power table (Table 16.2) using Russ Lenth's calculator. It is for the situation that we have been dealing with, one that involves means in two different groups. All calculations are for a two-tailed test using .05 level. Sample size refers to the total number of participants rather than to the number in each group. Equal numbers in both groups are assumed.

Observe that four of the *SMD* values in Table 16.2 are taken from Table 9.1 in Chapter 9. These values—0.20, 0.50, 0.80, and 1.30—were defined as *small*, *medium*, *large*, and *very large* size of relationship, respectively. The ">99" symbol in Table 16.2 conveys that power is greater than .99. For all areas of the table that are below or to the right of any ">99" symbol, power is also greater than .99. For readability, decimal points are not presented; for instance, "26" conveys power of .26.

TABLE 16.2 ■ Power Table for a Difference Between Two Means

| Sample Size | Standardized Mean Difference (SMD) in Population | | | | | | | | | |
|---|---|---|---|---|---|---|---|---|---|---|
| | .10 | .20 | .35 | .50 | .65 | .80 | 1.00 | 1.30 | 2.0 | 3.0 |
| 10 | 05 | 06 | 08 | 11 | 15 | 20 | 29 | 44 | 79 | 98 |
| 20 | 06 | 07 | 12 | 19 | 28 | 40 | 56 | 78 | 99 | >99 |
| 30 | 06 | 08 | 15 | 26 | 40 | 56 | 75 | 93 | >99 | |
| 50 | 06 | 11 | 23 | 41 | 61 | 79 | 94 | >99 | | |
| 70 | 07 | 13 | 30 | 54 | 76 | >99 | >99 | | | |
| 100 | 08 | 17 | 41 | 70 | 90 | | | | | |
| 150 | 09 | 23 | 57 | 86 | 98 | | | | | |
| 200 | 11 | 29 | 69 | 94 | >99 | | | | | |
| 400 | 17 | 51 | 94 | >99 | | | | | | |
| 600 | 23 | 69 | 99 | | | | | | | |
| 1,000 | 35 | 88 | >99 | | | | | | | |
| 2,000 | 61 | >99 | | | | | | | | |
| 4,000 | 88 | | | | | | | | | |
| 10,000 | >99 | | | | | | | | | |

Table 16.2 conveys the two key factors affecting power:

■ As sample size goes up, so does power; and

■ As size of relationship (the *SMD* in this example) goes up, so does power.

To see the first point, observe that power goes up as you read down the columns, that is, as sample size goes up. This is so for each column, that is, for each size of relationship (*SMD*).

To see the second point, observe that power goes up as you read across the rows from left to right, that is, as the size of relationship goes up. This is so for each row, that is, for each sample size.

Although Table 16.2 presents differences involving two means, the power values that it lists for the small, medium, large, and very large *SMD* values (.20, .50, .80, and 1.30) provide "rough" estimates for the corresponding size of relationship for the difference in percentages, the risk ratio, the odds ratio, and the correlation coefficient. For instance, a difference of percentages of 18% (*D%* = 18%) conveys a relationship of medium size (see Table 6.3). Table 16.1 informs us, for instance, that given sample size of 100 and a medium-sized *SMD*— one of .50—power equals .70. This provides a reasonable "rough" estimate of power in a similar-sized sample when the *D%* in the population is medium in size, that is, when it equals 18%. When precision is required, rather than using such an estimate, you will do better to use an online calculator.

As we close our discussion of power, remember that calculated power is, in essence, a best estimate of actual power. You may want to calculate power using several different estimates of the size of relationship in the population.

Power calculations are often performed to determine the needed sample size. Researchers adjust sample size until the desired power, often about .80 or greater, is achieved.

## 16.8 ■ NONRANDOM SAMPLES AND SIGNIFICANCE TESTS

Chapter 12, Section 12.2 stated that inferential statistical procedures are tools for drawing conclusions about populations based on observations from samples randomly selected from those populations. Section 12.3 stated specifically that inferential procedures should only be used with random samples.

Notwithstanding the discussion in Chapter 12, the reality of social science research is that statistical significance tests are often conducted in the absence of random sampling. For instance, the prevention of out-of-home placement example in Section 16.4.2 did not use random samples. Even so, significance tests were carried out.

When a significance test is conducted in the absence of random sampling, there is no *real* larger population—no real larger group of people beyond the study sample—to which study results may be generalized using the logic of inferential statistics. Suppose, for instance, that we reject the null that equal percentages of children in the two programs require out-of-home placement. Using statistically based logic, we can conclude that this null is likely false in the population from which the study sample was randomly selected. But, as there is no such population, this conclusion has dubious (if any) meaning.

On the other hand, whether or not a real study population exists, *the study sample consists of real people* and, hence, conclusions about it do have real-world meaning. In particular, the central question of statistical significance testing—whether the study sample result is due to chance alone—is important and viable even in the absence of random sampling. For instance, we rejected the null in our placement prevention example. This tells us that, *in our study sample*, chance alone is an unlikely explanation for the differing outcomes in the two programs. In the absence of random sampling, we cannot statistically generalize this conclusion beyond our sample but it does hold for the sample itself. We can be confident that something real made a difference in our sample.

In summary, even with nonrandom samples, most researchers carry out significance tests. You should do the same.

## 16.9 ■ REPORTING STATISTICAL SIGNIFICANCE

In reporting significance, the hypothesis testing model presented in Chapter 15, Section 15.2, differs from common practice in several ways. In the model, one chooses a significance level prior to carrying out the test. Further, one does not switch to another level after having carried out the test. For instance, in our second out-of-home placement study (see Section 16.4.2), we chose the .05 level. The probability of the study result ($p$) was .009. Even though .009 is less than .01, I did not switch to the .01 level but, instead, presented this result as significant at the .05 level. In actual research, however, researchers typically report significance at the lowest significance level that has been achieved. For instance, in an actual research situation, the researcher would report the study result ($p = .009$) as significant at the .01 level.

For most significance tests presented in this text, to make a decision on the hypothesis pair, we (a) compute the obtained statistic (for instance, for the large sample test of $\overline{X}$, we compute $z$), (b) reference a decision rule, and (c) make a decision. This process tells us whether $p$ (the probability of the result) is greater than or less than the probability associated with the selected significance level (.05 or .01). We do not, however, learn the exact value of $p$.

With the easy availability of computers, researchers use statistical software programs to carry out significance tests. Almost without exception, these programs provide the exact value of $p$. This being so, the preferred approach—preferred even to reporting the lowest significance level achieved as discussed earlier—is to report this value. For instance, for our out-of-home placement example, we would report that $p = .009$.[3]

## 16.10 ■ WHAT STATISTICAL SIGNIFICANCE IS (AND IS NOT)

Statistical significance is recognized as the most important concept in statistics and is clearly the cornerstone concept around which social science research revolves. A key problem, however, is that statistical significance is too often viewed as the *only* important concept. Because such extreme attention is focused on statistical significance, its meaning becomes blurred with other important but less recognized aspects of data analysis. Thus, when an association is statistically significant, some students (and professors) make the mistake of assuming that this association is also necessarily (a) large (strong), (b) causal, (c) generalizable to many settings, and (d) important. Statistical significance has one primary "nuts and bolts" meaning, that chance alone is not the likely explanation for an association or difference. Interpret it in this way and you will not go wrong. Do not make the mistake of blurring its meaning with these other distinct and important concepts.

We have already covered size of association (Chapters 6–9) and causality (Chapters 10 and 11). Section 16.8 in this chapter touched briefly on generalizability. Chapter 24 presents further discussion on how researchers generalize study results (Section 24.2) and discusses the distinction between the statistical significance (or lack thereof) of a study result and that result's importance (Section 24.3).

Having just emphasized that statistical significance has one primary meaning, you also know that it can be interpreted in many different ways. Table 16.3 presents valid conclusions pertaining to statistical significance or the lack thereof. Its left column lists valid conclusions when results are not significant; its right column lists such conclusions when results are significant. Table 16.3 presumes that an appropriate significance test was carried out. When this is not so, many of its conclusions do not hold.

This chapter and the prior two have presented the theory and logic of significance testing. The next six focus on the key statistical significance tests used in human services research.

## 16.11 ■ CHAPTER SUMMARY

The *statistical power* (*power*) of a significance test is the probability that it will reject a false null. Power and beta ($\beta$; the probability of Type II error) sum to 1.00 and also, Power $= 1 - \beta$. The most important factors influencing power are sample size and size of relationship in the population.

When sample size is small, power is often low. Conversely, when it is large, power is often high.

When sample size is very small, the size of the difference required to reject the null can be so large that the researcher does not have a realistic opportunity to do so. In such situations, power is almost always low, and the probability of Type II error is almost always high. As sample size increases, other things being equal and assuming that the null is false, so does power. When sample size is very large, even very small differences may be sufficient to reject the null. In such situations, power is almost always high and the probability of Type II error is almost always low.

Other things being equal, the larger the size of relationship or difference in the population from which the study sample is randomly sampled, the greater the power.

In addition to sample size and size of relationship in the population, five factors affect power: (a) reduced variability of independent or dependent variables, (b) control for third (extraneous) variables, (c) the significance level used, (d) whether the hypothesis pair is directional or nondirectional (one-tailed vs. two-tailed test), and (e) the particular significance test used.

Very low variability of either the independent or dependent variable reduces power. Control for extraneous variables reduces variability that is not central to the research question and, by so doing, increases power.

TABLE 16.3 ■ Valid Conclusions From Statistical Significance Tests

| Study Sample Result Is Not Statistically Significant | Study Sample Result Is Statistically Significant |
|---|---|
| **Fail to reject (accept) the null hypothesis; reject the alternative (research) hypothesis** | **Reject the null hypothesis; accept the alternative (research) hypothesis** |
| Chance alone (sampling error alone) is not a highly unlikely explanation for the study sample result (sufficiently unlikely for the null to be rejected). | Chance alone (sampling error alone) is an unlikely explanation for the study sample result. Chance alone is not a sufficient explanation for this result. |
| Study sample result does not provide strong evidence that the null is false. | Study sample result provides strong evidence that the null is false and, thus, that the alternative is true. |
| One cannot be confident that the null is false. | One can be confident that the null is false and, thus, that the alternative is true. |
| Study sample result is not highly inconsistent with the null (sufficiently inconsistent for it to be rejected). | Study sample result is inconsistent with the null. It is consistent with the alternative hypothesis. |
| Given a true null, the probability of obtaining the study sample result (or an even more extreme result) is greater than the probability associated with the selected significance level ($>\alpha$). | Given a true null, the probability of obtaining the study sample result (or an even more extreme result) is less than or equal to the probability associated with the selected significance level ($\leq\alpha$). |
| The probability of obtaining the study sample result (or an even more extreme result) due to chance alone (sampling error alone) is greater than the probability associated with the selected significance level ($>\alpha$). | The probability of obtaining the study sample result (or an even more extreme result) due to chance alone (sampling error alone) is less or equal to the probability associated with the selected significance level ($\leq\alpha$). |
| The probability that the difference between the condition stated in the null and the result obtained in the study sample is due to chance alone (sampling error alone) is greater than the probability associated with the selected significance level ($>\alpha$). | The probability that the difference between the condition stated in the null and the result obtained in the study sample is due to chance alone (sampling error alone) is less than or equal to the probability associated with the selected significance level ($\leq\alpha$). |
| If the .05 statistical significance level is used ($\alpha = .05$), one is less than 95% confident that the null hypothesis is false. (For the .01 level ($\alpha = .01$), one is less than 99% confident). | If the .05 statistical significance level was used ($\alpha = .05$), one is at least 95% confident that the null hypothesis is false (and that the alternative hypothesis is true). For the .01 level ($\alpha = .01$), one is at least 99% confident. |
| If the hypothesis pair pertains to an association, the study sample results do not provide sufficient grounds for concluding that variables are associated in the population from which the study sample(s) was randomly selected. The association in the sample may be due to chance alone. | If the hypothesis pair pertains to an association, it is likely that variables are associated in the population from which the study sample(s) was randomly selected. It is unlikely that the association in the sample is due to chance alone. |
| Study sample results do not prove that the null is true. | Study results do not prove that the alternative is true. |

Use of the .05 level rather than the .01 level increases power. Use of a directional hypothesis pair (one-tailed test) rather than a nondirectional one (two-tailed test) increases power. Generally speaking, significance tests for numeric variables have greater power than do those for categorical ones. This being so, the researcher should strive for interval/ratio-level measurement whenever possible.

By tradition, power of about .80 or more is regarded as high (good). When power is .80, the significance test has an 80% chance of rejecting a false null. Researchers use power tables or power calculators to determine power. Calculated power is an estimate of actual power.

Statistical significance testing is recommended even in the absence of random sampling. In the hypothesis testing model, the researcher selects the significance level prior to conducting the significance test. However, in actual research, it is common practice to report significance at the lowest level that has been achieved. Preferred over this is reporting the exact value of *p*.

Mistakenly, many regard statistical significance as the *only* important concept in data interpretation. In particular, many assume mistakenly that a statistically significant association is also necessarily (a) large, (b) causal, (c) generalizable to many settings, and (d) important. Statistical significance has one primary meaning—that chance alone is not the likely explanation for an association or difference.

## 16.12 ■ PROBLEMS AND QUESTIONS

### Section 16.2

1. Power is the _____ that a statistical test will reject a _____ _____ hypothesis, or, stated differently, that it will accept a _____ _____ hypothesis.

2. β (beta) is the probability of Type ____ error, that is, failing to _____ a _____ _____. Power and β (beta) sum to ____.

3. In each situation, β provided. *Calculate power.*
   a. β = .40
   b. β = .60
   c. β = .30
   d. β = .10

4. In each situation, power is provided. *Calculate β.*
   a. Power = .85
   b. Power = .50
   c. Power = .90
   d. Power = .40

5. In a given situation, power equals .80. *Assume that the null is false and respond to the following:*
   a. What is the probability of a Type II error?
   b. What does β equal?

## Section 16.3

6. When sample size is small, power is often _____. Conversely, when it is large, power is often _____.

7. (*True or False*) When sample size is small, the amount of sampling error is also almost always quite small.

8. (*True or False*) When sample size is small, the significance test can almost always easily distinguish between sampling error and a real difference.

## Section 16.4

9. $H_0$: $\mu = 100$, $s = 40$, $\alpha = .05$ (two-tailed test). For each of the following sample sizes, indicate (a) $s_{\bar{x}}$ (the estimated standard error of the mean) and (b) the approximate difference from the condition stated in the null that is necessary for rejection via the large sample test of $\bar{X}$. Hint: Study result must differ by about two standard errors for the null to be rejected.
   a. 100
   b. 400
   c. 1,600

10. Other things being equal, as sample size increases, increasingly _____ differences are sufficient to reject the null. Given that a null hypothesis is indeed false, as sample size increases, it becomes _____ to reject that null.

11. *Respond true or false to each statement.*
   a. When sample size is very small, small differences (small relationships) are typically sufficient for rejecting the null.
   b. When sample size is very small, even large associations in the study sample (large differences) may not achieve significance.
   c. When sample size is very small, sampling error alone can be the cause of very large differences.
   d. When sample size is small, the researcher often fails to reject the null not because the null is true but rather because power is low.
   e. As sample size increases (other things being equal and assuming that the null is false), power neither increases nor decreases.
   f. When sample size is very large, even small associations (small differences) are often sufficient to reject the null.
   g. When sample size is very large, even small associations (small differences) can often be discriminated from sampling error.

12. When sample size is huge, sampling error is reduced to almost _____ and, power can be close to _____ (numerical value).

**Section 16.5**

13. In a large scale survey of parenting skills ($N = 40,000$), a researcher establishes that for parents who emphasize Parenting Approach A, the mean score for closeness of parent–child relationship on the ABC scale is 50.00 (standard deviation equals 10.00). For those who emphasize Parenting Approach B, the mean score is 50.50 (standard deviation equals 10). A significance test reveals that this difference in means is statistically significant at the .01 level ($p \leq .01$). Respond to the following questions about this situation:
    a. The difference in means scores is likely to be caused by chance alone.
    b. The null of equal mean scores is rejected.
    c. (*True or False*) Because the difference in mean scores is statistically significant, we know that this difference is a large one.
    d. (*True or False*) Given the large sample size, there is likely a very large amount of sampling error.
    e. Calculate the *SMD*. (Consider Parenting Approach A to be the first group; see Formula 9.1.)
    f. The difference in mean scores is a large one (see Table 9.1).
    g. Comment briefly: Does this result suggest that one parenting approach is *much* preferred over the other. (*Bogus* hint: It must suggest this as the result is statistically significant. Correct?)

14. *Indicate whether power is greater for Situation #1 or Situation #2*. Assume that for each situation, sample sizes are equal, the .05 level is used, and the hypothesis pair is nondirectional (two-tailed test).
    a. #1:  correlation in population = .30; #2 correlation in population = .55
    b. #1:  *SMD* in population = $-0.20$; #2 *SMD* in population = 0.40
    c. #1:  Treatment 1   20% in population have successful outcome
            Treatment 2   40% in population have successful outcome
       #2:  Treatment 1   20% in population have successful outcome
            Treatment 2   30% in population have successful outcome
    d. #1:  correlation in population = .10; #2 correlation in population = .20

15. *Respond true or false to each.*
    a. Other things being equal, the larger the difference or relationship in the population, the greater the power.
    b. When the size of relationship or difference in the population is small, even small sample size is almost always sufficient to reject the null.
    c. In a given population, the *SMD* = 0.15. (True or False) A small sample size, say 15 in each group, will almost assuredly be sufficient to reject the null.
    d. When the size of relationship in the population is extremely large, even a moderate or small sample size may be sufficient to reject the null.
    e. When the size of relationship in the population is small, a large (rather than a small) sample size is often needed for good power.
    f. The power that a researcher calculates is, in essence, a best estimate of the actual power, which ultimately is unknown.

**16.** A researcher studies whether gender is associated with readmission to a psychiatric facility. In a random sample of 200 persons (100 women and 100 men) selected from Population A, 40% require readmission. In a random sample of 200 persons (100 women and 100 men) selected from Population B, 4% require readmission. In each sample, the researcher conducts a significance test on the association of gender to readmission. Assuming that the size of relationship between gender and readmission is equal in populations A and B, in which sample—that selected from Population A or that selected from Population B—will the researcher's test have greater power. Why?

**17.** A social worker teaches a course on child development to a group of new mothers ($N = 15$), *all* of whom are *very highly* motivated to learn about child development. Respond to each of the following:

    **a.** Do you think that motivation to learn new skills varies a great deal or only a little in this group of mothers?

    **b.** How will the amount of variability in motivation affect the power of a significance test that examines the relationship between motivation and knowledge? (Hint: The amount of variability is quite low.)

**18.** *The next group of questions are true or false.*

    **a.** Very restricted (low) variability in either the independent or dependent variable can lead to reduced (low) statistical power.

    **b.** Control for key extraneous third variables can reduce sampling error and, thus, increase power.

    **c.** Power increases substantially even when the controlled for variable is highly correlated with the independent variable of key interest and weakly correlated with the dependent variable.

    **d.** Other things being equal, rejecting the null is easier at the .05 level than at the .01 level.

    **e.** Other things being equal, power is greater at the .05 level than at the .01 level.

    **f.** When sample size is very small, this text recommends using the .01 level (rather than the .05 level).

    **g.** Other things being equal, when a one-tailed test rather than a two-tailed one is used, a smaller difference from the condition stated in the null is sufficient for rejecting the null.

    **h.** Assuming that the population parameter does indeed differ in the expected direction, power is increased by using a directional hypothesis pair and, therefore, a one-tailed test (rather than a nondirectional pair and two-tailed test).

    **i.** In general, the lower the level of measurement required by the significance test, the greater the statistical power.

**Section 16.6**

**19.** By tradition, social science has reached a consensus that power of about ____ or higher is good (high). When power is .80, the researcher has an ____% chance of rejecting a false null. In this situation, the risk of Type II error ($\beta$), failing to reject a _____ _____, is ____.

**Section 16.7**

**20.** Using Table 16.3, indicate the power for each combination of sample size (*N*) and *SMD*. Indicate also the probability of a Type II error. (This table assumes equal numbers in each group, use of the .05 level, and a two-tailed test.)
   **a.** $N = 20$, $SMD = .80$
   **b.** $N = 30$, $SMD = .80$
   **c.** $N = 50$, $SMD = .80$
   **d.** $N = 50$, $SMD = 1.00$
   **e.** $N = 50$, $SMD = 1.30$

**21.** Table 16.3 is based on the .05 level and a two-tailed test. Also, sample size is assumed to be equal in the two groups (50% in each group). *Indicate whether each change below would increase or decrease power from that listed in Table 16.3.*
   **a.** Using the .01 level rather than the .05.
   **b.** Using a one-tailed rather than a two-tailed test. Assume that the population parameter is in the expected direction.
   **c.** Splitting the two groups unevenly, say, 10% in one group and 90% in the other.
   **d.** Controlling for key third variables that introduce extraneous variation.
   **e.** Including a pretest.

**22.** (*True or False*) Power calculations are often performed to determine the needed sample size.

**Section 16.8**

**23.** *Respond true or false to each of the following:*
   **a.** It is a reality of social science research that statistical significance tests are often conducted in the absence of random sampling.
   **b.** In the absence of random sampling, there is no larger group of "real" people beyond the study sample to which study results may be generalized using the logic of inferential statistics.
   **c.** The central question of statistical significance testing—whether the study sample result is due to chance alone—is important and viable even in the absence of random sampling.
   **d.** This text advises that you carry out significance tests only with random samples.

**Section 16.9**

**24.** (*True or False*) In actual research, reporting the exact value of *p* is preferred to reporting the significance level.

**Section 16.10**

**25.** *Respond true or false to each of the following:*
   **a.** Statistically significant relationships are always large relationships.
   **b.** Statistically significant relationships are always causal relationships.
   **c.** Statistically significant results are always generalizable to many different settings.
   **d.** Statistically significant results are always important.
   **e.** Statistically significant results are unlikely to be caused by chance alone.
   **f.** Statistically significant results provide strong evidence that the null is false.

# 17

# THE *t* DISTRIBUTION AND ONE-SAMPLE PROCEDURES FOR MEANS

## 17.1 ■ CHAPTER OVERVIEW

Chapter 17 presents a new distribution—the *t distribution*—and two inferential statistical procedures based on it, confidence intervals (*CI*) for means and the *one-sample t test*. This chapter also introduces degrees of freedom.

## 17.2 ■ SMALL SAMPLE SIZE AND DISTRIBUTIONS

To this point, two inferential statistical procedures have been presented for sample means, confidence intervals (Chapter 13) and the large sample test of $\overline{X}$ (Chapter 15). Both procedures are based on the normal distribution and both require sample sizes of 100 or greater.

When sample size is less than 100 ($N < 100$), the estimate of the standard deviation of the sampling distribution of $\overline{X}$ ($s_{\overline{X}}$) can be inaccurate. This being so, when $N < 100$, inferential procedures involving means are not based on the normal distribution but instead on the *t* distribution. Prior to learning about the *t* distribution, degrees of freedom should be introduced.

## 17.3 ■ DEGREES OF FREEDOM

Most statistical procedures presented from this point forward require calculation of degrees of freedom. **Degrees of freedom** *(df)* are the number of independent values that remain after mathematical restrictions have been applied. For instance, suppose that you have 25 cases in a sample and compute the sample mean, $\overline{X}$. Suppose further that you inform a colleague of (a) the values of 24 of the 25 cases and (b) the value of $\overline{X}$. With this information, your colleague could figure out the value of the 25th case. As described, the value of the 25th case is not free to vary. Instead, it can be determined from the values of the other 24 cases and the mean. In this situation, there are 24 independent values (i.e., 24 *df*).

Generalizing from our example: For all samples, there are $N - 1$ opportunities for values to vary independently around the sample mean. In other words, there are $N - 1$ *df*.[1]

## 17.4 ■ THE FAMILY OF *t* DISTRIBUTIONS

Unlike the normal distribution, the **t distribution** is not a single distribution but instead is a **family of distributions**—that is, a group of distributions derived by a common set of procedures or formulas. Each distribution within a family, each *family member*, has a different shape and, often, other distinctive characteristics as well. For the family of *t* distributions, there is a different *t* distribution—a different family member—for each different *df*.

For confidence intervals for means and the one-sample *t* test, the two procedures based on the *t* distribution presented in this chapter, *df* equal sample size minus one (i.e., $df = N - 1$). For instance, if $N = 5$, $df = 5 - 1 = 4$.

The *t* distribution changes its shape as degrees of freedom change. When *N* is less than about 10 (*df* < about 9), the *t* distribution's shape differs markedly from that of the normal distribution. In particular, it has "heavier," more elongated tails than does the normal distribution. As *N* increases, its shape increasingly resembles that of the normal distribution. When *N* is about 100 or greater (*df* ≥ about 99), the shape of the *t* distribution and that of the normal distributions are almost identical.

Figure 17.1 presents *t* distributions with 4, 19, and 99 degrees of freedom. Observe the heavy, elongated tails when *df* = 4. Although Figure 17.1 does not present a normal distribution, if it did, it would be almost indistinguishable from the *t* distribution when *df* = 99.

In a normal distribution, the percentage of cases located between two given *z* scores is constant. For instance, 95% of cases are located between a *z* score of −1.96 and a *z* score of 1.96. This is so for all normal distributions. Indeed, because the normal distribution is not a family of distributions, there is, in essence, only one normal distribution.

For the *t* distribution, the value of *t* within which given percentages of cases are located varies according to the degrees of freedom. For instance, when *df* = 4, 95% of cases are located between a *t* score of −2.78 and a *t* score of 2.78. When *df* = 19, 95% are located between *t* scores of −2.09 and 2.09, and when *df* = 99, 95% are located between *t* scores of −1.98 and 1.98. Figure 17.2 presents visually the values of *t* within which 95% of cases are located for the three *t* distributions that have been discussed.

As mentioned earlier (see Section 17.2) when *N* < 100, the estimate of the standard deviation of the sampling distribution ($s_{\bar{x}}$) can be inaccurate. By changing its shape as degrees of freedom change, the *t* distribution adjusts for the likely amount of error involved in this estimate and, by doing so, yields accurate results.

### FIGURE 17.1 ■ *t* Distribution for Three Sample Sizes

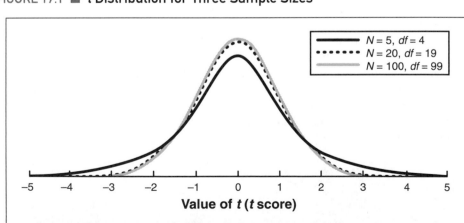

FIGURE 17.2 ■ Location of 95% of Cases for Three *t* Distributions

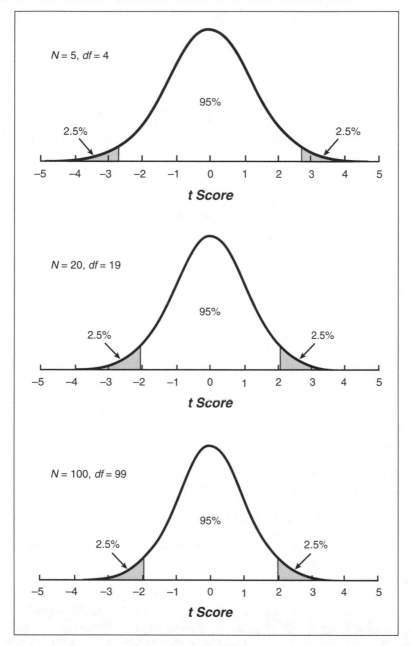

## 17.5 ■ CONFIDENCE INTERVALS FOR MEANS FOR SMALL SAMPLES (AND LARGE)

When sample size is less than 100, formulas based on the *t* distribution are used to form confidence intervals for means. These formulas may also be used when $N \geq 100$. Confidence intervals for means based on the *t* distribution yield highly accurate results when $N \geq 20$ and the study sample does not have an extreme skew (see Figures 5.4 and 5.6) and when $N \geq 100$ (even in the presence of extreme skew).

One confidence interval formula is

$$CI \text{ of } \mu = \overline{X} \pm t(s/\sqrt{N}) \qquad (17.1)$$

An alternative formula is

$$CI \text{ of } \mu = \overline{X} \pm t(s_{\overline{x}}) \qquad (17.2)$$

As you know, $s_{\overline{x}}$ is the estimate of the standard error of the mean (the estimate of the standard deviation of the sampling distribution of $\overline{X}$) and equals $s/\sqrt{N}$. In Formulas 17.1 and 17.2, $t$ is the value of $t$ in the $t$-distribution table (Table A.2 in Appendix A) that corresponds to the desired confidence interval and appropriate degrees of freedom. As stated earlier, $df = N - 1$.

Let us now calculate a confidence interval. Suppose that you select a random sample of 25 children in foster care and determine that they have experienced a mean of 4.35 placements with a standard deviation of 1.2 placements. That is, $N = 25$, $\overline{X} = 4.35$, and $s = 1.2$. Presume that your sample has a moderate positive skew. Because $N > 20$ and the skew is not extreme, results will be accurate and thus we may proceed.

**1.** Estimate $s_{\overline{x}}$.

$$\frac{1.2}{\sqrt{25}} = \frac{1.2}{5} = 0.24$$

**2.** Compute the degrees of freedom ($df = N - 1$): $df = 25 - 1 = 24$
**3.** Locate the appropriate value of $t$ in the $t$-distribution table (Table A.2)

The leftmost column in Table A.2 indicates $df$. Trace down it to find the row with 24. Trace across until you intersect the column labeled "Number of Standard Deviations Within Which 95% of Cases are Located." This $t$, 2.064, conveys for a $t$ distribution with 24 $df$, the number of standard deviations within which 95% of cases are located.

**4.** Multiply the $t$ from Table A.2 by $s_{\overline{x}}$ : 2.064 (0.24) = .495
**5.** Add and subtract from the sample mean:

95% $CI$ of $\mu = 4.35 \pm .495 = 3.855$ to $4.845$

Hence, we can be 95% *confident* that the population mean, $\mu$, is located within the interval that spans from 3.855 placements to 4.845 placements.

Sometimes, Table A.2 does not have a row corresponding to the exact number of $df$. In this case, one uses the row with the next smallest number. For instance, when $N$ is 70, $df = 70 - 1 = 69$. Table A.2 has no row for 69 $df$. It does, however, have a row for 60 $df$ and thus this is used.

For a 99% $CI$ rather than a 95% one, use the column labeled "Number of Standard Deviations Within Which 99% of Cases are Located." For $df = 24$, the $t$ in Table A.2 for a 99% $CI$ is 2.797. Computing the 99% $CI$ for our foster care example using Formula 17.1: $4.35 \pm 2.797(1.2/\sqrt{25} = 3.68$ to 5.02). As is always the case, this 99% $CI$ is wider than the 95% $CI$ calculated for the same situation.

Let us compare our 95% $CI$, 3.855 placements to 4.845 placements, with the 95% $CI$ that results from using the formula based on the normal distribution. Using the normal distribution formula, Formula 13.3: 95% $CI$ of $\mu = \overline{X} \pm 1.96$ $(s_{\overline{x}})$, results in a confidence interval that spans from 3.88 placements to 4.82 placements. Our confidence interval based on the $t$ distribution is slightly wider than this.

Other things being equal, confidence intervals based on the $t$ distribution are always wider than those based on the normal distribution. This is because they adjust for the error involved in estimating the standard error of the mean. For this same reason, confidence intervals based on the *t* distribution are more accurate than those based on the normal distribution. When $N \geq 100$, the degree of increased accuracy is so small that one may use a formula based on either distribution. My recommendation is to use the *t* distribution-based formulas even when $N \geq 100$. This is the common practice in research. (Even though I just did so for demonstration purposes, you should not use the formulas based on the normal distribution when $N < 100$.)

## 17.6 ■ INTRODUCTION TO THE ONE-SAMPLE *t* TEST

### 17.6.1 ■ Assumptions, Hypothesis Pairs, and Formula

Just as does the large sample test of $\overline{X}$, the **one-sample *t* test** examines whether the mean of a sample differs significantly from a hypothesized value. When $N < 100$, the large sample test of $\overline{X}$ can be inaccurate and thus the one-sample *t* test is used. When $N > 100$, the one-sample *t* test and the large sample test of $\overline{X}$ yield similar results, those of the one-sample *t* test being slightly more accurate. My recommendation is simply to use the one-sample *t* test even when $N > 100$; this is the common practice.

The one-sample *t* test assumes that the study sample is (randomly) selected from a population with a normal distribution. Stated more succinctly, it assumes normality. It is, however, quite robust to this assumption. Just as is the case for the just-presented confidence interval formulas, it yields highly accurate results when $N \geq 20$ except when the study sample has an extreme skew and when $N \geq 100$ (even in the presence of extreme skew). As it deals with means, it requires measurement at the interval/ratio level.

The hypothesis pairs for the one-sample *t* test are the same as those for the large sample test of $\overline{X}$. The nondirectional hypothesis pair states:

Null:         The mean of the population from which the study sample was randomly selected equals some value.

Alternative:  The mean of the population from which the study sample was randomly selected does not equal the value stated in the null.

Stated in mathematical symbols: $H_0: \mu = A; \quad H_1: \mu \neq A$

where $\mu$ is the mean of the population from which the study sample was selected and $A$ is a given value.

When the expected direction for the study result is positive (greater than the value stated in the null), the directional pair is:

Null:         The mean of the population from which the study sample was randomly selected is less than or equal to a given value.

Alternative:  The mean of the population from which the study sample was randomly selected is greater than the value stated in the null.

Or, using symbols: $H_0: \mu \leq A; \quad H_1: \mu > A$

When the expected direction is negative, the pair is: $H_0: \mu \geq A; H_1: \mu < A$

One formula for the one-sample *t* test is:

$$t = \frac{\overline{X} - \mu}{s/\sqrt{N}} \tag{17.3}$$

An equivalent formula is:

$$t = \frac{\bar{X} - \mu}{s_{\bar{X}}}$$
(17.4)

When the hypothesis pair is nondirectional, the one-sample $t$ test is two-tailed. When it is directional, it is one-tailed with the rejection region located in the direction stated in the alternative hypothesis.

### 17.6.2 ▓ Decision Rules

The decision rule for a nondirectional hypothesis pair and thus a two-tailed, one-sample $t$ test is

Fail to reject (accept) the null if the absolute value of the obtained $t$ is less than the value of $t$ in the $t$-distribution table (Table A.2 in Appendix A).

Reject the null if the absolute value of the obtained $t$ is greater than or equal to the value of $t$ in the $t$-distribution table.

For directional hypothesis pairs, the test is one-tailed. When the alternative hypothesis states greater than,

Fail to reject (accept) the null if the obtained $t$ is less than the $t$ in the $t$-distribution table (Table A.2).

Reject the null if the obtained $t$ is greater than or equal to the $t$ in the $t$-distribution table.

When the alternative hypothesis states less than,

Fail to reject (accept) the null if the obtained $t$ is greater than the "negative of" the $t$ in the $t$-distribution table (Table A.2).

Reject the null if the obtained $t$ is less than or equal to the negative of the $t$ in the $t$-distribution table.

I need to clarify the expression "negative of." First, observe that all of the values of $t$ in Table A.2 are positive numbers. To determine the negative of a positive number, simply add a minus sign to it. For instance, the negative value of 5 equals $-5$. The negative of 2.447 equals $-2.447$. ("Negative of" is an informal expression that, to my knowledge, is used only in this text.)

The values of $t$ in the $t$-distribution table (i.e., the critical values of $t$) vary according to whether the test is two-tailed or one-tailed and according to the selected significance level, .05 ($\alpha = .05$) or .01 ($\alpha = .01$). Just as for confidence intervals, when the exact number of $df$ is not listed, use the next-lowest listed number.

## 17.7 ▓ CARRYING OUT THE ONE-SAMPLE $t$ TEST

Suppose that all mental health centers in a large state administer an instrument that measures social functioning skills to all clients admitted during a given month and that the mean score for these clients is 50 points. Suppose that you work in a mental health center in a small neighboring state and are interested in comparing the level of functioning of clients at your center with that in the large state. Suppose further that you have sufficient resources to administer the instrument to 25 clients. As such, you select a random sample and do so. The mean score of these 25 clients is 45 points, with a standard deviation of 15 points. Stating your results using symbols: $N = 25$,

$\overline{X} = 45$, $s = 15$. Presume that the distribution of scores in your study sample has a strong negative skew.

You seek to determine whether your study sample mean differs significantly from 50, the mean of the client population in the neighboring state. The one-sample *t* test is the appropriate tool for doing so. Because $N \geq 20$ and the skew is not extreme, results will be accurate and you may proceed with the test.

1. State the hypothesis pair:   $H_0\colon \mu = 50$;   $H_1\colon \mu \neq 50$

You have chosen a nondirectional hypothesis pair. Presumably then, neither prior theory nor research indicates a compelling reason for thinking that the social functioning for clients at your mental health center differs in a particular direction from that of clients in the large neighboring state.

2. Choose a significance level.
   You choose the .05 level ($\alpha = .05$).
3. Carry out the test.
   First, we compute $s_{\overline{x}}$:

$$s_{\overline{x}} = \frac{15}{\sqrt{25}} = \frac{15}{5} =$$

   Next, we insert the appropriate values into Formula 17.1

$$t = \frac{45 - 50}{3} = \frac{5}{3} = -1.67$$

4. Make decision regarding the hypothesis pair.

Prior to making a decision, we need to determine the degrees of freedom:

$$df = N - 1 = 25 - 1 = 24$$

Because the hypothesis pair is nondirectional, the test is two-tailed. To locate the critical value of *t* in Table A.2, (a) trace down the *df* column to 24 and (b) trace across to the column for a two-tailed test where $\alpha$ equals .05. The *t* in Table A.2 is 2.064. The absolute value of the obtained *t* ($|t| = |-1.67| = 1.67$) is less than the *t* in the table (2.064). Hence, using the decision rule for a nondirectional pair (two-tailed test) at the .05 level, we fail to reject (accept) the null. As we fail to reject the null, we reject the alternative.

We conclude that chance alone is not a highly unlikely (sufficiently unlikely) explanation for the difference between the mean in your sample ($\overline{X} = 45$) and the value stated in the null ($\mu = 50$). More precisely, we conclude that

■ given a true null, the probability of obtaining your result or an even more extreme result is greater than .05, and that

■ the probability of obtaining your result or an even more extreme result due to chance alone is greater than .05.

Your result is not statistically significant at the .05 level (two-tailed test).

Figure 17.3 presents the sampling distribution of $\overline{X}$, the rejection regions and the study sample mean, $\overline{X} = 45$. For a two-tailed, one-sample *t* test, when $df = 24$ and $\alpha = .05$, the rejection regions include all sample means with *t* scores $\leq -2.064$ or $\geq 2.064$. The study sample mean was not located in a rejection region and hence we failed to reject the null.

Let us work through this example once more, this time presuming that you strongly expect to find lower social functioning at your clinic than in the neighboring state. Such an expectation

FIGURE 17.3 ■ **Study Sample Mean and Rejection Regions For Two-Tailed *t* Test,** $\alpha = .05$

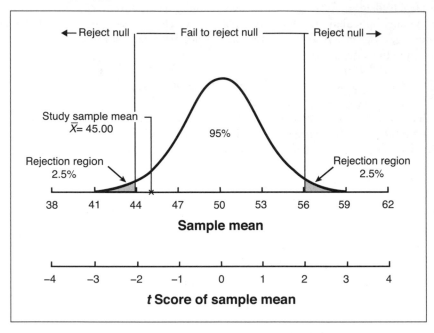

FIGURE 17.4 ■ **Study Sample Mean and Rejection Region For One-Tailed *t* Test,** $\alpha = .05$

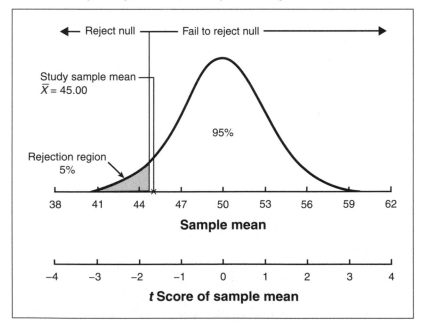

recommends a directional hypothesis pair. The alternative hypothesis conveys the direction of expectations. Hence, the hypothesis pair is

$H_0$: $\mu \geq 50$;        $H_1$: $\mu < 50$

Presume that you continue to use the .05 level ($\alpha = .05$). As the hypothesis pair is directional, the test is one-tailed. For a one-tailed *t* test with $df = 24$ and $\alpha = .05$, the value of *t* in Table A.2 is 1.711. As the alternative states less than or equal to, the decision rule calls for rejection when the obtained *t* is less than $-1.711$. ($-1.711$ is the negative of 1.711.) The obtained *t*, already calculated to be $-1.67$, just misses significance. Even with a one-tailed test, the probability that the study sample result is caused by chance alone (sampling error alone) exceeds .05, and thus we fail to reject the null. Figure 17.4 presents the sampling distribution of $\overline{X}$, the rejection region, and the study sample mean.

A comparison between the results with the directional and nondirectional pairs demonstrates again the increased power that accompanies the directional pair (one-tailed test). Thus, we just missed rejecting the null with the directional pair (see Figure 17.4) but came much less close to doing so with the nondirectional one (see Figure 17.3).

## 17.8 ■ CHAPTER SUMMARY

When sample size is less than 100, the estimate of the standard deviation of the sampling distribution of $(s_{\overline{X}})$ can be inaccurate. Because of this, when $N < 100$, inferential procedures that involve means are not based on the normal distribution but instead on the *t* distribution.

Degrees of freedom (*df*) are the number of independent values that remain after mathematical restrictions have been applied. For confidence intervals for means and for the one-sample *t* test, $df = N - 1$.

The *t distribution* is a *family of distributions* whose shape changes according to the degrees of freedom. When sample size is less than about 10, the *t* distribution has heavier, more elongated tails than does the normal distribution. As sample size increases, its shape increasingly resembles that of the normal distribution. When sample size is about 100, the shapes of the *t* and normal distributions are almost identical. For the *t* distribution, the value of *t* within which given percentages of cases are located varies according to the degrees of freedom. The *t* distribution adjusts for the likely amount of error involved in estimating $s_{\overline{X}}$ and, by doing so, yields accurate results.

Confidence intervals for means based on the *t* distribution yield sufficiently accurate results when $N \geq 20$ and the study sample does not have an extreme skew and when $N \geq 100$ (even in the presence of extreme skew). One formula is *CI of* $\mu = \overline{X} \pm t(s_{\overline{X}})$. Confidence intervals based on the *t* distribution are wider than those based on the normal distribution, although this difference is negligible when $N \geq 100$.

Just as does the large sample test of $\overline{X}$, the *one-sample t test* examines whether the mean of a sample differs significantly from a hypothesized value. It is robust to the normality assumption and yields accurate results when the conditions described earlier for confidence intervals for means are met. The researcher may state either a nondirectional (two-tailed test) or a directional (one-tailed test) hypothesis pair. The hypothesis pairs are the same as those for the large sample test of $\overline{X}$. The nondirectional pair is $H_0$: $\mu = A$; $H_1$: $\mu \neq A$. Critical values vary according to *df* and are accessed by consulting the *t*-distribution table. A formula is $t = (\overline{X} - \mu)/s_{\overline{X}}$.

When $N < 100$, confidence intervals and significance tests for means should be calculated using formulas based on the *t* distribution. When sample size is 100 or larger, formulas based on either the normal or *t* distribution may be used. In this situation, those based on the *t* distribution are slightly more accurate and are more commonly used.

## 17.9 ■ PROBLEMS AND QUESTIONS

### Section 17.2

1. (*True or False*) When $N < 100$, the estimate of the standard deviation of the sampling distribution of $\overline{X}$ ($s_{\overline{X}}$) can be inaccurate.

2. When $N < 100$, inferential procedures that involve means are not based on the _____ distribution but instead on the ___ distribution.

### Section 17.3

3. Define degrees of freedom in your own words.

4. $N = 5$. The sample mean equals 2. Four of the values are 1, 4, 0, 2. Respond to the following questions:
    a. What is the value of the fifth value, which is not provided?
    b. In this example, the sample mean is known. This being so, how many independent values are there?
    c. Given that the mean is known, how many *df* are there?

### Section 17.4

5. *The following questions are true or false:*
    a. There is only a single *t* distribution.
    b. The *t* distribution is a family of distributions.
    c. There is a different *t* distribution for each different *df*.
    d. When sample size is small (say, less than about 10), the shape of the *t* distribution and that of the normal distribution are almost identical.
    e. When sample size is very small (say, less than about 10), the *t* distribution has heavy, elongated tails.
    f. As sample size (*df*) increases, the shape of the *t* distribution increasingly resembles that of the normal distribution.
    g. When *N* is about 100 or greater (*df* ≥ about 99), the shape of the *t* distribution and that of the normal distributions are almost identical.
    h. For the *t* distribution, the percentage of cases located between two given *t* scores is the same for all sample sizes (all *df*).
    i. For the *t* distribution, the value of *t* within which given percentages of cases are located varies according to the *df*.
    j. As the *t* distribution only estimates the standard deviation of the sampling distribution of $\overline{X}$ ($s_{\overline{X}}$), inferential procedures based on it yield very inaccurate results.
    k. By changing its shape as *df* change, the *t* distribution adjusts for the likely amount of error involved in estimating $s_{\overline{X}}$ and thus yields accurate results.

**Section 17.5**

6. For purposes of calculating confidence intervals for means using the *t* distribution, indicate the *df* in each situation.
   a. Sample size equals 50
   b. $N = 50$
   c. $N = 67$

7. Confidence intervals for means based on the *t* distribution yield sufficiently accurate results when $N \geq$ ___ and the study sample does not have an _____ skew and when $N \geq$ ___ (even in the presence of _____ skew).

8. In each situation, based on the sample size and the degree of skew in the sample, indicate whether the requirements for computing a confidence interval using the *t* distribution are met.
   a. $N = 40$, skew is strong
   b. $N = 40$, skew is extreme
   c. $N = 140$, skew is extreme
   d. $N = 12$, skew = strong
   e. $N = 12$, skew = moderate

9. For each situation, calculate the degrees of freedom (*df*), the estimate of the standard error of the mean ($s_{\bar{x}}$), and the 95% *CI* of the mean (95% *CI* of $\mu$). Skew refers to the skew in the study sample. If requirements for computing the confidence interval are not met, indicate this and do not compute the interval. Hint: $s_{\bar{x}} = s/\sqrt{N}$. If the exact *df* is not provided in the *t*-distribution table, use the row for the next smallest number.
   a. $N = 49, \bar{X} = 40.0, s = 21.0$, skew = strong
   b. $N = 25, \bar{X} = 60.0, s = 30.0$, skew = moderate
   c. $N = 9, \bar{X} = 40.0, s = 21.0$, skew = extreme
   d. $N = 144, \bar{X} = 70, s = 24$, skew = extreme

10. For each situation in the prior problem, calculate the 99% *CI* of $\mu$. If requirements are not met, state this and do not calculate the confidence interval.

11. For the information presented in Question 9.d, calculate a 95% *CI* using the formula based on the normal distribution: 95% *CI of* $\mu = \bar{X} \pm 1.96(s_{\bar{x}})$. Is this confidence interval wider or smaller than that computed using the formula based on the *t* distribution?

**Section 17.6**

12. The one-sample *t* test assumes that the study sample is selected from a population with a normal distribution, that is, it assumes _____. It is quite _____ to this assumption.

13. The one-sample $t$ test yields accurate results when $N \geq$ ___ except when the study sample has an _____ skew and when $N \geq$ ___ (even in the presence of _____ skew).

14. *Respond true or false to each.*
   a. The hypothesis pair for the one-sample $t$ test is always nondirectional.
   b. The hypothesis pairs for the one-sample $t$ test are the same as those for the large sample test of $\overline{X}$.
   c. The one-sample $t$ test is recommended for use with very small samples ($N \approx 10$), particularly when the sample distribution is skewed.
   d. The one-sample $t$ test is used predominantly with ordinal-level variables.

15. When the hypothesis pair is nondirectional, the one-sample $t$ test is _____-tailed. When it is directional, it is _____-tailed with the _____ region located in the direction stated in the _____ hypothesis.

16. Calculate $t$ in each situation using Formula 17.4. Note that the value of the value of the standard error of the mean $s_{\overline{x}}$ is provided:
   a. $\overline{X}_1 = 20, \mu = 15, s_{\overline{X}} = 5$
   b. $\overline{X}_1 = 15, \mu = 20, s_{\overline{X}} = 5$
   c. $\overline{X}_1 = 25, \mu = 30, s_{\overline{X}} = 5$
   d. $\overline{X}_1 = 28, \mu = 18, s_{\overline{X}} = 4$
   e. $\overline{X}_1 = 33, \mu = 18, s_{\overline{X}} = 5$

17. Calculate $t$ in each situation using Formula 17.3.
   a. $\overline{X}_1 = 50, \mu = 40, s = 25, N = 25$
   b. $\overline{X}_1 = 50, \mu = 40, s = 25, N = 100$
   c. $\overline{X}_1 = 50, \mu = 60, s = 18, N = 36$
   d. $\overline{X}_1 = 20, \mu = 15, s = 16, N = 64$

18. For each situation, indicate whether you would fail to reject (accept) or reject the null.
   a. $t = 2.22$, nondirectional pair, .05 level, $df = 9$
   b. $t = 2.22$, nondirectional pair, .05 level, $df = 30$
   c. $t = 2.02$, nondirectional pair, .05 level, $df = 30$
   d. $t = 2.02$, directional pair (alternative states greater than), .05 level, $df = 30$
   e. $t = -2.02$, directional pair (alternative states greater than), .05 level, $df = 30$
   f. $t = -2.22$, nondirectional pair, .05 level, $df = 30$
   g. $t = -2.22$, nondirectional pair, .01 level, $df = 30$
   h. $t = -2.22$, directional pair (alternative states less than), .05 level, $df = 30$
   i. $t = -2.22$, directional pair (alternative states less than), .01 level, $df = 30$
   j. $t = -3.83$, directional pair (alternative states less than), .01 level, $df = 24$

**19.** Consider the following. $H_0$: $\mu = 80.0$, $N = 36$, $\bar{X} = 89.0$, $s = 18.0$, shape of distribution of study sample: moderate positive skew, .05 level is used ($\alpha = .05$).

   **a.** $H_1$ is not provided. What is it?

   **b.** What test should be used to test the null?

   **c.** Examine the sample size and skew. Should the test be carried out?

   **d.** Is the hypothesis pair directional or nondirectional?

   **e.** Is the significance test one-tailed or two-tailed?

   **f.** How many *df* are there?

   **g.** What is/are the critical value(s) of *t*?

   **h.** What is $s_{\bar{x}}$ (the estimated standard deviation of the sampling distribution)?

   **i.** What is the obtained *t* (the value resulting from the formula)?

   **j.** What is the decision regarding the null? The alternative?

   **k.** Given a true null, is the study result an unlikely one?

   **l.** Is chance alone an unlikely explanation for the study result?

   **m.** Is it likely that the null is true in the population?

   **n.** (*True or False*) One can be (at least) 95% confident that the null is false and that the alternative is true.

   **o.** Is the study sample result located in a rejection region?

   **p.** Does the study sample result provide strong evidence that the null is false?

**20.** $H_0$: $\mu \geq 60.0$, $N = 64$, $\bar{X} = 57.0$, $s = 16.0$, shape of distribution of study sample: moderate positive skew, .05 level is used ($\alpha = .05$). Respond to Questions 19.a to p, as presented in the prior problem.

# 18

# INDEPENDENT SAMPLES *t* TEST AND DEPENDENT SAMPLES *t* TEST

## 18.1 ■ CHAPTER OVERVIEW

Chapter 18 presents two statistical tests based on the *t* distribution: the *independent samples t test* and the *dependent samples t test*. The distinction between *independent samples* and *dependent samples* guides the researcher in choosing which of these tests to use.

## 18.2 ■ INTRODUCTION TO THE INDEPENDENT SAMPLES *t* TEST

### 18.2.1 ■ Purpose and Sampling Distribution

The one-sample *t* test determines the probability of obtaining the study sample mean under the null hypothesis that the population mean equals some stated value. The **independent samples *t* test** compare means in two samples, each selected randomly from a different population. It determines the probability of obtaining these means under the null hypothesis that means are equal in the populations. It is one of the two or three most commonly used statistical tests.

The sampling distribution of $\overline{X}$ has been the key distribution for the inferential procedures covered to this point—confidence intervals for means, the large sample test of $\overline{X}$, and the one-sample *t* test. The key distribution for the independent samples *t* test is the **sampling distribution of the difference between means**, (**sampling distribution of $\overline{X}_1 - \overline{X}_2$**). We will not cover the theory or formulas for this distribution (see Rosenthal, 2001, pp. 337–338).

A key idea underlying the sampling distribution of $\overline{X}_1 - \overline{X}_2$ is the fact that means are equal in two populations—that is, that $\mu_1 = \mu_2$—does not assure that means will also be equal in random samples selected from these populations—that is, that $\overline{X}_1 = \overline{X}_2$. Due to the luck of the draw, these means will, almost assuredly, differ. The sampling distribution of $\overline{X}_1 - \overline{X}_2$ conveys how luck (chance) affects differences between sample means.

### 18.2.2 ■ Hypothesis Pairs

The independent samples *t* test tests the null hypothesis that the means of two populations are equal. The hypothesis pair may be directional or nondirectional. The nondirectional hypothesis pair is

Null:     The mean of the population from which Sample 1 was selected equals the mean of the population from which Sample 2 was selected.

Alternative:    The mean of the population from which Sample 1 was selected is not equal to that of the population from which Sample 2 was selected.

Using mathematical symbols, this pair is $H_0$: $\mu_1 = \mu_2$; $H_1$: $\mu_1 \neq \mu_2$

When the alternative states greater than, the directional pair is

Null:    The mean of the population from which Sample 1 was selected is less than or equal to that of the population from which Sample 2 was selected.

Alternative:    The mean of the population from which Sample 1 was selected is greater than that of the population from which Sample 2 was selected.

Stated using mathematical symbols: $H_0$: $\mu_1 \leq \mu_2$; $H_1$: $\mu_1 > \mu_2$.

When the alternative states less than, the directional pair is

$$H_0: \mu_1 \geq \mu_2; H_1: \mu_1 < \mu_2$$

When the hypothesis pair is nondirectional, the independent samples $t$ test is two-tailed. When the pair is directional, it is one-tailed.

### 18.2.3 ▨ Assumptions and Formulas

In the discussion that follows, "$n$" conveys the number in a particular sample (Sample 1 or Sample 2) rather than the total number in the study.

The independent samples $t$ test assumes that the populations from which the study samples are selected are normally distributed. It is robust to this assumption. It yields quite accurate results when both sample sizes are about 10 or larger and neither sample has a strong or extreme skew, when both sample sizes are about 20 or greater and neither sample has an extreme skew, and when both samples are about 60 or greater, even in the presence of extreme skew. When either sample size is smaller than 10, it is not recommended.[1]

A second assumption of the independent samples $t$ test is the **equality (homogeneity) of variances assumption**, that is, that variances are equal in the populations from which samples are selected. Recall from Chapter 4, Section 4.8, that the variance is a measure of variability; it equals the standard deviation squared. When sample sizes are equal or nearly so, the independent samples $t$ test is robust to this assumption, that is, violations of it have minimal effects on the accuracy of results. On the other hand, when sample sizes differ, violations can lead to inaccurate results. This being so, there are two different formulas for the independent samples $t$ test: the **equal variances formula** and the **unequal variances formula**.

As the independent samples $t$ test is almost always carried out using a statistics software package, calculation formulas are not presented here. These packages typically implement an **equality of variances test** (*homogeneity of variances test*) to determine which formula is appropriate. The null for this test is that the samples have been selected from populations with equal variances ($\sigma_1^2 = \sigma_2^2$). When the equality of variance test fails to reject the null, the researcher uses the equal variances formula. When it rejects the null, the researcher uses the unequal variances formula.[2]

For the equal variances formula, calculation of degrees of freedom is straightforward: $df = n_1 + n_2 - 2$. The formula for degrees of freedom for the unequal variances formula is complex (see Rosenthal, 2001, p. 342). Decision rules are the same as those for the one-sample $t$ test presented in Chapter 17 (see Section 17.6.2). Data at the interval/ratio level is required.

A general formula for a *t* test with two samples is

$$t = \frac{\overline{X}_1 - \overline{X}_2}{s_{\overline{X}_1 - \overline{X}_2}} \tag{18.1}$$

where *t* is the test statistic; $\overline{X}_1$ is the mean of the first sample; $\overline{X}_2$ is the mean of the second, and $s_{\overline{X}_1 - \overline{X}_2}$ is the estimate of the standard error of the difference between means.[3]

## 18.3 ▩ CARRYING OUT THE INDEPENDENT SAMPLES *t* TEST USING THE SPSS SOFTWARE PACKAGE

An important dependent variable in Rosenthal and Groze's (1992) study of families who adopted children with special needs was the adoptive parents' perception of quality of relationship with the adopted child. This was measured by a five-item scale which we will term the "parent–child relationship scale." Scores on the scale can vary from a lowest possible score of 1.00 to a highest possible score of 4.00. The scale score was derived by summing responses to five individual questions and then dividing by five. Higher scores convey higher quality (e.g., greater closeness, trust, respect) in the relationship between parent and child. The authors compared the responses of parents in one- and two-parent families on this scale.

Because there was no compelling reason to think that perceptions of parent–child relationship would be more favorable in one type of family structure than in the other, the authors used a nondirectional hypothesis pair as follows:

Null:   The mean parent–child relationship scale score in the population from which respondents in one-parent families were randomly selected is not equal to the mean score in the population from which respondents in two-parent families were randomly selected.

Alternative: The mean parent–child relationship scale score in the population from which respondents in one-parent families were randomly selected is not equal to the mean score in the population from which respondents in two-parent families were randomly selected.

The just-stated hypothesis pair mentions random sampling from larger populations. In reality, the samples of one- and two-parent families were not random samples and, thus, no such populations exist. As discussed in Chapter 16 (Section 16.8), significance tests are often carried out on nonrandom samples. Because the samples are not random samples, statistically based conclusions will not generalize to any larger population. Stated differently, they only apply to the actual families in the study. Stating the hypothesis pair in symbols: $H_0$: $\mu_1 = \mu_2$; $H_1$: $\mu_1 \neq u_2$.[4]

Observe that both samples—respondents in one-parent families and those in two-parent families—are *subsamples* within the larger study sample that comprises all respondents. When this is so, researchers often use the term *group* to describe them. The discussion that follows does so. In this analysis, the one-parent family respondents compose Group 1 and the two-parent family respondents compose Group 2.

Table 18.1 presents independent *t*-test output from the SPSS statistical software program. Prior to interpreting this output, observe that both groups are large in size, $N = 114$ for the one-parent family group and $N = 633$ for the two-parent family group. Given these sizes, we need not be concerned about shape of distribution. Results will be accurate even if the distribution in one or both groups is highly skewed. Thus, we may proceed with the test. We will select the .05 level. We will also use this level for the equality of variances test.

TABLE 18.1 ■ Independent Samples *t* Test Results

| Group Statistics | | | | | |
|---|---|---|---|---|---|
| | One- vs. two-parent family | N | Mean | Std. Deviation | Std. Error Mean |
| Parent-child Relationship scale | One parent | 114 | 3.460 | .609 | .057 |
| | Two parent | 633 | 3.317 | .653 | .026 |

| Independent Samples Test | | | | | | | | | | |
|---|---|---|---|---|---|---|---|---|---|---|
| | | Levene's Test for Equality of Variances | | *t*-test for Equality of Means | | | | | | |
| | | | | | | | | | 95% Confidence Interval of the Difference | |
| | | F | Sig. | t | df | Sig. (2-tailed) | Mean Difference | Std. Error Difference | Lower | Upper |
| Parent-child relationshp scale | Equal variances assumed | 2.409 | .121 | 2.166 | 745.0 | .031 | .142 | .066 | .013 | .272 |
| | Equal variances not assumed | | | 2.273 | 163.3 | .024 | .142 | .063 | 0.19 | .266 |

*Note.* Table presents output from SPSS statistical package.

Some help in interpreting the SPSS output is in order. Observe that the mean scale score is higher for one-parent families than for two-parent families. Subtracting the mean for two-parent families from that for one-parent families yields what the output labels as the Mean Difference: 3.460 − 3.317 = .142. (This difference is .142 rather than .143 because of rounding off.)

Because the standard deviations in the two groups are quite similar—.653 and .609—our expectation is for the equality of variances test to fail to reject the null of equal population variances ($\sigma_1^2 = \sigma_2^2$). SPSS tests the equality of variances assumption using Levene's test. The probability given by Levene's test is .121 ($p = .121$). (SPSS labels $p$ as "Sig.," short for significance.) Because .121 is greater than .05 (our selected significance level), we fail to reject the null of equal population variances. This being so, the correct independent samples *t* test to use is that based on the equal variances formula. SPSS lists results for this test in the "Equal variances assumed" row and, thus, we reference this row from this point onward.

Degrees of freedom (*df*) equals 745. This was calculated using the *df* formula:

$$df = n_1 + n_2 - 2;\ 114 + 633 - 2 = 745.$$

The obtained *t*, 2.166, can be obtained using the general *t*-test formula: $t = \dfrac{\overline{X}_1 - \overline{X}_2}{s_{\overline{X}_1 - \overline{X}_2}}$ (Formula 18.1). Thus, we subtract the mean for two-parent families (Group 2) from that for one-parent families (Group 1) and divide by the estimate of the standard error of the difference between means, $s_{\overline{X}_1 - \overline{X}_2}$. SPSS labels the standard error of the difference between means as

*Std. Error Difference*, which equals .066. The calculation of $t$ is $t = (3.460 - 3.317) / .066 = .142 / .066 = 2.166$.

As mentioned in Chapter 16, Section 16.9, software programs almost always present the exact value of $p$. In this example, $p = .031$, which SPSS presents in the column labeled "Sig. 2-tailed." Because this probability is lower than that of our selected significance level ($\alpha = .05$), we reject the null and accept the alternative. Our result is statistically significant at the .05 level. We conclude that the difference in mean parent–child relationship scores between one-parent and two-parent families in the study sample is unlikely to be due to chance alone.

The just-presented example demonstrated the independent samples $t$ test using statistical software. If one knows the value of $t$ and wishes to use the table of critical values of $t$ (Table A.2 in Appendix A), the same decision rules as presented for the one-sample $t$ test apply (see Chapter 17, Section 17.6.2). In our example, the obtained $t$ equals 2.166 and $df = 745$. Because no row lists this exact degrees of freedom, one uses the row with the closest listed lower value. This is the row for $df = 500$. For a two-tailed test using the .05 level, the critical $t$ is 1.965. Because the absolute value of the obtained $t$ (2.166) is greater than the $t$ in the table (1.965), we reject the null.

The independent samples $t$ test is the first test that we have covered that assesses whether an association is significant. In addition to examining significance, the researcher often assesses size of association. Given that the independent samples $t$ test involves a difference between two means, the standardized mean difference (*SMD*) presented in Chapter 9, Section 9.2 is the preferred tool for assessing size of association. Chapter 9's formula—$SMD = (\overline{X}_1 - \overline{X}_2) / s_{wg}$—assumes that standard deviations in the two groups are equal, something that occurs hardly ever in actual research. In our example, the average standard deviation equals .631: $(.609 + .653) / 2 = .631$. This serves as a good estimate of the average standard deviation and, thus, we will use it to calculate the *SMD*: $SMD \approx (3.460 - 3.317) / .631 \approx 0.226$, where $\approx$ conveys approximately equal to. Hence, the mean family impact score in the one-parent family group is about 0.226 standard deviations higher than that in the two-parent family group. Referencing Table 9.1, this value is close to our guideline for a small relationship.[5]

In summary, the difference in means between the two groups is small in size. These results would be reported in a report as $t(745) = 2.166, p < .01$.

## 18.4 ▓ THE INDEPENDENCE ASSUMPTION

The independence of observations assumption asserts that pairs or groups of cases should not share some unmeasured factor that makes scores more similar than would otherwise be so. As applied to research studies involving two samples (groups), it asserts that observations in the samples should not be linked as pairs. In our recent special-needs adoption example, all observations in the first sample (the one-parent families) were independent from those in the second sample (two-parent families). In such a situation, one has two *independent samples*, and the independent samples $t$ test is the appropriate test for examining a difference between means. (See Chapter 12, Section 12.3 for more on the independence of observations assumption.)

Consider a different situation. Suppose that a group of parents participates in your parenting skills class and that you obtain parental "nagging" scores prior to your intervention (a *pretest*), and following it (a *posttest*). Observations in your pretest sample are not independent from those in the posttest sample but, instead, are logically linked. Suppose that one of the parents is named Cindy. Cindy's pretest score is not independent from her posttest score. Instead, her pretest and posttest scores form a logically linked pair. These two observations are said to be dependent. Stated differently, they form a **dependent pair** (*matched pair*).

Dependent observations occur most commonly when two measurements are taken for each study participant. This was the case in the just-provided pretest/posttest example. Some other situations that involve dependent observations include "naturally occurring pairs" (Toothaker, 1986, p. 406)—brothers and sisters, spouses, twins, roommates, and so on—and studies in which subjects have been *matched*. For instance, in some research designs, researchers identify pairs of persons with similar characteristics on key variables and then assign one member of each matched pair to one intervention and the other to a second. When the observations in two samples form dependent pairs, the samples are **dependent samples** (*paired samples, correlated samples, related samples, matched samples*).

The independent samples *t* test should be conducted only with independent samples. With dependent samples, the dependent samples *t* test is the appropriate significance test for examining a difference between two means.

## 18.5 ▪ THE DEPENDENT SAMPLES *t* TEST

### 18.5.1 ▪ Dependent Samples and Statistical Power

The **dependent samples *t* test** (**paired samples *t*-test**) examines whether a difference in means involving dependent samples is significant. Alternative names for this test include t *test for pairs*, t *test for matched samples*, t *test for correlated samples*, and t *test for related samples*.

When samples are dependent, the independence of observations assumption does not hold for the observations that form each pair. However, assuming that each pair is independent from (distinct from) each other pair, it does hold across the pairs. This being so, the dependent samples *t* test may be carried out.[6]

Although calculations are not shown, positive correlation between pairs of scores makes the standard error of the difference between means ($s_{\overline{X}_1 - \overline{X}_2}$) smaller in the *t*-test formula $t = \dfrac{\overline{X}_1 - \overline{X}_2}{s_{\overline{X}_1 - \overline{X}_2}}$, than is the case in the absence of such correlation. As positive correlation makes the *denominator* smaller, it makes the absolute value of the obtained *t* larger and, by so doing, increases the likelihood that it will exceed the critical value of *t* in the *t* distribution table. In summary, positive correlation between scores increases the likelihood of rejecting the null, that is, it increases statistical power.

The greater the positive correlation between scores in the two samples, the greater the increase in power. When the positive correlation is large, say, when $r \geq .50$, this increase can be substantial. As presented in Chapter 16, Section 16.5.4, pretest and posttest scores are often strongly and positively correlated. Hence, when a dependent samples *t* test involves a pretest and a posttest, statistical power is often much higher than what the researcher might assume to be the case based on the number of observations or pairs.

### 18.5.2 ▪ Requirements

The dependent samples *t* test uses the same general formula as presented for the independent samples *t* test (Formula 18.1). Decision rules are the same as for the independent samples *t* test and for the one-sample *t* test (see Chapter 17, Section 17.6.2). Degrees of freedom equals $N - 1$, where *N* is the number of *pairs*. Just as is so for the other *t* tests, normality is assumed but the test is quite robust to violations of this assumption. The dependent samples *t* test yields quite accurate results when the number of pairs is about 10 or greater and neither sample has a strong or extreme skew, when the number of pairs is about 20 or greater and neither sample has an extreme skew, and when the number of pairs is about 60 or greater even in the presence of extreme skew. When the number of pairs is less than about 10, the dependent samples *t* test is not recommended. Data should be at the interval/ratio level.[7]

### 18.5.3 ■ Example Demonstrating Increase in Power from Positive Correlation

Presume that we have the following data in which the dependent variable *X* represents the number of nagging behaviors by parents. Presume that, in both Samples 1 and 2, the degree of skew is moderate.

Sample 1: $n = 16$, $\overline{X} = 27.00$ behaviors, $s = 6.00$ behaviors

Sample 2: $n = 16$, $\overline{X} = 22.00$ behaviors, $s = 11.00$ behaviors

Presume that this data represents two different scenarios. First, presume that Sample 1 represents a group of parents who have not received a parenting skills intervention and that Sample 2 represents a group of parents who have received such an intervention. Because these samples are independent, an independent samples *t* test will be carried out. Second, presume that Sample 1 represents pretest data (prior to a parenting skills intervention) and that Sample 2 represents posttest data (subsequent to this intervention). Presume further that the correlation between pretest and posttest scores equals 0.70. Because these samples are dependent, a dependent samples *t* test will be conducted.

Observe that given that skew is moderate in both samples for both scenarios. This being so, the sample size guideline (10 or more) is met for the independent samples *t* test, and the guideline regarding the number of pairs (10 or more) is met for the dependent samples test. Hence, we may proceed with the tests. Presume that our hypothesis pair is nondirectional (two-tailed test) and that we use the .05 level ($\alpha = .05$).

For the independent samples *t* test, the denominator computes to 3.13 (calculations not shown). Thus, $t = (27.00 - 22.00) / 3.13 = 1.60$ (unequal variances formula). In this example, degrees of freedom equals 23.2. (As stated earlier, for the unequal variances formula, the calculation of degrees of freedom is complex and, thus, is not shown.) Consulting the *t* distribution table—Table A.2—for 23 degrees of freedom, the critical value of *t* is 2.069. The absolute value of our obtained *t* (1.60) is less than this and, thus, we fail to reject the null.

We now switch to the pretest–posttest situation and, thus, conduct a dependent samples *t* test. Assuming that the pretest/posttest correlation equals 0.70, the denominator calculates to 2.01 (calculations not shown) and, thus, $t = (27.00 - 22.00) / 2.01 = 2.49$. Degrees of freedom equals $N - 1$, where *N* is the number of pairs. Hence, $df = 16 - 1 = 15$. For $df = 15$ (two-tailed test, .05 level), the critical value is 2.131. Because the absolute value of the obtained *t* (2.49) exceeds 2.131, we reject the null.

In summary, although we used the same data in both scenarios, we rejected the null for the dependent samples *t* test but did not do so for the independent samples *t* test. Our example demonstrates that, given strong, positive correlation between pairs of scores—and this is often the case for pretests and posttests—the power of the dependent samples *t* test is often higher than the number of pairs would suggest.

Adding pretests almost always increases power. When convenient to do so, you should include pretests in your studies (see Chapter 16, Section 16.5.4).[8]

## 18.6 ■ CHAPTER SUMMARY

Based on the *sampling distribution of the difference between means*, the *t* tests presented in this chapter examine whether a difference between the means of two samples is statistically significant, that is, unlikely to be due to chance alone. Hypothesis pairs may be directional (one-tailed test) or nondirectional (two-tailed test). Decision rules are the same as those presented in the prior chapter for the one-sample $t$ test.

The *independent samples* t *test*, used with *independent samples*, is robust to the normality assumption. A second assumption is the *equality of variances assumption*, that the two samples are selected from populations with equal variances. With equal or nearly equal sample sizes, the independent samples $t$ test is robust to this assumption. However, with unequal samples sizes, violations of this assumption can produce inaccurate results. Because of this, the statistical software packages implement an *equality of variances test*. One uses the equal variances formula when the equality of variances test fails to reject the null of equal population variances ($\sigma_2^1 = \sigma_2^2$). One uses the unequal variances formula when it rejects this null. Degrees of freedom for the equal variances formula equals $n_1 + n_2 - 2$.

When the observations in two samples form linked pairs, one has *dependent (paired) samples* rather than *independent samples* and, thus, the *dependent (paired) samples* t *test* is used. When there is strong positive correlation between scores in the two samples, power is higher than would otherwise be expected. The dependent samples $t$ test is robust to the normality assumption. Degrees of freedom equals $N - 1$, where $N$ is the number of pairs.

## 18.7 ■ PROBLEMS AND QUESTIONS

### Section 18.2

1. The independent samples $t$ test is based on the sampling distribution of the _____ _____ _____, the symbol for which is _____.

2. *Respond true or false*
   a. Whenever the means of two populations are equal, one knows that the means of random samples selected from these populations will also be equal.
   b. The hypothesis pair for the independent samples $t$ test may be either directional or nondirectional.

3. The independent samples $t$ test assumes that the populations from which samples are selected are _____ distributed. It is _____ to violations of this assumption.

4. A second assumption of the independent samples $t$ test is the _____ (homogeneity) of variances assumption, that is, that variances are _____ in the populations from which samples are selected.

5. *Respond true or false.*
   a. When sample sizes are equal or nearly so, the independent samples $t$ test is robust to the equality of variances assumption.
   b. When sample sizes differ, violations of the equality of variances assumption can lead to inaccurate results.

6. Statistical packages typically implement an _____ of _____ test to determine which formula is appropriate. When this test fails to reject the null

of _____ population variances, the *t* test based on the _____ variances formula is used. When it does so, the *t* test based on the _____ variance formula is used.

## Section 18.3

7. The 50 clients at a mental health center who have problems pertaining to depression are identified. All agree to participate in an experiment. One half are randomly assigned to a cognitive behavioral intervention and one half to a psychosocial-based intervention. Following treatment, a depression scale is administered. The estimate of the standard error of the difference between means ($s_{\bar{X}_1 - \bar{X}_2}$) equals 3.12. Other results are

| Group | $\overline{X}$ | *s* | *n* | Shape of Sample Distribution |
|---|---|---|---|---|
| Cognitive behavioral | 49.0 | 10 | 25 | Moderate positive skew |
| Psychosocial | 58.0 | 12 | 25 | Moderate positive skew |

    a. What significance test should be used to assess whether the difference in means is statistically significant?

    b. What is the nondirectional null?

    c. Considering the degree of skew and the sample sizes, should we proceed to carrying out an independent samples *t* test?

    d. (*True or False*) The study samples are random samples from a larger population.

    e. (*True or False*) Given that the study samples are not random samples, most researchers (and this chapter) would recommend that no significance test should be carried out.

    f. Presume that the equality of variance test results in acceptance of the null ($p > .05$). Which formula for the independent samples *t* test should be used?

    g. Using Formula 18.1, what is the value of *t*? (Hint: The value of the denominator has been provided.)

    h. What is the formula for degrees of freedom? How many degrees of freedom are there?

    i. Given that $\alpha = .05$ (and that the test is two-tailed), what are the critical values of *t*?

    j. What is your decision regarding the null? The alternative hypothesis?

    k. Can you be confident that the null is false?

    l. Can you be certain that the null is false?

    m. Is the study sample result—that is, the difference between the sample means—likely to be caused by chance alone?

    n. Is the result statistically significant at the .05 level?

    o. Calculate the standardized mean difference (*SMD*) using 11 as an estimate for the standard deviation in the groups (11 is the average standard deviation; see Formula 9.1.)

    p. Referencing Table 9.1, how large is the size of the difference in means?

    q. (*True or False*) Participants were randomly assigned to groups.

    r. (*True or False*) The difference between the sample means may very well be caused by confounding variables.

    s. (*True or False*) Given the fact of randomization, the researcher can be confident that the difference in means is caused by the intervention; in other words, that the cognitive behavioral intervention was more effective than the psychosocial one in reducing depression.

8. Consider the following data:

   Group 1: $n = 50, \overline{X} = 40.00$ behaviors, $s = 8.00$ behaviors

   Group 2: $n = 25, \overline{X} = 45.00$ behaviors, $s = 20.00$ behaviors

   Presume that both samples have only a modest degree of skew, that the alternative hypothesis is $\mu_1 < \mu_2$, that the .05 significance level is selected ($\alpha = .05$), and that the equality of variances test rejected the null of equal population variances. The estimate of the standard error of the difference between means ($s_{\overline{X}_1 - \overline{X}_2}$) has been calculated and equals 4.16. Respond to the following:

   a. Are the sample results in the direction of expectations?
   b. Expressed in symbols, what is the null?
   c. Considering the sample size and the degree of skew, should the independent samples $t$ test be conducted?
   d. Which formula (equal variances formula or unequal variances formula) should be used?
   e. Use Formula 18.1 to calculate the obtained $t$.
   f. Degrees of freedom equals 27.9 (this calculation is not shown). What is the critical value of $t$ and what values of $t$ lead to rejection of the null?
   g. What is your decision on the null? On the alternative?
   h. Given a true null, is this study result a highly unlikely result?
   i. Is it highly unlikely that the study result is due to chance alone?
   j. Given that the null is accepted, may we be confident that it is indeed true?
   k. Does the study sample result provide strong evidence that the null is false?

## Section 18.4

9. Observations taken prior to intervention are termed a _____. Those taken subsequent to intervention are termed a _____.

10. When the observations in two samples form dependent (matched) pairs, the samples are _____ samples.

11. Each of the following lists two samples. Indicate whether these samples are dependent (paired) or independent.
    a. Brothers; sisters of the brothers
    b. Those who receive intervention X; others who receive intervention Y
    c. Clients take pretest; (same) clients take posttest
    d. A group of clients receive an intervention. Each member of the group is "matched" with someone of similar age, sex, and problem type who did not receive the intervention.
    e. Women in a class; men in that class
    f. Spouses and their partners

12. The independent samples $t$ test should be conducted only with _____ samples. With dependent samples, the _____ samples $t$ test should be used.

13. (*True or False*) Pretest and posttest scores are often positively correlated.

**Section 18.5**

14. Respond true or false with respect to the dependent samples *t* test.
    a. When samples are dependent, the independence of observations assumption does not hold for the individual observations that form each pair.
    b. Assuming that each pair is independent from (distinct from) any other pair, the independence of observations assumption does hold across the pairs.

15. Positive correlation between pairs of scores makes the standard error of the difference between means $(s_{\bar{X}_1 - \bar{X}_2})$ _____ and, by so doing, increases statistical _____.

16. Consider the following data:
    Pretest (Sample 1): $n = 36$, $\bar{X} = 20.00$, $s = 16.00$
    Posttest (Sample 2): $n = 36$, $\bar{X} = 15.00$, $s = 15.00$
    The estimate of the standard error of the difference between means equals 2.00. Scores in each sample have a moderate negative skew. The hypothesis pair is nondirectional, and the .05 level is used ($\alpha = .05$). For this data—
    a. Are the samples independent or dependent?
    b. What is the appropriate significance test for testing the difference between the sample means?
    c. Given the number of pairs and the degree of skew, may we proceed with the test?
    d. Using Formula 18.1, what is the obtained *t*?
    e. What is the number of degrees of freedom?
    f. Is the test one-tailed or two-tailed?
    g. What are the critical values of *t*?
    h. What is the nondirectional null?
    i. What is your decision regarding the null? Regarding the alternative?
    j. Is this result statistically significant at the .05 level?
    k. Given a true null, is the probability of obtaining the study sample result or an even more extreme result greater than or less than .05?
    l. Is the probability that the study result—the observed difference in means—is due to chance alone greater than or less than .05?
    m. Is chance alone a likely explanation for the study result?
    n. Can you be at least 95% confident that the null is false?
    o. Does this study provide strong evidence that the null is false?

# 19

# ONE-SAMPLE TESTS OF PROPORTIONS

## 19.1 ▧ CHAPTER OVERVIEW

Chapter 19 begins with the *one-sample test of a proportion* and then moves on to the *binomial test*. Both of these tests examine whether a sample proportion differs significantly from a stated value. Next, it introduces the *chi-square distribution* and a significance test based on this distribution, the *one-variable chi-square* ($\chi^2$) *test*. It discusses *expected* and *observed proportions* and *expected* and *observed frequencies*, all of which are important in the one-variable chi-square test.

## 19.2 ▧ ONE-SAMPLE TEST OF A PROPORTION

### 19.2.1 ▧ Introduction

The **one-sample test of a proportion** (**one-sample test of $p$**) examines whether a sample proportion, $p$, differs significantly from some stated value. For instance, suppose that a measure of child behavior problems is administered to a random sample of 25,000 children in the United States and that 10% obtain scores indicating the presence of serious behavior problems. Suppose further that you are a school social worker in a city that has experienced a sharp increase in unemployment. Teachers communicate to you that children's behavior is an increasing problem. You administer the behavior problems measure to 200 randomly sampled children in your school district and determine that 17% have serious problems. The one-sample test of $p$ can tell you whether chance alone is a likely explanation for difference in percentages between your school district (17% have problems) and the large sample (10%). The binomial test and the one-variable chi-square test, presented later in this chapter, can also be used to examine the difference between a proportion in a sample and that stated in the null.

### 19.2.2 ▧ Theory and Basics

Just as are confidence intervals for proportions, the one-sample test of the proportion is based on the sampling distribution of the proportion. The standard deviation of this distribution, the standard error of the proportion, $\sigma_p$, equals $\sqrt{\dfrac{P(1-P)}{N}}$ where $P$ is the proportion in the population (see Chapter 13; Section 13.4.1).

The hypothesis pair may be nondirectional (two-tailed test) or directional. The nondirectional pair is

Null:    The proportion in the population from which the study sample was selected equals some given value.

Alternative:  The proportion in the population from which the study sample was selected does not equal the value stated in the null.

In mathematical symbols, this pair is $H_0: P = A$; $H_1: P \neq A$
where $P$ is the proportion in the population from which the study sample was selected, and $A$ is some given value. In symbols, the directional hypothesis pairs (one-tailed test) are

$H_0: P \leq A$, $H_1: P > A$ and $H_0: P \geq A$, $H_1: P < A$

One formula for the one-sample test of $p$ is

$$z = \frac{p - P}{\sqrt{\dfrac{P(1 - P)}{N}}} \tag{19.1}$$

where $p$ is the proportion in the study sample, $P$ is the proportion stated in the null, and $N$ is the sample size. A mathematically equivalent formula is

$$z = \frac{(p - P)}{\sigma_p} \tag{19.2}$$

where $\sigma_p$ is the standard error of the proportion.

The one-sample test of $p$ yields sufficiently accurate results whenever both $NP$ and $N(1 - P)$ are greater than or equal to 5.[1] Decision rules are the same as those for the large sample test of $\overline{X}$ (see Chapter 15, Sections 15.8.2 [two-tailed, $\alpha = .01$], 15.9 [two-tailed, $\alpha = .01$], 15.11.1 [one-tailed, alternative states greater than, $\alpha = .05$], and 15.12 [other situations]).

### 19.2.3 ■ Carrying Out the Behavior Problems Example

**1.** State the hypothesis pair.

The solid explanation for the increase in behavior problems—the stress generated by the rise in unemployment—perhaps argues in favor of a directional pair. However, choice of the type of pair rests ultimately with the researcher. Because nondirectional pairs are more common and because I prefer these, our pair will be nondirectional.

Null:    The proportion of children with serious behavior problems in your school district equals .10.

Alternative:  The proportion of children with serious behavior problems in your school district does not equal .10.

In symbols, these hypotheses are    $H_0: P = .10$  $H_1: P \neq .10$

**2.** Choose the significance level: We will use the .05 significance level ($\alpha = .05$).
**3.** Carry out the test.

Prior to carrying out the test, let us see whether sample size is sufficient. Your sample comprises 200 children ($N = 200$), and the proportion stated in the null is .10 ($P = .10$). Hence, $NP = 200(.1) = 20$ and $N(1 - P) = 200(1 - .1) = 200(.9) = 180$. Because both $NP$ and $N(1 - P)$ are greater than or equal to 5, we may proceed with the test.

FIGURE 19.1 ■ Sampling Distribution and Study Result For Two-Tailed *z* Test of a Proportion, $\alpha = .05$

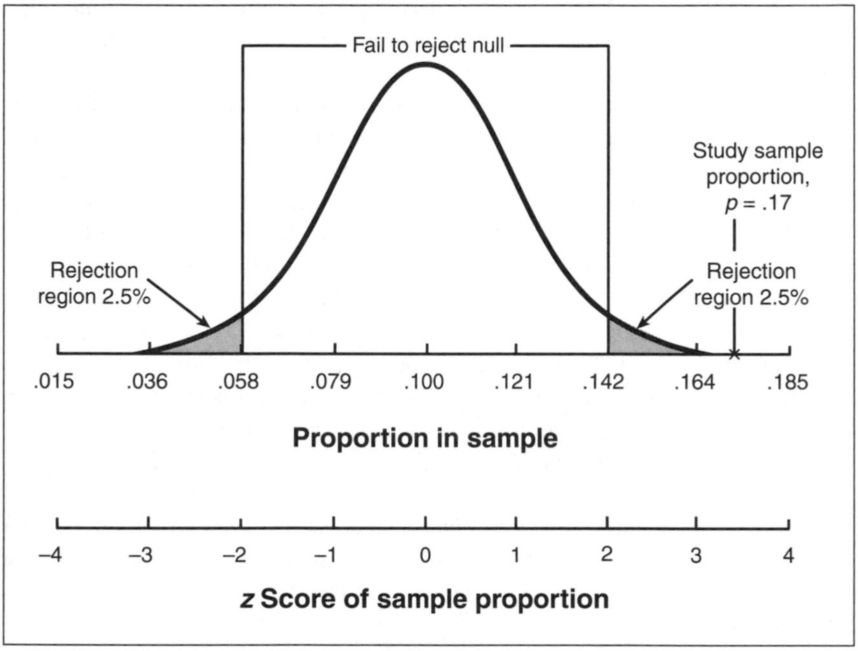

The first step is to calculate the standard error of the proportion.

$$\sigma_p = \sqrt{\frac{.10(1 - .10)}{200}} = \sqrt{\frac{.10(.90)}{200}} = \sqrt{\frac{.09}{200}} = \sqrt{.00045} = .021$$

Next, $\sigma_p$ is inserted into Formula 19.2: $z = (.17 - .10) / .021 = .07 / .021 = 3.30$

4. Make decision.

The decision rule (two-tailed test, .05 level) calls for rejecting the null when the absolute value of the obtained *z* is 1.96 or greater (see Chapter 15, Section 15.8.2). The absolute of the obtained *z*, 3.30, does indeed exceed 1.96 and thus, we reject the null and accept the alternative. Our result is statistically significant. The difference between the percentage of children in your school with serious problems (17%) and that in the large national sample (10%) is unlikely to be due to chance alone, $p < .05$. Because chance alone is an unlikely explanation, science gives you "permission" to think about the "real" factors causing this difference. Perhaps, for instance, the sharp rise in unemployment is indeed responsible. (See Chapter 14, Section 14.10 and Chapter 15, Section 15.13 for discussion on "permission" and "real" factors.) Figure 19.1 presents the results for our example.

## 19.3 ■ THE BINOMIAL TEST

### 19.3.1 ■ Background

The binomial test examines exactly the same question as does the one-sample test of *p*, whether the study sample proportion differs significantly—that is, by more than would be expected by chance alone—from the proportion stated in the null. The binomial test is often used when the sample size guideline for the one-sample test of *p* is not met, that is, when both *NP* and $N(1 - P)$

are not greater than or equal to five. It may also be used when the guidelines are met. It is based on the *binomial distribution*.

Let us continue to use the behavior problems example but change the sample size and your results. Presume that you administer the behavior problems measure to a random sample of five children and that three (60%) have serious problems. Can you conclude that the percentage in your school district, 60%, differs significantly from that in the large national sample, 10%?

Let us examine the sampling distribution assuming that the population proportion, $P$, equals .10. Figure 19.2, based on the binomial distribution, presents this distribution. Figure 19.2 conveys that the proportion of samples in which *exactly* three children experience serious problems equals .0081. To determine the proportion of samples in which three *or more* children experience problems, we sum the proportions for three, four, and five children: $.00810 + .00045 + .00001 = .00856$. Proportions are, in essence, probabilities (see Chapter 14; Section 14.3). Thus, given a population proportion of .10 ($P = .10$), the probability of selecting a random sample of size five in which three or more children have serious problems equals .00856; that is, $p = .00856$.

Observe that the distribution in Figure 19.2 differs from the normal distribution and the $t$ distribution in two ways: (a) it is "jagged" (composed of columns) rather than smooth, and (b) it is asymmetric. To calculate two-tailed probabilities in straightforward fashion, the researcher must create equal-sized tails on both sides of the distribution. When a distribution is both jagged and asymmetric, such tails (almost always) cannot be created. Except when the population proportion equals .50 ($P = .50$), the binomial distribution is both jagged and asymmetric and thus, calculation of two-tailed probabilities is problematic. In the interest of simplicity, this text covers only directional hypothesis pairs (one-tailed tests) for the binomial test.

The one-sample test of $p$ yields highly accurate probabilities when both $NP$ and $N(1 - P)$ $\geq 5$. In contrast, the binomial test yields *exact* probabilities. As just discussed, however, calculation of two-tailed probabilities is problematic when $P \neq .50$. Because its probabilities are exact,

FIGURE 19.2 ■ Binomial Sampling Distribution: $P = .10$, $N = 5$

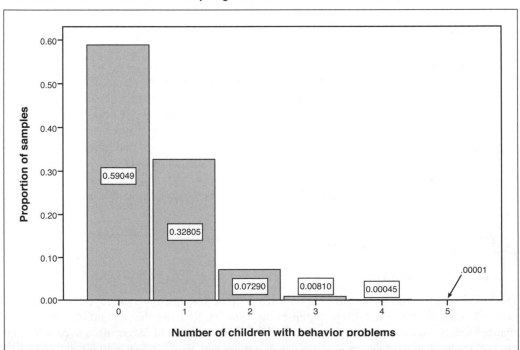

the binomial test is preferred for one-tailed tests (directional pairs). For two-tailed probabilities (nondirectional pairs), except when $P = .50$, the one-sample test of $p$ is the better choice.

Hypothesis pairs are the same as those for the one-sample test of $p$. As discussed, directional pairs (two-tailed tests) are problematic when $P \neq .50$.

We will not carry out computations for the binomial test but will instead reference a table of critical values for the binomial distribution, Table A.3 in Appendix A. When the alternative states greater than and the .05 significance level is used ($\alpha = .05$), the decision rule is to

Fail to reject the null when the frequency in the study sample is less than the number listed in the ">" (greater than) row in the binomial distribution table, Table A.3.

Reject the null, when this frequency is greater than or equal to the number listed in the table.

When the alternative states less than and the .05 significance level is used ($\alpha = .05$), the decision rule is to

Fail to reject the null when the frequency in the study sample is greater than the number listed in the "<" (less than) row in the binomial distribution table, Table A.3.

Reject the null, when this frequency is less than or equal to the number listed in the table.

In these decision rules, *frequency* refers to the number of cases that possess the characteristic of interest. For instance, in our example, three children have serious behavior problems.

In the binomial distribution table (Table A.3), a blank conveys that no study sample results will reject the null. For instance, when $N = 3$ and the proportion stated in the null equals .5, for both the ">" and "<" rows—that is both when the alternative states greater than and when it states less than—Table A.3 lists a blank. This conveys that *no* frequencies—not zero case, one case, two cases, nor all three cases possessing the characteristic of interest—will reject the null. In such a situation, statistical power equals 0.00, and there is no reason to conduct the test.

Some examples on how to use Table A.3 will be helpful. Suppose that sample size equals eight ($N = 8$), that the proportion stated in the null equals .25 ($P = .25$), and that the alternative states greater than. For this situation, Table A.3 lists "5." This conveys that the null is rejected for frequencies of five or greater. To give another example, when $N = 8$, $P = .8$, and the alternative states less than, the null is rejected for frequencies of three or lower.

Table A.3 lists critical values only for the .05 level. Given that the binomial test is most used often with small samples, power is often low. In such situations, use of the .01 level is not recommended because this reduces power still more. On the other hand, use of the .10 level is a good option because this increases power.

## 19.3.2 ■ Carrying Out the Test

1. State the hypothesis pair:
   Because our expectation is for increased behavior problems in your school district, we will use a directional pair. The alternative hypothesis states the direction of expectations.

   Null:      The proportion of children with serious behavior problems in your school district is less than or equal to .10.

   Alternative  The proportion of children with serious behavior problems in your school district is greater than .10.

   In symbols, this pair is      $H_0: P \leq .10$      $H_1: P > .10$

2. Select the significance level. We will use the .05 level.
3. and 4. Carry out the test and make a decision.

Three of the five students in your sample experienced serious behavior problems. Consulting the ">" row when sample size is five and referencing the column labeled ".1," Table A.3 lists the number "3." Because the frequency of children in the sample with serious problems, 3, equals the number in the table, 3, we reject the null and accept the alternative. We conclude that your study result is unlikely to be due to chance alone, $p < .05$.

Because we used a table to reach our decision, we did not learn the exact probability that our result is caused by chance alone. However, we determined this probability earlier, $p = .00856$ (see Figure 19.2). In real-world research, researchers carry out the binomial test with software packages and, thus, learn the exact probability of the study result, that is, the exact value of $p$.

## 19.4 ▦ THE ONE-VARIABLE CHI-SQUARE TEST

### 19.4.1 ▦ Background

The one-sample test of $p$ and the binomial test examine whether a single proportion in a sample differs significantly from the value stated in the null. The **one-variable chi-square test** (**one-variable $\chi^2$ test**, *goodness-of-fit chi-square test*) examines whether two or more proportions in a sample differ significantly from values stated in the null. "Chi" (pronounced "ki" as in kite) is symbolized by the lowercase Greek letter $\chi$.[3]

We need a working example to demonstrate the one-variable $\chi^2$ test: Suppose that you work in a mental health clinic in a medium-sized town and that 50% of the town's residents are White, 25% are Black, 15% are Hispanic, and 10% are from an ethnic background other than those mentioned. Suppose further that you take a random sample of 120 clients served at your clinic and find that 60% (72) are White, 20% (24) are Black, 10% (12) are Hispanic, and 10% (12) are of other ethnicity. The one-variable chi-square test can tell you whether chance alone is a likely explanation for the differences in percentages between your town and your sample. For our example, the hypothesis pair is

Null: In the population of clients served at your clinic, 50% of clients are White, 25% are Black, 15% are Hispanic, and 10% are from another ethnic background.

Alternative: In the population of clients served at your clinic, the percentage for at least one ethnic group differs from that stated for it in the null.

### 19.4.2 ▦ The Chi-Square Distribution

The one-variable $\chi^2$ test and the $\chi^2$ test of independence, presented in the next chapter, are based on the **chi-square ($\chi^2$) distribution**, the key distribution for most significance tests involving proportions. Just as is the $t$ distribution, the $\chi^2$ distribution is a family of distributions whose characteristics change according to the number of degrees of freedom. For the one-variable $\chi^2$ test, degrees of freedom equals the number of categories minus one, that is, $df = J - 1$ where $J$ is the number of categories. Because our example involves four categories of ethnicity, $df = 4 - 1 = 3$.

When the null is true, the researcher expects the value of $\chi^2$ resulting from the $\chi^2$ test (the obtained $\chi^2$) to be fairly close to the number of degrees of freedom. Such values often result in a decision to fail to reject the null. Values of $\chi^2$ considerably greater than the number of degrees of freedom are, generally speaking, inconsistent with the null. Such values often lead to its rejection.

### 19.4.3 ▓ Observed and Expected Frequencies

Expected and observed proportions and expected and observed frequencies are important in both the one variable $\chi^2$ test and the $\chi^2$ test of independence. Here, we define these terms for the one variable $\chi^2$ test.

A category's **observed frequency** equals the actual frequency of responses. For instance, the observed frequency of Black clients is 24. A category's **observed proportion** equals the actual proportion of responses. To calculate, divide the observed frequency (the actual frequency) by the sample size. For instance, the observed proportion of Black clients is: $24 / 120 = .20$.

A category's **expected proportion** is the predicted proportion given a true null. Expected proportion equals the proportion stated in the null. For instance, the expected proportion of White clients equals .50. A category's **expected frequency** is the predicted frequency of responses given a true null. To calculate, multiply the expected proportion (the proportion stated in the null) by the sample size $(N)$. For instance, the expected frequency for Hispanics is $.15(120) = 18$. Expressed as a formula:

$$f_e = p_e \times N \tag{19.3}$$

where $f_e$ is the expected frequency, $p_e$ is the expected proportion, and $N$ is the sample size.

### 19.4.4 ▓ Particulars for the Test

The hypothesis pair is always nondirectional. Stated generally,

Null:        Each proportion in the population from which the study sample was selected equals some given value.

Alternative: At least one proportion in the population from which the study sample was selected differs from the value stated for it in the null.

Chapter 15 (Section 15.6.2) stated that, with an exception to be discussed later, two-tailed tests are used with nondirectional pairs. This exception is that when *only* a nondirectional hypothesis pair is allowed, the significance test is one-tailed. Only a nondirectional hypothesis pair is allowed with the one-variable $\chi^2$ test. Hence, it is a one-tailed test. Its rejection region is located in the upper-tail.

One formula is

$$\chi^2 = N\left(\Sigma \frac{(p_o - p_e)^2}{p_e}\right) \tag{19.4}$$

where $\chi^2$ is the obtained chi-square, $N$ is the sample size, $\Sigma$ is the summation sign, $p_o$ is the observed proportion for a category, and $p_e$ is the expected proportion for a category. Study Formula 19.4 to see that the larger the differences between observed and expected proportions, the larger the obtained $\chi^2$ and, thus, the greater the likelihood of rejecting the null. An easier formula for hand calculations is presented shortly. As mentioned already, degrees of freedom equals the number of categories minus one, that is, $df = J - 1$. The decision rule is to

Fail to reject (accept) the null if the value of the obtained $\chi^2$ is less than the value listed in the chi-square distribution table, Table A.4 in Appendix A.

Reject the null if the obtained $\chi^2$ is greater than or equal to the value listed in Table A.4.

Given three or more categories $(J \geq 3)$, the one variable $\chi^2$ test yields sufficiently accurate results when the average observed frequency is at least four and the minimum expected frequency is at least one (see Roscoe & Byars, 1971). With two categories, the minimum expected frequency should be at least five.[4]

### 19.4.5 ■ Completing Our Example

1. State the hypothesis pair; the pair is stated above.
2. Select the significance level; we will use the .05 level.
3. Carry out the test.

The best formula for hand calculations is

$$\chi^2 = \Sigma \frac{(f_o - f_e)^2}{f_e} \tag{19.5}$$

where $\chi^2$ is the obtained chi-square, $f_o$ is the observed frequency in a category, and $f_e$ is the expected frequency.

Prior to carrying out the chi-square formula, we need to calculate each category's expected frequency using Formula 19.3. Thus, we multiply each category's expected proportion (the proportion stated in the null) by the sample size ($N$).

White clients: $f_e = .50(120) = 60$

Black clients: $f_e = .25(120) = 30$

Hispanic clients: $f_e = .15(120) = 18$

Other ethnicity: $f_e = .10(120) = 12$

Formula 19.5 directs one to carry out the following steps for each category: (1) subtract the expected frequency from the observed frequency, (2) square this difference, and (3) divide by the expected frequency. Finally (Step 4), the summation sign ($\Sigma$) directs one to sum the results from Step 3.

Prior to carrying out calculations, let us check that we meet the sample size guidelines. The average frequency equals the sample size ($N$) divided by the number of categories: $120 / 4 = 30$. This exceeds the recommended minimum of four. The minimum expected frequency was just calculated and is 12. This exceeds the recommended minimum of one. Hence, the guidelines are met.

Calculations are best carried out using a "grid" as in Table 19.1.

Our obtained $\chi^2$ equals 5.60. As already calculated, $df = 4 - 1 = 3$. Referencing the table of critical values for the chi-square distribution (Table A.4), for three degrees of freedom using the .05 level, the critical value of chi-square equals 7.81. Because the value of our obtained $\chi^2$ is less than this, we fail to reject the null and, thus, reject the alternative.

### TABLE 19.1 ■ Calculation of $\chi^2$ for the One-Variable Chi-Square Test

| Category | $f_o$ | $f_e$ | $(f_o - f_e)$ | $(f_o - f_e)^2$ | $(f_o - f_e)^2 / f_e$ |
|---|---|---|---|---|---|
| White | 72 | 60 | 12 | 144 | 2.40 |
| Black | 24 | 30 | −6 | 36 | 1.2 |
| Hispanic | 12 | 18 | −6 | 36 | 2.0 |
| Other ethnicity | 12 | 12 | 0 | 0 | 0 |
| | | | | | $\Sigma = 5.60$ |

FIGURE 19.3 ■ Chi-square Distribution With Three Degrees of Freedom

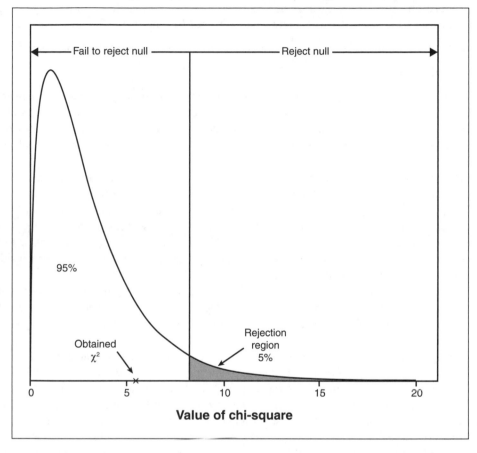

Given a true null, the probability of obtaining your study sample result is greater than .05. Chance alone is *not* an unlikely explanation for the differences between the proportions obtained in your sample and those stated in the null. Study results do not allow you to conclude that the proportions served at the clinic differ from those in the town.

Because we used a table to reach our decision, the exact probability of our result (i.e., *p*) is not provided. I used a software program to calculate this probability and it equals .133.

As already mentioned, the one-variable $\chi^2$ test is one-tailed with its rejection region located in the upper tail. Our example has three degrees of freedom. Figure 19.3 presents a chi-square distribution with three degrees of freedom. In Figure 19.3, the rejection region begins at 7.81, the critical value when the .05 level is used. The rejection region comprises the upper 5% tail of the distribution. Because our result was not in this region, we failed to reject the null.

## 19.5 ■ CHAPTER SUMMARY

The *one-sample test of a proportion* (*one-sample test of* p) examines whether a sample proportion, *p*, differs significantly from some stated value. The hypothesis pair may be directional (one-tailed test) or nondirectional (two-tailed). The nondirectional null states that the proportion in the population equals some given value. Decision rules are same as those for the large sample test of $\overline{X}$. Results are sufficiently accurate whenever both $NP$ and $N(1 - P)$ are greater than or equal to 5. One formula is $z = \dfrac{(p-P)}{\sigma_p}$ where $\sigma_p$ is the standard error of the proportion given a true null and equals $\sqrt{\dfrac{P(1 - P)}{N}}$.

Just as does the one-sample test of $p$, the binomial test examines whether a sample proportion, $p$, differs significantly from some stated value. It is often used when sample size guidelines for the one-sample test of $p$ are not met. The binomial test yields exact probabilities. When the proportion stated in the null does not equal .50 ($P \neq .50$), calculation of two-tailed probabilities can be problematic.

The *one-variable chi-square test* examines whether two or more proportions in a sample differ significantly from values stated in the null. It is based on the *chi-square ($\chi^2$) distribution*.

The $\chi^2$ distribution is a family of distributions whose characteristics change according to the number of degrees of freedom. For the one-variable $\chi^2$ test, degrees of freedom equals the number of categories minus one, that is, $df = J - 1$. Values of chi-square reasonably close to the number of degrees of freedom often result in a decision to fail to reject the null. Values considerably greater than this often result in a decision to reject it.

A category's *expected proportion* is the predicted proportion given a true null. Expected proportion equals the proportion stated in the null. A category's *expected frequency* is the predicted frequency given a true null. To calculate, multiply the expected proportion by the sample size, $f_e = p_e \times N$.

A category's *observed frequency* equals the actual frequency. A category's *observed proportion* is the actual proportion. To compute, divide observed frequency by the sample size.

The hypothesis pair for the one-variable $\chi^2$ test is always nondirectional. The null states that all proportions in the population equal those stated in the null. Although the hypothesis pair is nondirectional, the one-variable $\chi^2$ test is one-tailed. Its rejection region is in the upper tail. Given three or more categories, results are accurate when the average observed frequency is at least four and the minimum expected frequency is at least one. With two categories, this is so when the minimum expected frequency is at least five.

The preferred hand-calculation formula is $\chi^2 = \Sigma \dfrac{(f_o - f_e)^2}{f_e}$. The researcher rejects the null when the obtained $\chi^2$ exceeds the critical value in the $\chi^2$ distribution table.

## 19.6 ■ PROBLEMS AND QUESTIONS

### Section 19.2

1.  The one-sample test of $p$ examines whether a sample _____ differs significantly from some stated value.

2.  Calculate the standard error of the proportion, $\sigma_p$, for each situation. $P$ stands for the proportion in the population:
    a.  $P = .25, N = 100$
    b.  $P = .25, N = 25$
    c.  $P = .75, N = 25$

    **d.** $P = .10, N = 25$
    **e.** $P = .10, N = 100$

3.   For each situation in the prior question, calculate $NP$ and $N(1 - P)$ and indicate whether the smaller of these is large enough for the one-sample test of $p$ to yield accurate results. $P$ stands for the proportion stated in the null.

4.   (*True or False*) The hypothesis pair for the one-sample test of $p$ may be either directional or nondirectional.

5.   (*True or False*) The decision rules for the one-sample test of $p$ are the same as those for the large sample test of $\overline{X}$.

6.   In a very large population, the proportion of public welfare participants who secure jobs within 3 months that pay more than minimum wage is .15. Among 250 clients who participate in a demonstration program, this proportion is .25.
    **a.** What test should be used to examine whether the proportion in the demonstration program differs from that in the population?
    **b.** Using symbols, state the nondirectional hypothesis pair.
    **c.** Calculate $NP$ and $N(1 - P)$ and indicate whether the smaller of these is large enough for the one-sample test of $p$ to yield accurate results.
    **d.** Calculate $\sigma_p$, the standard error of the proportion.
    **e.** Calculate $z$ (carry out the test).
    **f.** Presume that you selected the .01 level ($\alpha = .01$, two-tailed test). What is your decision regarding the null? The alternative? (Hint: Decision rules are same as for the large sample test of $\overline{X}$.)
    **g.** Given a true null, is the probability of obtaining the study sample result or an even more extreme result greater than .01 or less than .01?
    **h.** Is the probability of obtaining the study sample result or an even more extreme result due to chance alone greater than .01 or less than .01?
    **i.** Is the study sample result likely to be caused by chance alone?
    **j.** Is the result statistically significant at the .01 level?
    **k.** Can you be confident that the null is false?
    **l.** Does the study provide strong evidence that the null is false?

7.   A community mental health program sets a goal that 80% of their clients will not be readmitted to a psychiatric hospital. The actual percentage for their first 100 clients is 90%. You wish to determine whether the actual percentage differs from the targeted percentage to a statistically significant degree, that is, by more than would be expected because of chance alone. You will carry out a nondirectional one-sample test of $p$ using the .05 significance level ($\alpha = .05$).
    **a.** Using symbols, state the nondirectional hypothesis pair for the test.
    **b.** Calculate $NP$ and $N(1 - P)$ and indicate whether the smaller of these is large enough for the one-sample test of $p$ to yield accurate results.

   **c.** Calculate $\sigma_p$.
   **d.** Calculate $z$ (carry out the test).
   **e.** Given that you selected the .05 level, what is your decision regarding the null? The alternative?
   **f.** Given a true null, is the probability of obtaining the study sample result or an even more extreme result greater than .05 or less than .05?
   **g.** Is the probability of obtaining the study sample result or an even more extreme result due to chance alone greater than .05 or less than .05?
   **h.** Is the difference between the actual percentage (90%) and the targeted percentage (80%) a statistically significant one?
   **i.** Can you be confident that the null is false?
   **j.** Does the study provide strong evidence that the null is false?

8. In a large state, girls are victims in 55% of reports of child maltreatment reports. In your very small rural county, girls are victims in 28 of 40 reports (70%). You wish to determine whether the percentage in your county differs significantly from the statewide percentage. Carry out a nondirectional one-sample test of $p$ using the .05 level.
   **a.** Is your sample a random or a nonrandom sample?
   **b.** (*True or False*) Given that your sample is nonrandom, this text recommends that you should not carry out a significance test.
   **c.** Using symbols, state the nondirectional hypothesis pair for the test.
   **d.** Calculate $NP$ and $N(1 - P)$ and indicate whether the smaller of these is large enough for the one-sample test of $p$ to yield accurate results?
   **e.** Calculate $\sigma_p$.
   **f.** Calculate $z$ (carry out the test).
   **g.** Given that you select the .05 level, what is your decision regarding the null? The alternative?
   **h.** Given a true null, is the probability of obtaining the study sample result or an even more extreme result greater than .05 or less than .05?
   **i.** Is the probability of obtaining the study sample result or an even more extreme result due to chance alone greater than .05 or less than .05?
   **j.** Is the difference between the actual percentage of reports for girls (70%) and the statewide percentage (55%) a statistically significant one?
   **k.** Can you be confident that the null is false?
   **l.** Does the study provide strong evidence that the null is false?

**Section 19.3**

9. *Respond true or false to each statement.*
   **a.** The binomial test yields exact rather than approximate probabilities.
   **b.** The binomial test examines whether a sample mean differs from some stated value.
   **c.** Hypothesis pairs for the binomial test are the same as those for the one-sample test of $p$.

**d.** The binomial test is often used with small samples (rather than with quite large ones).

**e.** When the proportion stated in the null differs from .50, calculation of two-tailed probabilities can be problematic for the binomial test.

**10.** The following "grid" lists: $N$ (sample size), $f$ (frequency observed), $P$ (proportion stated in the null), the direction stated in the alternative hypothesis (in $H_1$) and the selected significance level ($\alpha$).

| Situation | $N$ | $f$ | $P$ | $H_1$ states | $\alpha$ |
|---|---|---|---|---|---|
| #1 | 10 | 6 | 1/3 | > | .05 |
| #2 | 15 | 4 | .1 | > | .05 |
| #3 | 15 | 5 | .1 | > | .05 |
| #4 | 6 | 3 | .8 | < | .05 |
| #5 | 6 | 2 | .8 | < | .05 |
| #6 | 9 | 0 | .2 | < | .05 |

For each situation:

**a.** Indicate the critical value (frequency) listed in the binomial distribution table (Table A.3)

**b.** Describe the conditions that lead to rejection of the null.

**c.** Decide whether to fail to reject (accept) or reject the null.

**11.** In a large state, 20% of adoptions of high risk children have resulted in adoption disruption within 2 years of placement. A new service approach results in only 1 disruption in 20 placements (5%). Our interest is in whether one may conclude that the proportion ($p$) for the new program differs significantly from that for the state. Use the .05 level ($\alpha = .05$)

**a.** Using symbols, state the (directional) null and alternative hypotheses. Hint: The direction of expectations is for a lower percentage for the new service approach.

**b.** Calculate $NP$ and $N(1 - P)$ and indicate whether these are sufficiently large for the one-sample test of $p$ to yield accurate results. (Hint: Both must equal 5 or greater for this to be so.)

**c.** What is the best significance test to use in this situation?

**d.** What is the critical value (frequency) where $\alpha = .05$?

**e.** What is your decision regarding the null? The alternative?

**f.** Given a true null, is the probability of obtaining the study sample result greater than or less than .05?

**g.** Is the probability that the study sample result is caused by chance alone greater than or less than .05?

**h.** Can you be 95% confident that the null is false?

**i.** Does the result provide strong evidence that the null is false?

**j.** Is this result statistically significant?

**k.** In your own words, how can it be that the null is accepted when results for the new program (5% disrupt) represent such a substantial improvement over the situation statewide (20% disrupt)?

12. Historically, 75% of persons pass a social work licensing exam. In your group of 10 colleagues who study together for the exam, all 10 (100%) pass. You want to find out whether the percentage who pass in your group differs significantly from the historical rate. Presume that you use the .05 level.

   a. Using symbols, state a directional null. (Hint: The direction of expectations is greater than.)
   b. What is the critical value (if any) in the binomial distribution table?
   c. Describe the conditions under which the null is rejected.
   d. What is your decision on the null? The alternative?
   e. (*True or False*) In this situation, the probability of rejecting the null was 0.00.
   f. (*True or False*) In this situation, power was, in essence, 0.00.

13. Respond to the prior question again. All facts are the same except that the historical passing rate is 50% rather than 75%.

**Section 19.4**

14. The one-variable $\chi^2$ test examines whether _____ or more _____ in a sample differ significantly from values stated in the null.

15. The $\chi^2$ distribution is a _____ of distributions whose characteristics change according to the number of _____ of _____.

16. Each of the following lists the number of categories. Calculate the number of degrees of freedom for a one-variable $\chi^2$ test.
   a. five
   b. two
   c. ten

17. When the null is true, the researcher expects the value of $\chi^2$ resulting from the $\chi^2$ test (the obtained $\chi^2$) to be fairly _____ to the number of degrees of freedom. Such values often result in a decision to _____ to _____ the null. Values of $\chi^2$ considerably greater than the number of degrees of freedom often lead to a decision to _____ the null.

18. A category's _____ _____ equals the actual frequency of responses.
   A category's _____ _____ equals the actual proportion of responses.

19. A category's _____ _____ is the predicted proportion given a true null. Expected proportion equals the proportion stated in the _____. A category's _____ _____ is the predicted frequency of responses given a true null.

20. To calculate expected frequency, the researcher multiplies the expected proportion by the _____ _____.

**21.** Sample size ($N$) equals 100. The null states the following for four categories:

Category A: $P = .30$   B: $P = .40$   C: $P = .10$   D: $P = .20$

For each category, indicate the expected proportion and the expected frequency. (Use Formula 19.3 to calculate expected frequencies.)

**22.** Sample size ($N$) equals 50. The null states the following for four categories:

Category A: $P = .30$   B: $P = .40$   C: $P = .10$   D: $P = .20$

For each category, indicate the expected proportion and the expected frequency. (Hint: Use Formula 19.3 to calculate expected frequencies.)

**23.** Given three or more categories, the one variable $\chi^2$ test yields sufficiently accurate results when the average observed frequency is at least ___, and the minimum expected frequency is at least ___. With two categories, results are sufficiently accurate when the minimum expected frequency is at least ___.

**24.** The hypothesis pair for the one variable $\chi^2$ test is a _____ pair. This test is a ___ -tailed test with the rejection region located in the _____ tail.

**25.** Other things being equal, the larger the differences between observed and _____ proportions, the _____ the obtained $\chi^2$ and, thus, the greater the likelihood of _____ the null.

**26.** A new county social service agency begins service in a county in which the following percentages of residents are from each of three age groups: aged 17 or younger, 20%; aged 18–50, 45%; aged 51 or older, 35%. The percentages in these groups in the first 50 clients served by the agency are aged 17 or younger, 12% (6 clients); aged 18–50, 60% (30 clients); aged 51 or older, 28% (14 clients). You wish to examine whether the percentages served by the agency differ significantly from those in the county.
   **a.** What is the appropriate statistical significance test for this purpose?
   **b.** Is the hypothesis pair directional or nondirectional?
   **c.** State the null.
   **d.** What are the expected proportions?
   **e.** What are the expected frequencies?
   **f.** What are the observed proportions?
   **g.** What are the observed frequencies?
   **h.** What is the average observed frequency? Is it sufficient for carrying out the test?
   **i.** What is the minimum expected frequency? Is it sufficient for carrying out the test?
   **j.** Using Formula 19.5, calculate $\chi^2$?
   **k.** How many degrees of freedom are there?
   **l.** Presume that the .05 significance level was selected ($\alpha = .05$). What is the critical value of $\chi^2$?
   **m.** What is your decision regarding the null? Regarding the alternative hypothesis?

   **n.** Do the percentages served by the agency differ to a statistically significant degree from those for the county?

   **o.** Are the results statistically significant?

   **p.** Given a true null, are these results highly unlikely results (sufficiently unlikely for rejection of the null)?

   **q.** Is chance alone a highly unlikely explanation for the study results?

   **r.** (*True or False*) This is an example of a significance test being carried out in the absence of random sampling.

27. An agency operates programs A, B, C, and D. The director hypothesizes that one quarter of clients (25%) can best be served by each program. Among the first 80 clients served, 26 are evaluated as best served by A, 16 as best served by B, 23 as best served by C, and 15 as best served by D. Your task is to determine whether actual (observed) percentages differ from the hypothesized (expected) percentages to a statistically significant degree? Note: You select the .05 level ($\alpha = .05$).

   **a.** What are expected frequencies?

   **b.** What is the minimum expected frequency? Is it sufficient for carrying out the test?

   **c.** What is the average observed frequency? Is it sufficient for carrying out the test?

   **d.** What is the value of $\chi^2$?

   **e.** How many degrees of freedom are there?

   **f.** What is the critical value of $\chi^2$?

   **g.** What decision should be made on the null? The alternative?

   **h.** Is the probability that study sample result is due to chance alone greater than .05 or less than this?

   **i.** What is the probability—> .05 or < .05—that the differences between the percentages actually served and the director's hypothesized percentages are due to chance alone?

   **j.** Is this result statistically significant?

   **k.** Does the result indicate that it is likely that the null is true?

   **l.** Does this result provide strong evidence that the null is false?

28. Respond to the questions for the prior example but with the single change that observed frequencies are A, 28; B, 14; C, 25; D, 13.

# 20

# THE CHI-SQUARE TEST OF INDEPENDENCE

## 20.1 ▨ CHAPTER OVERVIEW

Chapter 20's focus is on the *chi-square* ($\chi^2$) test of independence, perhaps the best-known statistical significance test. This chapter presents this test's hypothesis pair, how to calculate expected and observed proportions and frequencies, and a computational formula. As an example at the end of the chapter demonstrates, it is important to remember that the $\chi^2$ test of independence is a significance test, not a measure of size of association.

## 20.2 ▨ INTRODUCTION TO THE CHI-SQUARE TEST OF INDEPENDENCE

The second test based on the chi-square distribution, the **chi-square test of independence** (**$\chi^2$ test of independence**), assesses the probability that an association between two categorical variables is due to chance. Among all significance tests, it may be the most used and best known. It is sometimes referred to simply as the *chi-square* ($\chi^2$) *test*.

To demonstrate the chi-square test, we will use an example first presented in Chapter 7 (Section 7.5). This example, taken from the special needs adoption study (Rosenthal & Groze, 1992), examined the association between the presence (vs. the absence) of serious behavior problems and family ethnicity. Family ethnicity defines three groups of adopting families: (a) minority inracial (minority [nonwhite] parents who adopt a child of the same race as at least one parent), (b) white inracial (white parents who adopt a white child), and (c) transracial (white parents who adopt a minority child). Table 20.1 displays the association between these variables.

In Table 20.1, the percentage of children with serious behavior problems differs by family ethnicity. Thus, 29% of minority inracial families, 47% of white inracial families, and 37% of transracial families reported such problems. As percentages differ, the variables are associated in the study sample. This association does not permit one to conclude that there is also an association in the population from which the sample was randomly selected. Perhaps the variables are unassociated in this population, and the association in the sample is due to sampling error, that is, chance.

## 20.3 ▨ SELECTED CHARACTERISTICS OF $\chi^2$ TEST

### 20.3.1 ▨ Hypothesis Pair

The hypothesis pair for the $\chi^2$ test may be presented in two ways. In the first, the null asserts an absence of association.

TABLE 20.1 ■ Family Ethnicity by Severity of Behavioral Problems

| | Minority Inracial | White Inracial | Transracial | |
|---|---|---|---|---|
| **Child has serious behavior problems** | 59<br>29% | 194<br>47% | 20<br>37% | 273<br>40.7% |
| **Child does not have serious behavior problems** | 142<br>71% | 222<br>53% | 34<br>63% | 398<br>59.3% |
| | 201 | 416 | 54 | 671 |

Null:      In the population from which the study sample was selected, two variables are unassociated.

Alternative:  In the population from which the study sample was selected, two variables are associated.

   With categorical variables, the absence of association is conveyed by equal percentages (equal proportions; see Chapter 6, Section 6.4.2). Hence, we may also state the hypothesis pair as

Null:      In the population from which the study sample was selected, percentages are equal.

Alternative:  In the population from which the study sample was selected, percentages differ.

   This text follows the practice of making the independent variable the column variable in a contingency table, that is, the variable at the top of the table (see Chapter 6, Section 6.4.1). With a table structured in this way, the just-stated hypothesis pair becomes

Null:      In the population from which the study sample was selected, column percentages are equal.

Alternative:  In the population from which the study sample was selected, column percentages differ.

### 20.3.2 ■ Distribution and Degrees of Freedom

Just as for the one-variable test, when the null is true, the researcher expects the obtained $\chi^2$ (the value yielded by the test) to be fairly close to the number of degrees of freedom. When the null is false, the researcher expects the obtained $\chi^2$ to be greater than this. Values of $\chi^2$ that are much larger than the number of degrees of freedom often indicate that the null is false. For the chi-square test of independence,

$$df = (R - 1)(C - 1) \tag{20.1}$$

where $R$ is the number of rows in the contingency table and $C$ is the number of columns. In our example, the contingency table (Table 20.1) has two rows and three columns. Hence, $df = (2 - 1)(3 - 1) = (1)(2) = 2$.

   As is the case for the one-variable $\chi^2$ test, the $\chi^2$ test of independence is always one-tailed. Its rejection region is (always) located in the upper tail.

### 20.3.3 ■ Observed and Expected Proportions

The cell percentages in Table 20.1 sum to 100 down the columns and, thus, are column percentages. If we divide these percentages by 100, they become proportions: across the top row, .29,

.37, and .47; and across the bottom, .71, .63, and .53. These are the *observed proportions* (or *observed column proportions*), the actual proportions in the cells.

A cell's *expected proportion* is the proportion predicted given a true null. The formula for *expected column proportion* is

$$p_e = \text{(row margin total)} / N \qquad (20.2)$$

where row margin total is the number of cases in the row in which the cell is located and $N$ is the number of cases in the table.

All cells in a given row have identical expected column proportions. For Table 20.1, the expected column proportion for each cell in the first row is $273 / 671 = .407$. For each cell in the second row, it is $398 / 671 = .593$.

Observe that a cell's expected column proportion equals the proportion of all cases that are in the row in which the cell is located. For instance, the proportion of all cases that are in the first row is .407; this is the expected proportion of each cell in this row.

### 20.3.4 ■ Formula, Observed and Expected Frequencies, Decision Rule, and Requirements

Chapter 19 presented two formulas (19.4 and 19.5) for the one-variable $\chi^2$ test, one based on expected and observed proportions and the other on expected and observed frequencies. These same formulas are used for the $\chi^2$ test of independence.

The formula based on proportions links well with the previously presented hypothesis pairs, thereby helping one to see that the $\chi^2$ test of independence examines whether observed proportions differ from expected proportions by more than would be expected from chance alone.

However, just as is the case with the one-variable $\chi^2$ test, the formula based on frequencies is easier for hand calculations. Formula 19.5 is repeated here for convenience.

$$\chi^2 = \Sigma \frac{(f_o - f_e)^2}{f_e}$$

where $\chi^2$ is the obtained chi-square, $f_o$ is observed frequency, and $f_e$ is expected frequency.

A cell's *observed frequency* is the actual frequency in the cell. A cell's *expected frequency*, that is, its predicted frequency given a true null equals

$$F_e = \frac{\text{(row margin total)} \times \text{(column margin total)}}{N} \qquad (20.3)$$

where row margin total is the number of cases in a case's row, and column margin total is the number of cases in the case's column.

One way to compute expected frequencies is to (a) create a contingency table with row and column totals and $N$ but with the cells left empty, and (b) for each cell, carry out the formula. Table 20.2 presents expected frequencies and the calculations involved. Observe that expected frequencies need not equal whole numbers.

Decision rules are the same as those for the one-variable $\chi^2$ test. The researcher fails to reject (accepts) the null if the obtained $\chi^2$ is less than the critical value in the chi-square distribution table, Table A.3 in Appendix A. She rejects it if the obtained $\chi^2$ is greater than or equal to the critical value.

With the exception of a $2 \times 2$ table (two dichotomous variables), the $\chi^2$ test of independence yields accurate probabilities whenever the average observed frequency is at least four and the

TABLE 20.2 ■ Calculation of Expected Frequencies for Family Ethnicity and Behavior Problems

| | Minority Inracial | White Inracial | Transracial | |
|---|---|---|---|---|
| Child has serious behavior problems | $\dfrac{(273)(201)}{671} = 81.78$ | $\dfrac{(273)(416)}{671} = 169.25$ | $\dfrac{(54)(273)}{671} = 21.97$ | 273 (40.7%) |
| Child does not have serious behavior problems | $\dfrac{(398)(201)}{671} = 119.22$ | $\dfrac{(398)(416)}{671} = 246.75$ | $\dfrac{(398)(416)}{671} = 32.03$ | 398 (59.3%) |
| | 201 | 416 | 54 | 671 |

minimum observed frequency is at least one. For a 2 × 2 table, the average observed frequency should be at least six and the minimum expected frequency should be at least one (see Roscoe & Byars, 1971).[1]

## 20.4 ■ CARRYING OUT THE $\chi^2$ TEST

### 20.4.1 ■ Hypothesis Testing Model and Calculations

We continue with our example involving family ethnicity and serious behavior problems. For our $\chi^2$ test to yield an accurate probability, the average observed frequency should be at least four and the minimum expected frequency should be at least one. To compute the average observed frequency, we divide the sample size by the number of cells: 671/6 = 111.8. The minimum expected frequency is 21.97 (upper right cell of Table 20.2). As the guidelines are met, we may proceed.

1. State the hypothesis pair.

   Null:         In the population from which the study sample was selected, family ethnicity and the presence of a serious behavioral problem are unassociated.

   Alternative:  In the population from which the study sample was selected, family ethnicity and the presence of a serious behavioral problem are associated.

   One may also state the hypothesis pair using percentages (proportions):

   Null:         In the population from which the study sample was selected, the percentage of children with serious behavior problems is equal in each of the three family ethnicity groups.

   Alternative:  In the population from which the study sample was selected, the percentage of children with serious behavior problems is not equal in all three family ethnicity groups.

2. State the significance level.

   The .01 statistical significance level is selected ($\alpha = .01$). With a large sample size such as this, use of the .01 level rather than the .05 level reduces the likelihood that an extremely weak association will achieve statistical significance. In general, with large samples, the .01 level is often a good choice (see Chapter 16, Section 16.5.5).

TABLE 20.3 ■ Calculation of $\chi^2$ for Family Ethnicity and Behavior Problems Example

| Cell | $f_o$ | $f_e$ | $f_o - f_e$ | $(f_o - f_e)^2$ | $(f_o - f_e)^2/f_e$ |
|---|---|---|---|---|---|
| Upper left | 59 | 81.78 | −22.78 | 518.93 | 6.35 |
| Upper middle | 194 | 169.25 | 24.75 | 612.56 | 3.62 |
| Upper right | 20 | 21.97 | −1.97 | 3.88 | 0.18 |
| Lower left | 142 | 119.22 | 22.78 | 518.93 | 4.35 |
| Lower middle | 222 | 246.75 | −24.75 | 612.56 | 2.47 |
| Lower right | 34 | 32.03 | 1.97 | 3.88 | 0.12 |
| | | | | | $\Sigma = 17.09 = \chi^2$ |

**3.** Carry out the test.

Because expected frequencies have already been calculated, we may proceed with the $\chi^2$ formula (Formula 19.5). For each cell in the contingency table, Formula 19.5 directs one to (1) subtract the expected frequency from the observed frequency, (2) square this difference, and (3) divide by the expected frequency. Finally (Step 4), the summation sign directs one to sum the results from Step 3. Calculations can be carried out using a grid (see Table 20.3).

**4.** Make decision.

Because Table 20.3 has two rows and three columns, $df = (2 - 1)(3 - 1) = (1)(2) = 2$. Referencing Table A.4 in Appendix A, the critical value for a $\chi^2$ distribution with two degrees of freedom at the .01 level ($\alpha = .01$) is 9.21. As the obtained $\chi^2$, 17.09, exceeds the critical value, the null is rejected. We accept the alternative hypothesis and conclude that family ethnicity and likelihood of serious behavior problems are indeed associated in the population.

Figure 20.1 presents our results visually. The obtained $\chi^2$ is in the rejection region and, hence, we reject the null.

FIGURE 20.1 ■ Chi-Square Distribution and our Test Result

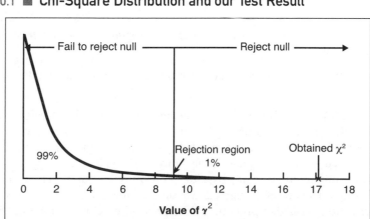

TABLE 20.4 ■ SPSS-Generated Table of Values of Obtained Chi-Square and Probabilities for Our Example

|  | Value | df | Asymp. Sig. (2-sided) |
|---|---|---|---|
| Pearson Chi-Square | 17.095[a] | 2 | .000 |
| Likelihood Ratio | 17.456 | 2 | .000 |
| Linear-by-Linear Association | 8.041 | 1 | .005 |
| N of Valid Cases | 671 | | |

[a]0 cells (.0%) have expected count less than 5. The minimum expected count is 21.97.

### 20.4.2 ■ Comments on the Example

As you know, statistical software packages calculate exact probabilities. Table 20.4 presents output from the SPSS *crosstabs* procedure. According to the *Pearson chi-square*—our formulas, Formulas 19.4 and 19.5, are formulas for this particular chi-square test—the probability (value of $p$) for our study sample result equals .00019. In other words, given a true null—equal proportions of serious problems in each of the three family ethnicity populations—the probability of obtaining our study sample proportions or proportions that differ from the null by even more than do these proportions equals .00019. Stated differently, given a true null, we would obtain our proportions or even more extreme proportions only 19 times in every 100,000 random samples. In sum, we can be extremely confident that the null is false and that the study result is not due to chance alone.

Now is a convenient time to provide the format for presenting $\chi^2$ results in journal articles. The current results would be reported as $\chi^2$ (2, $N = 671$) = 17.095, $p$ = .00019. The first number inside the parentheses conveys the degrees of freedom. If the exact probability was not known, these results would be expressed as $\chi^2$ (2, $N = 671$) = 17.095, $p < .01$.

## 20.5 ■ COMMENTS ON THE $\chi^2$ TEST

It was stated earlier that the hypothesis pair for the $\chi^2$ test of independence is always nondirectional. Yet, with two dichotomous (two-category) variables, one can formulate a directional pair. For instance, consider this pair:

Null:          The percentage of successful outcomes in Program A is less than or equal to that in Program B.

Alternative:  The percentage of successful outcomes in Program A is greater than that in Program B.

How does one test such a hypothesis pair given that the hypothesis pair for the $\chi^2$ test of independence is always nondirectional? The straightforward answer is that one does so by dividing the probability given by the $\chi^2$ test in half. So, suppose that in a given study, the $\chi^2$ test for our just-stated hypothesis pair yields a probability of .08, that is, $p$ = .08. By definition, this probability is for a nondirectional pair. To get the probability for our directional pair, we divide it by two: 08/2 = .04. Hence, presuming that we selected the .05 level and that our result is in the expected direction—a higher proportion of successful outcomes in A than B—we reject the null.[2]

When the minimum guidelines for a $2 \times 2$ table—average observed frequency of at least six and minimum expected frequency of at least one—are not met, **Fisher's exact test** is a good alternative to the $\chi^2$ test of independence (see Blalock, 1979, pp. 292–297). When the guidelines are met, the $\chi^2$ test of independence is preferred as the probability ($p$) given by Fisher's test can be higher than the actual probability that the result is caused by chance (Norušis, 1997, p. 305).[3]

Although sometimes used to do so, the $\chi^2$ test of independence is not recommended for examining directional association between categorical variables (see Chapter 7, Section 7.4). When directional association is present, the $\chi^2$ test may fail to reject the null in a situation in which a test designed for directional association would reject it. Recommended tests for directional association between categorical, ordinal-level variables include significance tests for tau$_b$ ($\tau_b$), tau$_c$ ($\tau_c$), gamma ($\gamma$), and Somers' $D$. We discuss these tests in Chapter 22, Section 22.6.2 (for more details, see Rosenthal, 2000, p. 414).

## 20.6 ■ THE $\chi^2$ TEST IS *NOT* A MEASURE OF SIZE OF ASSOCIATION

Suppose that two delinquency prevention experiments are conducted and that these are identical except for sample size. Presume that in the first experiment, 20 youth are randomly assigned to Method A and 20 to Method B and that in the second experiment, 200 are randomly assigned to each of these methods. Presume also that outcomes are identical in terms of the percentage of success (no delinquent act committed during follow-up period) and failure (one or more delinquent acts committed). Let us say that in both experiments, 80% of youth in Method A and 60% in Method B experience successful outcomes. Both studies then evidence the same size of association ($D\% = 80\% - 60\% = 20\%$) between method and outcome. The task of the $\chi^2$ test is to determine whether the association between method and outcome is statistically significant, that is, unlikely due to chance alone. Table 20.5 presents contingency tables for the two experiments. The rows labeled "Success" and "Failure" apply to both experiments.

Although the size of association in the two experiments is identical, the obtained $\chi^2$ differs. In the first (smaller) experiment, $\chi^2$ equals 1.90. With 1 $df$, this $\chi^2$ is not statistically significant ($p = .17$) and, thus, we fail to reject the null. On the other hand, the obtained $\chi^2$ in the second (larger) experiment equals 19.0, a value that is significant ($p = .0001$) and leads to rejection.

The differing values of $\chi^2$, despite the same size of association, demonstrate that the $\chi^2$ test is *not* a measure of size of association. It *is* a test of statistical significance. As such, its function is to determine the probability that study results are caused by chance. The probabilities (values of $p$) resulting from significance tests are highly dependent on sample size. Other things being equal, the greater the sample size, the greater the likelihood of rejecting the null. Or, to repeat a point from Chapter 16, the greater the sample size, the greater the statistical power (see Section 16.4).

TABLE 20.5 ■ Effect of Sample Size on Chi-Square Test of Independence

| Outcome | First Experiment | | Second Experiment | |
|---|---|---|---|---|
|  | Method A | Method B | Method A | Method B |
| **Success** | 16 | 12 | 160 | 120 |
|  | 80% | 60% | 80% | 60% |
| **Failure** | 4 | 8 | 40 | 80 |
|  | 20% | 40% | 20% | 40% |
| Number (total) | 20 | 20 | 200 | 200 |

## 20.7 ■ CHAPTER SUMMARY

Based on the $\chi^2$ distribution, the $\chi^2$ *test of independence* examines association between categorical variables. It may be the most used of all significance tests.

Its null is always nondirectional and may be stated in two ways: (a) variables are unassociated or (b) percentages are equal. It is a one-tailed test. Its rejection region is in the upper tail.

The $\chi^2$ test of independence examines whether *observed proportions* differ from *expected proportions* by more than would be expected from chance alone. A cell's *expected column proportion* is given by $p_e$ = (row margin total) / N. All cells in a given row have identical expected column proportions.

The preferred hand calculation formula uses *observed* and *expected frequencies*, $\chi^2 = \Sigma(f_o - f_e)^2/f_e$. To compute a cell's expected frequency, multiply its row margin total by its column margin total and divide by N.

With the exception of 2 × 2 tables, the $\chi^2$ test of independence yields accurate probabilities when the average observed frequency is at least four and the minimum expected frequency is at least one. For a 2 × 2 table, the average observed frequency should be at least six and the minimum expected frequency should be at least one.

The researcher rejects the null when the obtained $\chi^2$ is greater than or equal to the critical value of $\chi^2$ in the chi-square distribution table. Degrees of freedom equal $(R - 1)(C - 1)$.

With two dichotomous variables (2 × 2 table), one can obtain the probability (p) for a directional pair by dividing the p given by the $\chi^2$ test in half. With two dichotomous variables, *Fisher's exact test* is a good alternative to the $\chi^2$ test when the cell frequency guidelines are not met.

The $\chi^2$ test of independence is not recommended for examining directional associations. The $\chi^2$ test is a statistical significance test, not a measure of size of association.

## 20.8 ■ PROBLEMS AND QUESTIONS

### Section 20.2

1. *Respond true or false to each of the following:*
    a. When compared with most significance tests, the $\chi^2$ test of independence is seldom used.
    b. When percentages differ (as in Table 20.1), variables are associated in the study sample.
    c. The presence of association in the study sample is sufficient for concluding that there is also association in the population from which the sample was randomly selected.

### Section 20.3

2. (*True or False*) The hypothesis pair for the $\chi^2$ test is nondirectional.

3. The null states either (a) two variables are _____ or (b) percentages are _____.

4. When the null is true, the researcher expects the obtained $\chi^2$ to be fairly close to the number of _____ _____ _____. When the null is false, the researcher expects the obtained $\chi^2$ to be _____ than the number of degrees of freedom.

5. A cell's expected proportion is the proportion predicted given a _____ null.

6. Calculate degrees of freedom for $\chi^2$ tests based on contingency tables of the following sizes:
   a. $3 \times 4$
   b. $5 \times 2$
   c. $6 \times 4$
   d. $2 \times 2$

7. (*True or False*) All cells in a given row of a contingency table have identical expected column proportions.

8. Examine Table 6.2 in Chapter 6 (Section 6.2). What is the expected column proportion for
   a. each cell in the "Disrupted" row
   b. each cell in the "Stable" row

**Section 20.4**

9. One hundred students attend a school of social work. Fifty sign up to take part in a workshop on sexuality. Of the 50 students who take part in the workshop, 40 agree and 10 disagree with the statement "Sexual orientation is *not* predominantly a matter of choice." Of the 50 who do not attend, 32 agree and 18 disagree. Your task is to conduct a $\chi^2$ test of independence to examine whether workshop attendance (or lack thereof) and opinion (agree vs. any other response) on the statement have a statistically significant association.
   a. State the (nondirectional) null in terms of association or the lack thereof.
   b. State the (nondirectional) null using percentages. Do so by stating the percentages in the two attendance categories (attend and not attend) that agree with the statement.
   c. What are the expected frequencies for each cell? Hint: You may want to draw a $2 \times 2$ contingency table. Make "attend" (the independent variable) the column variable (the variable at the top of the table).
   d. Is the minimum expected frequency sufficient for conducting the $\chi^2$ test? (Note that two dichotomous variables are involved)?
   e. Although they are not used in computation of $\chi^2$, what are the observed column proportions? (Column proportions sum to 1.00 down the columns.)
   f. Are the two variables associated or independent in the sample?
   g. Although they are not used in computation, what are the expected column proportions? (These proportions sum to 1.00 down the columns.)
   h. Are the expected proportions identical to the observed proportions?
   i. What is the value of the obtained $\chi^2$? (*Calculate.*)
   j. How many degrees of freedom are there?
   k. Presuming that the .05 statistical significance level was selected, what is the critical value of $\chi^2$?
   l. Express results succinctly as they might appear, for instance, in a journal article.
   m. What is your decision regarding the null? The alternative?
   n. (*Yes or No*) Is this result a statistically significant one at the .05 level?
   o. (*True or False*) The probability that the study sample result is due to chance alone is less than .05.

**p.** (*True or False*) Chance alone is a highly unlikely explanation for the difference between expected and observed percentages.

**q.** (*True or False*) Chance alone is a highly unlikely explanation for the study sample result.

**r.** (*True or False*) One can be 95% (or more) confident that the association in the sample is not caused by chance alone.

**s.** (*True or False*) One can be confident that the null is indeed true.

10. Presume the same situation as in the prior question except that all numbers are doubled. Hence, of 100 students who take the workshop, 80 agree and 20 disagree with the statement. Of 100 students who do not take the workshop, 64 agree and 36 disagree. The value of $\chi^2$ computes now to 6.35 (double the value of 3.175 in the prior question). We continue to use the .05 level. Respond to the following questions:

   **a.** (*True or False*) The study sample has been randomly selected from a wider population.

   **b.** (*True or False*) Because the sample has not been randomly selected from a wider population, according to this text, a significance test should not be conducted.

   **c.** What is your decision regarding the null? The alternative? (Hint: the obtained $\chi^2$ equals 6.35.)

   **d.** Is the result statistically significant at the .05 level?

   **e.** (*True or False*) Chance alone is an unlikely explanation for the study sample result.

   **f.** (*True or False*) One can be 95% (or more) confident that the association in the sample is not due to chance alone.

   **g.** (*True or False*) One can be confident that the null is false.

   **h.** (*True or False*) The study provides strong evidence that the null is false.

   **i.** May one appropriately conclude that workshop attendance *causes* greater agreement? Why or why not?

TABLE 20.6 ■ Employment Status Five Years After Graduation by Concentration

| | Concentration | | | | |
|---|---|---|---|---|---|
| Employment Status | Children and Family | Mental Health | Health | Community Practice | Total |
| Employed in social work | 40 | 34 | 30 | 46 | 150 |
| Not employed in social work | 10 | 16 | 10 | 14 | 50 |
| Total | 50 | 50 | 40 | 60 | 200 |

11. Table 20.6 presents hypothetical data on the possible association between social work graduate students' choice of concentration and their employment status vis-à-vis social work 5 years after graduation. The value of $\chi^2$ (the obtained $\chi^2$) for this example computes to 2.06. Respond to the following:

   **a.** State the null in terms of the presence versus the absence of association.

   **b.** Calculate the percentage employed in social work for each of the four concentration areas. (These are the observed percentages for the "Employed in social work" row.)

c. What is the expected column proportion for each cell in the "Employed in social work" row? In the "Not employed in social work" row?

d. In the sample, are the variables associated?

e. Just from eyeballing the table, how would you characterize the size/strength of association? (Hint: Examine the size of the differences between the observed percentages.)

f. How many degrees of freedom are there?

g. Given that alpha (the significance level) is set to .05, what is the critical value of $\chi^2$?

h. What is your decision regarding the null? The alternative?

i. (*True or False*) Chance alone is a highly unlikely explanation for the difference in percentages in the different concentration areas?

j. (*True or False*) One can be confident that the null is true.

k. Is the obtained $\chi^2$ statistically significant at the .05 level?

l. (*True or False*) The data in Table 20.6 provide strong evidence that the null is false.

m. Express results succinctly, as they might appear in a journal article.

12. Fifty children who are placed in foster care participated in an experiment. Twenty-five are randomly assigned to a program that emphasizes enhanced extended family involvement. Twenty-five are randomly assigned to traditional intervention services. Twenty children in the enhanced family involvement group are reunited with their families within a year. Twelve children in the traditional group are reunited within this time. The .05 level is used. Table 20.7 (absent percentages) summarizes the data.

TABLE 20.7 ■ Association of Type of Program to Reuniting With Family

|  | Enhanced Family Involvement | Traditional |  |
|---|---|---|---|
| **Reunited within a year** | 20 | 12 | 32 |
| **Not reunited within a year** | 5 | 13 | 18 |
|  | 25 | 25 | 50 |

Respond to the following:

a. State the (nondirectional) null (in terms of association or the lack thereof).

b. State the (nondirectional) null using percentages. Do so by stating the percentages in the two groups (family involvement and traditional) who are reunited.

c. What are the expected frequencies for each cell?

d. Is the minimum expected frequency sufficient for conducting the $\chi^2$ test? (Note that two dichotomous variables are involved).

e. What is the average observed frequency? Is it sufficient for conducting the test?

f. Although they are not used in computation of $\chi^2$, what are the observed column proportions? (Column proportions sum to 1.00 down the columns.)

g. Although they are not used in computation, what are the expected column proportions? These proportions sum to 100 down the columns.

    **h.** Are the expected percentages identical to the observed percentages?

    **i.** Are the two variables associated or unassociated in the sample?

    **j.** What is the value of the obtained $\chi^2$? (*Calculate.*)

    **k.** How many degrees of freedom are there?

    **l.** Presuming that the .05 statistical significance level was selected, what is the critical value of $\chi^2$?

    **m.** What is your decision regarding the null? The alternative?

    **n.** Given a true null, the probability obtaining the study sample result or an even more extreme result is less than .05.

    **o.** (*True or False*) The probability that the study sample result is due to chance alone is less than .05.

    **p.** (*True or False*) Chance alone is a highly unlikely explanation for the difference between expected and observed percentages.

    **q.** (*True or False*) Chance alone is a highly unlikely explanation for the study sample result.

    **r.** (*True or False*) One can be 95% (or more) confident that the association in the sample is not due to chance alone.

    **s.** (*True or False*) One can be 95% confident that the null is false.

    **t.** (*Yes or No*) Is this result statistically significant at the .05 level?

    **u.** Express results succinctly as they might appear, for instance, in a journal article.

## Section 20.5

**13.** (*True or False*) The $\chi^2$ test of independence is highly recommended for examining directional association between categorical variables.

**14.** When the minimum frequency guidelines are not met in a 2 × 2 table (two dichotomous variables), _____ _____ _____ is a good alternative to the $\chi^2$ test of independence.

## Section 20.6

**15.** *Respond true or false to each of the following:*

    **a.** The $\chi^2$ test of independence is a measure of size of association.

    **b.** The $\chi^2$ test of independence is a statistical significance test.

    **c.** Other things being equal, the greater the sample size, the greater the likelihood of _____ the null.

# ANALYSIS OF VARIANCE

## 21.1 ■ CHAPTER OVERVIEW

Chapter 21 presents a key significance test for assessing differences between means and *analysis of variance* (*ANOVA*). It covers ANOVA theory, the *mean square within*, the *mean square between*, and the *F distribution*. We also examine *multiple comparison procedures* and close with a discussion of statistical *fishing*.

## 21.2 ■ INTRODUCTION TO ANALYSIS OF VARIANCE

The independent samples *t* test assesses differences in means between two independent samples. **Analysis of variance**, also known as **ANOVA**, assesses differences in means between two or more independent samples. Although ANOVA may be used when there are only two samples, most researchers prefer the *t* test in this circumstance. Hence, its typical use is with three or more samples. With two samples, a two-tailed independent samples *t* test (equal variance formula) and ANOVA yield identical probabilities. Although they appear different, these two tests are mathematically equivalent.

## 21.3 ■ THE LOGIC OF ANALYSIS OF VARIANCE

### 21.3.1 ■ Hypothesis and Overview

Our discussion uses the terms sample and group interchangeably. ANOVA's null states that all study samples (groups) have been selected from populations with equal means. In statistical symbols,

$$\mu_1 = \mu_2 = \ldots \mu_J$$

where $\mu_1$ is the population mean for the first group and $\mu_2$ is that for the second. The subscript $J$ stands for the last group. For instance, given five groups, $J = 5$. The ellipsis dots (. . .) convey the unlisted groups. For instance, with five groups, the null is:

$$\mu_1 = \mu_2 = \mu_3 = \mu_4 = \mu_5$$

The alternative hypothesis states that all population means are not equal.

Even when the null is true, group means can differ (vary) because of sampling error. ANOVA informs the researcher regarding whether the differences (variability) in group means in the sample (a) may be due to sampling error alone or (b) more likely reflect that all population means are not equal.

As our discussion proceeds, recall from Chapter 4 (Section 4.8) that the variance equals the standard deviation squared and, in turn, the standard deviation is the square root of the variance. The sample variance is symbolized by $s^2$ and the population variance by $\sigma^2$.

## 21.3.2 ▨ Two Estimates of the Population Variance

ANOVA generates two estimates of the population variance, $\sigma^2$. These estimates are key to its theory and logic.

ANOVA assumes that groups are selected from populations with equal variances, for instance, given five groups, that $\sigma_1^2 = \sigma_2^2 = \sigma_3^2 = \sigma_4^2 = \sigma_5^2$. Our discussion assumes equal group sizes and uses $n$ to convey that size. For instance, with five groups: $n_1 = n_2 = n_3 = n_4 = n_5$.

ANOVA's first estimate of the population variance, the $MS_W$: As the variance in a random sample ($s^2$) is the best estimate of the variance in the population ($\sigma^2$) from which that sample was selected (see Chapter 12, Sections 12.5 and 12.6), ANOVA's first estimate of $\sigma^2$ is simply the mean (average) variance in the groups: $MS_W = \Sigma\, s^2/J$, where $MS_W$ is the **mean square within**, $s^2$ is the variance of each group, and $J$ is the number of groups. The $MS_W$ is based on the variances *within* each group.

ANOVA's second estimate of the population variance, the $MS_B$: Given a true null ($\mu_1 = \mu_2 = \ldots\, \mu_J$), the means of the groups form a miniature sampling distribution of the mean (a miniature sampling distribution of $\overline{X}$). For instance, with five groups, the group means form a sampling distribution composed of five means. Recall from Chapter 13 (Section 13.3.1) that the researcher estimates the standard deviation of the sampling distribution of $\overline{X}$ ($s_{\overline{X}}$, the standard error of the mean) by dividing the standard deviation of the study sample ($s$) by the sample size ($n$): $s_{\overline{X}} = s/\sqrt{n}$. Let us carry out some algebra on this equation:

First, let us square both sides: $s_{\overline{X}}^2 = s^2/n$

Next, let us multiply both sides by $n$: $ns_{\overline{X}}^2 = s^2$

Finally, let us reverse the left and right sides: $s^2 = ns_{\overline{X}}^2$

As discussed earlier, $s^2$ provides the best estimate of the population variance. Thus, our second estimate of the population variance is: $MS_B = ns_{\overline{X}}^2$ where $MS_B$ is the **mean square between**, $n$ is the sample size, and $s_{\overline{X}}^2$ is the variance of the sample means (the variance of the miniature sampling distribution). Expressed in words, one estimates the population variance by multiplying the variance of the sample means by the sample size. The $MS_B$ is based on the variance *between* the group means.

When the null of equal population means is true, the only factor that causes the $MS_W$ and the $MS_B$ to differ is sampling error. Hence, one expects them to have quite similar values.

Suppose instead that the null is false, that is, that some population means differ. Differences *between* population means do not affect the $MS_W$ as this estimate is based on the variances *within* each group. On the other hand, differences between population means cause the group means to vary more (to be more spread out) than would be expected from sampling error alone. The $MS_B$ is based on the variance *between* the group means. When population means differ, the expected variance (spread) of the group means is greater and, thus, so also is the expected value of the $MS_B$.

In sum, when the null is true, one expects the $MS_B$ and the $MS_W$ to be similar in size. When it is false, one expects the $MS_B$ to be larger than the $MS_W$. This is the essential logic of ANOVA.

### 21.3.3 ■ The *F* Distribution

How much larger than the $MS_W$ does the $MS_B$ need to be to reject the null? The **F distribution** addresses this question. One calculates an **F ratio (F)** by dividing one estimate of population variance by another. In ANOVA, one divides the $MS_B$ by the $MS_W$:

$$F = \frac{MS_B}{MS_W} \tag{21.1}$$

When the null is true, we expect the $MS_B$ and the $MS_W$ to be similar in size, and thus we expect the *F* ratio to be close to 1.00. When the null is false, we expect the $MS_B$ to be larger than the $MS_W$, and thus we expect the *F* ratio to be larger than 1.00.

Like the *t* distribution and the $\chi^2$ distribution, the *F* distribution is not a single distribution but instead is a family of distributions that takes on different shapes and has different critical values depending on the degrees of freedom. Each *F* distribution has two different degrees of freedom, one corresponding to its numerator and one to its denominator. In ANOVA, degrees of freedom for the $MS_B$ (the numerator) equals the number of groups (*J*) minus 1: $df = J - 1$. Degrees of freedom for the $MS_W$ (the denominator) equals the total number of cases in the full study sample (*N*) minus the number of groups: $df = N - J$. Suppose that a study sample (*N* = 60) comprises six groups with 10 persons in each group: *df* for the $MS_B = 6 - 1 = 5$; *df* for the $MS_W = 60 - 6 = 54$. See Glass and Hopkins (1996, p. 430) for more on the *F* distribution.

## 21.4 ■ PARTICULARS OF ANALYSIS OF VARIANCE

### 21.4.1 ■ Assumptions and Level of Measurement

Formally, ANOVA assumes that samples have been selected from normally distributed populations. It is robust to this assumption. Given that $n \geq 10$ in each group, it yields accurate results whenever no group possesses a strong or extreme skew. Given that $n \geq 20$ in each group, results are accurate whenever no group possesses an extreme skew. Given $n \geq 60$ in each group, it yields accurate results even in the presence of extreme skew. See Glass and Hopkins for more on necessary sample size (1996).[1]

In addition to the normality assumption, ANOVA assumes that the populations from which samples have been selected have equal variances. This assumption, presented first in Chapter 18 (Section 18.2.3), is termed the *equality* (homogeneity) *of variances assumption*. Given equal sample sizes, ANOVA is robust to this assumption. In other words, with equal samples sizes, ANOVA provides accurate results even when population variances differ.

With unequal sample sizes, ANOVA is not robust to the equality of population variances assumption. The greater the disparity in sample sizes, the less robust it is. ANOVA is typically carried out by computer software programs, which provide a formal test of the equality of variances assumption.

When sample sizes are equal, because ANOVA is robust in this situation, the researcher may use ANOVA even when the test of the equality of variances rejects the null of equal variances. When sample sizes differ, the researcher should use ANOVA when the test does not reject the null of equal variances and use an alternative to ANOVA when it does reject it. The SPSS package, for instance, provides the Brown-Forsythe and Welch alternatives. The dependent variable should be at the interval/ratio level of measurement.[2]

### 21.4.2 ■ Hypothesis Pair

ANOVA's hypothesis pair is nondirectional. Expressed in words:

Null:        The means of all populations from which samples have been selected are equal.

Alternative:  All population means are not equal.

Expressing the null in symbols:

$$H_0 = \mu_1 = \mu_2 = \mu_3 = \ldots \mu_J$$

Recall that the hypothesis pair for the independent samples $t$ test can be either directional or nondirectional, an advantage when there are two groups.

### 21.4.3 ■ Critical Values and Decision Rules

Given the easy availability of computer software, we will not carry out ANOVA calculations. However, we will use a table of critical values of the $F$ distribution, Table A.5 in Appendix A.

To use Table A.5, find the critical value that corresponds to (a) the degrees of freedom for the $MS_B$ (numerator; listed across the top), (b) the degrees of freedom for the $MS_W$ (denominator; listed down the left column), and (c) the selected significance level ($\alpha$). When the exact number of degrees of freedom is not listed for the $MS_W$ (denominator), use the closest smaller number. The decision rule is to fail to reject (accept) the null when the obtained $F$ is less than the value of $F$ in the $F$ distribution table, Table A.5. Reject the null when the obtained $F$ is greater than or equal to the value of $F$ in the $F$ distribution table, Table A.5.

Although its hypothesis pair is nondirectional, the significance test for ANOVA, based on the $F$ distribution, is one tailed. The rejection region is located in the upper tail.

## 21.5 ■ CALCULATION EXAMPLE USING SPSS

Our example uses two variables from the special-needs adoption study (Rosenthal & Groze, 1992). The three family ethnicity groups are as follows: Group 1, minority inracial (minority parents who adopt a minority child of the same race with at least one parent); Group 2, White inracial (White parents who adopt a White child); and Group 3, transracial (White parents who adopt a minority child). Severity of behavioral problems is measured by a behavior problem scale filled out by parents. The higher the score, the greater the severity of problems (Achenbach, 1991).

The current example uses the SPSS statistical software program to assess whether mean behavior problems scores differ significantly among the three family ethnicity groups. The null is that all three groups have equal means: $H_0$: $\mu_1 = \mu_2 = \mu_3$. We will use the .01 significance level.

Table 21.1 presents the SPSS output. The "Descriptives" table conveys that the mean behavior problems score is highest in the White inracial group, intermediate in the transracial group, and lowest in the minority inracial group. Observe that the standard deviations in all three groups are similar.

TABLE 21.1 ■ SPSS-Generated ANOVA Results: Behavior Problems by Family Ethnicity Group

**Test of Homogeneity of Variances**

| | Levene Statistic | *df*1 | *df*2 | Sig. |
|---|---|---|---|---|
| Behavior problems score | .232 | 2 | 693 | .793 |

**Descriptives**

| | | | N | Mean | Std. Deviation | Std. Error | 95% Confidence Interval for Mean Lower Bound | 95% Confidence Interval for Mean Upper Bound |
|---|---|---|---|---|---|---|---|---|
| Behavior problems score | Family ethnicity | Minority, inracial | 208 | 31.13 | 25.80 | 1.79 | 27.60 | 34.66 |
| | | White-inracial | 433 | 40.21 | 26.23 | 1.26 | 37.74 | 42.69 |
| | | Transracial | 55 | 36.20 | 26.07 | 3.52 | 29.15 | 43.25 |
| | | Total | 696 | 37.18 | 26.37 | 1.00 | 35.22 | 39.14 |

**ANOVA**

| | | Sum of Squares | df | Mean Square | F | Sig. |
|---|---|---|---|---|---|---|
| Behavior problems score | Between groups | 11648.4 | 2 | 5824.2 | 8.559 | .000 |
| | Within groups | 471586.7 | 693 | 680.5 | | |
| | Total | 483235.2 | 695 | | | |

As would be expected given this similarity, the test of equality of population variances (see the "Test of Homogeneity of Variances" table) results in acceptance of the null of equal population variances: $H_0$: $\sigma_2^1 = \sigma_2^2 = \sigma_3^2$, $p = .793$. As the equality of variances assumption is met, our ANOVA results are accurate even with the unequal sample sizes. Had we rejected the null of equal variances, we would have used either the Brown-Forsythe or Welch alternatives provided by SPSS.

The table labeled "ANOVA" is typically termed an *ANOVA table*. It will be helpful to see how some of the numbers in this table were derived. The ANOVA table lists a sum of squares between groups and a sum of squares within groups. Without demonstrating ANOVA calculations, these terms are difficult to define, so I will simply state that the *sum of squares between* is used in calculating the $MS_B$, and the *sum of squares within* is used in calculating the $MS_W$. (See Rosenthal, 2000, pp. 395–397 for information on the sums of squares.) You should know that the $MS_B$ equals the sum of squares between ($SS_B$) divided by its degrees of freedom.

$$MS_B = \frac{SS_B}{df \text{ for } MS_B}$$

(21.2)

The $MS_W$ equals the sum of squares within $(SS_w)$ divided by its degrees of freedom.[3]

$$MS_W = \frac{SS_W}{df \text{ for } MS_W} \qquad\qquad (21.3)$$

Thus, the researcher calculates the appropriate mean square (between or within) by dividing the corresponding sum of squares by the degrees of freedom.

Continuing to focus on the ANOVA table, we direct our attention to the "*df*" column, which presents degrees of freedom. The degrees of freedom listed in the "Between groups" row is for the $MS_B$. This formula is $df = J - 1$, where $J$ is the number of groups: $df = 3 - 1 = 2$. The degrees of freedom listed in the "Within groups" row is that for the $MS_W$. This formula is $df = N - J$. The study sample size $(N)$ is 696. Hence, $df = 696 - 3 = 693$.

Each mean square is computed by dividing its sum of squares by its degrees of freedom.

$$MS_B = (11648.4)/2 = 5824.4; MS_w = (471586.7)/693 = 680.5$$

Finally, SPSS computes the $F$ ratio by dividing the $MS_B$ by the $MS_W$:

$$F = (5824.2)/(680.5) = 8.559$$

As listed in the "Sig." column in the ANOVA table, given a true null, the probability of obtaining an $F$ of 8.559 is .000. Because this probability is less than the selected significance level $(\alpha = .01)$, we reject the null and accept the alternative. We conclude that the differences between the group means are unlikely to be due to chance alone and instead reflect real differences. These ANOVA results would be reported as $F(2,693) = 8.559, p = .000$.

This example carries out ANOVA with statistical software. Let us see also how we would use the table of critical values of $F$, Table A.5 in Appendix A. The pertinent information is $df$ for $MS_B = 2$, $df$ for $MS_W = 693$, $F = 8.559$, and significance level $(\alpha) = .01$. Recall that when the exact $df$ for the $MS_W$ is not listed, one uses the next smallest number in the table. This number is 250. The critical value listed in Table A.5 is 4.69. As the obtained $F$ exceeds the critical value, the null is rejected.

Our use of Table A.5 demonstrates again an advantage of software. Software programs list the exact probability $(p)$ associated with the study result, whereas tables convey only whether this probability is greater than or less than the selected significance level. For greater detail on ANOVA, see Glass and Hopkins (1996), Toothaker and Miller (1996), or many other statistics books.

## 21.6 ■ MULTIPLE COMPARISON PROCEDURES

Suppose that an ANOVA with five groups yields statistically significant results. This informs us that it is unlikely that all population means are equal. The next step is to identify the particular pair(s) of means that differ to a statistically significant degree. One approach for doing so is to conduct an independent samples $t$ test for each pair. A disadvantage of this approach is that the number of tests needed increases rapidly with the number of groups. The number of $t$ tests necessary to compare all possible pairs of means is $[J(J - 1)]/2$, where $J$ is the number of groups. With five groups, for instance, 10 $t$ tests are needed: $[5(5 - 1)]/2 = 10$. As you recall, the probability of a Type I error, the error of rejecting a true null, equals the probability associated with the statistical significance level $(\alpha, \text{alpha})$. For instance, when the .05 level is used, this probability is .05. This probability applies to *each* statistical test, that is, to each comparison between means. (See Chapter 15, Section 15.10 to review Type 1 errors.)

When a series of comparisons is carried out, the probability of a Type I error for at least one comparison in the series is greater than that for any single comparison. For instance, given five groups and therefore 10 comparisons and using the .05 level (and also assuming a true null, that is, that all population means are equal), the probability of a Type I error on at least one comparison equals approximately 0.40.[4,5]

In sum, when multiple *t* tests are conducted, the probability of making at least one Type I error can greatly exceed the chosen significance level. Multiple comparison procedures were developed to deal with this problem. In essence, **multiple comparison** procedures adjust the risk of Type I error so that it applies to the whole series of comparisons rather than to each particular one. For instance, given five groups and therefore 10 possible comparisons, using an appropriate multiple comparison procedure, the researcher could set the risk of Type I error to .05 for the whole series of 10 comparisons. (Given that this risk is .05 for the series, it is less than this for any single comparison.)

Multiple comparison procedures reduce the likelihood that a comparison will reach significance simply because of sampling error and are clearly preferable to conducting multiple *t* tests. Most statistical packages have easy-to-use multiple comparison procedures. Each different multiple comparison procedure adjusts for the increased risk of Type 1 error in a slightly different way. Some of the better known multiple comparisons are the Student-Newman-Keuls (SNK), Tukey, and Bonferroni procedures. See Toothaker and Miller (1996, p. 483–512) for further discussion. In my opinion, the SNK procedure offers a well-balanced way of adjusting for the risk of Type I error, and thus I recommend it.

## 21.7 ■ FISHING EXPEDITIONS

### 21.7.1 ■ The Dangers of Fishing

Regarding comparisons between means, the prior section stated that "when a series of comparisons is carried out, the probability of a Type I error for at least one comparison in the series is greater than that for any single comparison." This same concept can be extended to all statistical tests and to research studies in general.

Suppose that in a given study, a researcher has five independent variables and three dependent variables. In such a study, she has 15 possible combinations of independent variables with dependent variables ($5 \times 3 = 15$ combinations). Thus, to examine each combination, she would need to conduct 15 statistical significance tests. Presume that the null is true for each combination. Stated differently, presume that, in the study population, each independent variable is unassociated with each dependent variable. Suppose that the .05 level is used for each test. We know that the probability that any given test in the series will yield a statistically significant result equals .05. This is the probability of a Type I error.

Another question is "What is the probability that *at least one* of the 15 tests will be significant?" This probability computes to about .54.[6] This example points out a key concept: When a series of statistical significance tests is carried out, the probability of a Type I error for *at least one* test in the series is greater than that for any single test.[7]

The basic message is that if enough tests are conducted, sooner or later one or more will achieve significance. Conducting many tests searching for a statistically significant result is sometimes referred to as a "fishing expedition" or, more simply, as *fishing*. Most researchers discourage such statistical fishing. In the worst cases, those who fish simply probe associations between all possible variables without guidance from theory and without critical thinking. Sooner or later, inevitably, they "catch a fish"—that is, they find a statistically significant association.

The number of tests conducted is only part of the problem. In addition to carrying out many tests, researchers sometimes selectively report only those test results that are statistically significant. In such a situation, the reader does not know that the reported significant results are the end product of a fishing expedition.

When a given study involves only a single significance test and the null is rejected at the .05 level, one can be 95% confident that it is false. When a study involves a reasonably small number of tests and these are well planned and based on theory, the reader may have basic confidence in results (although one should recognize that the likelihood of a statistically significant finding increases with the number of tests). When a researcher carries out many tests with scant attention to guiding theory—and particularly, when he or she reports results selectively—the reader should be skeptical. Here, the actual likelihood that a particular significant result is due to chance greatly exceeds the stated significance level. In such a situation (given the .05 level), the reader should have much *less than* 95% confidence that the null is false.

### 21.7.2 ■ The Dangers of Not Fishing

Having just discussed the dangers of fishing, now is a good time to point out problems associated with the opposite orientation, that is, of *only* investigating associations articulated by prior theory. The problem with such an orientation is akin to putting on blinders, that is, to seeing only what one wants to see. Suppose that a research study has three variables: *A*, *B*, and *C*. Suppose that the study's purpose is to assess the association of *A* and *B*, which is theorized to be large and highly significant. Suppose that *C* was considered an unimportant variable, perhaps one included in the study only as an afterthought. Now, suppose that study results show (a) no association between *A* and *B* and (b) a large, significant (and unexpected) association between *A* and *C*. If a researcher adopted the strictest possible stance against fishing, she would not report the association between *A* and *C*. Indeed, operating from such a stance, she would never even discover this association because her sole focus would be the association between *A* and *B*.

Many scientific discoveries involve discovery of the unexpected, and fishing can be a route toward such discovery. Indeed, with powerful computers that effortlessly crank out numbers and tests, it seems foolish not to exploit the full information in one's data set. Clearly, the situation today contrasts markedly with the first half of the 20th century when each significance test was computed by hand. On the other hand, excessive fishing without attention to theory calls to mind the phrase "garbage in, garbage out." So, the best approach is to find the right balance between (a) the key ideas conveyed by theory and (b) some amount of fishing.[8]

## 21.8 ■ CHAPTER SUMMARY

*Analysis of variance (ANOVA)* examines differences in means between two or more independent samples. The null states that all groups have been selected from populations with equal means. The hypothesis pair is nondirectional.

ANOVA generates two estimates of the population variance, the *mean square within* ($MS_W$), based on variances *within* groups, and the *mean square between* ($MS_B$), based on the variance *between* group means. When the $MS_W$ and the $MS_B$ have similar values, this suggests that differences between group means may be due to sampling error alone. When the $MS_B$ is considerably larger than the $MS_W$, this suggests that population means may indeed differ, in other words, that the null may be false.

ANOVA is based on the *F distribution*: $F = MS_B / MS_W$. When the null is true, one expects *F* to be close to 1.00. When it is false, one expects *F* to be larger than 1.00. The researcher fails to reject the null when the obtained *F* is less than the critical value in the *F* distribution table, Table A.5. She rejects it when the obtained *F* equals or exceeds this value.

To calculate the $MS_W$, divide the sums of squares within ($SS_W$) by the degrees of freedom for the $MS_W$ ($N - J$). To calculate the $MS_B$, divide the sums of squares between ($SS_B$) by the degrees of freedom for the $MS_B$ ($J - 1$).

ANOVA assumes that populations are normally distributed and have equal variances. It is robust to the normality assumption. With equal sample sizes, ANOVA is robust to the equal variances assumption. With unequal sample sizes, it is not. When sample sizes are unequal and the null of equal population variances is rejected, the researcher uses an alternative ANOVA formula available in many statistical software packages.

When a researcher carries out a series of comparisons of pairs using independent samples *t* tests, the probability of committing a Type I error for at least one comparison in the series exceeds that for any single comparison. *Multiple comparison procedures* adjust the risk of Type I error so that this risk applies to the series of comparisons.

Conducting many statistical tests searching for one to achieve significance is sometimes termed *fishing*. When many different significance test results are reported, the reader should be skeptical. Finding a balance between analyses guided by theory and some amount of fishing is a pragmatic approach—one that this author recommends.

## 21.9 ■ PROBLEMS AND QUESTIONS

### Section 21.2

1.  (*True or False*) When there are two (independent) groups, ANOVA and a two-tailed independent samples *t* test (equal variances formula) yield identical probabilities.

### Section 21.3

2.  ANOVA's null states that all study samples (groups) were selected from populations with _____ _____.

3.  State the null for ANOVA using symbols.

4.  ANOVA assumes that the populations from which samples have been selected are _____ distributed and have _____ variances.

5.  ANOVA generates two estimates of the population _____. When the null is true, these estimates are expected to be approximately _____.

6.  The first estimate of the population variance based on the variance _____ each group is termed the _____ _____ _____ and is symbolized by ___.

7.  Given equal sample sizes, the $MS_W$ equals the _____ variance in the groups.

8.  The second estimate of the population variance based on the variance _____ groups, is termed the _____ _____ _____ and is symbolized by ___.

9.  Given a true null ($\mu_1 = \mu_2 = \ldots \mu_J$) and given equal sample sizes, the means of the groups form a miniature sampling distribution of the _____.

**10.** When sample sizes are equal, the mean square between is derived by multiplying the variance of the "miniature" sampling distribution of $\overline{X}$ by the _____ _____, that is, by ___ (symbol).

**11.** The $MS_W$ is based on the variance _____ groups. The $MS_B$ is based on the variance _____ groups.

**12.** (*True or False*) When the null is true, one expects the $MS_W$ and the $MS_B$ to have very different values.

**13.** Differences between population means cause the sample means to " _____ out" more than would be expected due to _____ _____ (chance) alone.

**14.** When the null is false, one expects the mean square _____ to be larger than the mean square _____.

**15.** ANOVA is based on the ___ distribution. When one divides the $MS_B$ by the $MS_W$, they form (calculate) an ___ _____.

**16.** When the null is true, one expects the $F$ ratio to equal approximately _____. When the null is false, one expects the $F$ ratio to be _____ than 1.00.

**17.** What is the formula for $F$ (the $F$ ratio)?

**18.** What is the formula for degrees of freedom for the $MS_B$?

**19.** What is the formula for degrees of freedom for the $MS_W$?

**20.** Indicate the degrees of freedom first for the $MS_B$ and second for the $MS_W$ for the following situations.
   **a.** $N = 40, J = 5$
   **b.** $N = 100, J = 3$
   **c.** $N = 28, J = 4$
   **d.** $N = 60, J = 3$
   **e.** $N = 200, J = 6$
   **f.** $N = 75, J = 5$

**21.** A given study has three groups each with $n = 10$. The variances of these groups are as follows: $s_1^2 = 8.0$, $s_2^2 = 9.0$, $s_3^2 = 7.0$.
   **a.** What is the average variance within the groups?
   **b.** If one assumes equal variances in the populations from which samples were selected, what is the best estimate of the population variance?
   **c.** What is the $MS_W$?
   **d.** What is the $df$ for the $MS_W$?

22. Given the provided information, compute $F$ for each situation.
    a. $MS_B = 3.3, MS_W = 2.2$
    b. $MS_B = 7.8, MS_W = 2.6$
    c. $MS_B = 6.0, MS_W = 8.0$
    d. $MS_B = 6.0, MS_W = 1.5$
    e. $MS_B = 12.0, MS_W = 1.5$
    f. $MS_B = 3.0, MS_W = 1.5$
    g. $MS_B = 1.5, MS_W = 1.5$

23. Indicate for each of the following $F$ ratios whether one should fail to reject (accept) or reject the null at (a) the .05 significance level and (b) the .01 level.
    a. $F = 5.83, df = 2\ (MS_B)$ and $30\ (MS_W)$
    b. $F = 5.03, df = 2\ (MS_B)$ and $30\ (MS_W)$
    c. $F = 1.97, df = 5\ (MS_B)$ and $50\ (MS_W)$
    d. $F = 2.97, df = 5\ (MS_B)$ and $50\ (MS_W)$
    e. $F = 3.97, df = 5\ (MS_B)$ and $50\ (MS_W)$
    f. $F = 2.81, df = 3\ (MS_B)$ and $20\ (MS_W)$
    g. $F = 2.81, df = 3\ (MS_B)$ and $60\ (MS_W)$

**Section 21.4**

24. *Respond true or false to each of the following:*
    a. ANOVA is robust to the assumption that samples be selected from normally distributed populations.
    b. Even when sample sizes differ considerably, ANOVA is robust to the equality of variances assumption.
    c. When sample sizes are equal, ANOVA is robust to the equality of variances assumption.
    d. The hypothesis pair in ANOVA is always nondirectional.

25. ANOVA, based on the $F$ distribution, is a _____-tailed test. The rejection region is located in the _____ tail.

26. Given that $n \geq 10$ in each group, it yields sufficiently accurate results whenever no group possesses a _____ or _____ skew. Given that $n \geq 20$ in each group, results are sufficiently accurate whenever no group possesses an _____ skew. Given $n \geq 60$ in each group, it yields sufficiently accurate results even in the presence of _____ skew.

**Section 21.5**

27. To calculate the $MS_W$, one divides the $SS_W$ by the _____ of _____ for the $MS_W$, that is, by _____ (formula for $df$).

28. To calculate the $MS_B$, one divides the $SS_B$ by the _____ of _____ for the $MS_B$, that is, by _____ (formula for $df$).

**29.** A given study has 5 groups with 21 persons in each group. Respond to the following:

  **a.** Fill in the missing information for the ANOVA table.

| Source | Sum of Squares | df | Mean Squares | F Ratio |
|---|---|---|---|---|
| Between groups | 360.00 | | | |
| Within groups | 4,500.00 | | | |

  **b.** When alpha equals .05, what is the critical value of $F$?
  **c.** What is your decision regarding the null? The alternative?
  **d.** (*True or False*) These results are highly unlikely to be due to chance alone.
  **e.** (*True or False*) These results provide strong evidence that the null is false.
  **f.** (*True or False*) We can be confident that the differences in group means are not due to chance alone.

**30.** The questions for this problem are based on the following incomplete ANOVA table.

| Source | Sum of Squares | df | Mean Squares | F Ratio |
|---|---|---|---|---|
| Between groups | 300.00 | 3 | | |
| Within groups | 1000.00 | 100 | | |

  **a.** How many groups were there in this study?
  **b.** Assuming equal sample sizes, what was the sample size in each group?
  **c.** What is the $MS_B$, the $MS_W$, and $F$?
  **d.** When $\alpha = .01$, what is the critical value of $F$?
  **e.** At the .01 level, what is your decision regarding the null? The alternative?
  **f.** (*Yes or No*) Are these results likely to be due to chance alone?
  **g.** (*Yes or No*) Do these results provide strong evidence that the null is false?

**Section 21.6**

**31.** Assuming a true null, the probability of a Type I error equals the probability associated with the significance level, that is, equals ___.

**32.** When a series of comparisons is carried out, the probability of a Type I error for at least one comparison in the series is _____ than that for any single comparison.

**33.** Assuming a true null for all of the different tests, when multiple independent samples $t$ tests are conducted with $\alpha = .05$, the probability that the null will be rejected for at least one test is _____ than .05.

**34.** What is the name of the set of procedures that addresses the problem of increased probability of Type I error when many comparisons of pairs of means are conducted?

**Section 21.7**

**35.** *Respond true or false to each of the following:*

    **a.** (Assuming a true null for each of the tests), when many different significance tests are conducted, the probability of rejecting the null on at least one test exceeds that probability for any given (single) test.

    **b.** In general, one should be more skeptical when results of many varied tests are reported than when the result of a single, planned-for test is reported?

    **c.** This text advocates that researchers should *never* go fishing.

**36.** In your own words, what is/are the advantage(s) of fishing?

# MORE SIGNIFICANCE TESTS AND REASONING WITH TEST RESULTS

## 22.1 ■ CHAPTER OVERVIEW

Chapter 22 covers a broad range of content. It begins with the *significance test of Pearson's* r and presentation of a *correlation matrix*. Next, it demonstrates that the hypothesis testing model provides flexible rather than rigid guidelines and discusses how information from confidence intervals complements that from significance tests. It presents the distinction between *parametric* and *nonparametric* significance tests. Key nonparametric tests include the *Mann-Whitney U test*, the *Kruskal-Wallis test*, and *McNemar's test*. It introduces *single-case designs* and discusses statistical analyses of these designs. It demonstrates that statistical procedures are often carried out in qualitative research studies. Chapter 22 closes with an example that integrates many data analysis concepts presented to this point.

## 22.2 ■ STATISTICAL SIGNIFICANCE TEST OF PEARSON'S *r*

### 22.2.1 ■ Basic Logic

The Pearson correlation coefficient, $r$, measures the degree of linear association between two numeric variables. The nondirectional null hypothesis for the **significance test of Pearson's *r*** states that correlation between two variables in the population from which the study sample has been selected equals 0.00. The population correlation is symbolized by $\rho$ (*rho*, pronounced as in "row" your boat). Even when $\rho = 0.00$, due to sampling error, $r$ (the correlation in the study sample) differs from 0.00. For a nondirectional pair, the value of $p$ for a test of Pearson's $r$ conveys, given a true null ($\rho = 0.00$), the probability of obtaining an $r$ with an absolute value that is as large as or even larger than the $r$ in the study sample. The test of Pearson's $r$ is one of the two or three most frequently conducted statistical tests.

### 22.2.2 ■ Assumptions and Levels of Measurement

The test of $r$ presumes interval/ratio level measurement. It assumes that both variables are normally distributed in the population from which the sample is selected but is robust to this assumption. Even for strongly skewed distributions, it yields accurate results for samples as small as about 15 (see Havlicek & Peterson, 1977). The test of $r$ detects linear (straight line) relationships and, thus, is not appropriate for curvilinear relationships (see Chapter 8, Section 8.7).

### 22.2.3 ■ Hypothesis Pair

Both nondirectional and directional hypothesis pairs may be formulated. The nondirectional hypothesis states:

Null:            The correlation in the population from which the study sample was selected equals 0.00.

Alternative:  The correlation in the population from which the study sample was selected does not equal 0.00.

Using symbols, the nondirectional pair is: $H_0: \rho = 0$;  $H_1: \rho \neq 0$.

Two sets of directional hypothesis pairs—one for each direction—may be stated:

$$H_0: \rho \leq 0, \quad H_1: \rho > 0; \quad \text{and } H_0: \rho \geq 0, \quad H_1: \rho < 0.$$

### 22.2.4 ■ Decision Rules and Degrees of Freedom

When the hypothesis pair is nondirectional, the test of $r$ is two-tailed. In this case:

Fail to reject (accept) the null if the absolute value of the obtained $r$ is less than the $r$ in the table of critical values of $r$, Table A.6 in Appendix A.

Reject the null if the absolute value of the obtained $r$ is greater than or equal to the $r$ in Table A.6.

When the hypothesis pair is directional, the test of $r$ is one-tailed. When the alternative hypothesis states greater than, the rejection region is in the upper tail. In this case:

Fail to reject (accept) the null if the obtained $r$ is less than the $r$ in Table A.6 in Appendix A.

Reject the null if the obtained $r$ is greater than or equal to the $r$ in Table A.6.

When the alternative hypothesis states less than, the rejection region is in the lower tail. In this case:

Fail to reject (accept) the null if the obtained $r$ is greater than the negative of the $r$ in Table A.6. (For instance, the negative of 5 is $-5$.)

Reject the null if the obtained $r$ is less than or equal to the negative of the value in Table A.6.

Degrees of freedom for the test of $r$ equal the sample size minus two, that is, $N - 2$. When the exact degrees of freedom is not listed in the table of critical values of $r$ (Table A.6), one uses the next lower listed number. The values in the table vary by whether the test is one-tailed or two-tailed and by the significance level ($\alpha$; alpha).

### 22.2.5 ■ Carrying Out the Hypothesis Testing Model

The easiest way to carry out the test of Pearson's $r$ is with computer software. In Rosenthal and Groze's (1992) study of outcomes of special needs adoptions, the correlation between family income and closeness of relationship between parent and child was $-.21$ ($N = 635$, $df = 635 - 2 = 633$). Thus, as family income increased, closeness of parent–child relationship decreased. To carry out the hypothesis testing model:

**1.** State the hypothesis pair.

Null:            In the population from which the study sample was selected, the correlation of family income and closeness of parent–child relationship equals 0.00.

Alternative:  In the population from which the study sample was selected, the correlation of family income and closeness of parent–child relationship does not equal 0.00.

The hypothesis pair is nondirectional.

**2.** Select a statistical significance level.

The .01 level is selected. With large samples, researchers often choose the .01 level rather than the .05 level. Doing so reduces the likelihood that an association of trivial size will achieve significance (see Chapter 16, Section 16.5.5).

**3.** and **4.** Carry out the test and make a decision.

The SPSS statistical package calculated the probability of the study sample result as $p = .0000006$. This conveys that, given a two-tailed test (nondirectional pair) and a sample size of 635, and assuming that the null is true ($\rho = 0.00$), the probability of obtaining a Pearson's $r$ either $\leq -.21$ or $\geq .21$ equals .0000006. Clearly, chance alone is a highly unlikely explanation for the study result. Because $p \leq .01$, we reject the null.

If you are asking yourself how the value of $p$ can be so low for an $r$ that conveys a relationship that is small to medium in size ($r = -.21$; see Table 8.2), the answer rests with the large sample size; given that the sample size is large, even a small difference from the condition stated in the null ($\rho = 0.00$) can achieve significance. This is demonstrated in the next section. See also the discussion of power in Chapter 16, Sections 16.3 and 16.4.

The rejection of chance as a plausible explanation for the study correlation allows one to think about the *real* explanations for the negative correlation between family closeness and family income. The reader is invited to consider possibilities.

To this point, our discussion of the test of $r$ has focused on nondirectional hypothesis pairs and, therefore, two-tailed tests. By default, some computer programs compute probabilities for two-tailed rather than one-tailed tests of $r$. When the study sample $r$ is in the expected direction (the direction predicted in the alternative hypothesis), one may calculate the one-tailed probability (directional pair) by dividing the two-tailed probability by two. In our example, $p = .0000006 / 2 = .0000003$. (Note again that one may only carry out this procedure when the sample result is in the expected direction; see Chapter 15, Section 15.11.2.)

For learning purposes, let us carry out the same example using the table of critical values of $r$ (Table A.6). Let us presume a directional hypothesis pair with the alternative hypothesis stating our expectation of a *positive correlation* between income and closeness of relationship:

Null:       The correlation of income and closeness is less than or equal to 0.00.

Alternative:  The correlation of income and closeness is greater than 0.00.

(Pretending that we do not already know the study result), the expectation of a positive correlation between income and closeness is a sensible one. One might well reason that adequate income would lessen family stress and, therefore, facilitate closeness. We will use the .01 significance level.

Our obtained $r$ is .21. The table of critical values of $r$ (Table A.6) does not list 633 degrees of freedom ($df = N - 2 = 635 - 2 = 633$) and so we use the next closest lower listed number, which is 602. For a one-tailed test using the .01 level ($\alpha = .01$) with $df = 602$, the value of $r$ in Table A.6 is .095. For a directional hypothesis pair, when the alternative hypothesis states greater than, the decision rule is to fail to reject (accept) the null if the value of the obtained $r$ is less than the value of $r$ in the table. Our obtained $r$, $-.21$, is indeed less than the $r$ in the table, .095 and, hence, we fail to reject the null.

This is an example of a situation in which the study sample result (a negative value of $r$) is in the direction opposite to expectations (a positive value). We have already seen that a nondirectional pair resulted in rejection of the null.

The best recourse when one uses a directional pair and results are in the unexpected direction is to repeat the analysis with a nondirectional one (see Chapter 15, Section 15.11.2). However, doing so gives one *two* tries to reject the null. Some (including me) view this as "cheating." My advice is that you use a directional pair only when the expectation for a result in a particular direction is a strong, compelling one (see Chapter 14, Section 14.6.2).

### 22.2.6 ■ A Look at the Sampling Distribution of $r$

If one picked an unlimited number of random samples of a given size from a population in which rho ($\rho$, the population coefficient) equaled 0.00, one would build a sampling distribution of $r$. Without getting into formal theory, three things hold true about this distribution: (a) its mean equals 0.00; (b) except for highly skewed distributions used with very small sample sizes, its shape is normal or close to normal; and (c) as sample size increases, its standard deviation decreases.

Figure 22.1 presents the sampling distribution of $r$ for three different sample sizes, 20, 50, and 200. Notice that as sample size increases the spread/width (standard deviation) of the sampling distribution decreases. Figure 22.1 demonstrates that the larger the sample size, the smaller the absolute value of $r$ necessary to reject the null. When $N = 20$ (Distribution A), an absolute value of $r$ greater than or equal to .468 is required for rejection. When $N = 50$ (Distribution B), the requirement decreases to .276. Distribution C ($N = 200$) presents the rejection area for a one-tailed test in which the alternative hypothesis states the direction "less than." Here, the null is rejected whenever $r$ is less than or equal to $-.117$.

In summary, Figure 22.1 demonstrates that as sample size increases, it becomes easier to reject the null. To make the same point in a different way: As sample size increases, so does statistical power.

### 22.3 ■ A CORRELATION MATRIX

Sometimes, one wants to examine correlations among several variables. Table 22.1 is an SPSS-generated **correlation matrix** that presents correlations involving five variables in the special needs adoption study (Rosenthal & Groze, 1992).

Descriptions of these variables can help in interpreting the correlation matrix. Behavior problems are measured by a problem checklist, with higher scores conveying greater problems. Parent–child relationship is measured by a five-item scale; higher scores convey better relationship. The adoptive mothers' educational level is measured on a five-point scale; higher scores convey higher education level. Impact of adoption on the family is also measured on a five-point scale; higher scores convey more positive impact. Finally, family income is measured in $1,000 increments.

A correlation matrix lets the researcher explore correlations between various combinations of variables. Note that all the correlations in a straight line from the upper left corner of the matrix to the lower right corner equal 1.00. These correlations represent the correlation of each variable with itself. Such correlations always equal to 1.00.

Except for the correlation of each variable with itself, the matrix lists each correlation twice. For instance, the correlation between score on the behavior problems scale and that on

FIGURE 22.1 ■ Sampling Distribution of *r* for Three Different Sample Sizes

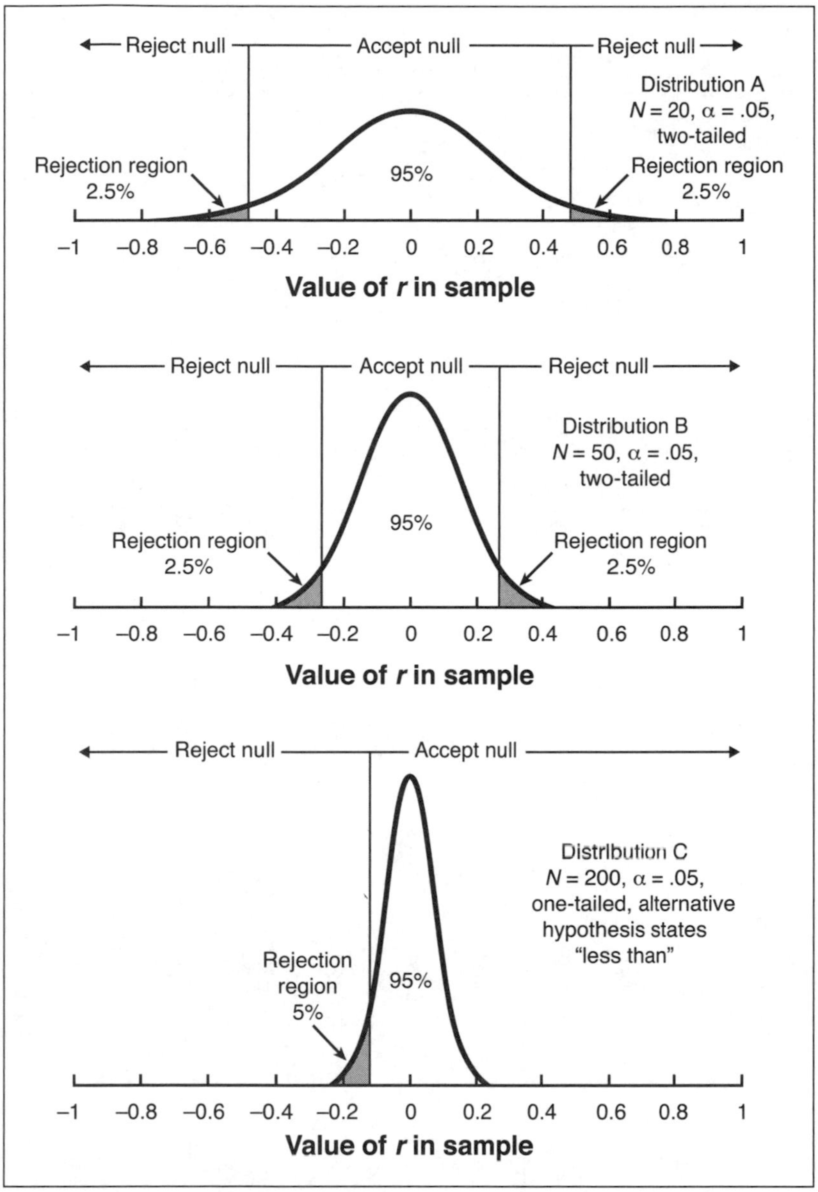

the parent–child relationship scale is listed in both the first row, second column and in the second row, first column. This correlation, −.609, conveys a large negative association between these variables. Of all the correlations, those involving family income may be most interesting. In addition to being negatively associated with the impact of adoption on the family, income is positively associated with behavior problems score, and negatively associated with closeness of parent–child relationship.

The asterisks flag statistically significant correlations. All correlations in the matrix achieve significance. As has been emphasized several times in this chapter and before, with large sample sizes, even small associations often achieve significance. Observe that all significance tests are two-tailed.

Table 22.1 ■ SPSS-Generated Correlation Matrix from Special-Needs Adoption Study (Edited)

| | | Behavior Problems Score | Parent-child Relationship Scale | Education Level of Adoptive Mother | Income in 1000s | Impact of Adoption on Family |
|---|---|---|---|---|---|---|
| Behavior Problems Score | Pearson's $r$ | 1 | −.609** | .094* | .092* | −.557** |
| | Sig. (2-tailed) | | .000 | .011 | 0.21 | .000 |
| | N | 757 | 738 | 732 | 633 | 747 |
| Parent-child Relationship scale | Pearson's $r$ | −.609** | 1 | −.199** | −.213** | .696** |
| | Sig. (2-tailed) | .000 | | .000 | .000 | .000 |
| | N | 738 | 773 | 744 | 635 | 755 |
| Education level of adoptive mother | Pearson's $r$ | .094* | −.199** | 1 | .327** | −.154** |
| | Sig. (2-tailed) | .011 | .000 | | .000 | .000 |
| | N | 732 | 744 | 768 | 634 | 753 |
| Income in 1000s | Pearson's $r$ | .092* | −.213** | .327** | 1 | −.170** |
| | Sig. (2-tailed) | .021 | .000 | .000 | | .000 |
| | N | 633 | 635 | 634 | 657 | 650 |
| Impact of adoption on family | Pearson's $r$ | −.557** | .696** | −.154** | −.170** | 1 |
| | Sig. (2-tailed) | .000 | .000 | .000 | .000 | |
| | N | 747 | 755 | 753 | 650 | 780 |

* Correlation is significant at the 0.05 level (2-tailed).
** Correlation is significant at the 0.01 level (2-tailed).

## 22.4 ▨ COMMENTS ON HYPOTHESIS TESTING AND CONFIDENCE INTERVALS

### 22.4.1 ▨ Hypothesis Testing

According to the hypothesis testing model, a researcher's study result is, *formally*, significant at the level that she selects rather than at some possible lower level. For instance, suppose that a researcher (a) selects the .05 level and (b) finds that the probability of her study result is .007 ($p = .007$). Formally, this result is statistically significant at the .05 level rather than at the .01 level.

Notwithstanding the formal model, the *reality* of real-world research is that, most researchers report significance at the lowest possible level. Thus, our researcher would almost assuredly report the result as significant at the .01 level rather than at the .05 level. Indeed, presuming that space is sufficient for doing so, the American Psychological Association (APA, 2010) recommends presenting exact values of *p*. Hence, our researcher would most likely report that $p = .007$.

Another reality is that, *formally*, researchers do not always follow all of the steps in the hypothesis testing model. For instance, many do not select a significance level (step 2) prior to carrying out the test. Why do so when, pragmatically, the exact value of *p* will most likely be reported?

Researchers often do not state the hypothesis pair explicitly. In such situations, the reader can, almost always, infer the pair. For instance, suppose that you read that "Pearson's *r* was statistically significant ($p = .028$, two-tailed test)." Because the test is two-tailed, you can infer that the hypothesis pair is nondirectional. Further, you know that the test of *r* examines whether the population correlation ($\rho$) differs from 0.00. Thus, it follows that the pair is $H_0$: $\rho = 0$; $H_1$: $\rho \neq 0$ (see Section 22.2.3). In summary, the hypothesis testing model functions more as a guide rather than as a blueprint to be followed rigidly.

### 22.4.2 ▨ Confidence Intervals

Chapter 13, Section 13.4 mentions that confidence intervals are often computed for statistics other than means and proportions. Now that we have covered significance tests, some additional comments on confidence intervals can be offered.

As an example, in the special-needs adoption sample, the correlation between internalizing (withdrawn, isolated, etc.) and externalizing (aggressive, acting out) behavior was .56, $p = .000$, $N = 746$. This significant value of *p* conveys that this correlation is unlikely to be due to chance alone; hence, we reject the null. The 95% confidence interval for this correlation ranges from .50 to .62. Thus, if we view the adoption sample as a random sample selected from an infinitely sized population, we can be 95% confident that the correlation between internalizing and externalizing in this population is located somewhere in the range from .50 to .62.

Significance test results (values of *p*) inform us about whether a study result is likely to be due to chance alone. Confidence intervals provide us with a range of likely values for that result. The information from confidence intervals complements that from significance tests and vice versa. Whenever possible, examine both test results (values of *p*) and confidence intervals (the likely range of values). This provides a richer perspective on results than does a narrow focus only on significance tests.

## 22.5 ▨ PARAMETRIC AND NONPARAMETRIC TESTS

Now is a good time to contrast parametric and nonparametric statistical significance tests: **Parametric tests** assume that the population from which the study sample was (randomly) selected has some particular distributional shape whereas **nonparametric tests** (*distribution-free tests*) make no such assumption.

Most commonly used introductory parametric tests assume normality, that is, that the population from which the study sample was selected has a normal distribution. Hence, pragmatically, a key distinction is that parametric tests assume normality whereas nonparametric tests do not. The following tests covered to this point are parametric: the large sample test of $\overline{X}$, the one-sample $t$ test, the dependent samples $t$ test, the dependent samples $t$ test, analysis of variance (ANOVA), and the significance test of $r$. Each assumes normality. The following can be characterized as nonparametric: the one-sample test of $p$, the binomial test, the one-variable $\chi^2$ test, and the $\chi^2$ test of independence. None of these assumes normality.

Observe that, for all of the just-mentioned parametric tests, the dependent variable is at the interval/ratio level of measurement. On the other hand, this is not the case for any of the nonparametric tests discussed to this point. This leads to another distinction.

For parametric tests, the dependent variable is at the interval/ratio level of measurement. For nonparametric tests, it can be at any level. However, when the dependent variable is at the interval/ratio level, the nonparametric test, in essence, treats it as being at a lower one. Consider, for instance, the following data which represents the number of out-of-seat behaviors without permission in two groups of elementary school children, each exposed to a different intervention:

Group 1:  1, 7, 6, 0, 5, 38, 9, 4, 8

Group 2:  5, 11, 15, 6, 17, 4, 67, 3, 10

This example involves two independent samples and an interval/ratio-level dependent variable. As such, it seems to call for an independent samples $t$ test to assess whether the mean number of out-of-seat behaviors differ between the groups. However, in both groups, the dependent variable is extremely skewed—this skew is caused by the outliers "38" and "67"—and, further, sample size is small ($n = 9$ in both groups). When both very strong skew and very small sample size are present, the independent samples $t$ test can yield inaccurate results and, thus, should not be used (see Chapter 18, Section 18.2.3).

Rather than carrying out an independent samples $t$ test, a better strategy is to carry out a nonparametric alternative to it, the Mann-Whitney $U$ test (discussed in greater detail in Section 22.6.3). Although the count of out-of-seat behaviors is at the interval/ratio level, the Mann-Whitney $U$ test, in essence, treats this data as a rank ordering. Ranked from highest (18) to lowest (1) and keeping the order of presentation the same as earlier, the Mann-Whitney $U$ test treats this data as follows:

Group 1:  2, 10, 8.5, 1, 6.5, 17, 12, 4.5, 11

Group 2:  6.5, 14, 15, 8.5, 16, 4.5, 18, 3, 13

(Observe that when two counts were equal, equal ranks were assigned. For instance, two counts of 5 were observed; each was assigned a rank of 6.5.)

It then evaluates whether, to a degree that is greater than would be expected by chance alone, ranks in the two groups differ. Summing up, although the count of out-of-seat behaviors is at the interval-ratio level, the information used—the ranks—is at a lower one (the ordinal level). This illustrates that although the dependent variable for a nonparametric test can be at any level of measurement, the actual information used—in essence, the variable actually analyzed—is almost always at the ordinal level (a rank ordering or a categorical ordinal-level variable) or the nominal level.

This example also illustrates that when a nonparametric test is not recommended, there is, almost always, a "handy" nonparametric alternative that can carry out a quite similar analysis. In such situations, the nonparametric test's results are, most often, more accurate than those of the parametric test that would otherwise have been conducted. We look now at various nonparametric tests, many of which are often used in situations in which parametric tests are not recommended.

## 22.6 ▓ SELECTED PARAMETRIC TESTS

### 22.6.1 ▓ Significance Test of Spearman's *r*

As presented in Chapter 8 (see Section 8.10), Spearman's *r* is the correlation between two rank orderings. The nondirectional null hypothesis for the **significance test of Spearman's *r*** is that the correlation between two rank orderings equals 0.00. The hypothesis pair may be either directional or nondirectional and the test itself may be either one-tailed (directional pair) or two-tailed (nondirectional pair). For interval-level data, a test of Spearman's *r* is an excellent alternative to a test of Pearson's *r* when skew is extreme and sample size is small and, thus, there is concern about the accuracy of a test of Pearson's *r*.

### 22.6.2 ▓ Tests of Association Between Two Ordinal-Level Categorical Variables

Chapter 7 (Section 7.4) introduced the concept of directional association between two ordinal-level variables. In a positive association, as one variable increases in value, so does the other. In a negative (directional) association, as one variable increases, the other decreases. Four measures of directional association between categorical, ordinal-level variables were presented in Chapter 7, Section 7.5: Kendall's tau-*b* ($\tau_b$), Kendall's tau-*c* ($\tau_c$), gamma ($\gamma$), and Somers' *D*. Each may vary between −1.00 and 1.00. For each, 0.00 conveys the absence of directional association.

Each measure may be tested for significance with either a directional or a nondirectional pair. In each case, the nondirectional null hypothesis is that the measure (tau-*b,* tau-*c*, gamma, or Somers' *D* as the case may be) equals 0.00 in the population from which the study sample was selected.

The easiest way to carry out these tests is with statistical software packages. The probabilities generated by software packages usually assume a two-tailed test. For a one-tailed test (directional pair), divide the two-tailed probability in half. (This assumes that results are in the expected direction.)

### 22.6.3 ▓ Tests for Independent Samples

***Mann-Whitney U test***. The nondirectional null of the Mann-Whitney *U* test states that ranks in two groups are equally "high," that is, that those in one group are not higher (or lower) than those in the other. The nondirectional alternative states these ranks are not equally high. The hypothesis pair may be either directional or nondirectional.

As discussed earlier, the Mann-Whitney *U* test is an excellent alternative to the independent samples *t* test in situations where that test can yield inaccurate results (see Section 22.5). This is its primary use.

A Mann-Whitney *U* test was carried out for the data presented earlier (see Section 22.5). The null was not rejected, $p > .05$. Hence, we do not have sufficient evidence to conclude that ranks in the two groups differ by more than would be expected by chance.[1,2]

***Kruskal-Wallis test***. The *Kruskal-Wallis* test is an extension of the Mann-Whitney *U* test to situations with two or more independent samples. It is an excellent alternative to ANOVA when violations of assumptions of that test can lead to inaccurate results. Its hypothesis pair is, in essence, the same as that for the Mann-Whitney *U* test, although the pair is always nondirectional.[3]

### 22.6.4 ▓ Tests for Dependent Samples

***Wilcoxon signed-ranks test and sign test***. The *Wilcoxon signed-ranks test* is used with two dependent samples. It is an excellent alternative to the dependent samples *t* test in situations when that test can be inaccurate. As you know, the dependent *t*-test results can be inaccurate when one or both samples is highly skewed and the sample size is very small (see Chapter 18, Section 18.2.3).

Table 22.2 ■ Appointment Keeping Prior to and Following Addition of Paraprofessionals

|  |  | Preintervention | | Total |
|  |  | Miss | Keep |  |
| --- | --- | --- | --- | --- |
| Postintervention | Miss | 10 | 5 | 15 |
|  |  |  |  | 30.0% |
|  | Keep | 15 | 20 | 35 |
|  |  |  |  | 70.0% |
| Total |  | 25 | 25 | 50 |
|  |  | 50.0% | 50.0% | 100.0% |

The dependent variable's level of measurement should be interval/ratio or nearly so. The hypothesis pair may be either directional or nondirectional. In essence, the nondirectional null states that values in the two groups are equally high.

The **sign test** is another alternative to the dependent samples *t* test. Like the Wilcoxon signed ranks test, it is used with two dependent samples. It is preferred over the Wilcoxon test when the dependent variable is a categorical ordinal-level variable.

*McNemar's test*. *McNemar's test* tests a difference in percentages (proportions) between two dependent samples. The nondirectional null hypothesis states that percentages in the two samples are equal.

As an example, presume that you have a caseload of 50 clients each of whom has a serious mental illness. Presume also that two paraprofessionals are assigned to help you manage this caseload. Let us say that in the month directly prior to the paraprofessionals beginning their work, 50% (25 of 50) of clients keep their monthly medication appointment and that in the month directly following this, 70% (35 of 50) do so. Presuming that the same clients compose your caseload at both occasions, the two samples—the "before" sample and the "after" sample—are dependent samples. You could use McNemar's test to examine whether the change in percentages (from 50% before to 70% after) was statistically significant, or on the other hand, plausibly due to chance. Table 22.2, a contingency table, presents your data.

Because the data is presented in a contingency table, you might be tempted to use a chi-square test of independence to conduct your significance test. However, this test is not appropriate as the pretest and posttest samples form dependent rather than independent samples (see Chapter 18, Section 18.4).

Carrying out McNemar's test on this data yields a *p* of .044 (two-tailed test). Presuming that you had selected the .05 level, you reject the null. You conclude that chance alone is an unlikely explanation for the improvement in appointment keeping.

## 22.7 ■ PARAMETRIC OR NONPARAMETRIC TEST?

The choice between a parametric and a nonparametric test can be difficult. Advantages of parametric tests include:

■ They are more commonly used and, hence, persons have greater familiarity with them.

■ In general, they are robust to violations of assumptions and, hence, probabilities are, typically, quite accurate.

- Other things being equal, they tend to have greater statistical power than do their nonparametric counterparts; hence, they are more likely to reject the null when the null is false. (This advantage is often modest and, further, differences in power can differ considerably from one situation to the next.)

- Often, they are more straightforward. (For instance, for some nonparametric tests, the hypothesis pair is less than straightforward.)

- They are often well connected to multivariate statistical procedures such as those that you will be introduced to in the next chapter. (Many nonparametric tests are a "dead end"; they do not set the stage for subsequent multivariate analyses.)

The chief advantage of the nonparametric test is greater accuracy of results in situations when a parametric test is not recommended.

My overall preference is to use parametric tests whenever possible. Others disagree. One alternative is to conduct both tests and compare results. More often than not, they are similar.[4]

## 22.8 ■ DATA TRANSFORMATION

**Data transformation** involves applying a mathematical "manipulation" to each score. Transformation from (raw) scores to $z$ scores is an example of data transformation. Some other examples of data transformation include: (a) adding a constant to each score, (b) multiplying each score by a constant, (c) squaring each score, (d) taking the square root of each score (e) taking the log of each score, and (f) computing each score's reciprocal.[5]

When sample size is very small and shape of distribution is highly skewed, parametric tests are, in general, not recommended. One strategy in such a situation is to carry out a nonparametric alternative to the parametric test; for instance, a Mann-Whitney $U$ test in lieu of an independent samples $t$ test. Another strategy is to transform the variable so that shape of distribution becomes close to normal, and then to carry out a parametric test on the transformed variable. For instance, consider this interval/ratio-level data which, let us say, represent scores in two groups of youth on a behavior problems measure; the higher the score, the greater the number of problems:

Group 1:  1, 2, 3, 3, 4, 5, 7, 8, 9, 9, 11, 13, 14, 16, 18, 23, 24, 29

Group 2:  1, 2, 3, 4, 6, 9, 9, 12, 12, 13, 15, 18, 22, 23, 26, 34, 38, 47

Figure 22.2 presents a box plot showing the distribution in each group. In both groups, the greater spread of the plot in the positive direction (upward) than in the negative (downward) conveys positive skew, enough so that, given the small sample sizes ($n = 18$), a $t$ test should not be conducted. The SPSS program implemented a square root transformation on the behavior problem scores; in other words, it computed the square root of each score. Figure 22.3 presents a box plot based on the transformed scores, that is, on the square roots. The plot now reveals much less positive skew; the upper and lower halves of the boxes are now spread out to about the same degree.

Given that the skew is now quite modest, we can carry out a $t$ test. This test does not reject the null of equal means in the two groups, $t$ ($df = 34$) $= -1.251, p = .219$ (equal variances test). These results apply to the square roots of the behavior problem scores rather than to the scores themselves.

Although the degree of skew was sufficient for recommending against carrying out a $t$ test on the nontransformed behavior counts, one was conducted for learning purposes. The two-tailed

FIGURE 22.2 ■ Box Plot of Nontransformed Scores

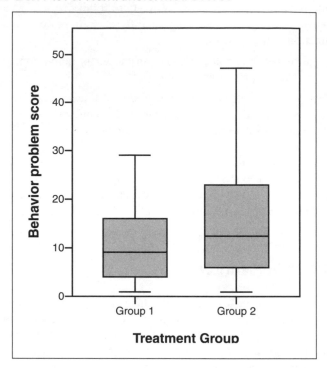

FIGURE 22.3 ■ Box Plot of Scores following Square Root Transformation

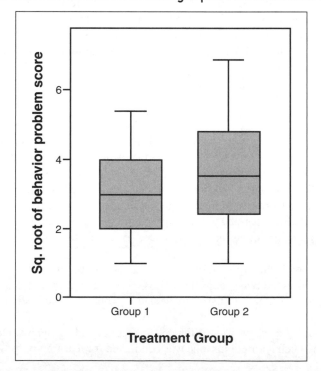

probability resulting from this test was .158. Hence, probabilities for the transformed and nontransformed sores did differ somewhat. The probability connected with the transformed scores ($p = .219$) is, almost assuredly, the more accurate of the two.

In addition, for learning purposes, a Mann-Whitney $U$ test was carried out on this data. As you know, this test uses ranks rather than actual scores. The probability yielded by the Mann-Whitney $U$ test was .281. It is difficult to choose between the results of this test and those of the $t$ test on the transformed data; both are good alternatives to a $t$ test based on the nontransformed data.[6]

In summary, when a test based on nontransformed data can yield inaccurate results, transforming that data to create a more normally shaped distribution is often a good strategy. In this regard, square root and log transformations are often used to transform positively skewed data. The next chapter demonstrates more uses of data transformation (see Section 23.2.2). See Cohen and Cohen (1983, pp. 260–272), Norušis (1997, pp. 432–433, 515–532), and Glass and Hopkins (1996, pp. 89–98) for more discussion of data transformation.

## 22.9 ■ SINGLE-CASE DESIGNS

### 22.9.1 ■ Basic Applications

In **single-case designs**, measurements are taken on at least several occasions both prior to and following an intervention. The **AB single-case design** consists of two "phases." The baseline phase, designated as A, comprises the preintervention observations and the intervention phase, designated as B, comprises the postintervention observations. Figure 22.4 displays the number of

FIGURE 22.4 ■ **Example of an AB Single Case Design**

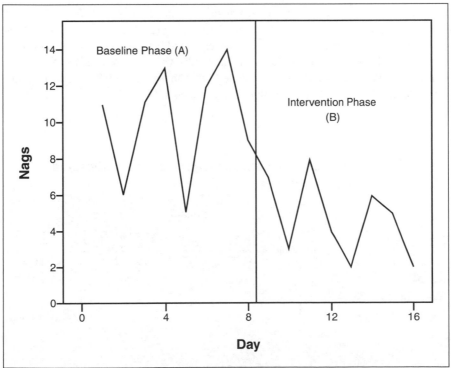

times that a parent "nags" her child on 8 days prior to and 8 days subsequent to an intervention. (Perhaps the intervention consists of participation in meditation or other stress-releasing activity.) Suppose that these counts of nags are

Baseline (A) phase: 11, 6, 11, 13, 5, 12, 14, 9

Intervention (B) phase: 7, 3, 8, 4, 2, 6, 5, 2

Let us focus first on the baseline phase. Observe that although the counts of nagging fluctuate considerably, the overall trend is neither upward nor downward, but instead is horizontal (parallel with the $X$ axis). Although a caution will be introduced subsequently, when there is no upward or downward trend, statistical procedures that have already been discussed in this text can often be used to analyze single-case design data.

In essence, the researcher thinks of the baseline phase as one group (say Group 1) and the intervention phase as the other (Group 2). In our current example, the data is at the interval-ratio level and, thus, suggests an independent samples $t$ test. However, with only eight cases per group, sample size is perhaps too small for this test and, hence, we will conduct a Mann-Whitney $U$ test. The Mann-Whitney $U$ test does indeed reject the null, $p = .006$. Hence, we conclude that the difference in counts between baseline and intervention phases is unlikely to be due to chance alone. When the baseline phase exhibits an upward or downward trend, neither the independent samples $t$ test nor the Mann-Whitney $U$ test is appropriate for analyzing an AB single-case design.[7]

Sometimes, the behavior being tracked is a nominal-level variable. For instance, we could track whether a client in a nursing home participates in socialization activities on a given day. In this example, participation is a dichotomous variable (yes, participates vs. no, does not participate). Table 22.3 presents data for a hypothetical client. The intervention phase consists of 10 observations and the client participates in socialization on 2 occasions (20%, 2 of 10). The intervention phase comprises 15 observations and the client participates 10 times (67%, 10 of 15).

The average observed frequency for the data in Table 22.3 is 6.25 (25 / 4 = 6.25) and the minimum expected frequency (upper left cell) is 4.8 [(12 × 10 / 25 = 4.8)]. These meet the requirements for a chi-square test of independence and, hence, we will conduct it. Because sample size is small, we will use the .05 level. Our results are: $\chi^2 (1, N = 25) = 5.235, p = .022$. Because $p \le .05$, we reject the null. We conclude that the improvement in participation from baseline to intervention is unlikely to be due to chance alone.

TABLE 22.3 ■ Participation in Socialization Activities in Baseline and Intervention Phases

|  |  | Phase | | |
|  |  | Baseline (A) | Intervention (B) | Total |
| --- | --- | --- | --- | --- |
| Participate in socialization | Yes | 2<br>20.0% | 10<br>66.7% | 12<br>48.0% |
|  | No | 8<br>80.0% | 5<br>33.3% | 13<br>52.0% |
| Total |  | 10<br>100.0% | 15<br>100.0% | 25<br>100.0% |

## 29.9.2 ■ Comments on Single-Case Designs

Most often, sample size in single-case designs is small. This being the case, statistical power is often limited. As you interpret significance test results for single-case designs, remember that failure to reject the null does not convey that the null is likely true but only that there is insufficient evidence to reject it.

A comment on causality is in order. Single-case designs are classified as quasi-experiments, conveying that, pragmatically, they have *some* characteristics that *may* allow the researcher to draw causal conclusions. Clearly, however, the ability to draw conclusions from these designs is far below that in a true experiment (a randomized trial; see Chapter 10, Section 10.6). When a result is statistically significant in a single-case design, you should be alert to the possibility that it may be due to some factor other than the intervention. Say, for instance, that a youth's behavior in school improves to a statistically significant degree from baseline phase to intervention phase. Perhaps, the treatment intervention is a points system that rewards good behavior. But this improvement may be due to something else. Perhaps, for instance, the youth's father began a new job just as the intervention phase commenced. Reduced financial stress in the family—not the points system—may explain the improved behavior. In summary, when results are significant, consider factors other than the treatment intervention that may be explanations.

We have explored only one single-case design—the AB design. Most other single-case designs are more sophisticated than the AB design and, thus, better suited for drawing causal conclusions. See Rubin (2010), or Rubin and Babbie (2008) for an introduction to single-case designs or Bloom, Fischer, and Orme (2009) for in-depth content.

## 22.9.3 ■ Serial Dependency

An important assumption for inferential statistical analyses is that each observation is independent of each other observation. Pragmatically, this means that pairs or groupings of observations should not be similar because of factors not taken into account in the analysis. (See Chapter 12, Section 12.3 for examples of violations of the independence of observations assumption.) Yet, for **time-series** data, that is, for data organized by time, adjacent observations are, more than occasionally, more similar than are those that are separated by many points in time. Suppose, for instance, that the following are 31 sequential measurements record whether a client participates in socialization activity. A Y conveys "Yes, participate" and an N conveys "No, not participate."

NNNNNYYYNNYYYYYYYYNNNYYYYYNNNNYY

Visual examination suggests that both "No" and "Yes" responses occur in "streaks" or "clusters." When a prior response is No, our best guess for the next response is No; when a prior response is Yes, our best guess for the next is Yes.

The just-presented observations are not independent, but rather dependent. More specifically, these observations are **serially dependent**, that is, they exhibit serial dependency. When observations exhibit **serial dependency** (*autocorrelation*), observations that occur close together in time have more similar values than those that do not.[8,9]

In Table 22.4, prior and subsequent observations are associated. When prior observation is "Yes, participate," subsequent observation is "Yes, participate" 81% of the time (13 of 16 times). On the other hand, when prior observation is "No, not participate," subsequent observation is "Yes, participate" only 29% of the time (4 of 14 times). This difference in percentages ($D\% = 81\% - 29\% = 52\%$) achieves significance, $\rho = .004$, affirming the serial dependency in our example.

When serial dependency is present, significance tests that do not take it into account can yield inaccurate results. More often than not, the $p$ yielded by such tests is lower than the actual $p$,

TABLE 22.4 ■ Association Between Prior and Subsequent Observation and Participation

| | | Prior Observation | | |
|---|---|---|---|---|
| | | Yes, Participate | No, Not Participate | Total |
| **Subsequent observation** | **Yes, participate** | 13<br>81.3% | 4<br>28.6% | 17<br>56.7% |
| | **No, not participate** | 3<br>18.8% | 10<br>71.4% | 13<br>43.3% |
| **Total** | | 16<br>100.0% | 14<br>100.0% | 30<br>100.0% |

*Note*: Although there were 31 observations in the original series, only 30 observations are presented in the table. This is because there is no prior observation for the first observation in the series.

that is, than the actual probability that the result is caused by chance. (For instance, the $p$ given by the test might be .08 and the actual $p$ might be .03). Tests that do not take serial dependency into account can create a high risk of Type I error, the error of mistakenly rejecting a true null (see Chapter 15, Section 15.10).

The small sample sizes often found in single-case designs reduce the power of significance tests designed to detect serial dependency. With small samples, it can be difficult to know whether serial dependency is affecting results. In such situations, significance tests should be supplemented with visual inspection.

The streaks/clusters of Yes and No responses revealed serial dependency in our example. This example involved a dichotomous dependent variable. When the dependent variable is numeric, serial dependency is revealed by a "snake-like," "serpentine-like" pattern of responses. Figure 22.5 presents such a pattern. Observe that adjacent observations tend to cluster together either above or below the horizontal line that splits the observations approximately at their mean. Data that is not serially dependent would not exhibit such a pattern. Instead, for such data, variability around a similar horizontal line will appear random.[10]

In Chapter 12 (Section 12.3), I advised that ignoring dependency between observations was sometimes the pragmatic solution. This advice does not hold well for serial dependency. If you detect serial dependency, either visually or statistically, you have two choices: (a) carry out an analysis that does not take serial dependency into account but explain in your discussion of results that it may have affected results or (b) carry out an analysis that appropriately deals with serial dependency. Unfortunately, such analyses can be complex and are beyond the scope of this chapter. See Bloom, Fisher, and Orme (2009, pp. 438–445) for more on serial dependency and single-case designs. See Yaffee and McGee (2000) for a highly technical discussion, one that is not recommended until after taking a statistics course with thorough coverage of multiple regression and related procedures.

## 22.10 ■ QUALITATIVE METHODS AND STATISTICS

As discussed in Chapter 1 (Section 1.3), quantitative research methods are characterized by objective measurement, whereas qualitative research methods "emphasize depth of understanding

FIGURE 22.5 ■ Figure Demonstrating Serial Dependency

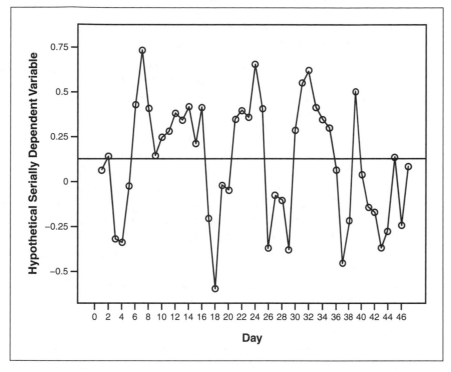

and the deeper meanings of human experience" (Rubin & Babbie, 2008, p. 643). Although their predominant use is in quantitative studies, statistical procedures are used in qualitative studies as well.

Suppose, for instance, that an online survey queries social work students about their experiences in their social work programs. One way to obtain responses would be to develop *close-ended questions*, ones for which students would, for instance, check a box to indicate their chosen response. Another would be to develop *open-ended questions*, ones that encourage students to respond in their own words. Because they ask for individualized responses—the student's own ideas and perceptions—open-ended questions represent a qualitative rather than a quantitative approach. Qualitative researchers often sift through responses to open-ended questions. They seek to find patterns, that is, common response themes among respondents. Having, hopefully, identified common themes, they, in essence, "switch hats" and become quantitative researchers. In particular, they count the frequency of the different themes. Suppose, for instance, that one theme is labeled "inadequate coverage of diversity content." Our "qualitative turned quantitative" researcher, in addition to counting the frequency of this theme, might analyze whether students with particular characteristics (e.g., minority vs. White, full-time vs. part-time program, female vs. male, etc.) are more or less likely to evidence the theme. A chi-square test of independence would likely be the preferred statistical test in these analyses.

In summary, many predominantly qualitative studies do indeed use the statistical methods presented here. Thus, even those whose primary interest is in qualitative approaches benefit from a basic knowledge of statistics and data interpretation. As you learn more about research methods, you will see that many studies combine quantitative and qualitative approaches, thereby drawing on the advantages of each.

## 22.11 ■ REASONING WITH DATA: A BRIEF REVIEW

Let us use an example to examine how the logic of statistical significance testing can be integrated with other topics presented to this point. Here is the example:

> Presume that 50 clients participate in Job-Training Program A and 50 clients participate in Job-Training Program B. Presume further that 60% (30 of 50) of those participating in A obtain jobs as compared to 40% (20 of 50) of those in B. Our hypothesis pair is nondirectional. We use the .05 significance level.

Is the difference in the percentage of successes in Programs A and B (60% vs. 40%) due to chance alone (sampling error, the luck of the draw of random samples) or is it due to an actual difference in the percentage of successes in the A and B populations? Because our example involves a difference in percentages, the appropriate significance test is the chi-square test of independence presented in Chapter 20. If the probability resulting from this test is less than or equal to the selected significance level (.05), we will reject the null. Otherwise, we will accept it. Prior to conducting the test, I will mention several things.

As we begin our discussion, recall that statistical significance and size of association are distinct concepts (see Chapter 16, Section 16.10). We can assess size of association by computing a difference in percentages ($D\%$) and then consulting Table 6.3, which lists qualitative descriptors for the $D\%$. The $D\%$ is $60\% - 40\% = 20\%$. Using the guidelines from Table 6.3, we characterize the association between Job-Training Program (A vs. B) and job obtainment (obtained vs. not obtained) as "medium" in size.

Second, notice that we are going to conduct a significance test even though the study samples are not random samples from a larger population (or, at least, none of the information provided in our example indicates that this is the case). Pragmatically, significance tests are conducted in the absence of random sampling. Do not let the absence of random sampling keep you from conducting significance tests (see Chapter 16, Section 16.8).

A primary focus of the current discussion is on the link between statistical significance and causality. Causality addresses whether we can be confident that one variable—in our example, Job-Training Program—is the cause of another (job obtainment). (Discussion draws on many of the ideas developed in Chapter 10, Section 10.6 on the role of random assignment in assessing causality). The information in our example says nothing about how participants were assigned to training programs. Accordingly, we will presume that this assignment was not random. (Note: Do not confuse random sampling and random assignment; see the end of Section 12.3 in Chapter 12.)

Carrying out the chi-square test (calculations not shown), probability computes to .046, $p = .046$. Because $p \leq .05$, our result is statistically significant at the .05 level and, thus, we: (a) reject the null and (b) conclude that the difference in percentages between the two programs is unlikely due to chance alone (sampling error alone). Given that the difference in percentages is unlikely due to chance alone, we conclude that it is likely due to something *real*, that is, to something other than chance.

When a study does not use random assignment, the "something real" that causes a statistically significant result may be a confounding variable. Thus, in our example, some factor other than the treatment intervention may be biasing results in favor of Job-Training Program A. In a nutshell, we (a) are confident that the results are caused by *something* real but (b) cannot logically rule out the possibility that this something is a confounding variable. Because of the second point, we cannot draw a *causal* conclusion about which job intervention program is more effective.

Now let us change our example: Let us presume that participants were randomly assigned to programs. All other facts stay the same (same sample sizes, same results, $p = .046$, etc.) In our revised example: (a) the fact of statistical significance lets us rule out chance as a plausible cause of the study result *and* (b) the fact of random assignment lets us rule out confounding variables as the something real that is causing the study result. (With random assignment, pragmatically, there are no confounding variables; see Chapter 10, Section 10.6.) The ruling out of confounding variables due to the random assignment allows us to conclude that the something real that is causing the study result is indeed the *treatment intervention*. In other words, we may conclude that Program A *causes* greater success than does Program B. In summary (and at the risk of oversimplifying), a statistically significant finding in a randomized design (a design with random assignment) permits a causal conclusion regarding the effect of the intervention on the dependent variable.

As we continue with the example, realize that our conclusions are probabilistic in this sense: Chance can never be ruled out with 100% certainty as an explanation for study results. We rejected the null that the percentage of successes is equal in Programs A and B. How confident can we be that the null is indeed false? To find out we can (a) multiply the probability given by the significance test by 100 and (b) subtract from 100: $100 - (.046 \times 100) = 95.4\%$. We can be 95.4% confident that the null is false (see Chapter 14, Section 14.9.4). But, viewed differently, there is, in essence, a 4.6% chance that our study sample results are due to the "luck of the draw of the random assignment process," that is, to chance.

As you continue to read, recognize that the language used to describe various conclusions is sometimes, too strong. For instance, in the paragraph that follows, I should, perhaps substitute *can be confident that* for *knows*. But I will not do so. Instead, I ask you to remember that all conclusions reached involving inferential statistics are probabilistic, at least to some degree.

With random assignment, given a statistically significant result, the researcher knows that the something real that is causing the study result is not external to the intervention, that is, is not a confounding variable. Stated differently, she knows that the something real is some characteristic of the treatment intervention *itself*. For instance, in our example, she knows that *something real* about Program A versus Program B causes better outcomes. Yet, even with random assignment, the researcher does not know what *particular* characteristic (what particular something is real) of the treatment intervention causes the study result. For instance, perhaps the persons delivering Program A have better intervention skills than those delivering Program B. In other words, the something real about A versus B may simply be the greater effectiveness of the persons delivering services rather than an actual program component. In summary, even with random assignment, the researcher does not know what particular component of the treatment intervention delivers the causal effect.

Recall that our study sample was not randomly selected from any wider population. What are the implications of this for the conclusions that we can reach? Basically, we cannot use inferential statistical logic to draw conclusions about any group other than the sample, per se. We can be confident that chance is not an explanation for our study result (and, if we presume random assignment, we can be confident that this result is caused by the treatment intervention), but we cannot use statistical logic to conclude that this same result will be found in any other group or population (see Chapter 16, Section 16.8).

Now let us put another twist on our example. Suppose that the data from our study had been different and that the probability yielded by the chi-square test had been greater than the statistical significance level ($p > .05$). In this instance, we (a) fail to reject (accept, retain) the null and (b) reason that the study sample result (the better outcome in A than in B) may be due to chance (sampling error) alone.

In our new scenario, issues connected with random assignment (or the absence thereof) do not even come up. We follow science's preference for the simplest possible explanation (see Chapter 14, Section 14.10 and Chapter 15, Section 15.13). As the results may be due to chance alone—the simplest possible explanation—we do not even begin to think about what real factors (what real "somethings") may or may not be involved. In essence, we would be (for lack of a better word) "foolish" to think too seriously about real explanations when chance alone is sufficient.

Now, still one final twist on our example. The just-presented scenario made no mention of sample size. A comment on sample size and statistical power can provide useful review.

In our initial example, sample size was moderate ($n = 50$ in each program) and, thus, statistical power was, let us presume, not extremely low. In other words, given a false null, we had a reasonable opportunity to reject that null.

Now, suppose that sample size is much smaller, say, that 10 persons participate in each Job-Training Program. Given the very small sample size, our power now is, presumably, extremely low. As such, only a very large difference (relationship) will be sufficient to reject the null.

Let us continue to presume the same percentages of successes in the two programs: Program A, 60% (6 of 10); Program B, 40% (4 of 10). Although the size of association is medium ($D\% = 60\% - 40\% = 20\%$, see Table 6.3.), the chi-square test (calculations not shown) no longer achieves significance, $p = .371$. Thus, we fail to reject (accept) the null.

When we fail to reject the null, the conclusions that follow are never correct. They are particularly misleading when power is low: "The null is *likely* true," "We can be *confident* that the null is true," "It is *likely* that results are due to chance alone," and (worst of all) "The null *is* true." When power is very low and the null is accepted, the following conclusion best expresses the state of affairs: "Because we did not have a genuine opportunity to reject the null, we cannot make an informed statement regarding which hypothesis—the null or the alternative—provides the better explanation for the study result." With very low power, the researcher fails to reject the null almost by default. In such a situation, there is no reason to carry out the study because the result is, in essence, a foregone conclusion.

Following discussion of multivariate procedures in Chapter 23, Chapter 24 continues this discussion of reasoning with data. In particular, it examines how the researcher determines whether a result—statistically significant or not—is *important* (see Section 24.3) and introduces *generalizability* (see Section 24.2).

## 22.12 ■ CHAPTER SUMMARY

The *statistical significance test of Pearson's* r examines whether the $r$ in the study sample differs significantly from 0.00. The hypothesis pair may be directional (one-tailed test) or nondirectional (two-tailed test). Although normality is assumed, the test of $r$ is robust to this assumption. In a nondirectional pair, the null states that the population correlation equals 0.00 ($\rho = 0.00$). A *correlation matrix* presents the correlations among several variables.

The steps of the hypothesis testing model provide flexible guidelines rather than a blueprint to be followed rigidly. Researchers often present the exact value of $p$. Confidence intervals add to and complement the information provided by significance tests.

*Parametric tests* assume that the population from which the study sample was selected has some particular distributional shape, whereas *nonparametric tests* make no such assumption. Most commonly used introductory parametric tests assume that this distribution has a normal shape, that is, they assume normality.

For parametric tests, the dependent variable is at the interval/ratio level of measurement. For nonparametric tests, it can be at any level. When it is at the interval/ratio level, the parametric test treats it as being at a lower level.

When a nonparametric test is not recommended, there is, almost always, a "handy" nonparametric alternative that can carry out a similar analysis. In such situations, the nonparametric test's results are, most often, more accurate.

The nondirectional null for a *significance test of Spearman's* r states that the correlation between two rank orderings equals 0.00. This test is an alternative to a test of Pearson's $r$. For tests of tau-*b*, tau-*c*, gamma, and Somers' *D*, the nondirectional null states that the measure equals 0.00.

The nondirectional null of the *Mann-Whitney* U *test* states that ranks in two groups are equally "high." The hypothesis pair may be directional or nondirectional. It is an alternative to the independent samples *t* test. The *Kruskal-Wallis test* is an alternative to analysis of variance.

*McNemar's test* tests a difference in percentages between two dependent samples. The non-directional null states that percentages in the two samples are equal.

Advantages of parametric tests include: more commonly used, robustness to violations of assumptions, greater statistical power, straightforwardness, and leading logically to multivariate analyses. In situations in which parametric tests should not be used, nonparametric tests are, most often, more accurate.

*Data transformation* involves applying a mathematical manipulation to each score. When a test based on nontransformed data can yield inaccurate results, transformation to create a more normally shaped distribution is often a good strategy.

In *single-case designs*, measurements are taken on at least several occasions prior to and following an intervention. In the *AB single-case design*, the *baseline phase (A)* comprises the preintervention observations and the *intervention phase (B)* comprises the postintervention observations. Straightforward statistical procedures can often be used to analyze single-case designs.

*Time-series data*, data arranged by time, exhibits *serial dependency* when observations that are close together in time have more similar values than do those that are not. Significance tests that do not account for serial dependency can yield inaccurate results.

Qualitative methods emphasize depth and meaning. Statistical procedures are often used in studies that are predominantly qualitative.

Statistical significance lets the researcher rule out chance, although never with certainty. When a result is statistically significant in a nonrandomized study, the researcher may conclude that the study result is unlikely due to chance alone and, thus, is likely due to something real. She may not, however, rule out confounding variables.

When a result is statistically significant in a randomized study, the researcher may rule out both chance (although never with certainty) and confounding variables. Thus, she may conclude that the treatment intervention *causes* the study result. Even in a randomized study, the researcher does not know what particular characteristic of the treatment intervention causes the study result.

When a result is not statistically significant, issues about causality do not even come up—we presume that the result is due to chance alone. When statistical power is very low, one does not have a genuine opportunity to reject the null and, thus, accepts it (fails to reject it) almost by default.

## 22.13 ■ PROBLEMS AND QUESTIONS

### Section 22.2

1. *r* measures the degree of _____ association between two numeric variables. The nondirectional null hypothesis for the test of Pearson's *r* states that correlation in the population from equals ___. The population correlation is symbolized by ___. Even when $\rho = 0.00$, because of _____ _____, *r* may differ from 0.00.

2. *Respond true or false to each of the following:*
   a. The test of Pearson's *r* is a very infrequently used (uncommon) significance test.
   b. The test of Pearson's *r* is designed for use with ordinal-level variables.
   c. The significance test of Pearson's *r* assumes that both variables are normally distributed.
   d. The significance test of Pearson's *r* is robust to the normality assumption.
   e. Both nondirectional and directional hypothesis pairs may be formulated for the test of Pearson's *r*.

3. Using symbols, state the nondirectional hypothesis pair for the test of Pearson's $r$.

4. Using symbols, state the directional pair for the test of $r$ when the alternative hypothesis states greater than.

5. A study finds that the greater the degree of health problems experienced by residents in a nursing home, the more frequent the visiting of family members: $r = .32, N = 102$. The hypothesis pair is nondirectional. Respond to the following questions:
   a. Is the correlation in the sample positive or negative?
   b. State the nondirectional null in words.
   c. How many degrees of freedom are there?
   d. Assuming that the .01 level is selected ($\alpha = .01$), what are the critical values of $r$?
   e. State the specific values of $r$ that result in rejection of the null?
   f. What is your decision regarding the null hypothesis? The alternative?
   g. How confident can you be that the null is false?
   h. Is the study sample result likely due to chance alone?
   i. Does the study sample result provide strong evidence that the null is false?
   j. Based on the provided information, are you ready to conclude that visiting causes increased health problems? If not, what is another explanation for the positive correlation between visiting and health problems?

6. Consider the information in the following grid:

| Situation | N | r | Alternative Hypothesis | α |
|---|---|---|---|---|
| #1 | 52 | −.26 | $r < 0.00$ | .01 |
| #2 | 52 | −.26 | $r < 0.00$ | .05 |
| #3 | 52 | −.26 | $r \neq 0.00$ | .05 |
| #4 | 72 | −.26 | $r \neq 0.00$ | .05 |
| #5 | 72 | −.26 | $r \neq 0.00$ | .01 |
| #6 | 1,002 | .07 | $r \neq 0.00$ | .05 |
| #7 | 14 | .49 | $r \neq 0.00$ | .05 |

For each situation in the grid:
   a. State the null using symbols
   b. Indicate the degrees of freedom
   c. Indicate the critical value(s)
   d. Indicate your decision on the null

7. A researcher studies the correlation between variables $X$ and $Y$. She formulates a hypothesis pair in which the alternative hypothesis states the direction greater than. That pair is $H_0: \rho_{xy} \leq 0, H_1: \rho_{xy} > 0$ where $\rho_{xy}$ is the hypothesized population

correlation. She uses the .05 level. Sample size equals 42 and correlation in the study sample is $r_{xy} = -.31$. Respond to the following:

    **a.** Formally, what decision should be made regarding the null? The research?

    **b.** Are study results in the expected direction?

    **c.** Was the use of a directional pair appropriate in this situation?

    **d.** In a situation such as this (results in a direction opposite to expectations), what does the text recommend?

**8.** In responding to the following, assume a nondirectional hypothesis pair.

    **a.** As sample size increases, the width of the sampling distribution of $r$ _____.

    **b.** As sample size increases, the absolute value of $r$ that is necessary to reject the null _____.

    **c.** Other things being equal, as sample size increases it becomes _____ to reject the null, in other words, power _____.

## Section 22.3

**9.** A table that displays the correlations between several variables is termed a _____ _____.

**10.** *Respond true or false to the following statements about the correlation between behavior problems score and mothers' educational level in Table 22.1:*

    **a.** This correlation equals .094.

    **b.** This correlation conveys a very strong association between behavior problems score and educational level.

    **c.** The significance test of this correlation presented in the matrix is two-tailed.

    **d.** This correlation is statistically significant at the .05 level.

    **e.** The probability that this correlation is due to chance alone is less than .05.

    **f.** One can be (at least) 95% confident that this correlation is not due to chance alone.

    **g.** This correlation is statistically significant at the .01 level.

    **h.** The probability that this correlation is caused by chance alone is less than .01.

    **i.** One can be 99% confident that this correlation is not caused by chance alone.

## Section 22.4

**11.** The following questions apply to this situation: A researcher selects the .05 level. The probability of the study result, as conveyed by the significance test is .003 ($p = .003$).

    **a.** *Formally*, using the hypothesis testing model, this result is statistically significant at the .01 level (rather than at the .05 level).

    **b.** In actual research, this result would likely be reported as significant at the .01 level (rather than at the .05 level).

    **c.** (Space permitting), the American Psychological Association recommends reporting the actual value of $p$ ($p = .003$ in this instance) rather than only the significance level.

## Section 22.5

12. *Respond true or false to each of the following:*
    a. Parametric tests assume that the population from which the study sample was (randomly) selected has some particular distributional shape whereas nonparametric tests make no such assumption.
    b. Most commonly used introductory parametric tests assume normality.
    c. When the dependent variable is at the interval/ratio level, nonparametric tests, in essence, treat it as being at a lower one.
    d. In situations in which parametric tests are not recommended, results of nonparametric tests are, most often, more accurate than those of the parametric tests that would otherwise have been conducted.

## Section 22.6

13. The nondirectional null for the test of Spearman's $r$ states that the correlation between two _____ _____ equals ___.

14. The nondirectional null for the significance tests of tau-$b$, tau-$c$, gamma, or Somers' $D$ states that the value of the (appropriate) measure equals ___.

15. The nondirectional null of the Mann-Whitney $U$ test states that ranks in two groups are equally "_____."

16. The Mann-Whitney $U$ test is an alternative to what commonly used parametric test?

17. The Kruskal-Wallis test is an extension of the _____-_____ ___ test to situations with ___ or more independent samples. It is an alternative to _____ of _____, also known as ___.

18. The Wilcoxon signed ranks test is used with two _____ samples. It is an alternative to the _____ samples $t$ test. The dependent variable's level of measurement should be _____/_____ or nearly so.

19. (*True or False*) For ordinal-level categorical dependent variables, the sign test is preferred to the Wilcoxon signed rank test.

20. McNemar's test tests a difference in _____ between two _____ samples.

## Section 22.7

21. Which of the following are advantages of parametric tests over nonparametric ones?
    a. More commonly used
    b. Often have more statistical power

c. Often more straightforward

d. In general, better connected to multivariate statistical procedures

**Section 22.8**

22. (*True or False*) One use of data transformation is to create a more normally shaped distribution so that (parametric) significance tests yield more accurate results.

23. What two data transformations are often used to transform positively skewed variables so that their shape becomes closer to normal?

**Section 22.9**

24. The ___ single-case design consists of two "phases." The _____ phase, designated as ___, comprises the preintervention observations and the _____ phase, designated as ___, comprises the postintervention observations.

25. You observe the following data which represent the number of times per day that a nursing home resident isolated from others participates in social activities. Within each phase, data are listed in chronological order.

    Baseline (A): 3, 5, 1, 6, 1, 5, 7, 2

    Intervention (B): 11, 6, 8, 13, 9, 5, 10

    Respond to the following questions. Assume that serial dependency is not a problem.
    a. Examine the baseline phase. Do you see a pronounced upward or downward trend across the baseline phase?
    b. Examine the intervention phase. Do you see a pronounced upward or downward trend across the intervention phase?
    c. Would an independent samples *t* test be appropriate here for examining the difference between baseline and intervention scores? Why or why not?
    d. Given that the independent samples *t* test is not appropriate, what test do you recommend?

26. (*True or False*) Even when there is a pronounced upward or downward trend in the baseline, the Mann-Whitney *U* test is still a recommended test for analyzing (interval-level) data in the AB single-case design.

27. During the 20-day baseline phase, a youth turns in her homework on 6 days and does not do so on 14 days. During the 20-day intervention phase, she turns in her homework on 12 days and does not do so on 8 days. Assume that the data do not exhibit serial dependency and that there is no pronounced trend in either the baseline or intervention phase. Respond to the following:
    a. During baseline, on what percentage of days does the youth turn in her homework?
    b. During intervention, on what percentage of days does the youth turn in her homework?

    **c.** Is there an association between phase (baseline vs. intervention) and turning in homework (turns in vs. does not turn in)?

    **d.** Calculate the difference in percentages ($D\%$) for turning in homework between the baseline and intervention phases. (Report this difference as a positive percentage.)

    **e.** Using the guidelines in Table 6.3, comment on size of association.

    **f.** What significance test would be a good one for examining whether the association between phase and turning in homework is statistically significant?

**28.** Observe the following time-series data which measures whether a youth turns in her homework on successive school days.

NYNNYNYNNYNYYNYNYNYNYNYNNYNNYYN

    **a.** Do the "Yes" and "No" responses tend to occur in (long) streaks/clusters?

    **b.** From visual inspection, does this data appear to evidence serial dependency?

    **c.** Would statistical procedures that do not address serial dependency be appropriate for this data?

**29.** Observe the following time-series data, which again measures whether a youth turns in her homework on successive school days.

NNNNNYYYYNNNNNYYNNNNYYYYYNNNYYYY

    **a.** Do the "Yes" and "No" responses tend to occur in streaks/clusters?

    **b.** From visual inspection, does this data appear to evidence serial dependency?

    **c.** Would statistical procedures that do not address serial dependency be appropriate for this data, that is, could you be confident that such procedures would yield accurate results?

**30.** When observations exhibit _____ _____, observations that occur close together in time have more similar values than those that do not.

**31.** *Respond true or false to each of the following:*

    **a.** When serial dependency is present, significance tests that do not take it into account can yield inaccurate results.

    **b.** A snake-like, serpentine pattern of dots around a horizontal line conveys that data do not exhibit a pattern of serial dependency.

    **c.** As sample size is often quite small in single-case designs, determining whether data exhibit serial dependency is, typically, easy and straightforward.

    **d.** This text highly recommends simply disregarding serial dependency as the best approach to analysis.

## Section 22.10

**32.** *Respond true or false to each of the following:*

    **a.** Statistical procedures are never used in predominantly qualitative studies.

    **b.** According to this chapter, those whose primary interest is in qualitative approaches do not need to know anything about statistics.

**Section 22.11**

**33.** *Respond true or false to each of the following:*

    **a.** When a relationship or result is statistically significant, we conclude that it is unlikely due to chance alone.

    **b.** When a relationship or result is statistically significant, it is likely to be caused by something real—something other than chance.

    **c.** Whenever we find a statistically significant relationship between the treatment intervention and the dependent variable, even in a study with nonrandom assignment, we can be confident that that relationship is a causal one (that the intervention is affecting the dependent variable).

    **d.** When we find a statistically significant relationship between the treatment intervention and the dependent variable in a study with random assignment, we can be confident that the relationship is a causal one (that the intervention is affecting the dependent variable).

    **e.** When we find a statistically significant relationship between the treatment intervention and the dependent variable in a study with random assignment, we can be confident about the *particular* characteristic of the intervention that has caused the study result.

    **f.** When a result is not statistically significant, this chapter encourages the researcher to think long and carefully about issues related to causality, that is, to about which particular independent variable(s) has affected the dependent variable.

    **g.** When power is extremely low, the researcher accepts the null almost by default.

# AN OVERVIEW OF SELECTED MULTIVARIATE PROCEDURES

## 23.1 ■ CHAPTER OVERVIEW

Chapter 23 overviews various multivariate statistical procedures, those that involve three or more variables. It begins with *multiple regression* analysis, focusing particular attention on how to interpret regression coefficients. Next, it presents *logistic regression*, a preferred approach when the dependent variable is dichotomous. The coverage of *two-way ANOVA* focuses on how to interpret *main effects* and interaction effects. The chapter closes with discussion of procedures that build on ANOVA and with "glimpses" at *structural equation modeling*, *multilevel modeling*, *survival analysis*, and *factor analysis*.

## 23.2 ■ MULTIPLE REGRESSION ANALYSIS

### 23.2.1 ■ Equation and Introduction

Multivariate statistical procedures involve three or more variables. The most commonly used multivariate procedure is multiple regression analysis. In **multiple regression analysis** (multiple regression), two or more **predictors** (independent variables) are entered into an equation that predicts an interval/ratio level dependent variable. The (unstandardized) multiple regression equation is

$$\hat{Y} = A + B_1X_1 + B_2X_2 + \ldots B_KX_K \tag{23.1}$$

where $\hat{Y}$ is the predicted value of the dependent variable, $A$ is the constant, $B_1$ is the regression coefficient for the first predictor, $X_1$ is the first predictor, $B_2$ is the regression coefficient for the second predictor, $X_2$ is the second predictor, $B_K$ is the regression coefficient for $K^{th}$ predictor, $X_K$ is the $K^{th}$ predictor, and ". . ." indicates the coefficients and predictors not explicitly listed in the equation.

Although the just-presented equation presents unstandardized coefficients, multiple regression analysis produces two sets of *regression coefficients*: $B$s and βs (betas, pronounced as [bait-ahs]). The $B$s are unstandardized and thus convey change in terms of original units of measurement (raw scores). The βs are standardized and thus convey change in terms of standard deviation units. The $B$s in multiple regression have much in common with the $B$s in bivariate regression. The βs have much in common with $r$, the correlation coefficient. (See Chapter 8, Section 8.9.2, for the contrast between B and $r$.) The βs in multiple regression are distinct from the β that conveys the probability of Type II error. (It is unfortunate that the same symbol is used for each.)

The key difference between $B$ and $\beta$ and their respective bivariate counterparts, $B$ and $r$, respectively, is that $B$ and $\beta$ convey change *controlling for other variables in the analysis*:

■ A predictor's unstandardized coefficient, $B$, conveys, controlling for other predictors in the analysis, the predicted change in original "raw score" units in the dependent variable as the predictor increases by 1.00 (1.00 original, "raw score" unit).

■ A predictor's standardized coefficient, $\beta$, conveys, controlling for other predictors in the analysis, the predicted change in standard deviation units in the dependent variable as the predictor increases by one (1.00) standard deviation.

Table 23.1, generated by the SPSS software program, presents a multiple regression analysis involving the special-needs adoption data. The dependent variable is score on the parent–child relationship scale. This score runs from a lowest possible score of 1.00 to a highest possible score of 4.00. It was derived by summing responses to five individual questions and then dividing by five. The behavior problems score can, theoretically, range from 0 to 236. In the adoption sample, the actual range is from 0 to 158. Income is measured in $1,000 increments (e.g., an income of $33,000 is recorded as 33). The adoptive mothers' education was *coded* as *less than high school* = 0, *high school diploma* or general education development (*GED*) = 1, *some college* = 2, *college graduation* = 3, *master's degree* or *higher* = 4. Finally, Foster_parent was coded as *not a prior foster parent to the adopted child* = 0; and *yes, prior foster parent* = 1.

When one category of a dichotomous variable is coded as 1 and the other as 0, then that variable is said to be *dummy-variable coded* and the variable is termed a **dummy variable** (*indicator variable, dummy*). Hence, Foster_parent is dummy-variable coded and is a dummy variable.[1]

As we begin our discussion, study Table 23.1 to see that whenever the $B$ for a predictor is significant, so also is the $\beta$. The same significance test tests each of these.

In discussing our regression results, I refer to the predictors by the names used for them in the SPSS-conducted analysis; these are the names in Table 23.1. Let us first focus attention on the unstandardized coefficients—the $B$s. For instance, the $B$ of $-.0153$ for Behavior_problems conveys that, controlling for the influence of Income_thousands, Education_mom, and Foster_parent, as Behavior_problems increases by 1.00, predicted parent–child relationship score decreases by .0153. As both Behavior_problems and parent–child relationship score are measured on unfamiliar scales, one cannot make intuitive sense of size of association from this coefficient.

TABLE 23. 1 ■ **Multiple Regression on Parent–Child Relationship Scale Score (*N* = 595)**

| Model | Unstandardized Coefficients | | Standardized Coefficients | | |
|---|---|---|---|---|---|
| | *B* | Standard Error | Beta | *t* | Sig. |
| (Constant) | 4.0554 | .062 | | 65.73 | .000 |
| Behavior_problems | −.0153 | .001 | −.592 | −18.69 | .000 |
| Income_thousands | −.0034 | .001 | −.114 | −3.34 | .001 |
| Education_mom | −.0434 | .019 | −.075 | −2.24 | .026 |
| Foster_parent | .1154 | .044 | .085 | 2.62 | .009 |

# 23

On the other hand, the βs do convey size of association. The β of −.592 for Behavior_problems conveys that, controlling for the influence of the other three predictors, as Behavior_problems score increases by one (1.00) standard deviation, parent–child relationship score is predicted to decrease by .592 standard deviations. One may use the qualitative descriptors for *r* to interpret size of association for β (see Table 8.2). Hence, the β for Behavior_problems conveys (controlling for the other variables in the analysis) a strong negative association between Behavior_problems and parent–child relationship. Continuing to focus on the βs and again using Table 8.2, we conclude that both family income and mothers' education level (controlling for other variables in the analysis) evidence weak negative relationships to parent–child relationship.

The beta (β) for Foster_parent is .085. Should we consult Table 8.2 and, having done so, conclude that Foster_parent (controlling for the other variables) has a weak positive relationship to parent–child relationship score? On balance, I recommend against interpreting the βs for dichotomous variables such as Foster_parent. At best, these βs approximate strength of relationship. Often, they underestimate strength of association.[2]

In regression analysis, I recommend coding dichotomous predictors as dummy variables. Doing so creates several advantages in interpreting results. The most important comes from the fact that one coding category is one (1.00) unit higher than the other. This being the case, the unstandardized coefficient, *B*, conveys the predicted difference between the two categories (groups). Hence, in our regression, the coefficient for Foster_parent, 0.1154, conveys that (controlling for other variables) the predicted parent–child relationship score is .1154 points higher for those who were prior foster parents than for those who were not. Given that parent–child relationship score ranges from 1.0 to 4.0, it is intuitive that 0.1154 units (about one tenth of a point) conveys a weak relationship. In sum, for a dichotomous predictor, I recommend (a) dummy-variable coding and (b) interpretation using *B* rather than β.

Perhaps the best way to interpret size of association for a dummy-variable coded dichotomous predictor coded is to transform the dependent variable into a *z* score. When parent–child relationship score is transformed into a *z* score, the *B* for Foster_parent equals 0.177. Hence, the regression analysis predicts that (controlling for other variables) for those who were prior foster parents, parent–child relationship score is 0.177 standard deviations higher than for those who were not. This difference is, in essence, a difference in standard deviation units (controlling for other variables). This being so, we may consult Table 9.1, which provides qualitative descriptors for differences in standard deviation units. Guided by this table, the difference of 0.177 standard deviations conveys a weak/small relationship between Foster_parent and parent–child relationship.

Observe that the constant (*A*) equals 4.0554. This conveys that when the value of all predictors equals 0, the predicted parent–child relationship score equals 4.0554. We may develop a multivariate (unstandardized) regression equation in much the same way as we did in the bivariate situation. Our multivariate equation is

Predicted parent–child relationship score = 4.0554 + (−.0153 × Behavior_problems) + (−.0034 × Income_thousands) + (−.0434 × Education_mom) + (.1154 × Foster_parent)

We can use this equation to calculate a predicted score for each case in the study sample. The SPSS output (not shown) informs us that the multiple correlation coefficient, symbolized by *R*, is equal to .645. The **multiple correlation coefficient** conveys the correlation between predicted scores (scores predicted by the regression equation) and actual scores. The guidelines in Table 8.2 for the correlation coefficient approximate the size of relationship conveyed by *R*.[3] Using these guidelines, we conclude that the relationship between predicted and actual scores is large to very large in size. (See Note 3 for this chapter when precise assessment of size of relationship is desired.)

Just as the correlation coefficient ($r$) is often interpreted by squaring it—$r^2$ conveys the proportion of shared variance—$R^2$, the **squared multiple correlation coefficient**, conveys the proportion of variance in the dependent variable explained by the multiple regression equation. For our regression, $R^2 = .645^2 = .416$. $R^2$ tends to be biased upward; it overestimates the $R^2$ that would be obtained if the full population (in other words, an infinite-sized population) rather than only a random sample was examined. The **adjusted $R^2$** provides a more accurate estimate of $R^2$ in the population. In our example, the adjusted $R^2$ equals .412.

## 23.2.2 ■ Assumptions of Multiple Regression

We have not discussed the assumptions of multiple regression analysis. Three important assumptions are as follows: (a) the dependent variable should be at the interval/ratio-level of measurement, (b) residuals should be normally distributed around predicted values (the values predicted by the equation), and (c) the variance of residuals around the predicted values should be equal (equality of variance). A **residual** is the difference between a case's actual score on the dependent variable and its predicted score (actual minus predicted equals residual). Figure 23.1 presents actual and predicted scores for our example. The dots convey the actual scores and the straight line conveys the predicted score. The vertical difference between each dot and the line conveys a case's residual. The second assumption earlier conveys that at each point along the line, the dots should be distributed normally around the line. The third assumption conveys that the spread (variance) of the dots should be approximately the same at different points along the line.[4]

**FIGURE 23.1. ■ Scatterplot of Residuals for Parent-Child Relationship Scale**

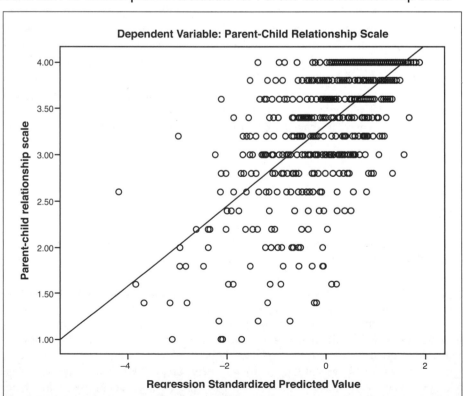

The plot in Figure 23.1 is not ideal. For instance, the dots tend to spread out more on the line's lower side than on its upper. This pattern of spreading violates the assumption that residuals should be normally distributed around the predicted values. Further, the dots tend to spread out more on the line's left side (lower predicted values) than on its right side (higher predicted values). This unequal spreading of residuals violates the assumption of equal variances of residuals.

When a plot such as in Figure 23.1 demonstrates violations (or potential violations) of assumptions, researchers often carry out data transformations, hoping to make the residuals "fit" better. Although transformations can be carried out on both the predictors and the dependent variable, the initial focus is often on the dependent variable. When the dependent variable is positively skewed, researchers often apply either square root or log transformations (see Chapter 22, Section 22.8). Parent–child relationship score is negatively skewed. When this is the case, transformation is more complex.[5,6]

I reran the multiple regression twice, each time using a different transformation of parent–child relationship score as the dependent variable. These transformations improved the fit of the residuals to some degree. Even so, values of *p* for the predictors changed hardly at all from those in the initial regression (see Table 23.1). This being so, and also because multiple regression is, on balance, robust to violations of the above-described normality and equal variances assumptions, I decided to stick with the initial regression. As the violations of these assumptions are more than modest, one should interpret the results with some caution.[7]

Figure 23.2 presents a residual plot for a hypothetical variable. The residuals in this plot fit the normality and equal variance assumptions quite well. The variance (spread) of the residuals perhaps appears wider in the center of Figure 23.2 than at the lower (left) and upper (right) areas, but this is a function of the fact that more data points are located in the center than at the sides, not

FIGURE 23.2. ■ Scatterplot of Residuals that Fit Well

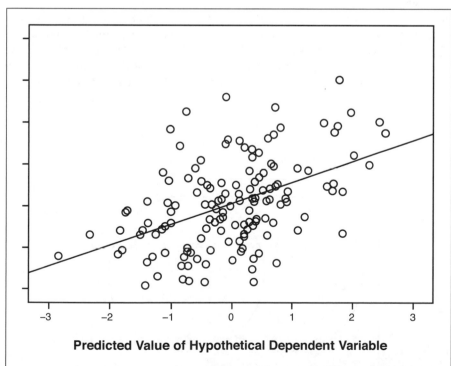

**Predicted Value of Hypothetical Dependent Variable**

of an actual difference in variance. The full process of checking assumptions and finding the best fit in multiple regression is beyond our scope. Excellent sources for this process include Abu-Bader (2010) and Norušis (2010). For further information on multiple regression, see Toothaker, and Miller (1996) or Glass and Hopkins (1996).

As you interpret the coefficients in Table 23.1, remember that variables not included in the analysis are not controlled for. Also, it is important to understand that when a predictor measures less than perfectly, that is, when it measures with some degree of error, multiple regression controls for *measured* score rather than for *actual* score.

For instance, our regression controls for *measured* behavior problems score. Just as a score on an exam only estimates a student's knowledge, this score only estimates a child's behavior problems. As such, our regression does not control *fully* for child behavior problems. This being so, child behavior may still be exerting some small effect (bias) on the coefficients of the other predictors in the equation. In sum, particularly when predictors measure with some degree of error, multiple regression controls well, but not perfectly, for the predictors in the equation.

## 23.3 ■ ADVANTAGES OF MULTIVARIATE ANALYSES

Chapter 16 (Section 16.5.4) discussed how introducing a third variable into an analysis can increase statistical power by making the "haystack" (sampling error) smaller and thus the "needle"—(the effect of the intervention or other kwy variable) easier to find. This section demonstrates these ideas and more in the context of multiple regression.

Figure 23.3 presents a visual representation of a correlation of .50 ($r = .50$) between two variables, $X$ and $Y$. If we presume that $X$ is the independent variable and $Y$ is the dependent, then $X$ explains 25% of the variance in $Y$ ($r^2 = .50^2 = .25 \times 100 = 25\%$; see Chapter 8, end of Section 8.5). The 75% of the variance that is not explained ($100\% - 25\% = 75\%$) is the sampling error (the haystack).

Figure 23.4 presents a multiple regression in which two predictors, $X$ and $Q$, are uncorrelated ($r = 0.00$)—this is the case because their circles do not overlap—and each predictor correlates, $r = .50$, with the dependent variable $Y$. As $r$ equals .50 for both $X$ and $Q$, each explains 25% of $Y$'s variance. As $X$ and $Q$ are uncorrelated, each explains separate (unique) variance in $Y$. As each predictor explains separate variance, the total percentage of explained variance in $Y$ can be found by summing: 25% + 25% = 50%. In Figure 23.3, 75% of the variance in $Y$ is unexplained. In Figure 23.4, this percentage

FIGURE 23.3. ■ **A Single Predictor**

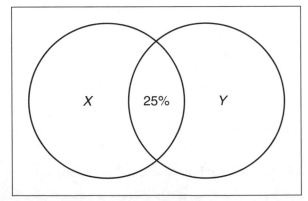

FIGURE 23.4. ■ Two Uncorrelated Predictors

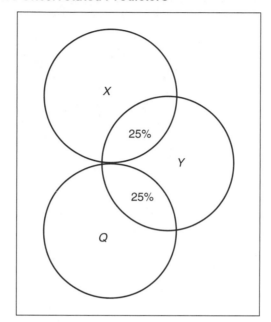

is 50% (100% − 50% = 50%). Continue to think of the unexplained variance as sampling error, that is, as the haystack. As the haystack is smaller, the power to detect whether $X$ is significantly related to $Y$ is greater in the multiple regression (Figure 23.4) than in the bivariate analysis (Figure 23.3).

Yet, it is unusual for predictors in multiple regression to be uncorrelated ($r = 0.00$). Figure 23.5 presents a more typical situation in which, as the overlap of their circles conveys, predictors $X$ and $Q$ are correlated. Because they are correlated, $X$ and $Q$ do not explain fully unique portions of the variance in $Y$, but instead some of the variance that each explains overlaps with that explained by the other. In Figure 23.5, $X$ and $Q$ each explain 25% of the variance but 5% of that variance is also explained by the other. In Figure 23.5, the total percentage of explained variance is 25% + 25% − 5% = 45%.

We want to explain as much variance as we can. The greater the percentage of explained variance, the greater the strength of association and, further, the better the predictions that we can make. Individually, $Q$ and $X$ each explain 25% of $Y$'s variance. Taken as a pair, they explain 45%. Taken as a pair rather than individually, $X$ and $Q$ (a) have a stronger relationship to $Y$ and (b) allow for better predictions of $Y$.

Let us shift our focus back to the relationship of $X$ to $Y$. Figure 23.3 presented the relationship of (only) $X$ to $Y$. In Figure 23.3, 75% of $Y$'s variance is unexplained. In Figure 23.5, this percentage is 55%. The unexplained variance is smaller in Figure 23.5 than in Figure 23.3. Should not this reduction in unexplained variance (the smaller haystack) increase our power to detect the relationship of $X$ to $Y$? In and of itself, the reduction in unexplained variance does increase our power. Yet this increase is counterbalanced by the fact that $X$ and $Q$ are correlated. As a general rule, the stronger the correlation between two predictors in a multiple regression, the lower is the power to detect the effect of each.

As the reduction in unexplained variance is counterbalanced by the correlation between $X$ and $Q$, the answer to the just-posed question is less than straightforward. However, two factors suggest that power is greater in the multiple regression (Figure 23.5) than in the bivariate analysis (Figure 23.3). First, the reduction in unexplained variance is substantial (75%–55%). Second, the

FIGURE 23.5. ■ Two Weakly Correlated Predictors

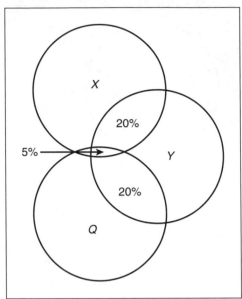

correlation between the predictors is low. In sum, power to detect the relationship of $X$ to $Y$ is, almost assuredly, greater in the multiple regression.

In Figure 23.5, the correlation between the predictors was low. At the other extreme, the correlation between two predictors can be so high that nearly all of the variance that each explains is also explained by the other. Figure 23.6 presents such a situation. In Figure 23.6, $X$ and $Q$ each explain 25% of $Y$'s variance but 23% of that variance is also explained by the other predictor. Hence, the total percentage of explained variance is 25% + 25% − 23% = 27%. In situations such as this, the addition of the second predictor almost assuredly reduces the power to detect the relationship of the first. For instance, the power to detect $X$'s relationship to $Y$ is, almost

FIGURE 23.6. ■ Two Very Strongly Correlated Predictors

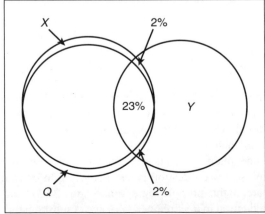

assuredly, greater in Figure 23.3 than in Figure 23.6. As Figure 23.6 also demonstrates, when two predictors are very highly correlated, the addition of the second predictor almost assuredly explains only a small amount of additional variance.

Let us sum up. In the "best" combination of predictors, each predictor has (a) a low correlation with each other predictor and (b) a high correlation with the dependent variable (Glass & Hopkins, 1996, p. 175). Such a combination explains a maximum amount of variance (or nearly does so) in the dependent variable and, at the same time, maximizes the power (or very nearly does so) to detect the relationship of each predictor to the dependent variable. On the other hand, when two predictors are very highly correlated, the addition of the second predictor almost always (a) explains little additional variance in the dependent variable and (b) reduces the power to detect the relationship of the first predictor to the dependent variable.

Figures 23.4, 23.5, and 23.6 present situations involving two predictors. Yet, multiple regression can be carried out with six or seven (or many more) predictors. In general, as more predictors are added, (a) the explained variance increases, but by decreasing amounts, and (b) the amount of overlapping variance—the variance explained by more than one predictor—increases. At some point, the regression reaches a point of diminishing returns where the addition of a new predictor explains little new variance. Further, as more and more predictors are added, it becomes increasingly difficult to detect the unique relationship of each to the dependent variable.

The "art" of multiple regression is to choose a parsimonious (reasonably small) number of predictors—preferably not highly correlated with one another—and, having done so, to explain as much variance as one can. Thoughtlessly adding many predictors, put simply, often creates a mess. Stated differently, adding "more" (predictors) often results in "less" (useful information).

Our discussion to this point may have created the misperception that a second (or subsequent) predictor that is highly correlated with an already included predictor should never be added to a multiple regression analysis. Although adding such a predictor often explains little new variance and often reduces the power to detect the relationship of the first predictor to the dependent variable, failure to do so can introduce bias. Stated differently, the second predictor may be an important confounding variable and thus including it may change the relationship (as conveyed by $B$ and $\beta$) of the first predictor to the dependent variable. The best way to find out whether this is the case is to introduce the second predictor and examine the results. (See Chapters 10 and 11 for more on confounding variables.)

Further, our discussion may have created the misperception that whenever two predictors are highly correlated, the unique relationship of each to the dependent variable is *always* small (or even nonexistent). One (or, occasionally, both) of these predictors can have a substantial unique relationship. Again, the best way to find out is to include both in the analysis and examine the results.[7]

This section and Chapter 16, Section 16.5.4, demonstrate that, by explaining variance that would otherwise be sampling error, including multiple independent variables (predictors) often increases statistical power. Chapters 10 and 11 demonstrated how confounding variables control for bias. In sum, two advantages from multivariate analysis are (a) often an increase in power and (b) improved control for bias (i.e., for the effects of confounding variables).

In closing discussion of multiple regression, the problem of multicollinearity (collinearity) should be mentioned. Problems of **multicollinearity** (*collinearity*) can occur when two predictors or some combination of predictors are *very* highly correlated. Severe problems of multicollinearity can cause a regression equation to "crash." Less severe problems reduce the power of the tests of the regression coefficients, the $B$s and $\beta$s. Although the exact correlation between $X$ and $Q$ in Figure 23.6 is not provided, this correlation is quite high, likely high enough to introduce the problem of multicollinearity.[8,9]

Although the points made in this section were made in the context of multiple regression analysis, most apply to other multivariate analytic approaches as well. We now overview a variety of multivariate approaches. For more on multiple regression, see the Notes at the end of this book.[10]

## 23.4 ■ LOGISTIC REGRESSION

Multiple regression examines the association of predictors to an interval/ratio-level dependent variable. **Logistic regression** examines the association of predictors to a dichotomous (binary, two-category) dependent variable. It draws on your knowledge of odds and odds ratios. The logistic regression formula is

$$\ln \left( \frac{p}{1 - p} \right) = A + B_1X_1 + B_2X_2 + \ldots B_KB_K \tag{23.2}$$

where ln is the natural logarithm, $p$ is proportion that experiences an event (the researcher designates one of the two categories as the event), and the other symbols are the same as in Formula 23.1.[11]

Recall from Chapter 7, Section 7.2.1, that $p / (1 - p)$ is a formula for the odds (Formula 7.3). Thus, Formula 23.2 predicts the natural logarithm of the odds of an event. The natural logarithm of the odds is often termed the *log of the odds* or the *logit*. The logit does not lend itself to intuitive interpretation. However, Formula 23.2 can be manipulated mathematically so that it predicts odds rather than the log of the odds:

$$\frac{p}{1 - p} = e^A \times e^{B_1X_1} \times e^{B_2X_2} \times \ldots e^{B_KX_K} \tag{23.3}$$

where $e$ is the base of the system of natural logarithms and equals approximately 2.71828. Other symbols are as in the prior equations.

Although the two just-presented equations may appear daunting, interpretation of logistic regression results by the second equation is straightforward. In particular, you do not need to understand either logarithms or "$e$" to make sense of results.

Using SPSS, let us carry out a logistic regression that predicts the odds that a respondent (an adoptive parent) in the adoption study will respond "very positive" (versus any other response) regarding the impact of adoption on the family. For simplicity, I use the same predictors used in the multiple regression example. Table 23.2 presents the results.

In Table 23.2, the $B$ coefficients apply to the regression on the *log of the odds* of a very positive impact, that is, to the logit (Formula 23.2). Our focus is on the $e^B$ coefficients, some-

TABLE 23.2 ■ **Logistic Regression on Responding "Very Positive" About the Adoption's Impact on the Family**

|  | B | SE | Wald | df | Sig. | $e^B$ |
|---|---|---|---|---|---|---|
| Behavior_problems | −.054 | .005 | 104.825 | 1 | .000 | .948 |
| Income_thousands | −.006 | .005 | 1.235 | 1 | .266 | .994 |
| Education_mom | −.178 | .088 | 4.035 | 1 | .045 | .837 |
| Foster_parent | .229 | .197 | 1.351 | 1 | .245 | 1.257 |
| Constant | 2.122 | .312 | 46.359 | 1 | .000 | 8.349 |

*Note.* SPSS uses the symbol Exp(B) to designate the $e^B$ coefficients. SE = standard error.

times termed the *exponentiated coefficients*.[12] These coefficients apply to the regression on the *odds* of a very positive impact (see Formula 23.3). The $e^B$ have much in common with odds ratios (see Chapter 7, Section 7.2). Each $e^B$ coefficient conveys, controlling for other variables in the analysis, the change in the odds as the predictor that corresponds to it increases by 1.00 (one). An $e^B$ coefficient greater than 1.00 conveys that as the predictor increases, so do the odds; an $e^B$ coefficient exactly equal to 1.00 conveys that the predictor has no relationship to the odds; and an $e^B$ coefficient less than 1.00 conveys that as the predictor increases, the odds decrease

To interpret the $e^B$ coefficients in Table 23.2, we need to consider how the predictors were coded. Recall that Foster_parent is dummy-variable coded (1 = *prior foster parent*, 0 = *not prior foster parent*). Thus, the $e^B$ for Foster_parent conveys that, controlling for the other variables, the odds of a very positive impact for prior foster parents are 1.257 times the odds for those who were not prior foster parents. We may also say that the odds of very positive impact are 25.7% higher for prior foster parents (1.257 − 1.00 = .257 × 100 = 25.7% higher). And further, we may say that the odds of very positive impact are higher for prior foster parents than for other parents by a factor of 1.257.

As Foster_parent is dummy-variable coded, the $e^B$ coefficient for Foster_parent is, in essence, an odds ratio, but one in which the effects of other predictors have been controlled for. As such, we may consult Table 7.2, which presents descriptors of size of association for the odds ratio (see Chapter 7, Section 7.2.2). Using Table 7.2's guidelines, the size of association is very small. Foster_parent is not a significant predictor of adoption impact, $p = .245$.

Recall that Education_mom was measured on a 5-point scale. Hence, as Education_mom increases by 1.00 point, the odds of very positive impact change by a factor of .837. Stated differently, as education increases by one point, the odds of a very positive impact decrease by 16.3% (1.00 − .837 = .163 × 100 = 16.3% lower). This association was significant, $p = .045$. Finally, let us interpret the $e^B$ for Behavior_problems: For each one (1.00) point increase in Behavior_problems score, the odds of very positive impact change by a factor of .948, that is, they decrease by 5.2% (1.00 − .948 = .52 × 100 = 5.2% lower).

Given that Behavior_problems score ranged from 0 to 158, the just-presented interpretation is less than straightforward. If we transform Behavior_problems to a $z$ score, it will be more straightforward. Rerunning the logistic regression with Behavior_problems transformed into a z score results in an $e^B$ of .246. Hence, as Behavior_problems increase by one standard deviation, the odds of a very positive impact change by a factor of .246, in other words, they decrease by 74.4% (1.00 − .246 = .744 × 100 = 74.4% lower).

We have only overviewed logistic regression. Good resources for logistic regression include Long (1997) and Hosmer and Lemeshow (2000). *Ordinal logistic regression* extends logistic regression to dependent variables with three or more ordered categories. (Binary logistic regression was presented here.) *Probit regression* is closely related to logistic regression and, almost without exception, yields highly similar outcomes. *Ordinal probit regression* extends probit regression to dependent variables with three or more ordered categories. Poisson and negative binomial regressions are specialized regression approaches for dependent variables that involve counts (see Long, 1997).

## 23.5 ■ FACTORIAL ANALYSIS OF VARIANCE

Chapter 21 introduced analysis of variance, also known as ANOVA. When only one variable defines groups (samples), the resulting ANOVA is a **one-way ANOVA**. The ANOVA presented in Chapter 21 was a one-way ANOVA in which family ethnicity defined the groups. In ANOVA, a variable that defines groups is termed a **factor**. The family ethnicity ANOVA, possessed one factor, that being family ethnicity. ANOVA designs can be expanded to include two or more fac-tors. An ANOVA with two factors is a **two-way ANOVA** (a **two-way analysis of variance**). Let us investigate the following questions with a two-way ANOVA:

■ Is handicap status (adopted child has a handicap vs. child does not have a handicap) asso-ciated with parent–child relationship score?

■ Does parent–child relationship score differ by whether the adopting parent(s) were (or were not) foster parents to the child?

In our two-way ANOVA, two factors, handicap status and prior foster parent status, define four groups:

**1.** Children with handicaps whose adoptive parents were prior foster parents to them
**2.** Children with handicaps whose adoptive parents were not prior foster parents to them
**3.** Children without handicaps whose adoptive parents were prior foster parents to them
**4.** Children without handicaps whose adoptive parents were not prior foster parents to them

A factor's categories are its **levels**. In our ANOVA, handicap status has two levels, children with handicaps and children without handicaps, as does prior foster parent status, those who were prior foster parents and those who were not. As our analysis has two factors, each with two levels, it is a 2 × 2 ANOVA (pronounced "2 by 2" ANOVA). Suppose that an ANOVA has three factors, the first with three levels, the second with two, and the third with four. This ANOVA is a 3 × 2 × 4 ANOVA. As it has three factors, this ANOVA is a *three-way* ANOVA). An ANOVA with two or more factors is a **factorial ANOVA** (*factorial design*).

Table 23.3 presents mean parent–child relationship scores for our two factors and four groups. Focusing on handicap status (i.e., disregarding foster parent status) the mean for children with handicaps is very slightly higher than is that for children without handicaps (3.38 vs. 3.33; see the table's rightmost row). Focusing on foster parent status (i.e., disregarding handicap status) those who were prior foster parents evidence a higher mean score than do those who were not (3.46 vs. 3.26; see the bottom row). The just-carried out comparisons focus on the main effects of the two study factors. A factor's **main effect** is its effect disregarding the presence of the other factor (or factors).

One advantage of two-way ANOVA over one-way ANOVA is that two main effects rather than one can be assessed. Yet, this advantage is a modest one. Indeed, it is just about as easy to conduct two one-way ANOVAs as to conduct one two-way ANOVA. A second advantage, but still a modest one, is that the statistical power to detect the effect of each factor often increases.[13]

TABLE 23.3 ■ **Means in Two-Way ANOVA With Factors Foster Parent Status and Handicap Status (Standard Deviations and Sample Sizes in Parentheses)**

|  | Prior Foster Parent | Not Prior Foster Parent | Total |
|---|---|---|---|
| **Child has handicap** | 3.59 ($s = 0.52, n = 81$) | 3.13 ($s = 0.76, n = 65$) | 3.38 ($s = 0.68, n = 146$) |
| **Child does not have handicap** | 3.41 ($s = 0.60, n = 250$) | 3.28 ($s = 0.68, n = 369$) | 3.33 ($s = 0.65, n = 619$) |
| Total | 3.46 ($s = 0.58, n = 331$) | 3.26 ($s = 0.69, n = 434$) | 3.34 ($s = 0.65, n = 765$) |

The key advantage of two-way ANOVA is that the researcher can assess whether two factors interact in predicting the dependent variable. When two factors *interact*—that is, when there is an *interaction* (*interaction effect*)—the association of each factor to the dependent variable differs according to the level of the other. Interactions between ANOVA factors involve the same concepts as were presented in Chapter 11, Section 11.5. Recall that interactions may involve size of, direction of, or presence of association.

Let us now run our two-way ANOVA using SPSS. Table 23.4 presents the results. Our focus is on the significance levels presented in the right-most column. The row for Foster_parent presents the main effect of prior foster parent status. This difference is significant, $p = .000$. This conveys that, disregarding the effect of handicap status, the overall difference in means between the two foster parent groups (3.46 vs. 3.26) is unlikely to be due to chance. On the other hand, the main effect for Handicap_status is not significant, $p = .824$. This conveys that the difference between the means for the two handicap status groups (3.38 vs. 3.33) may well be due to chance alone. Observe that the interaction effect between Foster_parent and Handicap_status is significant, $p = .008$. This interaction can be interpreted in two ways:

1. The *size* of association of prior foster parent status to parent–child relationship differs by handicap status:

   ■ For children with handicaps, outcomes are *much* more positive for adoptive parents who were prior foster parents (3.59 vs. 3.13)

   ■ For children without handicaps, outcomes are only *modestly* more positive for parents who were prior foster parents(3.41 vs. 3.28)

2. The *direction* of association of handicap status to parent–child relationship differs by prior foster parent status:

   ■ For children whose adoptive parents were prior foster parents, outcomes are more positive for children *with* handicaps (3.59 vs. 3.41)

   ■ For children whose adoptive parents were not prior foster parents, outcomes are more positive for children *without* handicaps (3.28 vs. 3.13)

As our example demonstrates, an interaction effect can typically be described in two different ways. In my view, each description in our example increases understanding of the results. In

TABLE 23.4 ■ Two-Way Factorial ANOVA: Foster Parent Status and Handicap Status Predict Closeness of Parent–Child Relationship

| Source | Type 3 Sum of Squares | df | Mean Square | F | Sig. |
|---|---|---|---|---|---|
| Corrected model | 10.41 | 3 | 3.47 | 8.37 | .000 |
| Intercept | 5220.15 | 1 | 5220.15 | 12595.40 | .000 |
| Foster_status | 10.03 | 1 | 10.03 | 24.19 | .000 |
| Handicap_status | .02 | 1 | .02 | .05 | .824 |
| Foster * handicap | 2.94 | 1 | 2.94 | 7.09 | .008 |
| Error | 315.40 | 761 | .41 | | |
| Total | 8871.20 | 765 | | | |
| Corrected Total | 325.81 | 764 | | | |

FIGURE 23.7. ■ Interaction of Handicap Status and Foster Parent Adoption

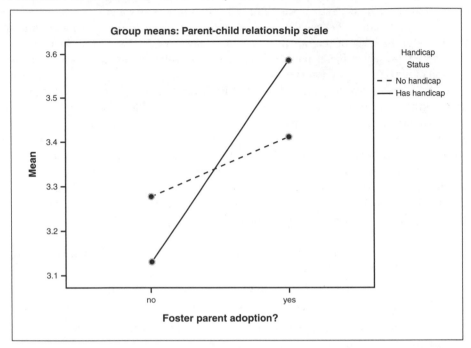

actual research, the researcher presents the description that, in her view, most effectively communicates the interaction's meaning to the reader. Figure 23.7 displays visually the interaction of handicap status and foster parent status. The markedly different slopes for the two lines convey the interaction.

When an interaction effect is significant in two-way ANOVA, interpretation of the main effects is not straightforward. This is because the main effects disregard the interaction and, by so doing, create an oversimplified, even misleading perspective on results. Hence, when there is a significant interaction, the main effects in ANOVA should be interpreted cautiously and only in the context of the interaction.

When the interaction in two-way ANOVA does not achieve significance, the ANOVA should, in most instances, be rerun with the interaction dropped from the analysis. (Software packages have straightforward means for doing so.) When the interaction is not significant, interpretation of the main effects is, most often, more straightforward.[14]

Two-way ANOVA assumes normality, but is robust to this assumption. It also assumes equal variances. It is robust to this assumption when group sizes are equal but not when they differ greatly. At a minimum, all group sizes should be at least 10 or so.

## 23.6 ■ MULTIVARIATE PROCEDURES RELATED TO ANALYSIS OF VARIANCE

**Analysis of covariance** (*ANCOVA*) builds on both one-way ANOVA and factorial ANOVA by adding *covariates*, that is, interval/ratio-level predictors. The addition of the covariates (predictors) can add power and also reduce bias. An important assumption in ANCOVA is that the covariate(s) evidence the same strength of association to the dependent variable in all of the different groups. This is termed the *homogeneity of regression* assumption.

See Glass and Hopkins (1996), Abu-Bader (2010), or other statistics books for more on ANCOVA.

*Multiple analysis of variance (MANOVA)* examines several dependent variables in a single analysis. MANOVA can test whether the overall variance explained for several dependent variables taken together is greater than would be expected by chance. The researcher goes on to analyze the individual dependent variables only when the overall variance explained in the MANOVA is statistically significant. MANCOVA adds covariates (interval/ratio-level predictors) to MANOVA.

*Repeated measures designs* analyze several or more different administrations of the same (interval/ratio-level) dependent variable. (The same measure is administered at multiple time points.) These designs, for instance, can examine whether better outcomes across time are observed in one group than in another. Serial dependency can be a problem in these designs (see Chapter 22, Section 22.9.3. This can manifest itself in violation of the compound symmetry assumption.) Abu-Bader (2010) and Norušis (2009) are good resources for the procedures discussed in this section.

## 23.7 ■ A GLIMPSE AT SELECTED PROCEDURES

**Structural equation modeling** (SEM) involves the building of causal models, typically much more complex than those presented in Chapters 10 and 11. These models may involve multiple dependent variables modeled simultaneously as well as variables that function as both predictors and dependent variables. In some models, multiple measures measure a common concept, thus building confidence that that concept is measured effectively. Two strengths of SEM models are (a) the ability to assess both direct and indirect effects and, often, (b) better assessment of causality than is the case in multiple regression analysis. *Path analysis* is similar to SEM. It can perhaps best be described as SEM but without the use of multiple measures to define concepts. Well-known SEM software packages included LISREL, Amos (an add-on feature within SPSS), and Mplus. A good reference for SEM is Kline (2011).

Consider a study of math achievement of fifth graders at, say, 100 different schools. Some potential predictors are at the level of the child. These might include the child's math skills as the study begins, support in the child's family for education, and the child's gender. Other potential predictors are at the level of the school. These might include the quality of teaching in the child's school, whether the school was a charter/magnet school, and the math ability of the child's classmates (perhaps where others are good at math, this "rubs" off on the individual child). The strength of **multilevel modeling** is its ability to examine contributions of variables at multiple levels of analysis. Multilevel modeling modules are found in some statistical software packages (in SPSS, see "Mixed Models") and in specialized packages, including HLM, MLWin, and Mplus. For more on multilevel modeling see Raudenbush and Bryk (2002).

Medical studies often measure the time from intervention (i.e., administration of a given procedure or drug) until death. A juvenile justice treatment program might want to measure the time from intervention until arrest. Note that, in this example, some youth may never be arrested. **Survival analysis** (*event history analysis*) is the preferred analytic method when the dependent variable is time to occurrence. It can accommodate both cases in which the event (i.e., death or arrest) occurs (in which case the amount of time until occurrence is assessed) and those in which it does not (in which case the amount of time during which the event did not occur is assessed). As it accommodates both types of cases, no cases are excluded and minimal information is lost. Most of the major statistical software packages include survival analysis programs. The most popular and straightforward survival analysis methodology is the *Cox* *proportional hazards model*. See Hosmer and Lemeshow (1999) or Norušis (2010) for more on survival analysis.

Consider an instrument that asks parents to respond to seven items pertaining to their child's behavior problems (hits others, isolated, fights, keeps to self, talks back, timid, swears). Looking at these problems, your mind perhaps separates them into two types. Let us call one type "aggressive"—hits others, fights, talks back, and swears fit well here. Let us call the other "withdrawn"—isolated, keeps to self, and timid fit here. In essence, we have reduced seven variables into two. **Factor analysis** searches for variables that "go together"—basically, it identifies variables that are highly correlated with one another—and groups these together into a *factor*. Reducing, say, seven pieces of information into two simplifies things. For instance, we can now assess what independent variables—gender, family structure, child's age, and so on—predict two dependent variables rather than seven. The major statistics software packages have factor analysis modules. Norušis (2009) is a good resource for factor analysis.

## 23.8 ■ CHAPTER SUMMARY

In *multiple regression analysis* (multiple regression), two or more *predictors* predict an interval/ratio-level dependent variable. The unstandardized multiple regression equation is

$$\hat{Y} = A + B_1X_1 + B_2X_2 + \ldots B_KX_K \tag{23.1}$$

The unstandardized coefficient, $B$, conveys, controlling for other variables in the analysis, the predicted change in "raw score" units in the dependent variable as a predictor increases by 1.00 "raw score" unit. The standardized coefficient, $\beta$ (beta), conveys, controlling for other variables, the predicted change in standard deviation units in the dependent variable as a predictor increases by one (1.00) standard deviation. $\beta$ conveys size of association but $B$ does not.

When one of its categories is coded as 1 and the other as 0, a variable is a *dummy variable*. The *multiple correlation coefficient*, $R$, conveys the correlation between predicted scores and actual scores. $R^2$ conveys the proportion of variance in the dependent variable explained by the multiple regression equation. The *adjusted $R^2$* provides a more accurate estimate of $R^2$ in the population. *Residuals* should be normally distributed and have equal variance.

In the "best" combination of predictors, each predictor has a low correlation with each other predictor and a high correlation with the dependent variable. On the other hand, failure to include a highly correlated predictor can introduce bias. *Multicollinearity* problems can occur when predictors are very highly correlated.

*Logistic regression* examines the association of predictors to a dichotomous dependent variable. The formula $\frac{p}{1-p} = e^A \times e^{B_1X_1} \times e^{B_2X_2} \ldots \times e^{B_KX_K}$ predicts odds. In this formula, coefficients convey, controlling for other variables, the change in the odds as a predictor increases by 1.00.

In ANOVA, a variable that defines groups is a *factor*. A *two-way ANOVA* has two groups. An ANOVA with two or more factors is a *factorial ANOVA*. A factor's categories are its *levels*. A 2 × 2 ANOVA, for instance, has two factors, each with two levels. A factor's *main effect* is its effect disregarding the presence of the other factor (or factors).

The key advantage of two-way ANOVA is that *interaction* can be assessed. When two factors *interact*, the association of each factor to the dependent variable differs according to the level of the other. When an interaction is significant, interpretation of the main effects is not straightforward.

*Analysis of covariance* adds interval/ratio-level predictors to ANOVA designs. This can improve power and reduce bias. *MANOVA* examines several dependent variables in a single analysis; *MANCOVA* adds covariates to MANOVA. *Repeated measures designs* analyze several different administrations of the same dependent variable.

*Structural equation modeling* (SEM) can be used to build complex causal models. *Multi-level modeling* examines contributions of variables at multiple levels of analysis. Researchers use *survival analysis* when the dependent variable is time to occurrence. *Factor analysis* reduces multiple pieces of information to a smaller number.

## 23.9 ■ PROBLEMS AND QUESTIONS

**Section 23.2**

1. A predictor's _____ coefficient, *B*, conveys, _____ for other _____ in the analysis, the _____ change in (original " _____ _____ " units) in the dependent variable as the predictor increases by 1.00 (1.00 original, " _____ _____ " unit).

2. A predictor's _____ coefficient, β, conveys, controlling for other _____ in the analysis, the _____ change in _____ _____ units in the dependent variable as the predictor increases by one (1.00) _____ _____.

3. The _____ _____ _____, symbolized by __, conveys the correlation between predicted scores and actual scores.

4. The _____ _____ _____ _____, symbolized by __, conveys the proportion of variance in the dependent variable explained by the multiple regression equation.

5. The _____ $R^2$ provides a more accurate estimate of $R^2$ in the population than does $R^2$.

6. When one category of a dichotomous variable is coded as 1 and the other as 0, that variable is a _____ variable.

7. (*True or False*) Multiple regression controls effectively for variables that are not included in the analysis.

8. The following questions pertain to the regression results in Table 23.1 and to additional information on these results that is presented in the text.
   a. (True or False) Whenever a predictor's *B* is significant, so also is its β.
   b. As income increases by $1,000—that is, as Income_thousands increases by one (1.00)—what is the predicted change in parent–child relationship score?
   c. As income increases by one standard deviation, what is the predicted change in standard deviation units in parent–child relationship score?
   d. Suppose that, for a given case, the value of each predictor equals 0.00? What is that case's predicted score?

382 Part 2 Inferential Statistics and Data Interpretation

e. (*True or False*) Given that the *B* for Behavior_problems ($B = -.0153$) is so close to zero (0.00), we may conclude that the relationship between Behavior_problems and parent–child relationship score is a very weak one.

f. As Education_mom increases by one point (on the 5-point education level scale), what is the predicted change in parent–child relationship score?

g. As Education_mom increases by one standard deviation, what is the predicted change in standard deviation units in parent–child relationship score?

h. What is the beta ($\beta$) for Education_mom? Does this convey small, medium, or large association?

i. The size of association of Education_mom to parent–child relationship score is very small. What is the most important reason why this very small association is statistically significant ($p = .026$).

j. (*True or False*) The coefficients (the *B* and $\beta$) for Education_mom reflect predicted change controlling for the effects of Foster_parent.

k. (*True or False*) The uncontrolled for effects of Income_thousands greatly affect the value of (size of) the coefficients for Education_mom.

l. (*True or False*) Severity of maltreatment is not included in the regression. Suppose that prior research indicates that it has a strong effect on parent–child relationship. Based on this information, we can be confident that the regression coefficients for Education_mom are not affected by severity of maltreatment.

m. (*True or False*) Controlling for the other predictors, Income_thousands demonstrates a negative relationship to parent–child relationship score. (As income goes up, predicted score goes down.)

n. What is the correlation between predicted parent–child relationship score (the scores predicted by the regression equation) and actual parent–child relationship score?

o. (*True or False*) Overall, the association between predicted and actual scores is extremely weak/small.

p. Assuming random sampling from an infinite-sized population, the adjusted $R^2$ ($R^2 = .412$) provides a better estimate of the $R^2$ in the population than does the unadjusted $R^2$ ($R^2 = .416$).

9. (*True or False*) Even when a predictor in multiple regression measures less than perfectly (measures with some degree of error), its effect (potential bias) on other predictors is controlled for fully.

10. A _____ is the difference between a case's actual score on the dependent variable and its predicted score.

11. *Respond true or false to each of the following:*
    a. A key assumption in multiple regression is that each predictor should be at the interval/ratio level of measurement.
    b. Multiple regression assumes that the dependent variable is at the interval/ratio-level of measurement.

c. Multiple regression assumes that residuals are normally distributed.

d. Multiple regression assumes that the variance of the residuals should be equal (equality of variance).

12. Problems of _____ occur when two predictors or some combination of predictors are very highly correlated.

**Section 23.3**

13. *Respond true or false to each of the following:*
    a. Typically, the predictors in a multiple regression are uncorrelated ($r = 0.00$).
    b. The predictors in Figure 23.4 are uncorrelated ($r = 0.00$).
    c. None of the variance explained by either predictor in Figure 23.4 overlaps with that explained by the other.
    d. The predictors in Figure 23.5 are uncorrelated ($r = 0.00$).
    e. None of the variance explained by either predictor in Figure 23.4 overlaps with that explained by the other.
    f. In Figure 23.5, 5% of the explained variance "overlaps"; in other words, 5% is explained jointly by both predictors.
    g. The predictors in Figure 23.6 are very strongly correlated.
    h. In Figure 23.6, neither predictor explains much unique variance (variance that is not also explained by the other predictor).
    i. When two predictors are highly correlated, the variance that each explains is fully unique (totally separate from that explained by the other).
    j. As a general rule, the stronger the correlation between two predictors, the lower is the power to detect the effect of each.
    k. Two predictors can be so highly correlated that including both in an analysis reduces the power to detect the effects of each.

14. Which of the following are characteristics of a "best" combination of predictors in multiple regression (*you may choose more than one*):
    a. Each predictor has a low correlation with each other predictor.
    b. Each predictor has a low correlation with the dependent variable.
    c. Each predictor has a high correlation with each other predictor.
    d. Each predictor has a high correlation with the dependent variable.

15. (*True or False*) Two advantages from multivariate analysis are, (a) quite often, an increase in power and (b) improved control for bias (i.e., for the effects of confounding variables).

16. *Respond true or false to each of the following:* (Note: "Second predictor" refers to the second predictor added to a multiple regression equation. "Highly correlated" refers to strong correlation between the second predictor and the predictor already in the equation.)
    a. The text recommends that the researcher should never add a highly correlated second predictor to a multiple regression equation.

**b.** A highly correlated second predictor can be a confounding variable.

**c.** If a highly correlated second predictor is a confounding variable, it can change the relationship (as indicated by $B$ or $\beta$) of the first predictor to the dependent variable.

**d.** Whenever two predictors are highly correlated, the relationship of each to the dependent variable is always small (or even nonexistent).

**e.** Problems of multicollinearity occur when two predictors or some combination of predictors have a very low correlation(s).

## Section 23.4

**17.** Logistic regression examines the association of predictors to a _____ dependent variable.

**18.** In logistic regression, the $B$s (the coefficients that are not exponentiated) predict the (natural) _____ of the _____ of an event. The $e^B$ coefficients (those that are exponentiated) predict the _____ of an event.

**19.** These questions apply to the logistic regression in Table 23.2.

**a.** As Income_thousands increases, do the predicted odds of very positive impact increase or decrease?

**b.** For each $1,000 increase in family income—in other words, as the variable Income_thousands increases by 1.00—the odds of very positive impact are predicted to decrease by _____%.

**c.** (*True or False*) Foster_parent is a dummy variable.

**d.** The odds of very positive impact for adopters who are foster parents are _____ (number) those for adopters who are not foster parents.

**e.** (*True or False*) The $e^B$ (exponentiated) coefficient for Foster_parent is in essence, an odds ratio, but one in which the effects of the other predictors has been controlled for.

**f.** (*True or False*) The coefficients for each predictor convey results controlling for the other predictors in the regression equation.

**20.** _____ logistic regression extends (binary) logistic regression to dependent variables with three or more (ordered) categories.

## Section 23.5

**21.** ANOVA is a shorter term for _____ of _____. In ANOVA, a variable that defines groups is termed a _____. An ANOVA with two factors is a _____-_____ ANOVA. An ANOVA with two or more factors is a _____ ANOVA. A factor's categories (groups) are its _____.

**22.** A factor's _____ effect is its effect disregarding the presence of the other factor (or factors). The key advantage of two-way ANOVA is that the researcher can assess whether two factors _____ in predicting the dependent variable.

**23.** *Respond true or false to each of the following:*

    **a.** When an interaction effect is significant in two-way ANOVA, interpretation of the main effects is less than straightforward.

    **b.** In Table 23.3, there is a statistically significant interaction between Foster_status and Handicap_status ($p = .008$).

    **c.** In our example (see Table 23.3), the relationship of Foster_status to parent–child relationship score is very similar for children with and children without handicaps.

    **d.** In our example (see Table 23.3), the relationship of Handicap_status to parent–child relationship score is very similar for children adopted by and not adopted by their prior foster parents.

    **e.** Interpretation of the main effects in Table 23.3 is straightforward.

**Section 23.6**

**24.** _____ of _____ (_____) builds on both one-way ANOVA and factorial ANOVA by adding _____, that is, interval/ratio level predictors.

**25.** _____ _____ of _____ (_____), examines several dependent variables in a single analysis.

**26.** _____ _____ designs analyze several or more different administrations of the same (interval/ratio level) dependent variable.

**Section 23.7**

**27.** _____ _____ _____ involves the building of causal models.

**28.** _____ modeling examines contributions of variables at multiple levels of analysis.

**29.** _____ _____ is the preferred analytic method when the dependent variable is time to occurrence. The most straightforward survival analysis methodology is the _____ _____ _____ model.

**30.** _____ _____ groups highly correlated variables together into a _____.

**31.** (*True or False*) In essence, factor analysis reduces a larger number of variables into a lesser number.

# 24

# GENERALIZABILITY, IMPORTANCE, AND A DATA INTERPRETATION MODEL

## 24.1 ■ CHAPTER OVERVIEW

Statistical methods provide a great deal of knowledge about study results, but researchers need to be able to go beyond that to determine how useful the results are. Chapter 24 begins by discussing how to assess *generalizability*, including the role of *degree of similarity* in this assessment. It emphasizes that *importance* and statistical significance are distinct concepts. Finally, it presents the *balanced model for data interpretation*.

## 24.2 ■ GENERALIZABILITY

### 24.2.1 ■ Inferential Statistics and Generalizability

All research studies are conducted in a particular setting, or, to use a fancier word, in a particular *context*. A dictionary definition of context is "the interrelated conditions in which something exists or occurs." The context of a research study represents the particular characteristics of that study—the time and place of the study, the study sample, the sampling method, the research design, the measurement instruments used, the intervention (if any), the persons (if any) who implement the intervention, those who gather the data (i.e., interviewers or observers), and the researcher(s) who conduct the study.

In our discussion, the larger population (if any) from which the study sample is selected is not considered to be part of the study context. This decision reflects the fact that, ultimately, those in the study sample, not those in the larger population, participate in research studies.

Researchers and practitioners alike are often interested in whether highly similar or quite different study results would be obtained were a given study to be carried out in a different context, that is, in a setting where one or more of its characteristics have changed. For instance, if you read a research report about an effective program serving unmarried mothers in a rural, southwestern state, you might wonder whether that program would also be effective with your caseload of unmarried mothers in, say, an urban setting in a northeastern state. Concerns such as this are addressed by the concept of generalizability. The **generalizability** of a study result is the expected degree of similarity between the study result and the result that would be obtained if the study was carried out in a different setting or context.

When similar results are expected, there is high generalizability or, one may say, the results are highly **generalizable**. When quite different results are expected, generalizability is low. The degree of generalizability is often difficult to assess. In some situations, one can do little more than make a best guess or conjecture. Typically, study results are highly generalizable to some settings but not generalizable to others.

Researchers assess generalizability using two sets of tools. The first set is the inferential statistical procedures that have been presented in the past 12 chapters (Chapters 12–23). Researchers use these tools to generalize study sample results to the population (if any) from which that sample was randomly selected. Confidence intervals for percentages illustrate this process. The researcher takes a random sample from a population, finds the percentage in the sample, and then establishes a confidence interval for the population. Thus, using the logic and tools of inferential statistics, the study's result has been generalized from one context or setting (the study sample) to another (the study population).

The researcher knows the precise degree of confidence to attach to generalizations made using inferential statistical tools. For instance, the researcher can state, "I am 95% confident that the true percentage for this population is located between 42% and 49%." Similarly, the researcher who rejects a null at the .01 statistical significance level can be 99% confident that this null is false in the population from which the study sample was randomly selected.

As you know, as sample size increases, the characteristics of random samples become increasingly similar to those of the populations from which they have been selected. Thus, given sufficient sample size, the researcher can make *accurate* statements about the study population; for instance, she can specify a narrow confidence interval. In summary, given sufficient sample size, the researcher can use inferential statistical tools to generalize to the study population with high confidence and accuracy. Let us call generalizations made using the logic and tools of inferential statistics, **statistical generalizations**. And let us say that when we make statistical generalizations, we are engaged in **statistical generalizability**.

What is the downside of generalizing using statistical tools and logic? The great limitation, of course, is that such generalizations can only be made to the population from which the study sample was randomly selected. This poses different problems depending on the sampling methodology.

As Chapter 16, Section 16.8, discusses, in many studies, one's sample is not a random sample from a wider population. In these studies, there is no real-world population to which statistical generalizations can be made. In other studies, the study sample is a random one, but the study population is limited in scope. For instance, suppose that a professor randomly selects 50 students from the 250 who attend her school and administers an intervention designed to reduce the anxiety experienced in statistics courses. The professor may (and indeed should) use the logic and tools of inferential statistics to generalize results from her study sample to the full population of students at her school. For instance, she could set a confidence interval for the mean level of anxiety that would be found if her intervention was administered to all 250 students.

Yet such statistically based logic may not be used to assess the results that would be obtained if the intervention was administered at, for instance, a nearby school. This is because the students in this school are not part of the population from which the study sample was (randomly) selected.

In my first statistics class, the professor admonished, "You may only generalize to the population from which the study sample was randomly selected." This admonition injected caution but at the same time paralyzed my thinking. I asked myself, "Does each study have relevance to only one specific population, that being the one (if any) from which the sample was randomly selected?" The answer is NO.

A more accurate admonishment is "the *tools and logic of inferential statistics* may only be used to make generalizations to the population (if any) from which the sample was randomly selected." Or, stated more succinctly, "statistical generalizations may only be made to the population (if any) from which the study sample was randomly sampled."

Pragmatically, the two just-presented statements are correct. In the interest of clarity, an exception will be pointed out. Occasionally, random methods are used to select more than just the study sample. For instance, presume that an educational experiment seeks to compare the impact of Curriculums A and B. Presume that in addition to randomly selecting students, (a) participating schools are randomly selected from a wider population of schools and (b) participating teachers are randomly selected from the population of teachers within the selected schools. As random methods were used to select both schools and teachers, the logic and tools of inferential statistics may be used to generalize results to (a) the population of schools from which the sample of schools was selected and (b) the population of teachers within those schools from which the sample of teachers was selected. Thus, a more technically correct admonishment is "statistical generalizations may only be made to those characteristics of a study that have been randomly selected."[1]

Researchers often do attempt to generalize study findings beyond both the study context and the study population (the population from which the sample was selected). For instance, they seek to generalize to different times and places, to different settings, and to different groups of people (cultural groups, gender-defined groups, different age groups, groups defined by social class or income, volunteers versus those ordered to participate, etc.). The logic and tools of inferential statistics may *not* be applied to this endeavor. Another kind of logic and set of tools are required. This second set of tools will be presented soon, but first a hypothetical vignette illustrates just how limited is the context of a study and, thus, how limited is the reach of statistical generalization:

> In January 1999, all 200 elementary students in Superrural, Oklahoma took part in a study on television violence. One hundred students were randomly assigned to a daily weeklong, 2-hour regimen of violent television consisting of the following (hypothetical) shows (*Shoot 'em Up, Blow 'em Up*; *Blow 'em Every Which Way*; etc.). Mr. Macho facilitated this group. One hundred were randomly assigned to nonviolent television shows (*Best Friends, Share With Your Neighbor, Best Friends II*, etc.). Ms. Peace facilitated this group. Both groups watched 20-in. television sets from 9 a.m. to 11 a.m. Observations of violent behavior during the lunchtime recess were made by trained observers using the (hypothetical) Playground Violence Observation Tool (PVOT). Statistical analysis indicated significantly more violent behavior in the violent television group than in the nonviolent television group ($p < .01$). Expressed in standard deviation units, the difference in means on the PVOT was .8 ($SMD = .8$).

Let us presume a carefully crafted study, accurate measurement, and that researchers had no "axe to grind" that may have biased results. Given the results as just described, we may conclude that the association between violent television and violent behavior is (a) unlikely to be due to chance (because it is statistically significant), (b) a reasonably large association (because a difference of .8 standard deviations is a large difference in means; see Table 9.1), and (c) almost assuredly a causal association (because the students were randomly assigned to groups; see Section 10.6).

Let us pose some questions pertaining to generalizability. Would we observe similar results—in other words, a similar size of association—if we carried out the study, say,

- in 2017 rather than 1999?
- in the junior high in Superrural?
- in the elementary school in a neighboring town?
- in New York City?
- with a predominantly African American population in the deep South?
- on a 70-in. television rather than a 20-in. one?

- with the viewing session in the afternoon rather than the morning and continuing for 2 weeks rather than 1?
- for a different selection of violent and nonviolent television shows?
- with facilitators other than Mr. Macho and Ms. Peace?
- using some instrument other than the PVOT?
- in outside play in the students' neighborhoods? and/or
- in the students' interactions with their family members?

The answers to the just-posed questions are beyond the reach of inferential statistical logic and tools. One cannot use statistical logic to generalize the study result to any wider real-world population, as no such population exists. One cannot use statistical logic to generalize to different times of the day, types of shows, group leaders, sizes of televisions, and so on because these aspects of the study were not randomly selected.

Some mistakenly assume that because an association is statistically significant, this same association will be observed in a different context or setting. Sometimes, this is the case. For instance, perhaps similar results would be obtained if Mr. Passive and Ms. Hottemp (rather than Mr. Macho and Ms. Peace) facilitated the study groups. Perhaps similar results would be obtained in New York City (perhaps not). The key point is that the logic and tools of inferential statistics do not address such issues. It is, indeed, easy to forget—or to simply never consider at all—just how *particular* and how *specific* is the context of each study and, thus, how limited is the reach of statistical inference, that is of statistical generalization.

## 24.2.2 ■ Generalization Using Nonstatistical Tools

The logic and tools of inferential statistics are used to assess generalizability to the population (if any) from which the sample was randomly selected and to any other aspects of the study that may have been selected randomly. For all other situations, a different logic is needed for assessing generalizability. This logic is grounded not in statistical concepts and procedures but instead in critical thinking and, ultimately, common sense.

A key tool for assessing generalizability beyond the study context and study population is the **degree of similarity** between the study context and the context to which one seeks to generalize. The greater that similarity, the greater the expected generalizability. The less that similarity, the less the expected generalizability. The fact that similarity is a key tool for assessing generalizability is so grounded in common sense that most texts make no mention of this. By failing to do so, they contribute to an impression that critical reasoning with careful attention to similarity is unscientific and has no role in understanding and interpreting data. My view is the opposite. I see such reasoning as central in scientific inquiry. Campbell's (1986) principle of "proximal similarity" makes explicit the importance of similarity, "As scientists we generalize with most confidence to applications most similar to the setting of the original research" (p. 75). (*Proximal* means "situated close to.")

Let us see how similarity guides us in assessing the generalizability of the results presented in the vignette. The concept of similarity would suggest that we would have greater reason to expect similar findings in, for instance, a neighboring school than in a school in a highly urbanized setting such as New York City. In general, the greater the similarity to that neighboring school—size, socioeconomic status, ethnicity, rural versus urban, and so on—the greater the expected generalizability of study findings.

Would the study results generalize to a different selection of television shows? A clever researcher might have randomly selected a sample of violent shows from the population of such shows and done the same for nonviolent shows. Then inferential statistics could have tackled this question and provided some reasonably definitive answers. In the absence of such a random selection process, our best strategy will be to compare the characteristics of the shows used in the study with "typical" violent shows. Perhaps the shows in the study do indeed share many characteristics with most other violent shows. This would nudge our thinking toward the conclusion that the study results could indeed be generalized across many television shows. On the other hand, perhaps the shows selected for the study were a particularly violent group. If "typical" violent shows tend to be much less violent than those in the study, we would presumably be cautious regarding possible generalizability to a broader selection of shows.

Suppose for the moment that the researcher was extra clever and did select a random sample of violent TV shows. This would indeed facilitate statistical generalization to the population of such shows. Yet, such generalization would be to the population of such shows in *1999*. This text was written in 2011. Do our results hold in 2011? In 2017? These are difficult questions to answer and statistical generalization cannot help with them.

The study results, based on the PVOT instrument, indicate that violent television viewed in the school setting leads to violent behavior in the school setting (at least during the lunchtime recess). May we conclude that watching violent television *at home* affects aggressive behavior in one's home and neighborhood? In other words, may we generalize the study's school-based results to home and neighborhood? There is no easy answer. My inclination is that such a conclusion stretches our results too far. Circumstances in one's home and neighborhood differ in important ways from those at school. Hence, we should perhaps recommend caution regarding such a generalization. For instance, in writing a journal article about the study, we might caution the reader not to jump to such a conclusion.

Perhaps I am being too cautious in this reasoning. Indeed, when one attempts to generalize outside of the study context, it is difficult to know whether one is being too cautious or too bold.

Let us term generalizations made using tools and logic other than those of inferential statistics' **nonstatistical generalizations**. And let us say that when we are engaged in making nonstatistical generalizations, we are engaged in **nonstatistical generalizability**. Similarity is, clearly, a driving force in nonstatistical generalizability but other considerations arc also important.

In general, nonstatistical generalizability is enhanced when the study sample represents a broad cross section of persons from diverse backgrounds rather than a homogeneous group. A good strategy for assessing generalizability to different groups is to see whether similar results are obtained in the different subgroups in one's study. For instance, suppose that Intervention X is more effective than Intervention Y for both women and men; both minority and nonminority participants; young, middle-aged, and older participants; and both highly and less educated participants. Such a pattern of results suggests that results may generalize well across these groups. On the other hand, when results differ markedly for subgroups—say for women versus men— this recommends caution in generalizing results for these groups. Observe that when one finds differing results in different subgroups, this is, in essence, an interaction (interaction effect; see Chapter 11, Section 11.5, and Chapter 23, Section 23.5). Hence, checking for interaction effects is useful in assessing generalizability.[2] Replication is at the heart of establishing generalizability. **Replication** refers to carrying out a study for a second (or third, fourth, fifth, etc.) time. In replicating, researchers do not carry out the study in the *exact* same way. Indeed, this is logically impossible as, even if nothing else differs, the date of a second study necessarily differs from that of a first. Rather than carrying out the exact same study, researchers strategically change key study characteristics.

When results differ sharply as some characteristic of a study changes, this suggests that study results do not generalize well across that characteristic. Suppose, for instance, that a replication of our study using a different selection of television shows yields quite different results from ours. Perhaps, for instance, no difference in violent playground behavior is observed between those watching violent and nonviolent shows. Such a result, when combined with our result, suggests that results do not generalize well across different shows.

On the other hand, when we see similar results when some study characteristic changes, our confidence in the generalizability of results increases commensurately. Clearly, for instance, the best way to find out whether our results generalize to the home and neighborhood is to replicate the study in this setting.

Given scarce resources, replication is often a luxury. There may be only one well-carried-out study on the intervention that you are planning to use with a client. In such a situation, you will not be able to compare the results of different replications to help determine the most likely results for your client. Your best assessment tool in this situation will be your informed judgment of the similarity (or difference) between your client's particulars and those of the clients in the research study. The greater that similarity, the greater the expected similarity of results (i.e., the greater the expected generalizability).

Generalization to the population from which one has randomly sampled is based on statistical logic. Given sufficient sample size, such statistical generalizations can be made with confidence and accuracy. Generalization outside of the study context and beyond the study population (to different populations, settings, study characteristics, etc.) is based on nonstatistical logic. Nonstatistical generalizations should be made with a healthy dose of caution (the knowledge that one may be wrong). In comparison to statistical generalizations, we make nonstatistical generalizations with much less confidence and with much greater caution. This is why many texts make no mention of this and why many professors admonish, "Do not do this."

Generalization outside of the study context requires a leap of faith—we use critical thinking skills, theory, common sense, and, sometimes, practice wisdom—to draw conclusions not merited by the research design per se. Although some admonish against this, there is no pragmatic alternative. All studies are lodged in a specific context. Without permission to generalize beyond that context, study results, by definition, have limited real-world applicability and relevance. Although we must make nonstatistical generalizations cautiously, we must, nevertheless, make them.

## 24.3 ■ IMPORTANCE

As you know, the search for relationships between variables is at the heart of social science research. So far, this text has discussed four key concepts in this endeavor: (a) *statistical significance*, whether a relationship is likely to be caused by chance; (b) *size (strength) of relationship*, the degree to which two variables tend to change or vary together; (c) *causality*, whether one variable affects the other; and (d) *generalizability*, the degree to which a similar relationship or study result is expected in a different context. A fifth concept is importance.

**Importance** may be defined as the importance that a relationship or study result has in the real world. Terms with similar meanings include *practical importance*, *practical significance*, and *substantive significance* (Rubin & Babbie, 1997, p. 518). The first four concepts bear on importance. Thus, associations that are statistically significant, strong, causal, and highly generalizable *tend to be* more important than those that are not. Even so, importance stands on its own as a distinct and separate issue.

An association that is statistically significant, strong, causal, and highly generalizable can be unimportant. An example would be a randomized study that demonstrates large and statistically significant differences in two interventions designed to improve scores in Tiddlywinks. Tiddlywinks, as I grew up in the 1950s, was associated with wasting one's time away in inconsequential activity. A human services professional's reaction to the just-presented Tiddlywinks study would likely be, "Who cares? Tiddlywinks scores have no relevance to the social issues that confront people and society." At least from a human services perspective, these results are unimportant.

An association or study result can be (a) not statistically significant and (b) important. For instance, consider a large-scale, randomized experiment with two treatment groups for at-risk youth. Presume that youth in one group are served in their own homes and that those in the other are served in placement settings (group homes, residential placements, etc.). Let us say that outcomes on various measures—delinquency rates, school performance, behavior problems, self-esteem—are similar in the two groups. Specifically, let us presume that the association of treatment approach (in-home versus placement) to each outcome measure is both (a) not statistically significant and (b) very weak in strength. Such findings suggest that neither intervention is more effective than the other.

Yet, such seemingly unremarkable results could have *important* implications for service delivery. From a public policy perspective, the in-home approach keeps families intact and, thus, is preferred. Presume also that the in-home approach is less expensive. This being so, our study results indicate that a program that is preferable from both policy and economic perspectives yields outcomes that are equivalent to one that is less preferable on both counts. In this context, these results are not so unremarkable after all. In summary, these statistically nonsignificant results could well lead to *important* changes, that is, to increased development of in-home services.

Do you see how misleading the term statistically *significant* is? Students often confuse *statistical* significance with *real-world* significance, that is, with importance. Many statistically significant results do indeed have real world significance. But these concepts are distinct. When a study result or association is statistically significant, we can be confident that it is not due to chance. Yet, it does not follow logically that it is important in the real world. It may or may not be.

The importance of an association or study result is determined, ultimately, by qualitative judgment. Although it is difficult to provide guidelines for assessing importance, some comments are in order.

Clearly, the researcher considers the particular result and the research design. Associations that are statistically significant, large, presumably causal, and/or highly generalizable stand a greater chance of having practical importance than do those that are not. Importance is not the same thing as newsworthiness. Yet, it is simply the nature of social science inquiry that the discovery that something makes a difference is more likely to be important than is the "discovery" that something does not.

The crux of importance is the presumed bearing that study results have for the real world. For instance, when a new intervention reduces depression among mental health clients to a greater degree than does a traditional one, the researcher or practitioner would try to assess whether switching to the new intervention would make an important (pragmatic, real) difference in clients' lives. Would their depression be reduced to a degree that would be meaningful to them and that would help them better carry out tasks of living? Such a question can be difficult to answer and requires assessment from varied perspectives.

Questions regarding importance are, ultimately, nonstatistical. For the most part, experts can agree on statistical questions. For instance, they can agree on whether a result is statistically significant. In part because there are no standards for establishing it, experts often disagree about questions of importance. Even if experts disagree, questions of importance cannot be avoided. Considerations of importance are, ultimately, the same as those of *meaning*. Ultimately, we must ask, "What is the meaning of this result in the real world?"

## 24.4 ■ THE BALANCED MODEL FOR DATA INTERPRETATION

This section builds the **balanced model for data interpretation** based on five factors: (a) statistical significance, (b) size of association, (c) causality, (d) generalizability, and (e) importance.

The term *balanced* reflects my belief that when each factor is accorded reasonably equal importance, data interpretation is balanced and begins to be comprehensive.

Typically, data interpretation is unbalanced. It tilts heavily toward statistical significance and pays scant attention to other concepts in the model. Statistical significance is the most misinterpreted concept in data interpretation.

Most misinterpretations of statistical significance follow a common pattern. Persons attach meanings to statistical significance that are only tangentially connected to it. These misinterpretations inevitably involve one of the other four factors in the model. Thus, persons conclude that statistically significant relationships are necessarily (a) large, (b) causal, (c) generalizable, and/or (d) important. Such reasoning does not follow logically and is incorrect.

Let us examine these illogical conclusions. First, some statistically significant associations represent large associations between variables but others do not. In particular, recall that when sample size is large, small associations often achieve statistical significance (see Chapter 16, Section 16.4). Regarding the second conclusion, recall that, for the most part, the assessment of causality hinges on the research design. In survey designs, the problem of confounding variables is persistent and, even when results are statistically significant, conclusions about causality cannot be reached. Third, some statistically significant associations have limited generalizability. Fourth, the connection between statistical significance and importance was just discussed. Some statistically significant associations—see, for instance, the Tiddlywinks study—are unimportant.

The same mistake is made in the other direction. Persons conclude that because an association is not statistically significant, it is necessarily (a) small in size, (b) not causal, (c) not generalizable, and (d) unimportant.

These (for the most part) illogical conclusions can also be examined. First, it does not follow that because an association is not statistically significant, it is small in size. In particular, when sample size is small, even large associations may not be statistically significant. The second conclusion holds reasonably well. When an association is not statistically significant, it may be due to chance factors. As such, one does not have solid grounds for concluding that it is causal. Third, generalizability is not the same as statistical significance. A result or association that is not statistically significant can be generalizable to many settings. Finally, as the own home services versus placement example demonstrated, an association can be both (a) not statistically significant and (b) important.

The key to balanced interpretation is to treat the five concepts as distinct. In particular, do not extend the meaning of statistical significance into areas that properly belong with the other concepts. To summarize, the key parts of the balanced data interpretation model are

1. *statistical significance*, whether the relationship is likely to be due to chance;
2. *size* (*strength*) *of association*, the degree to which the values of one variable vary, differ, or change according to the values of the other;
3. *causality*, whether one variable causes the other;
4. *generalizability*, the degree to which a similar relationship or study result will be found in a different context or setting; and
5. *importance*, the real-world implications of the study result.

In discussing the model, I sometimes interchange the words *study result* and *relationship* (*association*). Pragmatically, the study of relationship is at the heart of most of human services research. The key results of one's study are often one and the same as the relationships obtained.

The model makes several assumptions. Most basically, it assumes that the study of relationships is a key goal of the study. This holds for most studies. The occasional study reports purely univariate data. The model should not be applied to such studies. The model's third point pertains to causality. Some studies, notably some surveys, have a descriptive purpose; they describe results but do not seek to explain them. When a study's purpose is descriptive, questions pertaining to causality do not apply. In such a situation, drop causality from the model and work with a four-point model. For the most part, the model's steps are sequential. It typically makes most sense to begin with statistical significance and work your way through the other steps on to importance.

The model's steps move the researcher progressively from quantitative decision making yielding clear conclusions into qualitative decision making yielding those that are much less so. Books provide rules for statistical decision making. Rules cannot be provided for the more qualitative aspects of data interpretation. Reasoning in these areas is both difficult and important. This chapter can help you strike a balance between being so cautious that your thinking becomes paralyzed and reasoning recklessly. Careful, critical thinking—with a dash of creativity—is what is needed.

This text gave short coverage to confidence intervals, particularly to the fact these can be obtained for almost all of the inferential procedures presented. Confidence intervals are at the "cusp" between size of association and statistical significance. They build on and supplement what is learned from these concepts. Hence, I encourage you to incorporate confidence intervals into your data interpretation (see Chapter 13, Section 13.4, and Chapter 22, Section 22.4.1).

In closing, I note that this text has not discussed the quality of a study's *measures* (measuring instruments, instruments). For instance, suppose that a study examines self-esteem. Does its measure of self-esteem do a good job of measuring self-esteem? In your research methods class, you will learn about the *reliability* (consistency and repeatability) and *validity* (Does a measure measure what it intends to measure?) of measures. Issues of reliability and validity of measures are important in data interpretation. Poor reliability or validity can undermine conclusions that could otherwise be drawn.

## 24.5 ▧ CHAPTER SUMMARY

All research studies are conducted in a particular context. The *generalizability* of a study result is the expected degree of similarity between the study result and the result that would be obtained in a different context. When similar results are expected, there is high generalizability or, one may say, the results are highly *generalizable*. When quite different results are expected, generalizability is low.

The tools and logic of inferential statistics are used to make *statistical generalizations* to (a) the population (if any) from which the study sample was randomly selected and (b) the population (if any) from which any other aspect of the study was randomly selected. Given a large enough sample size, statistical generalizations can be made with confidence and accuracy. The logic and tools of inferential statistics may not be used to make generalizations beyond the study population or regarding any aspect of the study that has not been randomly sampled.

The logic for generalizing beyond the study context (and beyond the study population) is grounded in critical thinking and common sense. A key tool for assessing generalizability beyond the study context is the *degree of similarity* between that context and the context to which one seeks to generalize. The greater the similarity, the greater the expected generalizability.

In general, a broad, diverse study sample enhances generalizability. *Replication* in varied settings helps build generalizability. When replicating studies, researchers vary key study characteristics. Generalizations based on nonstatistical logic, that is, *nonstatistical generalizations*, should be made cautiously.

*Importance* is the importance that a relationship or study result has in the real world. Although statistical significance bears on importance, importance and statistical significance are distinct concepts. A relationship can be statistically significant and unimportant.

The *balanced model for data interpretation* includes five factors: (a) statistical significance, (b) size of association, (c) causality, (d) generalizability, and (e) importance. Statistical significance is often accorded too much importance. Many mistakenly conclude that a statistically significant association is also (necessarily) (a) large, (b) causal, (c) generalizable, and/or (d) important. Each factor in the model is distinct. When each is given reasonably equal consideration, data interpretation is balanced and has the potential to be comprehensive.

## 24.6 ■ PROBLEMS AND QUESTIONS

### Section 24.2

1. A near synonym for "particular setting" is _____ .

2. Define generalizability.

3. *Respond true or false to each of the following:*
   a. The tools of inferential statistics may be (appropriately) used to generalize to the population from which the study sample was randomly selected.
   b. The tools of inferential statistics may be (appropriately) used to make generalizations to populations different from that from which the study was randomly sampled.
   c. Statistical generalizations may be (appropriately) made to those characteristics of a study that have been randomly selected.
   d. Given a random sample of sufficient size, the researcher can use inferential statistical tools to generalize to the study population with both confidence and accuracy.
   e. In general, the greater the similarity between the setting/context to which one seeks to generalize and the setting/context of the research study, the greater the presumed generalizability.
   f. In general, greater generalizability is expected when one's study sample has diverse and varied characteristics than when it is homogeneous.
   g. When study results differ markedly for subgroups, this recommends caution in generalizing results across these groups.
   h. When different results (relationships) are observed for different subgroups, this is, in essence, an interaction effect.
   i. The most effective way to replicate is to keep all characteristics of the study *exactly* the same.
   j. A study's results may have high generalizability to one setting but low generalizability to another.
   k. Most statistics texts discuss explicitly and recommend enthusiastically the generalizing of study results beyond the study population.
   l. Generally speaking, one has greater confidence in generalizations made using inferential statistical logic to the population from which one has randomly sampled than in generalizations made using nonstatistical logic (to other populations, settings, etc.)

**m.** The text recommends making bold generalizations using nonstatistical logic, as, almost assuredly, these generalizations can be counted on to be accurate.

**n.** The text recommends never making any kinds of generalizations (statistical or nonstatistical) that go beyond the study population (or beyond any characteristic of the study that has not been randomly sampled).

4. Generalizations made out using the logic and tools of inferential statistics are termed _____ generalizations. Generalizations made using tools and logic other than those of inferential statistics are termed _____ generalizations.

5. A key tool for assessing the degree of generalizability beyond the study context (and beyond population from which sample was randomly selected) is the degree of _____ .

6. What is perhaps misleading about the statement, "Do not generalize beyond the population from which the study sample has been randomly sampled."

7. Give an example of a relationship or study result that is both statistically significant and unimportant for social work practice.

**Section 24.3**

8. _____ may be defined as the importance that a relationship or study result has in the _____ _____ .

9. *Respond true or false to each of the following:*
    **a.** Importance and statistical significance have essentially identical meanings.
    **b.** Importance and practical significance have similar meanings.
    **c.** A study that does not yield statistically significant results cannot be an *important* study.
    **d.** Statistical significance and real-world significance are one and the same.
    **e.** An association that is statistically significant, strong, causal, and highly generalizable can be unimportant.
    **f.** Questions regarding importance are, ultimately, nonstatistical rather than statistical questions.

**Section 24.4**

10. What are the five factors in the balanced interpretation model?

11. In typical "unbalanced" data interpretation, which factor is commonly accorded the greatest importance?

12. *Respond true or false to each completion of the following phrase:* Statistically significant associations are, necessarily
    **a.** large in size
    **b.** causal

   **c.** highly generalizable

   **d.** important

**13.** *Respond true or false to each of the following:*

   **a.** When a result is not statistically significant, it is necessarily small in size.

   **b.** When an association is not statistically significant, it may be due to chance factors.

   **c.** When an association is not statistically significant, one does not have solid grounds for concluding that it is causal.

   **d.** A result that is not statistically significant can be highly generalizable to many settings.

   **e.** When a result is not statistically significant, it is necessarily unimportant.

   **f.** The text recommends treating the five factors in the balanced model as highly overlapping (nearly synonymous) rather than as distinct and separate.

   **g.** Regarding the balanced model, the text recommends beginning with statistical significance and working through the steps to the final step, importance.

   **h.** As one proceeds through the model's five steps, decision making and thinking moves from the quantitative toward the qualitative.

   **i.** Rules are easily developed and applied for the qualitative aspects of decision making.

Integrative Problems: "Lower level" questions a. to cc. apply to questions 14–19, each of which is a research study vignette. In each vignette, assume that the hypothesis pair is nondirectional. (Question e. greatly oversimplifies the assessment of statistical power. It is based on the fact that, other things being equal, as sample size [$N$] increases, so does power.)

   **a.** What is the independent variable, that is, the intervention? What are its values? What is its level of measurement?

   **b.** What is the dependent variable? If it is a categorical variable, what are its values? What is its level of measurement?

   **c.** What statistical test, a chi-square test of independence or an independent samples $t$ test, should be used?

   **d.** What is the sample size ($N$, the total number of cases in the study)?

   **e.** Using the sample size-based guideline below, estimate (*very roughly*) the approximate statistical power.

   $N < 100 \rightarrow$ power likely low (only large associations will achieve significance).

   $100 < N < 399 \rightarrow$ power likely moderate

   $N > 400 \rightarrow$ power likely high (even small associations may achieve significance)

   **f.** What is the nondirectional null hypothesis?

   **g.** What is the nondirectional alternative hypothesis?

   **h.** Is the relationship statistically significant at the .05 level?

   **i.** What is your decision on the null?

   **j.** What is your decision on the alternative?

   **k.** Given a true null, is the probability of obtaining the study sample result or an even more extreme result greater than .05 or less than .05?

   **l.** Is the probability that the study sample result is due to chance alone greater than .05 or less than .05?

**m.** Can you be at least 95% confident that the null is false?

**n.** Does the study sample result provide (sufficiently) strong evidence that the null is false?

**o.** If you rejected the null, can you be *certain* that it is false? If you failed to reject it, can you be confident that it is true?

**p.** If the dependent variable is categorical, what is the difference in percentages (*D%*)? If it is numeric, what is the standardized mean difference (*SMD*)? Calculate so that the result comes to a positive rather than a negative.

**q.** How large/strong is the study result, that is, the relationship between the intervention and the dependent variable? For *D%*, see Table 6.3; For *SMD*, see Table 9.1.

**r.** Was random assignment used to assign persons to groups? (If not mentioned explicitly, assume not.)

**s.** Can you be confident that the intervention actually causes (affects) the dependent variable? Why or why not?

**t.** If you responded no to the prior question, suggest a confounding variable that may be involved.

**u.** Is the study sample a random sample? (If methods of chance not mentioned, assume not.)

**v.** Can statistical generalizations (generalizations made with statistical tools) be made beyond the study sample to any larger population? If one, which one? If not, why not?

**w.** For most of the questions so far—most specifically for h. to o. and for u. and v.—has your reasoning been largely statistical (quantitative) or largely nonstatistical (qualitative)?

**x.** Disregarding the population, if any, from which the study sample was randomly sampled, suggest another population/setting to which the study results may be highly generalizable; in other words, another population/setting in which highly similar results would likely be obtained.

**y.** Are you extremely confident that study results have high generalizability to the population/setting that you mentioned in the prior question? Why or why not?

**z.** Suggest a population/setting to which the study results may have low generalizability, in other words one in which quite different results might well be obtained.

**aa.** In your view, are the results important for the helping professions? Why or why not? (Hint: There is no right or wrong answer to this question.)

**bb.** For questions x. to aa., was your reasoning largely statistical (quantitative) or largely nonstatistical (qualitative)?

**cc.** In general, for questions x. to aa., do you have (a) very high confidence in all of your responses or (b) have only limited confidence in at least some responses?

The just-presented questions apply to each of the following vignettes.

**14.** Two community mental health centers serve clients with chronic and severe mental health problems in a large urban city in the northeastern United States. Mental health center A uses a model in which social workers make frequent visits to clients who live in their own residences. At mental health center B, clients live in "halfway houses" with social workers on these premises. Thirty of 200 (15%) clients at A versus 50 of 200 (25%) at B require psychiatric hospitalization within 12 months of beginning treatment. A significance test indicates that the difference in percentages in the two groups is statistically significant, $p \leq .05$.

15. At a private (highly exclusive) mental health clinic located on the beach in a wealthy suburb in Southern California, clients with issues related to depression are randomly assigned to one of two treatment approaches, A or B. On the Rainbow Depression Inventory, those in approach A evidence lower depression scores ($\overline{X}$ = 20.0, $s$ = 10, $n$ = 50) than do those in B ($\overline{X}$ = 30.0, $s$ = 10, $n$ = 50). A significance test indicates that this result is statistically significant, $p \le .05$.

16. Two large-scale welfare reform innovations are introduced in Oklahoma. The "search" approach emphasizes help with job searching, whereas the "education" approach emphasizes educational and vocational training. Four thousand clients are randomly assigned to each approach. Eighty percent of those in "education" versus 78% of those in "search" find jobs within a specified period. These results (the difference in percentages between the two groups) achieve significance, $p \le .05$.

17. A random sample of 600 11-year-old boys is selected from all such boys in a six-state region in the southeastern United States. They are asked to participate in a randomized study pertaining to which of two types of video game controllers provides more effective/realistic action. All agree to participate. Three hundred are randomly assigned to the "hand-motion" controller and 300 to the "body-motion" controller. Results are as follows on a multi-item scale that measures controller effectiveness (high score conveys greater effectiveness): hand-motion group, $\overline{X}$ = 40.0, $s$ = 10; body-motion group, $\overline{X}$ = 60.0, $s$ = 10.0. A significance test indicates a statistically significant difference in means, $p \le .05$.

18. A medium-sized midwestern town implements an experiment designed to test the effectiveness of an education program to prevent drug use among teens and preteens. From the 1,000 age-appropriate youth, 200 are randomly assigned to the education program (experimental group) and 800 are assigned to a control group. The education program involves components such as education, role play, video, and a celebrity advocating against drugs. One year after the program, students fill out a questionnaire that includes the question, "Have you used marijuana in the past 6 months?" Of the 200 youth who received the education program, 24% (48 of 200) respond affirmatively. This percentage is 25% (200 of 800) for youth in the control group. The difference in percentages between the groups is not significant, $p > .05$.

19. The juvenile justice agency in a large western state classifies its services into two basic types: (a) home-based and (b) placement-based. A large-scale follow-up study finds that those youth whose primary service was home-based were far less likely to commit offenses subsequent to services than were those whose primary service was placement-based. Specifically, during a 12-month follow-up period, only 10% of 1,500 youth in home-based services committed an offense as compared with 33% of 750 youth in placement-based services. This difference in percentages is statistically significant, $p \le .05$.

Portions of this chapter originally appeared in James Rosenthal's "Pragmatic Concepts and Tools for Data Interpretation." *Journal of Teaching in Social Work 15*(1/2), 1997, pp 115–130. Reproduced with permission.

# APPENDIX A

## TABLES

TABLE A.1 ■ Percentage of Cases in Selected Areas of the Normal Distribution

| z or −z | Cases Between Mean and z or −z | Cases > z or < −z | z or −z | Cases Between Mean and z or −z | Cases > z or < −z |
|---------|-------------------------------|-------------------|---------|-------------------------------|-------------------|
| 0.00 | 0.00 | 50.00 | 0.72 | 26.40 | 23.60 |
| 0.02 | 0.80 | 49.20 | 0.74 | 27.00 | 23.00 |
| 0.04 | 1.60 | 48.40 | 0.76 | 27.60 | 22.40 |
| 0.06 | 2.40 | 47.60 | 0.78 | 28.20 | 21.80 |
| 0.08 | 3.20 | 46.80 | 0.80 | 28.80 | 21.20 |
| 0.10 | 4.00 | 46.00 | 0.82 | 29.40 | 20.60 |
| 0.12 | 4.80 | 45.20 | 0.84 | 30.00 | 20.00 |
| 0.14 | 5.60 | 44.40 | 0.86 | 30.50 | 19.50 |
| 0.16 | 6.40 | 43.60 | 0.88 | 31.10 | 18.90 |
| 0.18 | 7.10 | 42.90 | 0.90 | 31.60 | 18.40 |
| 0.20 | 7.90 | 42.10 | 0.92 | 32.10 | 17.90 |
| 0.22 | 8.70 | 41.30 | 0.94 | 32.60 | 17.40 |
| 0.24 | 9.50 | 40.50 | 0.96 | 33.10 | 16.90 |
| 0.26 | 10.30 | 39.70 | 0.98 | 33.60 | 16.40 |
| 0.28 | 11.00 | 39.00 | 1.00 | 34.10 | 15.90 |
| 0.30 | 11.80 | 38.20 | 1.02 | 34.60 | 15.40 |
| 0.32 | 12.60 | 37.40 | 1.04 | 35.10 | 14.90 |
| 0.34 | 13.30 | 36.70 | 1.06 | 35.50 | 14.50 |
| 0.36 | 14.10 | 35.90 | 1.08 | 36.00 | 14.00 |
| 0.38 | 14.80 | 35.20 | 1.10 | 36.40 | 13.60 |
| 0.40 | 15.50 | 34.50 | 1.12 | 36.90 | 13.10 |
| 0.42 | 16.30 | 33.70 | 1.14 | 37.30 | 12.70 |
| 0.44 | 17.00 | 33.00 | 1.16 | 37.70 | 12.30 |
| 0.46 | 17.70 | 32.30 | 1.18 | 38.10 | 11.90 |
| 0.48 | 18.40 | 31.60 | 1.20 | 38.50 | 11.50 |
| 0.50 | 19.10 | 30.90 | 1.22 | 38.90 | 11.10 |
| 0.52 | 19.80 | 30.20 | 1.24 | 39.30 | 10.70 |
| 0.54 | 20.50 | 29.50 | 1.26 | 39.60 | 10.40 |
| 0.56 | 21.20 | 28.80 | 1.28 | 40.00 | 10.00 |
| 0.58 | 21.90 | 28.10 | 1.30 | 40.30 | 9.70 |
| 0.60 | 22.60 | 27.40 | 1.32 | 40.70 | 9.30 |
| 0.62 | 23.20 | 26.80 | 1.34 | 41.00 | 9.00 |
| 0.64 | 23.90 | 26.10 | 1.36 | 41.30 | 8.70 |
| 0.66 | 24.50 | 25.50 | 1.38 | 41.60 | 8.40 |
| 0.68 | 25.20 | 24.80 | 1.40 | 41.90 | 8.10 |
| 0.70 | 25.80 | 24.20 | 1.42 | 42.20 | 7.80 |

*(continued)*

TABLE A.1 ■ Percentage of Cases in Selected Areas of the Normal
Distribution *(continued)*

| z or −z | Cases Between Mean and z or −z | Cases > z or < −z | z or −z | Cases Between Mean and z or −z | Cases > z or < −z |
|---|---|---|---|---|---|
| 1.44 | 42.50 | 7.50 | 2.326 | 49.00 | 1.00 |
| 1.46 | 42.80 | 7.20 | 2.34 | 49.00 | 1.00 |
| 1.48 | 43.10 | 6.90 | 2.36 | 49.10 | 0.90 |
| 1.50 | 43.30 | 6.70 | 2.38 | 49.10 | 0.90 |
| 1.52 | 43.60 | 6.40 | 2.40 | 49.20 | 0.80 |
| 1.54 | 43.80 | 6.20 | 2.42 | 49.20 | 0.80 |
| 1.56 | 44.10 | 5.90 | 2.44 | 49.30 | 0.70 |
| 1.58 | 44.30 | 5.70 | 2.46 | 49.30 | 0.70 |
| 1.60 | 44.50 | 5.50 | 2.48 | 49.30 | 0.70 |
| 1.62 | 44.70 | 5.30 | 2.50 | 49.38 | 0.62 |
| 1.64 | 44.90 | 5.10 | 2.52 | 49.41 | 0.59 |
| 1.645 | 45.00 | 5.00 | 2.54 | 49.45 | 0.55 |
| 1.66 | 45.20 | 4.80 | 2.56 | 49.48 | 0.52 |
| 1.68 | 45.40 | 4.60 | 2.576 | 49.50 | 0.50 |
| 1.70 | 45.50 | 4.50 | 2.58 | 49.51 | 0.49 |
| 1.72 | 45.70 | 4.30 | 2.60 | 49.53 | 0.47 |
| 1.74 | 45.90 | 4.10 | 2.62 | 49.56 | 0.44 |
| 1.76 | 46.10 | 3.90 | 2.64 | 49.59 | 0.41 |
| 1.78 | 46.20 | 3.80 | 2.66 | 49.61 | 0.39 |
| 1.80 | 46.40 | 3.60 | 2.68 | 49.63 | 0.37 |
| 1.82 | 46.60 | 3.40 | 2.70 | 49.65 | 0.35 |
| 1.84 | 46.70 | 3.30 | 2.72 | 49.67 | 0.33 |
| 1.86 | 46.90 | 3.10 | 2.74 | 49.69 | 0.31 |
| 1.88 | 47.00 | 3.00 | 2.76 | 49.71 | 0.29 |
| 1.90 | 47.10 | 2.90 | 2.78 | 49.73 | 0.27 |
| 1.92 | 47.30 | 2.70 | 2.80 | 49.74 | 0.26 |
| 1.94 | 47.40 | 2.60 | 2.82 | 49.76 | 0.24 |
| 1.96 | 47.50 | 2.50 | 2.84 | 49.77 | 0.23 |
| 1.98 | 47.60 | 2.40 | 2.86 | 49.79 | 0.21 |
| 2.00 | 47.70 | 2.30 | 2.88 | 49.80 | 0.20 |
| 2.02 | 47.80 | 2.20 | 2.90 | 49.81 | 0.19 |
| 2.04 | 47.90 | 2.10 | 2.92 | 49.82 | 0.18 |
| 2.06 | 48.00 | 2.00 | 2.94 | 49.84 | 0.16 |
| 2.08 | 48.10 | 1.90 | 2.96 | 49.85 | 0.15 |
| 2.10 | 48.20 | 1.80 | 2.98 | 49.86 | 0.14 |
| 2.12 | 48.30 | 1.70 | 3.00 | 49.87 | 0.13 |
| 2.14 | 48.40 | 1.60 | 3.10 | 49.90 | 0.10 |
| 2.16 | 48.50 | 1.50 | 3.20 | 49.93 | 0.07 |
| 2.18 | 48.50 | 1.50 | 3.30 | 49.95 | 0.05 |
| 2.20 | 48.60 | 1.40 | 3.40 | 49.97 | 0.03 |
| 2.22 | 48.70 | 1.30 | 3.50 | 49.98 | 0.02 |
| 2.24 | 48.70 | 1.30 | 4.00 | 50.00 | 0.003 |
| 2.26 | 48.80 | 1.20 | 1.645 | 45.00 | 5.00 |
| 2.28 | 48.90 | 1.10 | 1.960 | 47.50 | 2.50 |
| 2.30 | 48.90 | 1.10 | 2.326 | 49.00 | 1.00 |
| 2.32 | 49.00 | 1.00 | 2.576 | 49.50 | 0.50 |

TABLE A.2 ■ Critical Values for the *t* Distribution and Values for
Confidence Intervals

| df | Number of *Standard Deviations* Within Which 95% of Cases are Located | Number of *Standard Deviations* Within Which 99% of Cases are Located | | |
|---|---|---|---|---|
| | **Two-Tailed Test** | | **One-Tailed Test** | |
| | α = .05 | α = .01 | α = .05 | α = .01 |
| 1 | 12.706 | 63.657 | 6.314 | 31.821 |
| 2 | 4.303 | 9.925 | 2.920 | 6.965 |
| 3 | 3.182 | 5.841 | 2.353 | 4.541 |
| 4 | 2.776 | 4.604 | 2.132 | 3.747 |
| 5 | 2.571 | 4.032 | 2.015 | 3.365 |
| 6 | 2.447 | 3.707 | 1.943 | 3.143 |
| 7 | 2.365 | 3.499 | 1.895 | 2.998 |
| 8 | 2.306 | 3.355 | 1.860 | 2.896 |
| 9 | 2.262 | 3.250 | 1.833 | 2.821 |
| 10 | 2.228 | 3.169 | 1.812 | 2.764 |
| 11 | 2.201 | 3.106 | 1.796 | 2.718 |
| 12 | 2.179 | 3.055 | 1.782 | 2.681 |
| 13 | 2.160 | 3.012 | 1.771 | 2.650 |
| 14 | 2.145 | 2.977 | 1.761 | 2.624 |
| 15 | 2.131 | 2.947 | 1.753 | 2.602 |
| 16 | 2.120 | 2.921 | 1.746 | 2.583 |
| 17 | 2.110 | 2.898 | 1.740 | 2.567 |
| 18 | 2.101 | 2.878 | 1.734 | 2.552 |
| 19 | 2.093 | 2.861 | 1.729 | 2.539 |
| 20 | 2.086 | 2.845 | 1.725 | 2.528 |
| 21 | 2.080 | 2.831 | 1.721 | 2.518 |
| 22 | 2.074 | 2.819 | 1.717 | 2.508 |
| 23 | 2.069 | 2.807 | 1.714 | 2.500 |
| 24 | 2.064 | 2.797 | 1.711 | 2.492 |
| 25 | 2.060 | 2.787 | 1.708 | 2.485 |
| 26 | 2.056 | 2.779 | 1.706 | 2.479 |
| 27 | 2.052 | 2.771 | 1.703 | 2.473 |
| 28 | 2.048 | 2.763 | 1.701 | 2.467 |
| 29 | 2.045 | 2.756 | 1.699 | 2.462 |
| 30 | 2.042 | 2.750 | 1.697 | 2.457 |
| 35 | 2.030 | 2.724 | 1.690 | 2.438 |
| 40 | 2.021 | 2.704 | 1.684 | 2.423 |
| 50 | 2.009 | 2.678 | 1.676 | 2.403 |
| 60 | 2.000 | 2.660 | 1.671 | 2.390 |
| 80 | 1.990 | 2.639 | 1.664 | 2.374 |
| 100 | 1.984 | 2.626 | 1.660 | 2.364 |
| 120 | 1.980 | 2.617 | 1.658 | 2.358 |
| 200 | 1.972 | 2.601 | 1.653 | 2.345 |
| 500 | 1.965 | 2.586 | 1.648 | 2.334 |

TABLE A.3 ■ Critical Values (Frequencies) for the Binomial Distribution:
One-Tailed Test, Alpha = .05

| Sample Size | Direction of Alternative Hypothesis | Proportion Stated in Null (*P*) | | | | | | | | |
|---|---|---|---|---|---|---|---|---|---|---|
| | | 0.10 | 0.20 | 0.25 | 0.3333 | 0.5 | 0.6667 | 0.75 | 0.80 | 0.90 |
| 2 | < | | | | | | | | 0 | 0 |
| | > | 2 | 2 | | | | | | | |
| 3 | < | | | | | | 0 | 0 | 0 | 1 |
| | > | 2 | 3 | 3 | 3 | | | | | |
| 4 | < | | | | | | 0 | 0 | 1 | 1 |
| | > | 3 | 3 | 4 | 4 | | | | | |
| 5 | < | | | | | 0 | 1 | 1 | 1 | 2 |
| | > | 3 | 4 | 4 | 4 | 5 | | | | |
| 6 | < | | | | | 0 | 1 | 2 | 2 | 3 |
| | > | 3 | 4 | 4 | 5 | 6 | | | | |
| 7 | < | | | | | 0 | 2 | 2 | 3 | 4 |
| | > | 3 | 4 | 5 | 5 | 7 | | | | |
| 8 | < | | | | | 0 | 1 | 2 | 3 | 5 |
| | > | 3 | 5 | 5 | 6 | 7 | 8 | | | |
| 9 | < | | | | | 0 | 1 | 3 | 4 | 5 |
| | > | 4 | 5 | 5 | 6 | 8 | 9 | | | |
| 10 | < | | | | | 0 | 1 | 3 | 4 | 6 |
| | > | 4 | 5 | 6 | 7 | 9 | 10 | | | |
| 11 | < | | | | | 0 | 2 | 4 | 5 | 7 |
| | > | 4 | 6 | 6 | 7 | 9 | 11 | 11 | | |
| 12 | < | | | | | 0 | 2 | 4 | 5 | 6 | 8 |
| | > | 4 | 6 | 7 | 8 | 10 | 12 | 12 | | |
| 13 | < | | | | 1 | 3 | 5 | 6 | 7 | 9 |
| | > | 4 | 6 | 7 | 8 | 10 | 12 | 13 | | |
| 14 | < | | 0 | 0 | 1 | 3 | 5 | 7 | 8 | 10 |
| | > | 4 | 6 | 7 | 9 | 11 | 13 | 14 | 14 | |
| 15 | < | | 0 | 0 | 1 | 3 | 6 | 7 | 8 | 10 |
| | > | 5 | 7 | 8 | 9 | 12 | 14 | 15 | 15 | |
| 18 | < | | 0 | 1 | 2 | 5 | 8 | 9 | 10 | 13 |
| | > | 5 | 8 | 9 | 10 | 13 | 16 | 17 | 18 | |
| 20 | < | | 0 | 1 | 2 | 5 | 9 | 11 | 12 | 15 |
| | > | 5 | 8 | 9 | 11 | 15 | 18 | 19 | 20 | |
| 25 | < | | 1 | 2 | 4 | 7 | 12 | 14 | 16 | 19 |
| | > | 6 | 9 | 11 | 13 | 18 | 21 | 23 | 24 | |
| 30 | < | 0 | 2 | 3 | 5 | 10 | 15 | 17 | 19 | 23 |
| | > | 7 | 11 | 13 | 15 | 20 | 25 | 27 | 28 | 30 |
| 35 | < | 0 | 2 | 4 | 6 | 12 | 18 | 21 | 23 | 27 |
| | > | 8 | 12 | 14 | 17 | 23 | 29 | 31 | 33 | 35 |
| 40 | < | 0 | 3 | 5 | 8 | 14 | 21 | 24 | 27 | 32 |
| | > | 8 | 13 | 16 | 19 | 26 | 32 | 35 | 37 | 40 |
| 50 | < | 1 | 5 | 7 | 10 | 18 | 27 | 31 | 34 | 40 |
| | > | 10 | 16 | 19 | 23 | 32 | 40 | 43 | 45 | 49 |
| 75 | < | 2 | 8 | 12 | 17 | 29 | 42 | 49 | 53 | 62 |
| | > | 13 | 22 | 26 | 33 | 46 | 58 | 63 | 67 | 73 |
| 100 | < | 4 | 13 | 17 | 25 | 41 | 58 | 67 | 72 | 84 |
| | > | 16 | 28 | 33 | 42 | 59 | 75 | 83 | 87 | 96 |

TABLE A.4 ■ Critical Values for the Chi-Square Distribution

| df | Significance Level | | | |
|---|---|---|---|---|
| | .10 | .05 | .01 | 0.001 |
| 1 | 2.71 | 3.84 | 6.63 | 10.83 |
| 2 | 4.61 | 5.99 | 9.21 | 13.82 |
| 3 | 6.25 | 7.81 | 11.34 | 16.27 |
| 4 | 7.78 | 9.49 | 13.28 | 18.47 |
| 5 | 9.24 | 11.07 | 15.09 | 20.52 |
| 6 | 10.64 | 12.59 | 16.81 | 22.46 |
| 7 | 12.02 | 14.07 | 18.48 | 24.32 |
| 8 | 13.36 | 15.51 | 20.09 | 26.12 |
| 9 | 14.68 | 16.92 | 21.67 | 27.88 |
| 10 | 15.99 | 18.31 | 23.21 | 29.59 |
| 11 | 17.28 | 19.68 | 24.72 | 31.26 |
| 12 | 18.55 | 21.03 | 26.22 | 32.91 |
| 13 | 19.81 | 22.36 | 27.69 | 34.53 |
| 14 | 21.06 | 23.68 | 29.14 | 36.12 |
| 15 | 22.31 | 25.00 | 30.58 | 37.70 |
| 16 | 23.54 | 26.30 | 32.00 | 39.25 |
| 17 | 24.77 | 27.59 | 33.41 | 40.79 |
| 18 | 25.99 | 28.87 | 34.81 | 42.31 |
| 19 | 27.20 | 30.14 | 36.19 | 43.82 |
| 20 | 28.41 | 31.41 | 37.57 | 45.31 |
| 21 | 29.62 | 32.67 | 38.93 | 46.80 |
| 22 | 30.81 | 33.92 | 40.29 | 48.27 |
| 23 | 32.01 | 35.17 | 41.64 | 49.73 |
| 24 | 33.20 | 36.42 | 42.98 | 51.18 |
| 25 | 34.38 | 37.65 | 44.31 | 52.62 |
| 26 | 35.56 | 38.89 | 45.64 | 54.05 |
| 27 | 36.74 | 40.11 | 46.96 | 55.48 |
| 28 | 37.92 | 41.34 | 48.28 | 56.89 |
| 29 | 39.09 | 42.56 | 49.59 | 58.30 |
| 30 | 40.26 | 43.77 | 50.89 | 59.70 |
| 35 | 46.06 | 49.80 | 57.34 | 66.62 |
| 40 | 51.81 | 55.76 | 63.69 | 73.40 |
| 50 | 63.17 | 67.50 | 76.15 | 86.66 |
| 60 | 74.40 | 79.08 | 88.38 | 99.61 |
| 70 | 85.53 | 90.53 | 100.43 | 112.32 |
| 80 | 96.58 | 101.88 | 112.33 | 124.84 |
| 100 | 118.50 | 124.34 | 135.81 | 149.45 |

## TABLE A.5 ■ Critical Values for the *F* Distribution

| *df* for $MS_w$ (Denominator) | Alpha (α) | Degrees of Freedom for $MS_B$ (Numerator) | | | | | | | | |
|---|---|---|---|---|---|---|---|---|---|---|
| | | 1 | 2 | 3 | 4 | 5 | 6 | 7 | 8 | 10 |
| 1 | .05 | 161.4 | 199.5 | 215.7 | 224.6 | 230.2 | 234.0 | 236.8 | 238.9 | 241.9 |
| | .01 | 4052 | 4999 | 5403 | 5625 | 5764 | 5859 | 5928 | 5981 | 6056 |
| 2 | .05 | 18.51 | 19.00 | 19.16 | 19.25 | 19.30 | 19.33 | 19.35 | 19.37 | 19.40 |
| | .01 | 98.50 | 99.00 | 99.17 | 99.25 | 99.30 | 99.33 | 99.36 | 99.37 | 99.40 |
| 3 | .05 | 10.13 | 9.55 | 9.28 | 9.12 | 9.01 | 8.94 | 8.89 | 8.85 | 8.79 |
| | .01 | 34.12 | 30.82 | 29.46 | 28.71 | 28.24 | 27.91 | 27.67 | 27.49 | 27.23 |
| 4 | .05 | 7.71 | 6.94 | 6.59 | 6.39 | 6.26 | 6.16 | 6.09 | 6.04 | 5.96 |
| | .01 | 21.20 | 18.00 | 16.69 | 15.98 | 15.52 | 15.21 | 14.98 | 14.80 | 14.55 |
| 5 | .05 | 6.61 | 5.79 | 5.41 | 5.19 | 5.05 | 4.95 | 4.88 | 4.82 | 4.74 |
| | .01 | 16.26 | 13.27 | 12.06 | 11.39 | 10.97 | 10.67 | 10.46 | 10.29 | 10.05 |
| 6 | .05 | 5.99 | 5.14 | 4.76 | 4.53 | 4.39 | 4.28 | 4.21 | 4.15 | 4.06 |
| | .01 | 13.75 | 10.92 | 9.78 | 9.15 | 8.75 | 8.47 | 8.26 | 8.10 | 7.87 |
| 7 | .05 | 5.59 | 4.74 | 4.35 | 4.12 | 3.97 | 3.87 | 3.79 | 3.73 | 3.64 |
| | .01 | 12.25 | 9.55 | 8.45 | 7.85 | 7.46 | 7.19 | 6.99 | 6.84 | 6.62 |
| 8 | .05 | 5.32 | 4.46 | 4.07 | 3.84 | 3.69 | 3.58 | 3.50 | 3.44 | 3.35 |
| | .01 | 11.26 | 8.65 | 7.59 | 7.01 | 6.63 | 6.37 | 6.18 | 6.03 | 5.81 |
| 9 | .05 | 5.12 | 4.26 | 3.86 | 3.63 | 3.48 | 3.37 | 3.29 | 3.23 | 3.14 |
| | .01 | 10.56 | 8.02 | 6.99 | 6.42 | 6.06 | 5.80 | 5.61 | 5.47 | 5.26 |
| 10 | .05 | 4.96 | 4.10 | 3.71 | 3.48 | 3.33 | 3.22 | 3.14 | 3.07 | 2.98 |
| | .01 | 10.04 | 7.56 | 6.55 | 5.99 | 5.64 | 5.39 | 5.20 | 5.06 | 4.85 |
| 11 | .05 | 4.84 | 3.98 | 3.59 | 3.36 | 3.20 | 3.09 | 3.01 | 2.95 | 2.85 |
| | .01 | 9.65 | 7.21 | 6.22 | 5.67 | 5.32 | 5.07 | 4.89 | 4.74 | 4.54 |
| 12 | .05 | 4.75 | 3.89 | 3.49 | 3.26 | 3.11 | 3.00 | 2.91 | 2.85 | 2.75 |
| | .01 | 9.33 | 6.93 | 5.95 | 5.41 | 5.06 | 4.82 | 4.64 | 4.50 | 4.30 |
| 13 | .05 | 4.67 | 3.81 | 3.41 | 3.18 | 3.03 | 2.92 | 2.83 | 2.77 | 2.67 |
| | .01 | 9.07 | 6.70 | 5.74 | 5.21 | 4.86 | 4.62 | 4.44 | 4.30 | 4.10 |
| 15 | .05 | 4.54 | 3.68 | 3.29 | 3.06 | 2.90 | 2.79 | 2.71 | 2.64 | 2.54 |
| | .01 | 8.68 | 6.36 | 5.42 | 4.89 | 4.56 | 4.32 | 4.14 | 4.00 | 3.80 |
| 20 | .05 | 4.35 | 3.49 | 3.10 | 2.87 | 2.71 | 2.60 | 2.51 | 2.45 | 2.35 |
| | .01 | 8.10 | 5.85 | 4.94 | 4.43 | 4.10 | 3.87 | 3.70 | 3.56 | 3.37 |
| 25 | .05 | 4.24 | 3.39 | 2.99 | 2.76 | 2.60 | 2.49 | 2.40 | 2.34 | 2.24 |
| | .01 | 7.77 | 5.57 | 4.68 | 4.18 | 3.85 | 3.63 | 3.46 | 3.32 | 3.13 |
| 30 | .05 | 4.17 | 3.32 | 2.92 | 2.69 | 2.53 | 2.42 | 2.33 | 2.27 | 2.16 |
| | .01 | 7.50 | 5.34 | 4.46 | 3.97 | 3.65 | 3.43 | 3.26 | 3.13 | 2.93 |
| 40 | .05 | 4.08 | 3.23 | 2.84 | 2.61 | 2.45 | 2.34 | 2.25 | 2.18 | 2.08 |
| | .01 | 7.31 | 5.18 | 4.31 | 3.83 | 3.51 | 3.29 | 3.12 | 2.99 | 2.80 |
| 50 | .05 | 4.03 | 3.18 | 2.79 | 2.56 | 2.40 | 2.29 | 2.20 | 2.13 | 2.03 |
| | .01 | 7.17 | 5.06 | 4.20 | 3.72 | 3.41 | 3.19 | 3.02 | 2.89 | 2.70 |
| 100 | .05 | 3.94 | 3.09 | 2.70 | 2.46 | 2.31 | 2.19 | 2.10 | 2.03 | 1.93 |
| | .01 | 6.90 | 4.82 | 3.98 | 3.51 | 3.21 | 2.99 | 2.82 | 2.69 | 2.50 |
| 250 | .05 | 3.88 | 3.03 | 2.64 | 2.41 | 2.25 | 2.13 | 2.05 | 1.98 | 1.87 |
| | .01 | 6.74 | 4.69 | 3.86 | 3.40 | 3.09 | 2.87 | 2.71 | 2.58 | 2.39 |
| 1000 | .05 | 3.85 | 3.00 | 2.61 | 2.38 | 2.22 | 2.11 | 2.02 | 1.95 | 1.84 |
| | .01 | 6.66 | 4.63 | 3.80 | 3.34 | 3.04 | 2.82 | 2.66 | 2.53 | 2.34 |

TABLE A.6 ■ Critical Values for Pearson's *r*

| N | df | Two-Tailed Test | | One-Tailed Test | |
|---|---|---|---|---|---|
| | | α = 0.05 | α = 0.01 | α = 0.05 | α = 0.01 |
| 3 | 1 | .997 | 1.000 | .988 | 1.000 |
| 4 | 2 | .950 | .990 | .900 | .980 |
| 5 | 3 | .878 | .959 | .805 | .934 |
| 6 | 4 | .811 | .917 | .729 | .882 |
| 7 | 5 | .754 | .875 | .669 | .833 |
| 8 | 6 | .707 | .834 | .621 | .789 |
| 9 | 7 | .666 | .798 | .582 | .750 |
| 10 | 8 | .632 | .765 | .549 | .715 |
| 11 | 9 | .602 | .735 | .521 | .685 |
| 12 | 10 | .576 | .708 | .497 | .658 |
| 13 | 11 | .553 | .684 | .476 | .634 |
| 14 | 12 | .532 | .661 | .458 | .612 |
| 15 | 13 | .514 | .641 | .441 | .592 |
| 16 | 14 | .497 | .623 | .426 | .574 |
| 17 | 15 | .482 | .606 | .412 | .558 |
| 18 | 16 | .468 | .590 | .400 | .543 |
| 19 | 17 | .456 | .575 | .389 | .529 |
| 20 | 18 | .444 | .561 | .378 | .516 |
| 21 | 19 | .433 | .549 | .369 | .503 |
| 22 | 20 | .423 | .537 | .360 | .492 |
| 23 | 21 | .413 | .526 | .352 | .482 |
| 24 | 22 | .404 | .515 | .344 | .472 |
| 25 | 23 | .396 | .505 | .337 | .462 |
| 26 | 24 | .388 | .496 | .330 | .453 |
| 27 | 25 | .381 | .487 | .323 | .445 |
| 29 | 27 | .367 | .471 | .311 | .430 |
| 32 | 30 | .349 | .449 | .296 | .409 |
| 37 | 35 | .325 | .418 | .275 | .381 |
| 42 | 40 | .304 | .393 | .257 | .358 |
| 47 | 45 | .288 | .372 | .243 | .338 |
| 52 | 50 | .273 | .354 | .231 | .322 |
| 62 | 60 | .250 | .325 | .211 | .295 |
| 72 | 70 | .232 | .302 | .195 | .274 |
| 82 | 80 | .217 | .283 | .183 | .257 |
| 102 | 100 | .195 | .254 | .164 | .230 |
| 142 | 140 | .165 | .216 | .139 | .195 |
| 202 | 200 | .138 | .181 | .116 | .164 |
| 302 | 300 | .113 | .148 | .095 | .134 |
| 402 | 400 | .098 | .128 | .082 | .116 |
| 602 | 600 | .080 | .105 | .067 | .095 |
| 1002 | 1000 | .062 | .081 | .052 | .073 |

# APPENDIX B

## REVIEW OF BASIC MATH

### B.1 ■ BASIC OPERATIONS, TERMS, AND SYMBOLS

When two numbers are added (or, one may say, summed) the result is a **sum**. For instance,

$3 + 3 = 6$ (the sum is 6).

When one number is subtracted from another, the result is a **difference**. For instance,

$5 - 4 = 1$ (the difference is 1).

When two numbers are multiplied, the result is a **product**. For instance,

$2 \times 4 = 8$ (the product is 8).

When one number is divided by another, the result is a **quotient**. For instance,

$6 \div 2 = 3$ (the quotient is 3).

Sometimes, symbols different from those used previously are used. A "slash" indicates division. For instance, $6 / 2 = 3$. A "horizontal bar" also conveys division.

$$\frac{6}{2} = 3$$

In expressions involving division, the number that is divided (the number above the bar) is termed the **numerator**, and the number by which one divides (the number below the bar) is termed the **denominator**.

When one or both of the two numbers are inside parentheses and there is no symbol between them, this indicates multiplication. For instance,

$(2)(4) = (2) \times (4) = 2 \times 4 = 8$

$2(4) = 2 \times (4) = 2 \times 4 = 8$

### B.2 ■ MORE SYMBOLS

Here is a list of symbols with which you may or may not be familiar and examples of how they are used:

| | |
|---|---|
| $<$ | less than ($5 < 7$, $-7 < -5$) |
| $>$ | greater than ($7 > 5$, $-5 > -7$) |

≤      less than or equal to $(3 \leq 5, 5 \leq 5)$

≥      greater than or equal to $(6 \geq 2, 6 \geq 6)$

≈      approximately equal to $(8.6532 \approx 8.6533)$

±      add and subtract $(5 \pm 3 = 5 - 3$ and $5 + 3 = 2$ and $8)$

Another symbol that you may not have encountered is the **summation sign**, $\Sigma$. The summation sign instructs one to sum whatever follows. Hence, the expression "$\Sigma$ (2,3,8,9,5)" directs one to sum 2, 3, 8, 9, and 5.

$$\Sigma (2,3,8,9,5) = 2 + 3 + 8 + 9 + 5 = 27$$

## B.3 ▪ ORDER OF OPERATIONS

An important rule to remember is to always carry out operations inside parentheses first. For instance,

$$(2 + 4) / (2 + 1) = 6 / 3 = 2$$

When more than one set of parentheses is needed, operations in the innermost parentheses should be carried out first. For instance,

$$(8 + (3 \times 4)) / 5 = (8 + 12) / 5 = 20 / 5 = 4$$

Assuming that operations within parentheses have been carried out, multiplication and/or division should be carried out prior to addition and/or subtraction. For instance,

$$7 + 3(5) = 7 + 15 = 22$$

## B.4 ▪ POSITIVE AND NEGATIVE NUMBERS AND ABSOLUTE VALUES

You will encounter both **negative numbers** (those with values less than 0) and **positive numbers** (those with values greater than 0). Negative numbers are designated by the negative sign. The **negative sign** (*minus sign*, $-$) is the same as the subtraction symbol and conveys subtraction from 0 (zero). Hence, $-5$ conveys the negative number "negative 5" which equals $0 - 5$ $(0 - 5 = -5)$. The **positive sign** (*plus sign*, $+$) is the addition symbol and conveys 0 plus a number. For instance, $+5$ conveys "positive 5" which equals $0 + 5$ $(0 + 5 = +5)$. When a number is a positive number, one need not designate this by a sign. For instance, 5 designates $+5$ (positive 5).

Two tips regarding addition and subtraction involving negative numbers are

Adding a negative number yields the same result as subtracting a positive number. Thus, to add a negative number, change its sign to positive and subtract. For instance,

$$4 + (-2) = 4 - 2 = 2$$

Subtracting a negative number yields the same result as adding a positive number. Thus, to subtract a negative number, change its sign to positive and sum. For instance,

$$-4 - (-2) = -4 + 2 = -2$$

Some rules to remember regarding multiplication and division are

A positive number multiplied by or divided by a positive yields a positive. For instance,

$4 \times 2 = 8$ and $4 / 2 = 2$

A negative number multiplied by or divided by a negative yields a positive. For instance,

$(-4)(-2) = 8$ and $(-4) / (-2) = 2$

A positive number multiplied or divided by a negative and, also, a negative number multiplied or divided by a positive yields a negative: For instance,

$(4)(-2) = -8$ and $(4) / (-2) = -2$

$(-4)(2) = -8$ and $(-4) / (2) = -2$

The **absolute value** of a number is its value disregarding its sign. Or stated differently, it is the positive value of the number. For instance, the absolute value of $-5$ is 5 (positive 5). Similarly, the absolute value of 5 is 5. Absolute value is symbolized by vertical bars on both sides of a number. Hence, $|-3|$ conveys the absolute value of minus 3, which is 3.

It may be helpful to clarify the meaning of a "less than" (symbolized by $<$) and a "greater than" (symbolized by $>$) in situations involving negative numbers. Obviously, for instance, $5 > 2$ and $2 < 5$. It may be less obvious whether the following expressions are true: $-5 < -2$, $-5 < 2$, $-2 > -5$, and $2 > -5$. All of these expressions are indeed true. In considering whether a given number is greater than or less than another, one considers actual values *not* absolute values. For instance, $-5$ is not greater than $-2$ but, instead, is less than this. On the other hand, the absolute value of negative 5 (which is 5) is greater than the absolute value of negative 2 (which is 2). Using symbols $|-5| > |-2|$.

This text occasionally uses the term the **negative of** to convey the negative number that is opposite in sign to a given positive number. For instance, as used in the text, $-7$ is the negative of 7, and $-1.87$ is the negative of 1.87. This term is not a formal term in mathematics but is useful for several applications that are presented.

## B.5 ■ SQUARES AND SQUARE ROOTS

The **square** of a number (or, one may say, a number squared) equals that number multiplied by itself. For instance, 6 squared $= 6 \times 6 = 36$. The symbol for a number squared is the superscript 2, that is, $^2$. Thus, 6 squared is symbolized by $6^2$. Expressed as an equation: $6^2 = 6 \times 6 = 36$.

The square root of a (first) number is the (second) number that when multiplied by itself yields the (first) number. For instance, the square root of 36 is 6 because $6 \times 6 = 6^2 = 36$. Square roots are designated by the radical symbol (the square root symbol). Hence, in symbols: $\sqrt{36} = 6$.[1]

## B.6 ■ FRACTIONS

Multiplication of fractions is straightforward. One simply multiplies the numerator of one fraction by that of the other and does the same with the denominators.

$$\frac{1}{4} \times \frac{3}{8} = \frac{3}{32}$$

To divide one fraction by another, invert ("flip") the second fraction and then multiply:

$$\frac{1}{4} \div \frac{3}{8} = \frac{1}{4} \times \frac{8}{3} = \frac{8}{12}$$

The denominator of any whole number is always one. For instance, 6 = 6/1. To solve the problem 5 × 2/3 = ?, it is convenient to express 5 as 5/1.

$$\frac{5}{1} \times \frac{2}{3} = \frac{10}{3}$$

It is often helpful to **reduce** a fraction, that is, to express with the lowest possible denominator. To reduce a fraction, find a number that divides evenly into both its numerator and denominator. For instance, 4 divides evenly into both the numerator and denominator of 8/12. Hence, 8/12 can be reduced to 2/3. Stated as an equation, 8/12 = 2/3.

To add and subtract fractions, one must find a **common denominator**. One way to do so is to multiply each fraction by 1 (one), with 1 expressed using the denominator of the other fraction. For instance, consider the problem: 1/3 + 2/5 = ?. The fraction 1/3 can be multiplied by 5/5: 1/3 × 5/5 = 5/15 (5/5 equals 1 and, thus, does not change the value of the fraction). Similarly, 2/5 can be multiplied by 3/3: 2/5 × 3/3 = 6/15. Now, both fractions have a common denominator (15) and they can be summed.

$$\frac{5}{15} + \frac{6}{15} = \frac{11}{15}$$

To calculate a number's **reciprocal**, divide 1 by that number. For instance, the reciprocal of 4 equals 1 ÷ 4 = 1/4. A number multiplied by its reciprocal equals 1. For instance,

$$4 \times \frac{1}{4} = \frac{4}{1} \times \frac{1}{4} = \frac{4}{4} = \frac{1}{1} = 1$$

## B.7 ■ ALGEBRA

To solve simple algebra problems, carry out the same operations on both sides of the equals sign. For instance, the following problem is solved by adding "5" to both sides:

$$X - 5 = 2$$
$$X - 5 + 5 = 2 + 5$$
$$X = 7$$

The next problem requires both addition and multiplication on both sides:

$$5X - 3 = 12$$
$$5X - 3 + 3 = 12 + 3$$
$$5X = 15$$
$$5X \div 5 = 15 \div 5$$
$$X = 3$$

## B.8 ■ RATIOS, PROPORTIONS, PERCENTAGES, AND PERCENTILES

Consider a classroom with 10 girls and 4 boys.
A **ratio** is the number in one group divided by that in the other.

- the ratio of girls to boys is 10/4 = 10 to 4 (or 5 to 2 or 2.5 to 1 or 2.5)
- the ratio of boys to girls is 4/10 = 4 to 10 (or 2 to 5 or 0.40)

Percentages and proportions convey the same information.

To calculate a **proportion,** divide the number in one group by the total number: the proportion of girls is 10 / 14 = 0.71; that of boys is 4 / 14 = 0.29.

To calculate a **percentage**, multiply the proportion by 100: the percentage of girls = 0.71 × 100 = 71%.

## B.9 ■ ROUNDING

It will be helpful to introduce some guidelines for **rounding**. Suppose that we have the number 518.428754". For most purposes, this number has more precision than is needed. We may wish to round it to, say, three decimal places. To see how to round, direct your attention to the number in the decimal place following the place to which you wish to round. If this number is 5 or greater, round up upward; if it is 4 or lower, round downward. For our example, the number in the fourth decimal place is 7. Seven is greater than 5. Therefore, we round upward to 518.429. As another example, to round 29.53468 to two decimal places, focus on the number in the third decimal place; 4 is less than 5 and, thus, we round downward to 29.53.

Whenever rounding is carried out, some **roundoff error** is introduced into the answer. With calculators and computers, this is much less of a problem than was the case when calculations were carried out by hand. The following guideline reduces (but does not eliminate) roundoff error: In all calculations, round to at least one more decimal place than you will use to express your answer. For instance, suppose that you need to multiply 8.45419 by 3.539682 and want to express your answer with two decimal places. According to the guideline, each number should be rounded to three decimal places (2 + 1 = 3). Hence, you would multiply 8.454 (note, that we rounded downward) by 3.540 (note that the third number, 9, is rounded up to 10) which results in 29.92716. Rounding this product to two decimal places, the answer is 29.93.

## B.10 ■ MATH REVIEW PROBLEMS

1. The result of addition is termed a _____; that of subtraction is a _____; that of multiplication is a _____; and that of division is a _____.

2. What does each symbol convey? $\geq$ _____; $\approx$ _____; $\pm$ _____.

3. What is $\Sigma(4,7,2,3,3)$? What is $\Sigma(4,4,5,0,2)$?

4. $(9 - 2) \times (3 / 4) = ?$; $10 \times [(2 + 6) / (3 \times 8)] = ?$

**5.** $8 - (-3) + (-2) = ?; 5 + (-3) - (-2) + 7 = ?$

**6.** $|-7| = ?; |12| = ?$

**7.** $5^2 = ?; \sqrt{49} = ?; 3^2 = ?$

**8.** $\dfrac{2}{1} \div \dfrac{3}{2} = ?; \dfrac{7}{4} \times \dfrac{5}{12} = ?$

**9.** $\dfrac{8}{3} - \dfrac{3}{9} = ?; \dfrac{2}{5} + \dfrac{3}{4} = ?$

**10.** What is the reciprocal of 2.5? Of 0.40?

**11.** Solve each for $X$: $X + (7 - 2) = 2X + 4$; $(10X)/5 = 20$

**12.** Round 3.42671 to two decimal places. Round it to four decimal places.

## B.11 ■ MATH REVIEW ANSWERS

**1.** sum, difference, product, quotient

**2.** $\geq$ greater than or equal to; $\approx$ approximately equal; $\pm$ plus or minus

**3.** 19, 15

**4.** 5.25, 3.33

**5.** 9, 11

**6.** $|-7| = 7, |12| = 12$

**7.** $5^2 = 25, \sqrt{49} = 7, 3^2 = 9$

**8.** $4/3 = 1.33, 35/48 = 0.73$

**9.** $21/9 = 7/3 = 2.33, 23/20 = 1.15$

**10.** $1/(2.50) = 0.40, 1/(0.40) = 2.50$

**11.** $X = 1, X = 10$

**12.** 3.43, 3.4267

# APPENDIX C

## APPROPRIATE MEASURES FOR
## DIFFERENT SITUATIONS

TABLE C.1 ■ Selected Univariate Measures and Measures of Association

| Measurement of First Variable | Univariate Measures | Measures of Association by Measurement of Second Variable | | | |
|---|---|---|---|---|---|
| | | Dichotomous | Nominal: Three or More Categories | Ordinal | Interval/Ratio |
| Dichotomous | Proportion ($p$) <br> Percentage (%) <br> Ratio <br> Frequency <br> Mode <br> Standard deviation of dichotomous variable ($s_{dich}$)[a] <br> 95% and 99% confidence intervals of the proportion | Difference in percentages ($D$%) <br> Risk ratio ($RR$) <br> Odds ratio ($OR$) <br> Phi ($r_{phi}$) | Cramer's $V$ <br> Lambda ($\lambda$)[a] | Same procedures apply as in ordinal/ordinal cell below | Standardized mean difference ($SMD$) <br> Eta ($\eta$)[a] <br> Eta squared ($\eta^2$) <br> Point-biserial correlation $r_{pb}$[a] <br> Exponentiated coefficient in logistic regression ($e^\beta$) |
| Nominal: three or more categories | Same as above cell but $s_{dich}$[a] and confidence intervals do not apply | — | Cramer's $V$ <br> Lambda[a] | Cramer's $V$ <br> Lambda[a] | Eta ($\eta$)[a] <br> Eta squared ($\eta^2$) |
| Ordinal | Same as above cell and also <br> Cumulative frequency <br> Cumulative percentage <br> Percentile rank <br> Median | — | — | If relationship is directional: <br> Spearman's $r$ ($r_{ranks}$) <br> Kendall's tau-$b$ <br> Kendall's tau-$c$ <br> Gamma <br> Somers' $D$ <br> If nondirectional: <br> Cramer's $V$ <br> Lambda[a] | No measures presented for this combination. <br> Measures in cell directly above, sometimes best choice; those in cell below, sometimes best choice |
| Interval/Ratio | Same as above and <br> Mean ($\bar{X}$) <br> Mean deviation ($MD$) <br> Standard deviation ($s$) <br> Variance ($s^2$) <br> Range <br> Interquartile range <br> 95% and 99% confidence intervals of the mean | — | — | — | Pearson's $r$ ($r$; in bivariate situation, $r$ is the standardized regression coefficient) <br> Standardized regression coefficient ($\beta$) <br> Unstandardized regression coefficient ($B$) <br> Coefficient of determination ($r^2$) |

[a]Procedure not discussed in text or discussed only briefly.

TABLE C.2 ■ Selected Statistical Significance Tests for Univariate, Bivariate, and Multivariate Situations

| Measurement of First Variable | Univariate Situations | Measurement of Second Variable: Bivariate and Univariate Situations | | | |
|---|---|---|---|---|---|
| | | Dichotomous | Nominal: Three or More Categories | Ordinal | Interval/Ratio |
| Dichotomous | One-sample test of the proportion ($p$) Binomial test (one-variable $\chi^2$ test is an alternative to one-sample test of $p$) | Chi-square ($\chi^2$) test of independence Fisher's exact test McNemar's test (dependent samples) | Chi-square ($\chi^2$) test of independence | Independent samples: Mann-Whitney $U$ test Kolmogorov-Smirnov test[a] Dependent samples: sign test Wilcoxon test tests in ordinal/ordinal cell below | Independent samples $t$ test Dependent samples $t$ test (Analysis of variance [ANOVA] is an alternative to independent samples $t$ test) In logistic regression, tests of coefficients ($e^B$) |
| Nominal: three or more categories | One-variable chi-square ($\chi^2$) test | — | Chi-square ($\chi^2$) test of independence | Kruskal-Wallis test (independent samples) Friedman test (dependent samples)[a] $\chi^2$ test of independence | Analysis of variance (ANOVA) |
| Ordinal | None presented One-variable $\chi^2$ test can be appropriate (will not pick up directional trend) | — | — | If relationship is directional: Spearman's $r$ ($r_{ranks}$) test of Kendall's tau-$b$ test of Kendall's tau-$c$ test of Gamma test of Somers' $D$ If nondirectional: test of Lambda[a] $\chi^2$ test of independence | Analysis of variance (ANOVA) is often appropriate (in particular, with linear polynomial contrast[a]) |
| Interval/Ratio | Large sample test of the mean ($\bar{X}$) One-sample $t$ test | — | — | — | Test of Pearson's $r$ ($r$) In multiple regression analysis, tests of unstandardized ($B$) and standardized ($\beta$) coefficients |

[a]Procedure not discussed in text or discussed only briefly.

# APPENDIX D

## SYMBOLS IN THE TEXT

| Greek Letters | Description |
|---|---|
| $\alpha$ | Alpha, probability connected with selected statistical significance level and probability of Type I error |
| $\beta$ | Beta, probability of Type II error (pronounced [bait-ah]) |
| $\beta$ | Beta, standardized regression coefficient (same symbol as for probability of Type II error) |
| $\eta^2$ | Eta squared (correlation ratio), measure of size/strength of association (pronounced [8-a]) |
| $\mu$ | Mu, population mean (pronounced [mew]) |
| $\rho$ | Rho, population correlation (pronounced [row]) |
| $\Sigma$ | Sigma (capital letter), summation sign |
| $\sigma$ | Sigma ("small" letter), population standard deviation |
| $\sigma^2$ | Population variance |
| $\sigma_{\bar{x}}$ | Standard error of the mean |
| $\sigma_p$ | Standard error of the proportion |
| $\chi^2$ | Chi-square statistic as used in both chi-square tests (pronounced [ki] as in "kite") |

| English Letters | Description |
|---|---|
| $A$ | Constant in regression equation |
| $B$ | Unstandardized regression coefficient |
| $D\%$ | Difference in percentages |
| $df$ | Degrees of freedom |
| $e^B$ | Coefficient in logistic regression conveying change in odds |
| $ES_{means}$ | Effect size for means |
| $F$ | $F$ ratio in analysis of variance |
| $f$ | Frequency |
| $H_0$ | Null hypothesis |
| $H_1$ | Alternative (research) hypothesis |
| $IQR$ | Interquartile range |
| $ln$ | natural logarithm |

| English Letters | Description |
| --- | --- |
| $M$ | Sample mean (for use in reports; this text more often uses $\overline{X}$) |
| $MD$ | Mean deviation |
| $MS_B$ | Mean square between (in ANOVA) |
| $MS_W$ | Mean square within (in ANOVA) |
| $n$ | Frequency (most often used to convey the number in a group) |
| $N$ | Number of cases in study sample |
| 95% $CI$ of $\mu$ | 95% confidence interval of the mean |
| 99% $CI$ of $\mu$ | 99% confidence interval of the mean |
| $n$ | Number of cases in a group (alternative symbol for frequency) |
| $OR$ | Odds ratio |
| $p$ | Proportion in sample |
| $p$ | Probability (including probability given by statistical significance test) |
| $P$ | Proportion in population |
| 95% $CI$ of $P$ | 95% confidence interval of the proportion |
| 99% $CI$ of $P$ | 99% confidence interval of the proportion |
| $r$ | Pearson correlation coefficient |
| $r_{phi}$ | Correlation between two (usually) dichotomous variables (phi is pronounced as in [five]) |
| $r_{ranks}$ | Spearman correlation coefficient |
| $r^2$ | Coefficient of determination (percentage of shared or explained variance) |
| $R$ | Multiple correlation coefficient |
| $R^2$ | Squared multiple correlation coefficient |
| Adjusted $R^2$ | $R^2$ adjusted to reduce bias |
| $RR$ | Risk ratio |
| $s$ | Sample standard deviation |
| $s^2$ | Sample variance |
| $s_C$ | Standard deviation in control group (used in $ES_{means}$ formula) |
| $s_E$ | Standard deviation in experimental group (used in $ES_{means}$ formula) |
| $SD$ | Sample standard deviation (for use in reports) |
| $s_p$ | Estimate of standard error of the proportion |
| $SS_B$ | Sum of squares between groups (used in ANOVA) |
| $SS_W$ | Sum of squares within groups (used in ANOVA) |
| $s_{wg}$ | Standard deviation within groups (used in $SMD$ formula) |
| $s_{\overline{X}}$ | Estimate of standard error of the mean |
| $SMD$ | Standardized mean difference |
| $s_{X_1 - X_2}$ | Estimate of the standard error of the difference between means |
| $t$ | Test statistic for $t$ tests |
| $X$ | The (raw) score of an individual case |
| $\overline{X}$ | Sample mean |
| $\hat{Y}$ | Predicted value of $Y$ (dependent variable) in unstandardized regression equation |
| $z$ | $z$ score (standard score) and test statistic for large sample test of $\overline{X}$ |
| $\hat{z}_y$ | Predicted $z$ score of $Y$ in standardized regression equation |

Note. ANOVA = analysis of variance.

# APPENDIX E

## FORMULAS IN THE TEXT

| | | |
|---|---|---|
| Percentage | $\% = (f/N) \times 100$ | 2.1 |
| Cumulative percentage | $\text{cumulative percentage} = \dfrac{\text{cumulative frequency}}{\text{sample size}} \times 100$ | 2.2 |
| Sample mean | $\overline{X} = \dfrac{\sum X}{N}$ | 3.1 |
| Range | $\text{Range} = X_{highest} - X_{lowest}$ | 4.1 |
| Interquartile range | $IQR = X_{75\%} - X_{25\%}$ | 4.2 |
| Mean deviation | $MD = \dfrac{\sum|X - \overline{X}|}{N}$ | 4.3 |
| Deviation score from the mean | $\text{Deviation score from the mean} = X - \overline{X}$ | 4.4 |
| Standard deviation | $s = \sqrt{\dfrac{\sum(X - \overline{X})^2}{N - 1}}$ | 4.5 |
| Variance | $s^2 = \dfrac{\sum(X - \overline{X})^2}{N - 1}$ | 4.6 |
| $z$ score (standard score) | $z = \dfrac{X - \overline{X}}{s}$ | 5.1 |
| Difference in percentages | $D\% = \%_1 - \%_2$ | 6.1 |
| Risk ratio | $RR = \dfrac{\%_1}{\%_2}$ | 6.2 |
| Risk ratio | $RR = \dfrac{p_1}{p_2}$ | 6.3 |
| Odds | $\text{odds} = \dfrac{\text{number that experience event}}{\text{number that does not experience event}} = \dfrac{n_e}{n_{ne}}$ | 7.1 |
| Odds | $\text{odds} = \dfrac{\text{percentage that experience event}}{\text{percentage that does not experience event}} = \dfrac{\%_e}{\%_{ne}}$ | 7.2 |
| Odds | $\text{odds} = \dfrac{\text{proportion that experience event}}{\text{proportion that does not experience event}} = \dfrac{p_e}{p_{ne}}$ | 7.3 |

| | | |
|---|---|---|
| Odds ratio | $OR = \dfrac{\text{odds for Group 1}}{\text{odds for Group 2}} = \dfrac{\text{odds}_1}{\text{odds}_2}$ | 7.4 |
| Pearson's $r$ (correlation coefficient) | $r = \dfrac{\Sigma(z_x \times z_y)}{N-1}$ | 8.1 |
| Standardized regression equation (predicted $z$ score on $Y$) | $\hat{z}_y = r_{xy}\, z_x$ | 8.2 |
| Unstandardized regression equation (predicted raw score on $Y$) | $\hat{Y} = A + BX$ | 8.3 |
| Standardized mean difference | $SMD = \dfrac{\overline{X}_1 - \overline{X}_2}{s_{wg}}$ | 9.1 |
| Effect size for means | $ES_{means} = \dfrac{\overline{X}_E - \overline{X}_C}{s_C}$ | 9.2 |
| $z$ score in a population | $z = \dfrac{\overline{X} - \mu}{\sigma}$ | 12.1 |
| Sampling error | sampling error = sample statistic − population parameter | 12.2 |
| Standard error of the mean | $\sigma_{\overline{X}} = \dfrac{\sigma}{\sqrt{N}}$ | 12.3 |
| Estimate of standard error of the mean | $s_{\overline{X}} = \dfrac{s}{\sqrt{N}}$ | 13.1 |
| 95% confidence interval of the mean | $95\%\ CI\ of\ \mu = \overline{X} \pm 1.96\left(\dfrac{s}{\sqrt{N}}\right)$ | 13.2 |
| 95% confidence interval of the mean | $95\%\ CI\ of\ \mu = \overline{X} \pm 1.96(s_{\overline{X}})$ | 13.3 |
| 99% confidence interval of the mean | $99\%\ CI\ of\ \mu = \overline{X} \pm 2.58\left(\dfrac{s}{\sqrt{N}}\right)$ | 13.4 |
| 99% confidence interval of the mean | $99\%\ CI\ of\ \mu = \overline{X} \pm 2.58(s_{\overline{X}})$ | 13.5 |
| Standard error of the proportion | $\sigma_p = \sqrt{\dfrac{P(1-P)}{N}}$ | 13.6 |
| Estimate of standard error of the proportion | $s_p = \sqrt{\dfrac{p(1-p)}{N}}$ | 13.7 |
| 95% confidence interval of the proportion | $95\%\ CI\ of\ P = p \pm 1.96\sqrt{\dfrac{p(1-p)}{N}}$ | 13.8 |
| 95% confidence interval of the proportion | $95\%\ CI\ of\ P = p \pm 1.96(s_p)$ | 13.9 |
| 99% confidence interval of the proportion | $99\%\ CI\ of\ P = p \pm 2.58\sqrt{\dfrac{p(1-p)}{N}}$ | 13.10 |

| | | |
|---|---|---|
| 99% confidence interval of the proportion | $99\% \ CI \ of \ P = p \pm 2.58(s_p)$ | 13.11 |
| Probability of event with given characteristic | $p = \dfrac{\text{number of events with that characteristic}}{\text{total number of events}}$ | 14.1 |
| Probability of event with given characteristic | $p = \text{proportion of events with that characteristic}$ | 14.2 |
| Large sample test of $\overline{X}$ | $z \approx \dfrac{\overline{X} - \mu}{\left(\dfrac{s}{\sqrt{N}}\right)}$ | 15.1 |
| Large sample test of $\overline{X}$ | $z \approx \dfrac{\overline{X} - \mu}{s_{\overline{X}}}$ | 15.2 |
| Power | $\text{Power} = 1 - \beta$ | 16.1 |
| Confidence interval of the mean | $CI \ of \ \mu = \overline{X} \pm t(s/\sqrt{N}) \quad \text{where } df = N - 1$ | 17.1 |
| Confidence interval of the mean | $CI \ of \ \mu = \overline{X} \pm t(s_{\overline{X}}) \quad \text{where } df = N - 1$ | 17.2 |
| One-sample $t$ test | $t = \dfrac{\overline{X} - \mu}{s/\sqrt{N}} \quad \text{where } df = N - 1$ | 17.3 |
| One-sample $t$ test | $t = \dfrac{\overline{X} - \mu}{s_{\overline{X}}} \quad \text{where } df = N - 1$ | 17.4 |
| General formula for a $t$ test with two samples | $t = \dfrac{\overline{X}_1 - \overline{X}_2}{s_{\overline{X}_1 - \overline{X}_2}} \quad \text{where } df = n_1 + n_2 - 2^a \text{ and } df = N - 1^b$ | 18.1 |
| One-sample test of a proportion | $z = \dfrac{p - P}{\sqrt{\dfrac{P(1 - P)}{N}}}$ | 19.1 |
| One-sample test of a proportion | $z = \dfrac{(p - P)}{\sigma_p}$ | 19.2 |
| Expected frequency for one-variable chi-square test | $f_e = p_e \times N$ | 19.3 |
| One-variable chi-square test and chi-square test of independence | $x^2 = N\left(\sum \dfrac{(p_o - p_e)^2}{p_e}\right) \quad \text{where } df = J - 1 \text{ for the one-variable chi-square test}$ | 19.4 |
| One-variable chi-square test and chi-square test of independence (calculation formula) | $x^2 = \sum \dfrac{(f_o - f_e)^2}{f_e} \quad \text{where } df = J - 1 \text{ for the one-variable chi-square test}$ | 19.5 |
| Degrees of freedom for chi-square test of independence | $df = (R - 1)(C - 1)$ | 20.1 |
| Expected column proportion for chi-square test of independence | $p_e = (\text{row margin total}) / N$ | 20.2 |

[a] *df for independent samples t test (equal variances formula)*
[b] *df for dependent samples t test*

| | | |
|---|---|---|
| Expected frequency for chi-square test of independence | $F_e = \dfrac{\text{(row margin total)} \times \text{(column margin total)}}{N}$ | 20.3 |
| *F* ratio | $F = \dfrac{MS_B}{MS_W}$ | 21.1 |
| Mean square between | $MS_B = \dfrac{SS_B}{df \text{ for } MS_B}$  where $df = J - 1$ | 21.2 |
| Mean square within | $MS_W = \dfrac{SS_W}{df \text{ for } MS_W}$  where $df = N - J$ | 21.3 |
| Unstandardized multiple regression equation | $\hat{Y} = A + B_1 X_1 + B_2 X_2 + \ldots B_K X_K$ | 23.1 |
| Logistic regression equation predicting log of the odds | $\ln\left(\dfrac{p}{1-p}\right) = A + B_1 X_1 + B_2 X_2 + \ldots B_K B_K$ | 23.2 |
| Logistic regression equation predicting odds | $\dfrac{p}{1-p} = e^A \times e^{B_1 X_1} \times e^{B_2 X_2} \times \ldots e^{B_K X_K}$ | 23.3 |

# APPENDIX F

## ANSWERS TO END-OF-CHAPTER PROBLEMS AND QUESTIONS

### CHAPTER 1

1. evidenced-based
2. theory, research
3. data
4. quantitative, qualitative
5. quantitative, qualitative
6. **a.** quantitative **b.** qualitative **c.** quantitative **d.** qualitative **e.** qualitative **f.** quantitative **g.** quantitative
7. **a.** applied **b.** pure **c.** applied
8. case
9. values
10. female, male
11. constants
12. constant
13. quantitative, qualitative (categorical)
14. quantitative
15. qualitative
16. categorical
17. **a.** quantitative **b.** qualitative **c.** quantitative **d.** qualitative **e.** qualitative
18. dichotomous, binary
19. random, probability samples
20. study sample
21. **a.** random **b.** nonrandom **c.** nonrandom **d.** random **e.** nonrandom
22. numerical summary
23. **a.** inferential **b.** descriptive **c.** descriptive **d.** inferential
24. **a.** incorrect **b.** incorrect **c.** correct **d.** incorrect **e.** correct
25. Note: independent listed first, dependent second:
    **a.** therapy, assertiveness
    **b.** exercise, blood pressure
    **c.** hours studied, grade
    **d.** cannot be classified as independent and dependent (in author's opinion)
    **e.** token economy, disruptive classroom behavior
26. **a.** bivariate **b.** univariate **c.** bivariate **d.** multivariate **e.** multivariate **f.** univariate
27. **a.** False **b.** True

**28.** statistical significance tests

**29.** confounding

**30.** **a.** perhaps volunteers had lower blood pressure to begin with or perhaps the volunteers simply got more exercise in general (not necessarily through the fitness program)

   **b.** perhaps volunteers were happier to begin with or perhaps they are more involved in many activities and these activities, not those of the student project led to greater happiness

   **c.** perhaps children with fewer behavior problems were more likely to be adopted by their foster parents whereas those with more problems were more likely to be adopted by "new parents"

**31.** assignment

**32.** random assignment (randomization), groups

**33.** **a.** no **b.** no **c.** no **d.** yes **e.** yes

**34.** **a.** False **b.** True **c.** True

**35.** classify, order, differences, ratio

**36.** ordinal

**37.** true, absence

**38.** The zero point is arbitrary; it does not indicate the absence of temperature. Thus, ratios do not make sense.

**39.** **a.** ordinal **b.** ordinal **c.** ratio **d.** nominal **e.** ordinal **f.** nominal

**40.** codes

**41.** highest

**42.** **a.** True **b.** False **c.** False **d.** False **e.** True **f.** True

## CHAPTER 2

**1.** $N$

**2.** frequency

**3.** $f$

**4.** $n$

**5.** **a.** 20 **b.** 10 **c.** 8 **d.** 40 **e.** 25 **f.** 80 **g.** 20

**6.** grouped frequency

**7.** **a.** 30

   **b.** 14

   **c.** because variable is at nominal-level, cumulative frequency cannot be calculated (because no values are higher or lower than other values, cumulative frequency does not "make sense")

**8.** distribution

**9.** tables, figures

**10.** **a.** nominal

   **b.** bar chart

   **c.** no; values are separated and distinct and there is no ordering to the values

**11.** about 350

**12.** arbitrary, because the level of measurement is nominal

**13.** **a.** True **b.** True

**14.** Histogram is preferred when the number of different values is reasonably small (say about 20 values or less) and frequency polygons are preferred when the number of values is reasonably high (say 20 or more).

**15.** 83 or 83rd percentile

16. **a.** 25th   **b.** 75th   **c.** 50th   **d.** whiskers   **e.** fences
17. **a.** 28%   **b.** 28%
18. **a.** about 15%   **b.** about 15%

## CHAPTER 3

1. central tendency, variability, shape
2. cluster, dispersed (spread out), shape of distribution
3. mode, median, mean
4. frequency, greater than, less than, middle, sum, number, sample size
5. **a.** 2   **b.** 4   **c.** 7
6. **a.** 3   **b.** 3   **c.** 4
7. all levels; nominal, ordinal, and interval/ratio
8. ordinal
9. There is no median because data are only at the nominal level.
10. **a.** 4, 6, 7, 8, 9   **b.** 7   **c.** 7
11. **a.** 13, 18, 29, 41, 62   **b.** 29   **c.** 29
12. 4
13. **a.** 8, 9, 12, 14, 15, 16   **b.** 12, 14   **c.** 13   **d.** 13
14. 6
15. **a.** short = 25%, medium = 40%, tall = 35%
    **b.** short = 25%, medium = 65%, tall = 100%
    **c.** 65%
    **d.** medium (or medium height)
    **e.** medium
    **f.** medium
    **g.** There is no mean because measurement is at ordinal level.
16. **a.** poor = 10%, fair = 20%, good = 30%, excellent = 40%
    **b.** poor = 10%, fair = 30%, good = 60%, excellent = 100%
    **c.** 60%
    **d.** good
    **e.** good
    **f.** excellent
    **g.** There is no mean because measurement is at the ordinal level.
17. 32 years
18. mean, $X$, $\overline{X}$, $M$
19. False
20. interval/ratio
21. **a.** False   **b.** False
22. 21.4
23. **a.** outlier (or extreme value)
    **b.** median
    **c.** 11.5
    **d.** positive (upward)
    **e.** 23 does not do a good job of conveying the common, typical value
24. **a.** False   **b.** False   **c.** True   **d.** True   **e.** True
25. upward, downward
26. **a.** 8   **b.** 3   **c.** median

**27.** **a.** 4
   **b.** 3
   **c.** Mean, because there is no longer an outlier (although the 9 has some effect on the mean and, in this sense, is "almost" an outlier; as such, the median would also be an acceptable measure).
   **d.** False
   **e.** True
**28.** 5%, 5%

# CHAPTER 4

**1.** dispersed (spread out), <u>central</u> <u>tendency</u>
**2.** b
**3.** a
**4.** have same variability
**5.** have same variability
**6.** **a.** True   **b.** True
**7.** c (same variability)
**8.** a (A has more variability)
**9.** **a.** high  **b.** low  **c.** high  **d.** low  **e.** high  **f.** low  **g.** constant (no variability)
   **h.** high  **i.** low  **j.** low
**10.** highest value minus the lowest value
**11.** True
**12.** **a.** 7  **b.** 33  **c.** 885  **d.** 10
**13.** **a.** 5  **b.** $7 - 5 = 2$   $4 - 5 = -1$   $6 - 5 = 1$   $3 - 5 = -2$
**14.** **a.** 3  **b.** $2 - 3 = -1$   $6 - 3 = 3$   $2 - 3 = -1$   $1 - 3 = -2$   $4 - 3 = 1$
**15.** **a.** True  **b.** True  **c.** True  **d.** False
**16.** **a.** 2  **b.** 2  **c.** 2.8  **d.** 1.43  **e.** 0
**17.** **a.** 2.58  **b.** 2.58  **c.** 3.94  **d.** 2.08  **e.** 0
**18.** for a through d, the best answer is "a little bit larger"; for e, "same size"
**19.** 1.58
**20.** 1.58
**21.** **a.** True  **b.** False  **c.** True  **d.** True  **e.** False  **f.** True
**22.** **a.** False  **b.** True  **c.** True  **d.** True
**23.** **a.** 9  **b.** 100  **c.** 36  **d.** 25  **e.** 4
**24.** **a.** 6  **b.** 11  **c.** 7  **d.** 10  **e.** 3
**25.** $s$, $s^2$, $SD$

# CHAPTER 5

**1.** shape, pattern, normal, bell
**2.** **a.** True  **b.** False  **c.** True  **d.** False
**3.** 50%, 50%
**4.** mean, median, mode, sixty-eight, standard deviation, symmetric, mirror
**5.** 95%, three
**6.** 95%

7. tails, negative (lower), positive (upper)
8. symmetry
9. **b.** upper (positive)
10. positive, negative
11. **a.** positive   **b.** negative   **c.** negative
12. outlier, positively
13. negative (downwards)
14. False
15. mean
16. median
17. False
18. peakedness
19. **a.** False   **b.** False   **c.** True   **d.** True   **e.** False
20. uniform (flat, rectangular), bimodal
21. **a.** close to normal
    **b.** bimodal
    **c.** close to uniform
    **d.** positively skewed (as a few persons can probably name many players)
    **e.** close to normal
    **f.** positively skewed (as the positive tail is probably extended more than the negative)
    **g.** positively skewed (a few families likely have many children)
    **h.** positively skewed
22. **a.** 50   **b.** 50   **c.** 34.13   **d.** 34.13   **e.** 47.72   **f.** 47.72   **g.** 49.87   **h.** 15.87
    **i.** 15.87   **j.** 2.28   **k.** 2.28   **l.** 0.13   **m.** 31.74   **n.** 4.56   **o.** 0.26
23. None of these questions can be answered as the distribution is not normally distributed.
24. about 47.72%
25. Cannot be determined because distribution does not have normal shape.
26. above, below, standard
27. 2.18
28. 0.38
29. 1.47 standard deviations below
30. 0.74 standard deviations above
31. b
32. 0.37 standard deviations below
33. insufficient information
34. 1.30
35. −0.60
36. **a.** 1.00   **b.** −0.50   **c.** 0.00   **d.** 0.75   **e.** −2.00   **f.** 1.50
37. **a.** 1.00   **b.** −0.50   **c.** 0.00   **d.** 0.75   **e.** −2.00   **f.** 1.50
38. **a.** 0.00   **b.** 1.00   **c.** −0.50   **d.** 1.00
39. **a.** 0.00   **b.** 1.00   **c.** mean = 0.00, standard deviation = 1.00
40. 0.00, 1.00, True
41. False
42. b
43. raw
44. **a.** 2.00   **b.** 0.33   **c.** a better high jumper
45. **a.** −0.50   **b.** 0.20   **c.** Test 2
46. **a.** 2.00   **b.** 0.00   **c.** 0.33   **d.** −0.75
47. **a.** 28.2   **b.** 28.2   **c.** 28.2   **d.** 28.2   **e.** 56.4   **f.** 56.4
48. **a.** 21.8   **b.** 21.8   **c.** 21.8   **d.** 21.8   **e.** 43.6   **f.** 43.6

**49. a.** 44.1　**b.** 44.1　**c.** 44.1　**d.** 44.1　**e.** 88.2　**f.** 88.2
**50. a.** 5.9　**b.** 5.9　**c.** 5.9　**d.** 5.9　**e.** 11.8　**f.** 11.8
**51. a.** 9.5　**b.** 9.5　**c.** 9.5　**d.** 9.5　**e.** 19.0　**f.** 19.0
**52. a.** 40.5　**b.** 40.5　**c.** 40.5　**d.** 40.5　**e.** 81.0　**f.** 81.0
**53. a.** 45.7　**b.** 50.0　**c.** 95.7　**d.** 45.7　**e.** 50.0　**f.** 95.7
**54. a.** 95.7　**b.** 4.3　**c.** 50
**55. a.** 23.9　**b.** 50.0　**c.** 73.9　**d.** 23.9　**e.** 50.0　**f.** 73.9
**56. a.** 73.9　**b.** 26.1
**57. a.** 50, 50　**b.** 2.7, 2.7　**c.** 97.3, 97.3　**d.** 81.1, 81.1　**e.** 18.9, 18.9
**58. a.** False　**b.** True　**c.** True　**d.** True　**e.** True　**f.** True　**g.** False
**59.** True
**60.** True

# CHAPTER 6

**1.** related (associated), values
**2. a.** R　**b.** R　**c.** R　**d.** U　**e.** R　**f.** I　**g.** I　**h.** R　**i.** U　**j.** R
**3. a.** False　**b.** False　**c.** False　**d.** False　**e.** True　**f.** True
**4. a.** contingency　**b.** type of mental health program　**c.** readmission to hospital (yes or no)
　　**d.** type of mental health program　**e.** readmission (yes or no)　**f.** True
　　**g.** Program 1, Program 2　**h.** yes, no　**i.** 2, 2, 2, 2　**j.** 160　**k.** margins　**l.** cells
　　**m.** 60　**n.** 60　**o.** 37.5　**p.** 60　**q.** 60　**r.** 40　**s.** 40　**t.** 20　**u.** 20　**v.** True
　　**w.** True　**x.** 40%　**y.** 40%　**z.** (40 / 100)100 = 40%.　**aa.** 33%　**bb.** 33%
　　**cc.** (20 / 60) × 100 = 33%　**dd.** False　**ee.** False　**ff.** True　**gg.** True　**hh.** No
**5. a.** True　**b.** True　**c.** True　**d.** True　**e.** True　**f.** False　**g.** True
**6.** True
**7.** effect size
**8.** The degree to which the values of one variable vary, differ, or change according to those of
　　the other.
**9. a.** 7%　**b.** −7%　**c.** −7%　**d.** 7%
**10.** 25%
**11.** 9%
**12.** Because only one variable is involved, there is no relationship and thus $D\%$ cannot be
　　calculated.
**13. a.** True　**b.** False
**14. a.** False　**b.** True　**c.** False　**d.** False　**e.** False　**f.** True
**15.** 10%, 90%
**16. a.** large　**b.** medium　**c.** small　**d.** very large　**e.** no association at all　**f.** small
　　**g.** very large
**17.** risk ratio, relative risk
**18. a.** 4　**b.** 2　**c.** 4　**d.** 0.25　**e.** 0.10　**f.** 10.0
**19. a.** Those in Program A are four times as likely as those in Program B to experience unsuc-
　　cessful treatment outcome. (Or: Risk of unsuccessful outcome in Program A is four times
　　that in Program B.)
　　**b.** Boys are twice as likely as girls to engage in aggressive playground behavior.
　　**c.** Men are four times as likely as women to pass the firefighters' physical exam.
**20. a.** large　**b.** between small and medium　**c.** large　**d.** large　**e.** very large
　　**f.** very large

**21.** False (no such thing as a negative risk ratio)
**22.** 0.25
**23.** Because they are reciprocals, they convey the same size of association.
**24.** **a.** 4.0   **b.** 0.20   **c.** 10.0   **d.** same size   **e.** 0.8
**25.** **a.** yes   **b.** no   **c.** no   **d.** no   **e.** 10%, 20%   **f.** 0.50   **g.** 2.0   **h.** same size
    **i.** small to medium
**26.** 30%
**27.** **a.** yes   **b.** no   **c.** no
**28.** $RR = 1.21$, may not be applied
**29.** False
**30.** **a.** *D%*   **b.** *RR*   **c.** *RR*   **d.** *D%*   **e.** both   **f.** neither

# CHAPTER 7

**1.** 0.00, infinity, 1.00
**2.** **a.** 3.0   **b.** 3.0   **c.** Only one variable cannot compute an odds ratio.
**3.** 1.00
**4.** **a.** 60, 25%   **b.** 30, 37.5%   **c.** 0.33   **d.** 0.33   **e.** 1.67   **f.** 1.67   **g.** 5.0   **h.** 5.0
    **i.** 0.20   **j.** 1.00, reciprocals
**5.** **a.** 1.50   **b.** 0.50   **c.** 3.00   **d.** 3.0   **e.** 0.33   **f.** 0.33   **g.** 0.33
**6.** 6.00. The odds of earning an A for students who study 20-plus hours are six times those of
    students who study less than this.
**7.** 2.25. The odds of not achieving for Intervention B are 2.25 those for Intervention A.
**8.** False
**9.** 0.00, positive infinity, 1.00, greater
**10.** reciprocals
**11.** **a.** 0.25   **b.** 0.125   **c.** 0.50   **d.** 0.167   **e.** 0.67
**12.** **a.** 4.00   **b.** 10.0   **c.** 3.00   **d.** 1.25   **e.** 1.50
**13.** **a.** 0.125   **b.** 8.00   **c.** 0.05   **d.** 2.50
**14.** **a.** 0.20   **b.** 0.80   **c.** 5.0   **d.** same size
**15.** **a.** very large   **b.** very large   **c.** very large   **d.** medium   **e.** small
**16.** Such an odds ratio is impossible; perhaps there was a typo.
**17.** **a.** *OR, D%*   **b.** *OR, RR%*   **c.** *OR*   **d.** *OR, D%, RR*   **e.** *OR, RR*   **f.** *OR, D%*
**18.** **a.** 0.50   **b.** 2.00   **c.** 2.00
**19.** **a.** False   **b.** False   **c.** True   **d.** False
**20.** **a.** 4%
    **b.** 11%
    **c.** 7%
    **d.** for a, very weak; for b, weak; for c, weak
    **e.** Because each of the three *D%*s conveys a weak or very weak association, the overall
       size of association is weak.
    **f.** True
**21.** Cramer's *V*
**22.** 0.00, 1.00
**23.** **a.** very large   **b.** medium   **c.** large   **d.** bogus, may not have value less than 0.00
    **e.** small   **f.** medium
**24.** **a.** positive   **b.** positive   **c.** negative   **d.** negative   **e.** nondirectional   **f.** no relationship
    **g.** nondirectional   **h.** negative   **i.** nondirectional   **j.** negative   **k.** nondirectional

**25. a.** True   **b.** True   **c.** False   **d.** True   **e.** False   **f.** False
**26. a.** Somers' $D$   **b.** tau-$b$   **c.** tau-$c$   **d.** gamma
**27. a.** strong positive   **b.** strong negative   **c.** weak negative   **d.** moderate positive
    **e.** no directional relationship at all; neither positive nor negative   **f.** strong negative
    **g.** medium negative   **h.** weak positive

## CHAPTER 8

**1.** Pearson's, linear, positive, negative, opposite, numeric, interval/ratio
**2.** similar, highs, lows, dissimilar, lows, highs
**3. a.** negative   **b.** positive   **c.** positive   **d.** positive   **e.** positive   **f.** negative
**4.** lower, upper, upper, lower
**5.** X (vertical) Y (horizontal)
**6.** Multiply each cases $z$ scores. Sum these products. Divide by $(N - 1)$
**7. a.** $-0.112$ on Test 1, $-0.614$ on Test 2
    **b.** Listed in the same order as in the text 0.07, 0.15, $-0.62$, 0.93, 1.70
    **c.** 2.23
    **d.** $r = .56$
**8. a.** True   **b.** True   **c.** False   **d.** False   **e.** False   **f.** False   **g.** True
**9.** $-.30$
**10.** $-.30$
**11. a.** negative, medium (moderate)   **b.** positive, medium (moderate)
    **c.** negative, very large (very strong)   **d.** positive, small (weak)
    **e.** negative, large (strong)   **f.** positive, very large (very strong)
    **g.** positive, large (strong)
**12.** There is such thing a correlation of 1.67 as this is outside of the range of possible values of $r$. So, it must be a typo or mistake in calculations.
**13. a.** .66   **b.** $-.66$   **c.** $-.66$   **d.** $-.92$   **e.** .8
**14.** narrower, straight line
**15.** determination, variance, shared
**16. a.** .16   **b.** .16   **c.** .81   **d.** .36   **e.** .36
**17. a.** .32   **b.** .27   **c.** .16
**18.** standardized
**19. a.** 0.12   **b.** $-0.12$   **c.** 2.00   **d.** $-2.00$   **e.** 0.60   **f.** 0.00
**20.** decrease by 0.70
**21. a.** increase by .22   **b.** decrease by .22   **c.** increase by .75   **d.** decrease by .38
    **e.** increase by 1.00
**22.** curvilinear
**23. a.** True   **b.** False   **c.** True   **d.** False
**24.** Pressure by a Little League coach and number of games won. If no pressure at all, kids may not be motivated. If extremely high pressure, kids will become anxious and not perform well. Medium pressure may produce the most wins.
**25.** lowers
**26. b.** $r > .20$
**27.** constant, 0.00, regression coefficient, 1.00
**28.** unstandardized, standardized
**29. a.** True   **b.** True   **c.** True   **d.** False
**30. a.** 3   **b.** 3   **c.** 2.5   **d.** 2.5   **e.** 2.5   **f.** 13   **g.** 3   **h.** $-7$   **i.** $-7$   **j.** 18
**31. a.** 6   **b.** 6   **c.** $-3$   **d.** $-3$   **e.** $-3$   **f.** $-6$   **g.** 6   **h.** 18   **i.** 18   **j.** $-12$

**32.** Cannot assess strength of association because regression equation is an unstandardized equation.

**33. a.** False   **b.** False   **c.** True   **d.** True   **e.** False   **f.** True   **g.** False

**34.** *phi*

**35.** Spearman's

## CHAPTER 9

**1.** Subtract mean of one group from the other and then divide by the standard deviation (which, in this text, is assumed to be equal in the two groups).

**2.** Cannot assess size of association because standard deviation information is not provided.

**3.** *SMD* $= -2.00$; size of association is very large

**4.** *SMD* $= 0.17$; size of association is small/weak

**5. a.** $-2.00$   **b.** 2.00   **c.** $-1.00$   **d.** $-3.00$   **e.** 0.00   **f.** 1.00   **g.** 0.50

**6. a.** large   **b.** large   **c.** very large   **d.** small/medium   **e.** medium   **f.** very large
   **g.** small

**7. a.** True
   **b.** False
   **c.** True
   **d.** True
   **e.** False
   **f.** False (Comment: For all of the measures, the qualitative descriptors convey size of association in the context of social science; relationships that are large or very large in this context are [almost always] not compelling strong in a strict mathematical sense.)

**8.** False

**9.** one third

**10. a.** no   **b.** yes   **c.** no

**11.** *ES* $= -0.40$, size of association is small to medium

**12. a.** *ES* $= -2.00$, very large   **b.** *ES* $= -2.00$, very large   **c.** *ES* $= 0.75$, large

**13.** $\eta^2$ (eta squared), variance

**14.** 0.17

**15. a.** medium   **b.** large   **c.** small   **d.** small to medium   **e.** large (or even larger)

## CHAPTER 10

**1.** causal

**2.** affect, influence, lead to, explain, and so forth

**3. a.** False   **b.** False

**4. a.** True   **b.** True   **c.** True

**5.** lurking variable, extraneous variable, control variable, nuisance variable, third variable

**6.** manipulates, measurements

**7. a.** True   **b.** False

**8.** true experiments, random assignment

**9. a.** no   **b.** yes   **c.** no   **d.** yes   **e.** no   **f.** no   **g.** yes   **h.** no

**10. a.** no   **b.** yes   **c.** no   **d.** yes   **e.** no   **f.** no   **g.** yes   **h.** no

**11. a.** low   **b.** high   **c.** low   **d.** high   **e.** low   **f.** low   **g.** high   **h.** low

**12. a.** False   **b.** True   **c.** True   **d.** False   **e.** True   **f.** True

**13.** Not willing to presume relationship is causal. Even though relationship between type of placement (foster vs. group) and behavior is still observed when age group is controlled for, this relationship may be caused by another confounding variable, which is not controlled for. Possible confounding variables include the level of behavior problems when placement has begun and the severity of maltreatment experienced.

## CHAPTER 11

**1.** constant
**2.** False
**3.** eliminated
**4.** constant
**5.** True
**6.** d
**7.** disappeared
**8.** **c.** disappears
**9.** **a.** True  **b.** False  **c.** True  **d.** False  **e.** True
**10.** **a.** yes
  **b.** $D\% = 26\%$
  **c.** medium to large
  **d.** Perhaps maltreatment of minority children is more often caused by neglect than abuse, and this leads to greater usage of kinship care. Perhaps minority children more often live in city environments, and this is conducive to kinship care.
**11.** **a.** 70%, 38%
  **b.** $D\% = 32\%$, yes
  **c.** 67%, 25%
  **d.** $D\% = 42\%$, yes
  **e.** yes
  **f.** yes
  **g.** city: $D\% = 15\%$; other than city: $D\% = 17\%$
  **h.** $D\%$ is smaller in the subgroups than was the case prior to control
  **i.** association weakens
  **j.** **b.** partially due to environment
  **k.** type of child maltreatment
  **l.** survey design
  **m.** no, may be due to an uncontrolled for confounding variable
**12.** causal model
**13.** that one variable directly affects/causes another
**14.** antecedent, antecedent
**15.** **a.** True  **b.** False  **c.** True  **d.** True  **e.** True  **f.** True  **g.** False  **h.** True
**16.** intervening, intervening
**17.** **a.** True  **b.** False  **c.** True  **d.** False  **e.** False  **f.** True  **g.** True  **h.** True  **i.** True
**18.** One way to draw this model would be as follows:

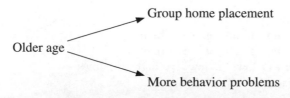

**19.** False

**20. a.** Perhaps youth at risk for not graduating were more likely to be assigned to mentors *and* were more likely not to graduate.

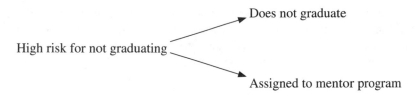

    Does not graduate

High risk for not graduating

    Assigned to mentor program

**b.** Perhaps being "smart" leads to playing chess *and* to doing better on achievement tests.

    Playing chess

Being smart

    Good achievement test scores

**c.** It may be that those served in the community support program had, on average, less serious mental health problems than those served in the transition program; less serious problems would lead to less recidivism.

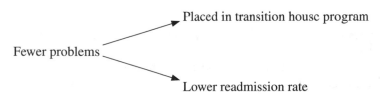

    Placed in transition house program

Fewer problems

    Lower readmission rate

**d.** Perhaps those served by A tended to have less serious behavioral problems than those served by B. Presuming that behavior problems lead to disruption, this would generate the observed results.

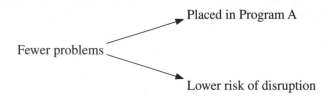

    Placed in Program A

Fewer problems

    Lower risk of disruption

**e.** Having low self-esteem leads persons into psychotherapy, so it is not suprising that those who are involved in psychotherapy tend to have lower self-esteem than those who are not.

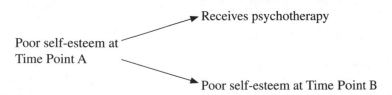

    Receives psychotherapy

Poor self-esteem at
Time Point A

    Poor self-esteem at Time Point B

**21. a.** False   **b.** True
**22. a.** True   **b.** False   **c.** False   **d.** True

**23. 1.** No

**2.** Yes. Men readmitted more often with traditional treatment; women readmitted more often with community treatment.

**3.** No

**4.** Yes. For men, community and traditional treatment have equal readmission rates; for women, traditional treatment has a much higher rate than does community treatment.

**5.** Yes. For men, readmission rate is *much* higher for traditional than for community treatment; for women, rates for these two approaches are very nearly equal.

## CHAPTER 12

**1.** populations, samples, randomly, populations
**2. a.** descriptive  **b.** inferential  **c.** descriptive
**3.** chance
**4. a.** no  **b.** no  **c.** yes  **d.** yes  **e.** no  **f.** no  **g.** yes
**5.** probability, nonprobability
**6.** equal
**7.** False
**8.** Say, when one child in a family is selected, his brothers and sisters are also selected.
**9. a.** no or not sure

**b.** yes

**c.** no

**d.** yes (All of these responses reflect my best judgment; often, this question cannot be answered definitively.)
**10.** Assume that it is met unless there is convincing evidence to the contrary.
**11.** assignment, sampling, assignment, sampling
**12. a.** False  **b.** True  **c.** True  **d.** False  **e.** False
**13. a.** True  **b.** False  **c.** False  **d.** True  **e.** True
**14. a.** False  **b.** True  **c.** False  **d.** False  **e.** True  **f.** True  **g.** False
**15. a.** correct  **b.** incorrect  **c.** incorrect  **d.** correct
**16.** Almost assuredly, the Young Republicans respondents will be less supportive of public welfare programs than the university population as a whole.
**17.** statistics, parameters
**18.** estimator, inferential statistic
**19.** Roman (English), Greek
**20. a.** $\bar{X}, \mu$  **b.** $s, \sigma$  **c.** $s^2, \sigma^2$  **d.** $p, P$
**21.** efficient, unbiased
**22.** minimum
**23.** underestimate, overestimate
**24. a.** unbiased  **b.** biased (by extremely small amount)  **c.** unbiased  **d.** unbiased
**25.** population mean = 10, population standard deviation = 6
**26.** $\mu = 10, \sigma = 6$
**27.** 28%
**28.** $P = .25$
**29.** point estimate, interval estimate
**30.** sampling error
**31. a.** $-2$  **b.** 2  **c.** .09  **d.** $-.09$
**32.** the distribution of a sample statistic that results from drawing an infinite number of random samples of a given size from the same population

33. statistics
34. flip a coin five times; count the number of heads; record this number; repeat the prior steps infinitely
35. select a random sample of given size; calculate the mean for that sample; record/plot that mean; repeat the prior process infinitely
36. central limit
37. mean is the population mean; standard deviation equals population standard deviation divided by size of random samples used to build distribution; shape approaches that of normal distribution as sample size increases
38. standard error of the mean, $\sigma_{\bar{x}}$
39. normal
40. False
41. **1.** 25, 1, close to normal
    **2.** 25, .5, close to normal
    **3.** 25, 2.5, unknown because $N < 100$ (In actuality, the shape would be a negative skew that was less pronounced than that in the population, but you are not responsible for this information.)
    **4.** 25, 2.5, close to normal
    **5.** 40, 1, close to normal
42. **a.** about 68%   **b.** about 95%   **c.** about 99.7%
43. 68% for Example 1, 95% for Example 2
44. 4, 2, 1, 0.5
45. decreases, decreases

# CHAPTER 13

1. confidence interval
2. the likely range within which the population parameter is located
3. 95% confidence interval, confident
4. 99% confidence interval, confident
5. error, standard deviation, square root, size
6. standard deviation, square root
7. $s_{\bar{x}} = \dfrac{s}{\sqrt{N}}$
8. **a.** False   **b.** True   **c.** False   **d.** True   **e.** False   **f.** True
9. 95% confidence interval of the mean
10. Select a random sample of given size; calculate its mean and its standard deviation. Divide standard deviation by square root of sample size to determine standard error (standard deviation of sampling distribution). Multiply the standard error by 2 and add and subtract from the sample mean.
11. 95%, 5%
12. False
13. 21.06 to 26.94
14. **#1.** 48.04 to 51.96   **#2.** 46.08 to 53.92   **#3.** 48.04 to 51.96   **#4.** 49.02 to 50.98   **#5.** 99.02 to 100.98   **#6.** 99.02 to 100.98   **#7.** sample size too small to compute
15. decreases
16. 95%
17. 99%
18. 95%, 99%, confidence level

**19.** **#2.** 44.84–55.16 **#3.** 47.42–52.58 **#4.** 48.71–51.29
**20.** narrower
**21.** wider
**22.** $p$, $P$
**23.** select a random sample of given size; find the proportion of cases with some given characteristic; record/plot this proportion; repeat the prior steps an infinite number of times
**24.** proportion, deviation, $\sigma_p$, standard error of the proportion, normal
**25.** **a.** .042 **b.** .042 **c.** .030 **d.** .040 **e.** .046 **f.** .050
**26.** $s_p$, $s_p = \sqrt{\dfrac{p(1-p)}{N}}$, 10
**27.** **a.** 40, 160, yes **b.** 20, 80, yes **c.** 80, 20, yes **d.** 40, 10, yes **e.** 5, 45, no
    **f.** 10, 90, yes **g.** 8, 792, no
**28.** **a.** .028 **b.** .040 **c.** .040 **d.** .057
**29.** **a.** .145 to .255 **b.** .122 to .278 **c.** .722 to .878 **d.** .688 to .912
**30.** **a.** 14.5% to 25.5% **b.** 12.2% to 27.8% **c.** 72.2% to 87.8% **d.** 68.8% to 91.2%
**31.** **a.** .128 to .272 **b.** .097 to .303 **c.** .697 to .903 **d.** .653 to .947
**32.** **a.** .011
    **b.** .058 to .102
    **c.** 95% confident
    **d.** .052 to .108
    **e.** 99% confident
    **f.** 95% *CI*
    **g.** 99% *CI*
    **h.** Neither is "better"; the 95% interval is more precise but we have greater confidence that the 99% interval includes the population mean.
**33.** 8% plus or minus 2.2% with 95% confidence
**34.** 58% to 70%
**35.** **a.** False **b.** True **c.** False **d.** True
**36.** nonresponse

# CHAPTER 14

**1.** hypothesis test
**2.** significance, inferential, chance
**3.** number of events with characteristic divided by total number of events
**4.** 0.00, 1.00
**5.** .40
**6.** $p$, $p$
**7.** **a.** 34% **b.** .34 **c.** .34 **d.** 47.7% **e.** .477 **f.** .477
**8.** **a.** .50 **b.** .68 **c.** .16 **d.** .16 **e.** .023 **f.** .023 **g.** .046 **h.** .046
**9.** Trick question: We have insufficient information to answer such questions for a positively skewed distribution.
**10.** null, alternative, research, opposite, hypothesis pair
**11.** False
**12.** False
**13.** percentages
**14.** means
**15.** correlation (Pearson's *r*), 0.00

**16.** False

**17.** False

**18.** equal, not equal

**19.** directional, greater than, less than

**20.** **a.** directional    **b.** nondirectional    **c.** nondirectional    **d.** directional

**21.** Null:          Women and men are equally likely to state that they like statistics.
Alternative:  Women and men are not equally likely to state that they like statistics.

**22.** Null:          Mean behavior problem scores of boys and girls are equal.
Alternative:  Mean behavior problem scores of boys and girls are not equal.

**23.** Null:          The correlation of enjoyment of brussels sprout and enjoyment of stats equals 0.00.
Alternative:  The correlation of enjoyment of brussels sprout and enjoyment of stats does not equal 0.00.

**24.** Null:          The percentage of women who choose salads over burgers is less than or equal to the percentage of men who do so.
Alternative:  The percentage of women who choose salads over burgers is greater than the percentage of men who do so.

**25.** Null:          The percentage of women who choose salads over burgers is greater than or equal to the percentage of men who do so.
Alternative:  The percentage of women who choose salads over burgers is less than the percentage of men who do so.

**26.** alternative, null

**27.** **a.** Truc    **b.** True    **c.** False

**28.** chance, sampling error, association

**29.** False

**30.** probability, extreme, true, population, randomly, *p*

**31.** null

**32.** rejects, accepts, fails to reject, unlikely

**33.** accepts, fails to reject, rejects

**34.** statistical significance level

**35.** statistical significance, *p*, greater than, rejects, accepts, less than

**36.** greater than .01, less than or equal to .01

**37.** alpha, α

**38.** .05, .01

**39.** False

**40.** **a.** fail to reject    **b.** reject    **c.** reject    **d.** fail to reject    **e.** fail to reject
**f.** fail to reject    **g.** reject    **h.** reject    **i.** fail to reject    **j.** fail to reject

**41.** greater than, rejects, less than or equal to

**42.** **a.** .0439    **b.** .0547    **c.** .0547    **d.** .1094    **e.** .1094

**43.** due to chance, sampling error, the luck of the draw—all of which are, in essence, the same thing

**44.** result, extreme, chance, sampling error, chance alone

**45.** difference, null, chance alone

**46.** **a.** True    **b.** True    **c.** True    **d.** False    **e.** False    **f.** False    **g.** True    **h.** True
**i.** False    **j.** True    **k.** False

**47.** **a.** True    **b.** False    **c.** False    **d.** False    **e.** False    **f.** False    **g.** False    **h.** False
**i.** False    **j.** True    **k.** False    **l.** True

**48.** **a.** False    **b.** True    **c.** True    **d.** False    **e.** True    **f.** True    **g.** False    **h.** False
**i.** False    **j.** False    **k.** False

**49.** **a.** Frue    **b.** False    **c.** False    **d.** True    **e.** False    **f.** True    **g.** True    **h.** False
**i.** False    **j.** True    **k.** True

**50. a.** 92%   **b.** 98%   **c.** 87%   **d.** 99.5%
**51.** e
**52.** 95%, 99%
**53.** null, unassociated, chance, sampling error
**54. a.** True   **b.** False   **c.** False
**55.** chance
**56.** statistically significant
**57.** rejecting, fails to reject
**58. a.** True   **b.** True   **c.** True   **d.** True   **e.** False   **f.** True   **g.** True   **h.** True
**59. a.** True   **b.** False   **c.** True   **d.** True   **e.** True   **f.** True   **g.** True   **h.** False

# CHAPTER 15

**1.** State hypothesis pair. Choose significance level. Carry out test. Make decision.
**2.** A condition that must be met for the test to yield an accurate probability (an accurate $p$).
**3.** normality, normally
**4.** robust
**5.** robust
**6.** False
**7.** random, independence
**8.** $H_0$, $H_1$
**9.** $\mu = 10$, $s_{\bar{x}} = .5$, shape is close to normal
**10. a.** .50   **b.** .16   **c.** .16   **d.** .32
**11.** two, rejection, both
**12** .05, 2.5%, 2.5%
**13.** .01, .5%, .5%
**14.** one, one, alternative
**15. a.** upper 5% tail   **b.** upper 1% tail   **c.** lower 5% tail   **d.** lower 1% tail
**16.** Again, my guidelines are arbitrary: The basic idea is that the lower the value of $p$, the less consistent the result is with the null.
   **a.** consistent, accept
   **b.** neither consistent nor inconsistent, fail to reject (accept)
   **c.** inconsistent, reject
   **d.** consistent, fail to reject (accept)
   **e.** neither consistent nor inconsistent, fail to reject (accept)
   **f.** inconsistent, reject
**17.** rejects, accepts, fails to reject, rejects
**18. a.** $z = -1.50$, 13.4%   **b.** $z = 1.50$, 13.4   **c.** $z = 2.00$, 4.6%   **d.** $z = 4.00$, .006%
**19. a.** nondirectional
   **b.** $\mu = 25.00$, $s$ is very close to 1.00, shape is close to normal
   **c.** $z = -1.60$
   **d.** 5.5%
   **e.** two-tailed
   **f.** two, 2.5%, 2.5%
   **g.** no
   **h.** fail to reject, reject
   **i.** $p = .055$
   **j.** $p = .11$

**k.** $p = .11$

**l.** $p = .11$

**m.** greater than

**n.** fail to reject, reject

**o.** fail to reject, absolute value, less than, greater than or equal to 1.96.

**p.** $-1.60, 1.60$

**q.** fail to reject, reject

**r.** no

**s.** $p = .11$

**t.** no

**u.** $p = .11$

**v.** $p = .11$

**w.** no

**x.** Although not consistent with the null, the result is not sufficiently inconsistent for the null to be rejected.

**y.** 89%

**z.** No, not strong enough; the key point is that the evidence that the null is false is not strong enough to justify rejecting the null.

**20. a.** nondirectional **b.** two **c.** 2.20 **d.** $p = .028$ **e.** True **f.** 1.96, reject, accept **g.** 2.58, fail to reject, reject

**21.** difficult, larger

**22.** rejects, true

**23. a.** 50 **b.** 50

**24. a.** 10 **b.** 10

**25.** .01, .05, lower

**26.** reduces (decreases), increases, Type II error, fails to reject, false

**27.** beta, $\beta$

**28. a.** True **b.** True **c.** False

**29.** 95%, 99%

**30.** 5%

**31.** Fail to reject (accept) the null if the obtained $z$ is less than 1.645. Reject the null if the obtained $z$ is 1.645 or greater.

**32. a.** directional **b.** one-tailed **c.** $H_1$ **d.** yes **e.** $z = 1.70$ **f.** .045 **g.** $p = .045$ **h.** $p = .045$ **i.** $p = .045$ **j.** yes it does exceed, reject, accept

**33. a.** True **b.** True **c.** False **d.** False **e.** True **f.** True **g.** True

**34.** one-tailed, increases, easier

**35.** double (two times), one-half

**36. a.** .03 **b.** .11 **c.** .20 **d.** .04

**37. a.** .04 **b.** .08 **c.** .32 **d.** .06

**38. a.** two-tailed **b.** $p = .088$ **c.** True **d.** no **e.** fail to reject, reject **f.** no

**39.** .01

**40.** Fail to reject (accept) the null if the obtained $z$ is less than 2.33. Reject the null if the obtained $z$ is 2.33 or greater.

**41. a.** $z = 1.70$ **b.** 2.33 **c.** fail to reject, reject **d.** no

**42.** True

**43. a.** directional **b.** one-tailed **c.** upper **d.** greater than (positive direction) **e.** less than (more negative) **f.** opposite to expectations **g.** $z = -3.00$ **h.** .13% **i.** greater than or equal to 1.645 **j.** fail to reject, accept **k.** True

**44.** chance alone, unlikely (insufficient), null, real

**45. a.** False **b.** True **c.** True **d.** False

## CHAPTER 16

1. probability, false null, true alternative
2. Type II, reject a false null, 1.00
3. **a.** .60 **b.** .40 **c.** .70 **d.** .90
4. **a.** .15 **b.** .50 **c.** .10 **d.** .60
5. **a.** .20 **b.** .20
6. low, high
7. False
8. False
9. **a.** $s_{\bar{x}} = 4$, about 8 **b.** $s_{\bar{x}} = 2$, about 4 **c.** $s_{\bar{x}} = 1$, about 2
10. smaller, easier
11. **a.** False **b.** True **c.** True **d.** True **e.** False **f.** True **g.** True
12. nothing (0.00), 1.00
13. **a.** False
    **b.** True
    **c.** False
    **d.** False
    **e.** $SMD = -0.05$
    **f.** False
    **g.** No, the *SMD* is very small, so small that the difference in means is almost nothing in practical terms. This difference is statistically significant because of the huge sample size that reduces sampling error, presumably, to practically nothing.
14. **a.** #2 **b.** #2 **c.** #1 **d.** #2
15. **a.** True **b.** False **c.** False **d.** True **e.** True **f.** True
16. that selected from A; the very low variability of readmission in B reduces power.
17. **a.** only a little (because all are very highly motivated)
    **b.** The low variability in motivation will reduce power.
18. **a.** True **b.** True **c.** False **d.** True **e.** True **f.** False **g.** True **h.** True **i.** False
19. .80, 80%, false null, .20
20. **a.** .40 **b.** .56 **c.** .79 **d.** .94 **e.** $>.99$
21. **a.** decrease **b.** increase **c.** decrease **d.** increase **e.** increase
22. True
23. **a.** True **b.** True **c.** True **d.** False
24. True
25. **a.** False **b.** False **c.** False **d.** False **e.** True **f.** True

## CHAPTER 17

1. True
2. normal, *t*
3. the number of independent values that remain after mathematical restrictions have been applied
4. **a.** 3 **b.** 4 **c.** 4
5. **a.** False **b.** True **c.** True **d.** False **e.** True **f.** True **g.** True **h.** False
   **i.** True **j.** False **k.** True
6. **a.** 49 **b.** 49 **c.** 66
7. 20, extreme, 100, extreme
8. **a.** yes **b.** no **c.** yes **d.** no **e.** no

9. **a.** $df = 48$, $s_{\bar{x}} = 3$, 95% *CI* of $\mu = 35.94$–$46.06$
   **b.** $df = 24$, $s_{\bar{x}} = 6$, 95% *CI* of $\mu = 47.62$–$72.83$
   **c.** $df = 8$, $s_{\bar{x}} = 7$, requirements for calculation not met
   **d.** $df = 144$, $s_{\bar{x}} = 2$, 95% *CI* of $\mu = 66.04$–$73.96$
10. **a.** 31.89 to 48.11
    **b.** 43.22 to 76.78
    **c.** requirements for calculation not met
    **d.** 64.77 to 75.23
11. 95% *CI* of $\mu = 66.08$–$73.92$, narrower when based on normal distribution
12. normality, robust
13. 20, extreme, 100, extreme
14. **a.** False  **b.** True  **c.** False  **d.** False
15. two, one, rejection, alternative
16. **a.** 1.00  **b.** $-1.00$  **c.** $-1.00$  **d.** 2.5  **e.** 3.00
17. **a.** 2.00  **b.** 4.00  **c.** $-3.33$  **d.** 2.5
18. **a.** fail to reject  **b.** reject  **c.** fail to reject  **d.** reject
    **e.** fail to reject (this result is in tail opposite to expectations)  **f.** reject
    **g.** fail to reject  **h.** reject  **i.** fail to reject  **j.** reject
19. **a.** $\mu \neq 80$  **b.** one-sample *t* test  **c.** yes  **d.** nondirectional  **e.** two-tailed
    **f.** $df = 35$  **g.** 2.030 and $-2.030$  **h.** $s_{\bar{x}} = 3.00$  **i.** $t = 3.00$
    **j.** reject the null; accept the alternative  **k.** yes  **l.** yes  **m.** no  **n.** True
    **o.** yes  **p.** yes
20. **a.** $H_1: \mu < 60.0$  **b.** one-sample *t* test  **c.** yes  **d.** directional  **e.** one-tailed
    **f.** $df = 63$  **g.** $-1.671$  **h.** $s_{\bar{x}} = 2.00$  **i.** $t = -1.50$
    **j.** fail to reject the null, reject the alternative  **k.** no*  **l.** no*
    *Key idea is not that the study result is likely but rather that it is not sufficiently unlikely
    for the null to be rejected.
    **m.** no (this conclusion is too strong)  **n.** False  **o.** no  **p.** no

## CHAPTER 18

1. difference between means, $s_{\bar{x}_2 - \bar{x}_2}$
2. **a.** False  **b.** True
3. normally, robust
4. equality, equal
5. **a.** True  **b.** True
6. equality of variances, equal, equal, unequal
7. **a.** independent samples *t*-test
   **b.** The mean depression score in the population from which the cognitive behavioral group
   was randomly selected is equal to the mean depression score in the population from
   which the psychosocial group was randomly selected.
   **c.** yes  **d.** False  **e.** False  **f.** equal variances formula  **g.** $t = 2.88$
   **h.** $df = n_1 + n_2 - 2$, $df = 48$  **i.** 2.021 and $-2.021$
   **j.** reject the null, accept the alternative  **k.** yes  **l.** no
   **m.** no  **n.** yes  **o.** $SMD = -0.81$  **p.** large
   **q.** True  **r.** False  **s.** True
8. **a.** yes  **b.** $H_0: \mu_1 \geq \mu_2$  **c.** yes  **d.** unequal variances formula  **e.** $t = -1.20$
   **f.** $-1.703$; reject null for all values $\leq -1.703$
   **g.** fail to reject the null, reject the alternative  **h.** no  **i.** no  **j.** no  **k.** no

**9.** pretest, posttest

**10.** dependent (or paired)

**11. a.** dependent  **b.** independent  **c.** dependent  **d.** dependent  **e.** independent
**f.** dependent

**12.** independent, dependent

**13.** True

**14. a.** True  **b.** True

**15.** smaller, power

**16. a.** dependent  **b.** dependent samples $t$-test  **c.** yes  **d.** $t = 2.50$
**e.** $df = 35$  **f.** two-tailed  **g.** 2.030 and $-2.030$
**h.** that the populations from which the pretest and posttest samples were selected have equal
means
**i.** reject the null, accept the alternative  **j.** yes  **k.** less than
**l.** less than  **m.** no  **n.** yes  **o.** yes

## CHAPTER 19

**1.** proportion

**2. a.** .043  **b.** .087  **c.** .087  **d.** .06  **e.** .03

**3. a.** 25, 75, yes  **b.** 6.25, 18.75, yes  **c.** 18.75, 6.25, yes
**d.** 2.5, 22.5, no  **e.** 10, 90, yes

**4.** True

**5.** True

**6. a.** one-sample test of $p$  **b.** $H_0: P = .15, H_1: P \neq .15$
**c.** $NP = 37.5, N(1-P) = 212.5$, yes  **d.** $\sigma_p = .023$
**e.** $z = 4.35$  **f.** reject the null, accept the alternative
**g.** $<.01$  **h.** $<.01$  **i.** no  **j.** yes  **k.** yes  **l.** yes

**7. a.** $H_0: P = .80, H_1: P \neq .80$  **b.** $NP = 80, N(1-P) = 20$, yes
**c.** $\sigma_p = .04$  **d.** $z = 2.50$  **e.** reject the null, accept the alternative
**f.** $<.05$  **g.** $<.05$  **h.** yes  **i.** yes  **j.** yes

**8. a.** nonrandom  **b.** False  **c.** $H_0: P = .55, H_1: P \neq .55$
**d.** $NP = 22, N(1-P) = 18$, yes  **e.** $\sigma_p = .079$  **f.** $z = 1.90$
**g.** fail to reject the null, reject the alternative  **h.** $>.05$
**i.** $>.05$  **j.** no  **k.** no, not sufficiently  **l.** no, not strong enough to reject it

**9. a.** True  **b.** False  **c.** True  **d.** True  **e.** True

**10. #1.** 7, reject if frequency is $\geq 7$, fail to reject
**#2.** 5, reject if frequency is $\geq 5$, fail to reject
**#3.** 5, reject if frequency is $\geq 5$, reject
**#4.** 2, reject if frequency is $\leq 2$, fail to reject
**#5.** 2, reject if frequency is $\leq 2$, reject
**#6.** no value results in rejection, null will never be rejected in this situation, fail to reject
(accept) the null

**11. a.** $H_0: P \geq .2; H_1: P < .2$  **b.** $NP = 4, N(1-P) = 16$, no  **c.** binomial test
**d.** 0  **e.** fail to reject the null, reject the alternative  **f.** greater than .05
**g.** greater than .05  **h.** no  **i.** no  **j.** no  **k.** The small sample size makes power low;
a very large difference is required for rejection.

**12. a.** $H_0: P \leq .75; H_1: P > .75$  **b.** There is no critical value listed.
**c.** The null can never be rejected given the described conditions.
**d.** fail to reject the null, reject the alternative  **e.** True  **f.** True

**13. a.** $H_0: P \le .50$; $H_1: P > .50$  **b.** 9  **c.** reject if frequency is 9 or higher
 **d.** reject the null, accept the alternative  **e.** False  **f.** False
**14.** two, proportions
**15.** family, degrees of freedom
**16. a.** four  **b.** one  **c.** nine
**17.** close, fail to reject, reject
**18.** observed frequency, observed proportion
**19.** expected proportion, null, expected frequency
**20.** sample size
**21. A:** .30, 30  **B:** .40, 40  **C:** .10, 10  **D:** .20, 20
**22. A:** .30, 15  **B:** .40, 20  **C:** .10, 5  **D:** .20, 10
**23.** four, one, five
**24.** nondirectional, one, upper
**25.** expected, greater (or larger), rejecting
**26. a.** one-variable chi-square  **b.** nondirectional  **c.** The population proportion ($P$) equals
 .20 for 17 and younger group, .45 for 18–50 group, and .35 for 51 and older group.
 **d.** .20, .45, .35  **e.** 10, 22.5, 17.5  **f.** .12, .60, .28  **g.** 6, 30, 14  **h.** 16.7, yes
 **i.** 10, yes  **j.** $\chi^2 = 4.80$  **k.** 2  **l.** 5.99  **m.** fail to reject the null, reject the alternative
 **n.** no  **o.** no  **p.** no  **q.** no  **r.** True
**27. a.** 20 for each program  **b.** 20, yes  **c.** 20, yes  **d.** $\chi^2 = 4.30$  **e.** 3  **f.** 7.81
 **g.** fail to reject the null, reject the alternative  **h.** greater than .05  **i.** >.05  **j.** no
 **k.** no (only indicates that we do not have strong grounds for concluding that it is false)
 **l.** no
**28. a.** 20 for each program  **b.** 20, yes  **c.** 20, yes  **d.** $\chi^2 = 8.70$  **e.** 3
 **f.** 7.81  **g.** reject the null, accept the alternative  **h.** less than .05  **i.** <.05
 **j.** yes  **k.** no, it indicates that the null is likely false  **l.** yes

## CHAPTER 20

**1. a.** False  **b.** True  **c.** False
**2.** True
**3.** unassociated (unrelated), equal
**4.** degrees of freedom, greater
**5.** True
**6. a.** 6  **b.** 4  **c.** 15  **d.** 1
**7.** True
**8. a.** .17  **b.** .83
**9. a.** In the population from which the study sample was randomly selected, workshop attendance and opinion are unassociated. Or, more simply, workshop attendance and opinion
are unassociated.
 **b.** Equal percentages of workshop attendees and nonattendees agree with the statement.
 **c.** attend/agree, 36; attend/not agree, 14; not attend/agree, 36; not attend/not agree, 14
 **d.** Yes, smallest expected frequency is 14.
 **e.** For those who attended: agree, .80; disagree, .20. For those who did not attend: agree, .64;
disagree, .36.
 **f.** associated
 **g.** For those who attended: agree, .72; disagree, .28. For those who did not attend: agree, .72;
disagree, .28.
 **h.** no  **i.** $\chi^2 = 3.175$  **j.** $df = 1$  **k.** 3.84

**l.** $\chi^2 (1, N = 100) = 3.175, p > .05$

**m.** fail to reject the null, reject the alternative

**n.** No  **o.** False  **p.** False  **q.** False  **r.** False

**s.** False (This conclusion is too strong; what we know is that the study does not provide strong evidence that the null is false.)

10. **a.** False  **b.** False  **c.** reject the null, accept the alternative

**d.** yes  **e.** True  **f.** True  **g.** True  **h.** True

**i.** No. Because there was no random assignment to groups, results may reflect the influence of confounding variables.

11. **a.** (In the population) concentration choice and employment in social work are unassociated.

**b.** children and family, 80%; mental health, 68%; health, 75%; community practice, 77%

**c.** employed row, .75; unemployed row, .25

**d.** yes  **e.** small/weak

**f.** $df = 3$  **g.** 7.81

**h.** fail to reject (accept) the null, reject the alternative

**i.** False  **j.** False  **k.** no  **l.** False

**m.** $\chi^2 (3, N = 200) = 2.06, p > .05$

12. **a.** Type of program (family involvement vs. traditional) and reuniting (yes or no) are unassociated.

**b.** Equal percentages in the family involvement and traditional programs are reunited with their families.

**c.** reunited/family, 16; reunited/traditional, 16; not reunited/family 9; not reunited/traditional, 9

**d.** yes (minimum is 9)  **e.** 12.5, yes

**f.** reunited/family, .80; reunited/traditional, .48; not reunited/family, .20; not reunited/traditional, .52

**g.** reunited/family, .64; reunited/traditional, .64; not reunited/family, .36; not reunited/traditional, .36

**h.** no  **i.** associated (related)  **j.** $\chi^2 = 5.56$  **k.** $df = 1$  **l.** 3.84

**m.** reject the null, accept the alternative  **n.** True  **o.** True  **p.** True

**q.** True  **r.** True  **s.** True  **t.** Yes  **u.** $\chi^2 (1, N = 50) = 5.56, p \le .05$

13. False

14. Fisher's exact test

15. **a.** False

**b.** True

**c.** rejecting

# CHAPTER 21

1. True
2. equal means
3. $\mu_1 = \mu_2 = ...\mu_J$
4. normally, equal
5. variance, equal
6. within, mean square within, $MS_W$
7. average
8. between, mean square between, $MS_B$
9. mean $(\overline{X})$
10. sample size, $N$

**11.** within, between
**12.** False
**13.** spread, sampling error
**14.** between, within
**15.** $F$, $F$ ratio
**16.** 1.00, larger
**17.** $F = MS_B / MS_W$
**18.** $J - 1$
**19.** $N - J$
**20. a.** 4, 35  **b.** 2, 97  **c.** 3, 24   **d.** 2, 57   **e.** 5, 194   **f.** 4, 70
**21. a.** 8.0   **b.** 8.0   **c.** 8.0   **d.** 27
**22. a.** 1.5   **b.** 3.0   **c.** 0.75   **d.** 4.0   **e.** 8.0   **f.** 2.0   **g.** 1.0
**23. a.** reject at both levels    **b.** reject at .05 level, fail to reject at .01 level
  **c.** fail to reject at both levels    **d.** reject at .05 level, fail to reject at .01 level
  **e.** reject at both levels    **f.** fail to reject at both levels
  **g.** reject at .05 level, fail to reject at .01 level
**24. a.** True   **b.** False   **c.** True   **d.** True
**25.** one, upper
**26.** strong or extreme, extreme, extreme
**27.** degrees of freedom, $N - J$
**28.** degrees of freedom, $J - 1$
**29. a.** Between groups: $df = 4$, $MS_B = 90$; Within groups: $df = 100$, $MS_W = 45$; the $F$ ratio is
  2.00
  **b.** 2.46   **c.** fail to reject the null, reject the alternative
  **d.** False   **e.** False   **f.** False
**30. a.** 4   **b.** 26   **c.** $MS_B = 100.0$, $MS_W = 10.0$, $F = 10.0$
  **d.** 3.98   **e.** reject the null, accept the alternative   **f.** No   **g.** Yes
**31.** alpha ($\alpha$)
**32.** greater
**33.** greater
**34.** multiple comparisons
**35. a.** True
  **b.** True
  **c.** False
**36.** do not have blinders on; might find something unexpected and interesting; makes effective
  use of data

## CHAPTER 22

**1.** linear, 0.00, $\rho$, sampling error (chance)
**2. a.** False   **b.** False   **c.** True   **d.** True   **e.** True
**3.** $H_0: \rho = 0$;    $H_1: \rho \neq 0$
**4.** $H_0: \rho \leq 0$, $H_1: \rho > 0$
**5. a.** positive   **b.** The correlation between visiting and health problems equals 0.00.
  **c.** 100   **d.** $-.254$ and .254   **e.** $\leq-.254$ and $\geq.254$
  **f.** reject the null, accept the alternative
  **g.** (at least) 99% confident   **h.** no   **i.** yes
  **j.** No, even though relationship is statistically significant, it may be caused by a confounding
    variable.

6. **#1. a.** $r \geq 0.00$ **b.** $df = 50$ **c.** $-.322$ **d.** fail to reject (accept) the null
**#2. a.** $r \geq 0.00$ **b.** $df = 50$ **c.** $-.231$ **d.** reject the null
**#3. a.** $r = 0.00$ **b.** $df = 50$ **c.** .273 and $-.273$ **d.** fail to reject (accept) the null
**#4. a.** $r = 0.00$ **b.** $df = 70$ **c.** .232 and $-.232$ **d.** reject the null
**#5. a.** $r = 0.00$ **b.** $df = 70$ **c.** .302 and $-.302$ **d.** fail to reject (accept) the null
**#6. a.** $r = 0.00$ **b.** $df = 1,000$ **c.** .062 and $-.062$ **d.** reject the null
**#7. a.** $r = 0.00$ **b.** $df = 12$ **c.** .532 and $-.532$ **d.** fail to reject (accept) the null

7. **a.** fail to reject (accept) **b.** no **c.** No, because direction of result is opposite to expectations.
**d.** rerun test as a two-tailed test (nondirectional hypothesis pair)

8. **a.** decreases **b.** decreases **c.** easier, increases

9. correlation matrix

10. **a.** True **b.** False **c.** True **d.** True **e.** True **f.** True
**g.** False (just misses) **h.** False (no just slightly more than this)
**i.** False (but can be 98.9% confident: $100\% - 1.1\% = 98.9\%$)

11. **a.** False **b.** True **c.** True

12. **a.** True **b.** True **c.** True **d.** True

13. rank orderings (two sets of ranks), 0.00

14. 0.00

15. high

16. independent samples $t$ test

17. Mann-Whitney $U$ test, two, analysis of variance, ANOVA

18. dependent, dependent, interval/ratio

19. True

20. proportions (percentages), dependent

21. all of these are advantages

22. True

23. square root transformation and log transformation

24. AB, baseline, A, intervention, B

25. **a.** no **b.** no **c.** no, sample size is too small **d.** Mann-Whitney $U$ test

26. False

27. **a.** 30% **b.** 60% **c.** yes **d.** 30%
**e.** large **f.** chi-square test of independence

28. **a.** No **b.** No **c.** Yes

29. **a.** Yes **b.** Yes **c.** No

30. serial dependency

31. **a.** True **b.** False **c.** False **d.** False

32. **a.** False **b.** False

33. **a.** True **b.** True **c.** False **d.** True **e.** False **f.** False **g.** True

## CHAPTER 23

1. unstandardized, controlling for other predictors, predicted, raw score, raw score
2. standardized, predictors, predicted, standard deviation, standard deviation
3. multiple regression coefficient, $R$,
4. squared multiple regression coefficient, $R^2$
5. adjusted
6. dummy
7. False

8. **a.** True   **b.** decreases by .0034 points   **c.** decreases by .114 standard deviations
   **d.** 4.0554   **e.** False   **f.** decreases by .0434
   **g.** decreases by .075 standard deviations   **h.** −.075, small
   **i.** the large sample size   **j.** True   **k.** False   **l.** False   **m.** True
   **n.** .645   **o.** False   **p.** True
9. False
10. residual
11. **a.** False   **b.** True   **c.** True   **d.** True
12. multicollinearity
13. **a.** False   **b.** True   **c.** True   **d.** False   **e.** True   **f.** True
    **g.** True   **h.** True   **i.** False   **j.** True   **k.** True
14. a and d
15. True
16. **a.** False   **b.** True   **c.** True   **d.** False   **e.** False
17. dichotomous (binary)
18. log of the odds, odds
19. **a.** decrease   **b.** $1.00 - .994 = .006 \times 100 = 0.6\%$
    **c.** True   **d.** 1.257   **e.** True   **f.** True
20. ordinal
21. analysis of variance, factor, two-way, factorial, levels
22. main, interact
23. **a.** True   **b.** True   **c.** False   **d.** False   **e.** False
24. Analysis of covariance (ANCOVA), covariates
25. Multiple analysis of variance (MANOVA)
26. Repeated measures
27. Structural equation modeling
28. Multilevel
29. Survival analysis, Cox proportional hazards
30. Factor analysis, factor
31. True

# CHAPTER 24

1. context
2. the expected degree of similarity between the study result and the result that would be obtained if the study was carried out in a different setting or context
3. **a.** True   **b.** False   **c.** True   **d.** True   **e.** True   **f.** True   **g.** True   **h.** True
   **i.** False   **j.** True   **k.** False   **l.** True   **m.** False   **n.** False
4. statistical, nonstatistical
5. similarity
6. In the author's opinion, careful reasoning based on degree of similarity can be used to make generalizations outside of this population. *Statistical* generalizations outside of this population are not appropriate.
7. Say, a physics experiment finds a statistically significant relationship among two categories of subatomic particles; this has little importance for social work practice.
8. Importance, real world
9. **a.** False   **b.** True   **c.** False   **d.** False   **e.** True   **f.** True
10. statistical significance, size of association, causality, generalizability, importance

**11.** statistical significance

**12. a.** False   **b.** False   **c.** False   **d.** False

**13. a.** False   **b.** True   **c.** True   **d.** True   **e.** False
**f.** False   **g.** True   **h.** True   **i.** False

**14. a.** mental health center (A vs. B), nominal

**b.** psychiatric rehospitalization (yes vs. no), nominal

**c.** chi-square test of independence   **d.** $N = 400$   **e.** power likely high

**f.** Percentages readmitted for A and B are equal (or center and readmission are unassociated).

**g.** Percentages readmitted for A and B are not equal (or center and readmission are associated).

**h.** yes   **i.** reject the null   **j.** accept the alternative

**k.** less than .05   **l.** less than .05   **m.** yes   **n.** yes   **o.** no

**p.** $D\% = 10\%$   **q.** small/weak   **r.** no

**s.** No. Because there is no random assignment, a confounding variable may be causing relationship.

**t.** Perhaps those served by B tend, on average, to have more serious mental health problems.

**u.** no   **v.** No, because sampling is not random.   **w.** statistical

**x.** other urban health centers mental health clients in urban areas of large United States cities in the Northeast

**y.** Not extremely confident; because logic for this generalization is nonstatistical, considerable caution is required.

**z.** say, rural clinics in southwestern United States (or, say, clinics in say rural areas outside of the United States)

**aa.** Yes, perhaps so. Finding effective programs for with chronic mental illness is an important program, and, further, the size of the difference observed (the *SMD*) was large.

**bb.** nonstatistical   **cc.** b, limited confidence

**15. a.** treatment approach (A vs. B), nominal

**b.** depression score on Rainbow Inventory, interval/ratio (or almost so)

**c.** independent samples *t* test   **d.** 100   **e.** power likely moderate

**f.** mean Rainbow Depression scores are equal for A and B

**g.** mean Rainbow Depression scores are not equal for A and B

**h.** yes   **i.** reject the null   **j.** accept the alternative

**k.** less than .05   **l.** less than .05

**m.** yes   **n.** yes   **o.** no   **p.** $SMD = 1.00$

**q.** large   **r.** yes   **s.** Yes, random assignment eliminated confounding variables.

**t.** there are no confounding variables

**u.** no   **v.** No, because there is no random sampling.   **w.** statistical

**x.** presumably to many exclusive mental health clinics that serve the well-to-do

**y.** Not extremely confident; because logic for this generalization is nonstatistical, considerable caution is required.

**z.** say, at a public clinic that served predominantly persons with very limited economic means

**aa.** Presumably yes. Finding effective treatments for depression is important. Further, one can draw causal conclusions in this study.

**bb.** nonstatistical   **cc.** b, limited confidence

**16. a.** type of intervention (search vs. education), nominal

**b.** find a job (yes vs. no), nominal   **c.** chi-square test of independence

**d.** $N = 8,000$   **e.** power likely high (indeed, likely extremely high because of a very large sample size)

**f.** Percentages in search and education who find jobs are equal (or type of intervention and finding a job are unassociated).

g. Percentages in search and education who find jobs are not equal (or type of intervention and finding a job are associated).

h. yes   i. reject the null   j. accept the alternative   k. less than .05

l. less than .05   m. yes   n. yes

o. no   p. $D\% = 2\%$   q. *extremely* small (almost no difference at all)

r. yes   s. Yes, random assignment eliminated confounding variables.

t. there are none   u. no   v. No, study is not a random sample.

w. statistical   x. perhaps to many of the states that border Oklahoma

y. No, as logic was nonstatistical and thus much caution is required.

z. say, perhaps highly urbanized states (or to other countries)

aa. Hard to say. Even though results are statistically significant, the two approaches are almost equal in their effectiveness ($D\% = 2\%$). Because finding work is highly important, I tend to think these results are important.

bb. nonstatistical   cc. b, limited confidence

17. a. type of controller (hand motion vs. body motion), nominal

   b. controller effectiveness, interval/ratio (or almost so)

   c. independent samples *t* test   d. $N = 600$   e. power likely high

   f. Controller effectiveness scores are equal for hand-motion and body-motion groups.

   g. Controller effectiveness scores are not equal for hand-motion and body-motion groups.

   h. yes   i. reject the null   j. accept the alternative   k. less than .05

   l. less than .05   m. yes   n. yes   o. no   p. $SMD = 2.00$

   q. very large   r. yes   s. Yes, random assignment rules out confounding variables.

   t. NA   u. yes   v. 11-year-old boys in the six-state region in the southeastern United States

   w. statistical   x. perhaps to all boys aged 10–12 years in the United States

   y. No, because logic was nonstatistical and thus much caution is required.

   z. say, perhaps girls aged 4–6 years

   aa. Probably not because video game skills is not a particularly important issue. (But perhaps so—perhaps can build self-esteem through better video game performance.)

   bb. nonstatistical   cc. b, limited confidence

18. a. education program (experimental vs. control group), nominal

   b. used marijuana in past 6 months (yes vs. no)

   c. chi-square test of independence

   d. $N = 1,000$   e. power likely high

   f. Equal percentages in experimental and control groups use marijuana (or group membership and marijuana use are unassociated).

   g. Percentage using marijuana differs in experimental and control groups (or group membership and marijuana use are associated).

   h. no   i. fail to reject (accept) the null   j. reject the alternative

   k. greater than .05   l. greater than .05   m. no   n. no   o. no   p. $D\% = 1\%$

   q. *extremely* weak (essentially no relationship)   r. yes

   s. Yes (in the sense that the random assignment ruled out confounding variables). On the other hand, the "tiny" effect size and the absence of statistical significance suggest that the intervention had little, if any, effect on marijuana use.

   t. NA   u. No   v. No, because there is no random sampling.   w. statistical

   x. say, to teens and preteens in medium-sized towns in midwestern states

   y. No, such nonstatistical reasoning requires considerable caution.

   z. Perhaps to elementary school students in urban settings in the Northeast

   aa. Perhaps so. Reducing drug use is important. Results suggest that it is not worthwhile to expend funds on this particular drug prevention model.

   bb. nonstatistical   cc. b, limited confidence

**19. a.** type of service (home based vs. placement based), nominal
   **b.** commit an offense (yes vs. no), nominal
   **c.** chi-square test of independence   **d.** $N = 2,250$   **e.** power is likely (very) high
   **f.** Equal percentages of home-based and placement-based youth commit an offense (or type of service and committing an offense are unassociated).
   **g.** Percentages of home-based and placement-based youths who commit an offense differ (or type of service and committing an offense are associated).
   **h.** yes   **i.** reject the null   **j.** accept the alternative   **k.** less than .05
   **l.** less than .05   **m.** yes   **n.** yes   **o.** no   **p.** $D\% = 23\%$
   **q.** medium to strong   **r.** no
   **s.** No, because of absence of random assignment, confounding variables may be affecting results.
   **t.** Those who were placed may have had lower-functioning families.
   **u.** No   **v.** No, not a random sample.   **w.** statistical
   **x.** Perhaps to other youth of similar ages in western states.
   **y.** No, because reasoning is nonstatistical.
   **z.** Perhaps to youth in states with juvenile justice delivery systems with much different characteristics than that in the state in which this study was conducted.
   **aa.** Question of importance is complicated because the relationship between the intervention and committing an offense may be due to confounding variables. Even so, knowing that fewer youth in home-based services commit and offence strikes me as important information that could be useful in program planning.
   **bb.** nonstatistical   **cc.** b, limited confidence

# NOTES

## CHAPTER 1

1. This text uses **bold font** to convey important (key) terms. It uses *italics* both for emphasis and to convey terms that are useful to know but are less important than those that are set in bold. Exceptions are that both in the Chapter Overview section at the beginning of each chapter and in the Chapter Summary section at the end of each chapter, important (key) terms are conveyed in *italics*.

2. Whether a given group of objects is a sample or a population depends, ultimately, on how that group is defined in a particular study. For instance, the students in your current statistics class are indeed the population of students in the class (they are *all* such students) but, at the same time, they are *some* of the students who attend your university and, thus, are a sample of the population of students at your university. And, similarly, (all of) the students at your university are, indeed, the population of students at your university. But at the same time, they are a sample of all university students in, say, your state. Practically, the issues raised in this note do not cause problems in actual research studies; the particulars of the study guide you in determining whether you are dealing with a sample or a population.

## CHAPTER 2

1. From this point forward, I refer to IBM SPSS Statistics simply as SPSS. This is the name by which it was known by for its 40 years or so of existence. Several years ago, SPSS switched its name to PASW but it switched back to IBM SPSS very recently.

2. The mathematical definition of percentile differs slightly from the definition given here, which is in essence a general definition. The mathematical definition deals with at least two issues: (a) how to count the individual cases (for instance, in our example, is Fred taller than himself?) and (b) how to count other cases that have the exact same value (if Fred is 5 ft. 9.38 in. tall, should we count him as taller than, equal in height to, or shorter than other persons who are the exact same height?). In today's world, computer software programs compute percentiles and the researcher can let the program use its own particular formula. Of course, percentiles should not be computed for nominal-level variables because their values cannot be ordered.

3. In most statistical programs, the software that generates histograms automatically combines values to produce a useful number of columns For instance, if respondents' ages range from 20 to 54, a histogram for age could contain, say, seven columns, each representing a different age range: 20–24, 25–29, 30–34, 35–39, 40–44, 45–49, and 50–54. Each of a histogram's columns must span the same range of values. In this example, each column spans five years. For instance, the second column contains all ages from 19.5 to 24.5.

## CHAPTER 3

1. This text presents the median of a categorical ordinal-level variable as the value of the category, for instance, as "Mostly positive" in Table 3.1. It is more common to present the median of such data using the assigned numeric code. Thus, most texts would present the median value in Table 3.1 as 4, the code assigned to Mostly positive. I think presenting the median as the actual value is more helpful and, thus, have done so.
2. For numeric data in which cases share common values, a more complex method for determining the median is often used. This more complex method is particularly appropriate for grouped frequency distributions. To see this method, you could google "median grouped frequency distribution" or consult many statistics books. (See, for instance, Toothaker & Miller, 1996, p. 156.)

## CHAPTER 4

1. See Pilcher (1990, pp. 155–156) for discussion of the index of dispersion and the index of qualitative variation—two measures that see occasional usage. Researchers sometimes do calculate the standard deviation (to be presented later in this chapter for numeric variables) of dichotomous variables, particularly those coded with 0s and 1s. Coded in this way, the standard deviation of a dichotomous variable is $s = \sqrt{p(1-p)}$, where s is the standard deviation and $p$ is the proportion coded with 1s. The mean of a variable coded in this way equals the proportion of 1s.

## CHAPTER 5

1. Distributions with high kurtosis are termed *leptokurtic* distributions. Those with low kurtosis are *platykurtic* distributions. Distributions with kurtosis similar to that of a normal distribution are *mesokurtic* distributions.
2. Where a distribution has the same degree of peakedness as the normal distribution, its kurtosis equals 0.00. When a distribution is more peaked than normal, its kurtosis will be greater than 0.00 (i.e., a positive number). When the distribution is flatter than the normal distribution, its kurtosis will be less than 0.00 (i.e., a negative number).

## CHAPTER 6

1. Differences that are small, other things being equal, are more likely to be caused by the luck of the draw than are those that are large. Chapter 16 demonstrates this. Chapters 14–16 focus on how researchers assess whether relationships may be due to luck alone. As discussed briefly in Chapter 1, they use statistical significance tests to do so.
2. The recommendation to use the percentages of the dependent variable that are closer to 0.00 was easy to implement in the chapter's example using vaccines given that the percentages for one category of the dependent variable (becoming ill, 1% and 8%) were much closer to 0.00 than were those of the other (not becoming ill, 99% and 92%). But sometimes, neither category has percentages that are markedly closer to 0% than the other. In such situations—particularly when no percentages are close to 0%—the *RR* is, almost always, less preferred than the *D%*.

3. The descriptors in Table 7.2 were designed primarily for the odds ratio, presented in Chapter 7. When both percentages for the event do not differ greatly from 0.00% (say are less than about 30%), the odds ratio and the risk ratio compute to fairly similar values, and thus the descriptors apply to the risk ratio. When the guideline is not met, the actual size of association conveyed by the risk ratio is often larger than that suggested by the descriptors. Although the descriptors should not be used when the percentage for either category exceeds 30%, the risk ratio itself may still be computed. For instance, for the example in the text, $RR = 60\% / 20\% = 3.00$.

## CHAPTER 7

1. The descriptors tend to underestimate size of association; In other words, the actual size of association is modestly larger than the descriptors suggest.
2. "Directional relationship" is used differently in this text than in most others. Most texts use this term to mean that the causal effect between two variables goes in a given direction—that is, Variable A affects Variable B rather than vice versa. In Chapter 10, this text uses similar language to describe the effect of one variable on another. As used in the current chapter, directional relationship means much the same thing as does *monotonic relationship*. A monotonic relationship is one that is either always increasing or always decreasing; in other words, direction of relationship never reverses itself (shifts from increasing to decreasing or from decreasing to increasing).
3. With the exception of gamma, the descriptors tend to underestimate size of association. In other words, the actual size of association is often modestly larger than the descriptors suggest.

## CHAPTER 8

1. The most important distinction between interval-ratio level variables and numeric variables involves rank orderings (see Chapter 1, Section 1.9.1). Rank orderings are numeric but not at the interval/ratio-level of measurement.
2. In the most formal sense, I should say that multiplication (or division) by any constant other than 0.00 does not affect the value of $r$. Multiplying all of a variable's values by 0.00 changes that variable from a variable to a constant, and a constant cannot be associated with any other variable. And, as you remember from earlier math, dividing by zero yields an undetermined result.
3. These examples express predicted change using standard deviation units. Change may also be expressed using $z$ scores. For instance, the $r$ of 0.80 in the high-jump/long-jump example conveys that as $z$ score in the high jump increases by 1.00, predicted $z$ score in the long jump increases by 0.80. And, regarding the long-jump/50-meter run example, the $r$ of $-0.78$ conveys that as $z$ score in the long jump increases by 1.00, predicted $z$ score in the 50-meter run decreases by 0.78.
4. When a relationship is curvilinear with one bend (as in Figure 8.7), it can be described by a quadratic equation. Such an equation typically uses two independent variables to predict the dependent variable. The first is the initial independent variable, say, $X$, and the second is that variable squared, $X^2$ (see Cohen & Cohen, 1983, pp. 224–242). Although not mentioned in this text, it is possible for a relationship to demonstrate an abrupt bend (a sharp angle) rather than a smooth curve. Pearson's $r$ is not appropriate in such a situation.
5. The regression line is also called the *least-squares line*. Thus, if you do the following: (a) for each case, subtract the predicted value for $Y$ (i.e., $\hat{Y}$) from the actual value of $Y$; (b) for each case, square this difference; and (c) add together all of the "squared differences," the result is the *sum of squares*. The regression line is the single line among all possible lines that minimizes the sum of squares, that is, makes its value as small as possible.

6. In calculations of phi, the numeric value 1 (1.00) is assigned to the category designated as higher and the value 0 (0.00) to that designated as lower. Although phi can be calculated when both variables are not dichotomous, Cramer's *V* is preferred in this situation (see Rosenthal, 2000, p. 121).

## CHAPTER 9

1. Just as did the prior one, this chapter uses "numeric variable" rather than "interval/ratio-level variable" for simplicity. The measures in this chapter should not be used for rank orderings even though, formally, these are numeric variables.

2. A disadvantage of the *standardized mean difference (SMD)* is that most statistical software packages do not calculate it. On the other hand, typing "effect size calculator" in Google yields calculators for Cohen's *d* and Hedges' *g*, both excellent measures of effect size. The formula for Cohen's *d*, is $d = \dfrac{\overline{X}_1 - \overline{X}_2}{\sqrt{\dfrac{(n_1 - 1)s_1^2 + (n_2 - 1)s_2^2}{n_1 + n_2 - 2}}}$ where $\overline{X}_1$ is the mean in Group 1, $\overline{X}_2$ is that in Group 2, $n_1$ is the sample size in Group 1, $n_2$ is that in Group 2, $s_1^1$ is the variance in Group 1, and $s_2^2$ is that in Group 2. Hedges's *g* removes a tiny amount of bias from Cohen's *d* and, thus, is preferred in analyses that synthesize data from many studies. Google "meta-analysis" or "systematic review" to learn about such studies.

## CHAPTER 10

1. This example is less than optimal because there are only two age groups. This being so, age still varies quite a bit within each group. In other words, age is not controlled well in this example. Chapter 11 presents several child welfare examples that break age into five groups and, thus, better control for its effects.

## CHAPTER 11

1. The computation of an average difference in percentages builds on the example presented in Chapter 7, Section 7.3.

2. Our discussion oversimplifies causality. This note brings up some points that we did not discuss. First, causality may be in the direction that is opposite to expectations; in other words, rather than *X* causing *Y*, *Y* may cause *X*. Also, causality effects can operate in both directions, that is, *X* causes *Y and Y* causes *X*. Further, multiple effects may operate simultaneously. For instance, *X* may cause *Y*, *Y* may cause *X*, and some third variable *Z* may be an antecedent variable that further affects the association between *X* and *Y*. In reading, you may see causal models in which two variables are connected by a double-headed curved arrow. Such an arrow conveys that two variables are correlated (related) and does not specify the reason for that association which may be any or all of the effects mentioned in this note or in the chapter.

## CHAPTER 12

1. A third quality of estimators is *consistency*. A *consistent* estimator yields an increasingly accurate estimate of the population parameter as sample size increases (see Glass & Hopkins, 1996, pp. 242–247).
2. All of this text's examples presume that the sampling distribution is built using statistical theory and that it is based on an infinite number of cases. Given the high speed of today's computers, researchers sometimes create sampling distributions by having a computer program randomly select a large number of samples. Google "bootstrapping statistics" to get a glimpse at some of this, although this topic is quite advanced.

## CHAPTER 13

1. When the degree of skew in the population is even more extreme than the extremely skewed distributions in Figures 5.4 and 5.6, the accuracy of the confidence interval might not be sufficient. In such a circumstance, $N = 500$ is perhaps a good guideline.
2. In our example, the population standard deviation ($\sigma$) is known. Had it not been known, we would have used the standard deviation of the sample ($s$) to estimate the standard error: $s_{\bar{x}} = \frac{s}{\sqrt{N}}$. As $N = 100$, doing so would have affected the resulting confidence interval hardly at all.
3. When either $Np$ or $N(1 - p)$ barely exceeds 10, the researcher may desire more accuracy than is provided by the formulas presented in this chapter. The Ghosh method (Glass & Hopkins, 1996, pp. 325–330) and confidence intervals based on the binomial distribution (Toothaker & Miller, 1996, pp. 257–260) can provide greater accuracy. Based on work by Samuels and Lu (1992), when either $p$ or $(1 - p)$ is less than .01, the formulas presented here should not be carried out if either $Np$ or $N(1 - p)$ is less than 25. The reader could google "confidence intervals proportions, small samples" to learn more.

## CHAPTER 14

1. As you know, when $r = 0.00$, there is an absence of linear association. It is possible that there is curvilinear association. See Chapter 8, Section 8.7.
2. In multivariate statistical applications, null hypotheses almost always state, in essence, that controlling for other variables in the analysis, there is no relationship between two variables. See Chapter 23, Section 23.2, on multiple regression analysis.
3. To express this interpretation in a longer form: Significance tests convey the probability of obtaining the difference between the value stated in the null and the study sample result or a difference even larger than this due to chance alone.

## CHAPTER 15

1. One percent of cases in a normal distribution are located 2.576 or more standard deviations from the mean. The text rounded to 2.58 to simplify calculations.
2. There are a few tests for which doubling the one-tailed probability may not result in the two-tailed probability. In particular, when the sampling distribution is neither symmetric nor smooth (this occurs most often in tests designed for very small samples), the probability of a two-tailed

result can be difficult to calculate and may not double that of a one-tailed one. This occurs, for instance, with the binomial test presented in Chapter 19, Section 19.3.1.

3. In general, it is not a good practice to change either the significance level or whether the test is one- or two-tailed subsequent to carrying out the test. Many researchers view this as manipulating the "rules of the game" in order to obtain the results that are desired.

## CHAPTER 16

1. Studies of identical twins raised apart provide an excellent example of control for extraneous variables. In many such studies, the researcher's central interest is in the effects of the environmental factors on development. Obviously, genetic factors also affect development. But each member of an identical twin pair is identical genetically. So, having identical twin pairs in the study, in essence, controls for genetic effects. This enhances the power of significance tests focused on the effects of the differing environments.

2. The discussion in this text oversimplifies. In some situations, six or seven (or more) third variables can be included in an analysis and each one will enhance power. In others, no variables affect power by more than a trivial amount. Further, indiscriminate adding of variables can actually reduce power (see Chapter 23, Section 23.3).

3. When researchers report results in tables, there is often not sufficient space for reporting the exact value of $p$. In this case, the researcher reports the lowest significance level, usually using an asterisk; for instance, a single asterisk next to a result ("*") often conveys significance at the .05 level and a double asterisk often conveys ("**") significance at the .01 level.

## CHAPTER 17

1. The fact that there are only $N - 1$ opportunities for values to vary around the sample mean is the key reason why the formulas for the standard deviation and the variance use $N - 1$ in the denominator rather than $N$ (see Formulas 4.5 and 4.6).

## CHAPTER 18

1. If the degree of skew in either sample is even larger than that in the extreme skew figures in Figures 5.4 and 5.6, a sample size larger than 60 could be required. You should use the independent samples $t$ test cautiously in situations such as this.

2. When sample size is small, say about 50 or less, the equality of variances test may fail to reject the null of equal population variances even when these variances differ considerably. This is caused by poor statistical power. In such a situation, it can be difficult to know which $t$ test formula is preferred. When sample sizes are equal, both formulas yield the same value of $t$ (although degrees of freedom differ) and, thus, use of the "wrong" formula is unlikely to affect the decision on the hypothesis pair. However, when sample sizes differ considerably, use of the wrong formula can affect results substantially. My recommendation is that you always use the unequal variance formula—regardless of whether or not the equality of variances test rejects the null—when all of the following conditions are present: (a) $N < 50$, (b) sample sizes are unequal, and (c) the larger sample variance is

50% or more larger than the smaller sample variance. Whenever all three conditions are not present, follow the recommendations in the body of this text: Use the equal variance formula when the equality of variance test fails to reject the null, and use the unequal variance formula when it does so.

3. Formula 18.1 does not demonstrate how $s_{\bar{X}_1 - \bar{X}_2}$ is calculated. This differs in different *t*-test formulas. This text has provided two equivalent formulas for several procedures, that is, formulas that yield identical results. The equal and unequal variances formulas are not equivalent. Except when sample sizes are equal, they yield different values of *t*. Thus, it is important to use the correct one. (See Rosenthal, 2001, pp. 340–342 for these formulas.)

4. As tests are so often carried out in the absence of random sampling and as random sampling is understood to be a requirement of tests, this text does not mention random sampling in hypothesis statements from this point forward.

5. When a precise measure of the standardized mean difference (*SMD*) is required, the formula

for Cohen's *d* may be used: $d = \dfrac{\bar{X}_1 - \bar{X}_2}{\sqrt{\dfrac{(n_1 - 1)s_1^2 + (n_2 - 1)s_2^2}{n_1 + n_2 - 2}}}$ . I used an online calculator

available at http://www.uccs.edu/~faculty/lbecker/ to calculate Cohen's *d* and obtained a value of .226, the same value as we obtained in our calculation. The calculator was developed by Lee A. Becker, University of Colorado at Colorado Springs (revised in 1999). See note 2 in Chapter 9.

6. Here is an example in which the independence of observations assumption does not hold across the pairs, in other words, where each pair is not independent from each other pair: 15 couples, wives and husbands, participate in a communication workshop. These couples form 15 different pairs. Two of the wives in the sample are sisters. Each pair of observations that includes one of these sisters is not independent from the other pair of observations that includes the other sister. In this situation, the researcher might want to drop, at random, one of the two pairs prior to conducting a dependent samples *t* test.

7. If the degree of skew in either sample is even stronger than the "extreme skew" figures in Figures 5.4 and 5.6, more than 60 pairs could be required. You should use the dependent samples *t* test cautiously in situations such as this.

8. In some situations, taking a pretest can affect responses on the posttest, potentially introducing bias. This is called *pretest sensitization*. My opinion is that the increase in power that comes with the pretest almost always outweighs concerns related to pretest sensitization, hence, my recommendation in this text is to include pretests whenever it is possible to do so.

## CHAPTER 19

1. When the proportion stated in the null is between .01 and .05 or between .95 and .99, then both $NP$ and $N(1 - P)$ should be greater than or equal to 10. When this proportion equals .01 or .99, both $NP$ and $N(1 - P)$ should be greater than or equal to 25. When this proportion is less than .01 or greater than .99, the one-sample test of $p$ is not recommended.

2. The one-variable $\chi^2$ test may be used with dichotomous variables, those with two categories. For instance, rather than having used the one-sample test of $p$ for our first behavior problems example, we could have used a one-variable $\chi^2$ test. In contrast to the formula for the one-sample test of $p$ which uses the proportion for only one (selected) category, the one-variable $\chi^2$ test's formula (Formula 19.4) uses proportions for both categories. The advantage of the one-sample test of $p$ with a dichotomous variable is that one may use either a nondirectional pair (two-tailed test) or a directional one (one-tailed test). In contrast, the hypothesis pair for

the one-variable $\chi^2$ test is always nondirectional. For dichotomous variables, a one-sample test of $p$ based on a nondirectional pair (two-tailed test) and a one-variable $\chi^2$ test yield identical values of $p$. This being so, one may calculate a one-tailed probability for a one-sample test of $p$ by dividing the probability for a one-variable $\chi^2$ test in half. This may come in handy if your statistical package does not include the one-sample test of $p$. (Prior to calculating, be sure that your study result is in the direction stated in the alternative hypothesis.)

3. Given two categories, if the expected proportion (the proportion stated in the null) for either category is less than .05 but greater than .01, the minimum expected frequency should be at least 10; if the expected proportion equals .01, the minimum expected frequency should be at least 25; if the expected proportion is less than .01, the test should not be used. Given many categories, say six or more, guidelines for both average and minimum expected frequency can be relaxed. In such a situation, an average frequency of three and a minimum expected frequency of .5 are sufficient. In general, however, one wants to avoid very small expected and average frequencies. Often, both of these can be increased by combining categories that have similar values.

## CHAPTER 20

1. When the sample size guidelines are just barely met, the accuracy of the probability given by the $\chi^2$ test of independence can be described as adequate rather than precise. In this situation, however, this probability tends to be conservative. In other words, the probability given by the test tends to be higher than the actual probability that the result is caused by chance. Hence, there is little concern that the researcher will mistakenly reject the null because of inaccuracy in the test (Roscoe & Byars, 1971). This conservative bias does not hold for the 2 × 2 table (Roscoe & Byars, 1971). The just-made point notwithstanding, the $\chi^2$ test can often be used with 2 × 2 tables with average observed frequencies as low as two (see Camilli & Hopkins, 1978, 1979; Glass & Hopkins, 1996, p. 335).

2. Glass and Hopkins (1996, p. 337) discuss the $z$ test of a difference in proportions. This test tests differences in proportions for situations involving two dichotomous variables. An advantage of the $z$ test over the $\chi^2$ test is that one may formulate either a directional (one-tailed) or a nondirectional (two-tailed) hypothesis pair. A nondirectional $z$ test of a difference in proportions and an $\chi^2$ test of independence yield identical probabilities. If one divides the $p$ from the $\chi^2$ test in half, one, in essence, conducts a directional (one-tailed) $z$ test of a difference in proportions. As many software packages do not present the $z$ test, the pragmatic way to conduct it is to (a) carry out a $\chi^2$ test and (b) divide $p$ by two if a one-tailed (directional pair) probability is desired.

3. For a 2 × 2 table (two dichotomous variables), most statistical packages compute Yates's continuity correction. Many researchers recommend this correction. Glass and Hopkins (1996, p. 335) do not recommend it because it often makes the probability yielded by the $\chi^2$ test higher than the actual probability that the result is caused by chance. My recommendation is not to use Yates's correction.

## CHAPTER 21

1. As with all guidelines regarding test assumptions, those for analysis of variance (ANOVA) are approximate. The guidelines in this text work even when the number of groups is only two. As the number of groups increase, they can be relaxed. For instance, with four or more groups, none of which possesses strong or extreme skew, a minimum sample size of about 8 is sufficient. For four or more groups, none of which possesses extreme skew, sample size of

about 15 is sufficient. For four or more groups, one or more of which possesses extreme skew, sample size of about 40 is sufficient. (These are simply my best estimates.) If you find that you do not meet these guidelines, you might still conduct an ANOVA but you should recognize that the probability that it yields can be less accurate than would be desired. When the degree of skew is considerably stronger than the "extreme" skew in Figures 5.4 and 5.6, the sample size guidelines in this text may not be adequate. In general, one must be more careful about meeting guidelines when the .01 level is used than when the .05 level is used. Chapter 22, Section 22.6.3, presents the Kruskal-Wallis test, an alternative to ANOVA.

2. When sample sizes are nearly equal (say, when the largest is no more than about 20% larger than the smallest) and sample variances do not differ markedly (say, when the largest variance is no more than 33% larger than the smallest), then the results of ANOVA will be quite accurate even if the equality of variance test rejects the null of equal variances.

3. Formally, degrees of freedom are for the sums of squares rather than for the mean squares. I have taken the liberty of characterizing them as for the mean squares because this text only overviews sums of squares.

4. There is intuitive logic behind this result. On any given comparison, the probability that sampling error will result in rejection is .05. Even though this probability is small for any single comparison, given enough comparisons, sampling error may well prevail at least once.

5. The approximate probability of at least one error equals $1 - (1 - \alpha)^c$ where $c$ is the number of comparisons. For 10 comparisons using the .05 level, $1 - (1 - .05)^{10} = .40$. This probability is approximate because the formula for calculation assumes that each comparison is independent of each other comparison; this is likely not the case for real-world data.

6. In other words, even though the null is true in each instance, our researcher stands about a 50/50 chance of finding at *least one* statistically significant association.

7. Using the formula from the prior footnote: $1 - (1 - .05)^{15} = .54$.

8. Try googling "data mining" and you will learn about various sophisticated tools for mining through data for the purpose of finding relationships to guide decision making.

## CHAPTER 22

1. The *Kolgomorov-Smirnov* test is another alternative to the independent samples *t* test (Blalock, 1979, p. 276).

2. The Mann-Whitney *U* test is not recommended when the variability of ranks differs markedly in the two groups. For instance, presume that the following ranks are assigned: Group 1, "1, 2, 4, 8, 10, 11" and Group 2, "3, 5, 6, 7, 9." In this example, mean ranks are equal ($\overline{X} = 6$) but variability differs. Clearly, ranks in Group 2 are clustered much more closely together than are those in Group 1. In a situation such as this, the Mann-Whitney *U* test should not be used.

3. The prior note also applies to the *Kruskal-Wallis test*; this test should not be used when the variability of ranks differs greatly between groups.

4. Conducting two different significance tests is, for the most part, an acceptable practice. When results are similar, each test validates the other. On the other hand, one should not conduct two (or more) tests for the purpose of trying to find one that will yield significant results. This, clearly, is cheating. It is akin to "shopping" for many doctors until you find one who delivers an opinion that you agree with. See also Chapter 21, Section 21.7, on statistical fishing.

5. See note 5 in Chapter 23 on how to transform a negatively skewed variable.

6. My modest preference is for the *t* test on the transformed data. Typically, this test has greater power than does the Mann-Whitney *U* test. Hence, other things being equal, it is more likely to reject a false null.

7. If you see an upward or downward trend in the baseline, one alternative is to (a) calculate a regression line for the baseline phase, (b) extend this line through the intervention phase, (c) count the number of cases in the intervention phase that are above or below the extended line (whichever of these conveys a positive outcome), (d) count the total number of observations in the intervention phase, and (e) carry out a binomial test setting the expected proportion, $p$, to .50 (see Chapter 19, Section 19.3).

8. When a time series involves a dichotomous variable, one can check for serial dependency by constructing a contingency table displaying prior and subsequent observations. Table 22.4 presents this data for our example.

9. Very occasionally, adjacent observations are less similar than are those separated by many time points. Basically, there are three explanations for serial dependency: (a) prior observations influence/affect subsequent ones; (b) some external factor affects close-together observations, making them more similar than would otherwise be so; or (c) there is an upward or downward trend in the data.

10. The most straightforward way to assess whether a numeric time series variable exhibits serial dependency is to have a software program compute the correlation between scores on prior and subsequent observations. Such a correlation is termed an *autocorrelation*. In the SPSS software program, one uses the "lag" function to compute autocorrelations. (Click "Transform" and then "Compute" and then use the arrow to move the "lag [1] function" to the proper spot in the dialog box.) The autocorrelation ($r$) for the data in Figure 22.4 equals .50, which is statistically significant, $p = .000$. This affirms the presence of serial dependency.

## CHAPTER 23

1. Suppose a variable has three categories. For instance, suppose that treatment intervention comprises Treatment A, Treatment B, and Treatment C. We may develop three dummy variables (dummies) from treatment intervention. These are, with suggested names for the dummies: Treatment_A: 1 = assigned to Treatment A, 0 = assigned to B or C; Treatment_B: 1 = assigned to Treatment B, 0 = assigned to A or C; and Treatment_C: 1 = assigned to Treatment C, 0 = assigned to A or B. The researcher often develops as many dummy variables for a variable as there are categories. Here, our original variable has three categories and, thus, we developed three dummies. Although the researcher often develops as many dummies as there are categories, the number of dummies that can be entered into a multivariate analysis equals (at most) the number of categories minus one ($K - 1$, where $K$ is the number of categories). For instance, in the example in the text, Foster_parent status has two categories (prior parent and not prior parent), but only a single dummy is entered into the analysis. If you try to enter as many dummies as there are categories, the regression will crash (or the software program will pick one dummy and exclude it from the analysis). Attempting to enter as many dummies as there are categories creates a problem of total multicollinearity (Section 23.3 discusses multicollinearity).

2. As described, $\beta$ conveys the predicted change in standard deviation units for the dependent variable as the independent variable increases by one standard deviation. Recall, however, that dichotomous variables are at the nominal level of measurement. Do such variables even have a standard deviation? Formally, any variable with numeric values has a standard deviation. The standard deviation of a dummy variable coded dichotomous variable is: $s = \sqrt{p(1 - p)}$, where $p$ is the proportion assigned with the value of 1.00. Observe that the standard deviation varies according to the value of $p$. When $p$ is close to .50, the standard

deviation is larger; when it is close to 0.00 or to 1.00, it is smaller. For instance, when $p = .50 = \sqrt{.50(1.00 - .50)} = .50$ ; when $p = .10$, $s = \sqrt{.10(1.00 - .10)} = .30$. As the proportions in each category affect the standard deviation, they also affect β. This is a major reason why the βs for dichotomous variables should be interpreted with caution. The text mentions that for dichotomous variables, β often underestimates size of association. The degree of underestimation increases as $p$ gets closer to 0.00 or to 1.00. Particularly, when $p > .9$ or $< .1$, the degree of underestimation is pronounced and, thus, you should not interpret strength of association from β. (On the other hand, if you do so, recognize that the actual strength of association is larger than suggested by Table 8.2.)

3. $r$ measures the association of a single predictor to a dependent variable. Multiple $R$ measures the relationship of several predictors. As such, Cohen (1988) recommends modestly larger guidelines for assessing size of relationship (effect size) for $R$. He recommends small, $R = .14$; medium, $R = .36$; and large, $R = .51$. When precision is required, the *adjusted R* rather than $R$ should be used in comparisons. The adjusted $R$ can be found by taking the square root of the adjusted $R^2$. In our example: *adjusted R* $= \sqrt{.412} = .642$.

4. As a rule of thumb, the ratio of cases to predictors in a multiple regression analysis should be less than 10 to 1. For instance, if you have 50 cases, you should have no more than five predictors. In general, the lower the ratio of cases to predictors, the greater the difference between $R^2$ and the adjusted $R^2$.

5. For negatively skewed variables, Abu-Bader (2010) recommends (a) subtracting the constant "$K$" from each score, where $K$ equals the value of highest score plus 1 ($K$ = highest score + 1) and then (b) carrying out either a square root or log transformation. These are the transformations that I carried out as I reran the analysis.

6. On balance, multiple regression is robust to violations of assumptions related to normality and equality of variance. In other words, modest violation of these assumptions is unlikely to introduce serious inaccuracy. One motivation in transforming variables is not, per se, to have the most accurate possible $p$ values but rather for the model to do the best possible job—indeed, the most elegant job—of modeling the data.

7. As transformation of the dependent variable improved the fit of the residuals only moderately, the next step would be transformation of predictors. Both Income_thousands and Behavior_problems are positively skewed. Square root (or, possibly, log) transformations of these would make their shapes closer to normal. These transformed predictors could then be used in the regression, hopefully improving the residuals' fit. In multiple regression analysis, the researcher wants the dependent variable to have a shape that is close to normal; when this is not the case, residuals will hardly ever fit well. The problem in our regression is that no data transformation can make the shape of Relationship_scale close to normal. This is because fully 25% of respondents (190 of 773) obtained the highest possible score (4.0) on this scale—in essence, the distribution of Relationship_scale has no positive tail at all. In a situation such as this, tobit analysis, a highly specialized procedure, is the optimal analytic tool (Long, 1997).

8. When the correlation between two predictors is extremely high, say, $r = .90$ or above (or $-.90$ or below), it is almost assuredly the case that neither has a unique relationship to the dependent variable that is more than nontrivial in size. It rarely makes sense to include two predictors that are this strongly correlated. When the correlation between two predictors is high but not extremely so, say, $r =$ about .50–.80 (or about $-.50$ to $-.80$), then it is more likely that the unique relationship of one or both to the dependent variable is more than nontrivial. Recognize that this section summarizes a great deal of material, and, as such, has not discussed many issues. In particular, parts of the discussion assume that all variables are positively correlated; when this is not the case, some points hold approximately at best.

9. To reduce problems in multicollinearity (a) try not to use predictors that are very highly correlated and (b) limit the number of predictors strategically; in particular, do not add predictors that explain only a very small amount of additional variance.

10. Most statistical software programs issue warning messages related to multicollinearity; so, in this sense, you can let the package take the lead in assessing whether this problem is present. On the other hand, you will do well to examine correlations between predictors and to be cautious about entering highly correlated predictors in an equation.

11. In our example (see Table 23.1), we simply entered all designated predictors into our multiple regression equation. The SPSS software package terms this the *enter* approach. There are several different approaches (methods) for entering predictors in multiple regression. For instance, in the *forward* approach (a) the predictor that explains the greatest amount of variance in the dependent variable is entered; (b) the first predictor already in the equation, the predictor that most increases the explained variance is added; (c) the first two predictors already in the equation, the predictor that most increases the explained variance is added; (d) the first three predictors already in the equation, the predictor that most increases the explained variance is added; (e) and so on. This process continues until the addition of a new variable does not result in a statistically significant increase in the amount of explained variance, that is, in the value of $R^2$. It is possible that no predictors (or combination of predictors) explain significant variance in the dependent variable; in such a situation, no predictors at all are entered into the equation. (In essence, there is no equation.) The *stepwise* approach is similar to the forward approach, but it is possible for a variable already in the equation to be removed at a subsequent step. The *backward* approach is, in essence, the reverse of the forward. In the backward approach, all variables are initially entered. The variable whose removal reduces the explained variance by the least amount is then removed. That variable having been removed, the variable whose removal reduces the explained variance by the least amount is removed and so on. This process stops when a predictor's removal reduces the explained variance by a statistically significant amount. It could be the case that the removal of the first predictor results in a statistically significant decrease in the explained variance. In this case, no predictors at all would be removed. In choosing between forward, stepwise, and backward, the stepwise approach is perhaps most common and is an excellent choice (Abu-Bader, 2010). Finally, the *hierarchical* approach enters variables in an order that the researcher prescribes. In SPSS, the researcher can implement a hierarchical method by specifying the first variable to be entered as "Block 1," the second as "Block 2," the third as "Block 3," and so on. The precise way in which a particular software program implements these regression approaches can differ some from the descriptions provided in this text.

   A researcher may want several variables to be added (or removed) together at the same step in a regression. This is accomplished by designating these variables as a *block*. For instance, a researcher might want all sociodemographic variables entered at the same step; she can accomplish this by designating these variables as a block. Some regressions involve more than two dummy variables created from a given multicategory categorical variable (see note 1 in this chapter). All such dummies should be added (or removed) together, that is, that they should be in the same block. By (a) using the hierarchical approach (researcher controls entry order) and (b) designating blocks (combinations of variables to be entered at the same step), the researcher can assume near full control over the regression process. Note that as the "enter" approach in SPSS enters all variables, one does not need to be concerned about issues related to blocks; the enter approach essentially designates all variables in the regression as being in the first block (and only the first block) that is entered.

12. Though you don't need to understand logarithms to interpret logistic regression, this note provides an overview. An exponent is the power to which a number is raised. Consider the exponential expression $10^2 = 100$. In this expression, the exponent is 2. Logarithms are, in

essence, exponents. The basic difference between an exponent and a logarithm is that exponents appear in exponential expressions and logarithms appear in logarithmic ones. The dictionary defines logarithm as "the exponent of the power to which a base number must be raised to equal a given number" (The Random House Dictionary of the English Language 1987, page 1130). Consider the logarithmic expression $\log_{10}(100) = 2$. The base (base number) in this expression is 10 and the logarithm is 2. The expression conveys that the base number 10 must be raised to the 2nd power to equal 100. Consider the logarithmic expression $\log_{10}(1000) = 3$. Here the base is 10 and the log (logarithm) is 3. This expression conveys that 10 must be raised to the 3rd power to equal 1000. In the system of natural logarithms, the base is not 10 but instead is $e$. $e$ equals approximately 2.71828. Rather than using "log," natural logarithmic expressions use "ln". Consider the expression $\ln_e(7.39) = 2$. In this expression, the base is $e$ and the logarithm is 2. The expression conveys that $e$ must be raised to the 2nd power to equal 7.39. Logarithmic expressions and exponential expressions can be viewed as different ways of expressing the same information. For instance, $\ln_e(7.39) = 2$ (logarithmic expression) and $e^2 = 7.39$ (exponential expression) convey the same information. Natural logarithmic expressions can be written with the $e$ dropped. For instance, $\ln_e(7.39)$ can be written as $\ln(7.39) = 2$. Here are some natural logarithmic expressions: $\ln(2.72838) = \ln(e) = 1$; $\ln(1.00) = 0.00$, $\ln(.50) = -.694$ I note that $\ln(0)$ is undefined as is the natural log of a negative number.

13. The antilog (or antilogarithm) is the number that corresponds to a given logarithm. For instance, operating in base $e$, the antilog of 2 is 7.39 as $\ln_e(7.39) = 2$ (and also $e^2 = 7.39$). The $e^B$ coefficients in Table 23.2 are the antilogs of the $B$ coefficients. For instance as just stated, regarding Education_mom, the antilog of .229 is 1.257, that is $\ln_e(1.257) = .229$ (and also, $e^{.229} = 1.257$). When one takes the antilog of number (of a logarithm), that number (logarithm) is *exponentiated*. Observe that the $B$s in Table 23.1 are the logarithms that correspond to the $e^B$ coefficients (to the antilogs). For instance as just stated, $\ln_e(1.257) = .229$. Stated in words, .229 is the logarithm that corresponds to the antilog 1.257 (in base $e$).

14. If both factors explain significant variance, and if the factors are not highly associated, then power typically increases, at least to some degree. The next note discusses association between factors.

15. Even in the absence of an interaction effect, interpretation of main effects can be problematic. Interpretation is straightforward in designs in which sample sizes in the groups are equal and in other balanced designs (designs in which the factors are unassociated). This interpretation can be problematic when the factors are associated. For instance, if 40% of children with handicaps versus 80% of children without handicaps are placed with prior foster parents, then (because these percentages differ) handicap status and prior foster parent status are associated. Assuming that both factors in an ANOVA are indeed associated with the dependent variable, then their association with each other affects the main effects. When factors are associated, the use of the regression (unique)—sums of squares approach—is strongly recommended. This approach can eliminate the effects of association between factors on the main effects. In SPSS, this is termed the Type III Sum of Squares approach.

# CHAPTER 24

1. In analysis of variance (ANOVA), a *random factor* is a factor whose levels have been randomly selected. For instance, if one randomly selects seven classrooms from, say, 100 classrooms, "classroom" is a random factor. When a researcher carries out a significance test with a nonrandom sample, she treats that sample as a random sample. Similarly, ANOVA factors that are not selected randomly are sometimes treated as random. For instance, if all seven

classrooms in a given school participate in a study, the researcher might treat classroom as a random factor even though, in reality, the selection of classrooms was not random. (See Glass & Hopkins, 1996, pp. 536–571 to learn more about random effects ANOVA.)

2. In this section, this text presents interaction effects as part of a discussion of nonstatistical generalizability. But, as the researcher can conduct significance tests of interaction effects (see Chapter 23, Section 23.5), the examination of these effects is mostly within the domain of statistical generalizability.

## APPENDIX B

1. Formally speaking, positive numbers have two square roots, one of which is a positive number and the other of which is a negative. For instance, the two square roots of 36 are 6 and $-6$ ($6^2 = 36$ and $(-6)^2 = 36$). In common usage and as used in this text, square roots are positive numbers.

# REFERENCES

Abu-Bader, S. H. (2010). *Advanced and multivariate statistical methods for social science research with a complete SPSS guide*. Chicago, IL: Lyceum Books.

Achenbach, T. M. *Manual for the child behavior checklist 4/18 and 1991 profile*. Burlington, VT: Department of Psychiatry, University of Vermont.

American Psychological Association. (2010). *Publication manual of the American Psychological Association* (6th ed.). Washington, DC: Author.

Berzin, S. C. (2008). Difficulties in the transition to adulthood: Using propensity scoring to understand what makes foster youth vulnerable. *Social Service Review, 82*(2), 171–196. doi:10.1086/588417

Blalock, H. M., Jr. (1979). *Social statistics* (2nd ed.). New York, NY: McGraw-Hill.

Bloom, M., Fischer, J., & Orme, J. G. (2009). *Evaluating practice: Guidelines for the accountable professional* (6th ed.). Boston, MA: Pearson Higher Education.

Camilli, G., & Hopkins, K. D. (1978). Applicability of chi-square to $2 \times 2$ contingency tables with small expected cell frequencies. *Psychological Bulletin, 85*(1), 163–167.

Camilli, G., & Hopkins, K. D. (1979). Testing for association in $2 \times 2$ contingency tables with very small sample sizes. *Psychological Bulletin, 86*(5), 1011–1014.

Campbell, D. T. (1986). Relabeling internal and external validity for applied social scientists. In W. M. K. Trochim (Ed.), *Advances in quasi-experimental design analysis* (New Directions for Program Evaluation No. 31, pp. 66–77). San Francisco, CA: Jossey-Bass.

Cohen, J. (1988). *Statistical power analysis for the behavioral sciences* (2nd ed.). Hillsdale, NJ: Lawrence Erlbaum Associates.

Cohen, J., & Cohen, P. (1983). *Applied multiple regression/correlation analysis for the behavioral sciences* (2nd ed.). Hillsdale, NJ: Lawrence Erlbaum Associates.

Comstock, G., & Strasburger, V. C. (1990). Deceptive appearances: Television violence and aggressive behavior. *Journal of Adolescent Health Care, 11*(1), 31–44.

Fisher, P. A., Gunnar, M. R., Dozier, M., Bruce, J., & Pears, K. C. (2006). Effects of therapeutic interventions for foster children on behavioral problems, caregiver attachment, and stress regulatory neural systems. *Annals of the New York Academy of Sciences, 1094*, 215–225. doi:10.1196/annals.1376.023

Fleiss, J. L. (1994). Measures of effect size for categorical data. In H. Cooper & L. V. Hedges (Eds.), *The handbook of research synthesis* (pp. 245–260). New York, NY: Russell Sage Foundation.

Glass, G. V, & Hopkins, K. D. (1996). *Statistical methods in education and psychology* (3rd ed.). Boston, MA: Allyn & Bacon.

Havlicek, L. L., & Peterson, N. L. (1977). Effect of the violation of assumptions upon significance levels of the Pearson *r*. *Psychological Bulletin, 84*(2), 373–377.

Hosmer, D. W., Jr., & Lemeshow, S. (1999). *Applied survival analysis: Regression modeling of time to event data*. New York, NY: John Wiley & Sons.

Hosmer, D. W., Jr., & Lemeshow, S. (2000). *Applied logistic regression* (2nd ed.). New York, NY: John Wiley & Sons.

Kline, R. B. (2011). *Principles and practice of structural equation modeling* (3rd ed.). New York, NY: The Guilford Press.

Lazar, B. A. (1994). Why social work should care: Television violence and children. *Child and Adolescent Social Work Journal, 11*(1), 3–19.

Lenth, R. V. (2006). *Java applets for power and sample size* [Computer Software]. Retrieved from http://www.stat.uiowa.edu/~rlenth/Power/index.html

Long, J. S. (1997). *Regression models for categorical and limited dependent variables*. Thousand Oaks, CA: Sage.

McDonald, J. H. (2009). *Handbook of biological statistics*. Baltimore, MD: Sparky House. Retrieved from http://udel. edu/~mcdonald/statancova.html

Moore, D. S. (1997). *Statistics: Concepts and controversies* (4th ed.). New York, NY: W. H. Freeman.

Norušis, M. J. (1991). *The SPSS guide to data analysis for SPSS/PC+*. Chicago, IL: SPSS.

Norušis, M. J. (1997). *SPSS 7.5 guide to data analysis*. Upper Saddle River, NJ: Prentice Hall.

Norušis, M. J. (2009). *PASW statistics 18: Statistical procedures companion*. Upper Saddle River, NJ: Prentice Hall.

Norušis, M. J. (2010a). *PASW statistics 18: Advanced statistical procedures companion*. Upper Saddle River, NJ: Prentice Hall.

Pilcher, D. M. (1990). *Data analysis for the helping professions: A practical guide (SAGE sourcebooks for the human services)*. Newbury Park, CA: Sage.

*Random House Webster's dictionary* (2nd ed.). (1987). New York, NY: Random House, Inc.

Raudenbush, S. W., & Bryk, A. S. (2002). *Hierarchical linear models* (2nd ed.). Thousand Oaks, CA: Sage.

Robinson, T. N., Wilde, M. L., Navracruz, L. C., Haydel, K. F., & Varady, A. (2001). Effects of reducing children's television and video game use on aggressive behavior: A randomized controlled trial. *Archives of Pediatrics & Adolescent Medicine, 155*(1), 17–23.

Roscoe, J. T., & Byars, J. A. (1971). An investigation of the restraints with respect to sample size commonly imposed on the use of the chi-square statistic. *Journal of the American Statistical Association, 66*, 755–759.

Rosenthal, R. (1994). Parametric measures of effect size. In H. Cooper & L. V. Hedges (Eds.), *The handbook of research synthesis* (pp. 231–244). New York: Russell Sage Foundation.

Rosenthal, J. A. (2001). *Statistics and data interpretation for the helping professions*. Belmont, CA: Brooks/Cole.

Rosenthal, J.A., and Groze, V. K. (1992). *Special Needs Adoption: A Study of Intact Families*. New York, NY: Praeger

Rubin, A. (2010). *Statistics for evidence-based practice and evaluation* (2nd ed.). Belmont, CA: Brooks/Cole.

Rubin, A., & Babbie, E. (1997). *Research methods for social work* (3rd ed.). Pacific Grove, CA: Brooks/Cole.

Rubin, A., & Babbie, E. (2008). *Research methods for social work* (7th ed.). Belmont, CA: Thomson Higher Education.

Samuels, M. L., & Lu, T. C. (1992). Sample size requirements for the back-of-the-envelope binomial confidence interval. *The American Statistician, 46*(3), 228–231.

Toothaker, L. E. (1986). *Introductory statistics for the behavioral sciences*. New York, NY: McGraw-Hill.

Toothaker, L. E., & Miller, L. (1996). *Introductory statistics for the behavioral sciences* (2nd ed.). Pacific Grove, CA: Brooks/Cole.

Webster's New Collegiate Dictionary. (1979). Springfield, MA: G. & C. Merriam Company.

Wikipedia. (2010a). *Social work*. Retrieved from http://en.wikipedia.org/wiki/Social_work

Wikipedia. (2010b). *Statistics*. Retrieved from http://en.wikipedia.org/wiki/Statistics

Yaffee, R. A., & McGee, M. (2000). *An introduction to time series analysis and forecasting: With applications of SAS® and SPSS®*. San Diego, CA: Academic Press.

# INDEX

*Note.* f refers to a figure; t refers to a table.

## A

α (significance level), 202–203. *See also* statistical significance levels
  .01 and .05, 202–203
  choice on, in decision making, 228–230, 229f, 401–402
  statistical power and, 256
AB single-case design, 349–350, 349f, 350t
absolute values, 411
acceptance of null hypothesis
  definition and theory, 202
  example, 205
  meaning, 207–208
adjusted $R^2$, 368
algebra, 412
alternative hypothesis, 196–197
  acceptance of, 202
  decision making and, 231, 231t
  rejection of, 202
  in scientific inquiry, 208
analysis of covariance (ANCOVA), 378–379
analysis of variance (ANOVA), 323–330
  calculation example, SPSS, 326–328, 327t, 406
  definition and use, 323
  factorial, 375–378, 376t, 377t, 378f
  fishing expeditions
    dangers of fishing, 329–330
    dangers of not fishing, 330
  logic, 323–325
    $F$ distribution, 325, 406
    hypothesis and overview, 323–324
    two estimates of population variance, 324–325
  multiple comparison procedures, 328–329
  one-way, 375
  one-way *vs.* two-way, 376–377
  particulars
    assumptions and level of measurement, 325–326
    critical values and decision rules, 326, 406
    hypothesis pair, 326
  three-way, 376
  two-way, 376–378, 376t
  two-way factorial, 376–377
answers, to end-of-chapter problems and questions, 425–452
antecedent variable, 147
antecedent variable model, 147, 148f
applied research, 4
arbitrary zero, 10
assignment, random, 162–163, 354
  causality and, 139–140
  on confounding variable, 354–355
  definition, 8–9, 138
  to groups, 138
  systematic bias and, 140
association, 6–7, 75–84. *See also* relationship
  causal, 7
  definition, 75–76
  directional (ordinal)
    definition, use, and example, 98–100, 99t
    measure, between categorical variables, 100
  disappearance, 137t, 145, 146–147, 147t
  linear, 107
  negative, 98
  nondirectional, 98–99
  persistence, 145–146
  positive, 98
  size (strength) of, 80, 354, 392
    balanced model for data interpretation, 393–395
    chi-square test of independence, 317, 317t
    definition, 80, 392
    qualitative descriptors, 81–82, 81t
    statistical power and, 252–254, 253t

association (*cont.*)
  between two ordinal-level categorical variables,
      test, 345
  variation by subgroup, 145
  weakening, 145, 146, 146t
assumptions
  normality, 220
  of statistical significance tests, 220
attributes, 5
attribution, causal. *See* causality
autocorrelation, 351–352, 352t
average, 29


**B**

*B* (regression coefficient)
  meaning, 118
  multiple regression analysis, 365–367, 366t
  *vs. r*, 119–120
balanced model for data interpretation, 393–395
bar, 21
bar charts, 21–22, 21f, 22f
baseline (A) phase, 349–350, 350t
bell-shaped curve, 51
best fit line, 118–119
β (regression coefficient), 365–367
bias
  nonresponse, 163, 187
  sampling, 163
  systematic, random assignment and, 140
bimodal distribution, 58, 59f
binary variable, 5
binomial distribution, 298, 298f
  critical values: one-tailed test, alpha = .05, 404
  theory, 167
binomial statistical significance, 203
binomial test, 297–300
  behavior problems example, 298–299, 298f, 404
  carrying out, 298f, 299–300
  function and use, 297–298
bivariate standardized regression equation, 115
bivariate statistics
  key concepts, 6–7
  tests, 417
bivariate unstandardized regression equation, 118


**C**

case, 4
categorical variables, 77. *See also specific variables*
  definition, 5
  direction association between, measure, 100
  two ordinal-level, tests of association between, 345
  variability, 40–41, 40t

causal attribution. *See* causality
causal conclusion, 354
causality, 7, 354
  balanced model for data interpretation,
      393–395
  correlation and, 115
  definition, 135, 392
  introduction, 135
  multiple variables, control for, 149–150
  random assignment and, 139–140
  randomization and, 9
  social science, 135
  statistical significance and, 354–356
causal models
  antecedent variable model, 147, 148f
  effects, 148–149
  intervening variable model, 147–148, 148f
causal relationship (association), 7, 135
  direct, 149
  indirect, 149
causation. *See* causality
cause, in social science, 135
cell, table, 77t, 78
cell frequencies, 77t, 78
cell percentages, 77t, 78
central limit theorem *(CLT)*, 168–170, 169f,
      179–180
central tendency, 29–33, 52, 52f
  definition, 29
  key univariate statistic concepts, 29
  measures, 54f–56f, 55–57
    skewness on, 54f, 55–57, 56f
    tails and, 52, 52f
  measures, three key, 29
    choosing between, 32–33, 32t
    mean, 29, 31–32
    median, 29, 30–31, 31t
    mode, 29, 30
chance, 355
charts
  bar, 21–22, 21f, 22f
  pie, 24–25, 25f
chi-square ($\chi^2$) distribution, 300, 405
chi-square ($\chi^2$) test, one variable
  completing example, 302–303, 302t, 303f, 405
  formula, 423
  function and use, 300
  observed and expected frequencies, 301, 423
  test particulars, 301–302, 405
chi-square ($\chi^2$) test of independence, 311–317
  carrying out, 314–316
    comments on example, 316, 316t
    hypothesis testing model and calculations,
        314–315, 315f, 315t, 405

comments, 316–317
decision rule and requirements, 313–314, 404
degrees of freedom, 312, 423
description and use, 312t
distribution and degrees of freedom, 312
expected column proportion, 423
formula, 313, 423
hypothesis pair, 311–312
*not* a measure of size of association, 317, 317t
observed and expected frequencies, 313, 314t, 424
observed and expected proportions, 312–313, 312t
classification, of variables, 9
clinical trials
nonrandomized, 8
randomized, 8
closed-ended questions, 353
codes, 11
coefficient
exponentiated, 375
Pearson's correlation (*see* Pearson's correlation
coefficient (Pearson's *r*))
regression *(B)*
meaning, 118
in multiple regression analysis, 365–366
*vs. r*, 119–120
regression (β), 365–367, 366t
standardized, 119
unstandardized, 119–120
coefficient of determination ($r^2$), 114
collinearity, 373
column, 21
column totals, 77, 77t
column variable, 77, 77t
common cause model, 147, 148f
common denominator, 412
confidence intervals, 179–189
comments, 343
definition, 179
margin of error and, 187
if $N < 100$, 271–273
if $N \geq 100$, 271–273
95%, 179–181, 181f, 403
99%, 179, 183
nonresponse on, 187
other applications, 188
population size on, 187
proportions and percentages, 184–187
formulas and application, 185–187
theory, 184–185, 185f
random selection, 187
values, 403
confidence intervals of the mean, 179–184
formulas and computation, 181–184, 403, 423
95%, 181–183, 403, 422

99%, 183–184, 403, 422
small samples, 271–273, 403
*t* distribution
theory and calculation, 271–272, 403
*vs.* normal distribution, 272–273
theory, 179–181, 181f
confidence level, 184
confounding variable, 7, 9, 136–138, 137t
controlling for, 143–152
basic concepts, 143–145, 144t
causal models
antecedent variable model, 147, 148f
effects, 148–149
intervening variable model, 147–148, 148f
different patterns following control, 145
initial relationship disappears, 137t, 145,
146–147, 147t
initial relationship weakens, 145, 146, 146t
interaction effects, 150–151, 150t, 151t
multiple variables and causality, 149–150
random assignment, 140, 354–355
constant, 5
constant, holds, 143–145
context, 387
contingency table
assessing relationship using, 78–79, 78t, 79t
odds ratio in, 93–95, 94t
reading, 77–78, 77t
$> 2 \times 2$, relationship in, 97–98, 97t
contingency table analysis, 77
control group, 130–131, 139
control variable, 137
conversion
scores, 61
*z* scores, 61–62
correlated samples
definition, 288
*t* test, 288–289
correlation
causality and, 115
curvilinear relationship and, 116–117, 117f
negative (inverse), 107, 108–109, 109f
nominal-level variables, 120
ordinal-level variables, 120
perfect, 111–112, 112f
positive, 107, 108–109, 109f
scatterplots
negative, 108–109, 109f
positive, 108–109, 108f, 109f
correlation coefficient (Pearson's *r*). *See* Pearson's
correlation coefficient (Pearson's *r*)
correlation matrix, 340–341, 342t
correlation ratio ($\eta^2$), 131
counts, 10, 21f, 22

Cox proportional hazards model, 380
Cramer's *V,* 97–98, 99–100, 113t
critical regions, 225
critical values, 228. *See also specific values*
  binomial distribution: one-tailed test,
    alpha = .05, 404
  chi-square distribution, 405
  *F* distribution, 406
  Pearson's *r,* 407
  *t* distribution, 403
crosstabs (cross tabulation) tables
  for assessing relationship, 78–79, 78t, 79t
  reading, 77–78, 77t
cross tabulation, 77
cumulative frequency, 19–20, 20t
cumulative percentage, 20, 421
curve, bell-shaped (normal), 51
curvilinear relationship, 112, 116–117, 117f

**D**
*D%* (difference in percentages)
  definition and use, 80–81
  formula, 421
  *vs.* risk ratio, 84
*D,* Somers', 100, 345
data, 4
data presentation, 19–25. *See also specific topics*
  figures, 21–25
    bar charts, 21–22, 21f, 22f
    box plots, 23–24, 24f
    definition, 21
    frequency polygons, 23, 23f
    histograms, 22, 22f
    pie charts, 24–25, 25f
  frequency distributions and tables, 19–21
    grouped frequency distribution, 20, 21t
    table cell, 77t, 78
    table cell frequencies, 77t, 78
    table cell percentages, 77t, 78
    table column totals, 77, 77t
    table margins, 77–78, 77t
data transformation, 347–349, 348f
decision making
  choice on significance level, 228–230, 229f, 403
  null and alternative hypotheses, 231, 231t
decision rules. *See also specific measures*
  inferential statistics, 227–228, 401–402
  more, for one-tailed, 234–236, 234f, 235f,
    401–402
degree of similarity, 390
degrees of freedom *(df),* 269. *See also specific tests
  and measures*
  *t* distribution and, 270, 270f

denominator, 409
denominator, common, 412
dependent observations, 288
dependent pair, 287–288
dependent samples
  definition, 288
  tests, 345–346, 346t
dependent samples *t* test
  example, increased power from positive
    correlation, 289, 403
  requirements, 288–289
  statistical power and, 288
dependent variable, 7–8, 254–255
descriptive statistics, 6, 161
deviation score, 42, 43
deviation score from the mean, 42, 43, 421
dichotomous measures, 416
dichotomous variable, 5
difference, 409
difference in percentages *(D%)*
  definition and use, 80–81
  formula, 421
  *vs.* risk ratio, 84
difference in population, statistical power and,
    252–254, 253t
differences, measurement, 10. *See also
    specific types*
direct causal relationship, 149
direct effect, 147
directional association (relationship)
  definition, use, and example, 98–100, 99t
  measure, between categorical variables, 100
directional hypotheses, 199–200, 256–257
directional hypothesis pairs, 225–226, 225t
  definitions and examples, 199–200
  guidelines, 200–201
  one-sample *t* test, 274
disappearance of association, 137t, 145,
    146–147, 147t
distribution, 19. *See also specific types*
  binomial, 298, 298f
  binomial, critical values: one-tailed test,
    alpha = .05, 404
  chi-square, 300, 405
  definition, 51
  empirical, 51
  frequency, 19, 20t
  frequency, grouped, 20, 21t
  normal *(see* normal distribution)
  sample size and, 269
  sampling *(see* sampling distribution)
  sampling distribution of the mean, 168–170
    definition and example, 168–170, 169f
    sample size and, 170–172, 171f, 171t

distribution-free tests, 343–344
distribution shape, 29, 51–66
  bimodal, 58, 59f
  central tendency and tails, 52, 52f
  definition, 51
  kurtosis, 57, 57f
  normal, 51–52, 52f (*see also* normal
    distribution)
    percentages, 58–61, 59f, 60f
    standard deviations, 52, 53f
  skewed, 53–57
    characteristics, 53–55, 54f, 55f
    skewness and measures of central tendency,
      54f, 55–57, 56f
  symmetric, 51, 52f
  theoretical, 51
  uniform (flat, rectangular), 58, 58f
  *z* scores, 61–66 (*see also z* score)


**E**
effect
  direct, 147
  indirect, 148
  interaction, 150–151, 150t, 151t
effect size, 80
effect size for means ($ES_{means}$), 130–131, 422
efficient estimator, 165
empirical distribution, 51
end notes, 453–466
English letter symbols, 419–420
equality of variances
  assumption, 284
  formula, 284–285
  test, 284
equal variances formula, 284
error
  at .05 level
    type I, 257
    type II, 257
  margin of, 187
  roundoff, 413
  sampling, 166
    formula, 422
    null hypothesis and, 201
  standard error of the mean ($\sigma_{\bar{x}}$), 168, 272, 422
  standard error of the proportion *(p)*, 184–185,
    185f, 422
  type I, 230–231, 231t, 257
  type II, 230–231, 231t, 257
$ES_{means}$, 130–131
estimate. *See also specific measures*
  interval, 165
  point, 165

estimators, 165
  characteristics, 165
  definition, 164
  efficient, 165
  unbiased, 165
(eta)$\eta^2$, 131
eta squared ($\eta^2$), 131
event history analysis, 379–380
evidence-based practice, 3, 4
expected frequency, in chi-square ($\chi^2$) test
  of independence, 313, 314t, 424
  one variable, 301, 423
expected proportion, in chi-square ($\chi^2$) test
  of independence, 312–313, 312t, 423
  one variable, 301
experiment, 138
  preexperiment, 138
  quasi-experiment, 138
  true, 138
experimental designs, 138. *See also specific types*
  random assignment to groups, 138
  types, 138
experimental group, 130–131, 139
exponentiated coefficient, 375
extraneous variable, 137, 255–256
extreme value, 32


**F**
factor analysis, 380
factorial analysis of variance, 375–378, 376t,
    377t, 378f
factorial design, 376
failure in rejection (acceptance) of null hypothesis
  definition and theory, 202
  example, 205
  meaning, 207–208
family member, 270
family of *t* distributions, 270–271, 270f, 271f
*F* distribution, 325, 406
fences, 23–24, 24f
figures, 21–25
  bar charts, 21–22, 21f, 22f
  box plots, 23–24, 24f
  definition, 21
  frequency polygons, 23, 23f
  histograms, 22, 22f
  pie charts, 24–25, 25f
Fisher's exact test, 317
fishing
  dangers of, 329–330
  dangers of not, 330
flat distribution, 58, 58f
formulas, 421–424

fractions, 411–412
*F* ratio, 424
frequency, 19
   binomial distribution: one-tailed test,
      alpha = .05, 404
   binomial test, 299
   cumulative, 19–20, 20t
   expected
      chi-square test, one variable, 301, 423
      chi-square test of independence, 313, 314t, 424
   observed
      chi-square test, one variable, 301
      chi-square test of independence, 313
frequency distribution, 19–21, 20t
frequency distribution, grouped, 20, 21t
frequency distribution table, 19, 20t
frequency polygons, 23, 23f

**G**
gamma ($\gamma$), 100, 345
generalizability, 387–392
   balanced model for data interpretation, 393–395
   definition, 387, 392
   inferential statistics and, 387–390
   nonstatistical, 391
   nonstatistical tools in, 390–392
   statistical, 388
   tools for assessment, 388
generalization
   nonstatistical, 391
   statistical, 388
goodness-of-fit chi-square ($\chi^2$) test, 300–303
   chi-square distribution, 300, 405
   completing example, 302–303, 302t, 303f, 405
   function and use, 300
   observed and expected frequencies, 301
   test particulars, 301–302, 405
Greek letter symbols, 419
group, 285
grouped frequency distribution, 20, 21t
grouped frequency distribution table, 20, 21t

**H**
histograms, 22, 22f
holds constant, 143–145
homogeneity of variances
   assumption, 284
   formula, 284–285
   test, 284
hypothesis
   directional, 199–200
   nondirectional, 199

hypothesis pairs
   ANOVA, 326
   chi-square test of independence, 311–312
   common pattern, 197–199
   definition and example, 197
   directional
      definitions and examples, 199–200,
         203–205, 204f
      guidelines, 200–201
      large sample test of the means,
         225–226, 225t
      one-sample *t* test, 274
   large sample test of the mean
      directional, 225–226, 225t
      nondirectional, 224–225
   nondirectional, 224–225
      definitions and examples, 199–200,
         203–205, 204f
      guidelines, 200–201
      one-sample *t* test, 274
      in one-sample *t* test, 274
   statistical significance tests, 197–201
      common pattern, 197–199
      definition and example, 197
      directional and nondirectional, 199–201,
         203–205, 204f
   *t* test, independent samples, 283–284
   *t* test, one-sample
      assumptions and formula, 273–274
      decision rules, 274, 403
hypothesis testing (model), 219–220. *See also*
         statistical significance tests
   chi-square test of independence, 314–315, 315f,
      315t, 405
   comments, 343
   large sample test of the mean ($\bar{X}$), 219–221
   Pearson's correlation coefficient *(r)*,
      338–340, 407

**I**
importance, 392–393
   balanced model for data interpretation, 393–395
   practical, 392
independence
   of observation, 162
   of selection, 162
independent samples, 287
   parametric tests, 345
   tests, 345
   *t* test, 283–288
      assumptions and formulas, 284–285, 423
      formula, 423
      hypothesis pairs, 283–284

independence assumption, 287–288
  purpose and sampling distribution, 283
  SPSS software package, 285–287,
    286t, 403
independent variables. *See also* relationship
  definition, 75–76
  reduced variability of, statistical power and,
    254–255
indirect causal relationship, 149
indirect effect, 148
inferential statistics, 6, 161–172
  central limit theorem, 168–170, 169f
  definition, 164
  estimators
    characteristics, 165
    definition, 164
    efficient, 165
    unbiased, 165
  generalizability, 387–390
  procedures, 161
  random samples
    advantages, 163–164
    definition, 159, 161
    percentages and normal distribution, 61
    random assignment, 162–163
    random samples, 161–163
    random selection, 162–163
    skew, 56
    *vs.* descriptive statistics, 161
  sampling distribution of the mean
    definition and example, 168–170, 169f
    sample size and, 170–172, 171f
  sampling distributions, 166–170
    building, 166–167, 167f
    concepts, 166
    definition, 166
    histogram of coin flips, 166–167
  sampling error, 166
  statistics and parameters, 164, 164t
interaction, 150–151t, 150t, 151t, 377
interaction effects, 150–151, 150t, 151t, 377
interquartile range *(IQR)*, 41, 421
interval estimate, 165
interval level of measurement, 10
interval/ratio-level of measurement, 10
interval/ratio measures, 416
intervening variable, 147–148
intervening variable model, 147–148, 148f
intervention, 8, 138
intervention (B) phase, 349–350, 350t
inverse correlation
  definition, 107
  scatterplots, 108–109, 109f
*IQR,* 41

K
Kendall's tau-b $(\tau_b)$, 100, 345
Kendall's tau-c $(\tau_c)$, 100, 345
Kruskal-Wallis test, 345
kurtosis, 57, 57f

L
large sample test of the mean $(\overline{X})$, 219–237
  choice on significance level in decision making,
    228–230, 229f, 401–402
  decision making and null and alternative
    hypotheses, 231, 231t
  decision rules, more, for one-tailed, 234–236,
    234f, 235f, 401–402
  definitions and assumptions of, 220
  formula, 423
  hypothesis pairs
    directional, 225–226, 225t
    nondirectional, 224–225
  hypothesis testing model for, 219–221
  rejecting the null and "real" things, 236–237
  sample distribution
    significance test using, 226
    statistical tests and, 221–224, 222f–224f,
      401–402
  statistical significance test
    carrying out, 227
    decision rules, 227–228, 401–402
    making decision, 228
  two-tailed *vs.* one-tailed tests in
    carrying out example, 226f, 232, 233f, 401–402
    determining exact value of study sample
      result, 233–234
  type I and II errors, 230–231, 231t
  use, 219
level, 376. *See also* significance level
levels of measurement, 9–11
  interval, 10
  interval/ratio, 10
  nominal, 9, 10
  ordinal, 9, 10–11
  ratio, 10
linear association, 107
linear relationship, 116
logic. *See also specific tests*
  of science, 208
logistic regression, 374–375, 374t
logistic regression, ordinal, 375
logistic regression equation formulas
  predicting log of odds, 424
  predicting odds, 424
logit, 374–375, 374t, 424
log of the odds, 374–375, 374t, 424

lower tail, 52, 52f
lurking variable, 137


**M**
main effect, 376
Mann-Whitney *U* test, 344, 345
margin of error, 187
margins, table, 77–78, 77t
matched pair, 287–288
matched samples
   definition, 288
   *t* test, 288–289
math review, 409–413
   absolute values, 411
   algebra, 412
   fractions, 411–412
   operations
      basic, 409
      order of, 410
   percentages, 413
   percentiles, 413
   positive and negative numbers, 410–411
   proportions, 413
   ratios, 413
   rounding, 413
   roundoff error, 413
   squares and square roots, 411
   symbols, 409–410
   terms, basic, 409
McNemar's test, 346, 346t
*MD*, 41–42
mean *(X̄)*, 31–32, 164t
   definition, 29
   difference between, sampling distribution, 283
   normal distribution, 51–52, 52f
   sample, 421
   skewed distribution, 56–57, 56f
   skewness on, 54f, 55f, 56
   trimmed, 33
mean deviation *(MD)*, 41–42, 421
mean difference, standardized *(SMD)*, 127–130
   caution, 130
   definition and applications, 127–128, 128t
   formula, 127
   graphical interpretation, 128–129, 128t, 129f
   qualitative descriptors of size and strength
      association of, 128, 128t
mean square between, 424
mean square within, 424
measurement. *See also specific types*
   levels (scales), 9–11
   objective, 4
   variables, 4–5

measures. *See also specific measures*
   association, 416
   choosing, 32
median, 30–31, 31t
   definition, 29
   normal distribution, 51–52, 52f
   skewed distribution, 56–57, 56f
   strongly skewed distributions, 54f, 55f, 56
mediating variable, 147–148
mediation model, 147–148, 148f
midrange, 41
minus sign, 410
mode
   definition, 29, 30
   normal distribution, 51–52, 52f
   skewed distribution, 56–57, 56f
moderation, 150–151t, 150t, 151t
multicollinearity, 373
multi-item scale, 11
multilevel modeling, 379
multiple analysis of variance (MANOVA), 379
multiple comparison procedures, in ANOVA, 328–329
multiple correlation coefficient *(R)*, 367
multiple correlation coefficient, square *(R²)*, 368
multiple regression analysis, 150. *See also*
      multivariate regression analysis
multiple regression equation, unstandardized, 424
multivariate analysis, 149–150. *See also specific types*
   advantages, 370–374, 370f
   related to ANOVA
      analysis of covariance, 378–379
      multiple analysis of variance, 379
      repeated measures designs, 379
   tests, 417
multivariate regression analysis, 365–374
   advantages
      multicollinearity, 373
      review, 373
      two modestly correlated predictors,
         371–372, 372f
      two uncorrelated predictors, 370–371, 371f
      two very highly correlated predictors,
         372–373, 372f
   assumptions, 368–370, 368f, 369f
   equation and introduction, 365–368, 366t
multivariate statistics
   key concepts, 7
   tests, 417


**N**
*N*, 19
*N* < 100, confidence intervals and significance test
      for means, 271–273

$N \geq$ 100, confidence intervals and significance test
    for means, 271–273
nanrandom samples, significance tests and, 260
negative association, 98
negative (inverse) correlation
    definition, 107
    scatterplots, 108–109, 109f
negatively skewed distribution
    definition and examples, 53–54, 55f, 56
    mode, median, and mean, 56–57, 56f
negative numbers, 410–411
negative of, 411
negative outlier, 32
negative relationship, 98
negative sign, 410
negative tail, 52, 52f
95% confidence interval, 179–181, 181f, 401–402
95% confidence interval of *P*, 185–186
95% confidence interval of the mean, 181–183,
    401–402, 422
95% confidence interval of the proportion,
    185–186, 422
99% confidence interval, 183
99% confidence interval of *P*, 186–187, 422, 423
99% confidence interval of the mean, 183–184,
    401–402, 422
99% confidence interval of the proportion,
    186–187, 422, 423
nominal level of measurement, 9, 10
nominal-level variables, correlation, 120
nondirectional association, 98–99
nondirectional hypothesis, 199
nondirectional hypothesis pairs, 224–225
    definitions and examples, 199–200, 203–205,
        204f
    guidelines, 200–201
    one-sample *t* test, 274
nondirectional relationship, 98–99
nonparametric tests. *See also specific tests*
    definition, uses, examples, 343–344
    *vs.* parametric, choice, 346–347
nonprobability sample, 5, 161–162
nonrandomized clinical trials, 8
nonrandomized studies, 8
nonrandom sample, 5, 161–162
nonrandom sampling, 5
nonresponse bias, 163, 187
nonstatistical generalizability, 391
nonstatistical generalization, 391
normal curve, 51
normal distribution, 51–52, 52f
    definition, 51
    mean, median, and mode, 51–52, 52f
    percentage of cases in selected areas, 401–402

percentages, 58–61, 59f, 60f
    areas above and below mean, 53f, 59, 59f
    cases >1 *SD* above mean, 53f, 59, 60f
    cases >1-3 *SD* below mean, 53f, 60
    inferential statistics, 61
    probability, 196, 401–402
    standard deviations, 52, 53f
    *z* scores and percentages of cases
        with both sides of distribution, 64–65, 65f,
            66f, 401–402
        with one side of distribution, 63–64, 64f,
            401–402
normality assumption, 220
notes, 453–466
not statistically significant, 209
nuisance variable, 137
null hypothesis, 196–197
    decision making and, 231, 231t
    failure in rejection (acceptance)
        definition and theory, 202
        example, 205
        meaning, 207–208
    rejection
        definition, 202
        example, 203–204, 204f
        meaning, 206–207
        "real things," 236–237
    scientific inquiry, 208
    significance tests, 201
    statistical significance tests, 196–197
numerator, 409
numeric variable, 5


**O**
observation
    dependent, 288
    independence of, 162
observational studies, 138
observed frequency
    chi-square test, one variable, 301
    chi-square test of independence, 313
observed proportion
    chi-square test, one variable, 301
    chi-square test of independence, 312–313,
        312t
obtained statistic, 227
odds, 421
    logistic regression equation, predicting, 424
    log of, 374–375, 374t, 424
    variations, 93–94
odds ratio *(OR)*, 93–96
    advantages, 96
    basics and formula, 93–95, 94t

odds ratio *(OR) (cont.)*
  contingency table, 93–95, 94t
  definition, 93
  formula, 422
  interpretation, 95–96, 95t
  qualitative descriptors, 95–96, 95t
one-sample test of a proportion *(p),* 295–297
  carrying out behavior problems example,
      296–297, 297f
  definition and application, 295
  formula, 423
  theory and basics, 295–296
one-sample *t* test, 273–277
  assumptions, hypothesis pairs, and formula,
      273–274
  carrying out, 274–277, 276f, 403
  decision rules, 274, 403
  formula, 423
one-tailed test, 225–226
  large sample test of the mean, more decision
      rules, 234–236, 234f, 235f, 401–402
  statistical power and, 256–257
  *vs.* two-tailed tests
    carrying out example, 226f, 232, 233f,
        401–402
    determining exact value of study sample
        result, 233–234
one variable chi-square ($\chi^2$) test, 300–303
  chi-square distribution, 300, 405
  completing example, 302–303, 302t, 303f, 405
  function and use, 300
  observed and expected frequencies, 301, 423
  test particulars, 301–302, 405
one-way ANOVA, 375–377
open-ended questions, 353
operations, math
  basic, 409
  order of, 410
*OR,* 93–96. *See also* odds ratio *(OR)*
ordering
  rank, 9
  variables, 9
ordinal association
  definition, use, and example, 98–100, 99t
  measure, between categorical variables, 100
ordinal level of measurement, 9, 10–11
ordinal-level variables, 9, 10–11
  categorical, tests of association between
      two, 345
  correlation, 120
ordinal logistic regression, 375
ordinal measures, 416
ordinal probit regression, 375

ordinal relationship
  definition, use, and example, 98–100, 99t
  measure, between categorical variables, 100
outlier, 32
  negative, 32
  positive, 32


**P**
*p. See* proportion
*p* < .05, 202–203, 207, 209
pair
  dependent (matched), 287–288
  hypothesis (*see* hypothesis pairs)
  *t* test, 288–289
paired samples, 288
paired samples *t* test, 288–289
parameters, 164, 164t
parametric tests. *See also specific tests*
  of association between two ordinal-level
      categorical variables, 345
  definition, uses, examples, 343–344
  for dependent samples, 345–346, 346t
  for independent samples, 345
  significance test of Spearman's *r,* 345
  *vs.* nonparametric, choice, 346–347
Pearson chi-square, 316, 316t
Pearson's correlation coefficient (Pearson's *r*)
  correlation matrix, 340–341, 342t
  critical values, 407
  definition, 107
  formula, 109–111, 110t, 422
  interpreting, caution, 117–118
  multiple, 367
  multiple, squared, 368
  multiple correlation, 367
  multiple correlation, squared, 368
  predicted change, 115–116
  sampling distribution of *r,* 340, 341f
  squared multiple, 368
  statistical significance, 337–340
    assumptions and level of measurement, 337
    basic logic, 337
    decision rules and degrees of freedom,
        338, 407
    hypothesis pair, 338
    hypothesis testing, 338–340, 407
  understanding, 111–115
    absolute value of *r,* 113
    coefficient of determination, 114–115
    0.00 correlation, 112
    negative correlation, 114, 114f
    perfect correlations, 111–112, 112f

positive correlation, 113–114, 113f
    size and strength of association, 113, 113f
    *vs.* regression coefficient *(B),* 119–120
percentage, 413, 421
    cell (table), 77t, 78
    confidence intervals, 184–187
        formulas and application, 185–187
        theory, 184–185, 185f
    cumulative, 20, 421
    normal distribution and, 58–61, 59f, 60f
        areas above and below mean, 53f, 59, 59f
        cases >1 *SD* above mean, 53f, 59, 60f
        cases >1-3 *SD* below mean, 53f, 60
        inferential statistics, 61
    row (table), 77t, 78
percentage difference *(D%)*
    definition and use, 80–81
    *vs.* risk ratio, 84
percentile, 23–24, 24f, 413
percentile rank, 23–24, 24f
perfect correlation, 111–112, 112f
persistence, of association, 145–146
phi *(r_{phi})*, 120
pie charts, 24–25, 25f
plot, box (whisker), 23–24, 24f
point estimate, 165
polygon, frequency, 23, 23f
population
    definition, 5
    difference in, statistical power and, 252–254, 253t
    size, on confidence intervals, 187
population distribution
    nonnormal shape, 168–169, 169f
    normal shape, 169–170, 169f
population variance, two estimates, 324–325
positive association, 98
positive correlation
    definition, 107
    scatterplots, 108–109, 109f
positively skewed distribution
    definition and examples, 53, 54f, 55–56
    mode, median, and mean, 56–57, 56f
positive numbers, 410–411
positive outlier, 32
positive relationship, 98
positive sign, 411
positive tail, 52, 52f
posttest, 287
power. *See also* statistical power
    definition, 247
    formula, 423
practical importance, 392
practical significance, 392

predictors, 365
preexperiment, 138
preintervention (A) phase, 349–350, 350t
pretest, 255–256, 287
probabilistic conclusions, 206, 355
probability *(p)*
    definition and formula, 195–196
    event with given characteristic, 423
    normal distribution and, 196, 401–402
probability sample. *See* random (probability)
        samples
probit regression, 375
probit regression, ordinal, 375
problems, answers to, 425–452
product, 409
proof, 206
proportion
    expected
        chi-square test, one variable, 301
        chi-square test of independence, 312–313,
            312t, 423
    observed
        chi-square test, one variable, 301
        chi-square test of independence, 312–313, 312t
proportion *(P)*
    95% confidence interval of, 185–186, 422
    99% confidence interval of, 186–187, 422, 423
proportion *(p),* 164t, 413
proportion *(p)*
    confidence intervals for, 184–187
        formulas and application, 185–187
        theory, 184–185, 185f
    one-sample test of, 295–297
        carrying out behavior problems example,
            296–297, 297f
        definition and application, 295
        theory and basics, 295–296
    sampling distribution of, 184
    standard error of, 184–185, 185f, 422
proximal, 390
*p* value (statistical significance), 202–203
    definition and theory, 201
    examples, 203–205, 204f
    failure in rejecting (accepting) the null and,
        207–208
    more interpretations, 205–206
    rejecting the null and, 206–207


**Q**

qualitative descriptors
    odds ratio, 95–96, 95t *(see also* odds ratio *(OR))*
    size and strength of relationship, 81–82, 81t

qualitative methods and statistics, 4, 352–353
qualitative variables
  definition, 5
  variability, 40–41, 40t
quantitative research methods, 4
quantitative variable, 5
quasi-experiments, 138
questions, answers to, 425–452
quotient, 409

**R**
$R^2$, 368
*r* (Pearson's correlation coefficient). *See* Pearson's
    correlation coefficient (Pearson's *r*)
$r^2$ (coefficient of determination), 114
$R^2$ adjusted, 368
random assignment, 162–163, 354
  causality and, 139–140
  on confounding variable, 354–355
  definition, 8–9, 138
  to groups, 138
  systematic bias and, 140
randomization. *See* random assignment
randomized clinical trials, 8
randomized studies, 8
random (probability) samples, 161–163
  definition, 5, 161
  independence of observation, 162
  independence of selection, 162
  inferential statistics, 6
  random assignment *vs.*, 162–163
  random selection, 161–162
  sampling, 162–163
  selection, 161
  simple random sample, 162
random sampling (selection), 162–163, 354
  assumption, 220
  confidence intervals, 187
  definition, 5
range, 41, 421
range, interquartile, 41
rank(ing)
  percentile, 23–24, 24f
  variables, 9
rank ordering, 9
ratio, 413
ratio level of measurement, 10
raw score, 61
real explanations, 208
reasoning, with data, 354–356
reciprocal, 412
rectangular distribution, 58, 58f
reduce (fraction), 412

regression, 115, 118–120
  logistic, 374–375, 374t
  probit, 375
  regression equation, 118
  regression line, 118–119, 119f
  scatterplot, 118, 119f
regression analysis
  multiple, 150
  multivariate (*see* multivariate regression
    analysis)
regression coefficient
  *B*
    meaning, 118
    multiple regression analysis, 365–366
    *vs. r*, 119–120
   β, 365–367, 366t
regression equation, 118
regression line, 118–119, 119f
rejection of null hypothesis
  definition, 202
  example, 203–204, 204f
  meaning, 206–207
  "real" things, 236–237
rejection regions, 225
related samples
  definition, 288
  *t* test, 288–289
related variables, 6–7
relationship, 75–84. *See also* association
  categorical variables, 77
  causal, 7, 135
    direct, 149
    indirect, 149
  comments, 76–77
  contingency tables
    assessing relationship using, 78–79,
      78t, 79t
    reading, 77–78, 77t
  contingency tables > 2 × 2, 97–98, 97t
  curvilinear, 112, 116–117, 117f
  definition, 75–76
  difference in percentages, 80–81
  difference in percentages *vs.* risk ratio, 82
  directional (ordinal)
    definition, use, and example, 98–100, 99t
    measure, between categorical variables, 100
  linear, 116
  negative, 98
  nondirectional, 98–99
  positive, 98
  risk ratio, 82–84
  size (strength)
    definition, 80
    qualitative descriptors, 81–82, 81t

size (strength), statistical power and, 252–254, 253t
  between variables, 208
relative risk *(RR)*, 82–84
repeated measures designs, 379
replication, 391
research, 4. *See also specific topics*
research hypothesis, 196–197
  acceptance, 202
  decision making, 231, 231t
  rejection, 202
  scientific inquiry, 208
residual, 368–370, 368f, 369f
risk ratio *(RR)*, 421
  definition and use, 82–84
  *vs.* difference in percentages, 82
robust, 220
rounding, 413
roundoff error, 413
row percentages, 77t, 78
row totals, 77t, 78
row variable, 77, 77t
$r_{phi}$, 120
$r_{ranks}$, 120


**S**
*s. See* standard deviation *(SD, s)*
$s^2$, 44–45, 164t
sample, 5. *See also specific types*
  correlated
    definition, 288
    *t* test, 288–289
  dependent, 288
    definition, 288
    tests, 345–346, 346t
  independent *(see* independent samples)
  large, test of the mean $(\bar{X})$, 219–237 *(see also* large sample test of the mean $(\bar{X})$)
  matched
    definition, 288
    *t* test, 288–289
  nonrandom (nonprobability)
    definition, 5
    significance tests and, 260
  paired, 288
  random (probability) *(see* random (probability) samples)
  related
    definition, 288
    *t* test, 288–289
  simple random, 162
  study, 5
sample mean, 421

sample size *(N)*, 19
  distributions, 269
  sampling distribution of the mean, 170–172, 171f
  small, confidence intervals for means, 271–273, 401–402
  statistical power, 247–252
    examples, 248–252, 249f, 251f
    necessary size, 257–259, 259t
    theory, 247–248
sampling
  definition, 5
  nonrandom, 5
  random, 5, 162–163
sampling bias, 163
sampling distribution, 166–170
  binomial, 298, 298f
  binomial, critical values: one-tailed test, alpha = .05, 404
  building, 166–167, 167f
  definition, 166
  of difference between means, 283
  of *p*, 184
  of the proportion, 184
  of *r*, 340, 341f
  of significance tests, 222
  significance test using, 226, 226f
  statistical tests and, 221–224, 222f–224f, 401–402
  and 2.5 tails, 223, 223f
  of $\bar{X}$, 170–172, 171f, 171t, 222–223, 222f
sampling distribution of the mean, 168–172
  definition and example, 168–170, 169f
  sample size and, 170–172, 171f, 171t
sampling error, 166
  formula, 422
  null hypothesis, 201
scale. *See also specific scales*
  measurement, 9–11
    nominal, 9
    ordinal, 9
  multi-item, 11
scatterplots, 108–109, 108f, 109f
science
  logic, 208
  research, 4
scientific inquiry, null and alternative hypotheses in, 208
score(s), 5. *See also specific types*
  raw, 61
  transformation (conversion) of, 61
  *z,* 61–66 *(see also z* score)
*SD* (standard deviation), 42–44, 43t, 164t
  formula, 421
  within groups, 127

*SD* (standard deviation)(*cont.*)
  normal distribution, 52, 53f
  predicted change in units, 115–116
selection
  independence of, 162
  random, 161–163, 187, 354 (*see also* random
      (probability) samples)
    assumption, 220
    confidence intervals, 187
    definition, 5
serial dependency, 351–352, 352t, 353f
shape of distribution, 29, 51–66
  bimodal distribution, 58, 59f
  central tendency and tails, 52, 52f
  definition, 51
  kurtosis, 57, 57f
  normal distribution, 51–52, 52f
  percentages and normal distribution, 58–61,
      59f, 60f
  skewed distributions, 53–57
    characteristics, 53–55, 54f, 55f
    skewness and measures of central tendency,
        54f, 55–57, 56f
  standard deviations of normal distribution, 52, 53f
  uniform distribution, 58, 58f
  *z* scores, 61–66 (*see also z* score)
significance
  practical, 392
  statistical *vs.* real-world, 393
  substantive, 392
significance level (α), 202–203
  .01 and .05, 202–203
  choice, in decision making, 228–230, 229f, 401–402
  statistical power and, 256
significance test. *See also* statistical significance
      tests; *specific types*
  basic job, 221–222
  decision making, 195
  estimation, 195
  nanrandom samples and, 260
  of null hypothesis, 201
  sampling distributions, 222, 226, 226f
significance test for means
  *N* < 100, 271–273
  *N* ≥ 100, 271–273
significance test of Spearman's *r,* 345
sign test, 346
similarity, degree of, 390
simple bivariate Venn diagram, 370, 370f
simple random sample (SRS), 162
single-case designs, 349–352
  basic applications, 349–350, 349f, 350t
  comments, 351
  serial dependency, 351–352, 352t, 353f

size of association (relationship), 80, 354, 392
  balanced model for data interpretation, 393–395
  chi-square test of independence, 317, 317t
  definition, 80, 392
  qualitative descriptors, 81–82, 81t
  statistical power and, 252–254, 253t
skewed distributions, 53–57
  characteristics, 53–55, 54f, 55f
  on measures of central tendency, 54f, 55–57, 56f
  negative, 53–54, 55f, 56
  positive, 53, 54f, 55–56
  positive *vs.* negative, distinguishing, 55
skewness (skew), 55–57
  definition, 55
  on mean, 54f, 55f, 56
  on measures of central tendency, 54f, 55–57, 56f
social work
  definition, 3
  evidence-based practice, 3, 4
  science and research, 4
  statistics and, 3–4
Somers' *D,* 100, 345
Spearman's *r* ($r_{ranks}$), 120
Spearman's *r* ($r_{ranks}$) significance test, 345
SPSS software package, 285–287, 286t, 403
  analysis of variance, 326–328, 327t, 406
  *t* test independent samples, 285–287, 286t, 403
squared multiple correlation coefficient ($R^2$), 368
square roots, 411
squares, 411
SRS (simple random sample), 162
standard deviation *(SD, s),* 42–44, 43t, 164t
  formula, 421
  within groups, 127
  of normal distribution, 52, 53f
  predicted change in units, 115–116
standard error of the mean ($\sigma_{\bar{x}}$), 168, 272, 422
standard error of the proportion *(p),* 184–185,
      185f, 422
standardized coefficient, 119
standardized equation, 115
standardized mean difference *(SMD),* 127–130
  caution, 130
  definition and applications, 127–128, 128t
  formula, 127, 422
  graphical interpretation, 128–129, 128t, 129f
  qualitative descriptors of size and strength
      association of, 128, 128t
standardized regression equation, 115, 422
standard score, 421. *See also z* score
statistical generalizability, 388
statistical generalizations, 388
statistically significant, 209
statistically significant result, 209

statistical power, 247–259
  amount, necessary, 257
  definition, 247
  dependent samples and, 288
  directional hypotheses and one-tailed tests and, 256–257
  formula, 423
  low, 354–356
  reduced variability of independent/dependent variable and, 254–255
  sample size on, 247–252
    examples, 248–252, 249f, 251f
    necessary size, 257–259, 259t
    theory, 247–248
  significance level and, 256
  size of relationship or difference in population and, 252–254, 253t
  statistical significance test and, 257
  third variables and, controlling for, 255–256
statistical significance
  balanced model for data interpretation, 393–395
  binomial, 203
  causality and, 354–356
  definition, 392
  reporting, 260
  *vs.* real-world significance, 393
  what it is and isn't, 261, 262t
statistical significance levels, 202–203
.01 statistical significance levels, 202–203
.05 statistical significance levels, 202–203, 257
statistical significance tests, 7, 195–210. *See also null hypothesis; specific tests*
  alternative (research) hypothesis, 196–197
    acceptance, 202
    rejection, 202
    scientific inquiry, 208
  assumptions, 220
  bivariate, 417
  carrying out, 227
  decision rules, 227–228, 401–402
  definition, 195
  examples, 203–206
  fail to reject (accept) the null
    example, 205
    meaning, 207–208
  hypothesis pairs, 197–201
    common pattern, 197–199
    definition and example, 197
    directional and nondirectional, 199–201, 203–205, 204f
  low statistical power, 354–356
  making decision, 228
  more interpretations of *p,* 205–206
  multivariate, 417

null hypothesis, 196–197, 208
  probability *(p),* definition and formula, 195–196
  reasoning with data, 354–356
  reject the null
    definition, 202
    example, 203–204, 204f
    meaning, 206–207
    "real things," 236–237
  sampling error and null hypothesis, 201
  statistically significant result, 209
  statistical power and, 257
  statistical significance levels, 202–203
  univariate, 417
  use, 159
statistical tests, sample distribution and, 221–224, 222f–224f, 401–402
statistics. *See also specific topics*
  bivariate
    key concepts, 6–7
    tests, 417
  definition, 6, 164
  descriptive, 6, 161
  inferential *(see inferential statistics)*
  levels of measurement, 9–11
  multivariate
    key concepts, 7
    types, 417
  obtained, 227
  qualitative, 4, 352–353
  random assignment (randomization), 8–9
  samples and populations, 5
  social work, 3–4
  test, 227
  univariate
    key concepts, 6, 29
    tests, 417
  univariate descriptive
    key concepts, 6, 29
    tests, 6, 417
  variables and measurement, 4–5
straight-line pattern, 116
strength of association (relationship)
  balanced model for data interpretation, 393–395
  definition, 80, 392
  qualitative descriptors, 81–82, 81t
structural equation modeling (SEM), 379
studies. *See also specific types*
  nonrandomized, 8
  randomized, 8
study sample, 5
subsamples, 285
substantive significance, 392
sum, 409

summation sign, 410
survey designs, 138
surveys, 138
survival analysis, 379–380
symbols
    English letter, 419–420
    Greek letters, 419
    math, 409–410
symmetric distribution, 51, 52f
systematic bias, random assignment and, 140


**T**
table, 19–21
    cell, 77t, 78
    cell frequencies, 77t, 78
    cell percentages, 77t, 78
    column totals, 77, 77t
    margins, 77–78, 77t
tails, 52, 52f
tails, measures of, 52, 52f
tau-b ($\tau_b$), 100, 345
tau-c ($\tau_c$), 100, 345
*t* distribution
    confidence intervals for means based on,
        271–273, 401–402
    critical values, 403
    degrees of freedom, 270, 270f
    family, 270–271, 270f, 271f
tests. *See specific types*
test statistic, 227
theoretical distribution, 51
theory, 4
third variables
    controlling for, and statistical power, 255–256
    definition and use, 137
three-way ANOVA, 376
time-series data, 351
totals (table)
    column, 77, 77t
    row, 77t, 78
transformation of scores, 61
treatment, 8, 138
trimmed mean, 33
true experiments, 138
true zero, 10
*t* test
    correlated samples, 288–289
    dependent samples
        example, increased power from positive
            correlation, 289, 403
        requirements, 288–289
        statistical power and, 288
    dependent (paired) samples, 288–289

independent samples, 283–288
    assumptions and formulas, 284–285, 423
    hypothesis pairs, 283–284
    independence assumption, 287–288
    purpose and sampling distribution, 283
    SPSS software package, 285–287, 286t, 403
matched samples, 288–289
one-sample, 273–277
    assumptions, hypothesis pairs, and formula,
        273–274, 423
    carrying out, 274–277, 276f, 403
    decision rules, 274, 403
    formula, 423
    pairs, 288–289
two-tailed tests, 224, 226
    *vs.* one-tailed tests
        carrying out example, 226f, 232, 233f,
            401–402
        determining exact value of study sample
            result, 233–234
two-way ANOVA, 376–378, 376t
two-way factorial ANOVA, 377, 377f
type I error, 230–231, 231t
type I error at .05 level, 257
type II error, 230–231, 231t
type II error at .05 level, 257


**U**
unassociated variables, 7, 75–76. *See also*
        relationship
unbiased estimator, 165
unequal variances formula, 284
uniform distribution, 58, 58f
univariate descriptive statistics
    key concepts, 6, 29
    tests, 6, 417
univariate measures, 416
univariate statistics
    key concepts, 6, 29
    tests, 417
unrelated variables, 7, 75–76. *See also*
        relationship
unstandardized coefficient, 119–120
unstandardized multiple regression equation, 424
unstandardized regression equation, 118, 422
upper tail, 52, 52f


**V**
*V,* Cramer's, 97–98, 99–100, 113t
value(s)
    definition, 5
    extreme, 32

variability, 29
  concept, 39–40
  independent/dependent variable, statistical
      power and, 254–255
variability measures, 39–45
  categorical variables, 40–41, 40t
  concept of variability, 39–40
  interquartile range, 41
  mean deviation, 41–42
  range, 41
  standard deviation, 42–44, 43t
  variance, 44–45
variable(s)
  antecedent, 147
  categorical (qualitative), 5, 77
    directional association between, measure, 100
    variability of, 40–41, 40t
  classification, 9
  column, 77, 77t
  confounding, 7, 9, 136–138, 137t (*see also*
      confounding variable)
    control for, 143
    controlling for, 143–152
    random assignment on, 140
  control, 137
  control for, 143
  definition, 5
  dependent, 7–8
  dichotomous (binary), 5
  extraneous, 137, 255–256
  independent, 7–8, 75–76 (*see also* relationship)
  interval/ratio level, 10
  intervening (mediating), 147–148
  lurking, 137
  in measurement, 4–5
  multiple, and causality, control for, 149–150
  nominal-level, 120
  nuisance, 137
  numeric (quantitative), 5
  ordering, 9
  ordinal level, 10–11
  ordinal-level, 120
  ranking, 9
  related (associated), 6–7, 75–84 (*see also*
      relationship)
    causal, 7
    definition, 75–76

relationships between, 208
  row, 77, 77t
  third, 137
  unrelated (unassociated), 7, 75–76 (*see also*
      relationship)
variance ($s^2$), 44–45, 164t
  analysis of (*see* analysis of variance (ANOVA))
  equal, formula, 284
  equality (homogeneity) of
    assumption, 284
    formula, 284–285
    test, 284
  formula, 421
  population, two estimates, 324–325
  unequal, formula, 284
  unequal variances formula, 284
variation of association by subgroup, 145
Venn diagram, simple bivariate, 370, 370f

**W**
weakening of association, 145, 146, 146t
whisker plots, 23–24, 24f
whiskers, 23–24, 24f
Wilcoxon signed-ranks test, 345–346
within groups standard deviation, 127

**Z**
zero
  arbitrary, 10
  true, 10
$z$ score, 61–66
  basics, 61–62
  calculation, 61, 62f
  formula, 164
    population, 422
    standard score, 421
  normal distribution and, 63–66
    percentages of cases, both sides of
        distribution, 64–65, 65f, 66f, 401–402
    percentages of cases, one side of distribution,
        63–64, 64f, 401–402
    reminders and cautions, 65–66
  predictions, 115
  raw, 61, 62f
  transformation, 61–62, 62f
  uses, 62–63